# HOMEBREWING
## VOLUME I

### Beginner Basics to Creating Your Own
### Award-Winning Recipes

## AL KORZONAS

## Sheaf & Vine
### Palos Hills, Illinois

Technical Review: A. J. deLange
Copy Editors: Raymond Korzonas, Karen Korzonas

Printed in the United States of America

10 9 8 7 6 5 4 3 2 1

Published by Sheaf & Vine
PO Box 1673, Bridgeview, IL 60455
korz@xnet.com (orders and distribution information only)
http://www.brewinfo.com/brewinfo/
Voice/fax: 708-430-HOPS

Cover design: Al Korzonas and Karen Korzonas
Interior design: Al Korzonas and Karen Korzonas
Cover photography by Michael Lichter, Michael Lichter Photography
Interior photography and illustration: Al Korzonas and Karen Korzonas
Figure 4-9 courtesy of Dan McConnell, reprinted with permission from *Zymurgy*

ISBN: 0-9655219-0-7
Library of Congress Catalog Card Number: 97-91922

# DEDICATION

*This book is dedicated to my loving wife, Karen,*
*a woman of endless patience, support, and help.*

# TABLE OF CONTENTS

# New Yeasts, Updates and Errata
## as of 3 December 1998

See also:  http://www.brewinfo.com/brewinfo/

p.85   In Table 5-1, under "honey," "25 cup" should be "2/5 cup."

p.108  "plenty or headspace" should be "plenty of headspace"

p.113  "Tadcaster Brewery" should be "The Old Brewery - Tadcaster."

p.130  The formulas for converting between SRM and EBC are based on the old (pre-1987) method for measuring EBC degrees. Since about 1987, EBC = 1.97 SRM.

p.157  "Tadcaster Brewery" should be "The Old Brewery - Tadcaster."

p.182  "Tadcaster Brewery" should be "The Old Brewery - Tadcaster."

p.163  I said that Burton Water Salts are a blend of gypsum, magnesium sulfate and table salt, but I've since found out that at least one distributor's (L. D. Carlson) is simply gypsum and papain (a proteolytic enzyme, which, incidentally would be denatured [made inactive] if added in the boil as I suggest – I disapprove of the use of papain so I recommend that you continue to add the BWS in the boil if you choose to use it).

p.184  The last sentence should read: "While the synthesis of fatty acids and sterols cannot occur in the absence of oxygen, yeast are capable of utilizing unsaturated fatty acids found in cold break, thereby reducing the yeasts' oxygen requirements."

p.432  Under Oktoberfest/Märzen, "1810" should be "1840." (Oktoberfest itself began in 1810, but the beer was not introduced by Sedlmayr till the 1840's.)

pp.461-464  The table headings should be "Alpha Acid %," "Beta Acid %," and "Cohumulone % of Alpha Acid."

Since sending the book to the printer, I have developed a spreadsheet that calculates potential FG and ABV, and after plugging in all the values for each style, I found that there were a number that I had initially calculated wrongly:

p.427  Under Pre-prohibition American Lager, the ABV should be 4.7 to 5.8%

p.430  Under Eisbock, the ABV should be 7 to 13+%.

WLP008- East Coast Ale Yeast: Our "Brewer Patriot" strain can be used to reproduce many of the American versions of classic beer styles. Similar neutral character of WLP001, but less attenuation, less accentuation of hop bitterness, increased flocculation, and a little tartness. Very clean and low esters. Great yeast for golden, blonde, honey, and German alt style ales. Attenuation is 70-75%. Flocculation is Medium to High. Optimum fermentation temperature is 68-73 degrees. [I question the usefulness of this yeast for Altbier; it would be a good choice for Samuel Adams' or Baltimore Brewing Company's ales]

WLP023- Burton Ale Yeast: From the famous brewing town of Burton upon Trent, England, this yeast is packed with character. It provides delicious subtle fruity flavors like green apple, clover honey and pear. Great for all English styles, IPA's Bitters, Pales. Excellent in Porters and Stouts. Attenuation is 69-75%. Flocculation is Medium. Optimum fermentation temperature is 68-73 degrees. [a good choice for emulating Marston's or Burton Bridge ales]

WLP028- Edinburgh Ale Yeast: Scotland is famous for its malty, strong ales. This yeast can reproduce these complex, flavorful Scottish style ales. Attenuation is 70-75% . Flocculation is medium. Optimum fermentation temperature is 65-70 degrees. [my first choice for Caledonian or McEwan's clones]

WLP029- German Ale/Kölsch Yeast: From a small brewpub in Cologne, Germany, this yeast works great in Kölsch and Alt style beers. Slight sulfur produced during fermentation will disappear with age and leave a super clean, lager-like ale. Attenuation is 72-78% Flocculation is medium. Optimum fermentation temperature is 65-69 degrees. [a good choice for emulating PJ Früh or Mühlen Kölsches]

WLP300- Hefeweizen Ale Yeast: This infamous German yeast is a strain used in the production of traditional, authentic wheat beers. It produces the banana and clove nose traditionally associated with German wheat beers. Attenuation is 72-76% Flocculation is low which leaves the desired cloudy look of traditional German wheat beers. Optimum fermentation temperature is 68-72 degrees. [most German Hefeweizens are filtered, then bottled with lager yeast which is intentionally stirred up during the pour – these beers are not cloudy because of unflocculent yeast]

# ACKNOWLEDGMENTS

First and foremost, I must thank God for blessing me with the skills needed to brew and enjoy beer. Beer and brewing are my passion – I really feel that they are my calling in life and this book is an effort to share what I've learned with others who have similar passions.

If we didn't brew, we would not be brewers. Without my cousin and friend, Dr. Linas Bartuska, and his tireless help, accurate palate, and love of beer, I would not have gained the knowledge required to undertake this series of books. Thanks, Bôbs, for your help and constructive criticism.

Thanks also to my wife, Karen, for reviewing the book, trying (and successfully learning) to share in my love of beer and, most importantly, for putting up with me during this and my other beer-related endeavors.

Thanks to my parents: to Dad for reviewing the book and for helping with some of the physics and materials sciences that I stumbled over and to Mom for saying, "Is this what we sent you to college for?" and inspiring me to continue this project.

A huge thanks must go to the entire membership of the Homebrew Digest, the Brewer's Forum, Lambic Digest, JudgeNet, and Advanced Topics in Brewing, five electronic forums, without which I wouldn't know half of what I know about brewing.

Initially, I had most of the people who helped me together in one huge list. On giving this a bit more thought, I realized that some of those who helped me really should get a special thanks. Some of these people reviewed either sections or the entire book. Others provided me with volumes of information. Clearly their help was instrumental in the completion of this book. A special thanks goes to: Steve Alexander, Dr. Tracy Aquilla, Peter Blum at The Stroh Brewery Company, Jim Busch, Pierre Celis and Peter Camps at Celis Brewing Company, A. J. deLange, Dave Draper, Dr. George Fix, Michael Jackson, Pierre Jelenc, Mark Kellums founder of Just Hops, Finn Knudsen at the New Zealand Hop Marketing Board, Dan McConnell at the Yeast Culture Kit Company, Ralph Olson and Dr. Greg Lewis at HopUnion USA, Dr. Maribeth Raines, Cindy Renfrow, Glenn Tinseth, Andrew Walsh, and Ed Westemeier.

Thanks also to (in a sort of alphabetical order):
Tony Babinec, Ed Basgall, Harlan Bauer, Tesa Brainard, Mark Bridges,
Russ Brodeur, Jan de Bruyne and Daisy Claeys at Brugs Beertje, Jacques
Bertens, Dave Burley, Char at Northwestern Extract Company, Chuck Burkins,
everyone at Caledonian Brewing Company Ltd., everyone at L. D. Carlson
Company, Seth Cohen at Saccharomyces Supply Company, Conn Copas,
everyone (especially Seth) at Crosby and Baker Ltd., Ray Daniels, Dennis
Davison, Tim Dawson, Armand & Guido DeBelder at Drie Fonteinen, George
De Piro, Ken Don and everyone at Young & Company – The Ram Brewery,
Helmut Donhauser at Paulaner Bräuhaus, Mark Dorber of the White Horse at
Parsons Green, Bob Dougherty, Richard Drake, Mary Anne Gruber and Carl
Siebert at Briess Malting Company, Paul Edwards, Jim Ellingson, Brad Fabbri,
Massimo Faraggi, Tim Foley at J. E. Siebel Sons' Company, Jeff Frane at
Advanced Brewers Scientific, Dennis Franz at Anheuser-Busch, Rob Gardner,
George, Perry and John at Mainstreet, Michael Gerholdt, Steve Hamburg, Dr.
John Harrison, Geoff Cooper, and the Durden Park Beer Circle, Craig Hartinger,
Jay Hersh, Jeff Hewit, Jim Hodge, Stefan Jakob at Forschungsbräurei, Larry
Johnson, Scott Kaczorowski, Steve Kamp, Jonas Kazukauskas, Edmundas
Korzonas, Dave LaRocque, Jeff Lemon at Lemon Creek Winery, Jim Liddil, Dr.
Johann Maier at the Hans-Pfulf Hop Research Institute, Jeff Mellem at Brewer's
Resource, Russell Mast, Dave Mercer, Terry Murphree, Ray McNeill at
McNeill's Pub, Chris Neuss, Michael Newman, Tim Norris, Dr. Brian Nummer
at Head Start Brewing Cultures, everyone at The Old Brewery – Tadcaster
(Samuel Smith's), Jim Overstreet, Charlie Papazian, Joe Power and Bill Siebel at
the Siebel Institute of Technology, Rob Reed, Brad Reeg, Randy Reichwage at
G.W. Kent, Jeff Renner, Dave Ritchie at Grain Millers, Joe Rolfe, Alex Santic,
Jack Schmidling, Charlie Scandrett, Olin Schultz, Phil Seitz, Tad Seyler, Paul
Sovcik, Tim Stover at J. E. Siebel Sons' Company, Jeff Stuecheli, Steve Stroud,
Tom Testwuide, Jr. at Schreier Malting Company, Spencer Thomas, Dr. Fred
Tumac at Zapata Technologies, Mike Uchima, Jean-Pierre and Claude Van Roy
at Cantillon, Paul Vanslyke, Don Van Valkenburg, Domenick Venezia, Chuck
Wettergreen, Sabine Weyermann at Mich. Weyermann Malzfabrik, Terry
Winningham at Widmer, and Julian Zelazny.

Finally, I would like to thank my close personal friends for putting up with me
during this project (again, in a sort of alphabetical order): Bob & Renata, Linas
& Kim, Marius & Dalia, Paulius & Audrone, Povilas & Loreta, and last but not
least, Vidas & Beth.

# 1

# INTRODUCTION

There are a great many books on homebrewing, so how is this one different? Some books are very quaint and folksy. Others are very technical. There are even books about brewing that don't say anything about procedures but rather describe the science of brewing. I have all these books and many more in my brewing library and I've gained lots of valuable information from all of them.

The primary focus of this book is on the *procedures* of beginning and intermediate homebrewing. On occasion, I will provide a little scientific background for the procedures, but this book is primarily on the "how-tos" of brewing and not the "whys." Many books this size cover *all* aspects of homebrewing. I've chosen instead to dedicate more space to the equipment, ingredients and procedures of *beginning* and *intermediate* brewing here and cover advanced brewing in volume II, rather than try to fit it all into one book.

## How is this book different?

*Homebrewing - Volume I:*

- doesn't force you to read it cover-to-cover before you begin brewing,

- contains the most comprehensive information on ingredients and equipment,

- teaches you how to create your own, *original*, award-winning recipes, and

- has more pages dedicated to troubleshooting and frequently asked questions than all other current homebrewing books *combined*.

I'd like you to view this book in three distinct parts. Part one consists of chapters one and two and is on brewing your very first batch of beer. I encourage you to read these first two chapters and then go and brew some beer – ***don't read any further until you have that first beer in the fermenter.*** The reason I suggest you do this is because of what happened to me when I tried to start homebrewing. After buying my first homebrewing book and ingredients, I quickly proceeded to read the book from cover to cover. I was so excited about this newly found hobby that I think I read the 400 page book in one week. Was I ready to brew? No. My head was swimming with information and it all sounded so complicated that I ended up re-reading the book before starting that first batch. I now know that I made at least three big mistakes on that first brew but the beer turned out surprisingly drinkable.

Part two explains the basics of homebrewing equipment, intermediate homebrewing procedures, ingredients, and recipes. It is in these chapters that I will also cover everything that you need to know to graduate from being a "beginner" to being an "intermediate" homebrewer.

Part three consists of the "reference" section of the book: Troubleshooting, Frequently Asked Questions, and Recipe Formulation. The appendices contain detailed descriptions of the world's beer styles along with commercial examples, descriptions of nearly 100 hop varieties, tables on recommended hop varieties for various beer styles, and information about most of the yeasts that are currently available to homebrewers. I hope that the information in these chapters and appendices will be useful throughout your homebrewing endeavors and that you find them a helpful reference even as you continue to advanced brewing.

If you follow the procedures I describe in this book chances are pretty good that your first beer will at least be drinkable. It may taste as good as (or better than) commercial beer or it may taste a bit "off." Don't be discouraged if your first attempt doesn't turn out to be as good as you had expected. Take a bottle of the beer that you have brewed to a more experienced homebrewer and have them suggest improvements. There are many homebrewers around and I've never met one who was not willing to help a peer. Clubs are a great way to meet fellow brewers. Consider joining or even forming a club.

## What's Important?

First, I'd like to answer a few commonly asked questions about homebrewing and then go on to what's important.

*Is it legal?* Yes. At the time of publication, homebrewing is legal in the United States except for a handful of states. Contact the American Homebrewers Association at (303) 447-0816 for the most current status, because the list of states in which it is illegal to homebrew is shrinking rapidly. In the states in which it is legal, adults of legal drinking age are permitted to brew up to 100 gallons of beer per adult in the household with a limit of 200 gallons per household per year. It is, however, illegal to sell beer without a license.

*Is it safe?* Yes. The alcohol and chemical composition of beer keeps it safe for you to drink. In fact, historians tell us that beer and wine production was crucial to peoples' survival. In many places, potable water was not easy to come by and fermented beverages were safer to drink than water.

*Is it strong?* Not necessarily. You can make beer of any strength (limited only by your yeast's endurance), but most homebrew is in the same range as comercially available beers.

*Is it expensive?* No. Homebrewed beer costs much less than its comercially available counterparts. It costs between one-half and one-quarter of what you might pay for a commercial version of the style.

*How long does it take?* That depends on the style, but a simple ale (the easiest style) will take about 20 days till it's ready to drink. Most of this time is spent waiting. The total time that you actually have to work on the batch is perhaps 7 hours: approximately four hours to brew and perhaps three more to bottle.

*Must I start from grain?* No. You can if you wish, but it's far easier if you brew from malt extract, at least until you learn the mechanics of homebrewing. Malt extract is a syrup or powder, made from grain, in which the first step of making beer has already been done for you at a factory. Many prize-winning beers have been made from malt extract and for most styles, if you use fresh ingredients, you can brew as good a beer from extract as from grain.

*Where do I get equipment and ingredients?* Look in your yellow pages under "Beer Homebrewing Supplies and Equipment" for a local store. Failing that, there are many fine mailorder stores that can ship the supplies to you. Even if you end up paying a few pennies more, support your local store. Supplies at a moment's notice and the fact that you can get instant, free feedback on your beer are two good reasons for trying to ensure that your local store stays in business. In the Further Reading section at the back of Chapter 17 there is a list of several homebrewing magazines. In addition to being great sources of the latest brewing information, they also contain ads for local shops and mailorder suppliers.

*What's important?* Finally! The most important thing is sanitation! Although there's nothing that can live in beer that is harmful to you, certain bacteria and yeast can get into your beer uninvited and make it taste bad. Sour flavors, sour smells, or off aromas are the result of sloppy sanitation. Make sure that everything that comes in contact with the beer or wort (unfermented beer) has been sanitized. Follow the procedures for sanitation outlined in this book and you should have no problems. Keep track of what's sanitized and what's not and don't cut corners when it comes to sanitation.

# BREWING YOUR FIRST BATCH

## Basic Equipment

hapter 4 describes equipment in detail, but here I'll just list the very basics for getting started (the next page has a photograph illustrating the items which may be new to you):

- two food-grade plastic buckets (ideally 7.5 gallons or larger)
- one tight-fitting lid for one of the buckets (this will be the fermenter)
- an airlock (and a stopper if the bucket lid needs one)
- a large kettle (12 quarts or larger)
- a long-handled spoon for stirring the kettle
- a thermometer (40 to 220° F or 4 to 104° C, ideally a floating one)
- a racking cane (preferably the curved, 30" version)
- $5/16$" inside diameter, food-grade hose for siphoning
- a plastic hose clamp for regulating the siphon hose
- 48 empty, non-twist-off, glass, beer bottles (preferably brown)
- bottle capper and 55 bottlecaps
- a Pyrex® measuring cup or some other, small, heat-tolerant container
- a few tablespoons of household chlorine bleach

Equipment that is not mandatory, but does make things much easier:
- a bottle filler (makes bottling easier)
- a small pot or saucepan (1 quart or so)
- bottle brush (helps clean out dirty bottles)

**Figure 2-1***: (back row, l to r) 12-ounce bottle, bottlecaps, measuring cup, 7.5-gallon fermenter with lid, stopper, and airlock, 12-quart enamel kettle, and 7.5 gallon bottling bucket, (front row, l to r) wooden spoon, bottle brush, bottle filler, racking cane and hose with hose clamp, bottle capper, and chlorine bleach.*

It is often more economical to buy a complete kit from a homebrew supply store than trying to buy all the equipment separately. Some kits contain other non-essential items like hydrometers, glass carboys or hop and grain bags. These will certainly be useful as you progress forward from being a beginner, so it does not hurt to get them in your first kit. Chapter 4 has more details on equipment.

# Ingredients

For your first kit, I recommend that you get one that contains pre-hopped malt extract. If a kit contains dry yeast but has not been refrigerated or recently packaged, you may want to get some fresh dry yeast from the refrigerator at the store. Some kits also contain crystal malts, hop pellets and/or liquid yeast. These are great, but for your first batch, I recommend that you begin with as basic a kit as possible so you have less to worry about until you learn the mechanics of brewing.

There are hundreds of kits available, but usually boxed kits tend to make better beer than just the simple, single-can kits, although I've tasted some excellent homebrewed beer made from the Cooper's Kits, even if you do add 1 kg (2.2 lb.) of corn sugar as recommended. Among the better kits are the ones from Brewer's Best, Munton & Fison's Gold "All Malt" line, John Bull's Master Class line, Glenbrew's Premium "All Malt" line, and Cooper's. In addition to the kit, you will also need 3/4 cup (175 ml) dextrose (corn sugar) unless the kit includes it. This will be used to carbonate the beer.

# The Day Before Brewing

24 hours or so before brewing, we need to make some cool, sanitized brewing water and sanitize the fermenter. Hopefully the equipment kit included two buckets - one for a fermenter and the other for bottling. If both are the same size, then just pick one. If not, we'll use the larger one for the fermenter. We will be pouring concentrated, hot wort (unfermented beer) into the cool, sanitized water and the result will be 5 gallons of wort ready for yeast. I don't recommend that you simply use plain, cool tapwater since municipal water usually contains chlorine and all water (especially well water) has some bacteria in it. Boiling will evaporate much of the chlorine and will kill most of the bacteria that can harm your beer. Even if we use bottled water, there's no guarantee that it is free of wild yeasts and bacteria. If your water tastes good (i.e. doesn't have too much iron, sulfur or off smells), then it will make fine beer. Do not use softened water - bypass your softener if you have one. If your water tastes or smells bad, you may try installing a filter (I use a Brita system in the summer when my water smells like algae) or, you can use bottled spring water from the grocery store or a home delivery company.

We will need four gallons (about 15 liters) of water for today and one and a half gallons (about 5 3/4 liters) of water on brewing day. If you have a 5 gallon (or larger) kettle, we can boil all four gallons at once. If you only have a 12 quart (about 12 liters) kettle, we will have boil one half first and then the other half. There has been some debate about whether an aluminum kettle is all right to use, but they are perfectly fine as long as you don't scrub the layer of aluminum oxide that forms on the inside of the kettle.  Other alternatives are enameled steel and stainless steel.  Mild steel (the kind that rusts) and cast iron are not recommended.  More information on kettles is detailed in chapter 4.

While the water is coming to a boil, we should sanitize your fermenter.  Pour 5 gallons (about 19 liters) of warm water into the fermenter and add 5 tablespoons (about 65 ml) of household chlorine bleach.  If your kit came with a sanitizing powder, follow the instructions on the package (metabisulfite is *not* a sanitizer - use bleach).  Be careful to not splash this sanitizing solution on good clothes because it will bleach them.  Use a very clean, non-abrasive sponge or a soft cloth to gently rinse the inside of the lid and the inside walls of the fermenter with the sanitizing solution.  Always be careful to not scratch the inside of the fermenter.  Scratches will give places for bacteria and other microbes to hide from the sanitizing solution.  Resist the temptation of storing brewing equipment in the fermenter.

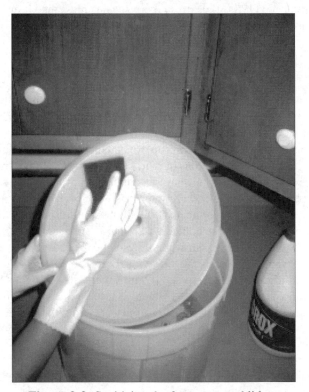

**Figure 2-2:** Sanitizing the fermenter and lid.

Take apart the airlock (if it comes apart) and put all the pieces along with the stopper into the sanitizing solution. Let the sanitizing solution sit in the fermenter for 15 minutes, remove the airlock and stopper and pour the solution down the drain. Rinse the airlock, stopper, lid and fermenter in tapwater.

Once the water has come to a boil, carefully pour the water into the sanitized and rinsed fermenter. The boiling water will also help sanitize the fermenter, but only up to the level of the water, so don't bypass the bleach solution sanitation step. If you are using a glass fermenter, let the water cool before you pour it in - otherwise the glass is likely to shatter. Affix the lid onto the fermenter.

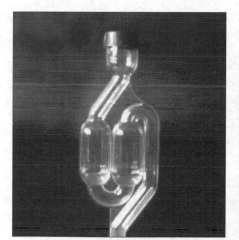 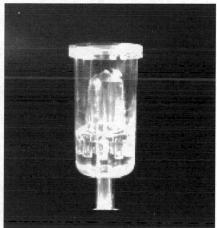

**Figure 2-3:** *Properly filled airlocks of various types.*

Attach the airlock and fill it with one inch of clean water. Some airlocks are made up of three parts: the body, the "thimble" and the cap. The "thimble" should rest inside the body, it's bottom 5/8 of an inch submerged in the water and you should put the cap onto the body after filling. Be careful to not overfill the airlock. The purpose of the airlock is to allow carbon dioxide (which is made by the yeast) to escape while keeping air out. As the boiling water (or tomorrow's warm wort) cools, the air in the headspace will cool and contract. If we overfill the airlock, the water will be sucked into the fermenter ("suckback"). Ideally, you would rather it didn't, but if it does, don't worry about it. S-shaped airlocks are better in this respect because they can run in both directions without risk of suckback.

Put the fermenter in a cool place (65-70° F or 18-21° C is ideal) and don't go peeking inside unnecessarily.

## Brewing Day

On brewing day, now that the four gallons of sanitized brewing water have cooled to about 70⁰ F (21° C), we are ready to make the wort (that's what brewers call the unfermented beer and pronounce it "wert"). There's nothing wrong with waiting longer than 24 hours between making the sanitized brewing water and making the concentrated wort - we can delay brewing for several days with no problems. If you are really impatient and must brew the same day, we can put your sanitized floating thermometer along with the four gallons of boiling water into your plastic fermenter and stick it into a refrigerator (or a snow bank) till it cools down to 65° F (18° C) or so. Don't try cooling hot water or wort in a snow bank if you are using a glass fermenter - it is guaranteed to crack.

Bring one and a half gallons (5 ½ liters) of tapwater (or bottled water) to a boil. Pour eight ounces (about 250 ml) of this boiling water into a Pyrex measuring cup or another, small, heat-tolerant container, insert your thermometer, cover with plastic wrap and set aside to cool.

**Figure 2-4:** *Cooling the water to be used for rehydrating the yeast.*

Turn off the heat and pour in the malt extract (and dextrose if the kit calls for it). Stir until it has dissolved. If we try stirring in the malt extract while the heat is on, the extract will scorch and the beer will have a burnt flavor. Turn on the heat, partially cover the kettle with its lid and bring the wort to a boil. Don't cover the kettle completely because it is necessary for unwanted gases to escape and completely covering the kettle increases the likelihood that the wort will foam up and make a mess. Watch the wort carefully, keeping an eye out for the foaming.

If the foam begins to rise, we can subdue it by blowing on it, stirring, lowering the heat or by dumping in a half cup of cool water (blowing rarely works, but all four combined will work for sure). Don't boil completely uncovered either because we will lose too much water. Ideally, we would like to have about one gallon of wort after the one hour boil.

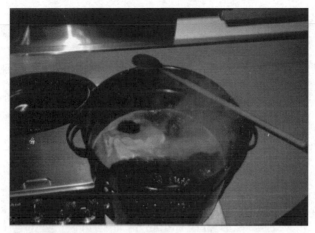

**Figure 2-5**: *Boiling wort.*

After boiling for an hour, remove the lid from the fermenter and set it someplace clean (making sure to not touch the sanitized inside to anything unsanitary). Take the kettle off the heat and gently (minimizing splashing) pour the wort into the four gallons of cool water in the fermenter. Hopefully, the 8 ounces of boiled water that we put in the Pyrex container will have cooled to between 90 and 110° F (32 and 43° C). A refrigerator will help, but don't overcool.

Once the 8 ounces of water has cooled to between 90 and 110° F, remove the thermometer, sprinkle the dry yeast into the container and re-cover it with the plastic wrap. Let the yeast re-hydrate for 15 to 30 minutes. It does not help to rehydrate in wort or sugar water, in fact it is more stressful on the yeast[73]. If we are using liquid yeast instead of dried, follow the directions on the yeast package and omit the instructions about rehydrating dry yeast. Note that liquid yeast requires us to start the yeast several days before brewing day.

**Figure 2-6**: *Rehydrating yeast.*

After the yeast has rehydrated (15 to 30 minutes), pour the yeast into the fermenter. Swirl the wort with a sanitized tube such as the racking cane or bottle filler. If you happen to have a plastic or stainless steel, long-handled spoon we can use that, but don't use a wooden spoon – bacteria and wild yeast are certain to be hiding in the wood. To sanitize an item, pour a gallon or two of warm water into the second plastic bucket and add one tablespoon of household chlorine bleach per gallon. Soak the tube or spoon for 10 to 15 minutes and then rinse well with tapwater. If your tapwater is known to be infected, we can pre-boil your rinse water. If we put any sanitized item on an unsanitized surface, we must re-sanitize it.

The purpose for the swirling is not so much for distributing yeast, but rather for introducing air into the wort. Whip the wort for several minutes so you work up a good froth. The yeast need the oxygen from the air at this stage for good health. Once fermentation starts, introducing more air will give us undesirable (in most cases) aromas and flavors. Therefore, avoid splashing the wort throughout the entire process, once fermentation begins. This holds true up to and including bottling.

**Figure 2-7**: *Aerating the cooled wort.*

Press the lid firmly onto the fermenter and carefully move it into a cool, dark place. For making ales, the ideal temperature is between 65 and 70° F (18 and 21° C). Don't let the temperature drop too much below 65° F or rise too much above 75 or 80° F (24 or 27° C). Try to choose a place where the temperature stays relatively constant from day to day. The yeast don't like it when the temperature changes suddenly.

If a dark place is not available, cover the fermenter with a dark-colored plastic garbage bag or a cardboard box. If you live with a non-brewer, you might want to put a note on the bag or box covering the fermenter, so they don't accidentally knock it over or try to move it somewhere. I used to put a "YEAST AT WORK — PLEASE DO NOT TOUCH" note on my garbage bags so my mom wouldn't try to "clean it up."

You may be tempted to make more than 5 gallons, thinking that there's enough space in the fermenter for 7.5 gallons, but I urge you to not exceed 5 gallons. As the yeast ferments the wort, it will create a foam which needs space in the fermenter. If we overfill the fermenter it can clog the airlock and eventually the whole thing will go "FOOP!" and shower the room with brown foam. This happened to me twice, most recently with my raspberry/cherry "Karinos & Algio Nuptial Ale." It's not pretty.

## Fermentation

Depending on the yeast, temperature, and how well we aerated the wort, fermentation should start between 6 and 48 hours. The airlock will begin to bubble. The most common question I get from new brewers is: "It's been three days and my airlock never bubbled... what shall I do?" The most common reason for this is that they added the yeast in the evening put the fermenter in a warm place and did not check the fermenter till later the next day. The ferocious part of the fermentation took place while they weren't looking.

**Figure 2-8**: *Fermentation!*

One tell-tale sign that the main part of the fermentation has completed is a brown ring around the fermenter, just above the level of the beer. Once the main fermentation is complete, small leaks in the lid and/or near the airlock can be big enough so that there is no airlock activity.

While the beer is fermenting, it is a good idea to start collecting and cleaning 48 beer bottles. They should be non-twistoff and make sure that they work with your bottlecapper. Some brands of bottles don't work with some cappers. You can try capping with a straightened-out used bottlecap, just to make sure. Ideally, they should be brown, but green and clear bottles will work – they will just require us to be a little more careful about exposure to light. The insides of the bottles should be "squeaky" clean. Soaking in chlorine bleach solution helps remove gunk and labels too. Reject any bottles that cannot be cleaned out well or have chips around the mouth of the bottle. Recycling centers are great sources for bottles.

Again, depending on the type of yeast, the temperature, how much malt and sugar we put in and how well we aerated the wort, the fermentation should begin to subside after about 2 to 7 days. Healthy, dried yeast, fermenting average-strength wort at 70° F (21° C) will certainly begin to subside in 2 days. Many factors can slow the fermentation and make it take longer. Fermenting at a colder temperature will slow fermentation. Old, weak or unrehydrated yeast can make your fermentation take longer. If we are making a very strong beer it will take longer to complete fermentation. You must wait until the fermentation is effectively over before we bottle because if we don't, our beer will be overcarbonated (have you ever seen "Old Faithful" in Yellowstone Park?) and in extreme cases, the bottles may even burst.

**Figure 2-9**: *The brown ring which indicates that the volcanic part of the fermentation has come and gone.*

I tend to be conservative and wait till the bubbles in the airlock are two minutes apart. Again, if there is a small leak, the airlock may not move at all. Sometimes, there are small colonies of yeast floating on top of the beer – don't worry about them. You can tell that the beer is ready to bottle when the yeast has settled: the beer will stop looking like chocolate milk and will be much darker and quite clear... it will look like... beer!

## Preparing for Bottling

Normally, if we are fermenting between 65 and 70° F (18 and 21° C), the beer should be ready to bottle in about 10 days, but it's better to wait a few days longer than to make two cases of gushers. Waiting too long (much more than two weeks) after the beer is done fermenting can cause off flavors, but around two weeks is nothing to worry about.

When we are ready to bottle, first we need to prepare the priming sugar – it will give the beer carbonation. For most styles, the amount of priming sugar will vary from $1/2$ cup to $3/4$ of a cup. Note that's $3/4$ of a CUP, NOT pound. Pour the priming sugar into a small pot with 8 ounces (250 ml) of tapwater and bring it to a boil, stirring occasionally. Boil the priming sugar and water for 5 minutes (just to sanitize it) and then cover the pot with its lid for another two minutes (so the steam sanitizes the lid too).

**Figure 2-10**: *Priming the beer while racking (note: lid covering fermenter to prevent things from falling in).*

Sanitize the priming bucket (the other bucket) just like we sanitized the fermenter, but don't pour out the solution just yet. We will use it to sanitize the racking cane (siphoning pickup tube) and siphon hose. "Racking" is the transfer of wort or beer (usually via siphon) from one container to another.

Starting the siphon is often the hardest part of brewing. The easiest way to start a siphon is to never let the siphon run dry. Read on and you'll see what I mean. Slide the hose clamp onto the hose 2 inches from the outlet end of the hose. Attach the racking cane the other end of the hose. If you have a plastic bottle filler, attach it to the hose. If your racking cane has a removable tip (that keeps it from drawing from the very bottom), put the tip onto the cane. If you have attached a plastic bottle filler, remove the valve at the tip being careful to put all the parts someplace safe for now. If you have a brass bottle filler (these are good for bottling but shouldn't be used for racking) or if you don't have one at all, slide the hose clamp so it is about 18 inches from the outlet end of the hose.

Fill the whole racking cane/racking hose/bottle filler setup with tapwater, close the hose clamp so the water does not run out and lower the cane into the bleach solution in the priming bucket. Lower the outlet of the hose so that it is below the level of the solution in the bucket (the flow of the liquid in the racking setup will always run "downhill"), point the bottle filler tube (or outlet of the hose) into the sink or a bucket and open the hose clamp. We must always make sure that we keep the outlet of the siphon setup lower than the level of the liquid in the source container. Let the siphon run for a minute, shut off the hose clamp and quickly dunk the bottle filler (or the outlet-end of the hose), right up to the hose clamp, into the bleach solution. Now both the outside and inside surfaces that will come into contact with the beer are in contact with the sanitizer and are being sanitized.

**Figure 2-11**: *"Ceiling clip" holding a sanitized racking cane.*

After soaking for 15 minutes, remove the racking setup from the sanitizer and rinse off the outside with water. Make sure to not touch the sanitized parts of the setup (the parts that will contact the beer) with your hands or anything else that is unsanitized. This is where a brewing partner helps. I've screwed two "butterfly" binder clips to the basement ceiling so I can safely hang my sanitized racking setup from them when I'm brewing alone.

Dump the sanitizing solution down the drain and rinse the priming bucket. Pour three gallons of tapwater into the priming bucket and put the priming bucket up on the counter again. Recall that the racking setup is still full of sanitizing solution. Lower the racking cane into the water in the priming bucket, lower the outlet end of the setup into the sink or a bucket (below the level of the water in the priming bucket) and open the hose clamp. Siphon water down the drain for a minute.

Close the hose clamp and remove the cane from the priming bucket. Don't let the areas of the racking cane and hose that will touch the beer touch anything that has not been sanitized (including your hands!). Dump the water out and place the priming bucket on the ground. Pour the priming sugar/water solution (which you boiled earlier) into the bucket. If you can, try to avoid splashing. Splashing will aerate the solution and now that the beer is done fermenting, you want to avoid aeration. Carefully bring the fermenter over and place it on a counter, table or washing machine (anyplace that is significantly higher than the priming bucket).

## Racking the Beer

Remove the lid from the fermenter and set it aside. There may be small colonies of yeast still floating on the top of the beer – that's normal – don't worry about them. Lower the racking cane into the fermenter and hold the outlet of the hose below the level of the beer and over the sink or some kind of container. Note that there is dormant yeast at the bottom of the fermenter, so be careful to not stir it up while carrying the fermenter and while inserting the cane. We will now use the water that is in the racking cane and hose to start the beer siphon.

Open the hose clamp and let the liquid run until all the water has left the hose and beer is flowing. Don't let the bottling tube (or hose end) touch the sink or container unless you have sanitized it. Close the hose clamp and lower the hose into the priming bucket. Slowly open the hose clamp and let the beer flow gently into the priming bucket. Try to not splash the beer into the bucket or you may get off flavors. As soon as there is enough beer in the priming bucket, try and keep the end of the bottling tube (or hose end) submerged in the beer. If the flow is too intense to avoid splashing, either partly close the hose clamp or raise the priming bucket (the rate of flow is dependent on the difference in the heights of the levels in the source and destination containers.

We should avoid transferring the yeast into the priming bucket. It's not a big deal if we transfer some – it will eventually sink to the bottom of the bottle along with most of the yeast that's still in suspension (it's the yeast in suspension that will carbonate the beer for us).

Watch the level of the beer in the fermenter so that you don't run out of beer and break the siphon (i.e. don't let all the beer run out of the racking setup). If we do accidentally let all the liquid out of the hose, we will have to restart the siphon before we can bottle. Always keep in mind what is sanitized and what is not. One way to restart the siphon is to insert the end of a sanitized turkey baster into the outlet end of the hose. Be careful to not blow air back through the hose/racking cane into the beer (this would aerate the beer). Another way to restart the siphon is to fill it with water and then use that water to draw the beer back through the cane/hose. Starting the siphon by sucking on the hose is NOT recommended.

If we had to touch any item that comes in contact with the beer while restarting the siphon or if while we were restarting the siphon, a sanitized part touched something unsanitized, we should resanitize that part. If we forget to sanitize something or something falls into the beer, don't despair – chances are it will be all right. We just want to minimize the chance that wild yeast or bacteria will get in and spoil the flavor of your beer.

Once we've siphoned all we can out of the fermenter (without the racking cane running dry), close the hose clamp and remove the cane. You may want to rinse excess yeast off the cane if there is a lot, but actually, it may be simply safer to just let it be. If the cane has a removable tip, we should remove it now, keeping the inlet end of the cane higher than the rest. Be careful to not touch the part of the cane that will be going back into the beer. Quickly insert the cane into the priming bucket (so the beer doesn't run out when you point the cane downwards) but try not to splash. Gently stir the beer with the cane to mix the priming sugar with the beer. Try to keep from splashing. The priming sugar will give the yeast more to eat and the resulting carbon dioxide ($CO_2$) they produce will carbonate the beer.

Clean out the fermenter and fill it with five gallons (about 19 liters) of water. Add five tablespoons (about 65 ml) of household chlorine bleach. Soak 48 clean bottles and the bottle filler valve (the whole bottle filler if it's not already attached to the racking setup) in the bleach solution for 15 minutes and then rinse them well in cold tapwater. Naturally, you will have to sanitize the bottles in groups of about 12. Alternatively, you could have sanitized the bottles at the same time as you sanitized the priming bucket, but don't let sanitized bottles sit around for more than a few hours because the likelihood of wild yeast or bacteria floating into the bottles. Rinse out the filler valve (and the filler if it's not already attached to the racking setup). Press the bottle filler valve firmly onto the end of the filler tube. Soak the end of the bottle filler in the sanitizing solution for 5 minutes (note: you have to do this because you had to touch the valve with your fingers while putting it on the tube). Rinse the sanitizing solution off the filler tube with cold tapwater. Rinse all the sanitized bottles with cold water.

Press the bottle filler tube into the end of the siphon hose if it's not already attached, touching only the parts of the filler that will not go into the bottles. Pour 55 bottlecaps into the sanitizing solution (the extra ones are in case we drop any or if any crimp crookedly onto a bottle. Let them sit in the sanitizer for 15 minutes. Rinse the bottlecaps in cold tapwater. Keep refilling the container with cold tapwater and then dumping it out. Fill and dump at least five times. Finally, drain as much water as you can without pouring the caps down the drain and put the container next to your capper.

Lift the priming bucket (which now contains primed beer) up onto a table, counter, or washing machine and place the priming sugar pot or some other sanitized container below the priming bucket. Open the hose clamp. Pressing the filler valve against the bottom of the pot or container will start the flow of beer. Letting go will stop the flow. On some fillers you will have to lift up on the filler tube because the tube's own weight is enough to start the beer flowing.

We first need to purge the air from the bottle filler tube and then we need to run the unprimed beer out of the racking cane and hose. Press the filler tube down into a sanitized "slop bucket" (I usually use the priming sugar pot). Let the beer run in to the slop bucket for 5 seconds and then stop the flow. Now we are ready to bottle.

# Bottling

Select a clean, sanitized and rinsed bottle and carefully slip the bottle filler tube into the bottle. Do not let the bottle filler tube touch the outside of the bottle. Raise the bottle so you can see the level of beer in the bottle, but not so high that the bottle is above the level of the beer in the priming bucket.

**Figure 2-12**: *Filling a bottle.*

If we do accidentally raise it too high, the beer will flow backwards (from the bottle to the bucket) and if it runs dry, we will have to restart the siphon. Press down on the tube and watch the beer level rise in the bottle. When the level of the beer in the bottle has reached the very top, release pressure on the tube (or lift up, depending on your filler) to shut off the flow of beer.

When the tube is removed, the level of the beer in the bottle will drop. Ideally, you would like the level of the beer to be about 1 inch below the top of the bottle, but anything from 3/4 inch to 1 1/2 inches is fine. Too much airspace in the neck of the bottle is another invitation for our beer to become oxidized and develop off flavors. Too small an airspace slows carbonation.

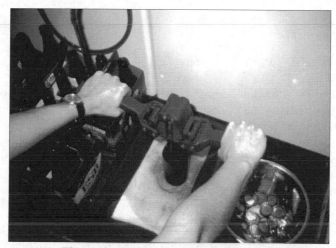

**Figure 2-13**: *Capping with a two-handled capper.*

Select a sanitized cap from the container, being careful to only touch the one we will be using and only touch the caps by the edges (don't touch the plastic liner). Place the cap into the capper (a magnet may hold it in place – some double-handled cappers do not have a magnet. If you have this type of capper, you should place the cap onto the bottle instead of into the capper.

Place the capper onto the bottle. A low-sided tray lined with several layers of paper towels is a good idea. It's a non-slip surface and will catch the spillage if we happen to tip the bottle over (I have). Slowly, carefully press the handles down till the cap crimps onto the bottle. There will be distinct point where the cap crimps onto the bottle. Raise the handles and inspect the cap. Make sure it has sealed well. Repeat this procedure until we've bottled all the beer. Five gallons is approximately 48 12-ounce bottles.

# Waiting

Place the bottles in a room-temperature (65-70° F or 18-21° C), dark place (exposure to light will cause our beer to smell like a skunk – brown bottles give better protection than green or clear, but keeping them dark is a good idea whatever the color of the bottles). The yeast will take from 10 days to two weeks to carbonate the beer. Stronger beers will take longer to carbonate.

After the beer has carbonated, it will improve in flavor for a few weeks, perhaps four or eight (depending on the strength). It will then begin to slowly decline in quality. This decline can be reduced by refrigeration, but since this beer is not pasteurized, unless our sanitation was super-human and if we were very careful to not aerate, it will probably eventually develop some minor off flavors. Some very strong beers can improve in flavor for up to 25 years. The alcohol and yeast help preserve them.

## Tasting

When you're ready to drink the beer, chill it to 50-55° F (10-13° C), the proper serving temperature for ales. Make sure not to shake up the yeast that has settled on the bottom of the bottle. Open the bottle and carefully pour the beer into a large glass. Choose one that is big enough to hold the 12 ounces of beer plus a few ounces of foam. Don't tip the bottle back and forth or you will stir up the yeast. If you do accidentally get a little yeast into the glass, don't worry about it – a small amount will not affect the flavor significantly, it will just make the beer a little cloudy. You will have to leave a bit of the beer behind to avoid pouring out the yeast. Enjoy the beer – you made it!

**Figure 2-14**: *Beer you made yourself!*

# BEGINNING HOMBREWING QUESTIONS

In this chapter, I will try to answer the most common questions you may have when you are just starting out. If you have a question that is not answered here try looking in chapter 16, "Frequently Asked Questions," and chapter 14, "Troubleshooting." Some answers can be rather lengthy, so to avoid duplication, I will point you to the appropriate section in the Troubleshooting chapter.

## Why hasn't my fermentation started?

This is by far the most common question asked by beginning homebrewers. Most often, fermentation has started and actually you only didn't see the "volcanic" part of the fermentation – it occurred during the first night. See "Fermentation didn't start" in chapter 14.

## Why does my beer smell/taste odd?

The most common cause for odd smells and flavors is sloppy sanitation. See "Review Sanitation Procedures" in chapter 14. Stale ingredients are another source of odd smells and tastes. Alas, this is more common than it should be – if possible, look for kits that have expiration dates.

## Should I use the dry yeast that comes with the kit?

If the yeast envelope or kit box is within its expiration date it should be all right to use. Let's just hope that your supplier hasn't been storing it at 90° F (32° C). If you are suspicious of the yeast that comes with the kit, go ahead and buy some refrigerated dry yeast or even liquid yeast (all yeast should be refrigerated: both liquid and dry). You can toss the yeast that came with the kit into the boil – it will provide nutrition for the live yeast you add later.

## Where do I get empty bottles?

The easiest place to get empty bottles is to buy them from your homebrew supply store, but this is also the most expensive way to get empties. Recycling centers and taverns are good places to get used bottles. Some homebrewers have wondered if the bottles have to be returnable/refillable bottles or if the thinner glass bottles used by most commercial brewers are okay to use. While the heavier returnable bottles are the most indestructible, regular, non-twistoff commercial bottles are perfectly fine.

**Figure 3-1**: *Various types of bottles (the group on the left are non-competition bottles, that is, they are unsuitable for most competitions because they are either larger than 14 ounces, smaller than 10 ounces, have raised brand lettering, or have bale-top closures).*

## Can I use twistoff bottles?

Twist-off bottles can be used, but there are two problems with them that will result in a significant number of loss. Firstly, they are much thinner glass so up to 15% of the bottles will break during capping. Secondly, they are made to be capped with special caps and therefore you will get some bottles that simply will not cap right (although you may not know it) and eventually all the carbonation will escape.

## How can I avoid boilover?

Boilover is caused by a thick head of foam being created by proteins in the boiling wort trapping the escaping water vapor. One way to minimize your chances of a boilover is to stand by with a sieve as the wort is coming to a boil and to skim the hot break scum that forms on the top of the wort. Other ways to fight-off an impending boilover are to blow on the foam, stir, lower the heat, and splash a little cold water on the foam – a spray bottle would be ideal. Depending on the vigor of the boil and the amount of protein in the wort, some of these techniques may not work, but together they are certain to stop boilover.

## Why can't I get a rolling boil?

While you are heating the kettle from the bottom, heat is also escaping from the kettle sides and top and in the evaporating water vapor. One solution, although an expensive one, is to increase the size of your burner. Another solution is to cover your pot partly – do not cover it completely (see "Cooked corn aroma" in chapter 14). A third solution is to insulate your kettle, or at least the lid of the kettle, but be sure to use flameproof and heat-resistant insulation and don't use insulation (like fiberglass) that can accidentally fall into the wort.

## Why does my fermenting beer look like egg-drop soup?

Sometimes, during fermentation you will see chunks of white blobs rising and falling inside the fermenter. This is cold break which is made up of proteins. For now, don't even worry about it – it won't affect your beer significantly.

## Why does my fermentation just go on and on?

Most likely it is because you used weak yeast (perhaps you didn't rehydrate it or maybe it was old or mishandled) or you are fermenting far too cold for the yeast you are using. See "Fermentation doesn't stop" in chapter 14 for more suggested solutions.

## Why is my fermentation weak?

Most commonly, there's absolutely nothing wrong – see "Why hasn't my fermentation started" above. However, just as with long fermentations, it could also be weak yeast or too cold a temperature. See "Fermentation weak" in chapter 14.

## Why does my fermenting beer smell like rotten eggs?

It is not uncommon for yeast to produce hydrogen sulfide ($H_2S$) during fermentation. It smells exactly like rotten eggs. Lager yeasts are more likely to produce it than ale yeasts, but in most cases, the aroma will dissipate either by the end of fermentation or after a few weeks of aging.

## Why did my fermentation stop early?

It probably didn't. Everything is probably all right. If you are really worried, see "Stuck fermentation" in chapter 14.

## Why does my siphon keep stopping?

See "Siphon keeps stopping" in chapter 14.

## Why is my beer overcarbonated?

The most common causes for overcarbonation are bottling too early and wild yeast infections. You really need to wait till the fermentation is over before bottling. If you suspect an infection see "Review Sanitation Procedures" in the Troubleshooting chapter. Also see "Overcarbonated" in chapter 14 for a couple more possible causes.

## Why is my beer undercarbonated?

Most likely, you simply need to wait a little longer or you are keeping the bottles too cold. Unless you forgot to add the priming sugar or your bottlecapper is defective, time is usually all you need.

## Why does my beer smell liked cooked corn?

The most common reasons for this is that you either boiled with the cover completely on the kettle or you took too long to cool the wort. See "Cooked corn aroma" in chapter 14.

## Why does my beer smell like medicine?

Medicine-like, clove-like and plastic-like aromas are most commonly caused by a wild yeast infection (although some yeasts, like Bavarian Weizen yeasts, are chosen for this quality). See "Clovey aroma" in chapter 14.

## Why does my beer smell nutty/sherry-like?

Sherry-like aromas are the result of Hot-Side Aeration (HSA) which is quite simply the aeration of the wort while it is hot. The cooler the temperature, the less oxidation that takes place. Note that there is a difference between oxygenation and oxidation. Oxygenation is the dissolving of oxygen in a liquid. Oxidation is a chemical reaction between oxygen (or other electron donors) and another compound. Cooling the wort to below about 80° F (27° C) before aeration minimizes the amount of oxidation to a level that is not noticeable in the finished beer. Oxygen in the finished beer can also sometimes give sherry-like aromas, but HSA is the most common cause.

## Why does my beer smell like a skunk?

When hopped wort or beer are exposed to light, chemical reactions take place in certain hop compounds (isohumulones) forming chemicals called mercaptans. Mercaptans are the actual compounds that give skunks their aroma. The energy of the light effects the rate of the reaction, sunlight taking as little as five minutes through clear glass, fluorescent light taking a few hours and incandescent light taking quite a bit longer. The color of the glass does reduce the rate of the reaction, dark brown glass being the best at protecting the beer. Green and clear glass provide virtually no protection. There is a large American brewery that uses clear glass for their bottles, but their beer does not get skunky. Why? Because they use specially modified hop extracts that are not sensitive to light. "Lightstruck" is another name for "skunky."

## Why does by beer smell like wet cardboard?

This is due to oxidation of finished beer. To avoid this, don't let the finished beer sit in a plastic fermenter too long, minimize splashing during bottling and try to fill the bottles within an inch of the top. See "Cardboard aroma" in chapter 14 for more details.

## Why is my beer too dark?

Usually, only pale styles of beer such as Pilsner or Witbier are criticized for being too dark. Undoubtedly you have already used only pale malt extract but your beer is still too dark. What's the problem? Well, there are several other factors that you need to consider. Firstly, the wort will darken during the boil. You can reduce this darkening by doing a full boil (all 5 gallons in the kettle) instead of a partial boil (a $1^{1}/_{2}$ - or $2^{1}/_{2}$-gallon boil added to 4 or $3^{1}/_{2}$ gallons of cold water). See chapter 5 for more details on doing a full boil. Secondly, oxidation increases color. Especially in pale beers, it is important to avoid aerating hot wort and to minimize the aeration during racking and bottling. Also, remember that not all extracts are created equal. Some labeled "Pale," "Gold" or "Light" are much darker than others. Those labeled "Extra Light" tend to be some of the palest. Finally, as malt extract syrup ages it darkens. Dried malt extracts are more immune to this darkening, so they keep better.

## Why does my beer have a burnt flavor?

The most likely source of a burnt flavor is scorching the malt. Always remove the kettle from the heat before adding the extract and make sure it is well dissolved before restarting the heat. One wheat extract that I've used has a strong burnt flavor. The first time I used it, I blamed my technique. The second time, I realized that it was the malt - it smells burnt right from the can. This extract does make an interesting Rauchweizen however...

## Why is my beer sour?

Sourness is due to acids. For beginners (since you are not adjusting your water with salts or acids or adding dark grains) acidity is most likely from bacterial sources. See "Review Sanitation Procedures" in chapter 14.

## Why is my beer not sweet enough?

The usual reason that a beer is too dry is a bacterial or wild yeast infection. Most cultured yeasts will not eat all the sugars in the wort, leaving a slight sweetness. *Lactobacillus* and *Pediococcus* bacteria, *Saccharomyces diastaticus* and yeasts of the *Brettanomyces* genus, for example, can ferment sugars that most brewing yeasts cannot. The resulting beer is much too dry, usually overcarbonated and often tastes too bitter. See "Review Sanitation Procedures" in chapter 14.

One other source for the beer coming out too dry is the use of amylase enzyme (sometimes labeled "special Pilsner enzyme"). Adding amylase enzymes at fermentation time can cause too much of the unfermentable sugars and dextrins to be broken down into fermentable ones and leaving the beer too dry. I recommend against the use of enzymes in the fermenter.

## Why does my beer have a yeasty flavor?

Most commonly, the cause for a yeasty flavor is that you stirred-up the yeast from the bottom of the bottle while pouring or you did not let the bottles sit long enough for the yeast to settle. Some yeasts (particularly those dry yeasts simply labeled "Beer Yeast") take a very long time to settle. If the beer has already carbonated you can refrigerate it to help speed the settling of the yeast.

## Why does my beer taste thin?

When a beer comes out too thin, especially if it is also overcarbonated, bacterial or wild yeast infections are usually to blame. See "Review Sanitation Procedures" in chapter 14. The use of refined sugars such as cane, corn, or candi sugars reduces body. Replacing refined sugars with dried malt extract will increase the body. Finally, it can be that the kit you used didn't contain enough malt extract. To get a beer of a similar strength to American Microbrewed or Imported beers, you will need to use at least 6 pounds of malt extract syrup or 5 pounds of dried malt extract for a 5-gallon batch. If you used only one 3.3-pound can of extract syrup in a 5-gallon batch, the resulting beer will taste watery.

# 4

# EQUIPMENT

This chapter will describe virtually all homebrewing equipment commonly in use today. Because this book is primarily on beginning and intermediate brewing procedures, I will not discuss advanced equipment (that which can only be used for all-grain brewing) in great detail. However, since you may encounter advanced equipment in your further reading, it's a good idea that you know a little about it. Much of the equipment described in this chapter is optional, so I urge you to read about the benefits of each item and decide whether or not to add it to your arsenal.

## MEASUREMENT, CALCULATION, RECORD KEEPING AND STORAGE

### Thermometers

A thermometer, although left out of many beginners' equipment kits, is quite important. Yeast are living creatures and don't like sudden temperature changes any more than we humans do. I always use a thermometer to check the temperature of the water into which I'm rehydrating dry yeast (it should be between 90 and 110° F (32 and 43° C)). Also, I always check the temperature of the wort before I pitch the yeast so the

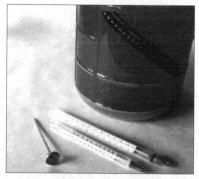

**Figure 4-1:** *Various types of thermometers used in homebrewing.*

temperature difference is no more than 5 or 10° F (3 or 6° C). A floating thermometer may not be as accurate as a lab thermometer, but if you accidentally drop it into your wort, you'll either be happy you bought a floating one or wish you had. Dial thermometers are notorious for being inaccurate, but several Chicago Beer Society members have brewed some very tasty beer with them. If you do get one that can be calibrated, do so often. Calibrate your thermometers against fever thermometers – make up some 99° F (37° C) water and check all your thermometers against the fever thermometer. Digital thermometers are fast and precise, but expensive and they don't float (always have spare batteries on hand).

There is one other type of thermometer that is for a completely different use. It is a liquid crystal strip with an adhesive on the back. I have attached these on several of my fermenters and they really are accurate on glass and stainless steel. They tend to show a degree or two cooler than the wort on plastic fermenters. Yeast give off heat during fermentation and the wort can be as much as 10° F (5° C) warmer than the room so these liquid crystal thermometers do serve a practical purpose. Note that when you read a homebrewer's recipe and the fermentation temperature is given as 68° F (20° C), chances are that this was the air temperature surrounding the fermenter. On the other hand, when a commercial brewer tells you they ferment at a particular temperature, most likely this is actually the temperature of the fermenting beer. Since the temperature of the fermenting wort can be quite a bit warmer than the room temperature, this can be a significant difference. If you do get one of these liquid crystal thermometers, I recommend that you still record the air temperature in your brewing log in addition to what the thermometer is displaying.

## Hydrometers

A hydrometer (also called a saccharometer) is an instrument for measuring the specific gravity (how heavy something is relative to water) of wort, beer, sugar solutions, whatever. It is a glass or plastic tube that has a scale inside. You float the hydrometer in the wort or beer and read the level of the hydrometer off the scale. The heavier the liquid, the higher the hydrometer floats. The importance of the specific gravity (also known as "gravity" or "SG") is that it is a very good measure of how much fermentable and unfermentable solids are dissolved in the

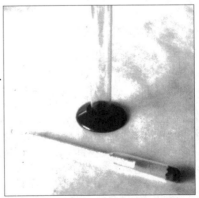

**Figure 4-2:** *Hydrometer and test jar.*

solution. The gravity of the wort just before you add the yeast is called the "original gravity" or "OG" and the gravity of the beer after fermentation is complete is called the "final gravity" or "FG." The difference between the OG and FG allows you to calculate, quite closely, the approximate alcohol level of the finished beer. Simply multiply the difference between the OG and FG by 105 to get the alcohol by weight (ABW):

$$\% \ ABW = (OG - FG) \times 105$$
$$= (1.055 - 1.013) \times 105$$
$$= 0.042 \times 105$$
$$= 4.41$$

Multiply 1.25 times the percent alcohol by weight to get percent alcohol by volume (ABV):

$$4.41 \ \% \ ABW = 4.41 \times 1.25 = 5.51 \ \% \ ABV$$

A hydrometer is not mandatory for extract brewers but it is a good idea to record the OG and FG in your brewing log, if for no other reason than to help you decide what subcategory to enter the beer in at a homebrew competition. When you start doing all-grain brewing, a hydrometer lets you know how efficient your procedures are and helps you predict the original gravity on subsequent batches. Since there can be quite a bit of variation between brands of malt and brewing systems, you need to know the OG so you know if you just made a Bitter or a Barleywine and can hop accordingly. A hydrometer can also help determine if your fermentation is complete – whether you have reached your intended FG or if the yeast still needs more time. Sometimes, the yeast are having difficulty with the fermentation (alcohol level too high or perhaps not enough nutrients). By knowing the specific gravity and comparing it to the expected final gravity, you can tell if the fermentation is "stuck" (see "Attenuation" in Chapter 10).

Some hydrometers have multiple scales. Virtually all beer hydrometers have the specific gravity scale. Another scale commonly found on hydrometers is the Balling or Plato scale which is the density of the solution as if it was a percentage of weight as sucrose. 12° Plato (usually written as 12 P) is the density of 100 pounds of sucrose/water solution of which 12 pounds are sucrose. The third common scale is the potential alcohol scale. Not commonly used commercially, it makes it easy to determine the alcohol content by volume by simply taking a reading before and after fermentation. If, for example, the wort read 10% before fermentation and 4% after, the approximate alcohol would be 10 - 4 = 6, or 6% alcohol by volume (ABV).

Reading a hydrometer can be tricky. Due to surface tension, the wort has a tendency to "climb" up the hydrometer. When you look closely, you will see that the point at which the wort contacts the hydrometer is quite a bit higher than the surrounding wort. What you want to do is ignore the wort that is "climbing" the hydrometer and read the level of the hydrometer in the *surrounding* wort. Perhaps a drawing will make this easier to understand:

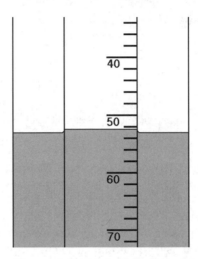

**Figure 4-3**: *This hydrometer reads 1.053.*

Make sure that you have mixed the wort well before taking a sample. This is especially true if you have just poured thick wort into a fermenter partially filled with water. The heavy wort will tend to sink to the bottom and only partly mix with the water. A sample taken from the unmixed wort can be off by more than 50%! Also, it is important to note that the gravity will read higher than it should if the wort is cloudy from suspended proteins – use only the clear part of the wort for specific gravity measurements. If a cloudy sample is all that is available, make sure you save 50% more than you need to take the measurement, so that when the proteins settle (in an hour or so), you will have enough clear wort in which to measure the specific gravity.

Another factor that must be considered is that the thickness of the wort and, therefore, the gravity changes with temperature. At higher temperatures, the gravity will read lower than it really is and at lower temperatures it will read higher than it really is. "Higher or lower than *what?*" you may ask. Each hydrometer has been built and calibrated for use at a particular temperature. Currently, among hydrometers intended for homebrewing use, this is usually 60° F (15.5° C), but my first hydrometer was calibrated for use at 70° F and recently, hydrometers calibrated to 68° F (20° C) are becoming more and more common. Also, the compensation is not quite linear with gravity, so that you need to consider the range of gravity that you are measuring. Since most hydrometers are calibrated to either 60° F or 68° F, I'll provide tables from which you can read the compensation. The curves from which these compensation factors are derived are actually smooth (averages of my own experimental data), but the fact that only three digits to the right of the decimal point are being displayed is why there appear to be several discontinuities.

Note that you should not plunk a room-temperature hydrometer into boiling wort – it will shatter. Even though I provide temperatures well above 100° F, you should at least heat the hydrometer under hot tapwater so the shock is not so great. To use the following tables, measure the temperature of the wort or beer. Next, quickly measure the specific gravity. Now pick the table that corresponds to the calibration of your hydrometer and the "Approximate Wort or Beer Gravity" column that is closest to the specific gravity measured. Follow the row of the temperature that you measured over to the column you picked and read the compensation. The left side is the specific gravity adjustment and the right side is the Plato degree adjustment. Simply add the adjustment that you read in the table from the gravity measurement you read off the hydrometer. For example if you have a hydrometer calibrated at 60° F and read 1.068 at 90° F, you would add 0.004 to 1.068 and your temperature-corrected specific gravity is 1.072.

**Table 4-1: Temperature Adjustments for a Hydrometer that is calibrated at 60° F (15.5° C).**

| Temp. | Temp. | Approximate Wort or Beer Gravity | | | | | |
|---|---|---|---|---|---|---|---|
| | | 1.040 | | 1.070 | | 1.100 | |
| 40° F | 4.4° C | -0.002 | -0.50 P | -0.002 | -0.50 P | -0.002 | -0.50 P |
| 50° F | 10.0° C | -0.001 | -0.25 P | -0.001 | -0.25 P | -0.001 | -0.25 P |
| 60° F | 15.5° C | 0.000 | 0.00 P | 0.000 | 0.00 P | 0.000 | 0.00 P |
| 70° F | 21.1° C | +0.001 | +0.25 P | +0.001 | +0.25 P | +0.001 | +0.25 P |
| 80° F | 26.7° C | +0.002 | +0.50 P | +0.003 | +0.75 P | +0.003 | +0.75 P |
| 90° F | 32.2° C | +0.004 | +1.00 P | +0.004 | +1.00 P | +0.005 | +1.25 P |
| 100° F | 37.8° C | +0.005 | +1.25 P | +0.006 | +1.50 P | +0.007 | +1.75 P |
| 110° F | 43.3° C | +0.007 | +1.75 P | +0.008 | +2.00 P | +0.009 | +2.25 P |
| 120° F | 48.9° C | +0.008 | +2.00 P | +0.011 | +2.75 P | +0.011 | +2.75 P |
| 130° F | 54.4° C | +0.010 | +2.50 P | +0.013 | +3.25 P | +0.014 | +3.50 P |
| 140° F | 60.0° C | +0.013 | +3.25 P | +0.016 | +4.00 P | +0.016 | +4.00 P |
| 150° F | 65.6° C | +0.015 | +3.75 P | +0.019 | +4.75 P | +0.019 | +4.75 P |
| 160° F | 71.1° C | +0.017 | +4.25 P | +0.022 | +5.50 P | +0.022 | +5.50 P |
| 170° F | 76.7° C | +0.020 | +5.00 P | +0.025 | +6.25 P | +0.026 | +6.50 P |

**Table 4-2: Temperature Adjustments for a Hydrometer that is calibrated at 68° F (20° C)**

| Temp. | Temp. | Approximate Wort or Beer Gravity | | | | | |
|-------|-------|--------|--------|--------|--------|--------|--------|
| | | 1.040 | | 1.070 | | 1.100 | |
| 40° F | 4.4° C | -0.002 | -0.50 P | -0.003 | -0.75 P | -0.003 | -0.75 P |
| 50° F | 10.0° C | -0.002 | -0.50 P | -0.002 | -0.50 P | -0.002 | -0.50 P |
| 60° F | 15.5° C | -0.001 | -0.25 P | -0.001 | -0.25 P | -0.001 | -0.25 P |
| 68° F | 20° C | 0.000 | 0.00 P | 0.000 | 0.00 P | 0.000 | 0.00 P |
| 80° F | 26.7° C | +0.001 | +0.25 P | +0.001 | +0.25 P | +0.001 | +0.25 P |
| 90° F | 32.2° C | +0.002 | +0.50 P | +0.003 | +0.75 P | +0.003 | +0.75 P |
| 100° F | 37.8° C | +0.004 | +1.00 P | +0.004 | +1.00 P | +0.005 | +1.25 P |
| 110° F | 43.3° C | +0.005 | +1.25 P | +0.006 | +1.50 P | +0.007 | +1.75 P |
| 120° F | 48.9° C | +0.007 | +1.75 P | +0.008 | +2.00 P | +0.009 | +2.25 P |
| 130° F | 54.4° C | +0.008 | +2.00 P | +0.011 | +2.75 P | +0.011 | +2.75 P |
| 140° F | 60.0° C | +0.010 | +2.50 P | +0.013 | +3.25 P | +0.014 | +3.50 P |
| 150° F | 65.6° C | +0.013 | +3.25 P | +0.016 | +4.00 P | +0.016 | +4.00 P |
| 160° F | 71.1° C | +0.015 | +3.75 P | +0.019 | +4.75 P | +0.019 | +4.75 P |
| 170° F | 76.7° C | +0.017 | +4.25 P | +0.022 | +5.50 P | +0.022 | +5.50 P |

Finally, it's usually recommended that hydrometer samples be discarded after measurement. Sanitation is the concern. Resist the temptation of floating your hydrometer in your fermenter during fermentation. The kräusen will stick the hydrometer and throw-off your readings. Before fermentation, you can resanitize the sample by boiling it for a few minutes and then you can safely add it back to the fermenter. During and after fermentation I recommend against this. You can, however, dilute the sample with water and then compensate for the dilution. For example, if you dilute 50 ml of beer with 150 ml of water and it reads (after temperature correction) 1.008, the actual specific gravity of the 50 ml is 1.032. Your gravity measurement will only be as accurate as your volume measurements, so don't expect high accuracy with a simple kitchen measuring cup.

## Hydrometer Sample Jars

For many years, when I measured the gravity of my beers, I put the sample in the plastic cylinder in which I bought the hydrometer. After knocking over the full cylinder one time too many, I finally bought a hydrometer sample jar. A hydrometer sample jar is a tall, clear plastic cylinder which holds a sample of beer or wort while you take the hydrometer reading.

## Scales

A scale is needed for measuring hops, grain and even brewing salts (while you can use measuring spoons for brewing salts, it is much better to use a scale). Unless you are willing to spend hundreds of dollars for a scale that both has the resolution needed to weigh grams of brewing salts and the capacity to handle 10 pounds of grain, you will have to get several scales. I have three:

- one that weighs up to 10 pounds and has a resolution of $1/4$ ounce (for grain),
- one that weighs up to 1 pound and has a resolution of $1/16$th of an ounce (for hops), and
- one that weighs up to 10 grams and has a resolution of 0.1 grams (for brewing salts).

## Measuring Cups

A low-tech item, but it has its place. Ideally, you would like to weigh every ingredient, but a measuring cup works well enough 90% of the time. When it comes to measuring grain, using a cup will result in a recipe that is not nearly as reproducible as one based upon weight, but it won't make your beer undrinkable. I've often fielded questions from homebrewers asking how many cups of a particular grain are in a pound. The fact is… it depends. It depends on the type of grain, its moisture content and how much you pack it. Therefore, when it comes to reproducing a recipe that says "3 cups DeWolf-Cosyns Caravienne malt," you can get pretty close, but if the recipe says "1 pound of 60L crystal malt," I really can't give you a reasonable conversion to cups.

## Measuring Spoons

Another important low-tech item is the measuring spoon. Ideally, you would like to use a gram scale for water salts, yeast nutrients and other powders, but for the most part, a measuring spoon will get you close enough. One use of measuring spoons that I'd like to discourage is for adding priming sugar to individual bottles. This is neither sanitary nor is it accurate enough for reliable carbonation.

## Graduated Cylinders

For some measurements, kitchen-grade measuring cups are satisfactory – measuring priming sugar, for example. The reason is that a 5% error is not going to make a significant difference in the result. On the other hand, if you are diluting a hydrometer sample, kitchen-grade measuring cups are not good enough. Note also that the markings on laboratory beakers and Erlenmeyer flasks are only approximations. To really measure accurately, you need a graduated cylinder. These can be quite expensive, but you can save a lot of money on items like these at science surplus stores.

## Wine Thieves

A wine thief is a device for taking a sample of wine or beer from the fermenter. It is usually a 12- or 14-inch glass or plastic tube with a narrow opening at each end. You dip it into the fermenter, put your thumb over the end and withdraw the device. When you release your thumb, the sample pours out. A wine thief is a fast way to get a hydrometer sample and is easy to sanitize.

**Figure 4-4:** *Wine thief.*

## pH Meters and Papers

pH meters and papers are primarily used by all-grain brewers to measure the acidity or alkalinity (pH) of the mash, but can be used by extract brewers to measure the pH of steeping grain or wort. Personally, I recommend against getting a pH meter. They are expensive, unless you go professional you will use it infrequently, they can foul easily (especially given all the proteins in wort), should be calibrated before use, need to have their expensive electrodes replaced every few years, and many require special storage conditions. pH papers are not as accurate or precise, but they are accurate and precise enough and are far cheaper. If you get narrow-range pH papers (roughly 5 to 6 pH for brewing), they will be easier to read. The inexpensive pH papers (about $3 to $4 US) tend to be hard to read and inaccurate – the more expensive ones ($10 to $15 US) are more accurate, but make sure to still get narrow-range ones. Unless your pH meter is solid state (ISFET) or has a potassium chloride (KCl) reference electrode, you must *not* dip it into the actual mash or wort (take a sample and discard it after measurement)[1]. Note that pH changes with temperature and if you use a pH meter with ATC (automatic temperature compensation) *at* the steeping, mash, or boiling temperature this is taken into account. However, if you cool your sample to room temperature (as I recommend) and then measure it with pH papers or a meter, you must subtract a few tenths from the value you get to account for the fact that the pH is actually lower in the hot liquid. The amount of pH decrease due to temperature is dependent on the mineral content of the water. It can vary from as little as 0.1 to as much as 0.5 pH[232]. How much you have to subtract depends on your water chemistry, but I recommend that you should subtract 0.3 from the value you measure at room temperature (68° F / 20° C) to get the actual pH at steeping temperature (170° F / 77° C)[1].

## Homebrew Color Guide

Invented by Dennis Davison, the Homebrew Color Guide is very accurate and useful if you want to get the color of your beer just right. It is a translucent, plastic card which you hold up to the light next to an ounce or so of the test beer. You match up the beer with one of the cells and read the color off that cell. It is meant to be used with the standard judging cups whose base is 2 1/8" (5.4 cm) in diameter. Therefore, if you use cups with a larger or smaller diameter, the readings will not be accurate.

## "Hop-Go-Round"

This is an ingenious circular slide-rule invented by Randy Mosher which helps you estimate the amount of hops you need to get a particular bitterness. For my system, the utilization values from the graph on the back are too optimistic, so I use the utilization values that are listed in Chapter 15.

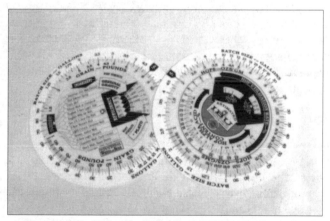

**Figure 4-5**: *"Wheel of Beer" and "Hop-Go-Round"*

## "The Wheel of Beer"

Another circular slide-rule invented by Randy Mosher, "The Wheel of Beer" helps you calculate what the original gravity will be for a particular addition of grain, extract or sugar. It is quite accurate, but you need to know your efficiency, which you can only determine from trial and error. Each extract will have a particular value on the scale also, for which you can use the efficiency value again. For example, when you add one brand of extract you may need to use 90% on the efficiency scale whereas a different brand may require you to use 87%. Note that when you are mashing, you would get slightly better efficiency than when you simply steep specialty grains in water for 30 minutes. Start with 80% efficiency when you are steeping roasted barley, crystal, chocolate and black malts. After a few batches, you will be able to determine the proper efficiency for your system. While this may all sound confusing, when you have one of these in your hands, you'll see the efficiency scale and this will make perfect sense.

## Timers

This can be anything from a wristwatch to a grandfather clock. The main things you will be timing are the boil and the hop additions. I have an alarm watch which allows me to do other things while I'm waiting for the boil or other steps to complete and frees me from having to look at my watch continuously.

## Brewing Logbooks

Keeping good records is extremely important for improving your homebrewed beer. You should keep a logbook and take detailed notes on your recipes and procedures so that you can repeat the good recipes and so that you can learn from both the good and the bad batches. I recently learned that a particular odd flavor I was getting was the result of adding too much flavor hops. I determined this by comparing recipes of beers that had this flavor in common. I use spiral notebooks for taking notes during brewing, but plan to transfer all these recipes onto my computer. I enter a lot of competitions and it would be much easier if I could simply print out a recipe when I need one for a competition.

## Computer

There are a number of software packages available to help with recipe formulation or at least for helping keep a brewing log. Describing and comparing them is beyond the scope of this book, so if you are interested in getting more information on brewing software, see "Scroll Through Brewing Software" by Ray Daniels and Steve Hamburg in the Spring 1994 issue of Zymurgy[2]. One important warning: some homebrewing software packages allow the user to select among a variety of utilization values – one of the three has very low utilization values and therefore can result in beer that is *severely* overhopped. Some later versions of SUDS Version 3.x default to these very low utilization values so I recommend changing to either the Rager or Tinseth values. If the software package allows for inserting your own utilization values, you may want to start with the ones in chapter 15 and then adjust them based upon your actual results.

## Tape Recorder

A number of homebrewers use a small tape recorder for taking "notes" during a brewing session. These are later transcribed into a notebook or computer. An extremely innovative use of technology was posted in Homebrew Digest #1857 (an Electronic "Newsletter" on the Internet - see Further Reading at the end of Chapter 17) by Spencer Thomas, who proposed using the "memo" feature of his digital answering machine as a brewing log. Every entry is timestamped so upon playback, he can transcribe the exact times at which every step in the procedure was performed.

## Food-Grade Buckets

I buy my grain in bulk. It always comes in plastic-lined paper bags. These are not very good for long-term storage especially over the summer when the humidity can get pretty high. Therefore, as soon as I receive an order of grain, I pour it into white, HDPE, food-grade buckets with gasketted lids. Stored like this, the malt will be good for years.

## Protective Masks

If you handle a lot of grain, you will breathe a lot of grain dust. If you have respiratory problems this can aggravate them, so I recommend getting a cheap, $1 protective mask from the hardware store. Sure, it makes you look like Dancing Bear, but it's a good idea to be safe.

## Heat Sealers

You can buy a "food vacuum sealer" for less than $30 and it really comes in handy for resealing half-used bags of hops and grain (plus you can use it to make your own boil-in-bag vegetable medleys). This is far from being an essential piece of equipment, but I wouldn't part with mine now that I've got it.

# GRAIN PREPARATION AND MASHING

## Grain Mills

Grain mills are not essential for extract brewers because the amount of grain used is usually not more than a pound or two. Using a rolling pin (or beer bottle) and a zipper-closure plastic bag doesn't take that long to crush a few pounds. All-grain homebrewers, on the other hand, can often use more than 10 pounds of grain for a 5-gallon batch. Obviously, a mill is needed for such quantities.

Ideally, you would like to peel each grain and crush the rest of the grain into a fine powder[3]. Unfortunately, this is impractical even on a commercial level. Our most reasonable compromise is to break both the husk into three or four pieces and the endosperm (the starchy part of the insides) into five to ten pieces. This strikes a balance between breaking the husk up too much (which results in excessive extraction of compounds called polyphenols (a.k.a. tannins) and silicates which increase haze potential and can cause astringent flavors) and not breaking the endosperm up enough (which results in poor yield from your grain).

It used to be that the only choices a homebrewer had were a rolling pin or a Corona mill. The Corona grain designed for making tortillas not beer and, as a result of its design, to get the insides relatively well crushed, the husk ends up getting shredded. A company called Mercato makes a hand-cranked mill labeled Marga Mulino which can crush malt to a reasonably good size, however, the mill has opposing diagonal knurling which twists each grain as it crushes it, splintering the husk. Jay Hersh has reported in The Homebrew Digest that he has successfully modified his Marga Mulino to work for milling malt. He used a grinder to add cuts into the rollers lengthwise, to pull the grain through without twisting. Kitchenaid makes a grain milling attachment for one of their mixers, but it is made for making bread and not beer – it crushes the grain much too finely for brewing (I've heard that it is possible to modify it to mill the grain more coarsely, which might make the crush satisfactory). Coffee mills that have a spinning steel blade are completely unacceptable for crushing grain. If you are going to buy a grain mill, trust me: buy a roller mill. There are nearly a half dozen roller mills available to homebrewers and they range in price from about $75 to $150.

Finally, I'd like to mention a few points regarding buying pre-crushed grain. Crushed grain attracts moisture immediately and begins to degrade in a relatively short time. If you do buy grain pre-crushed, ask your supplier how long it has been crushed or look to see how long the bags of crushed grain have been sitting around. If they were crushed more than a week ago, unless the bags are airtight, I would recommend passing on that grain.

## Mash Tuns

A mash tun is a vessel used by all-grain or partial-mash brewers to hold the mash while the starches are converted to sugars. Ideally, it is insulated, may have a means for heating via direct or indirect heat and may be combined with a lauter tun into a single unit. I will not go into any more detail because this is not a piece of extract brewing equipment.

## Lauter Tuns

A lauter tun is a vessel used by all-grain or partial-mash brewers to separate the wort from the grain husks and other insoluble parts of the grain. There are many different designs of lauter tuns used by homebrewers, many of them function as both a mash and a lauter tun. Again, this is strictly for brewing from grain and is not a piece of extract brewing equipment.

## Sparging Bags

A sparging bag is really a piece of all-grain equipment. I imagine you could build a hop back from one, however (see "Hop Backs" below). Usually, they are inserted into a bucket which has a spigot mounted at the bottom. Typically, a sparging bag will have a drawstring at the top to help secure it to the top of the bucket. One style of sparging bag has canvas sides and a mesh bottom. This is the type I feel is pretty good. The type I don't recommend is the one that is all mesh, both the sides and the bottom.

# BOILING AND COOLING

## Kettles

A large kettle is probably the first piece of brewing equipment you need to get. For 5-gallon batches (18.9 liter), you might think that you need a 5-gallon kettle. As a matter of fact, you'll see that either a smaller or larger one is much more practical. First of all, your kettle must have room in it for the foam that always rises when you boil. Secondly, when brewing from extract (as long as you compensate for the thickness of the wort), you don't have to boil all 5 gallons. You can boil just 2 gallons (7.6 liters) and then later add water to reach the 5-gallon mark. Therefore, if you are on a budget (and who isn't), a 3-gallon (11.2 liter) kettle is just fine. Two or three gallons of headspace are recommended for full boils (where you boil all 5 gallons) so you would need at least an 8-gallon (31 liter).

Enamel-on-steel, stainless steel, and aluminum are the most common types used by homebrewers. Each one has its advantages and disadvantages. Enamel-on-steel is inexpensive and conducts heat pretty well. However, it chips easily (which eventually results in rust coming into contact with your wort) and these pots' handles are just not made for carrying a full load. If do you get an enameled kettle, be extra careful to not bang it around – dents on the outside cause cracks on the inside which allows wort to contact the steel and rust to form. Stainless steel will not rust (unless you soak it in strong bleach solution or let it get too hot) and the handles on most stainless steel kettles are strong enough to support the weight of a batch of beer. On the down side, stainless steel kettles are expensive and don't conduct heat very well. It is for this reason that the better stainless steel kettles will have copper or aluminum cladding on the bottom – to distribute the heat more evenly. If you are thinking about stainless steel, I recommend you scrape up the extra money for the cladding. Don't scrub the inside of the pot till it shines – the gray oxide layer that protects the steel from rusting also protects the wort from picking up metallic flavors. If you do have to scrub the oxide layer off for some reason, just don't use the pot for a week or two and the oxide layer will re-form.

Many brewing books have said bad things about aluminum kettles. However, an experiment which was written up in Brewing Techniques proved that beer made in an aluminum kettle had no higher aluminum levels than did another batch made in a stainless steel kettle[4]. It is important if you do use aluminum around the brewery to not let it touch chlorine bleach since aluminum is quite reactive. Also, as with stainless steel, since it is the gray oxide layer that protects the wort from the aluminum, you should take care to not scrub this protective layer off of the pot. I've heard brewers report metallic flavors from beer made in aluminum kettles that have been scrubbed till the aluminum shined. I don't know if anodized aluminum is better or worse than plain aluminum.

There are advantages to doing full boils (all 5 gallons together), you may want to brew larger batches some day and most brewers eventually do start brewing all-grain (at which time you will need to boil about 7 or eight gallons), so a 10-gallon kettle should be your next step up from the 3-gallon one. I know some brewers who started with a 10-gallon kettle, right from the start.

Where do I get kettles this size? 3-gallon enamel kettles are available at any housewares store – I've even seen them at the local supermarket for under $20. Flea markets are good places to try. Scrap dealers often will get some stainless kettles or small tanks that could be made into kettles. Restaurant supply stores (especially those that have used equipment) are great sources for big stainless steel kettles at affordable prices. Remember that both aluminum and most stainless steels are not magnetic, so bringing a magnet to the store won't help you determine from which metal they are made. Aluminum is much lighter than Stainless Steel and is much softer (will scratch quite easily with a key).

## Stirring Spoons

A wooden spoon is great for stirring boiling wort, but you certainly don't want to stir chilled wort with it (the wood is a great hiding place for bacteria and wild yeasts). Plastic spoons are better, but not as safe as stainless steel ones. I simply use a wooden spoon for the boil and then put it away as I turn off the boil. If I need to stir during or after cooling, I'll use a sanitized racking cane or bottle filler.

There is another important use for the stirring spoon: as a dipstick for measuring the volume of the wort in the kettle. What I've done is notch my wooden spoon with a pocket knife at 1-gallon marks. You must take into account the fact that water expands upon heating, so to get 1 gallon of cooled wort, you need 1.04 gallons of boiling wort. Since we will typically either be shooting for 1 gallon at the end of the boil (partial boil method) or 5 gallons, minimally, you need only these two marks. Bring a gallon of cold water to a boil and mark the level on the spoon. Start again with 5-gallons of cold water, bring that to a boil and mark the spoon again. If you have a stainless steel spoon, you may want to get a wooden dowel for use as a dipstick. Don't forget that if you change kettles, you will have to re-calibrate your dipstick.

## Garden Hoses

If you brew outdoors, you may be getting your water from a garden hose. Most garden hoses are not made from food-grade plastic and can impart unpleasant flavors/aromas to the water. I recommend that you purchase a garden hose labeled "drinking water safe." This type of hose will be lined with food-grade plastic.

## Grain Bags

A grain bag is used to help you add grains to extract batches. Basically, it is just a mesh bag with a rather loose weave. You pour your crushed grain into it, tie a knot in the top and toss it into the kettle when the water is the right temperature. Don't heat the kettle with the grain bag in there – the heat can scorch or even melt the grain bag. The alternative to using a grain bag is to scoop the grain out with a sieve after steeping (soaking) the grain but this is quite a chore. The grain bag makes it much easier to remove the spent grains from the kettle than a sieve. Some homebrewers pour the hot water/grain mixture through a sieve into another container after steeping. This procedure is nothing but an invitation for Hot-Side Aeration (more about that later) and should be avoided. Although you could probably get away with it, I really don't recommend using a grain bag for mashing grain (note – don't confuse "grain bag" with "sparging bag"). Although it is true that you can put crushed pale ale or pilsner malt into a grain bag and soak it in water and the starches will convert to sugars, the problem occurs when the time comes to separate the wort from the spent grain. In a proper lautering system, the grain bed acts as a filter to strain out tiny particles which, if left in the wort, can cause clarity and other problems in the finished beer.

## Hop Bags

Not to be confused with a hop *back* (see below), a hop bag is used to simplify the removal of hops after boiling. Instead of adding the hops directly into the kettle (which means you will have to use a sieve or strainer to remove them after the boil), I recommend using a hop bag for pellets, plugs, and whole hops. It does reduce hop utilization a little, but we can compensate for that. When the time comes to remove the hops, the hop bag is far easier than using a sieve. I don't like the disposable ones – I prefer to compost the hops and reuse the bag. I have several hop bags and use one for each addition of hops. If I'm adding hops at the beginning, middle and end of the boil, I'll measure out each addition, put them in separate bags and then make sure to add the right bag at the right time in the boil. I don't use hop bags for dryhopping – they are difficult to get into and out of the narrow neck of a carboy. I have heard of some homebrewers using pantyhose for hop bags. I recommend against that: the dyes are somewhat soluble in boiling wort.

## Oven Mitts

Not very high-tech, but a good idea when working around boiling wort. Incidentally, the steam coming out of the kettle takes but a second or two to give you a first degree burn so be very careful when removing the lid from a boiling kettle.

## Stoves

Gas stoves are preferred over electric ones, simply because they have more heat output, but for several years all I had was an electric stove and I still brewed some very good beer. The main problems with the electric stove were the long time it took for the water or wort to come to a boil and the fact that I had to keep the lid partly on the kettle just to maintain a rolling boil. If I removed the lid completely, too much heat was lost and the rolling boil was reduced to a simmer, which is insufficient. One hour boils at full heat with a very large kettle can really take a toll on the heating elements and it certainly can shorten their life. An alternative, depending on the model of your stove, may be to buy what is known as a "canning element" which is heavier-duty, stands off from the top of the stove (so it doesn't overheat the enamel), and will hold up longer.

An alternative to a stove is to get a plastic electric boiler such as the BruHeat™ which will allow you to set up your home brewery someplace other than the kitchen. These come in 110 and 220 volt versions. The 220 volt version is recommended if you have a 220 volt outlet available (the type used for electric stoves, dryers, or older air conditioners) because it will be much faster and will maintain a rolling boil much easier.

## Portable Cookers

When you begin to do full boils or if you decide you want to make 10- or 15-gallon batches, you might find that your stovetop burner just doesn't produce enough heat. One alternative is to buy a portable cookers;. These usually start at about 35,000 BTUs and some can crank out even 200,000 BTUs. The typical stovetop, natural gas burner is about 10,000 BTUs, so you can see that you can get to a rolling boil quite fast with one of these monsters. When choosing a cooker, two important factors should be considered: jet configuration and air intake adjustability. There are two main types of jet configurations: 1) single-jet burners (sometimes called "rocket engines") and 2) multi-jet burners. If the cooker allows you to adjust the air intake, you can get a clean-burning flame at all gas pressures. If the air intake is preset, it will be optimized for a particular gas pressure and you can get lots of soot on your kettle if you use too much or too little gas. The least expensive cookers are single-jet, fixed air intake ones. The most expensive ones have multiple jets and adjustable air intakes, but I think they are worth the extra cost.

Most of the portable burners available are set up for propane. They can be converted to natural gas, but if you don't know what you are doing, get someone who knows to help you. Heating contractors are a good source of information on these types of conversions. If you are mechanically inclined, you have two more options open to you regarding burners: water heaters and wok burners. When a water heater winds up in the trash, 9 times out of 10 the problem is a water leak – the burner is still in perfect shape. I know a lot of homebrewers who have built themselves a stand and mounted a recycled water heater burner under it. Most water heaters are set up for natural gas, but again, many can be converted. Don't try to run a burner that is jetted for one gas with the other. It will run inefficiently, can produce lots of soot and an excessive amount of dangerous carbon monoxide.

Wok burners are great high-BTU heat sources and usually run on less-expensive natural gas. One Chicago Beer Society member got his at a store in Chicago's Chinatown. Usually, these burners simply come as a big cast-iron ring with a dozen or so brass gas jets. I would imagine that propane jets would be available as replacements. Of all the homebrew-sized burners I've seen, these wok burners are the most impressive.

Before we leave the topic of cookers, I have three safety tips. First, the heat generated by these burners is quite intense and they can easily melt or burn the surface on which they are standing. Therefore, cement or bricks are the surface of choice. I strongly recommend that you not use the cooker on a wooden, vinyl tile or roofing paper surface. If you must, lay down a layer of bricks or a steel garbage can lid to reflect the heat. Secondly, make sure you have adequate ventilation. This probably means brewing indoors is out of the question unless you build yourself some additional forced-air ventilation like a restaurant stove hood). These burners generate not only a lot of carbon monoxide (which will kill you at high enough concentrations) but they use lots of oxygen so you need a fresh air supply or you can suffocate. Finally, for safety's sake, don't store your propane tank in the house.

## Hop Backs

A hop back is basically a large strainer for removing whole hops (most designs will not work with pelletized hops) and hot break (coagulated protein, formed during the boil) from the boiled wort. Some commercial breweries even put additional whole hops into the hop back for adding hop aroma during the straining process. Home-built hop backs can be made from two food grade buckets, one inside the other, with a spigot on the outer one and several hundred tiny holes drilled into the bottom of the inside one. I've heard of one homebrewer that has made a stainless steel hop back from an old soda syrup keg. Since the wort is still hot at this time, you must be careful to not splash the wort going into, or coming out of the hop back. Using hop bags eliminates part of the need for a hop back but it can still help remove hot break – you will have to put some whole hops in it to act as a filter bed.

## Whirlpools

A whirlpool is a tank into which hot wort is pumped to remove pelletized hops and hot break before sending the wort to the chiller. The wort enters the tank tangentially so that it starts to spin around. The hops and hot break pile up in the center of the tank and the wort is then drawn off to be cooled. Now, this may sound like a recipe for Hot-Side Aeration. You're right – in fact, this is a big problem for many brewers. Although this is primarily a piece of equipment used by professional brewers, I know that Jim Busch has built one into his homebrewing system. If you are using an immersion chiller to cool your wort (see Wort Chillers below), a very simple adaptation of this concept is to give your cooled wort a swirl with a sanitized spoon and then either siphon from the edge of the kettle or drain the kettle through a spigot.

## Sieves

I use a sieve for only two reasons: removing hot break from the wort during the boil and for a method of brewing from grain called a decoction mash. Virtually all other uses of sieves are invitations for Hot-Side Aeration or sanitation problems. There is a sieve-like device on the market called the SureScreen™. It is a cylindrical, stainless steel tube which slips over a racking cane, copper tube or keg dip tube and keeps things like fruit or hops from being

**Figure 4-6**: *The SureScreen™ (foreground) and a SureScreen™ on the end of a copper racking cane.*

sucked up the tube. I've used one for a very difficult batch of Flanders Brown Ale with peaches – there's no way I could have siphoned that without the SureScreen. SureScreens can be also used for siphoning (hot or cooled) wort from the kettle, screening out whole hops and/or break.

## Water softeners and filters

If you have an ion-exchange water softener (the type into which you have to load a block of salt or salt crystals), you should bypass it for your brewing water. Hard water is rough on pipes and water heaters and makes it difficult to get soap to lather, but all it means is that your water is high in calcium. For brewing, high-calcium water is usually a blessing (see chapter 9). Ion-exchange water softeners simply replace calcium with sodium. Besides the fact that you probably don't want all that extra sodium in your diet, sodium can give your beer off-flavors and even be harmful to the yeast.

The other type of water softener is called a "reverse osmosis" or "RO" system. This type of system makes virtually mineral-free water so it gives you a lot of flexibility when it comes to matching water to beer styles (see chapter 9). There are three disadvantages to RO systems, however. They are expensive, they use many gallons of supply water to make one gallon of RO water, and the water they produce is very corrosive, so you must use plastic pipe for delivering the water.

If your water is pretty decent and all you want to do is get rid of chlorine, you can get an activated carbon water filter. These are available as filters you build-into your kitchen/brewery or self-contained pitchers, like the Brita system.

## Coolships

A coolship is a very shallow, open-topped tank into which hot wort is pumped for cooling. The risk of infection is extremely high with this kind of cooling method so all but a handful of commercial brewers have abandoned it. Unless you are

very daring and are trying to make traditional Lambic/Lambik, I strongly urge you to use some other method of chilling the wort.

**Figure 4-7**: A "beer's-eye" view of the coolship at Cantillon Brewery.

## Wort chillers

A wort chiller is a device for cooling the boiling wort to the proper temperature for adding yeast. If you do a partial boil you can get away without a wort chiller. If you only boil 1 1/2 gallons of wort down to 1 gallon and then gently add it to 4 gallons of boiled, chilled water, you don't have to chill the wort at all. The resulting mix will be between 80 and 90° F (27 and 32° C). If you boil 2, 3 or more gallons of wort, you will have to chill the wort somehow. While it is possible to chill the wort reasonably well by putting the kettle into a sink full of running tapwater or ice water, the faster you cool the wort, the better. When you do a full boil, you are really much better off, in terms of the quality of the finished beer, using a wort chiller.

There are four main types of chillers that use water as a coolant which you can build or buy. The simplest type is called an immersion chiller and is basically a 20- to 50-foot (6- to 15-meter) coil of copper or stainless steel tubing which you dip into the wort and then run cold tapwater through it. Ed Hitchcock has come up with an interesting twist on the immersion chiller design. Instead of the standard spool-shaped coil, he has coiled his tubing into a flat coil, like an electric stove element[5]. This flat coil is suspended just below the level of the wort and Ed reports very fast cooling without the need to stir or move the chiller.

The second type is called a counterflow chiller and is usually constructed from a copper tube inside a larger diameter hose (often a garden hose). Hot wort flows through the copper tube and cold water runs through the space between the outside of the copper tube and the inside of the larger diameter hose. The last two designs are variations on the counterflow design. In place of the hose one design uses a 6-inch diameter (approximately) plastic tube, roughly a foot in length. In the other counterflow variant, the hose is replaced by a bucket of ice water.

**Figure 4-8**: *Immersion chiller.*

You can purchase either type of chiller or you can build one from scratch. If you choose to build a counterflow chiller, Listerman Manufacturing Company distributes something called "Philchill Phittings" which is basically a counterflow chiller without any of the tubing or hoses - you supply those yourself and assemble the whole device.

**Figure 4-9**: *Counterflow wort chiller.*

While the hose-type counterflow chiller is the most efficient, I prefer the immersion chiller. I feel that it is easier to keep clean, easier to get the wort to a predictable temperature (even if you overshoot, you can run warm water through it to warm the wort back up again) and you can separate the wort from the cold break (coagulated protein, formed during the cooling of the wort) without an additional transfer of the wort. Personally, I use an immersion chiller made from 35 feet (about 11 meters) of 1/2-inch (13 mm) outside diameter soft copper tubing.

If you brew outdoors, you can use the chiller water on plants, but don't use the first few gallons until they have cooled or you will kill them. I save the first 5 gallons in a bucket and then let the rest water the grass. By the time I've used those 5 gallons for cleaning up equipment, they have cooled down to a reasonable temperature. If you brew indoors, near the laundry room, you may want to fill your washing machine with the chiller water.

There are many other inventive ways that homebrewers have devised to cool wort. One very inexpensive one is to freeze several 2-liter bottles of water (leave a little headspace for expansion). When you are ready to chill your wort, you clean the outsides of the bottles and dunk them into the hot wort. The boiling wort will sanitize the outsides of the bottles. This method is not as fast as the immersion or counterflow wort chillers and scratches in the plastic can harbor bacteria.

## Floatation Tanks

A floatation tank is used by some commercial breweries to aerate their cooled wort and to remove some of the hot and cold break  They are basically a tank with one or more aeration stones (diffusers) in the bottom.  As the air or oxygen rises up through the cooled wort, it causes some of the break to float.  The wort is then drained out of the tank leaving much of the break behind.

# FERMENTATION

## Fermenters

The most popular fermenter among beginners is the plastic pail.  Low cost and lots of headspace are two plusses, but they do get scratched up eventually and these scratches can harbor bacteria, molds and wild yeasts.  Another problem with plastic fermenters in general is that some can have poorly-fitting lids which allow air into the fermenter.  This is not a problem if you don't leave the beer sitting in the fermenter for more than two weeks or so, but if your schedule is erratic and you are unsure if you will be able to bottle when the batch is ready, a glass carboy might be a better choice.  Not all plastic pails are created equal either.  Make sure your fermenter is made from food grade plastic, most commonly high-density polyethylene (HDPE).  I've read about homebrewers making beer in garbage cans made from non-food grade plastic which resulted in beer that smelled like plastic.

Glass carboys are not without problems.  Besides the obvious (they break when you drop them), they also can break if you expose them to sudden temperature changes and rarely do they have enough headspace to handle all the kräusen (foam) that most beers will generate.  Unless you either leave at least 2 gallons of headspace or use a blowoff hose (see below), you will have foam coming out of your airlock and maybe worse (clogged airlock!).  I have read about one homebrewer who traced an infection problem to a hairline crack in a glass carboy, so inspect your carboys regularly.  Standard water cooler carboys are 5 gallons (18.9 liters) but you can also get 3-, 6-, 6 1/2- and 7-gallon carboys (11.4, 22.7, 24.6, and 26.5 liters). Some lucky homebrewers have even found stainless steel tanks that serve as fermenters.  Soda syrup kegs are a risky choice for fermenters for two reasons: 1) if you seal the lid and try to blow off the kräusen through the fittings (even if you remove the connectors) the small openings can clog with coagulated protein and hop resins and 2) they are so much taller than they are wide that some yeast strains perform very poorly in them.

On the subject of carboy safety, Jim Hodge posted a very good suggestion on the Internet.  When carboys break, they don't shatter into millions of little pieces like tempered glass does. It breaks into large, sharp shards. Jim's suggestion is to wrap electrical tape around the carboy, several inches apart. If the carboy breaks, the tape will keep all the pieces together.

## Blowoff hoses

When beer ferments, it inevitably produces some foam, called kräusen. Either your fermenter must have enough headspace to hold the kräusen or you need to provide a path for it to exit the fermenter safely while maintaining the airlock and sanitary conditions. A blowoff hose or tube is a large diameter hose, one end of which you attach securely to the top of the fermenter and the other end of which goes into a smaller bucket into which you have poured some water. Some brewers insist on putting sanitizing solution into the blowoff bucket, but plain water (boiled and cooled if you prefer) is a far better idea. When the wort is cooling, the air in the headspace of the fermenter is cooling. As it cools it contracts and, if the headspace is big enough, can suck liquid from your blowoff bucket into the fermenter. I would much rather have water sucked into my fermenter than bleach or iodophor which is why I recommend plain water in the blowoff bucket.

**Figure 4-10**: *Blowoff setup.*

There are homebrewing books that recommend that you use your siphon hose for blowoff. There are two reasons that I insist you avoid this practice. First, it's very hard to clean the inside of the blowoff tube and you will be forced to siphon your delicious beer through that gunked-up tube. Secondly, siphon hoses are typically 5/16-inch (8 mm) inside diameter. This is far too small and can easily clog. Take it from me – I've made this mistake personally… twice. When my 5/16-inch tube clogged, I got some 1/2-inch (12.7 mm) inside diameter hose to use just for blowoff. This worked fine until I tried making a raspberry/cherry ale. The pulp clogged the blowoff tube, the pressure built up and eventually the rubber stopper blew out of the fermenter. That was four ago and I'm still finding bits of pink fruit pulp in the basement. After that incident, I purchased several three-foot lengths of 1 1/4-inch (31.75 mm) outside diameter vinyl hose and just stick that right into the neck of the carboys – no stopper required.

## Airlocks and stoppers

An airlock allows $CO_2$ to escape from the fermenter while preventing air (which contains oxygen) from entering the fermenter. Glass airlocks are the best, but they are fragile and expensive, so I have several of them and reserve them for starters where sanitation is most important. While I put a blowoff tube on all my fermenters for the first few days, I switch to an airlock when the threat of blowoff is over. Stoppers are available in many different sizes. Make sure to use a white (cream-colored, really) gum rubber stopper or a silicone stopper, not one made from a smelly rubber which can give your beer an off aroma.

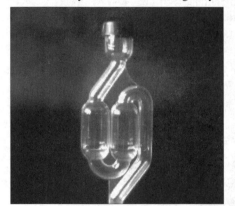 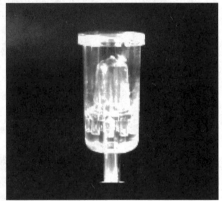

**Figure 4-11**: *Properly filled airlocks.*

For years I've been using the three-piece style of airlock. Lately, I've noticed that this type of airlock tends to dry out faster than the s-shaped style. The s-shaped type of airlock also has the advantage of running both forwards ($CO_2$ coming out of the fermenter) and backwards (headspace in the fermenter contracting, drawing air into the fermenter) with much less risk of "suckback" (the airlock liquid being sucked into the fermenter). With either style of airlock, suckback is a problem if you overfill. It's just that with the s-shaped type, there is a larger range of proper fill levels.

There is some debate as to what is the proper liquid to put into the airlock. In the event that the pressure in the fermenter drops (for example, as the wort cools or if the temperature of the room drops) and the airlock is overfilled, the liquid in the airlock can be sucked back into the fermenter. Some homebrewers use bleach solution, others use iodophor, alcohol or even salt water. I prefer to use plain water. The only disadvantage to using water is that if you leave it in the light, you can grow a colony of algae in the airlock (which is not a serious problem from the beer's perspective). Contrary to popular belief, gases bubbled through sanitizing solutions are not sanitized, so the sanitizer doesn't help in that respect. If you must use something other than plain water, use cheap vodka.

## Carboy handles

Carboy handles really help you lift carboys more safely, but you must be sure that they fit well. The orange plastic-coated carboy handles I have fit my 3-, 5- and 6-gallon carboys perfectly. They do not fit 6 $1/2$ and 7 gallon carboys. I've read in many places that you should not lift full carboys by the handle (that you should lift them from the bottom) but I have yet to have a mishap, even with full carboys. Liquid Bread makes a carboy dolly which is much safer and easier than carrying around full carboys by the handle. 5- and 6-gallon carboys fit into plastic milk crates which will allow you to lift the carboy more safely (from the bottom) with handles.

## Funnels

If you use a carboy, unless you siphon the chilled wort into it, you will have to use a funnel. First of all, it has to be big enough. A kettle full of wort is pretty heavy and you need a wide mouth on the funnel or only a fraction of the wort will make it into the fermenter. I have used two different types of large funnels and neither is ideal. I prefer the "Anti-splash" funnel which gives you the option of two different brass mesh screens (fine and coarse). The screens are useful in some cases, but I usually just leave both of them out. Please note that you *must* chill the wort before you pour it through a funnel. Aeration of hot wort (such as pouring through a funnel into a carboy or splashing of any kind) will give your beer off-aromas and flavors.

## Aeration/oxygenation systems

A typical aeration system consists of an aquarium pump, some plastic tubing, an optional submicron filter (for filtering out bacteria, wild yeasts and molds) and an optional airstone or diffuser (which creates many tiny bubbles instead of fewer large ones). An oxygenation system replaces the aquarium pump with a tank of oxygen. These types of systems are not absolutely necessary, but the higher the original gravity of the wort (i.e. the higher the expected alcohol level) the more important it is to use one. Yeast use oxygen to build strong cell membranes and with insufficient initial oxygen levels in the wort, the yeast will have low alcohol tolerance. Basically, if there is not enough dissolved oxygen for the yeast, they will poop-out from the alcohol they made while there is still some sugar left. Not only does this mean that the beer will be too sweet, but that it will not naturally carbonate. Simply shaking a partially filled carboy or the action of pouring through a funnel should be enough aeration for worts below about 1.050 (12.5 P) or so. Above this gravity, an aeration or oxygenation system becomes increasingly important. Another simple aeration device is a metal or plastic tube, with a few extra holes drilled in it, which attaches to the end of your racking setup. As you siphon the beer through this "aeration tube," the passing cooled wort sucks air in through the holes and aerates the wort. While this may be better than nothing, it is not a very good method for adding oxygen to wort. See "Aeration vs. Oxygenation" in chapter 6 for more on the various aeration and oxygenation methods.

**Figure 4-12**: *Oxygenation system (left) and aeration system (aquarium pump, in-line submicron filter, tubing, and diffuser).*

How do you sanitize an airstone? I recommend against using chlorine bleach because it is difficult to get all the sanitizer out of the stone. I've used iodophor, but unless you make sure that the stone is permeated with the sanitizer, there may be places that bacteria or wild yeasts can hide. I've heard that some of the cheap airstones from pet stores (used for aquariums) will actually dissolve in alcohol. I recommend that you get a stainless steel airstone which you can safely boil for 10 minutes to sanitize it. I have replaced the vinyl tubing on mine with silicone tubing (available from supply companies such as McMaster-Carr and US Plastics) which I can boil along with the stone.

If you wish to filter out bacteria, wild yeasts and molds you need to use a submicron filter available from many homebrew suppliers. Several articles have been published in homebrewing magazines in which the authors presented a system which they claimed would sanitize the air used for aeration. They consist of a flask or jar into which alcohol, hydrogen peroxide or some other sanitizer had been added. The air from an aquarium pump is bubbled through the liquid and then travels out of the flask or jar via tubing to the wort. This kind of setup *does not* sanitize the air! Since only the walls of the bubbles are in contact with the sanitizer, the wild yeasts, bacteria and molds simply ride up inside a bubble safely out of harm's way. When the bubble pops, it releases its airborne cargo into the headspace of the flask or jar after which it travels through the tubes to the wort.

## Carboy brushes

A carboy brush is virtually essential for cleaning out carboys. It is L-shaped so you can clean the bottom and the "ceiling" of the carboy – where all the gums and resins from the blowoff stick. I remember wrestling with a bent-up bottle brush, trying to scrape off that crud. When I finally got the carboy brush, I kicked myself for not getting one sooner.

## Pyrex® measuring cups

Any heat-proof container will work, but I prefer glass and since it will be holding boiling water, that means that it needs to be Pyrex or another heat-resistant glass. Besides the obvious, my primary use for the Pyrex measuring cup is for rehydrating dried yeast.

## Erlenmeyer flasks

Erlenmeyers are those triangular glass laboratory flasks and are perfect for making starters. I put a gum rubber stopper and an empty glass airlock in mine and boil the starter wort right in the flask. The escaping steam sanitizes the airlock and then the airlock fills up with condensing steam[6]. Recently, for extra security, I've started to put a sterile cotton ball into the top of the glass airlock. This is so that as the starter cools and sucks air into the flask, some of the dust/bacteria/mold/yeast get filtered out by the cotton ball. I've had no problems putting the flask on my gas stove, but I've read that you need a trivet (a metal spacer) if you plan to use an electric stove. Although they are made from borosilicate glass (e.g. Pyrex®, Kimax), it's still a good idea to not go straight from the flame to an ice bath – I put the flask into a big bowl of hot tapwater and then slowly add ice. Finally, these flasks are prone to boilover – don't fill them more than half-way.

**Figure 4-13**: *Erlenmeyer flask, stopper and glass airlock.*

## *Temperature control*

If you are planning to make a lager, but you are not blessed with a cellar that is a steady 50° F (10° C) all winter long, you will need a refrigerator. Bohemian Pilsners should be aged (lagered) close to 33° F (1° C). Again, unless you are blessed with an area of your house or garage where the temperature is that cold and relatively stable, you will need a refrigerator. Similarly, if you live in a warm climate, you many need a refrigerator simply to keep your ales below 75° F (24° C) in the summer.

Rarely will the standard thermostat of a typical home refrigerator allow you to set it any higher than about 50° F, so for ale temperatures you will need a replacement thermostat. If you are electrically inclined, you can replace the internal thermostat with a wider-range one. Alternatively, many homebrew supply stores sell external replacement thermostats which are easy to use: simply plug the thermostat into the wall outlet, plug the refrigerator into the thermostat outlet and place thermostat sensor inside the refrigerator.

Dennis Davison (Beer Barons of Milwaukee and Chicago Beer Society) has built a temperature control box out of plywood and a window air conditioner. It has four compartments connected by baffles, each at a different, predictable temperature (50, 55, 60, and 65° F or 10, 13, 16, and 21° C)[7].

If you live in a relatively dry climate and you only need about 5 or 10° F (3 or 6° C) of cooling, you can use evaporative cooling. Place the fermenter into a large pan or bucket, slip an old T-shirt over it and dip the bottom of the shirt into a few inches of water. The evaporating water will cool the fermenter. You should watch carefully for molds and replace the water if they begin to grow.

Not all temperature control is cooling. In colder climates, cellars can be far too cold for many ale yeasts. I know of only one commercially available device specifically sold for heating fermenters. It is called the "Brew Belt" but I have not used it personally so I cannot comment on its effectiveness. I've read the accounts of many inventive homebrewers who have built their own heated fermentation boxes. Usually, they use a light bulb for a heat source (careful to protect the beer from direct light somehow) and often use an old refrigerator for the insulated enclosure. If you do choose to build some kind of heating system yourself, be careful and consider all potential fire hazards.

## Inverted-carboy fermenters

There are some other pieces of brewing equipment that you may be considering. One that comes to mind is one of those setups that allows you to flip a glass carboy over and ferment "upside down." The originator of this kind of device, Kinney Baughman, is a good friend of mine and says that literally thousands of batches of beer have been brewed using the Brewcap™ with no problems. On some designs, the tube that allows $CO_2$ to escape is very small in diameter and I'm afraid that it will clog during fermentation and lead to big problems if the batch begins to blow-off. Do not use a system like this with dryhops or fruit.

## Wooden casks

Wooden casks (barrels) for fermentation or dispensing are being used by some homebrewers. The important thing to consider is the type of wood from which the cask is made and whether or not the cask is lined. If it is lined, it really doesn't matter what type of wood it is - also, you don't have any of the benefits or drawbacks of wood (i.e. you might as well be fermenting in glass). If it is unlined, the type of wood is extremely important. Charred casks are used in making whiskey and I've tasted some very delicious stouts brewed in used whiskey casks. Casks made from American oak are going to impart an incredible amount of oaky flavors the first several times you use them. You can try to remove some of these flavors by filling the cask with baking soda solution and letting it soak several times. Casks used by British and Belgian brewers are made from European or Russian oak which imparts very little if any oaky character or Chestnut which is reported to impart no woody character at all. India Pale Ale recipes that call for oak chips for "authenticity" are not very authentic. The only currently produced (Ballentine's IPA used to taste very oaky) commercial beers that I know of that have a significant oak flavor and aroma are Rodenbach Grand Cru and Petrus Oak Aged Dark Beer. Rodenbach Grand Cru is aged for nearly two years in huge unlined oak tuns on which a fine layer of wood is scraped off the inside to expose fresh wood every two batches or so. Even so, the oakiness of Rodenbach is less than what you would get from even a few weeks in a new American oak cask.

I've tried to reduce the oakiness imparted by a new American oak cask by filling it with water, soaking for a few weeks and then draining. I repeated this procedure four or five times till the aroma of the water coming out of the cask was virtually oak-free. Beer extracts far more oakiness than water, however, and a subsequent beer that I put into that cask was excessively oaky after only 2 weeks.

In a conversation with a vintner on the use of oak casks, he said that they taste the wine periodically to determine if it has taken on enough oak character. For new casks, it can be a short as a few weeks, whereas for older casks, the wine can age in the oak for up to a year[8].

Sanitation of wooden casks is a nightmare unless you are trying to make something resembling one of the Belgian sour ales, in which case you invite infections. Since the wood is porous, bacteria, wild yeasts and molds can hide in the pores and make it virtually impossible to sanitize the cask completely.

Some commercial breweries still use wooden casks for dispensing ("beer from the wood"), but due to the high cost of maintenance and the aforementioned sanitation worries, few breweries are willing to put up with the hassles.

## Scissors

When brewing, there's often a lot of packages that need opening: yeast, hops, grains. Scissors help make sure that you don't rip the bag in half and spill 5 pounds of grain on the floor.

## Butane lighters

A disposable butane lighter is a handy way to flame sanitize glass and metal items. I have a refillable butane pipe lighter which I use to flame the tops of bottles and flasks before I pour yeast out of them. I also use it to flame my scissors before I use them to cut open yeast packages.

## Microwave ovens

Microwave ovens are good for getting a cup or two of water boiling (but frankly, my stove is faster than my microwave when it comes to this) but they are not good for sanitizing dry surfaces. There have been rumors going around in the homebrewing community that microwaves kill bacteria and wild yeast, but in fact both yeast and bacteria are so small that it's virtually impossible to hit every one. Boiling some wort in the microwave will sanitize it, but make sure there is plenty of room for foam or it will coat the inside of your oven with sticky, brown goo.

# BOTTLING, KEGGING AND DISPENSING

## Siphon hoses, hose clamps and racking canes

Initially, I hadn't included a racking cane in the basic equipment list but added it later because when I tried to assemble the most basic brewing steps, I found myself recommending the racking cane every other sentence. It really makes siphoning easier, especially if you must homebrew solo. The hose and hose clamp are essential equipment. Some homebrewing setups utilize spigots mounted in the bottom of buckets and there is even a glass carboy available which allows you to avoid siphoning. I have never used one of these "siphonless fermenters" and they might make things easier, but remember that you still have to deal with the trub (dead/dormant yeast and coagulated protein – it's pronounced TROOB) at the bottom of the fermenter. Make sure that the tubing you use is food-grade: most commonly Tygon®, silicone, beer line (such as Foxx SuperFlex™) or labeled "FDA-approved." Polyethylene (milky white) tubing is food-grade, but is very stiff and hard to use, but is acceptable from a flavor perspective. Don't use the regular vinyl tubing you get at the hardware store – it will make your beer taste like plastic!

## Priming (a.k.a. bottling) "buckets"

In the old days, the way you carbonated your homebrew was by bottling before the beer was done fermenting. This was very risky since you can never be quite sure how much more the beer was going to ferment and you could bottle yourself two cases of gushers. A big improvement in technique was the introduction of priming. Not too long ago, the way homebrewers primed their beer was to add $1/4$-teaspoon of corn sugar to each bottle. This is not as risky as the old days, but you can introduce bacteria or wild yeast by adding the unsanitized sugar to the bottles. Also, the carbonation can vary from bottle-to-bottle.

The most reliable and safe method of carbonation (outside of force-carbonation with either a kegging system or a device called a Carbonater™) is bulk priming. This is where you take a measured amount of priming sugar, boil it in a cup of water and mix it with the entire batch of beer in the priming (a.k.a. bottling) bucket. Some have spigots at the bottom so you don't have to siphon the beer, but I've had some difficulty with these in the past, so I stick to using a carboy for priming. As with fermenters, if the bucket is scratched, it can harbor microbes that can spoil your beer. If you have a kegging system, you can prime the beer in a keg and then use $CO_2$ to push the uncarbonated, primed beer into the bottles.

## Ceiling clips

Ideally, you would like to brew
with a friend. Very often, you
will need an extra hand or two,
especially when bottling. In the
event that you must brew alone, it
really helps to have some safe
place to put sanitized items
temporarily. What I've done is
that I've twisted a couple of
screw-eyes into the basement
ceiling over my bottling area. To
these, I've attached binder clips
which I use to hold sanitized
hoses, racking canes and funnels.
Mounting these over the sink is

**Figure 4-14**: *"Ceiling clip."*

usually a good idea since what you hang up there is often dripping either sanitizer
or beer.

## Bottle brushes

Ideally, you would like to rinse used bottles immediately after pouring, but
sometimes they do sit unrinsed for a couple of weeks. Also, used bottles from
recycling centers are usually pretty dirty inside. When the time comes to clean
out these bottles, a bottle brush really comes in handy. Note that they are
available in beer bottle and wine bottle lengths. There are two main types that
I've seen, ones with a straight tuft at the end and ones without the straight tuft at
the end. I feel that the ones with the tuft do a better job scrubbing out the bottom,
but only rarely have I seen them in homebrew supply stores.

## Bottle fillers

A bottle filler is a long, straight tube with a valve that eases bottle filling.
Generally, the valve opens when you push the filler tube down against the bottom
of the bottle. While there may be more designs, I've seen three: the orange,
spring-loaded valve filler, the green gravity-close filler and the Listerman Phil's
Philler.

**Figure 4-15**: *Various types of bottle fillers.*

## Cappers

Basically, there are three types of cappers: 1) hammer cappers, 2) double-lever cappers and 3) bench cappers. Hammer cappers are, well... to be avoided. They work by holding a bottlecap on top of a bottle while you bash down on it with a hammer. Not very safe. Double-lever cappers are less expensive than bench cappers and modern ones are quite reliable. Bench cappers are the very best available – they are fast, reliable, easiest to use, not that much more expensive and work on virtually all bottles from tiny 6-ounce bottles to sparkling wine bottles (note that most European sparkling wine bottles take larger diameter caps than a standard beer bottle cap and thus don't work with standard bottle cappers). Among bench cappers, some are easy to adjust for different height bottles and others are not easy. I feel that this should be an important consideration when selecting a capper – it makes it much easier than grouping all your similarly sized bottles before starting a bottling session.

**Figure 4-16**: *Various types of bottle cappers.*

## Bottle rinsers

A bottle rinser is what I call a device that squirts liquid into bottles. I suppose you could use it to squirt water, but it is most useful for sanitizing bottles. As far as I know, there is only one manufacturer of such a device and they call it a Viniator. All you need to do to sanitize clean bottles is pour a quart (about a liter) of your favorite sanitizer into the bowl, slip a bottle over the nozzle and push down on the bottle. Each push pumps a squirt of sanitizer into the bottle. I usually use between 15 and 25 pumps per bottle. The one I have mounts securely on top of my bottle tree.

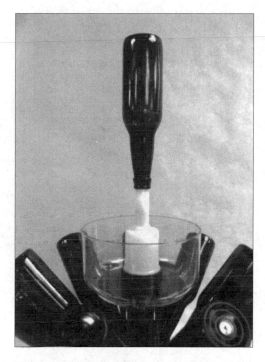

**Figure 4-17**: *The "Viniator" bottle rinser.*

## Bottle washers

Not to be confused with what I call a bottle rinser, a bottle washer screws onto a sink faucet and squirts a strong stream of water into a bottle when you push a bottle down on the device. These devices are great for rinsing sanitizer out of bottles and it does it so quickly and conveniently that you regret not having gotten one sooner.

## Bottle trees

Bottle trees are plastic stands for holding your bottles in preparation for bottling. When I finally got one, I was overjoyed. My standard procedure is to sanitize 50 bottles, placing each on the tree (still dripping with sanitizer). Once all 50 are done, I rinse a bottle with water, fill it with primed beer, cap it, repeat. Since I've gotten the bottle tree, bottle rinser, Jet bottle washer and bench capper, I can bottle a 5-gallon (18.9-liter) batch in about two hours, by myself!

**Figure 4-18**: *Bottle tree.*

## Corkers

Actually, a winemaking tool, but since there are some commercial beers that come in corked bottles, you might want to cork some homebrew bottles. I have a two-handled corker which I used with regular straight corks. #9 x 1 3/4" corks work for 75cl Chimay bottles. Just don't push the cork in all the way - I left about 3/8-inch of cork sticking out of the bottle, put on a metal cap (I have collected many of these from Chimay, Tres Monts, Affligem and Champagne bottles) and then twisted-on a new wire bale I got from the homebrew supply store. I sanitized the corks (and made them easier to insert) by soaking them in some boiling water. I took two

**Figure 4-19**: *A bottle of homebrewed Abbey Ale in a corked bottle, a wire bale, metal cap, cork, and corker.*

large plastic cups (you could use two plastic bowls too) put the boiling water and corks in one and used the other one to weigh-down the corks.

## Kegging systems

Most homebrewers hate bottling. I happen to be in the minority. If you hate bottling, kegging may be a viable option. A kegging system consists of a keg (Cornelius and Firestone soda syrup canisters are popular and are available in 3-, 5- and 10-gallon sizes), a $CO_2$ tank with a regulator, a hose with a gas-in connector to go from the regulator and the keg, a hose with a liquid-out connector to go from the keg to the faucet and the faucet (usually what's called a Cobra faucet). Not only does kegging eliminate the need to bottle (unless you want to enter a competition, although there is a keg-only competition every year organized by the Blotarian Brewing League) but it also allows you to force-carbonate your beer. If you do need several bottles for a competition, you can use a counterpressure bottle filler. Kegging systems will be covered in detail in volume II of this series.

**Figure 4-20**: A "Cornelius keg" kegging system (note that this $CO_2$ tank is set up to run up to four kegs and currently has a spray nozzle attached to purge air from bags of hops - most systems are not this complicated).

## Counterpressure bottle fillers

Counterpressure bottle fillers are devices that allow you to bottle carbonated beer. They are called counterpressure fillers because they allow you to first pressurize the bottle with $CO_2$ and then let the beer flow into the pressurized bottle, thereby reducing foaming, oxidation and carbonation loss. You must have a kegging system to use one of these devices. If you are going to get one, my one piece of advice is to get one that has good valves. Don't even consider one that has those cheap needle valves. Counterpressure bottle fillers will be covered in detail in volume II of this series.

## Beer engines

Also known as a handpump, a beer engine is one of the two traditional ways of dispensing English Real Ale (the other being by gravity, straight from a cask). It is quite amazing how different a beer tastes when dispensed with a beer engine or gravity. Handpumped and gravity-dispensed beer is smoother – the bitterness (which can be very high in an English Bitter) is so much more rounded and softer than when the same beer is dispensed under $CO_2$ pressure. Traditionally, real ales were drawn from wooden casks and are still used by some breweries such as the Tadcaster Brewery (Samuel Smith's), but most breweries now use stainless steel casks. The system I have in my basement consists of a twin-pump beer engine mounted on my bar counter and uses 5-gallon soda syrup canisters.

**Figure 4-21**: *A dual beer engine set up to use Cornelius kegs.*

## Filters

There are a number of types of filters that have been advertised in magazines and sold in stores. I'm not going to go into detail on filters here because each different kind has special requirements for operation. If you do get one, hopefully it will have come with instructions or the person who sold it to you will explain how to use it. One important note is that only filtration with very small pore sizes leads to losses in bitterness[9]. This must be considered when formulating the recipe.

## Further Reading

Broderick, H. M., ed., *The Practical Brewer* (Master Brewers Association of America, Madison, Wisconsin, 1977).

Daniels, R. and S. Hamburg, "Scroll Through Brewing Software," *Zymurgy,* 17 (1) 46-50 (Spring 1994).

DeClerck, J., *A Textbook of Brewing*, Vol. 1 (Chapman and Hall, London, 1957).

deLange, A. J., "How to Gain Maximum Control over Wort Chilling Operations," Brewing Techniques, 4 (4) 42-53 (July/Aug 1996).

deLange, A. J., "pH Meters and Automatic Temperature Compensation," *Brewing Techniques,* 3 (3) 9-12 (May/June 1995).

Donaghue, J., " Testing Your Metal - Is Aluminum Hazardous to Your Beer?," *Brewing Techniques*, 3 (1) 62-65 (Jan/Feb 1995).

Hitchcock, E., "Planispiral Wort Chiller," *Brewing Techniques*, 2 (3) 9 (May/Jun 1994).

Hough, J. S., D. E. Briggs, R. Stevens, and T.W. Young, *Malting and Brewing Science,* Vol. 1 and 2 (Chapman and Hall, London, 1982).

Hough, J. S., *The Biotechnology of Malting and Brewing*, (Cambridge University Press, Cambridge, 1985).

McConnell, D. S. and K. D. Schramm, "Cool Coils: Immersion Chiller Road Test," *Zymurgy,* 19 (3) 54-60 (Fall 1996).

McConnell, D. S. and K. D. Schramm, "From Hot to Cold: A Cool Brew Cruise," *Zymurgy,* 19 (1) 42-49 (Spring 1996).

Van Zyle, P., "Tips and Gadgets: Constant Temperature Bath," *Zymurgy,* 17 (5) 31 (Winter 1994).

*Zymurgy Special Issue 1992* "Gadgets & Equipment" 15 (4), (Special 1992).

# INTERMEDIATE BREWING

To me, a homebrewing beginner is defined as a person who simply brews from hopped extract. Once you begin to add grains and hops to the extract, I feel you are an intermediate. In fact, when you begin to formulate recipes yourself, I would have to say that this is beyond intermediate brewing. The final step is allgrain brewing where you no longer use extracts at all, but many very good brewers still brew a significant percentage of their beers from extract.

Why move on to intermediate brewing? Mostly, for more control over the flavor and aroma of the finished product, for more grain and hop character in the beer and for the satisfaction of being more involved in the brewing process. The manufacturing of extract from wort drives off many grain aromas that can be replaced (in part) by the addition of crystal and dark malts.

## Sanitation

The most important part of making good beer is sanitation. You can add double the hops, half the hops, double the malt extract, half the malt extract, the wrong hops, the wrong extract, the wrong crystal malt, the wrong yeast or ferment at the wrong temperature and 99 times out of 100, you will still make drinkable beer. But, if you don't have good sanitation techniques, you can do everything else right and get sour or odd-smelling beer. Luckily, nothing dangerous can live in beer so it is always safe to drink. One time, I went ahead and drank a whole glass of a pretty foul-smelling beer after a homebrew competition in Kansas City and spent the next day recovering from a pretty bad stomach ache.

First, the equipment you are sanitizing needs to be clean. Actually, you should think of cleaning and sanitizing as separate steps. Don't use soap for cleaning since it will leave a film on the equipment which will later interfere with head retention. I recommend that you use plain old Washing Soda (sodium carbonate) for cleaning, but you can use automatic dishwasher powder (not liquid dishwashing soap). Try to get some that doesn't have perfumes or rinse agents (anti-spotting additives) since they can carry-over into your beer. What you want to make sure is that all dirt, oils and grime are washed off your equipment before sanitizing because they can provide places for bacteria and wild yeasts to hide from the sanitizer.

There are three basic types of sanitizers used by homebrewers: household bleach, iodophor and percarbonate based sanitizers. Whenever I can, I try to use the percarbonate-based sanitizers, such as One-Step[TM], because it is the least insulting to the environment. The chlorine in bleach and the iodine in iodophor are not very good for the environment, so I try to use them as little as possible.

The proper concentration for sanitizing with fresh household bleach is one tablespoon per gallon of cool water. The proper concentration for sanitizing with iodophor depends on the manufacturer, but the brand I currently have in the brewery is $1/2$ ounce per 5 gallons of cool water. A working solution of One-Step is one tablespoon of the powder per gallon of cool water. Another advantage to using iodophor and percarbonate-based sanitizers is that they do not have to be rinsed (although you can if you want to as long as your rinse water is sanitary) if you let most of the sanitizer drip off or out of whatever you are sanitizing. You must rinse when you use chlorine bleach as a sanitizer. If you know that your water is a source of bacteria or wild yeast, you can rinse with boiled and cooled water or cheap commercial beer, which will always be sanitary.

Contact times for the various sanitizers are between 10 and 15 minutes, but I usually stick with 15 minutes, just to be on the safe side. All items must first be clean or caked-on dirt can protect bacteria and wild yeast from being killed by the sanitizing solution.

Contrary to what has been written in countless brewing books, a solution of potassium metabisulfite or sodium metabisulfite (campden tablets) is *not* a sanitizing solution! First of all, for these to be effective at all, they need to be in an acidic solution, like fruit juice (wort does not have a low enough pH). Secondly, while they do kill some of the bacteria and wild yeast, all we can be assured of is that the metabisulfites *inhibit* their growth. They are used by vintners (winemakers) to give their cultured yeast a head start over other microorganisms, but they are really only inhibitors, *not* sanitizers.

Keep track of what's sanitized and what's not. Don't put sanitized items on unsanitized countertops or hanging against an unsanitized wall. I've attached a few large "butterfly" binder clips to the ceiling above my work area and hang sanitized items from them.

There has been some debate as to whether cold water or hot water is better for rinsing. It seems that hot water would be a better sanitizer, no? The argument against hot water is that some bacteria can withstand the temperatures of a hot water heater and that the heater itself can be a breeding ground for bacteria. Since I rinsed brewing items with hot water from the tap for ten years with no infections that were traced to the water, at least for my house, this is not a problem. Some brewers raise the temperature of the hot water heater for brewing day, but this can increase the chance of scalding, especially if you have children in the house.

Many homebrewing books suggest it's okay to start your siphon with your mouth. Nothing could be further from the truth! Your saliva contains many bacteria which can spoil your beer. Some have suggested that you can sanitize your mouth by gargling with whiskey or vodka. While this may be true, the contact time for sanitation with alcohol is 15 minutes. If you were to gargle with a shot of whiskey for 15 minutes, chances are you would forget all about brewing for a while.

# A Partial-Boil Intermediate Batch

A partial-boil intermediate batch is probably the next step for most homebrewers. It doesn't take much more equipment than does a beginning batch and the improvement in the finished beer is quite dramatic. "Partial-boil" refers to the fact that only part of the water is boiled with the extracts. The primary differences between this type of batch and a beginning batch is the addition of hops, crystal and/or dark malts, possibly the addition of fining agents which make the beer clearer (less cloudy) and possibly the use of liquid yeast instead of dry yeast.

## The Recipe

Here's a typical partial-boil intermediate recipe (there are nearly 30 more in chapter 12). Note that it differs from a full-boil intermediate recipe (presented later in this chapter) only in that the hop utilization is less for a partial boil since the wort is much thicker. I've given the hops in terms of ounces and then included the % Alpha Acids of the hops I used followed by the Alpha Acid Units (AAUs). Alpha Acids are the primary bittering compounds in hops. If a package of hops says "4% Alpha Acid" that means that 4 percent of those hops (by weight) are Alpha Acids. The higher the percentage, the more bittering potential the hops have. "Alpha Acid Units" are a value created by the late Dave Line. They are simply the % AA times the ounces. Two ounces of 4.3% Alpha Acid hops are 8.6 AAUs.

AAUs are handy because they make it easier to substitute hops of a different % Alpha Acid (AA). If, for example the hops you buy are 4% AA and the recipe calls for 11 AAUs, divide 11AAU by 4 to get the number of ounces you should use, namely 2.75 ounces. If you don't want to mess with the math, you can simply use whatever %AA Fuggle pellets are at the store (Willamette or Goldings are acceptable substitutes) and the resulting beer may have a slightly different bitterness, but it will still turn out just fine. Neither the %AA nor the AAUs are given for the dryhops since virtually no bitterness is imparted by dryhops.

"Lovibond" is a color scale which is used more by homebrewers than by commercial brewers for beer, but it is still the most common color designation used by American maltsters (European brewers and maltsters use EBC degrees and American brewers use SRM which is close enough to Lovibond for our purposes). In any event, I've specified a range the color of the crystal malt – the higher the number, the darker the grain and, therefore, the darker the beer.

"OG" is the original gravity, "FG" is the final gravity, ABV stands for "Alcohol by Volume" and "estimated IBUs" is an approximation of how bitter the beer will be. "IBU" stands for "International Bittering Unit." For a beer of *average* maltiness, below 20 IBUs is a mild bitterness, 20 – 40 IBUs is an assertive bitterness and above 40 IBUs is strongly bitter. The maltier the beer, the more IBUs you will need to give the same perception of bitterness.

**Easy English Bitter** - *1 1/2 gallon Partial-Boil Version* makes 5 gallons

6 pounds Northwestern Gold malt extract syrup (unhopped)
1/2 pound crystal malt (20 to 40 degrees Lovibond)
2 ounces Fuggle pellets (4.4% AA - 9 AAU) boiled 60 minutes for bittering
3/4 ounce Fuggle pellets (4.4% AA - 3.3AAU) boiled 15 minutes for flavor
1/4 teaspoon Irish Moss (optional)
1 package Nottingham dry yeast OR Wyeast London Ale yeast (#1028)
1 ounce Fuggle or Willamette whole hops for dryhopping
1/2 cup corn sugar (dextrose) for priming
50 bottlecaps

OG: 1.042-1.046 (10.5-11.5P)
FG: 1.011-1.014 (2.8-3.5P)
approximate ABV: 4%
estimated IBUs: 25

If Northwestern extract is not available, you can substitute 6 to 6.6 pounds of any high-quality pale, unhopped malt extract syrup or 5 pounds of high-quality, pale, unhopped dried malt extract (*not* Laaglander, "Dutch," "Hollander," or Northwestern "European" dried malt extracts, since these will result in very sweet beer – good for some recipes, but not this one). If you buy more dry malt extract than you need, store the unused portion in an airtight bag or container to keep it from absorbing moisture and turning into something resembling a large piece of brown glass.

## The Equipment

Intermediate brewing will take a few more pieces of equipment than beginning brewing. There are several ways of handling the grains and hops, but the easiest and (I feel) the best is by the use of mesh grain and hop bags. Alternatively you can use a sieve as some other brewing books suggest, but using a sieve aerates the hot wort and is more difficult than using mesh bags. If must use a sieve, you really should cool the wort before running it through the sieve (note that you will not want the water in the fermenter to be very cold if you force-chill your wort).

For this recipe, you will need one mesh grain bag and two mesh hop bags. Some recipes call for three or even four additions of hops and in those cases you will need a mesh hop bag for each hop addition. Also, if you are making a very, very big (strong) beer and will be using many pounds of grains, you may need to use multiple grain bags (otherwise you may overfill a single mesh grain bag and not get as much goodness out of the grains). I recommend never filling a bag more than half-full.

## The Preparation

If you are using Wyeast liquid yeast, you need to start the package several days in advance of brewing. Inside the gold package there is another, inner pouch. The inner pouch contains food and nutrients for the yeast and the outer package contains the yeast in liquid form. When you want to start the yeast, you pop the inner pouch and knead the package until the food and nutrients are distributed throughout the outer package. A day or two after you pop the inner pouch, the outer package will begin to swell. At the bottom of the package, there is a date code which is the packaging date. 25NOV96 means that the package was filled on November 25th, 1996. Different strains of yeast will take varying amounts of time to fully swell and the older the package, the longer it will take to be ready. To figure out how many days in advance of brewing you should pop the inner pouch, count the number of months since the packaging date and add two (Wyeast Labs recommends adding only one, but I feel that it is better to wait an additional day). Ideally, you should make a starter (see chapter 10), but I've made lots of great batches simply by using a fully puffed package of Wyeast. Note that you *must* use a starter if you plan to use liquid yeast from The Yeast Culture Kit Company, BrewTek, Advanced Brewers Scientific or Head Start Brewing Cultures.

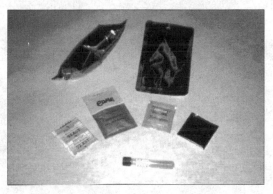

**Figure 5-1**: *Various ways you can buy yeast (note puffed and unpuffed Wyeast packages in the top row).*

Another thing that you need to do in preparation for brewing is boil and chill four gallons of brewing water. This is just like the beginning procedures. Boil up four gallons of brewing water, pour it into your sanitized fermenter, seal up the fermenter, put it into a cool place. You should do this 24 hours before brewing to give the water time to cool to room temperature (around 65° F or 18° C). If you are using a glass carboy for a fermenter, don't pour boiling water into it or it may crack from the temperature shock. Cool the water so it is no hotter than about 60 or 70° F (30 or 38° C) warmer than the glass.

Finally, if you are going to use Irish Moss (a fining agent which helps reduce haze in the finished beer), it's best to rehydrate it in warm water overnight. Measure out 1/4 teaspoon of Irish Moss, put it into a cup of warm water, cover the container (so nothing falls in while it's rehydrating) and put it in a safe place.

## The Water, the Grain and the Hops

On brewing day, measure out 1 1/2 gallons (6 liters) of brewing water put it into your kettle, put the kettle on the stove and fire up the heat. While the water is heating, crush the crystal malts and dark grains (if applicable to your recipe). If you have a grain mill, use it, but if not, you can use a rolling pin and a plastic bag. If you don't have a rolling pin, a beer or wine bottle will work. Measure out the crystal malts and dark grains, put them into the plastic bag about 1/2 pound (1 kg) at a time and crush the grain with the rolling pin. You don't want to pulverize the grains, you just want to crush them enough to allow the water to reach the goodness inside. Breaking each kernel into three to five pieces is enough. Once you have the grain crushed place it into the mesh grain bag and tie a knot in the top to keep the grains in.

**Figure 5-2**: *Crushing crystal malt in a zipper-lock plastic bag with a beer bottle for a rolling pin - just keep rolling till at least 90% of the kernels are cracked in half.*

When the water reaches 170° F (77° C), turn off the heat and place the mesh grain bag into the water. Let the grain steep (soak) in the water for 30 minutes, stirring gently about once every five or ten minutes. I once noticed that some powder was leaking through the mesh grain bag on the way to the kettle and thought that it was pulverized husks (which are bad). So, I shook the bag over the sink until the powder stopped coming out of the bag. Later, after tasting what I had shaken out of the bag, I realized that this was merely very small crystals from the inside of the malt. There was absolutely no benefit to shaking this powder out of the bag and it would have been better to have left it in the bag.

During the steep, you should weigh out your bittering, flavoring, and finishing hops. You won't be using your dryhops at this time, so you don't have to weigh them out until much later. If you don't have a scale, you can get pretty close by simply subdividing a package of hops of a known weight. If you do use this method, make sure you label the package with the remaining weight of hops so you will know next time the weight with which you are starting. Place each addition of hops in its own mesh hop bag and tie a knot in the top (or draw the string closed if there is a drawstring). Make sure you know which hop bag contains each addition of hops (bittering, flavoring, finishing/aroma) so you don't mix them up.

## The Boil

After the 30 minute steep, fish the mesh grain bag out of the kettle with a long spoon, but before you pull it out, twist up the bag around the spoon by rotating the spoon. Press the bag against the side of the kettle as you twist and slowly pull it out of the kettle. Don't raise the bag up too high or the falling drops will aerate the wort. Once you've squeezed most of the wort out of the bag, pull it completely out and set it aside. If you are using a recipe that calls for several pounds of crystal and dark malts you may lose a significant amount of your boil water. If that is the case, add some tapwater to bring the water volume back to 1 $1/2$ gallons.

**Figure 5-3**: *Squeezing steeping water out of the grain bag – try to keep it low to minimize splashing (aeration).*

If you are using dry yeast, boil up a cup of water for rehydrating the yeast and set it aside to cool before you add the yeast. I put a cup of boiling water and my floating thermometer into a Pyrex® measuring cup and cover it with plastic wrap.

Add the extracts (and sugars if the recipe calls for them) and stir them gently into solution. Turn on the heat and stir gently to prevent the wort from scorching. Don't set the heat too high at first or scorching will be inevitable. Watch for boilover – a condition in which the foam head of the boil overflows out of the kettle. This is why you need a kettle considerably larger than the volume of wort you intend to boil. If you see boilover about to occur, there are several things you may try, but you had better try them fast. First of all, you can try stirring faster. If that doesn't work, blowing on the foam can sometimes stop it from rising. If neither of these two methods work, a few ounces of cold water splashed onto the head always works. After about ten minutes into the boil, the proteins that cause the boilover have coagulated into globs and the risk of boilover is considerably lower (but it can still occur, so don't leave the kettle unattended). As the hot break forms, it will create a brown film on the top of the wort which I recommend you skim off, being careful to not aerate the wort. I use a stainless steel sieve, but a slotted spoon can be used.

**Figure 5-4**: *Skimming hot break.*

Once the wort begins to boil, wait ten minutes before adding the bittering hops This gives the hot break (coagulated proteins which could, if left in the beer, cause problems later) a chance to form and reduces the risk of boilover when you add the hops. I have only a few datapoints, but I believe that waiting ten minutes before adding the boiling hops increases the amount of bitterness you get from them (hop utilization rate). I hypothesize that, since the hops help form the hot break, some of the hot break will coat the hops interfering with the extraction of their bitterness.

It is common practice by commercial brewers to add a small amount (less than 10%) of the bittering hops before the boil begins to minimize foaming. If you are not using hop bags, you may want to consider this option. Until you build yourself some kind of hop back, I recommend that you stick to using hop bags.

Once you've added the mesh hop bag containing the bittering hops, start your timer or log the time of day. You will be boiling for 45 minutes until the next addition to the kettle. Adjust the heat so that you get a rolling boil, but not any higher. Higher temperatures will cause more caramelization of sugars and possible scorching of the wort. It will also increase the amount of water that is boiled off. Don't put the lid completely on the kettle, but don't leave it off completely either. Leaving the lid on completely will not allow some unwanted compounds, such as dimethyl sulfide (DMS), to evaporate. Leaving the lid off completely will result in too much water boiling off. I usually keep the lid between 50 and 75% closed. Keeping the lid on will also retain heat and result in a more vigorous boil if you have a low-output stove burner.

If your kettle has volume markings in it, you can sort of see what volume of wort you have. My kettles don't so I've marked my wooden spoon with notches every quart. Note that the wort will contract when it cools. Boiling wort has about 4% more volume than the same wort cooled to room temperature. Also, the hops will displace some volume and retain some wort when you remove them. So, in general, you want 1.2 gallons (4.5 liters) in the kettle just before adding the Irish Moss and flavor hops.

**Figure 5-5**: *Measuring the volume in the kettle with a notched wooden spoon.*

If you find that you have too much wort (i.e. have not boiled-off enough water), you should notice this before you have added the flavor and/or aroma (finishing) hops. It's okay to boil uncovered for 10 or 15 extra minutes *before* you add the flavor and aroma hops. The additional bitterness you get from the bittering hops will not be too great. You *cannot* increase the boil time *after* adding the flavor and/or aroma hops – you will get significantly more bitterness from them and lose most of the flavor/aroma you wanted.

If you find that, with 15 minutes left in the boil, you have only boiled-off $^1/_2$ gallon and were expecting to boil-off a whole gallon in the 1-hour boil, you may be able to increase the evaporation rate by uncovering the kettle, but if your burner is underpowered, you may not be able to maintain a rolling boil. You may be forced to boil 15 minutes longer (i.e. 60 minutes before adding the flavor hops) with the pot partially covered.

After boiling for 45 minutes, add the hop bag containing the flavor hops and pour in the rehydrated Irish Moss if you are using it. If the recipe calls for aroma/finishing hops, you will be adding them with 3 minutes or so left in the boil, so set your timer for 12 minutes. If there are no finishing hops in the recipe, you will be boiling the flavor hops and Irish Moss for 15 minutes, so set your timer for that duration.

If the recipe calls for aroma/finishing hops, add the hop bag containing them with 3 minutes left in the boil. Once the boil is complete, turn off the heat and remove the hop bags in the same way that you removed the mesh grain bag – by twisting the bag around the spoon and squeezing the wort out of the bag against the side of the kettle.

**Figure 5-6**: *Squeezing wort out of the hop bag.*

You may need to add a little water now to bring the volume up to 1 gallon (in the event that more than $^1/_2$ gallon was boiled off). Alternatively, you can wait till you add the hot wort to the cold water, but then remember that any topping-off water needs to be sanitized first by boiling. If you are only adding a few cups, you need not cool the topping-off water because it won't change the temperature of the wort too much, but you should still sanitize it. If you need to add a lot of water, you had better cool the boiled water before adding or the wort may be too hot for the yeast.

If you are using a wooden spoon, put it aside now since wood is porous and is therefore a great place for bacteria and wild yeast to hide. During the boil any wort-spoiling life that does make it out of your spoon and into the wort will be killed by the heat. Now that you've turned off the heat and are about to cool the wort, it's best to put the wooden spoon away to avoid using it accidentally.

## The Chilling and Aeration

The advantage to the partial-boil method is that you can cool the wort to the proper temperature for adding yeast by mixing the hot wort with cold water. If you do a full boil, you will have to force chill the wort somehow (ice bath, wort chiller, etc.). Gently pour the wort (minimizing splashing) into the 4 gallons of boiled, chilled water you prepared earlier. Never pour hot wort directly into an empty glass container unless it is made of borosilicate (Pyrex® or Kimax). Take a sanitized stainless steel or plastic, long-handled spoon, or sanitized bottling tube and stir gently. If the temperature of the wort is above 80° F (27° C) cover the fermenter and let it sit in a cool place until it cools. If the temperature is very high, a cool water bath or a wet tee-shirt draped around the fermenter will speed the cooling. An ice bath can really chill the wort quickly, but if you are using a glass fermenter and the wort is quite hot, the sudden temperature change can crack the glass.

It is important to minimize splashing until the wort is below 80° F (27° C) or so. If you splash the wort when it is hot, you will aerate it and the oxygen will oxidize certain compounds in the wort. Air introduced into the wort while the wort is hot is referred to as Hot-Side Aeration (HSA) and can lead to sherrylike flavors in the finished beer and significantly shorten shelf life. Furthermore, very little oxygen is soluble in hot water or wort so that not only will aerating hot wort cause HSA, but it will not even dissolve the needed oxygen into the wort[14].

Once the temperature of the wort is below 80° F (27° C), you can take a hydrometer sample if you wish and then aerate the wort (dissolve oxygen into the wort). Aeration increases in importance as the original gravity (the amount of dissolved sugars) of the wort increases and is more important when you use liquid yeast than dry yeast. If you are using a carboy or if you can get a reliable seal between your lid and your fermenter you can aerate by rocking the fermenter and sloshing the wort around. Otherwise you can aerate by splashing the wort between two sanitized containers or by whipping air into the wort with a sanitized spoon or bottle filling tube. See "Aeration vs. Oxygenation" in chapter 6 for more on this and other means for adding oxygen to the wort.

## The Yeast

By the time the boil is over, the cup of boiling water has cooled to between 90 and 110° F (32 and 43° C), the ideal temperature range for rehydrating dry yeast. Simply sprinkle the yeast into the water – don't stir. The yeast should be rehydrated for 15 to 30 minutes. You may be tempted to rehydrate the yeast in wort, but this is not recommended. The dry yeast needs to first absorb water and plain water is far better than wort for the yeast due to the pressures on the cells.

If you are using liquid yeast, try to wait until the temperature of the wort and the starter (or yeast package) are the same temperature or at least within 10° F (6° C), then swirl the yeast and pour it into the fermenter. If you used a starter and it has completely fermented out (all the yeast has settled on the bottom of the container, you may choose to pour off most of the spent wort in the starter before swirling up the yeast. See chapter 10 for more on the use of starters.

**Figure 5-7**: *Pitching (adding) yeast.*

Seal up the fermenter, fill the airlock with clean water (see figure 4-11) and affix it onto the fermenter. If you are making a 5 gallon batch and using a 5 gallon glass carboy, you should use a blowoff tube. As the beer ferments, it will create a foam called the kräusen (pronounced KROY-zen and spelled kraeusen if you can't type an umlaut). Unless you leave a gallon or two of headspace (depending on the yeast and the protein content of your wort) the kräusen will foam right out of the top of your fermenter. A blowoff tube is simply a hose that directs this foam into a bucket. The best kind of blowoff tube is one that fits into the neck of the carboy without a stopper (1 1/4 inch outside diameter). There is virtually no chance of this clogging. Place the other end of the blowoff tube into a bucket or wide-mouthed jug of water and put enough water into the bucket to cover the end of the blowoff tube. This creates a water-seal and prevents air, dust and insects from getting to your beer while allowing $CO_2$ and kräusen to exit the fermenter.

Put the fermenter in a dark place (or cover it with a black garbage bag) where the temperature stays a fairly constant 65 to 70° F (18 to 21° C). A little warmer is all right, but cooler than that can slow some yeasts to a crawl.

## *The Fermentation*

If you used fresh dry yeast and if the temperature of the wort was not extremely hot or extremely cold, you should begin to see activity in the airlock or blowoff bucket within about 12 to 24 hours. This is about the same amount of lag time (the time it takes to see fermentation activity) that you would typically experience when using liquid yeast *with a starter*. If you have chosen to use Wyeast in place of dry yeast but have *not* used a starter, you can expect to wait up to three days for fermentation to begin.

**Figure 5-8**: *High kräusen.*

Depending on the yeast strain, the health of the yeast, the level of nutrients in the wort, the amount of oxygen you dissolved into the wort, the original gravity of the wort, the fermentability of the wort (how much of the sugars in it are fermentable and how much are not) and the room temperature, fermentation can be complete in as little as 24 hours or may take as long as several weeks. I isolated a yeast from a bottle of Belgian beer that is incredibly slow – it took three months to ferment a medium-strength beer.

I judge the completion of the fermentation by the activity of the airlock on most batches and by the specific gravity on strong beers. The alcohol in strong beers can slow or even kill the yeast and you may need to add more to finish the job. If you are making a medium-gravity beer, such as the example recipe above, the airlock should be a sufficient indicator. Once the airlock begins to slow the beer should start to clear (the yeast will be settling). Wait until the airlock has slowed to about one bubble every two minutes. By this time, most of the yeast will have settled and the beer will be noticeably darker than it was during fermentation (it will look like chocolate milk during fermentation). In the above recipe, with well-aerated wort and a room temperature of about 65° F (18° C) using rehydrated Nottingham dry yeast, fermentation will take about 3 to 7 days. Note that plastic fermenters often don't have a very good seal between the lid and pail and there may be enough leakage of $CO_2$ that the airlock doesn't have enough pressure to move after the first day of fermentation. You should still wait for at least 7 days to allow fermentation to complete and for the yeast to settle.

Often, especially in summertime when the room temperature is in the low 80's Fahrenheit, many new homebrewers complain that their beer isn't fermenting. Actually, what has happened is that the violent part of the fermentation occurred during the first night that the brewer missed all the airlock activity. A tell-tale indicator that the exciting part of the fermentation has already occurred is a brown ring of gunk stuck to the sides of the fermenter just above the level of the beer. If you see this, you can be sure that the main part of the fermentation is over. Still, you should wait at least 7 days before bottling. Bottling too early can result in overcarbonation (excessive foaming when you open and try to pour the beer) or even exploding bottles in extreme cases. If in doubt, let the beer sit in the fermenter for a few extra days.

**Figure 5-9**: *Here's a close-up of the brown ring formed during fermentation.*

When using plastic fermenters there can be a problem with allowing the beer to sit around too long. Finished beer contains alcohol and oxygen reacts with alcohols to create aldehydes which give beer off aromas and off flavors. Plastic fermenters often have a poor seal on the lid are therefore notorious for allowing oxygen to enter the container and react with the beer. If you know that you will not be able to bottle for a few weeks, I recommend that you use a glass fermenter and make sure that you keep the airlock filled to the right level (the water evaporates with time).

## The Dryhopping

If your recipe calls for dryhops, you should wait until the fermentation is almost complete to add them to the fermenter. There are three reasons for this: sanitation, aromatic scrubbing, and airlock clogging. For many years I was afraid to add dryhops because of sanitation concerns. If you wait until the fermentation is almost over, then sanitation problems are much less likely. The yeast has made alcohol, the pH of the beer has dropped, there is little oxygen, and there is far less sugar for any wild yeasts or bacteria to eat. Experiments were done several years ago regarding this very issue and although some bacteria were found on whole hops, they were killed by the beer during dryhopping. Personally, I have never had an infected beer in which the problem was due to dryhops.

The second reason for waiting until fermentation is almost over is because evolving $CO_2$ will scrub the hop aromatics that we desire right out of the beer.. Waiting until there is little activity will minimize the loss of the hop aromatics. Finally, even if you use a blowoff tube, there is a good chance of the dryhops being pushed up by the kräusen and blocking the blowoff tube or airlock.

**Figure 5-10**: *Adding dryhops to a batch in a carboy (note that both the funnel and the 3/8" OD stiff, polyethylene tubing were sanitized).*

I prefer to use whole hops for dryhopping because they float for weeks, which makes it much easier to separate the finished beer from them. Pellets will float for a few days and then they will begin to sink. You sort of have to wait for them to all sink because it is virtually impossible to siphon the beer out of the fermenter without picking up some of the pellets. Another reason for using whole hops is that the heat that is generated during the pelletizing process causes some of the hop aromatics to evaporate. It is true, however, that dryhopping with pellets seems to produce a stronger hop aroma in the finished beer. This may be because pelletization breaks open the lupulin glands on the hop petals and makes the essential oils more accessible. Still, in view of the increased ease of siphoning and the "higher quality" aroma, I choose to use whole hops or plugs for dryhopping.

Even if you use whole hops, when the time comes to bottle, it is still inevitable that you will get a few hop bits into the priming bucket or carboy, but this should not be of too much concern. Only a small fraction of the hop bits will make it into the priming bucket and then only a fraction of those will make it up the siphon into the bottle filler. Most of what makes it up the siphon will be blocked by the bottle filler valve. If these hop bits are still a concern, consider using a SureScreen™ on the pickup-end of the siphon to screen out virtually all the dryhop bits.

## The Bottling

The procedure for bottling is exactly the same as described in chapter 2. There are a few details, that I omitted for simplicity, which I will cover here.

## Priming

The most common way to prime homebrewed beer is by adding a measured amount of dextrose to the entire volume of beer and then bottling the primed beer. This is called "batch priming." An older technique was to prime each bottle individually with a spoonful of sugar. This is neither sanitary nor is it very accurate and often resulted in unevenly carbonated bottles. I recommend against using this older technique.

In most beginner's instructions it simply says to measure 3/4 cup (175 ml) of dextrose and use that for carbonation in 5 gallons. This is the recommended amount of dextrose for the level of carbonation you would expect in most American lagers. For British-style ales, where a lower level of carbonation is expected, 1/2 cup (120 ml) of dextrose is recommended. Belgian ales and German Wheat beers are more highly carbonated and therefore 7/8 cup (205 ml) of dextrose should be used. American ales and European lagers tend to vary in

carbonation somewhere between English ales and American lagers. I usually use
$^2/_3$ cup (160 ml) of dextrose for the American ales I brew.

In this table, I have also included the volumes and weights for a number of other
possible priming sugars. Note that all the measurements in ounces are by weight
and not fluid ounces.

### Table 5-1: Priming Amounts for a 5-gallon Batch

| Sugar | British Ale | American Ale or European Lager | American Lager | Belgian Ale or German Wheat |
|---|---|---|---|---|
| **dextrose** (corn sugar) | $^1/_2$ cup (120ml) $2^1/_2$ oz (70g) | $^2/_3$ cup (160ml) $3^1/_3$ oz (95g) | $^3/_4$ cup (175ml) $3^3/_4$ oz (105g) | $^7/_8$ cup (205ml) $4^3/_8$ oz (125g) |
| **dried malt extract** | $^2/_3$ cup (160ml) 4 oz (115g) | $^7/_8$ cup (210ml) $5^1/_3$ oz (150g) | 1 cup 9235ml) 6 oz (170g) | $1^1/_8$ cup (275ml) 7 oz (200g) |
| **sucrose** (table sugar) | $^7/_{16}$ cup (115ml) $2^1/_3$ oz (65g) | $^5/_8$ cup (150ml) $3^1/_4$ oz (90g) | $^2/_3$ cup (160ml) $3^1/_2$ oz (110g) | $1^3/_{16}$ cup (195ml) $4^1/_8$ oz (115g) |
| **honey** | $^1/_3$ cup (65ml) $4^1/_8$ oz (120g) | 25 cup (95ml) $5^1/_2$ oz (115g) | $^7/_{16}$ cup (105ml) $6^1/_8$ oz (175g) | $^1/_2$ cup 9120ml) $7^1/_4$ oz (205g) |
| **molasses** | $^2/_3$ cup (160ml) $8^7/_8$ oz (250g) | $^7/_8$ cup (210ml) $11^3/_4$ oz (335g) | 1 cup (235ml) $13^1/_4$ oz (375g) | $1^1/_8$ cup (275ml) $15^1/_2$ oz (440g) |

There are several important notes. Weights are better to use than volumes for the
dry measures because volumes can vary based upon how firmly you pack the
powder. Also, not all dried malt extracts are equally fermentable. The above
values are for dried malt extracts with 75% fermentability (therefore more would
be needed if you used Laaglander, "European," "Hollander," or "Dutch" DME.).
The same is true for different honeys and brands of molasses. Not only is the
fermentability a variable in the honey and molasses, but also the water content, so
that there will be some additional variability in terms of weight, so it is even more
important to remember that these should just be starting points for your own
experimentation with alternative priming sugars. Actually, you can prime
with anything that has sugar in it (Coffee liquor, for example), but you will have
to experiment to determine the proper amount.

One final note regarding priming with dried malt extract versus dextrose.
Several years ago, in an effort to keep my beer "all malt," I switched to priming
with dried malt extract. Shortly thereafter, I noticed what I thought were
infections in my bottles. Rings had formed right at the level of the beer in the
bottles. Through experimentation, I determined that this was not an infection,
but rather protein from the dried malt extract primings. When I switched back to
dextrose, the rings went away. Ever since, I've stayed with dextrose simply
because it is easier. I have not noticed any lack of "fineness" in the carbonation
as reported by some. If you choose to use dried malt extract for priming, boil it

in 16 fluid ounces (approximately 500 ml) of water for at least 15 minutes and then force-chill the priming solution to cause the cold break to form. Leave this cold break behind when you prime the beer. This procedure will reduce the chances that you will get a ring around the collar from the DME primings.

## Fill Level

There are books that say that underfilling results in overcarbonation. While the fill level does affect the carbonation, it is not as great an effect as some have suggested. Experiments I've performed have shown that a high fill level ($1/2$ of an inch or less) takes much longer to carbonate and never quite reaches the carbonation level of a lower fill. A very low fill was found to be equivalent to a low or a "normal" fill (about 1 inch of headspace) in terms of carbonation. If you overprime, a low fill may be overcarbonated while a normal fill may have the carbonation level limited by the smaller headspace. Don't be fooled by the bigger "ffffft" you hear upon opening a bottle with a bigger headspace – the sound is dependent mostly on the headspace and is not an indication of over- or under-carbonation. Finally, if you are concerned that lower fill levels will result in oxidized beer, fear not. Research has shown little correlation between fill levels and air levels[224].

**Figure 5-11**: *One underfilled bottle (l), two properly filled bottles, and one overfilled bottle.*

## *The Conditioning*

Conditioning is the time period during which the beer carbonates, the yeast settles to the bottom and certain other chemical reactions take place (e.g. polyphenol reactions, reabsorption of diacetyl and acetaldehyde, etc.). It will take some time for the yeast to eat the primings and carbonate the beer. How long this will take depends on many things: the yeast strain, the health of the yeast, the alcohol level, the temperature, the amount of oxygen you dissolved during wort aeration and the type of priming sugar you used. High-alcohol beers will take longer to carbonate than regular-strength beers. If the bottles contain ale yeast, but you immediately put the beer into a refrigerator, a cold cellar or even on the cement floor of a warm cellar, it can take months to carbonate. Some ale yeasts don't ferment at all when the temperature gets too cold and your beer may never carbonate. Dried malt extract, honey, and molasses will take longer to carbonate the beer than will dextrose or sucrose.

Depending on the yeast, your procedures and fermentation temperature, the various reactions that take place may improve your beer over the next several weeks. Polyphenols (a.k.a. tannins) extracted from the malt will complex, reducing astringency. The yeast will re-absorb diacetyl and acetaldehyde (two compounds that they created during the fermentation). Diacetyl lends a buttery flavor to the beer and acetaldehyde has a green apple flavor. Higher alcohols tend to give beer a harsh flavor (they sort of "burn" the back of the throat), but will esterify (combine with acids to create esters) with time, in the presence of yeast.

The appropriate aging time for properly-made ales (low in polyphenols and higher alcohols) depends on the original gravity. I usually serve low-gravity ales (less than 1.040 OG) after two weeks in the bottle or keg. For medium-strength ales (1.040 to 1.055 OG), I think that four weeks of aging is about right. For strong ales (1.055 to 1.080 OG), you want to condition at least 6 or 8 weeks. Very strong beers will improve a lot for 9 months and can continue to improve for decades.

Lagers will improve similarly, but this conditioning is above and beyond any lagering time (see chapter 6). After bottling lagers, I will store them at cellar temperature for at least three weeks for the carbonation to form. If I haven't lagered them in the secondary enough, I will slowly chill the bottles to lagering temperatures and store them for a few more weeks. For more on lagers, see chapter 6.

## The Enjoyment

Now that your beer is carbonated and (if you made a lager) properly lagered, you are ready to chill and serve. The proper serving temperature is 50 to 55° F (10 to 13° C) for ales and 45 to 50° F (7 to 10° C) for lagers. Choose a glass that is large enough to hold the entire contents of the bottle and still have some room for the head. Pour the beer in a single movement (don't slosh it back and forth) or you will stir up the yeast on the bottom. With practice, you will be able to pour all but the last 1/2 ounce of beer/yeast. Some yeasts are very powdery and even an expert pourer may have to leave an ounce in the bottle.

# A Full-Boil Intermediate Batch

In this section, I will not repeat all details of the procedures that are common to the partial-boil method, but rather I will simply give the highlights and the differences. A "full-boil" is one where all 5-gallons of wort are boiled at the same time. Before I start describing procedures, let me mention some of the benefits of a full boil. The main physical difference between a partial boil and a full boil is the thickness of the wort. This affects primarily three things: hop utilization, darkening of the wort, and wort loss trapped in the hops.

In a high-gravity (thick) wort, the hop utilization is considerably lower than in a low-gravity (thin) wort. We can easily compensate for the difference in utilization when formulating our own recipe, but it is not always so easy when we are trying to work from someone else's recipe. If the author of the recipe has told us that they only boiled two gallons of wort, then we can either duplicate their procedure and use two gallons of water or we can scale the recipe to whatever boil volume (and therefore gravity) we choose. See "Converting Partial-boil to Full-boil Recipes" in chapter 15.

Besides better hop utilization (which saves you hops and, therefore, money) a lower-gravity boil will also reduce the amount that the wort darkens during the boil. If you are trying to make a really pale beer, you will have to start from grain (the process of making extract darkens it), but you can make relatively pale beers from extract. You just need to use extra light extract and should do a full boil.

After the boil, you will remove the hop bag and drain as much wort from the hops, but some amount will always be trapped. You lose a lot less extract if you have a cup of 1.045 wort trapped in the hops than if you have a cup of 1.120 wort! Incidentally, I've read that you can get a better hot break (better protein coagulation during the boil, which results in less chance of a hazy beer and better shelf life) with a full boil, but I have not noticed a significant difference, in my experience.

## The Recipe

A very common mistake that homebrewers make is to try to use a recipe that has been developed for a partial-boil as a full-boil recipe or vice versa. The problem is mostly with the hop utilization. Let's consider the Easy English Bitter recipe presented earlier in this chapter. Here it is again, but the full boil version:

**Easy English Bitter** - *Full-Boil (6-gallon boil) Version*     makes 5 gallons

6 pounds Northwestern Gold malt extract syrup (unhopped)
$1/2$ pound crystal malt (20 to 40 degrees Lovibond)
$1^1/4$ ounces Fuggle pellets (4.4% AA - 5.5 AAU) boiled 60 minutes for bittering
$1/2$ ounce Fuggle pellets (4.4% AA - 2.2 AAU) boiled 15 minutes for flavor
$1/4$ teaspoon Irish Moss (optional)
1 package Nottingham dry yeast   OR   Wyeast London Ale yeast (#1028)
1 ounce Fuggle or Willamette whole hops for dryhopping
$1/2$ cup corn sugar (dextrose) for priming
50 bottlecaps

OG: 1.042-1.046 (10.5-11.5P)
FG: 1.011-1.014 (2.8-3.5P)
approximate ABV: 4%
estimated IBUs: 25

## The Equipment

The only additional equipment that you must have for a full-boil in addition to the equipment for a partial-boil batch is a larger pot (or, you could use several medium-sized pots, but make sure you split your hops proportionately). The pot should hold at least 7 gallons so you have room for the foam that will rise from the boiling wort. You also will need some way to cool the hot wort after the boil because you will not have the 4 gallons of cold water to help you out. There are many methods for chilling the wort to pitching (yeast addition) temperatures (from cheapest to most expensive): time, a sink full of ice, 2-liter bottles full of ice, an immersion chiller, or a counterflow chiller (see chapter 4 for more details on chillers).

**Figure 5-12**: *Using an immersion chiller to cool the wort.*

Time is a bad choice for cooling.  The obvious reason for the importance of cooling quickly is to get the yeast into the wort before bacteria and wild yeasts have a chance to spoil the wort.  A big, healthy yeast starter will quickly use up the oxygen in the wort, produce alcohol and drop the pH, making what is now called "green beer" less susceptible to damage from wort spoiling bacteria. Bacteria and wild yeasts are unavoidable – there will be some in the wort.  If your cultured yeast outnumber the spoilers a zillion to one, the resulting beer will have no detectable problems.  But, if you give the undesirable microorganisms a head start, then their byproducts can reach flavor thresholds.  However, this is a less-likely source of a problem due to a long cooling period than the production of dimethyl sulfide which gives the beer a "cooked-corn" aroma.

When wort is above 158° F (70° C),  S-methyl methionine (SMM) in the wort rapidly breaks down to dimethyl sulfide (DMS)[10].  As long as the wort is boiling, the SMM that is converted to DMS is boiled off (allowing DMS to evaporate is one of the reasons why it's important to not cover the kettle completely).  When you turn off the heat and the boiling stops, DMS begins to increase in the wort. If you cool quickly, the DMS created will be below the flavor threshold and the finished beer will not have a detectable amount.  However, if the wort spends a long time between boiling and room temperature (where DMS production is virtually nil), then the DMS level becomes excessive.  This is the primary reason that cooling the wort quickly is important.

Another reason for chilling quickly is that it produces a better cold break, which is made of clumped protein-polyphenol complexes that begin to form as the wort drops below 140° F (60° C).  If you don't get a good cold break the protein remaining in the wort can later cause problems for the yeast during fermentation[11] and contribute to haze in the finished beer.

Soaking the kettle in a sink full of ice is a simple, yet effective way to cool hot wort.  It is inexpensive, requires no additional equipment and, if you add more ice as it melts, should not take so long that DMS becomes a problem.  It is not very fast, however, since the only the walls of the kettle are cooling the wort and because if you have a stainless steel kettle, the heat transfer is not very efficient. Nonetheless, it works and is better than simply letting the air cool the wort.

A slightly faster way to cool the wort is to partially fill four or five very clean (labels removed) 2-liter soda bottles with water, freeze the water, clean the outsides of the bottles, and then dunk the bottles into the hot wort.  The boiling wort will sanitize the outsides of the bottles.  This works a little faster because there is more cooling surface area and it can be used along with the "sink full of ice" method. Unfortunately, the plastic is not a good conductor of heat (worse than stainless steel) and as the ice in the bottles melts, the water layer between the bottle and the ice actually insulates the ice from the wort. The more you keep the bottles moving (making sure to maintain good sanitation) the faster the wort will cool. Scratches in the plastic can harbor bacteria, so try to not scratch the bottles. Also, if your kettle does not have enough room for you to put all the bottles in at once, you will have to sanitize the outsides of the bottles before you dunk them in because, for all but the first bottle, the wort will not be hot enough to sanitize the plastic.

Wort chillers, whichever design you choose, are the very best way to cool the wort. They are fast, easy to sanitize and easy to use. Chapter 4 discusses them in more detail, but I'd just like to add that if you are serious about homebrewing, build or buy a wort chiller – you won't regret it.

## The Preparation

In preparation for the full-boil batch, you still need to start the yeast and make a starter if you choose to do so. Also, if you choose to use Irish Moss, ideally you should rehydrate it overnight, but rehydrating an hour is better than not rehydrating at all. You will not need to make the four gallons of boiled/chilled water.

## The Boil

When moving up to full-boil batches, the natural thing to do is to bring 5.5 to 6 gallons (21 to 23 liters) of water to 170° F (77° C) and steep the crystal and dark malts in the entire volume. I made this mistake and brewed quite a few astringent beers until I figured out what I was doing wrong. When you soak a pound of crystal malt in 1 1/2 gallons (6 liters) of reasonably low-carbonate water, the pH stabilizes at around 5.2 to 5.5 (after subtracting 0.35 to compensate for the temperature if you measure at room temperature). If you put that same pound of crystal malt into 6 gallons (23 liters) of water, the pH can be well above 7 and this is far too high for steeping grains. This high a pH will extract lots of polyphenols (a.k.a. tannins) from the grain and result in an astringent beer. The solution is to steep the grain in no more than 1 gallon of water per pound (no more than about 1 liter per 500 g). After the 30 minute steep at 170° F (77° C), remove the grains and add the rest of the water to the kettle. Resist temptation to rinse the grains with the water you add. You may extract a small amount of additional sugar, but you will also extract a lot of polyphenols (a.k.a. tannins) which will give your beer an unpleasant astringency.

You would like to begin with 6 gallons to 61/2 gallons (23 to 25 liters) of wort because you will lose between 1/2 and 1 gallon (2 to 4 liters) of water to steam, a quart or so (around 500 ml) will be lost to the grains and hops, and  you will lose another quart to hot and cold break.  "Hot break" is "cooked" protein, protein-polyphenol complexes, hop resins, insoluble salts, and a good portion of the lipids (fat-like substances) that forms during the boil[12]. "Cold break" is more coagulated protein and protein-polyphenol complexes that clump when the wort is chilled. Much of this break is removed during the making of the extract, but there will still be a small amount.  Oddly, these terms are also used in brewing literature to identify the point of formation of the break, for example, "Wait until after the hot break to add the hops."

**Figure 5-13**: *Hot break.*

Heat the water to a boil, turn off the heat (so you don't scorch the extract), and add the extracts and sugars.  If you are trying to make a pale beer and are using cane or corn sugar, you may want to wait until the last 15 minutes of the boil to add these refined sugars.  All they need is to be sanitized so you might as well leave them out until the end and reduce the amount of caramelization and darkening of the wort that occurs.

Make sure the extracts and sugars are well-dissolved before you fire up the heat again.  Bring the wort to a boil again, watching out for boilover.  Once the wort reaches a boil, let it boil without hops for 10 minutes (skimming hot break as it forms – I use a stainless steel sieve) and then add your bittering hops in a hop bag.  45 minutes later, add the flavor hops (if your recipe calls for them) in another hop bag and the Irish Moss if you have chosen to use it.  If your recipe calls for finishing hops, add them with 3 minutes left in the boil, using a third hop bag.

When the boil is over, remove the hop bags and drain as much wort out of them as practical without aerating the hot wort. It is important to minimize splashing until the wort is below 104° F (40° C)[13], but most homebrewers cool down to at least 80° F (27° C) before aerating. If you splash the wort when it is hot, you will aerate it and the oxygen will oxidize certain compounds in the wort. Air introduced into the wort while the wort is hot is referred to as Hot-Side Aeration (HSA) and can lead to sherrylike flavors in the finished beer and significantly shorten shelf life. Furthermore, more oxygen will dissolve in cooler wort than in warmer wort[14]. Before you cool the wort, you may need to add a little water to bring the volume of the wort to 5.3 gallons (which would be 5 gallons after cooling and removing cold break) if more water boiled off than expected.

## The Chilling and Aeration

The importance of chilling the wort quickly was described in the section about equipment above. Whatever method for chilling you choose, be sure to maintain good sanitation as soon as you start cooling because the wort will soon be susceptible to infection from wild yeast, molds and bacteria. Also, as mentioned before, avoid aeration until the wort is below 104° F (40° C). If you want to take a hydrometer reading, this is the time to do it. After you aerate, there will be a thick head of foam on top of the wort and reading the hydrometer will be impossible. Some books say to always take a sample of the wort and measure the specific gravity of that. I find it much easier to measure the specific gravity by simply putting the sanitized hydrometer into the kettle after I've cooled the wort with my immersion chiller. If you use a counterflow chiller, you will either have to take a sample and force cool it or cool the whole batch and then draw a sample. Don't just dunk the hydrometer into hot wort – chances are pretty good that it will shatter from the temperature shock. Wait at least until the wort is below 150° F (66° C) or so before taking a reading.

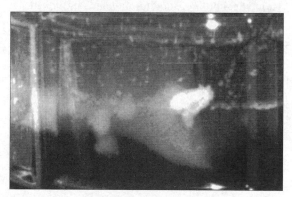

**Figure 5-14**: *This cold break happens to have made it into the fermenter and although this can be avoided, it's not a problem.*

Note that the hotter the wort, the lower the specific gravity. Most hydrometers are designed to be used at either 60° F (15.5° C) or 68° F (20° C), but some are meant to be used at 70° F (21° C). If you want to take a hydrometer reading at a temperature other than the temperature at which the hydrometer was calibrated, see tables 4-1 and 4-2 in chapter 4.

Once the wort has been cooled, it needs to be aerated because yeast need oxygen during the lag phase (more about this in chapter 10). I usually cool to 70° F (21° C) for ales and 50° F (10° C) for lagers. There are many ways to aerate the wort. If you are using a carboy or if you can get a reliable seal between the lid and the fermenter you can aerate by rocking the fermenter and sloshing the wort around. Otherwise you can aerate by pouring the wort between two sanitized containers or by whipping air into the wort with a sanitized spoon or bottle filling tube. See "Aeration vs. Oxygenation" in chapter 6 for more on this and other means for adding oxygen to the wort.

Note that during the summertime, there is a lot more life in the air (molds, wild yeast, bacteria) than during the winter. Sanitation techniques that worked fine during the winter can make infected beer in the summertime. One thing that I found I cannot do in the summertime is rely on room air for aeration. I get a slight phenolic (clove-like) aroma, presumably from wild yeast, in all my beers if I do. This past summer I put a ball valve on the bottom of my kettle (so I could drain it into the fermenter without aerating), started using a filtered-air aeration system (see chapter 4) and it seems to be helping: none of the beers I made during the summer have developed that phenolic aroma.

## The Rest

The rest of the procedures are the same as in a partial boil: adding yeast, fermentation, dryhopping, bottling, conditioning and enjoyment..

# Further Reading

Fix, G., "The Detriments of Hot Side Aeration," *Zymurgy*, 15 (5), 34-40 (Winter 1992).
Foss, G., "The Dirt on Brewery Cleaning: A Review of Procedures and Chemicals," *Brewing Techniques*, 5 (1) 64-74 (Jan/Feb 1997).
Johnson, D., "Applications of Chlorine Dioxide: A Postrinse Sanitizer that Won't Leave a Bad Taste in Your Mouth," *Brewing Techniques*, 5 (1) 76-81 (Jan/Feb 1997).

# OTHER BREWING CONSIDERATIONS

Now that we've covered the basics of extract brewing, there are a few other methods and procedures that are more complicated or improve upon the basics. This chapter will cover some that you may want to consider incorporating into your brewing. Although all of these are optional, if the benefits of the procedure are not self-evident, I will explain the pros and cons so you can decide if it is worth the effort.

## Lagers

From the beer drinker's perspective, there are primarily three differences between ales and lagers:

- ales are fruity whereas lagers are not,
- ales often have noticeable levels of diacetyl (which lends a buttery or butterscotch aroma and flavor) whereas in most lagers this is usually considered a fault, and
- lagers often have a slight DMS aroma (grain-like at low levels, like cooked corn at higher levels) whereas in most ales DMS is unacceptable.

From a brewing perspective there are three differences between ales and lagers: yeast, fermentation temperature, and cold conditioning. Some lager yeasts make really great ales. Few ale yeasts, however, are capable of still fermenting at the low temperatures at which lagers are fermented. Lager yeasts can ferment some sugars that ales yeasts cannot, but the percentage of these larger sugars in typical worts are rather small so that I, personally, would not say that lager yeasts are significantly more attenuative (result in a beer with a lower final gravity) than ale yeasts.

Lagers are fermented colder than ales. Typical lager fermentations are done at 45 to 55° F (7 to 13° C) whereas typical ale fermentations are done at 60 to 70° F (15.5 to 21° C). This colder fermentation means that the yeast produce smaller quantities of esters, the chemical compounds that give fruit their aroma/flavor.

**Figure 6-1**: *Fermenting in a chest freezer which has been fitted with an external thermostat to allow better temperature control (note that the carboy is standing in a bucket just in case there isn't enough headspace and the beer blows-off).*

The word "lagern" means "to store" in German. The fact that lagering (storing at cold temperatures) improved beer flavor was discovered by accident. During this cold conditioning (maturing at cold temperatures), which is typically done between 33 and 45° F (1 and 7° C), proteins combine with polyphenols (a.k.a. tannins) and sink to the bottom of the lagering tanks, the yeast reabsorbs the diacety and acetaldehyde it created during the primary fermentation and numerous other chemical reactions take place. I once made a Traditional German Bock which initially smelled like home perm solution. Miraculously, after four months, the sulfury aroma suddenly disappeared and the Bock took first place at several homebrew competitions.

There are two basic methods for homebrewing lagers. In the first method, a large starter is made and fermented at a cool, but not necessarily cold temperature. As the brewing day approaches, hopefully the starter is at high kräusen and you can begin to cool it down to the temperature at which you plan to ferment the wort, let's say 50° F (10° C). If you cool the starter too quickly, the yeast will be shocked and may take several days to recover. Some books say cool no faster than one degree per day, but most yeasts will tolerate 5° F (3° C) per day. Once the wort is made, it is cooled down to the temperature at which fermentation is to be performed (50° F / 10° C in our example). The yeast is pitched (added to the wort) and the fermenter is kept refrigerated at the fermentation temperature.

The second method for making lagers involves cooling the wort only to about 60 to 65° F (16 to 18° C) and pitching the yeast starter which is also at this temperature. Next, the brewer waits for the yeast to begin showing activity and then slowly cools the green beer down to lager fermentation temperatures. This method has the advantage of being much faster than the first method and reduces the time taken to complete fermentation. There are two important notes associated with this method. First, the cooling still cannot be too abrupt or the yeast will be shocked (the subsequent fermentation being sluggish and possibly even being incomplete). Second, this method for making lagers requires a well-behaved yeast – one that does not produce a lot of esters at warmer temperatures.

The first method is the recommended way of brewing a lager. The main concern with the first method is the longer lag time than the second method. However, as long as you use a large starter (or double the amount of dry yeast you might use for an ale – 10 to 20 grams rather than the usual 5 to 10 grams), the lag time will not be much longer than the second method and the resulting beer will be much less likely to have unwanted esters.

Speaking of esters, second only to lowering fermentation temperature, pitching a large starter is important to minimize their production. Some researchers believe that ester production is greatest during yeast reproduction, therefore, since oxygen plays such a strong role in reproduction, it has been suggested that to minimize ester production, dissolved oxygen levels (i.e. post-cooling wort aeration/oxygenation) should be reduced in lagers[15,16]. However, other research overwhelmingly indicates that decreased dissolved oxygen levels *increase* ester production[87,88,89,90,91]. I feel that possibly yeast strain and wort composition (cold break amounts, for example) could be the complicating factors. The safest practice for us is to pitch large starters, aerate normally, and ferment cold.

One way to reduce the amount of time required for lagering is to perform what's called a "diacetyl rest." This is a method of increasing the rate that the diacetyl (which the yeast produced during fermentation) is reabsorbed by raising the temperature of the fermenting lager to between 55 and 65° F (13 and 18° C) for two to ten days. Typically this is done when the specific gravity of the fermenting lager has dropped 2/3 of the way from the original gravity to the anticipated final gravity. Performing the diacetyl rest too early will increase ester production. After the diacetyl rest, don't chill the beer too fast or you may shock the yeast (no more than a few degrees per day).

For most of us, a refrigerator is the only way to make a lager, but you may be blessed with a cellar or crawlspace that is at lager fermentation temperatures. As long as the temperature stays relatively constant (doesn't change more than 5° or so throughout the day) you can use this space for fermentation. Sudden temperature changes are what we're concerned about for two reasons:

1) the yeast can get shocked and
2) the headspace can contract on cooling and suck air or, in some cases, even airlock liquid into the fermenter (suckback).

**Figure 6-2**: *Fermenting in the crawlspace (note cardboard insulating the carboys from the cement floor). I've been blessed with a house that has a 50 F (10 C) crawlspace.*

After the fermentation is complete, it's time to lager. It is recommended that you rack (transfer) the beer to a secondary for lagering to get the beer away from the hot and cold break and the settled yeast. Be careful to not splash or otherwise aerate the beer when racking. Slowly cool the beer down to your lagering temperature. While the beer may look clear, there is still quite a bit of yeast in suspension. Chilling too quickly can cause the yeast to drop out of the beer and you may have difficulty getting it re-suspended. It may be tempting to top-up the secondary with water or wort, but I suggest that you resist temptation. The risks are numerous and there are virtually no benefits. The beer will give off a little $CO_2$ during the racking so the headspace in the secondary will pretty much be oxygen-free. You may see a little airlock activity in the secondary, but this is most likely due to the $CO_2$ coming out of solution due to the agitation from racking and a slight temperature rise.

I usually lager at 40° F (4° C). Not every beer will undergo a dramatic change during lagering – it depends somewhat on the malts and original gravity, but mostly on the yeast. That Traditional Bock was made with Wyeast Munich Lager (#2308). For four months I cursed that yeast, but in the end, I believe that it was worth the wait. The time and temperature of lagering depends on the yeast and the gravity of the beer. Try four to eight weeks at 40° F (4° C) and then evaluate the beer. Is the beer still cloudy? Is there still a lot of acetaldehyde (does it smell like green apples)? Are there some sulfury aromas? Is there still too much diacetyl (characterized by a butterscotch aroma)? If so, then try a couple more weeks of lagering.

Typically, I will lager in the secondary for 8 to 12 weeks and then bottle. Some authors recommend adding more yeast at bottling time, but I have yet to have any problems with carbonation without any additional yeast. I store the bottles at cellar temperature for three or four weeks for the carbonation to form. If the lagering in the secondary was not sufficient (some remaining acetaldehyde, for example) I will slowly cool the bottles to lagering temperatures and then store them for several more weeks.

It's important to note that airlocks on cold fermentations bubble much more slowly than on warm fermentations. If you are planning to do all the lagering in the bottle (although you will have considerably more sediment in the bottles than if you lagered in bulk), you should wait till the bubbles are 4 minutes apart before you even think about bottling. At 40° F, one bubble every 2 minutes is still a relatively active fermentation and bottling at this point will surely lead to overcarbonated beer.

## Clarity and Finings

Since the Bohemians started making crystal clear beers, beer clarity has grown to be an important factor in beers of most types. Only in a few wheat and rye beers is any amount of cloudiness deemed acceptable by the consumer. Most commercial breweries achieve clarity through filtration, but there are quite a few other ways to clarify beer, many of which are used by professional brewers in addition to filtering.

"Finings" are compounds that, when added to the wort or beer, help improve clarity in one way or another. Some are added in the boil and others after fermentation has completed. Finings don't become part of the finished beer – they settle out, taking various things (like polyphenols, proteins, or yeast) out of the beer with them.

First, let's consider what can cause cloudiness in beers. While there are many sources of haze in beer, the most common among homebrewed beers are chemical haze, biological haze, and chill haze.

**Figure 6-3**: *Crystal clear, slightly hazy, and very hazy beers.*

## Chemical Haze

Chemical haze is usually caused by a deficiency of calcium in the boil (oxalate haze), by iron or copper levels in the water exceeding 1 part-per-million (ppm), or by tin levels exceeding 0.1 ppm. It's a good idea to get a water analysis from your water supplier, whether it is municipal or bottled, or have your water tested if you have a well. Note that the mineral content of all water will change from season to season or even after a strong rain. You would like to have at least 50 ppm of calcium in your water, but you may be able to get by with 25 ppm with no problems. If have a permanent haze and you find that your water is very low in calcium, you can add it via gypsum, calcium chloride, or chalk, but don't just add it haphazardly – see chapter 9 and don't forget that gypsum may add unwanted sulfate or that chalk may add unwanted carbonates (depending on the style these other ions may be desirable). If your water has excessive levels of iron, copper, or tin, certain types of water filters may help or you may have to dilute your water with bottled spring or distilled water.

## Biological Haze

Biological haze can come from either bacterial sources or from yeast. If the cause of the haze is bacterial, the solution is, obviously, better sanitation. When yeast is the source, this can be from a wild yeast, a cultured yeast that has mutated into a form that has lost the ability to flocculate (in fact, this is a common mutation), ion concentrations in your water or simply due the use of a cultured yeast that is a poor flocculator[17]. If the source is a wild yeast, it may have infected your batch due to poor sanitation techniques or, if you were reusing yeast, may have come into the batch via your yeast culture. If this is the case or if your yeast has mutated, the end effect is the same: you should obviously avoid reusing the yeast from this batch. Proper levels of calcium are important to yeast flocculation but, ironically, excessive levels can impede yeast growth[18].

Some yeast strains are very slow to flocculate without the help of some kind of finings. Finings are additives that improve clarity. Isinglass and gelatin are the two finings commonly used to help yeast flocculate but I had heard that the use of Irish Moss can also improve the flocculation of yeast[19]. My only explanation of this is perhaps that higher protein levels in the wort may interfere with the processes the yeasts use to flocculate. I did a small experiment to test if Irish Moss really does improve yeast flocculation. The results were quite impressive: the batch without Irish Moss took nearly two weeks for the yeast to settle whereas with Irish Moss the yeast settled three days after fermentation. If you are making a lager don't fine the beer till after lagering. First of all, the yeast may settle on its own and secondly, the yeast is important to some of the chemical reactions taking place during lagering. Forcing the yeast to settle before lagering is not a good idea.

Isinglass is the traditional fining used in cask-conditioned "Real Ales" and is available to homebrewers as either a powder or as a liquid. The liquid form is far easier to use because it does not require preparation – just be sure that it has been refrigerated – liquid isinglass becomes totally useless after a day or so above 68° F (20° C). Liquid isinglass should be rather thick (when it spoils, it loses viscosity and looks like water). Isinglass works by electrostatically attracting yeast cells to its long molecules and then sinking to the bottom of the fermenter. It works most effectively at a pH of 4.4. To prepare a working solution from the powder, the isinglass should be dissolved in boiled (to sanitize) water chilled to between 50 and 60° F (10 and 16° C) in water which has been made mildly acidic, usually with the addition of tartaric, citric, malic, or sulfurous acid. Some brands of isinglass are now available in powdered form with the proper amount of tartaric acid already added, therefore, you must follow the directions supplied with the type of isinglass you purchase. Since the preparation of the isinglass is difficult, I recommend that you get the ready-to-use liquid form, if possible.

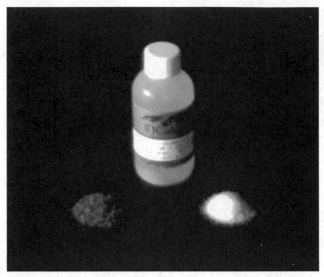

**Figure 6-4**: *Flaked Irish Moss, liquid isinglass, and gelatin.*

The proper amount of isinglass solution to be added varies depending on which book you read, but this may be due to the fact that the proper rate depends on the concentration of the working solution and on the amount of yeast remaining in the beer. Again, follow the directions that come with the isinglass. If you get isinglass without any directions, for 5 gallons of beer, add $1^1/_2$ grams of isinglass into 50 ml of cold, sterile water (plus enough citric, malic, or tartaric acid to acidify the solution to between 2.4 and 3.0 pH, unless the acid is already included with the isinglass) and allow it to sit for 48 hours in the refrigerator[21]. Mix the isinglass solution with 12 ounces (about 360 ml) of the beer to be fined and then add this solution to the total volume of beer. The time taken for the yeast to settle depends on the strain, but in my experience, most yeasts take between one and four days. In addition to helping settle yeast, isinglass also can remove some polyphenols (a.k.a. tannins) and proteins (via hydrogen bonds) from the beer (helping prevent chill haze) and can improve head retention by removing lipids (fat-like substances) and other compounds that interfere with head retention[20,21,22,23]. Fining at cooler temperatures increases the amount of proteins and polyphenols that are removed[70].

Adding isinglass to a beer destined for bottling should be reserved for beers with which you are having trouble getting the yeast to settle. I don't recommend making the use of isinglass part of your regular brewing procedure. In Britain, it is typically used for cask-conditioned beers (which are shipped from the brewery with yeast in the cask) to reduce the settling time and make the yeast pack more firmly in the bottom of the cask. Using isinglass in beers to be bottled can lengthen the time it takes for the beer to carbonate and if done too early in the fermentation can result in high levels of diacetyl and/or acetaldehyde. If you have given the yeast a week or two to settle and you must use isinglass, add the prepared finings to the beer two to three days before bottling.

Gelatin does not work as effectively or as quickly as isinglass, but works sufficiently well and at a fraction of the cost. Physically, it functions in the same way as Isinglass. The proper dosage again depends on the amount of yeast to be settled, but typically a rate of $1/2$ to 1 teaspoon per 5 gallons. To prepare a working solution, add the gelatin to a cup of water and heat it gently to between 170° F (77° C) and boiling for one minute to pasteurize and then add it to the beer. Clarification time depends on the yeast strain, but should take between three and six days. Every book which describes the use of gelatin in beer fining says to not boil the solution, but this warning originated in cookbooks where the gelatin is added to fruit juices which are acidic. Boiling in water for a short time will not affect the fining properties of the gelatin unless your water is very acidic or alkaline[24].

As with isinglass, I don't recommend using gelatin for bottled beers unless you are having trouble with the yeast. Add the gelatin solution two to three days before bottling.

Another option for removing unflocculent yeast is Sparkolloid®. See below for preparation and usage.

Finally, filtering is a possible method for removing unflocculent yeasts or if you are impatient. As long as the pore size of the filter is not unreasonably small (3 to 7 microns, typically) yeast mass can be significantly reduced without removing the proteins and dextrins that give beer its body and head retention This is often called "polish" or "rough" filtering, although there are no definitive rules on this nomenclature. Volume II of this series covers filtering in detail.

## Chill Haze

Chill haze is probably the most common cause of clarity problems. Proteins and polyphenols (a.k.a. tannins), both primarily from the malt, combine to form protein-polyphenol complexes which are soluble at warmer temperatures, but become insoluble as the beer cools, forming chill haze. Reducing chill haze is a matter of reducing either the protein, the polyphenols, or both. I recommend first trying to reduce the protein and polyphenols in the wort (including the use of Irish Moss). If that is insufficient, try using one of the post-fermentation finings that removes polyphenols. Finally, if you still have chill haze, try one of the post-fermentation finings that removes proteins.

Moll reports that headspace air, protein, iron content, and the pH of the beer (in that order) are the four most important variables found in one study[145]. Note that this study was presumably done on filtered, commercially-packaged beer, which may mean that the importance of air in the headspace for our bottle-conditioned beers is less than in this study. Protein content was no surprise, but the fact that increased beer iron content and pH actually decreased the tendency for chill haze development is opposite of what would be expected.

## Reducing Protein

The best way to solve the problem is to attack it at its source. Protein in the wort comes in many sizes. Small- and medium-sized proteins are what give the beer head retention and body. Only the large proteins complex with the polyphenols to cause chill haze  Protein in the wort can be reduced by:

1)   selecting low-protein grains,
2)   using a mash schedule that converts the large proteins to small- and medium-sized ones,
3)   boiling well to get a good hot break[25],
4)   making sure the boil pH is above 5.0 (when the wort pH is below 5.0 break formation is decreased)[25],
5)   chilling well to get a good cold break,
6)   using kettle finings, and
7)   using finings in the finished beer.

It would appear that extract brewers have no control over 1 and 2 but, in fact, they do!  The extract brewer has control over these factors when selecting the brand of extract that is used.  In other words, if you've tried 3 through 7 and you still have chill haze, try a different brand of extract.

Note that one study found that removing cold break did a good job of minimizing chill haze, while another study found no such correlation[148].

## Irish Moss

The kettle fining agent that is most commonly used by homebrewers is Irish Moss. Irish Moss is actually a red seaweed that is available in various forms, but research has shown that refined flakes are the best and that a 24-hour rehydration of the Irish Moss substantially improved performance[26].  In my opinion, this same research showed that the best results (when considering tradeoffs between break formation, attenuation, clarity, and head retention) was 1/8 gram per liter.  This rate is approximately equivalent to 1 teaspoon for a 5 gallon batch.  However, it is important to note that this is for an all-malt, all-grain wort and that since much of the hot break has already been removed during extract production, the rate should, theoretically be lower for extract beers.

Experiments that I conducted (see Figure 6-5, below) indicated that for a typical 1.048 all-malt, extract wort, the proper amount of Irish Moss is only 0.033 grams per liter or 0.63 grams for a 5 gallon batch. This is equivalent to just under 1/4 teaspoon of refined Irish Moss flakes for a 5 gallon batch. For higher-gravity worts, I recommend adding proportionately more Irish Moss (for example, use 3/8 teaspoon for a 1.072 wort). My experiments also showed that adding too much Irish Moss resulted in a slightly hazy beer, which was clearer, however, than if none was used.

The Irish Moss should be rehydrated in a cup of clean water for 12-24 hours and then added in the last 15 minutes of the boil. If you forgot to rehydrate it, go ahead and use it dry, but it will make a much bigger difference if you rehydrate it first. Irish Moss can smell a little "fishy" (it's seaweed, after all!), but that will dissipate during the boil, so the aroma is nothing to worry about.

**Figure 6-5**: *Experiment using various amounts of Irish Moss.*

## Bentonite (in the boil)

Research has shown that adding bentonite to the boil can significantly reduce haze in the finished beer[147]. It works by adsorbing tannins and proteins and I recommend adding it in the last 15 minutes of the boil. Scaling down from the amounts research has shown to work for commercial operations (50 to 200 grams/hectoliter[147]), the recommended amount for a 5-gallon batch would be about 10 to 40 grams. I suggest sticking to the lower end of the range for two reasons:

- quite a bit of the protein has already been removed during the extract production, and
- bentonite absorbs 6 to 10 times it's volume in water so losses can be significant.

## Papain

Papain is a proteolytic (protein-degrading) enzyme derived from papaya. The only usage rate I could find was 1/2 gram per 5-gallon batch[27], but since papain breaks proteins down indiscriminately, it can negatively affect head retention and body by breaking down too many proteins. I would advise against the use of papain for this reason.

## Silica gel

Silica gel is a polymeric hydrogel (or xerogel) made from sodium silicate and works by absorbing proteins as it sinks down in the fermenter. The pore sizes of the silica gel can be made to very consistent dimensions thereby making the absorption of proteins very selective. Scaling down from the rates shown to work for commercial operations (50 to 100 grams/hectoliter[148]), the recommended amount for a 5-gallon batch would be 10 to 20 grams. While silica gel has been available to commercial brewers for quite some time, it has only recently begun to be available to homebrewers. A word of caution: the FDA has not yet approved the use of silica gel in unfiltered beer and thus packages of silica gel are required to state that beer made with it must be decanted before consumption[28]. It takes but a few hours for the silica gel to absorb the proteins (some xerogels are made for long-term conditioning and may take considerably longer), but I would give the silica gel two to three days to settle. Actually, there is very little data on the use of silica gel on unfiltered beer (all the commercial brewers who use it, filter after dosing) so you are treading on uncharted territory here[29].

## Colloidal silicon dioxide, silica sol, or kieselsol

Similar to silica gel, colloidal silicon dioxide is said to be one of the most powerful clarifying agents available to brewers[71]. Usage is 1 teaspoon per 5 gallons (5 ml per 18.9 liters) of beer, added to the fermenter two to four days before bottling or kegging[71]. As with silica gel, it is not FDA approved for unfiltered beer, so similar precautions to the use of silica gel apply. Kieselsol is available to homebrewers as "Claro K. C.® Beer Finings" and comes with a package of chitin (basically, a very large carbohydrate). Follow package directions *after fermentation is complete.*

## Bentonite (post-fermentation)

Bentonite has been suggested for use along with PVPP (see below) as the primary method for reducing chill haze[30]. Make a working solution of bentonite by blending two ounces (60 grams) into a quart of boiling water, using a sanitized blender. Two tablespoons of this slurry (which has to be stirred up before use) will give 0.1 parts-per-trillion (ppt) of bentonite in 5 gallons of wort. The proper rate for bentonite is typically 0.1 to 0.5 ppt. The slurry should be added 48 hours before racking or adding PVPP, a.k.a. Polyclar.

## *Reducing Polyphenols*

As with proteins, it is better to solve the polyphenol problem at its source. Reducing the amount of polyphenols that are extracted from the malt can be done by being mindful of the time, temperature, and especially the pH of the steeping water (or in the case of all-grain brewing, the mash). Don't steep the grain longer than you have to (30 minutes is plenty) and don't exceed 170° F (77° C) or so. It also helps to not overcrush the malts. Unless your water is very high in carbonates, as long as you don't use more than a gallon of water per pound of grain, the pH should be low enough. You can buy pH testing papers and check the pH if you are having problems with astringency or chill haze. Get the narrow-range pH papers (roughly 4 to 7 pH). You want the pH of the water *after adding the grain* to be between 5 and 5.5 pH. If it is much higher, you can try using less water (say 3/4 gallon per pound) or you can aerate, boil, chill and decant the water (leave behind the white precipitate) before adding the grain. This will reduce the carbonates in the water and lower the pH. If, after boiling and decanting your water, the pH of the steeping grains is significantly higher than 5.5, you should probably use some lactic or phosphoric acid to lower the pH. Make sure you get food-grade acids and add them in very small amounts – a little goes a long way.

Many books say that polyphenols (a.k.a. tannins) come from primarily from the malt husks. This is not quite right. Polyphenol and silicate levels were measured in laboratory mashes of normal and dehusked malt. While the silicate content of the wort from the dehusked malt drops to nil relative to normal malt, the polyphenol content of wort is only slightly lower when dehusked malt is used[229].

There is evidence that only oxidized polyphenols will complex with proteins to form chill haze[228]. This would indicate that avoiding splashing during transfer and other situations where hot wort or finished beer may pick up oxygen is important not only regarding off-flavors but also haze formation.

Surprisingly, only about 2/3 of the polyphenols come from the malt which means that 1/3 of them come from the hops (primarily from the woody parts of the hop cones)[146]. In fact, beer made without hops had less than half or even $1/3$ of the chill haze relative to lightly and moderately hopped beers, respectively[158]. Therefore, there are a few things you may want to keep in mind during recipe formulation if you are creating a beer that is supposed to be quite bitter:

1.  small amounts of high-alpha hops will add less polyphenols than large amounts of low-alpha hops,
2.  pay particular attention to minimizing large proteins (see above), and
3.  plan on using finings.

The most reliable post-fermentation fining for reducing polyphenols is PVPP, a.k.a. Polyclar. Sparkolloid® is another option for removing polyphenols although it has been used primarily by wine and mead makers to settle yeast. Gelatin and Isinglass help remove polyphenols somewhat (see above under Biological Haze).

## PVPP

PVPP (polyvinylpyrrolidone – trade named Polyclar) is a good choice for a fining because it removes polyphenols as opposed to proteins, so it will have no effect on head retention. PVPP works by electrostatically attracting polyphenols (tannins) as it sinks to the bottom of the fermenter. It also reduces the bitterness of the beer slightly and lightens the color of the beer a shade. There seems to be some discrepancy in the homebrewing literature regarding its proper usage rate (2 grams per 5 gallons by one author, as much as $1/4$ cup by another)[23,30,31,32]. The range of rates may reflect various amounts of polyphenol in the beer depending on the grain bill and water pH. Scaling down from the rates shown to work for commercial operations (20 to 25 grams/hectoliter[149]), the recommended amount for a 5-gallon batch would be about 3 to 5 grams (4 to 6 teaspoons) for a pale beer – darker beers would probably need less due to the lower pH and subsequent lesser polyphenol extraction. Mix the PVPP with a cup of water, boil it a minute to sanitize (watch out for boilover – leave plenty or headspace), add it to the fermenter, and give the PVPP two to five days to settle to the bottom of the fermenter.

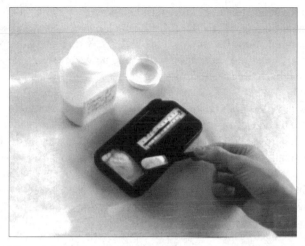

**Figure 6-6**: *Weighing out PVPP.*

Two types are available: Polyclar SB100 (a.k.a. Polyclar AT) and Polyclar 10. The SB100 is for general use and settles more rapidly than the finer Polyclar 10[71]. Note that if your excessive polyphenol levels are due to your water having a high pH and high levels of carbonates, it is best to solve water problem rather than try to eliminate a symptom (the excessive polyphenols) later with the addition of PVPP.

## Sparkolloid®

This is a polysaccharide in a diatomaceous earth carrier which is used quite commonly by wine makers. It removes yeast cells and polyphenols as it sinks to the bottom of the fermenter. For 5 gallons (18.9 liters) of beer, boil 3 grams of Sparkolloid in 8 ounces (about 250 ml) of water for 15 minutes and then mix it thoroughly with the beer 48 hours before bottling or kegging[71]. It can do such a good job of settling yeast that you may want to consider adding more yeast at bottling time.

## *Fermentation considerations*

In commercial-sized batches, higher pitching rate (2 liters of yeast slurry per hectoliter versus 1 liter, versus 0.5 liters) were found to result in slightly less hazy beer than lower pitching rates[149]. These rates, scaled-down to a 5 gallon batch, correspond to about 375 ml, 190 ml, and 95 ml of yeast slurry. I'd like to point out that for 375 ml of yeast slurry, you would probably need to make up at least an 16-liter yeast starter (see chapter 10) or use part of the settled yeast from a previous batch.

Research has shown that warmer lager fermentations (beginning at 46° F / 8° C with a maximum limit of 54° F / 12.2° C) resulted in beer that was less hazy than colder lager fermentations (beginning at 41° F / 5° C with a maximum limit of 47° F / 8.2° C)[149]. For ales, no correlation was found between fermentation temperature and haze.

When it comes to conditioning, lagering at 32° F (0° C) has shown to result in much less haze than lagering at 37° F (3° C)[149]. Furthermore, regarding haze reduction, my interpretation of the research data indicates that the difference between one month of lagering and two months was far greater than between two months and three[149] (the law of diminishing returns). Don't forget that haze reduction is but one purpose for lagering and that a three-month (or longer) lagering period would be preferable for other reasons.

### Filtering

Although I am not a proponent of it, I should, for the sake of completeness, mention filtering as a method for removing chill haze . The "cold filtering" that is proudly mentioned in many beer advertisements is just that – chilling the beer to where chill haze is formed and then filtering out the haze. The reason I am opposed to filtering is because it is not very selective – filtering removes much of the proteins that give beer its body and head retention. Overfiltered beer has no mouthfeel or head retention unless they are chemically re-introduced into the beer.

### Packaging

Dissolved oxygen levels in the beer during bottling/kegging have a slight effect on chill haze, but significantly increases permanent haze after about two months storage[150]. So, in addition to keeping your beer's aroma smelling fresh and hoppy, here's another reason to minimize aeration during bottling.

# Single-stage vs. Two-stage Fermentation

There is some debate as to whether single-stage or two-stage fermentation is better. In single-stage fermentation, you use only one fermenter, sometimes called a "primary." In two-stage fermentation, you have two fermenters, the "primary" and the "secondary." There are advantages and disadvantages to both methods. The advantages to using only a primary are:
* eliminating the risk of oxidation during transfer,
* eliminating the risk of infection during transfer,
* eliminating the time and effort of the transfer, and
* eliminating the need to sanitize another container.

The disadvantages of using only a primary are:
- if you use a plastic fermenter and let the finished beer sit too long, oxygen entering through an ill-fitting lid (or, during very long periods of time, permeating through the plastic) can oxidize the beer – note that this can be avoided by the use of a glass primary,
- if you want to reuse the yeast and plan to dryhop the beer you will be forced to pitch the used dryhops along with the yeast (not recommended, due to risk of airlock or even blowoff hose clogging),
- if you want to use finings you will stir up the settled yeast when stirring them in,
- you end up with more yeast in the bottom of each bottle after conditioning, and
- some yeast strains are very prone to autolysis (see chapter 10) from the beer sitting on a large yeast cake too long giving your beer excessively yeasty or even rubbery aromas.

I feel there is little advantage to using a plastic secondary fermenter or using a secondary if you are using a glass primary, so I will assume that we are debating the use of a glass secondary after using a plastic primary. The advantages of using a glass secondary are:
- reducing the risk of oxidation due to oxygen entering through an ill-fitting lid (or, during very long periods of time, permeating through the walls of the plastic primary),
- allowing reuse of the yeast from the primary without interference from dryhops (assuming you are dryhopping),
- allowing better distribution of finings such as Bentonite, gelatin, or PVPP without the stirring up as much settled yeast,
- reducing the amount of yeast in the bottom of each bottle after conditioning, and
- reducing the risk of autolysis.


The disadvantages of using a secondary are:
- increased risk of oxidation during transfer,
- increased risk of infection during transfer,
- increased time and effort, and
- increased use of sanitizer for sanitizing the secondary.

Personally, I use glass primaries for most batches and don't use secondaries except for lagers (where I plan to keep the beer in the fermenter for months) or fruit beers (where I often need to make room for the fruit). Normally, I will even dryhop in the primary unless I want to reuse the yeast. In this case, I'll rack the beer to a secondary, pour new wort onto the yeast cake in the primary and add the dryhops in the secondary.

## Open Fermenters vs. Closed Fermenters

"Open" fermenters don't necessarily mean that they are always open to the air, but rather that you can open the lid and remove the "dirty head," the brown residue that floats up on top of the kräusen during fermentation. Closed fermenters are simply fermenters in which you cannot get to the kräusen. However, using the blowoff method of fermentation with a closed fermenter has a similar (albeit less selective) effect. Most commercial fermenters are closed, but there are still a great many world class beers that are brewed using open fermentation techniques, for example all the Samuel Smith's beers, and the beers from Anchor, Liefmans, and Young's breweries, just to name a few. As long as you maintain sanitation (which, naturally, is slightly more difficult with open fermenters) and if you don't let the beer sit too long (try to transfer or bottle within 10 days) after fermentation is complete, there are no problems with using this technique. It is important to note that skimming the dirty head reduces bitterness so this must be calculated into the recipe during formulation (chapter 15). There are some commercial brewers that use closed fermenters that are designed in such a way that the dirty head rides upward upon the kräusen and sticks to the ceiling of the fermenter. When the kräusen settles, the dirty head remains stuck to the ceiling of the fermenter and is removed in this way.

Why would you want to remove the dirty head? There are some brewers who believe that removing the dirty head results in a cleaner beer. I'm not one of them. I was unsure of whether beer in which the dirty head was removed was better, worse, or the same as beer in which the dirty head was allowed to drop back into the ferment, so I did an experiment. I brewed two batches of beer using two different yeasts and split the wort into four fermenters. Half of each wort was put into a fermenter set up to blow the dirty head off the kräusen and half into a fermenter where the dirty head would drop back into the beer. The resulting beers were compared double-blind by BJCP judges and sent to the Siebel Institute of Technology for laboratory analysis. The bottom line: the only truly significant difference was in the level of bitterness, both perceived and measured. The non-blowoff beers were not harsher or rougher than the blowoff beers. Furthermore, the differences between the split batches in terms of protein content, head retention, ester content, and levels of higher alcohols were not large enough to be noticeable by tasters. This was confirmed by the lab analysis. A complete write-up of my experiment can be found in reference 33.

**Figure 6-7**: *The Yorkshire Stone Squares used at the Tadcaster Brewery (Samuel Smith's).*

## Stainless Steel Fermenters

Since most commercial brewers use stainless steel fermenters, many home brewers wish they could too. A tempting possibility is to use soda-pop syrup canisters as fermenters. There are two problems with this. Firstly, unless you leave the lid off and cover the fermenter with plastic to keep bugs and dust out, you will have to vent $CO_2$ through the connectors which are very small. It would not take much blowoff to clog these tiny openings. Secondly, these canisters are tall and thin. Some yeasts do not perform well in tall, thin fermenters, dropping out of suspension early and leaving a high final gravity[34].

Quarter- and half-barrel kegs are possible candidates, but the main problem is that you cannot see inside to make sure it's clean enough. A penlight and inspection mirror can be used, but be very careful when removing the tapping assembly – make sure to vent all the pressure before attempting it. Don't forget that an airlock can clog just as easily on a 15.5-gallon fermenter as on a 5-gallon one. Be sure to leave enough room for the kräusen or use a large diameter blowoff tube.

Extended contact with bleach will pit stainless steel, so iodophor or peroxide-based sanitizers are recommended. If you must use chlorine bleach, limit exposure to 15 minutes, do not exceed 200 ppm of chlorine (1 tablespoon per gallon) and rinse immediately with sanitary water or inexpensive commercial beer[35].

## Blowoff vs. Non-blowoff

This debate has raged among homebrewers for quite a while. The blowoff method is a closed fermentation technique in which the kräusen is directed out of the fermenter via a tube (called a blowoff tube). It achieves the same thing as skimming the dirty head, but it is done automatically and without the increased risk of infection. Its supporters claim that it reduces an abrasive bitterness and results in a cleaner-tasting beer with fewer higher alcohols. Opponents of the technique point to the loss of beer (sometimes as much as 1/2 gallon from a 5 gallon batch) and suggest that perhaps there is some loss of head retention.

I've done some experiments comparing the two methods in which I split a single wort between two fermenters having similar geometry, but one was set up for blowoff and the other was set up so that the dirty head fell back into the beer. I had the resulting beers tasted by experienced Beer Judge Certification Program (BJCP) judges and analyzed by the Siebel Institute of Technology. The judges found little difference other than a lower bitterness in the blowoff beer. The lab analyses showed that there was very little change in either the protein levels (indicating that there should be no difference in head retention) or the higher (fusel) alcohol levels. What the lab did find was that there was a significant loss of bitterness (13 to 17%)[33]. Therefore, as with skimming in an open fermenter, you must compensate for this loss when you formulate your recipe (chapter 15).

## Dropping

There is a procedure used by some British commercial brewers and homebrewers called "dropping." Dropping is nothing more than siphoning or draining the fermenting beer out from under the kräusen before fermentation subsides and the kräusen drops back into the beer. It is similar to using a blowoff tube or skimming the kräusen off the fermenting beer if you are using an open-topped fermenter (although it also has the benefit if removing any break that may have settled). Again, note that all three of these procedures reduce the bitterness of the beer significantly so this should be taken into account during the recipe formulation (chapter 15). Also, it is important to remember that this transfer must be done during fermentation and that you should avoid transferring both the trub (hot break, cold break, and dead yeast at the bottom of the fermenter) and the "dirty head" (the brown part of the kräusen) into the secondary fermenter.

There is one other option associated with dropping and that is aeration during the dropping. Yes, everything you've read before has said that you should not aerate the beer after fermentation has begun. Well, this is an exception. It works well with some yeasts (such as Yeast Culture Kit Company A42 or Wyeast London ESB, #1968) and poorly with others. Aeration *during* fermentation causes an increase in the production of diacetyl and helps some yeasts achieve better attenuation (drier beer with a lower final gravity).  Samuel Smith's beers are not dropped, but their yeast is so flocculent that they need to mechanically resuspend it.  In the process, which utilizes pumps and sprayers, the fermenting beer gets aerated.  This is part of the reason that Samuel Smith's beers have such high diacetyl levels (the other reason is that their highly-flocculent yeast doesn't stay in suspension long enough to reabsorb the diacetyl it produces).  If you do choose to aerate during dropping, I recommend that you do it just after the dirty head forms.  If you wait longer into the fermentation, more alcohols will be produced and the risk of oxidizing alcohols to noticeable levels of aldehydes will be higher.

# Aeration vs. Oxygenation

Before we talk about aeration and oxygenation, let me clarify that there's a big difference between "oxygenation" and "oxidation."  The former is the addition of oxygen (either via air or pure oxygen).  The latter (in terms of this discussion) is the reaction between oxygen and chemical compounds in the hops, malt extract, wort, or beer.  Anytime there is oxygen present, there is some amount of oxidation taking place in the wort, but when the wort is cool (so that the oxidation reactions are taking place slowly) and there is yeast present (which absorb oxygen quite quickly) very little oxidation actually takes place.  Consider it a necessary evil to provide the yeast with the oxygen they need.

Different strains of yeast can have very different oxygen requirements.  In one study, initial dissolved levels above 20% of saturation did not significantly increase growth or fermentation rate[36].  Other yeasts can have initial dissolved oxygen requirements approaching 100% of saturation[37, 215].  The yeast will absorb virtually all the oxygen you provide, so providing more than the yeasts' minimum needs is not harmful.  Very high levels of oxygen can be toxic to yeast, but these levels can only be achieved with pure oxygen bubbled through the wort for a long time under pressure.

## Aeration/oxygenation methods

There are many different ways to dissolve oxygen into the cooled wort.  They include:

- whipping,
- pouring,
- aerating tube,
- shaking,
- compressed air, and
- oxygen.

While I don't have data on whipping air into the wort with a plastic spoon or bottling wand, A. J. deLange performed a series of tests which he posted to the Homebrew Digest in January of 1996.  The results were quite surprising.  In all these tests, the values are in terms of the % saturation of oxygen. The amount of oxygen that will dissolve in water or wort is a function of the temperature. At room temperature, using air (not oxygen), water will hold about 8 milligrams per liter (mg/l) and as the temperature approaches freezing, it is possible to dissolve nearly 15 mg/l. Higher gravity worts have lower saturation limits[38, 215]. Up to 30 mg/l of oxygen can be dissolved in room temperature wort if you use pure oxygen[215].

In one experiment, A. J. ran deoxygenated water through an aerating tube (a short tube at the outlet end of a siphon hose into which several small holes have been drilled perpendicular to the flow of the liquid). The resulting water had only 14% saturation. He took this water and poured it about three feet into another container.

### Table 6-1: Aeration by pouring

| Number of pours | Saturation |
|:---:|:---:|
| 0 | 14% |
| 1 | 49% |
| 2 | 71% |
| 3 | 82% |
| 4 | 91% |
| 5 | 96% |

In another experiment, posted in Homebrew Digest #1937, A. J. ran water that had been de-aerated to 22% saturation through an aeration tube (see "Aeration/oxygenation systems" in chapter 4). The resulting water had 49% saturation, which shows that it is pretty much equivalent if not worse than simply pouring wort from one container to another.

In a third experiment, A. J. compared shaking a half-filled carboy, bubbling compressed air through an airstone with gentle swirling and bubbling oxygen through an airstone with gentle swirling. He measured the % saturation at one-minute intervals. (Note that unless the carboy was sealed with an airlock, that 145% saturation would eventually drop to 100%).

**Table 6-2: Various methods of introducing dissolved oxygen**

| Time | Shaking | Compressed air | Oxygen |
|------|---------|----------------|--------|
| 0 min | 7 % | 7 % | 7 % |
| 1 min | 55 % | 40 % | 85 % |
| 2 min | 70 % | 62 % | 145 % |
| 3 min | 75 % | 75 % | |
| 4 min | 80 % | 82 % | |
| 5 min | 82 % | 90 % | |
| 6 min | 84 % | 92 % | |
| 8 min | 87 % | 98 % | |

## Yeast oxygen needs

How much oxygen is enough? This depends on four factors: the yeast strain, the size of the starter, the original gravity, and whether you are using dry or liquid yeast. Some yeast strains can ferment normal gravity wort well with less than 2 mg/l of dissolved oxygen. Other strains, such as the Ringwood strain, really don't perform well unless it has nearly 8 mg/l (which corresponds to 100% saturation with air). The Ringwood strain happens to produce excessive diacetyl in under-oxygenated wort. The oxygen needs of various yeasts can range from 2 mg/l to as much as 30 mg/l (which corresponds to 100% saturation with pure oxygen at 68° F / 20° C)[215]. If you use a large starter, especially if you have aerated the starter wort well, you can get away with less than the ideal amount of dissolved oxygen. As the original gravity of the wort climbs, so do the yeasts' oxygen needs. Dry yeast is grown under aerobic conditions so they have had a lot of oxygen available to them before being dehydrated. Therefore, dry yeasts have lower dissolved oxygen needs than liquid yeasts.

The oxygen is used by the yeast to create sterols for building cell membranes. If the cell membranes are weak (i.e. if the yeast did not have sufficient oxygen or sterols available in the wort) the yeast will have low alcohol tolerance and will expire before consuming all the sugar in the wort. Yeast can get by with less oxygen if they have some cold break available, which provides some of the necessary sterlols[215].

One thing to consider is that if you have wild yeast or bacteria in the air surrounding your wort and you aerate your wort via whipping, aeration tube, pouring or shaking, you will be infecting the wort with these unwanted microbes. In the summertime, I have a particularly nasty wild yeast in my house. I must use a filtered air aeration system or oxygen to aerate/oxygenate my wort or I get a medicinal/plastic aroma in my beer a week or two after bottling.

I have gone from using a filtered air aeration system to oxygen for one reason: foaming. I usually use 6-gallon glass carboys for fermenters and put 5 gallons of wort in them. After about a minute of bubbling with an airstone, that one gallon of headspace is all foam and I have to shut off the compressor. 10 minutes later, the foam has settled and I can aerate again. Let's look at the table above again: 90% saturation requires 5 minutes of aeration. That's 40 minutes of waiting for foam to settle! With oxygen, I get the same amount of foaming, but can get 85% saturation without ever waiting for the foam to settle.

You shouldn't fear adding too much oxygen to the wort. Unless you use oxygen and continuously oxygenate the wort under pressure, you can't add too much. On November 11, 1996, A. J. deLange reported in the Homebrew Digest that he periodically oxygenated pitched wort for several days to maintain a dissolved oxygen level of 30 to 35 ppm and the yeast continued to flourish. It's better to err on the side of too much aeration/oxygenation than not enough, but without pressurization, it is clearly impossible to over-oxygenate the wort.

## Saturation levels in wort

Please note that all the above saturations were based upon tests on water. As it has been noted before, the solubility of oxygen in wort is a function of specific gravity and can be considerably lower. In Homebrew Digest #1446, Dr. George Fix posted the results from some tests he performed using oxygen and verified that the dissolved oxygen (DO) levels (unless held artificially high with constant oxygen flow) are strongly dependent on the specific gravity (SG) of the wort:

**Table 6-3: Oxygen solubility in wort**

|  | Dissolved Oxygen at Various Temperatures | | |
|---|---|---|---|
| SG | 54.5° F (12.5° C) | 59° F (15° C) | 68° F (20° C) |
| 1.030 (7.5P) | 8.1 ppm | 7.5 ppm | 6.5 ppm |
| 1.040 (10P) | 7.7 ppm | 7.1 ppm | 6.2 ppm |
| 1.060 (15P) | 6.9 ppm | 6.3 ppm | 5.6 ppm |
| 1.080 (20P) | 5.7 ppm | 5.5 ppm | 5.0 ppm |

## Summary

So what should we learn from all this data? Here are the most important points you should remember from the above discussion:

1.  Aeration tubes are no better than simply pouring the wort into the fermenter.

2.  Some yeasts will perform well with a single pour; shaking the carboy for a minute or a minute and a half of compressed air.

3.  Other yeasts require several pours, several minutes of shaking, several minutes of compressed air, or a minute of pure oxygen.

4.  As the OG of the wort goes up, not only do the oxygen needs of the yeast increase, but so does the difficulty of dissolving oxygen into the wort. Therefore, for very high-gravity worts, 5 pours, more than 8 minutes of shaking, 5 minutes of compressed air or 2 minutes of oxygen is recommended for the best yeast performance.

5.  You can't over-oxygenate wort under normal conditions.

## Priming More Precisely

The guidelines for priming in the previous chapter don't take an important factor into account: there is already some $CO_2$ dissolved in the beer. How much is dissolved depends on the temperature of the beer. The following table indicates the number of volumes of $CO_2$ are typical for various styles. 2.3 liters of $CO_2$ dissolved in a liter of beer is "2.3 volumes." Note that handpumped British Ales will have only 1.25 to 1.5 volumes of $CO_2$, with the odd exception reaching 1.75 volumes.

**Table 6-4: Typical carbonation levels for various styles**

| Style | Volumes of $CO_2$ |
|---|---|
| British Ales | 1.25 - 1.75 |
| American Ales and European Lagers | 2.0 - 2.7 |
| American Lagers | 2.0 - 3.0 |
| Belgian Ales and German Wheat Beers | 2.5 - 4.5 |

The following table will allow you to account for the dissolved $CO_2$ in the beer at bottling time. Note that fermentation must be complete. It is necessary to use less priming sugar when priming colder beer due to the fact that more $CO_2$ will dissolve in beer when it is colder than when it is warmer. Beer that has been fermenting at 39° F (4° C) will have more dissolved $CO_2$ in it than beer that has been fermenting at 68° F (20° C). To determine how many ounces (weight) of dextrose to use, simply select the column which most closely matches the temperature of the beer you are priming, choose a carbonation level from the vertical scale and read the proper priming rate from the intersection of the column and row. If you choose to prime with sucrose (table sugar), just multiply the value you get from the table by 0.94.

If you prefer to use metric measures, after you find the proper priming rate in the table in ounces-per-gallon, multiply that value by 7.53 to get grams-per-liter.

**Table 6-5: Ounces (weight) of dextrose per gallon for various levels of carbonation (multiply by 7.53 to get priming rates in grams/liter of dextrose).**

| | | 32F 0C | 36F 2C | 39F 4C | 43F 6C | 46F 8C | 50F 10C | 54F 12C | 57F 14C | 61F 16C | 64F 18C | 68F 20C | 72F 22C | 76F 24C |
|---|---|---|---|---|---|---|---|---|---|---|---|---|---|---|
| | 4.50 | 1.37 | 1.42 | 1.47 | 1.52 | 1.57 | 1.62 | 1.66 | 1.69 | 1.72 | 1.75 | 1.77 | 1.80 | 1.82 |
| | 4.25 | 1.25 | 1.30 | 1.35 | 1.40 | 1.45 | 1.49 | 1.53 | 1.57 | 1.60 | 1.63 | 1.65 | 1.68 | 1.70 |
| | 4.00 | 1.13 | 1.18 | 1.23 | 1.27 | 1.32 | 1.37 | 1.41 | 1.45 | 1.47 | 1.50 | 1.53 | 1.55 | 1.57 |
| | 3.75 | 1.00 | 1.05 | 1.10 | 1.15 | 1.20 | 1.25 | 1.29 | 1.32 | 1.35 | 1.38 | 1.41 | 1.43 | 1.45 |
| Volumes | 3.50 | 0.88 | 0.93 | 0.98 | 1.03 | 1.08 | 1.13 | 1.17 | 1.20 | 1.23 | 1.26 | 1.28 | 1.31 | 1.33 |
| of | 3.25 | 0.76 | 0.81 | 0.86 | 0.91 | 0.96 | 1.00 | 1.04 | 1.08 | 1.11 | 1.14 | 1.16 | 1.19 | 1.21 |
| $CO_2$ | 3.00 | 0.64 | 0.69 | 0.74 | 0.78 | 0.83 | 0.88 | 0.92 | 0.96 | 0.98 | 1.01 | 1.04 | 1.06 | 1.08 |
| | 2.75 | 0.51 | 0.56 | 0.61 | 0.66 | 0.71 | 0.76 | 0.80 | 0.83 | 0.86 | 0.89 | 0.92 | 0.94 | 0.96 |
| | 2.50 | 0.39 | 0.44 | 0.49 | 0.4 | 0.59 | 0.64 | 0.68 | 0.71 | 0.74 | 0.77 | 0.79 | 0.82 | 0.84 |
| | 2.25 | 0.27 | 0.32 | 0.37 | 0.54 | 0.47 | 0.51 | 0.55 | 0.59 | 0.62 | 0.65 | 0.67 | 0.70 | 0.72 |
| | 2.00 | 0.15 | 0.20 | 0.25 | 0.29 | 0.34 | 0.39 | 0.43 | 0.47 | 0.49 | 0.52 | 0.55 | 0.57 | 0.59 |
| | 1.75 | 0.02 | 0.07 | 0.12 | 0.17 | 0.22 | 0.27 | 0.31 | 0.34 | 0.37 | 0.40 | 0.43 | 0.45 | 0.47 |
| | 1.50 | | | 0.00 | 0.05 | 0.10 | 0.15 | 0.19 | 0.22 | 0.25 | 0.28 | 0.30 | 0.33 | 0.35 |
| | 1.25 | | | | | | 0.02 | 0.06 | 0.10 | 0.13 | 0.16 | 0.18 | 0.21 | 0.23 |

# Bottles: Labeling and De-labeling

If you are going to enter your beer in a competition, removing the old label from a commercial beer bottle is mandatory, but most brewers remove the labels anyway, just to make the bottles look neater and so they could put their own label on the bottle. Some commercial beers' labels float off in plain water, but most need something to dissolve the glue. A tablespoon of chlorine bleach per gallon of warm water works well for most labels, but for some (especially the foil labels), you still need to scrub the labels off with a wire brush or razor blade.

What I usually do is soak the bottles in bleach solution for a week and then use a razor blade and holder (usually used for scraping paint and available at any hardware store) to scrape off the label. I then use a kitchen scrubbing pad to get all the glue off. Washing soda works well for removing some brands' labels, but don't soak bottles in washing soda or One-Step™ longer than an hour or two because you will get a carbonate residue on the bottles that you can only remove with acid (lemon juice or vinegar, for example).

**Figure 6-8**: *You can label your bottles as simply or as elaborately as you want (note that in competitions, you cannot have any labels on the bottle or distinguishing marks on the cap).*

When putting your own labels on the bottles, you have several choices. Obviously, you don't want them to be difficult to remove. There are plastic stick-on labels that are reusable, but you are limited to several designs. What most homebrewers do is make up some labels by hand or with a computer drawing program (possibly including clip-art) and then either print a bunch on the printer or on a copier. The two best (easily removable) adhesives are the glue stick and milk. Yes, regular kitchen-variety milk (whole, skim… it doesn't matter) – simply dip the label in and stick it on. It will dry clear. There are two disadvantages to milk as a label adhesive:

1. even the sweating of the cold bottle can cause the label to slide off (so don't put a dozen, various, milk-labeled bottles into a cooler full of ice or you will be guessing which is the Pilsner and which is the California Common) and

2. many printer inks are soluble in milk (HP 600-series inkjet inks, for example, are milk-soluble and water-soluable; most laserjet toners are not).

## Oxygen-absorbing vs. Regular Bottlecaps

Personally, I always use oxygen-absorbing bottlecaps. While it is far more important to keep from oxidizing your hot wort (the oxygen absorbing caps won't help you here), I feel that every little bit helps. Side-by-side blind tastings have been done by the Chicago Beer Society, comparing oxygen-absorbing versus regular bottlecaps and the most striking difference was that the beer bottled in oxygen-absorbing caps retained its hop aroma longer. Other research has shown that the oxygen-absorbing caps not only virtually eliminates oxygen that is in the bottle headspace, but also significantly reduces oxygen permeation through the liner and the amount of oxygen that reacts with the beer[225].

Some manufacturers make both oxygen-absorbing and oxygen-barrier caps. The former type both serves as a barrier and absorbs oxygen. I'm not sure about the designations used by other manufacturers, but Zapata oxygen-absorbing caps are labeled with "PureSeal® 'A.'"

It is important to note that moisture activates the oxygen absorbing properties of the caps so that they should be stored in a dry environment, ideally in a sealed moisture-proof bag or container. Note also, that once you've sanitized the caps, you should use them within an hour or so. Some books and articles will tell you that you must turn over the bottles to activate the absorption, but this is not true – the sanitizing and rinsing of the caps as well as the moisture in the headspace of the bottle is enough. Finally, the caps should be sanitized via bleach or iodophor solution – boiling and oxygen-based sanitizers (like OneStep™ and B-Brite™) will ruin the caps' absorbing capabilities.

## Hop Bags vs. SureScreens™

I used to use pelletized hops and hop bags for the boil, but recently, I've mounted a pair of SureScreens™ (see under "Sieves" in chapter 4) attached to a valve at the bottom of my boiling kettle and now I usually use whole hops without hop bags. Since I can now easily drain the cooled wort from my kettle, I prefer to have the whole hops loose so that they form a filter bed for removing more of the hot and cold break from the cooled wort. The disadvantage of this setup is that it's difficult to squeeze the wort out of the hops while maintaining good sanitation and therefore I lose a bit more wort than when I used pellets and hop bags.

The main attraction for me to this new method was not so much the break removal. I added the valve to the kettle so that I could drain cooled wort into the carboy without aeration. During the summer, I have a lot of wild yeasts floating around my house. By draining the cooled wort into a carboy purged with oxygen and then using an Oxynater™ to add additional oxygen, I protect my wort from wild yeast infections. In effect, I have built a hop back and a sort of whirlpool into my kettle. Alas, pellet hops clog the screens almost immediately, so I'm limited to using plugs and whole hops.

You might think that late additions of hops would contribute slightly more bitterness using this method because they stay in contact longer (during the cooling) than if they were removed immediately after the boil. I have read, however, that the alpha acids dissolve quite quickly in the wort and that it is the isomerization that takes some time. If this indeed is the case, then there would be no difference between leaving the hops in or taking them out during cooling. Tasting of the several batches I've made using this new method confirms that the hop utilization in late additions is not significantly improved.

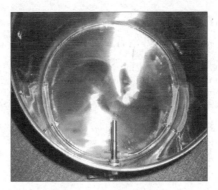

**Figure 6-9**: *While not a good design for a lauter tun (too much sparge water will channel along the sides of the tun – the screens need to be farther from the sides), the screens near the walls allow me to stir easily to avoid scorching and then run off through a bed of hops (similar to a hop back).*

## Hot and Cold Break Removal

Frankly, until recently, I have not put much effort into removing the hot and cold break. As of yet, I have not noticed any difference between the beer made from wort in which little effort was made in removing the hot or cold break and the more recent batches where most (not all) was removed. There is universal acceptance among brewers that the wort should be separated from the hot break but there is some disagreement as to whether the cold break should be removed[39,40,41]. In addition to the nutritional benefits (to the yeast) of cold break, it has been theorized that cold break provides nucleation sites for $CO_2$ bubbles to form[40,41]. High levels of dissolved $CO_2$ have a negative affect on fermentation.

One method for removing hot break is to run the hot wort through a bed of hops (making sure to minimize oxidation) on the way to a counterflow chiller. If an immersion chiller is used before running the cooled wort through a bed of hops, then both hot and cold break will be removed. Another method is the use of a whirlpool tank (see "Whirlpools" in chapter 4). A fourth break-removal method is to allow the break to settle and then rack the clarified wort off the break material before fermentation (which will stir up the break) begins. Finally, a floatation tank may be used (see "Floatation tanks" in chapter 4).

So what does all this mean to the homebrewer? My advice is to not be overly concerned with hot or cold break removal. If you do choose to modify your equipment or procedures in such a way that allows the removal of break material and your fermentation suffers, consider if perhaps slightly less-efficient break removal may be better.

## Further Reading

Bickham, S., "Floatation Tanks Can Remove Trub at Any Scale of Brewing," *Brewing Techniques*, 5 (1) 17-18 (Jan/Feb 1997).

Daugharty, P., "A Manual Oxygenation Technique," *Brewing Techniques*, 5 (1) 16 (Jan/Feb 1997).

DeClerck, J., *A Textbook of Brewing*, Vol. 1 (Chapman and Hall, London, 1957).

Fix, G. J., *Analysis of Brewing Techniques* (publication pending by Brewers Publications, 1997).

Foster, T., "Clear Beer Please," *Beer and Brewing Vol. 9* (Brewers Publications, Boulder, Colorado, 1989), 60.

Hough, J. S., D. E. Briggs, R. Stevens, and T.W. Young, *Malting and Brewing Science*, Vol. 1 and 2 (Chapman and Hall, London, 1982).

Hough, J. S., *The Biotechnology of Malting and Brewing*, (Cambridge University Press, Cambridge, 1985).

Johnson, D., "Noncaustic Cleaners and Elbow Grease," *Brewing Techniques*, 4 (5) 10-12, (Sept/Oct 1996).

Knull, G. W., "Trouble With Trubless Fermentations," *Brewing Techniques*, 4 (5) 14-19, (Sept/Oct 1996).

Korzonas, A. R., "When Fermentation Rears Its Dirty Head," *Brewing Techniques*, 4 (3), 50-54, (May/Jun 1996).

Stroud, S., Homebrew Digest #2123 post.

# MALTS, GRAINS, AND EXTRACTS

alt, hops, water, and yeast are the four main ingredients in beer. The Bavarian Beer Purity Law of 1516, "Reinheitsgebot," decreed that only barley, hops, and water may be used in the production of beer sold in Bavaria (brewers didn't know the importance of yeast in brewing until 1841, when Mitcherlich discovered the role of yeast in fermentation)[42]. However, there are a great many other ingredients that are often used in the production of beer, for example, other grains such as wheat, rye, corn (maize), or rice. Cane, corn, and beet sugars are often added and are essential for some styles. Virtually anything that contains starch or sugar can be a source of fermentables, such as potatoes or fruits. Furthermore, other ingredients can simply add flavor, for example spices.

In the next few chapters, the ingredients commonly used for making beer will be described. At times, it may sound a little complicated, but don't panic, there won't be a test on this. I just want to give you enough background information about the ingredients so that you can choose your ingredients more intelligently. It is important to understand the tradeoffs between different types of ingredients and have an idea of some of the options available to you as a brewer. This chapter will cover malts, grains, and malt extracts. Subsequent chapters describe hops, water, yeast, and other ingredients.

## Barley and Barley Malt

The most common source of fermentable sugars used in the production of beer is from barley malt. It is made from raw barley via a process called malting. Malting begins with wetting the grain and keeping it at the proper temperature till it germinates (sprouts). After the correct amount of growth, the grain is kilned (heated and dried in a kiln). Finally, it is cleaned (i.e. the malt is separated from the rootlets that grew during germination). Malting is important because it releases enzymes stored in the barley kernels which are later used by the brewer to convert proteins, starch, and other compounds into nutrients and sugar essential for the yeast during fermentation. Furthermore, the starch in barley is bound up very tightly in a protein matrix. Malting makes this starch more easily available for making beer.

## Malt Extracts

In the brewery, the brewmaster crushes the malt, mixes it with water forming what is called "the mash," heats the mash to specific temperatures, and holds (rests) it at these temperatures for specific times. During these temperature rests, various enzymes break down complex molecules into simpler molecules. Depending on the types of malt (or, additionally, other grains and/or starch sources) used in the mash, some rests may be omitted.

**Figure 7-1**: *Mashing. In extract brewing, this has been done for you by the extract manufacturer.*

The simplest mashing schedule is where the mash is rested at a single temperature roughly between 149 and 158° F (65 and 70° C). During this rest, the starch in the mash is converted into sugars. Next the sweet liquid (called wort, pronounced WERT) is separated from the grain husks in a process called läutering (technically, pronounced LOY-ter-ing, but more commonly LAW-ter-ing). The wort is then boiled with hops, cooled, yeast is added and, after fermentation, the result is beer.

An option both to homebrewers and commercial brewers, is to purchase the wort in a dehydrated form. Malt extract manufacturers take the wort and then evaporate water under a vacuum. This dehydrated wort is called malt extract and is available in either powdered (where virtually all of the water is removed) or syrup (which is about 80% malt extract and 20% water). The powdered form is called "Dried Malt Extract" (DME) or "Spray Malt Extract" and contains about 3% water.

**Figure 7-2**: *Malt extract syrups and dried malt extract.*

Malt extracts are available in various colors and may be hopped (bittered with hops) or unhopped. Some malt extracts tend to make a sweeter beer and others result in a drier beer. As long as the malt extract is not diluted with corn syrup or other refined sugars its quality should be high and you can make excellent beer from it. Some recipes call for a particular brand of extract. In most cases you can substitute a similar product from a different manufacturer with little or no difference in flavor. What I recommend is that you experiment with the same recipe using several different malt extracts and get to know the different brands. I've used about 30 different extracts from roughly 10 different manufacturers and now I pretty much stick to five manufacturers' extracts.

In the Winter 1994 issue of Zymurgy, there was an article comparing malt extracts. Incidentally, the same issue contains a very detailed article on malt extract production. In summary, all the extracts tested were of at least "acceptable" quality although some were better than others. The article provides some important information for the formulation of recipes, namely the specific gravity of a gallon of wort made from a pound of the particular extract. This is very useful, but is not the entire picture. The fermentability of the wort (which is tied to the sweetness of the resulting beer) is almost as important.

As I mentioned above, when I brew an extract batch (yes, about 15% of my batches are still from extract), I currently use one of five brands: Northwestern, Munton & Fison (syrup and dried), Alexander's, Ireks, or Laaglander (dried). It's not that other brands are not as good, but I have a better idea of how the beer will turn out since I have lots of experience with these five brands. From using these brands, I've found that the Northwestern dried malt extract (DME) tends to result in a slightly sweeter beer and the Laaglander DME makes for a very sweet beer. DME labeled "Dutch Dried Malt Extract," "Hollander Dried Malt Extract," and Northwestern's "European Dried Malt Extract " ferment very much like Laaglander, leaving a very sweet, high finishing gravity, beer. These DME's have fooled many brewers into thinking they have a stuck ferment (where the yeast stops working prematurely). A beer made entirely from Laaglander DME or these other two similar DME's will have only 45 to 55% apparent attenuation (which means that a 1.048 wort would stop fermenting somewhere between 1.026 and 1.022, depending on your yeast's attenuation). This is not a negative if you use it to your advantage – if you are brewing a beer in which you want a higher finishing gravity (e.g. Bitter or Scottish Ale) and sweetness (e.g. a Sweet Stout), then you may want to use 1 or 2 pounds of Northwestern European DME in place of the same amount of a more fermentable extract. One final word of warning: the unfermentable sugars in Laaglander, European, and Dutch DME's can be eaten (albeit slowly) by some yeasts. Therefore, don't be surprised if beers made with these extracts have a tendency to overcarbonate after several months.

## 2-row Versus 6-row Barley Malt

There are two main varieties of barley grown for malting: 2-row and 6-row. 2-row barley has 2 rows of kernels on each ear of barley whereas 6-row has 6. Because of the way the kernels are organized on the ear, two thirds of all the 6-row kernels have a slight "twist" in the barley corn (seed). The remaining one third of the 6-row kernels are straight as are all 2-row kernels.   This is one way (besides the obvious difference in size) to distinguish 2-row from 6-row malts. There is also barley which is called "4-row," but this is actually a type of 6-row barley in which two pairs of the rows have twisted so far that they overlap, giving the appearance of there only being four rows of kernels. From the brewer's perspective, 4-row barley is equivalent to 6-row. Virtually all European malts are made from 2-row barley whereas in the US and Canada, both 2-row and 6-row malts are made. The following chart compares malts made from 2-row and 6-row barleys.

### Table 7-1: Comparing 2-row and 6-row malts.

| characteristic | 2-row | 6-row | brewing implications |
|---|---|---|---|
| **protein levels** | lower | higher | higher protein levels in the base malt require either the addition of low-protein adjuncts like rice and corn (maize) or more complicated mashing schedules; higher protein levels increase the likelihood that the finished beer will have haze; |
| **starch percentage** | higher | lower | you get slightly more extract per pound of grain with higher starch percentages; |
| **haze** | lower | higher | beer made from 2-row barley malt has been found to be less likely to be hazy than that made from 6-row barley malt; |
| **husk percentage** | lower | higher | a higher percentage of husk material means the extraction of silicates (and other undesirable compounds) is more likely; a higher percentage of husks also means less difficulty in brewing with huskless grains such as wheat; |
| **enzyme levels** | lower | higher | higher enzyme levels mean that larger amounts of non-enzymatic adjuncts, such as corn (maize), rice or potatoes can be used; |
| **price** | higher | lower | cost (while you can typically get more bushels per acre from 6-row malts, supply and demand affects malt prices far more than yield – some years 6-row can be more expensive); |

Note that the differences described above apply primarily to the base malts (the malts that must be mashed) and not the crystal or color malts. Also, in my experience, the difference between various maltsters' (manufacturers') malts is striking and this contrast is even more pronounced when it comes to crystal and dark malts (I'll tell you about these shortly) than in the case of base malts such as Pilsner or Pale Ale malt.

## Color: Lovibond, SRM and EBC

There are several methods used for determining malt and beer color. The oldest surviving method uses the Lovibond scale. Brewing grains made in the US come to us with their color given in degrees Lovibond ("degrees" is usually left off and you will see a malt listed as 60 Lovibond or 60 L). SRM is a newer method and scale (it stands for Standard Research Method), but it is close enough to Lovibond for our purposes. SRM used by American brewers and brewing scientists and usually only for beer color. EBC stands for European Brewing Convention and EBC color measurement is used for both grains and beer by most European brewers and brewing scientists. You can convert EBC to SRM for lighter colors by first adding 1.2 to the EBC degrees and then dividing by 2.65. To convert back the other way, first multiply SRM degrees by 2.65 and then subtract 1.2. These formulas are only accurate for SRM degrees below about 4.

## Specific Gravity and "points/pound/gallon"

The yeast convert sugars to $CO_2$, alcohol, and various flavor compounds. The more sugar there is in the wort, the stronger the resulting beer will be. Also, since the yeast cannot eat every type of sugar in the wort, the more sugar there is in the wort, the "heavier" or "thicker" the beer will be. The way that brewers determine the amount of sugar in the wort or beer is by measuring its specific gravity with a hydrometer. The specific gravity of the wort before yeast is added is called the "original gravity" (usually written as OG) and the gravity of the finished beer is called the "final gravity" or "terminal gravity" (usually written as FG or TG).

But how do we predict what the OG and FG will be? The FG is a bit more complicated and will be covered later, but brewers estimate the OG by adding up the contributions of each of the ingredients. The most common unit in these predictions among extract brewers is "points/pound/gallon" or "pts/lb/gal." It literally translates to "the number of points contributed by a pound of an ingredient in a gallon of wort." "Points" are the rightmost part of the specific gravity measurement (e.g. 1.057 wort contains 57 points).

If you add 6 pounds of an ingredient that contributes 35 pts/lb/gal in to the wort that will become 5 gallons of beer, the wort is expected to have:

$$(35 \times 6) / 5 = 210 / 5 = 42 \text{ points}$$

which means the OG of the wort will be approximately 1.042.

## Lager, Pilsner and Pale Ale Malts

When the germinated barley is simply dried at relatively cool temperatures, the result is a light-colored malt with most of its enzymes intact. At homebrew supply stores you will always see grain labeled "pale ale" malt. You may also see grain labeled "lager" or "pilsner" malt. The names "lager" and "pilsner" malt are used interchangeably by various maltsters. The difference between these malts and pale ale malt is in the time and temperature of the kilning (drying). Lager or pilsner malts are kilned at lower temperatures, are therefore paler and are slightly higher in enzymes and certain compounds that are driven-off during the kilning process. There is also a type of malt called "wind malt" which is even paler than pilsner malt, but I have been unable to find any commercially. If you find it somewhere, send me a note.

Pale ale malts are slightly darker, may be higher in "toasty" and/or "caramelly" flavors, and slightly lower in enzymes and other compounds. A few maltsters let their lager or pilsner malts germinate a shorter time (brewers refer to this as "undermodified" malt) which means that a more complicated mashing schedule is necessary to get all the extract out of the malt and to break down haze-forming proteins. Lager, pilsner and pale ale malts (also sometimes simply called "2-row malt" or "6-row malt") cannot be used in making beer without being mashed. If you add these types of malts to a simple extract batch, you will have a permanent haze in the finished beer from the unconverted starch.

## Crystal or Caramel Malts

"Crystal" malts (also known as "caramel" malts, or by trade names such as "Cara Pils," "Caravienne," "Caramunich," and "Special B") are a type of malt that can be used without mashing so they are often used by extract brewers. While the germinated barley is still wet, the maltster will heat the malt into the range of 150 to 170° F (66 to 77°C) and hold it there for 1 1/2 to 2 hours with very little ventilation[43]. The malt essentially "mashes" right in the husk (the enzymes in the malt convert the starches to sugars) and the interior of the grain liquefies. The temperature is then raised and the grain is ventilated so the excess moisture is driven off. When the malt cools the liquefied center hardens into an amber crystal-like solid. Depending on the time and temperature, the color of the crystal malt can vary from about 1.5 Lovibond to over 200 Lovibond.

**Figure 7-3**: *Various crystal malts (top row, center is Weyermann Wheat Caramel Malt, a crystal malt made from wheat).*

Some homebrewing books say that crystal malts need to be mashed. While this may have been true years ago, most modern crystal malts (except for Dextrine malt and several other very pale crystal malts) don't need to be mashed. The very pale crystal malts can have a considerable percentage of unconverted starch, which will give a slight haze. See the tables below to see which malts shouldn't be used unless mashed. If the crystal malt you plan to use is not listed, you can check for a starch haze by steeping a tablespoonful of the malt in a cup of 170° F (77° C) water. If it results in a hazy liquid, don't use it unless you mash.

Different maltsters' crystal malts can vary quite widely in flavor. Some tend to be very fruity, others caramelly, and even some have biscuity flavors. The differences are stunning and do carry over to the finished beer. You should pick your crystal malts as carefully as you pick your hops and yeast – considering how you want the finished beer to taste. The subtle "undertones" of the crystal malt flavors and aromas add complexity and life to the beer, especially extract beers in which a lot of the malt aroma has evaporated during the manufacturing process.

In the following table, the points/lb/gal are not the "theoretical" maximums that can be achieved in a laboratory, but rather realistic values which you can expect to get in your recipes. They are based upon gravities I've measured from a pound of the grain steeped for 30 minutes in a gallon of 160 to 170° F (71 to 77° C) water. Remember that 27 points/lb/gal means that 1 pound of this grain in a gallon of wort will produce a specific gravity of 1.027. Note that this value assumes that you are going to boil away some of the water. You see, steeping a pound of crystal malt in a gallon of water will give you about 17 to 22 points (1.017 to 1.022), but when you reduce the volume during the boil, you concentrate the wort, so you get more points.  In the following table, I'm assuming you will be losing between $1/2$ and 1 gallon of water for a 5-gallon batch size (its always important to remember that all calculations need to be relative to the batch size not boil size).  This is a 10 to 20% volume reduction.  You may also get slightly more or slightly less points depending on the freshness of your grain, the efficiency of your methods, and the fineness of your crush.  As always, there is a tradeoff when it comes to the crush: a fine crush means better extraction and more gravity points but it can also mean more polyphenol (a.k.a. tannin) extraction which can lead to astringency and chill haze.

**Table 7-2 (sheet 1 of 5): Crystal malts.**

| Crystal Malt | Color | points lb/gal | Aroma/Flavor |
|---|---|---|---|
| **Hugh Baird & Sons - Witham, Essex, England** | | | |
| Cara Malt | 10 - 13°L | 25 - 28 | light biscuity and mildly fruity aroma; aroma reminiscent of French pastry; neutral, nicely caramelly flavor; not currently available in the homebrewing market; |
| Carastan Malt | 30 - 39°L | 25 - 28 | biscuity and fruity aroma; stronger French pastry-like aroma;  caramelly flavor; |
| Crystal Malt | 50 - 60°L | 25 - 28 | more intense biscuity and fruity aroma; aroma reminiscent of French pastry; sweeter, raisiny flavor; considerable caramelly flavor; not currently available in the homebrewing market; |
| Crystal Malt | 70 - 80°L | 25 - 28 | strong biscuity aroma; slight toasty notes in aroma and flavor; caramel flavor strong; raisiny; |
| Crystal Malt | 90 - 110°L | 24 - 27 | biscuit aroma dominant; stronger toasty aroma and flavor;  very caramelly and raisiny flavor;  very slight roasty flavor; not currently available in the homebrewing market; |
| Dark Caramel Malt | ~130°L | n/a | samples unavilable; not currently available in the homebrewing market; |

## Table 7-2 (sheet 2 of 5): Crystal malts.

| Crystal Malt | Color | points/ lb/ga | Aroma/Flavor |
|---|---|---|---|
| **Beeston Malting Company - Arbroath, Tayside, Scotland** | | | |
| Pale Crystal Malt | 26°L | 24 - 27 | slightly biscuity, toasty aroma; neutral flavor – gentle toasty/caramel flavor; |
| Caramalt | 45°L | 24 - 27 | mild grainy aroma; slight toasty aroma; quite fruity flavor; mild Darjeeling tea flavor; |
| Crystal Malt | 60°L | 24 - 27 | woody, slightly biscuity, and some ripe fruit aromas; slight dark malt flavor; lots of raisin and ripe fruit flavors; |
| Dark Crystal Malt | 93°L | 24 - 27 | biscuity aroma; plum flavor; some dark malt flavor; burnt toffee flavor; hints of apple; |
| **Briess Malting Company - Chilton, Wisconsin, USA** | | | |
| Dextrine / Carapils® | 1.5°L | 10 - 14 | *this crystal malt should be mashed – it will lend a slight haze if not; if it is mashed, it will give 23 - 26 points;* pleasant, mild grainy aroma; very neutral grainy flavor; |
| Caramel 10 | 8 - 12°L | 24 - 27 | pleasant milk chocolate aroma; slight toasty aroma; toasty flavor with a milk chocolate note; very malty flavor; |
| Caramel 20 | 15 - 25°L | 24 - 27 | sweet pastry aroma (not unlike gingerbread); very caramelly flavor; holiday cookie flavor; |
| Caramel 30 | 25 - 35°L | 24 - 27 | very light milk chocolate aroma; very caramelly flavor; slight toasty aroma and flavor; |
| 2-row Caramel 40 | 35 - 45°L | 24 - 27 | biscuity aroma; mild caramelly flavor; slight Darjeeling tea finish; |
| Caramel 40 | 35 - 45°L | 24 - 27 | pleasant milk chocolate aroma; very caramelly flavor; rich pastry-like flavor – a hint of chocolate cake; |
| Caramel 50 | 45 - 55°L | 24 - 27 | sweet, rich, pastry-like aroma; pleasant plum and raisin flavor; |
| 2-row Carmel 60 | 55 - 65°L | 24 - 27 | mild Munich malt and caramel nose; strong caramel and plum flavors; |
| Caramel 60 | 55 - 65°L | 24 - 27 | pleasant milk chocolate aroma; dark caramel flavor; soft dark malt flavor; |

**Table 7-2 (sheet 3 of 5): Crystal malts.**

| Crystal Malt | Color | points/lb/gal | Aroma/Flavor |
|---|---|---|---|
| 2-row Caramel 80 | 75 - 85°L | 23 - 26 | resiny aroma; rich caramel and ripe fruit flavors; very fruity flavors; |
| Caramel 80 | 5 - 85°L | 23 - 26 | English Christmas Pudding aroma with slight fresh tobacco notes; rich, dark pastry flavor; toasty flavor with lots of dark caramel; |
| Caramel 90 | 85 - 95°L | 23 - 26 | toasted sweet pastry aroma; ripe fruit flavor: plums; mild milk chocolate flavor; |
| Caramel 120 | 100 - 120°L | 23 - 26 | resiny aroma; dark malt flavor; not very sweet (will add little sweetness); very little fruitiness; decided black malt flavor with some sharpness (can be used as a substitute for dark malt when less sharpness is desired); |
| **Crisp Maltings - Great Ryeburg, England** | | | |
| Crystal | 90°L | 25 - 28 | rather strong caramel flavor, with slight toasty overtones; ripe fruit aroma in the finish; |
| **DeWolf-Cosyns Maltings - Aolst, Belgium** | | | |
| Caramel Pils | 4 - 8°L | 25 - 28 | biscuity aroma; light malty/biscuity flavor; |
| Caravienne | 19 - 23°L | 26 - 29 | Munich malt aroma; caramelly, Munich malt flavor; |
| Caramunich | 53 - 60°L | 25 - 28 | mildly fruity aroma with some toasty notes; very fruity flavor: ripe fruit, plum-like flavor strong; |
| Special B | 75 - 150°L | 24 - 27 | strong raisin and dark malt aroma; raisin and dark caramel flavors; ripe fruit hints and a slight sharpness; |
| **Durst Malz - Bruchsal, Germany** | | | |
| Helles Crystal | 8 - 10°L | 25 - 28 | grainy aroma with a hint of fruit; very neutral Pils malt flavor; very little caramel flavor; |
| Cara-Munich Munich Crystal | 40 - 50°L | 25 - 28 | dark bread aroma; strong Munich malt flavor; mild dark bread and caramel flavors; slight citrus/orange flavor; |

Table 7-2 (sheet 4 of 5): Crystal malts.

| Crystal Malt | Color | points/ lb/gal | Aroma/Flavor |
|---|---|---|---|
| Dunkel Crystal | 80 - 90°L | 24 - 27 | definite apricot aroma; strong dried apricot flavor with hints of dark bread crust character; |
| **Ireks Arkedy - Kulmbach, Germany** | | | |
| Light Crystal | 2 - 3°L | - | *this crystal malt should be mashed – it will lend a slight haze if not; if it is mashed, it will give 25 - 28 points;* very neutral aroma – almost like a pilsner malt;  very neutral flavor; |
| Dark Crystal | 38 - 45°L | 25 - 28 | ripe fruit/plum aroma;  clean caramel flavor; |
| **Malteries Franco-Belges (Grain Millers), Nogent-Sur-Seine, France** | | | |
| CaraPilsner | 8 - 11.8°L | 24 - 27 | hard;  bready, biscuity nose (like fresh Pale Ale malt);  does not add a lot sweetness;  neutral malt flavor; |
| CaraViena | 19.2 - 23°L | 24 - 27 | slightly toasty nose; lightly caramelly; slightly fruity – faintly like apricots; |
| CarAmber | 30.5 - 38°L | 24 - 27 | quite toasty nose – like French pastry; solid caramel flavor;  very slightly melon-like flavor;  a very distinctive malt; |
| CaraMunich | 43 - 50°L | 24 - 27 | rather strongly caramelly/toasty nose; adds quite a bit of sweetness;  slightly raisiny and very clean caramel flavor; very slight chocolate flavor; |
| CaraWheat | 22.5 - 31°L | 25 - 28 | very toasty and slightly resiny aroma; adds quite a bit of sweetness;  very interesting caramel flavor – unlike barley crystal malt;  slight cognac flavor; |
| **Munton & Fison PLC - Stowmarket, Suffolk, England** | | | |
| Cara Pils | 15 - 25°L | 25 - 28 | grainy aroma; very neutral, English Pale Ale malt flavor with just a hint of Darjeeling tea; |
| Crystal 60L | 55 - 65°L | 25 - 28 | very neutral caramel flavor;  slightly biscuity; |

## Table 7-2 (sheet 5 of 5): Crystal malts.

| Crystal Malt | Color | points/ lb/gal | Aroma/Flavor |
|---|---|---|---|
| Dark Crystal | 135 - 165°L | 24 - 27 | raisiny aroma; deep caramel flavor; very toasty and roasted character; |
| **Schreier Malting Company - Sheboygan, Wisconsin, USA** | | | |
| Caramel 10 | 8 - 12°L | 24 - 27 | very slight biscuit aroma; neutral flavor with very slight biscuity note; |
| Caramel 20 | 17 - 23°L | 24 - 27 | mild biscuit aroma; clean, crisp, light caramel flavor; |
| Caramel 30 | 26 - 34°L | 24 - 27 | biscuity aroma with a hint of toastyness; sweet, raisin/ripe fruit flavor; mild caramel flavor; |
| Caramel 60 | 55 - 65°L | 23 - 26 | clean, light caramel aroma; very neutral, clean caramel flavor with a restrained sweetness; very light mixed-fruit undertones; absolutely no burnt or sharp flavors; |
| **Mich. Weyermann Malzfabrik - Bamberg, Germany** | | | |
| Carapils® | 1.8 - 2.3°L | - | *this crystal malt should be mashed – it will lend a slight haze if not;* very slight caramel aroma; light malty with just a hint of biscuit flavor; |
| Carahell® | 8 - 16°L | 25 - 28 | neutral, grainy aroma; slight fruity/melon-like flavor; |
| Caramünch® I | 38 - 48°L | 25 - 28 | very hard; light raisiny aroma; smells faintly of Christmas pudding / fruitcake; slight caramel flavor – otherwise very neutral; |
| Caramünch® II | 55 - 65°L | 25 - 28 | very hard; toasty/bready/malty aroma; slight caramel flavor with some toasty notes; |
| Caramünch® III | 70 -75°L | 25 - 28 | very hard; Munich malt, some caramel, and hints of apple and freshly cut pine; deep caramelly and strong toasty flavor; slightly roasty; |
| Wheat Caramel Malt | 76 - 102°L | 17 - 20 | great toasted bread aroma; unique toasted bread flavor with deep caramel notes; very dextrinous; unlike any barley-based crystal malt; |

Carapils®, Carahell® and Caramünch® are registered trademarks of Mich. Weyermann GmbH & Co. KG.

## High-kilned Malts

Instead of kilning the germinated barley at cooler temperatures, some malts are kilned at higher temperatures. Examples of such malts are "Vienna," "Munich," "Amber," "Aromatic," "Melanoidin," and "Brown." malts. These malts, although lower in enzymes, can still convert themselves and the lighter- and medium-colored ones are often used to make up the majority of the mash. The darkest ones are usually used in smaller quantities to add complexity to the flavor and aroma. These malts result in more malt flavor and aroma than their paler cousins. Alas, they must be mashed so they cannot be used in simple extract batches.

## Smoked Malts

Hundreds of years ago, all kilns were fired by wood fires (or in Scotland, by peat fires). The resulting malts had a smoky character. There are still some maltsters that make such malts. Rauch (pronounced rouh) malt from Bamberg is used to make the Bamberger Rauchbiers. Rauch malt as well as peat-smoked malt (called "Peated Malt") from Britain are available to homebrewers. While these malts must be mashed, you can make smoked crystal malt by smoking it yourself so that you can add smoky aromas and flavors to your extract beers without the need for mashing (see "Smoked Malt" in chapter 15).

## Roasted Malts and Roasted Barley

Roasted malts are made from pale (pale ale or pilsner) malts. Kiln-dried malts are put into a slowly rotating cylindrical roaster for 2 to 2 1/2 hours. These roasted malts can vary in the amount of roasting. The malts with the least roasting and therefore the lightest colors have names such as "toasted," "biscuit," and "Victory™" malt. They should always be used only in small amounts since their flavor contribution is quite strong. Naturally, they add toasty and biscuity flavors. Despite what several other homebrewing books say, these malts *must* be mashed so they cannot be used by extract brewers or they will give the beer a permanent starch haze if they are simply steeped in water. The same is true for home-toasted pale malts. [Victory™ is a trademark of the Briess Malting Company.]

Darker roasted malts are simply heated in the roaster at higher temperatures for longer periods. These malts include "Kiln Coffee," "chocolate," "black patent," "black" and "roasted" malt. Paler roasted malts will give a slight starch haze, but the darker ones can be used without mashing, like chocolate malt. Black malt, black patent malt, and roasted malt are essentially equivalent ("roasted malt" is a name used by several Belgian maltsters for their black malt). These darker malts can be used in extract recipes without mashing and add dark malt flavors and varying amounts of sharpness.

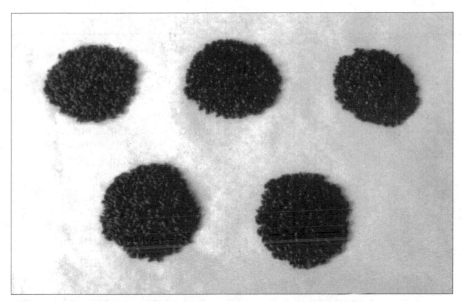

**Figure 7-4**: V*arious roasted malts and unmalted grains (l to r: chocolate, Kiln Black, roasted wheat, roasted barley, roasted rye).*

Roasted barley is made just like black malt except it is made from unmalted barley and can also be used in extract recipes without mashing. Roasted barley imparts the coffee-like flavor and aroma found in Dry Stouts and can be used in very small amounts to add a reddish color to a pale beer.

In the following table, the points/lb/gal are not the "theoretical" maximums that can be achieved in a laboratory, but rather realistic values which you can expect to get in your recipes. They are based upon gravities I've measured from a pound of the grain steeped for 30 minutes in a gallon of 160 to 170° F (71 to 77° C) water. Remember that 25 points/lb/gal means that 1 pound of this grain in a gallon of wort will produce a specific gravity of 1.025. Note that this value assumes that you are going to boil away some of the water. You see, steeping a pound of chocolate malt in a gallon of water will give you about 15 to 21 points (1.015 to 1.021), but when you reduce the volume during the boil, you concentrate the wort, so you get more points. In the following table, I'm assuming you will be losing between 1/2 and 1 gallon of water for a 5-gallon batch size. This is a 10 to 20% volume reduction. You may also get slightly more or slightly fewer points depending on the freshness of your grain, the efficiency of your methods and the fineness of your crush. With the dark malts, you need not have much concern for polyphenol (a.k.a. tannin) extraction due to too-fine a crush because dark malts are naturally acidic and thus lower the pH considerably, even with higher-carbonate water.

## Table 7-3 (sheet 1 of 3): Dark malts and roasted barleys.

| Dark Grain | Color | points/ lb/gal | Aroma/Flavor |
|---|---|---|---|
| **Hugh Baird & Sons - Witham, Essex, England** | | | |
| Chocolate Malt | 450 - 500°L | 23 - 26 | strong roasty aroma; lots of dark malt aroma; strong roasty flavor; low bitterness for a dark malt, but higher than some other chocolate malts; very neutral – like a mild black patent – no chocolaty flavors; |
| Black Malt | 500 - 550°L | 23 - 26 | strong roasty aroma; lots of dark malt aroma; slight ripe fruit aroma; very smooth for a black malt – among the lowest in bitterness for black malts; very smooth – not sharp; |
| Roasted Barley | 500 - 550°L | - | samples unavailable; not currently available in the homebrewing market; |
| **Beeston Malting Company - Arbroath, Tayside, Scotland** | | | |
| Pale Chocolate Malt | 202°L | 24 - 27 | smooth dark malt aroma; quite a bit of dark malt flavor; nice blend of smooth and sharp flavors with toasty character; |
| Chocolate Malt | 429 °L | 23 - 26 | more dark malt aroma with some woody notes; very slight smoky aroma; very smooth; minimal sharpness; |
| Roasted Barley | 493 °L | 23 - 26 | woody, slightly smoky notes; a very soft roasted barley – not as sharp as most others; smooth coffee-like flavor; |
| Black Malt | 499 °L | 23 - 26 | lots of dark malt aroma with some woody notes; very slight smoky aroma; less sharp than some other black malts; immense dark malt flavor; |
| **Briess Malting Company - Chilton, Wisconsin, USA** | | | |
| Chocolate Malt | 350 °L | 19 - 23 | dark malt and ripe fruit aroma; very slight coffee aroma and flavor; deep chocolate flavor; no sharpness; |
| Roasted Barley | 300 °L | 19 - 23 | coffee-like aroma and flavor; adds a slight "dryness" to the mouthfeel, but not as much as the Black Barley; |
| Black Malt | 500 °L | 19 - 23 | dark bread crust aroma; slight burnt aroma; dark bread crust flavor with some sharpness; |

**Table 7-3 (sheet 2 of 3): Dark malts and roasted barleys.**

| Crystal Malt | Color | points/ lb/gal | Aroma/Flavor |
|---|---|---|---|
| Black Barley | 525 °L | 19 - 23 | strong coffee-like aroma and flavor; adds a "dryness" to the mouthfeel; |
| **Crisp Maltings - Great Ryeburg, England** | | | |
| Chocolate Malt | ~700 °L | 24 - 27 | rather sharp, coffee-like flavor; less chocolaty than other chocolate malts; |
| Roasted Barley | ~800 °L | 22 - 24 | a very smooth roasted barley; low bitterness; slight coffee flavor – less than most roasted barleys; |
| Black Patent Malt | ~800 °L | 23 - 26 | very smooth, very neutral black malt; very low bitterness for a black patent malt of such intensity; |
| **DeWolf-Cosyns Maltings - Aolst, Belgium** | | | |
| Chocolate Malt | 375 - 450 °L | 23 - 26 | slightly resiny aroma; woody aroma; very biscuity flavor; dark malt flavor; slight sharpness; |
| Roasted Barley | 450 - 600 °L | 23 - 26 | coffee-like aroma and flavor; adds some "dryness" to the mouthfeel; slight sharpness; |
| Roasted Malt (a.k.a. (Black Malt) | 525 - 600 °L | 23 - 26 | dark bread crust aroma; burnt aroma; dark bread crust flavor with medium sharpness; |
| **Malteries Franco-Belges (Grain Millers), Nogent-Sur-Seine, France** | | | |
| Kilncoffee | 57 - 71°L | 19 - 24 | very distinctive flavor; *will impart a slight starch haze in pale and amber beers so it should be mashed or used only in dark beers*; lends a tan head to the beer; slight roasted malt aroma with woody notes; unique toasted marshmallow flavor; |
| Roasted Rye | 94°L | 20 - 25 | *will impart a slight starch haze in pale and amber beers so it should be mashed or used only in dark beers*; very soft; slightly resiny nose; clean dark malt aroma with hints of rose; dark rye bread flavor; smooth, soft, no harshness or sharpness at all; |
| Chocolate | 368 - 375°L | 19 - 24 | roasty; slightly woody/smoky nose; very smooth, soft, dark malt flavor; |

## Table 7-3 (sheet 3 of 3): Dark malts and roasted barleys.

| Dark Grain | Color lb/gal | points/ | Aroma/Flavor |
|---|---|---|---|
| Roasted Wheat | 375 - 565°L | 19 - 23 | dark roasted grain aroma; slight resiny flavor; mild ripe fruit flavor; smooth – not sharp; |
| Kilnblack | 375 - 565°L | 19 - 23 | dark malt aroma; very slightly resiny; very smooth dark malt flavor; sweeter than most black malts; a hint of toasted marshmallow flavor; |
| Roasted Barley | 375 - 565°L | 19 - 23 | very restrained aroma; faint coffee-like aroma; smooth, roasted flavor with hints of coffee; |
| **Munton & Fison PLC - Stowmarket, Suffolk, England** | | | |
| Chocolate Malt | 300 - 350 °L | 23 - 26 | dark malt and black bread crust aroma; toasty aroma; smooth dark malt flavor; no sharpness; very toasty flavor; slightly biscuity flavor; |
| Black Barley | 450 °L | 23 - 26 | strong coffee-like aroma; adds a "dryness" the mouthfeel; |
| Black Patent | 450 °L | 23 - 26 | black bread crust aroma; strong dark malt aroma; dark malt/dark bread crush flavor; medium sharpness; |
| **Mich. Weyermann Malzfabrik - Bamberg, Germany** | | | |
| Carafa® I | 300 - 340 °L | 23 - 26 | dark bread crust aroma; rich, smooth dark malt aroma and flavor; dark bread crust flavor; no sharpness; just a hint of smokiness and unsweetened chocolate flavor; |
| Carafa® II | 370 - 500 °L | 23 - 26 | dark bread crust aroma; a hint of smokiness; very smooth flavor with a restrained sharpness and some unsweetened chocolate flavor; |
| Carafa® III | 500 - 570 °L | 23 - 26 | dark bread crust aroma; very smooth flavor for this level of roasting; does not taste burnt, but rather deeply toasted; |

Carafa® is a registered trademark of Mich. Weyermann GmbH & Co. KG

# Other Grains and Malts

As mentioned earlier, virtually anything that contains starch can be used as a source of fermentables in beer. Corn (maize) and rice are commonly used in American Lagers. They are very low in protein and are often used to counteract the problems encountered with the use of high-protein malts. Corn and rice do make slight flavor contributions but their effect is mostly to lighten the body and mouthfeel of the beer.

Other grains commonly used in brewing include wheat, rye and oats Wheat is certainly the most popular of the three among brewers, but rye and oats are gaining favor. In some African nations, sorghum is used for making beer. Other grains which, as yet, have minimal use among commercial brewers are spelt, triticale, buckwheat, and quinoa.

The flavor that wheat adds is rather difficult to describe, but is easily identified. Malted wheat is used in American Wheat beers, Bavarian Weizens and Berliner Weissbiers. Unmalted wheat is used in many Belgian ales including Witbiers and Lambieks/Lambics although the extreme flavors of these styles make it difficult to identify the contribution of the raw wheat.

Rye has been said to impart a wide variety of flavors including "spicy," "phenolic," "minty," and even "wintergreen"[44]. Personally, I feel that its contribution is mostly in terms of mouthfeel, lending an oily character to the beer. As for flavor, I feel that it imparts a flavor similar to that of rye bread (without caraway seeds). It is quite impossible to put this flavor character into

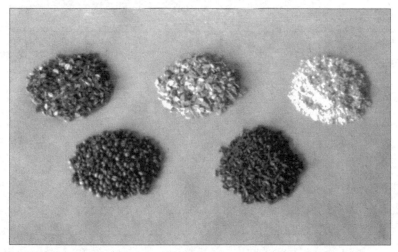

**Figure 7-5**: *(l to r) Flaked rye, torrified wheat, flaked oats, malted rye, and flaked corn.*

words so it is best that you go buy some rye malt or flaked rye and crunch on it. The flavor it imparts to the beer is quite similar to the taste of the grain, although not as intense.

Oats seem to impart a creamy, slightly oily mouthfeel more than any particular flavor. They are an essential part of Oatmeal Stouts and are sometimes used in Witbiers.

There are six main forms in which the grains can be found commonly: raw (unmalted), malted, torrified, flaked, grits and flour. Raw grains are self-explanatory and malting has been covered earlier. Torrified grains have been puffed like breakfast cereal. Flaked grains have been micronized (cooked via microwaves) and then pressed through heated rollers[45]. Grits are basically the starchy parts of the grain after removal of the husk, bran and the rest of the outer layers. Flour is made from the whole grain and then can be used as-is or further processed to increase its starch percentage[45].

The bad news for extract brewers is that all these grains must be mashed and that only wheat malt extract iscommonly available. Oatmeal stout extract is available (to the best of my knowledge) only from William's Brewing in California. Wheat malt extract can be purchased in various mixes with barley malt: 55%-45%, 60%-40%, 65%-35% and even a 100% wheat malt extract.

**Table 7-4: Wheat malt extracts.**

| Wheat malt extract | % wheat malt | Comments |
|---|---|---|
| Alexander's Sun Country | 60 | this is one of the palest extracts; |
| Briess | 65 | |
| Edme "Superbrew Gold" Weizenbier | 55 | |
| Ireks | 100 | strong smoky flavor and dark; |
| Ironmaster Wheat Beer Kit | 55 | |
| Morgan's | 55 | |
| Munton's "Connoisseurs" Wheat Beer | 55 | |
| Munton's (Munton & Fison) | 55 | both the syrup and the DME; |
| Northwestern Extract Company | 65 | |
| Premier Reserve Gold | 55 | |

## Malt and Grain Storage

I've often been asked if freezing grain is the best way to store it. While cold temperatures may slow the degradation of grains, what is most important is protecting the grain from absorbing moisture and keeping the aromatics from evaporating. In fact, unless you have put the grain in a well-sealed, moisture-proof bag or container, the cold grain can actually frost-up in the freezer and then get damp when you take it out to use. I buy my grain in bulk and the sacks in which the grain comes are not particularly good for either protecting the grain from moisture or sealing-in their aromatics. What I do is immediately transfer the grain into gasketted polyethylene buckets (a 5-gallon bucket will hold about 25 pounds of malt) and heat-sealed 6-mil polyethylene bags (a 1-gallon bag holds about 5 pounds). These I store at cellar temperatures. I've used three-year-old grain stored like this and the resulting beer showed absolutely no ill effects from the older grain. One of the reasons that malt was originally made (back in ancient times) was because people found that it kept much better than raw grain.

## Extract Fermentability

Earlier, I mentioned that Laaglander DME, Northwestern "European" DME, "Dutch" DME, and "Hollander" DME tend to leave very high final gravities (FGs). "Fermentability" is the term brewers use to refer to how far a particular wort will ferment, i.e. what the FG will be for a given original gravity (OG). Depending on the temperatures used during the mash, a wort can vary in fermentability. An extract made from a wort with high fermentability will result in a beer with a lower FG, whereas an extract made from a wort with a low fermentability will result in a beer with a higher FG. Another name for fermentability is apparent attenuation (see "Attenuation" in Chapter 10). Most extracts (besides the ones I have listed above) tend to have fermentabilities between 75 and 80%, meaning that the specific gravity will *drop* between 75 and 80% during fermentation. Note that adding crystal malts will decrease the fermentability and thus raise the FG whereas certain yeasts and bacteria can ferment sugars too complex for normal yeast and will result in a beer with a lower FG.

Therefore, unless you use one of the four very unfermentable extracts mentioned above, the FG you get is much more a function of the yeast you use than the brand of extract. To illustrate this, I fermented a wort made with only Munton & Fison DME (no crystal malts) with Wyeast American Ale #1056 and American Lager #2035. The 1.040 OG wort fermented with the #1056 had an FG of 1.010 (an apparent attenuation or fermentability of 75%) whereas the same wort fermented with the #2035 had an FG of 1.008 (an apparent attenuation or fermentability of 80%). Most other extracts I've used (except for the four very unfermentable extracts above) resulted in very similar fermentabilities. Using the

Using the same two yeasts, Alexander's Pale Malt Extract Syrup and Northwestern's Gold Syrup had apparent attenuations of 76% and 81% and Northwestern's Gold DME had apparent attenuations of 73% and 78%. While traditional differences may seem significant, note that I used a precision laboratory hydrometer to measure the final gravities. With a typical homebrewer's hydrometer, the differences would not have been measurable.

## Light, Amber and Dark Malt Extracts

"Light," "pale," and "gold" are the various names given by the manufacturers for their standard, light-colored extract. This is generally made from pale malt (either pilsner or pale ale malt) and may also contain a little light-colored crystal malt. Most extract manufacturers also make several other colors of malt extract. "Extra light" and "extra pale" are even lighter than the standard extract. "Amber," "dark," and "extra dark" have varying amounts of crystal malts and dark grains added. Some manufacturers use crystal malt to create "amber" extract, others use small amounts of dark grains. "Dark" extracts can contain chocolate, black patent, roasted barley, or some combination of the three in addition to some crystal malt too.

Currently, when I create recipes from extract, I use only light (also called "pale" or "gold" by some manufacturers) malt extracts. Because of the various ways that extract manufacturers make their amber and dark extracts, substituting one brand for another can result in noticeable changes in the flavor of the finished beer. I feel that there is less variation in the flavor of light extracts so that makes it easier to substitute one brand for another without large differences in the final flavor.

Another benefit to sticking with light malt extracts is that you can add more crystal and dark malts which gives you more control over the finished beer and adds more fresh malt aroma than you get from simply using colored extracts. You will notice, however, than many of my recipes in chapter 12 do use colored extracts. Many of these recipes have served me faithfully for nearly 10 years so I'm hesitant to re-formulate them using light extracts.

Suppose you have a recipe that calls for amber or dark malt extract and you only have light available. As I mentioned earlier, it's difficult to predict which grains a particular manufacturer uses to create their version of colored extract, but the following table gives some suggestions for making substitutions. Each line in the table represents one "recipe" for the additions you need to make *per pound* of light extract to substitute for one pound of colored extract (there are five *different* "recipes" for amber, three for dark, and one for extra dark). Note that these amounts of malts are *in addition to* any currently in the recipe.

### Table 7-5: Duplicating colored malt extract

| Extract to be duplicated | 40 to 60° L crystal malt | chocolate malt | black malt | roasted barley |
|---|---|---|---|---|
| amber | 2 ounces | – | – | – |
| | – | $1/2$ ounce | – | – |
| | – | – | $1/2$ ounce | – |
| | 1 ounce | – | – | $1/2$ ounce |
| | 1 ounce | $1/2$ ounce | – | – |
| dark | – | 2 ounces | – | – |
| | 1 ounce | 1 ounce | – | – |
| | – | – | $1/2$ ounce | $1/2$ ounce |
| extra dark | – | 1 ounce | 1 ounce | – |

# Malt Summary

So now you should have a pretty good idea of how all the different malts are made and how malt extracts fit into the homebrewing picture. Since I've presented an awful lot of information here that may be new to you, I'll summarize the important factors for extract brewers. Malted barley is the base of most beer made in the world today. It is made from barley by a process called malting. Malted barley can be further processed to make various other types of malts. Some malts must be mashed to convert their starches to sugars that yeast can eat. These include Pilsner malt, Lager malt, Pale Ale malt, Amber malt, and Biscuit malt.

If you add malts that must be mashed to an extract batch, the starch will give your beer a permanent haze. As an extract brewer, you should only be using crystal (a.k.a. caramel) malts, dark roasted malts (such as chocolate and black patent) and roasted barley. These may be used without mashing.

# Further Reading

DeClerck, J., *A Textbook of Brewing*, Vol. 1 (Chapman and Hall, London, 1957).
Farrell, N., "The Enchanting World of Malt Extract," *Zymurgy*, 17 (5) 34-41 (Winter 1994).
Fix, G. J., *Analysis of Brewing Techniques* (publication pending by Brewers Publications, 1997).
Hough, J. S., D. E. Briggs, R. Stevens, and T.W. Young, *Malting and Brewing Science*, Vol. 1 and 2 (Chapman and Hall, London, 1982).
Hough, J. S., *The Biotechnology of Malting and Brewing*, (Cambridge University Press, Cambridge, 1985).
Lodahl, M., "Malt Extracts: Cause for Concern," *Brewing Techniques*, 1 (2) 26-28 (Jul/Aug 1993).
O'Neil, C., "Extract Magic: From Field to Kettle," *Zymurgy*, 17 (5) 46-51 (Winter 1994).
Schwarz, P. and Horsley, R., "A Comparison of North American Two-Row and Six-Row Malting Barley," 4 (6) 48-55 (Nov/Dec 1996).

# HOPS

oday, we couldn't imagine beer without hops, but it was not always so. Many spices were used in the production of malt beverages. In the 7th or 8th century, hops began to be used in beer production. The use of hops in beer spread quickly, but as late as the 14th century there were still wide areas of Europe in which gruit (a blend of bog myrtle, yarrow, St. John's wort, coriander, rosemary and/or wormwood) was used for making malt beverages in the role that hops play today[46]. Hops became popular partly due to their flavor but also because they help clarify the wort, improve head retention and help keep it from spoiling. This last effect was most important to their growing popularity in the time before refrigeration.

## Hop Basics

Hops are used primarily to provide bitterness which balances the sweetness of the malt, but they also add their own distinctive flavors and aromas. They are the flowers of a perennial climbing vine (*Humulus lupulus*). Hops are either added in the boil, just after the boil and/or in the fermenter, after most of the fermentation has subsided. When they are added determines what character they will add.

Hops added in the fermenter (which is called dryhopping) as well as hops added to a device called a hop back (see chapter 4), through which the wort is filtered, impart only aroma to the beer. Those that are added within the last five minutes of the boil are called finishing hops and add primarily aroma, but can also add some hop flavor. The aroma added by the finishing hops is slightly different than that contributed by dryhops or hops in the hop back. Finishing hops are

**Figure 8-1**: *Hops on the vine in my back yard.*

also sometimes referred to as "aroma hops" (although when German brewers say "aroma hops" they probably are referring to what we call "Noble hops"). Personally, I feel that dryhopping lends a more complex aroma than either finishing or hop back hops. Boiling hops for much longer than five minutes boils off virtually all their aroma. Hops added with 5 to 15 minutes left in the boil are called flavor hops because their primary contribution to the beer is hop flavor. It is difficult to generalize the flavor of hops because each variety has a slightly different flavor profile. As the hop boiling time increases beyond 15 minutes, the flavor contributions of the hops begin to boil away and the hops contribute mostly bitterness. The following table summarizes the contributions.

| **Addition** (boil time) | **Aroma** | **Flavor** | **Bitterness** |
| --- | --- | --- | --- |
| dryhopping | very strong | very little | very little |
| hop back | strong | very little | very little |
| finishing (0-5 min) | medium | mild | little |
| flavor (5-15 min) | very little | strong | mild |
| bittering (30+ min) | virtually none | very little | strong (increases with boil time) |

Note that there is some research that indicates that "first wort hopping" may result in a superior hop aroma[47]. The experiments with first wort hopping were done on Pilsner beers and the results were based upon preferences by experienced tasters. The process involves the adding of the aroma hops (the addition normally reserved for the end of the boil) and putting them into the kettle as the wort is being introduced from the lauter tun. Now, normally, you would think that the hop aroma would evaporate during the boil. Researchers theorize that when the hops spend time in contact with the wort before the boil, some hop aroma compounds complex with wort compounds and in this way are carried through to the finished beer.

My experience with first wort hopping is that it contributes less bitterness than hops added after the boil has started, adds a small amount of hop aroma and an incredible amount of hop flavor. My (as yet untested) hypothesis as for why there is less bitterness from first wort hops than hops added at the beginning of the boil is that the hops may be coated with hot break which interferes with the extraction of alpha acids from the hops. Personally, I believe my tests indicate that first wort hopping is not a good substitute for aroma hops.

## Hop Forms

The three most common forms in which hops are available are whole, pellets, and plugs. Whole hops are also commonly called raw hops, hop cones, hop flowers, or leaf hops. This last title is a misnomer: the leaves of hops are not used in brewing. Plugs (Type 100 hops) are compressed whole hops and are virtually equivalent to whole hops. Exposure to the oxygen in air causes degradation in the various hop components (bittering, flavoring, and aromatic) so protection from air is an important consideration when storing hops. Compressing the whole hops into plugs protects the hops somewhat from exposure to air and reduces the amount of space needed for storage. Hop pellets are made by grinding whole hops and then extruding the paste through a die. There are two types of hop pellets available: Type 90 and Type 45. Type 90 are simply pelletized whole hops, whereas Type 45 hops are also known as concentrated pellets and are made from enriched hop powder. As long as the package of hops you buy has the Alpha Acid percentage listed, it is not really important if they are Type 90 or 45. Because the surface to weight ratio in pelletized hops is much smaller than in either whole hops or plugs, they have the best storageability.

**Figure 8-2**: *(l to r) Hop pellets, whole hops, and hop plugs.*

The choice of whole hops versus pellets used to be a matter of freshness. Whole hops were virtually unavailable fresh, so to get relatively fresh hops you had to buy pellets. Since the use of proper packaging has become common among homebrew supply stores in the last five years, fresh hops are available as both pellets and whole hops. So, how do you choose? Personally, I've been using pellets in the boil (I put them in mesh hop bags – one for each addition) and whole hops for dryhopping. The reason I have been using pellets is partly because they give better utilization (the fraction of the bittering potential that actually makes it into the finished beer), but mostly because (until recently) I had a wider selection of varieties available in pellet form and because they take up far less space in the freezer. I use only whole hops for dryhopping because they float and that makes siphoning the beer out of the fermenter much easier than waiting for all the pellets to sink (which they eventually do).

Two other hop products that you may encounter are hop extracts and hop oils. Hop extracts are available in isomerized and unisomerized forms. When you add hops during the boil, the alpha acids in hop resins are changed in structure (isomerized) by the heat which makes them soluble in cooled wort. Therefore, the isomerized hop extracts do not need to be boiled and can be added directly to the wort after the boil or even at bottling time. Unisomerized hop extracts need to be boiled, just like whole or pellet hops. Depending on the method of extraction, the extracts may also contain polyphenols (a.k.a. tannins), waxes, fats, and chlorophyll. The best hop extracts are made by using liquid carbon dioxide at 41 to 59° degrees F (5 to 15° C) and 50 atmospheres of pressure[48]. Hop oils impart only aroma and must be added only after the boil (otherwise, their contribution will be boiled away).

## Hop Packaging

The issue of storageability brings us to hop packaging. Commercial brewers are actually at a disadvantage to homebrewers in this respect. Because they use hundreds or thousands of pounds of hops each year, the best they can do is keep the hops cold and in the compressed bales in which the hops come from the growers. Homebrewers have the ability to buy and store their hops in oxygen-barrier packages which have had the oxygen purged from them with carbon dioxide or nitrogen gas. Because much of the cost of hops for the homebrewer is in the labor of packaging, using oxygen-barrier plastic in the packages and purging the packages before sealing, results in only a small increase in price. The improvement in storageability is phenomenal. I urge you to buy hops only in purged, oxygen-barrier packages. Oxygen-barrier plastic is either aluminized or crystal-clear but is always crisp and shiny. Polyethylene bags are soft, slightly milky in color, and are not oxygen-barrier. One way to tell that a package is not oxygen-barrier is to smell it. If you can smell hops through the package, then it's not an oxygen-barrier package. Because there is some amount of degradation in the hops even in proper packaging, ideally you should keep the hops below 32 degrees F (0 C).

**Figure 8-3**: *(l to r) Pellets in an oxygen-barrier bag, pellets in a non-oxygen-barrier bag, and whole hops in an oxygen-barrier bag.*

Some people insist that hops must also be kept dark. Actually, while long-term exposure to light does change the color of the hops to a slightly lighter, yellow-green, their brewing properties are unaffected[49]. It is not until the alpha acids are isomerized in the boil that they are affected by light (see "Skunky aroma," chapter 15).

Heat sealers are outstanding. I just bought another one for home use (in addition to the two I had for the homebrew supply shop, that I recently sold). I paid $37.99 for it at a Service Merchandise store. I've seen them for $29.99 in mailorder catalogs. Because all the hops I get either come in oxygen-barrier bags or I immediately package them in oxygen-barrier bags, I can always rely on my hops being fresh if, after using some hops from a package, I repurge the package with $CO_2$ and reseal it with the heat sealer. If you have the space in your freezer, glass jars with tight seals are a great alternative for storing hops. Purge with $CO_2$ or nitrogen if you can.

## Hop Constituents

Roughly 84% of the hop flower is vegetive matter and 16% is lupulin. The vegetive matter consists of cellulose and lignin, proteins, water, ash, polyphenols, lipids and waxes, pectin, monosaccharides, and amino acids. The lupulin is made up of soft resins (alpha acids, beta acids, and other soft resins), hard resins and essential oils. Although there are many chemical reactions that take place in the boil that involve the vegetive matter, for simplicity's sake, we'll just consider the soft resins and essential oils here.

The alpha acids in the soft resins consist primarily of humulone, cohumulone, and adhumulone. Alpha acids are responsible for the bitterness hops impart in beer. In the past, high levels of cohumulone have been associated with harsh, unpleasant bitterness and have been implicated in the reduction of head retention. My own personal experience tends to contradict this. In an experiment, I judged four beers made with exactly the same recipe except for the hops. Three of the hops were high in cohumulone (Eroica, Galena, and Olympic) and one was low (Mount Hood). The amounts of hops used were adjusted to account for the varying alpha acid percentages so that the bitterness of all three beers was the same. The beers made with the three high-alpha hops had a smoother bitterness than the Mount Hood beer. Recent work by Narziss at Weihenstephan and others at Oregon State University indicates that perhaps high cohumulone levels correlate with smoother bitterness[50]. Low cohumulone hops have been associated with improved head retention[51].

Alpha acids are soluble in hot wort, but not very soluble in cold wort. Boiling converts (isomerizes) alpha acids into iso-alpha acids which are more soluble in cold wort and therefore will pass on into the finished beer. This is why boiling is important to getting bitterness from the hops into the beer. As alpha acids oxidize, their potential for imparting bitterness to the beer decreases.

**Figure 8-4**: *Hop fields in the Hallertau region of Germany.*

The beta acids in the soft resins consist primarily of lupulone, colupulone, and adlupulone. Beta acids are not particularly bitter, but oxidized beta acids are. Therefore, as hops age, the losses in bittering potential from the alpha acids can be balanced by increased bitterness provided by the oxidized beta acids[52]. Hops that are very old will impart very little bitterness as evidenced by the almost total lack of bitterness in Lambiek/Lambic-style beers which are made with very large quantities of hops which are intentionally aged three years or more.

Essential oils are the component of the hops that adds aroma to the finished beer. There are dozens of compounds that make up the essential oils and in many cases the oxidized forms of some of these compounds are desirable. Noble hops are said to give better hop aroma after a certain amount of aging, which is undoubtedly the result of the oxidation of some of the essential oil compounds. Severely aged hops never smell particularly good and just as every hop smells different fresh (because they all have different distributions of those various compounds), every hop smells different stale. Aged Fuggle hops often smell cheesy whereas aged Cascade hops can smell piney.

## Hop Age

Hops grow during the summer and are harvested in the fall. Therefore, the most recent crop of hops will be dated from the previous summer. With proper packaging (purged, oxygen-barrier packages) and storage conditions, hops can retain both their aromatic and bittering potential for several years. In fact, because hop quality varies from year to year due to weather differences, the previous year's or two-year-old hops may be superior in quality to the most recent crop. The bottom line is that if the hops are packaged and stored well, you should have no reservations about purchasing even three-year-old hops. With imported varieties, some crop years are so poor that they are simply not imported – this is another case where you may see older hops at your retailer's store. The bottom line is: don't judge the hops simply by their crop year – judge them by their aroma. If the hops don't smell right (grassy, moldy, or cheesy, for example), take them back to your supplier and ask for your money back.

## Dryhopping Versus Finishing Hops

Dryhopping is primarily a British (and subsequently an American) practice. With the exception of Sticke (a special version of Düsseldorfer Altbier) and a rare few Belgian Ales (most notably Orval), dryhopping is uncommon among German, Bohemian, and Belgian brewers.

Studies have shown, however that the aroma imparted by dryhopping is preferred over that from finishing hops[53]. Furthermore, a more intense aroma is possible with dryhopping if the hops are in contact with the beer for a sufficient length of time. Because there is no boiling involved, less oxidation compounds of the essential oils end up in the finished beer and therefore the aroma of the beer tends to more closely resemble that of the raw hops. Finally, the hop nose imparted by dryhopping tends to be more stable than that resulting from finishing hops. It is important to note that while dryhopping may sound "better" than finishing hops, the two are far from equivalent. Once, I tried dryhopping a Bohemian Pilsner. This was a big mistake. The beer had an odd aroma and didn't smell anything like a traditional Bohemian Pilsner.

If you want to, you can add both finishing hops and dryhops to a beer, but I usually don't. I usually dryhop British and American Ales, Orval clones, and Sticke and use finishing hops for German and Bohemian styles (like Pils) in which a hop nose is appropriate.

## When to Dryhop?

The time to add the dryhops is when most of the fermentation is over. This is important for three reasons, namely sanitation, blowoff, and retaining aromatics. The former is addressed in the next section and the risk of hops clogging your blowoff hose or airlock is obvious, but to understand the theory behind the third reason, you need to understand $CO_2$ scrubbing. As the carbon dioxide, produced by the yeast, bubbles through the fermenting beer, it takes many undesirable (and some desirable) aromatic compounds with it. If you add something like fruit or dryhops while the beer is still very active, the evolving $CO_2$ will scrub out much of the desirable aroma which we seek. Waiting till the fermentation is almost still will help maximize the fragrance of the beer. I prefer to use whole hops or plugs for dryhopping because they float, but if you do use pellets, it's even more important to wait till most of the yeast has settled. Pellets sink within a few days and I believe that yeast settling on top of them tends to reduce the amount of aroma the pellets contribute.

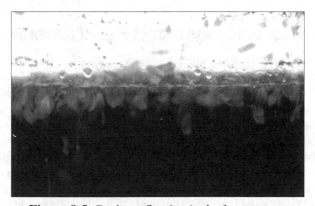

**Figure 8-5**: *Dryhops floating in the fermenter.*

## Dryhopping and Sanitation

Many homebrewers are afraid to dryhop because they are concerned that it will introduce infections. I was afraid of this too, at first, but after some reading and pondering, I tried it and loved the results. In well over 100 dryhopped batches, I've never had any infections – the handful of batches in which I had minor wild yeast infections were, in fact, all un-dryhopped. There are three reasons why sanitation regarding dryhops should not be a big concern:
1. when you add the dryhops, fermentation should be mostly complete so there is alcohol in the beer,
2. because fermentation is almost over, there are virtually no sugars or nutrients for any wild yeast or bacteria to eat, and
3. while there may be stray wild yeast or bacteria on the hops, it's not a fruitful environment in which to grow microbes – i.e. a colony is unlikely to form on a hop.

## Dryhopping and Airlock Activity

Often when a homebrewer adds dryhops to a batch of recently-fermented beer, they will notice that the airlock (which had been silent) has restarted to bubble. Their first thought is: "Oh no… I've infected my beer." This is very rarely the case. Firstly, even if you did infect the beer it would take at least a few days for the infection to multiply enough to show airlock activity – remember, there is very little sugar left, no nutrients, and virtually no oxygen. It will take more than an hour for a wild yeast to multiply enough to even create one bubble, let alone a steady series of bubbles. No, the reason that the airlock begins to move again is because the beer is saturated with $CO_2$. Adding the hops causes some of this $CO_2$ to come out of solution, bubble out of the beer, and move the airlock. This activity is nothing to worry about.

## Dryhopping, Bitterness, and Head Retention

Most homebrewing texts say that dryhopping does not affect bitterness. While it is true that boiling is required to isomerize the hop alpha acids, Don Van Valkenburg hypothesized in a Homebrew Digest post that perhaps oxidized beta acids in the dryhops could be contributing bitterness. This was based partly on the fact that the experiment his local club (Long Beach Homebrewers) performed found that the bitterness varied for a single split batch which was dryhopped with a large number of different hop varieties, but that no correlation was found between the alpha acid level and the increase in bitterness[152]. It is important to note, that in his post, Don said that between the Hallertauer and Hallertauer triploid hops (Mt. Hood, Liberty, Crystal, and Ultra), the Liberty and Hallertauer increased the bitterness most, yet Mt. Hood has the highest beta acid levels of all the hops in this group. Note that Don's hypothesis could still be correct, but this would highlight that the extent to which the beta acids were oxidized could be a bigger factor than the beta acid percentage in the hops.

Another interesting result from the experiment was that the dryhops appeared to improve head retention and that the extent to which the head retention was increased, differed among hop varieties.

## How Much to Dryhop?

The dryhopping potential of a particular batch of hops is dependent not only on the amount of essential oil, but also on how much of the aromatic compounds of that oil will make it to the finished beer. This second factor is the percentage of a particular hop's essential oils that is made up of compounds so volatile that they don't even make it into the glass, such as myrcene (which varies widely from year to year and even farm to farm)[49]. Therefore, hop oil ratings on packages are not the cure-all some would like us to believe. Anyone who tells you that you *must* have the essential oil percentage of the hops to dryhop consistently is either unaware of all the other important variables (for example, what percentage of the oil is myrcene?) or simply chooses to ignore them because they cloud the pretty picture they are trying to sell you.

**Figure 8-6**: *The casking room at the Tadcaster Brewery (Samuel Smith's).*

A good starting point for average hop aroma in ales is one ounce of hops in a five gallon batch. At ale fermentation temperatures (say, 60 to 70° degrees F / 16 to 21° C), 10 days to two weeks is about the right amount of time. You then rack the beer off the dry hops and bottle or keg. In Britain, commercial brewers typically dryhop two to three weeks (with or without periodic agitation), but remember that British cellar temperatures are quite a bit lower than ours in the US (typically the beer conditions at 55 to 60° F). British commercial brewers also use only about 1/4 to 1/2 oz (7 to 14 grams) of dryhops per gallon, but do not remove the hops before serving from the cask. Although I've never successfully dryhopped a lager (few are, commercially) it is my best guess that the lagering temperatures would slow the process and I would dryhop for four to six weeks.

## Hop Tea

Hop tea is a possible alternative to dryhopping. The procedure for making the hop tea is simply boiling a few cups of water, taking the water off the heat, and then soaking hops in it. This method can be more comfortable to those brewers who are still afraid of infections from dryhopping. After cooling the hop tea and then soaking for another hour or so, the hops are gently removed (minimizing splashing, and therefore, aeration) the liquid is added to the finished beer. Using whole hops in a hop bag is the easiest way to gently remove them from the cooled tea. There is a risk, however, of adding astringency to your beer with this method. You see, the pH of the wort is quite a bit lower than that of your tapwater and the higher the pH, the more polyphenols are extracted from the hops. If your water has a pH above 7, you may be better off adjusting the pH with some lactic or phosphoric acid so it is below 6, just to be on the safe side. Note that it may only take a fraction of a drop of acid to lower the pH of a few cups of water significantly. Exactly how much you need depends on the minerals in your water, especially carbonates.

**Figure 8-7:** *Cooling hop tea in an ice bath.*

A fellow member in the Brewers of South Suburbia homebrew club, Terry Murphree, did an experiment comparing dryhopping to adding a hop tea. He made a split batch, half of which was dryhopped. At kegging time, the dryhopped half was separated from the hops and the other half was dosed with hop tea. The same amount of hops was used in each half. For the first two weeks, the hop tea half had a fresher and more intense hop nose. Curiously, after about two weeks, the dryhopped half (although the beer had been separated from the hops), had a stronger hop nose than the hop tea half. This experiment should be re-done several times to be statistically significant, but having smelled and tasted these two beers over the course of two months, I was amazed at the difference. My only explanation could be that perhaps some oxygen was introduced as the hop tea was added. Oxygen contact with the essential oils reduces hop aroma and this could be why the dryhopped half overtook the hop tea half as time passed.

## Hop Varieties

Hopefully, the information presented here and in appendix B will help demystify hop selection and substitution. Although you will often see hops grouped as "bittering" or "aroma" in other books and articles, I prefer to not make such generalizations for most hops. Any hop can be used for bittering and most can be used for flavoring and aroma. It does make a difference if you bitter with Saaz or Olympic. While it's true that most of the flavor and virtually all of the aroma are boiled off after a 60-minute boil, there are hop components that carry through and make the beer taste smooth or rough, spicy or herbal, etc. If you do substitute one variety for another, don't forget to add more or less depending on their relative alpha acid percentages. So if you are substituting a 4% alpha acid (AA) Tettnanger for a recipe that calls for two ounces of 3% AA Saaz (or just Saaz with no AA% given), you should use 1 1/2 ounces of Tettnanger because:

$$\frac{3\% \text{ AA}}{4\% \text{ AA}} \times 2 \text{ ounces} = \frac{3}{4} \times 2 \text{ ounces} = 1 \tfrac{1}{2} \text{ ounces}$$

There has been some debate about what are Noble hops and what varieties are included in this respected group. Even among German and Czech brewers (the originators of the expression "Edelhopfen" which we translate as "Noble hops") there appear to be two different opinions of which hops belong to this group. Noted hop researcher, Dr. Alfred Haunold is one of the few hop researchers to have actually ascribed quantitative characteristics to the Noble hop group. According to Dr. Haunold[140], they have:

- relatively low percentages of alpha and beta acids,
- balanced alpha and beta acid levels,
- relatively poor storage stability,
- low cohumulone content (about 20 to 25%),
- less than 50% myrcene in the oil of freshly harvested hops,
- a relatively high level of humulene in the oil (20% or more), and
- a humulene/caryophyllene ratio above 3.

The only varieties that consistently meet these specifications are Hallertauer Mittelfrüh, Tettnang Tettnanger, Czech Saaz, Polish Lubelski, and US Liberty. Over the years, I had heard from various sources that only the first three were considered to be Noble, so I tried to get confirmation of this assertion.

During discussions about Noble hops with Ralph Olson and Dr. Greg Lewis at HopUnion USA, it was suggested that Dr. Haunold's Noble hop characteristics were not universally accepted, that some German researchers (at Hüll Research Institute) had not included Hallertauer Mittelfrüh, and that only Czech Saazer, Tettnang Tettnanger, and Spalt Spalter are considered to be Noble hops. Dr. Greg Lewis suggested that I contact Dr. Johann Maier at the Hans-Pfulf Institute for Hop Research and discuss Dr. Haunold's Noble hop characteristics. I sent Dr. Maier a letter and in his reply he said that he agrees with the characteristics and that he does indeed consider Hallertauer Mittelfrüh a Noble hop[55].

Finally, I talked to two brewmasters in Bavaria to get their perspective. Stefan Jakob at Forschungsbrauerei in Perlach said that he considers Hallertauer Mittelfrüh, Tettnanger Tettnang, and Czech Saazer to be Noble hops[54]. On the other hand, Helmut Donhauser at Paulaner Bräuhaus in Munich feels that only Tettnanger Tettnang, Czech Saazer, and Spalt Spalter are Noble hops[77].

There you have it: two different views of Noble hops. As much as I had hoped to find a single standard, it wasn't possible. So, while we still don't have complete agreement among brewmasters as to the characteristics that define Noble hops, we at least have a set of specifications that have buy-in from both German and American hop researchers.

Appendix B contains descriptions of as many hop varieties as I could find. It also contains suggested hop varieties for many beer styles.

# Further Reading

DeClerck, J., *A Textbook of Brewing*, Vol. 1 (Chapman and Hall, London, 1957).

Grant, B., "Hop Varieties and Qualities," *Zymurgy*, 13 (4) 24-26 (Special 1990).

Guzinski, G., "Hop Oil Equals Aroma and Flavor," *Zymurgy*, 13 (4) 35-37 (Special 1990).

Haunold, A. and G. B. Nickerson, "Development of a Hop with European Aroma Characteristics," *ASBC Journal*, 45 (4) 146-151.

Haunold, A. and G. B. Nickerson, "Factors Affecting Hop Production, Hop Quality, and Brewer Preference," Brewing *Techniques*, 1 (1) 18-21 (May/June 1993).

Haunold, A. and G. B. Nickerson, Mt. Hood, a New American Noble Aroma Hop, *ASBC Journal*, 48 (3) 115-118.

Haunold, A., "Development of Hop Varieties," *Zymurgy*, 13 (4) 15-23 (Special 1990).

Haunold, A., S. T. Likens, C. E. Horner, S.N. Brooks, and C. E. Zimmermann, "One-Half Century of Hop Research by the U.S. Department of Agriculture," *ASBC Journal*, 43 (3) 123-126.

Hilton, J. F. and G. H. Salazar, *Hops - The Essence of Beer and The U.S. Hop Market Report*, (S. S. Steiner, Inc., Milwaukee, Wisconsin, 1993).

Hop Variety Specifications, HopUnion, USA.

Hough, J. S., D. E. Briggs, R. Stevens, and T W Young, *Malting and Brewing Science*, Vol. 2 (Chapman and Hall, London, 1982).

Hough, J. S., *The Biotechnology of Malting and Brewing*, (Cambridge University Press, Cambridge, 1985).

Kenny, S.T., "Identification of U.S.-Grown Hop Cultivars by Hop Acid and Essential Oil Analyses," *ASBC Journal*, 48 (1) 3-8.

Laws, D. R. J., P. V. R. Shannon, and G. D. John, "Correlation of Congener Distribution and Brewing Performance of Some New Varieties of Hops," *ASBC Journal*, 34 (4) 166-170.

Lemmens, G. W. Ch., "Hops in America: A 20-Year Overview," 4 (6) 56-65 (Nov/Dec 1996).

Nickerson, G. B. and P. A. Williams, "Varietal Differences in the Proportions of Cohumulone, Adhumulone and Humulone in Hops," *ASBC Journal*, 44 (2) 91-94.

Olson, R., "Processing Hops into Bales and Pellets," *Zymurgy*, 13 (4) 29-30 (Special 1990).

Protz, R., *The Real Ale Drinker's Almanac*, (Lochar Publishing Ltd., Moffat, Scotland, 1990).

Protz, R., *The Real Ale Drinker's Almanac*, (Neil Wilson Publishing Ltd., Glasgow, Scotland, 1993).

Rager, J., "Calculating Hop Bitterness in Beer," Zymurgy, 13 (4) 53-54 (Special 1990) [Note there is an error in the formula for GA: 0.050 should be 1.050].

Rajotte, P., "Growing Hops at Home," *Zymurgy*, 13 (4) 38-40 (Special 1990).

Rajotte, P., "Multiplying Hop Plants," *Zymurgy*, 13 (4) 40-43 (Special 1990).

Ramsey, M., "Factors Influencing Hop Utilization," *Zymurgy*, 13 (4) 46-52 (Special 1990).

Smith, Q. B., "Matching Hops with Beer Styles," *Zymurgy*, 13 (4) 55-60 (Special 1990).

Van Valkenburg, D. "A Question of Pedigree - The Role of Genealogy in Hop Substitutions," *Brewing Techniques*, 3 (5), 56-57, (Sep/Oct 1995).

Wills, D., "Assessing Hop Quality," *Zymurgy*, 13 (4) 27-28 (Special 1990).

# WATER

I t's easy to forget the importance of water in making beer. You can't make good beer from bad water. What's bad water? High iron content, sulfury aromas, musty smells, fishy odors, algae aromas – any of these problems, and many more, can make for beer that is unpleasant to drink. High chlorine levels can be problematic too, but boiling drives off the chlorine, which is one of the reasons I recommend that you boil all your brewing water.

Not all waters are created equal. The mineral content of the water you use has a strong effect on the flavor of the finished beer. When you are brewing from extract, the mineral content of the water you use is not as important as if you were mashing.

If you have very hard water you probably have a softener. Bypass it for your brewing water. Simple saline water softeners work by replacing the calcium in your water with sodium. You are much better off with excess calcium in your water than excess sodium. In fact, when you eventually move on to all-grain brewing, your high-calcium water may be a blessing (depending on what other minerals are in your water). A reverse-osmosis (RO) system will reduce hardness (and other minerals) without adding sodium. You should see if you can get an analysis of both raw and processed water. Then, depending on the style you are brewing, you may sometimes want to use raw water and sometimes processed water. The tables below will show you what minerals you want in your water for each style.

Water (also called "liquor" by brewers) is the last of the four main ingredients that I addressed in my brewing. I wasn't sure why my beer would taste very authentic in some styles but was missing something in others. Back then, I was routinely adding Burton Water Salts to my beers as a habit, not even thinking about how it may be improving or detracting from my beer. Once I started paying attention to mineral content, my beers started tasting more like the commercial examples I was trying to imitate.

Burton Water Salts, since I've mentioned them, are a blend of gypsum (calcium sulfate), magnesium sulfate, and table salt (sodium chloride), which is supposed to make your water similar to the water in Burton-upon-Trent, a town famous for its water and hoppy pale ales. The problem is that everyone's water is different so how can one blend of three salts be right for everyone? Ideally, you would like to add only what you need for each style and I'll teach you how to do that, but if you want simplicity, you can go ahead and use Burton Water Salts – just don't do what I did – use them only for hoppy pale British ales.

One thing that often causes confusion is that sometimes the concentrations are given in ppm (parts per million) and other times in mg/l (milligrams per liter). The two units are equivalent, which explains why they are often used interchangeably.

**Figure 9-1**: *Some of the buildings of the oldest working brewery in the world (1040), Weihenstephan, near Munich.*

If you read more about water, you will often find statements such as "sulfate levels should be below 150 ppm" or "we must make sure that carbonate levels are kept below 100 ppm." Unless the author is talking about a particular style of beer, these statements are incorrect. How much you need of a particular mineral is dependent on the style of beer you are brewing. As you'll read later in the Famous Brewing Waters section, in many styles the sulfate levels must be higher than 150 ppm and in others you may need to have carbonate levels many times higher than 100 ppm.

## How to Use This Chapter

Personally, I feel that water chemistry is the most difficult part of brewing and if you get confused while reading this chapter, don't worry too much about it. Firstly, read "Is Your Water Good for Brewing?" You can then skim "The Effects of Certain Ions" and "What Are pH, Alkalinity and Hardness?" and come back to them later as references. When you are brewing a particular style, you don't necessarily need to understand how each ion affects the beer, but rather look at the table in "Matching Waters to Styles" and simply follow the directions. It's no more difficult than that unless you want it to be. If you want, you can skip "Famous Brewing Waters" and "Adjusting Your Water" completely for now and come back to them when you want to fine-tune your brewing.

## Is Your Water Good for Brewing?

You are entitled to a water analysis from your water supplier, be it a municipal supplier or a bottled water company. Call your water department or the bottled water company and ask for the most recent water analysis report. I've heard that some water departments can be hesitant to give you the report if they aren't sure why you want it, that's why I think that it's best to reassure them that you are a homebrewer and just would like to know the mineral content of your water. If you have a well, you will have to get it tested if you want to know your ion levels. Your local University Agricultural Extension office should be able to direct you to a water analysis company.

Some cities now rely on chloramine (sometimes added directly, sometimes created indirectly) for sanitation. If your water is sanitized via chloramine, which is not removed simply by boiling as is chlorine, you will have to use a carbon filter to get it out of your water before brewing. Chlorine combines with various compounds in the finished beer to give medicinal and/or plastic-like aromas and flavors, which is why it is important that we get rid of it.

There are many minerals that are important to brewing, but for extract brewers there are primarily two ions that need consideration. They are carbonate and sulfate.

Unless your water is high in carbonates (let's say over 150 ppm), you need not worry about reducing the carbonate levels. High levels of carbonate/bicarbonate ions will result in a high pH which, in turn, will extract excessive levels of polyphenols (a.k.a. tannins) from grain and hops in pale beers. This will result in an unpleasant astringency in the finished beer. Luckily, in most waters, carbonates/bicarbonates can be reduced simply by aerating the water, boiling it, and then decanting it off the precipitated calcium carbonate. The acidity of dark grains is balanced by the alkalinity of the carbonate ions, so if you are making a dark beer, don't pre-boil the water, thus keeping the carbonate levels high.

**Figure 9-2**: *Inside one of the open fermenters at Young's Ram Brewery, London, England.*

Unless you are trying to imitate the brewing waters of Burton-upon-Trent, Vienna, or Dortmund, high levels of sulfate ions are not a good idea. If you are trying to make a Bohemian Pilsner, you would like to have sulfate level below 10 ppm. Alas, if your sulfate levels are too high for style, there is no easy way to reduce then. You will either have to dilute it with bottled water, buy an RO system, or resign yourself to brewing styles that work well with high-sulfate water.

As long as the levels of these two ions are low and your water doesn't taste like iron or smell like fish, you have been blessed with versatile water and can brew many different styles of great beer with it. I suggest that you simply try brewing with your usual drinking water and chances are your beer will taste great. If your beer is very astringent (puckering, drying, like chewing on a grape skin or red apple peel) then you probably have high carbonate levels. If your beer has a long, lingering bitterness in the finish, then your water is probably high in sulfates. Just follow the table in "Matching Waters to Styles" and your beer will be fine.

# The Effects of Certain Ions

In the following sections, many of the effects are only important to all-grain brewing. For example, when effects on enzymatic reactions are noted these would not affect extract brewing, but have been included for completeness. Also, these ions are not independent – they all work together in the mash, boil, fermentation and beyond – adding one can upset the balance of another. An entire book could be written about brewing water so I'm afraid that I can only touch upon the most important points here.

## *Calcium*

Calcium is probably the most important ion in all-grain brewing. It lowers mash pH, assists in starch gelatization, is important to many enzymatic reactions, helps the extraction of hop bitterness, and lightens wort color. Calcium protects alpha amylase (an important enzyme in the conversion of starch to sugar) from destruction in the mash[56]. It stimulates yeast growth, but is not absolutely necessary for it[215]. A concentration between 50 and 100 ppm has been said to be optimal[57]. However, the calcium concentration in Burton-upon-Trent is over 200 ppm and that water has been envied and imitated by Pale Ale brewers around the world. A calcium deficiency in the boil can result in what is called "oxalate haze." Normally calcium oxalate forms during the boil and cakes up on the inside of the kettle. If you have very high levels of carbonates in your water and you pre-boil it to remove the carbonates you can also precipitate too much of your calcium  and may have to add some back before the boil. A concentration of less than about 10 ppm would be considered a calcium deficiency[58].

## Carbonate and bicarbonate

Carbonate and bicarbonate are treated together because they are intimately tied. The balance of carbonate ions ($CO_3^{-2}$), bicarbonate ions ($HCO_3^-$), and carbonic acid ($H_2CO_3$) shifts with the pH of the water. In a water analysis, they will often be lumped together as "alkalinity as $CaCO_3$" which means that this is the amount of carbonate and bicarbonate ions as if there was this amount of calcium carbonate in the water. For our purposes, what's important is that they increase grain steeping and boil pH, impede starch gelatinization, and can interfere with yeast flocculation.

Many books claim that carbonates can impart a harsh, bitter flavor at higher levels. This is only partly correct. The carbonates themselves don't actually cause the harsh, bitter flavor – if that were true, all beers from Dublin (where the water has very high levels of bicarbonate) would be undrinkably bitter and harsh, but they are not. No, carbonates indirectly cause harsh and bitter flavors in beer if you are not careful. You see, high levels of carbonates (or bicarbonates) raise the pH of the mash (if you are doing all-grain brewing) or the steeping grains (if you are simply steeping crystal malts in water). The high pH water extracts polyphenols (a.k.a. tannins) which give the finished beer harsh, astringent flavors and can lead to chill haze. Similarly, high pH water increases hop utilization, and therefore can increase the bitterness of the beer. Carbonates themselves are not particularly bitter – taste calcium carbonate – it tastes like chalk (because it is).

Depending on the style (see below) 50 ppm may be too much and 200 may not be enough (see Famous Brewing Waters). Usually, concentrations above 200 ppm are only acceptable if balanced by the acidity of dark malts.

## Chloride

Chloride accentuates sweetness, increases palate fullness, helps clarification and smoothes bitterness, although it can interfere with yeast flocculation[175]. Typical levels in brewing water are below 150 ppm, but some British brewers' water has more than double that[65].

## Copper

Copper is required in small amounts for yeast nutrition but levels in the water exceeding 1 ppm can cause a haze in the beer[59]. Higher levels can even be fatal to yeast. Some types of water filters remove copper.

## Fluoride

Brewing with fluoridated water appears to have no effect on brewing or the flavor of the resulting beer[60].

## Iron

Iron levels above 0.05 ppm give a metallic/blood-like flavor and can affect yeast in higher concentrations. Levels exceeding 1 ppm can cause a haze in the beer[59] and can promote gushing[61]. Some types of water filters remove iron.

## Lead

Lead levels should definitely be below 0.1 ppm[62]. Some types of water filters remove lead.

## Manganese

A very small amount of manganese is important to some enzymatic reactions, but malt should provide plenty. Excessive levels can lend a metallic taste. Levels above 0.5 ppm are considered excessive[62].

## Magnesium

At low levels (10 to 20 ppm) magnesium is a yeast nutrient and is important in some enzymatic reactions[63, 215]. At high concentrations, it has a diuretic effect. Malt usually provides sufficient magnesium so brewing water is rarely deficient. Magnesium carbonate is quite a bit more soluble than calcium carbonate so that if you have high levels of magnesium in your water, you may not be able to precipitate out as much carbonate via boiling as you might expect. Excessive amounts are a laxative, however, you would have to consume upwards of 2000 mg (20 liters, if the beer contains 100 ppm!) to have a significant effect[156].

## Nickel

Excessive nickel levels play a role in gushing and haze formation[64].

## Nitrate and nitrite

Nitrate and nitriteare tied together as we will see below. Nitrite is the troublesome one both from the yeast's perspective and the possibility of the formation of carcinogenic nitrosamines[62]. Nitrates are not a problem in beer, but can easily be converted to nitrites by various bacteria so that concentrations above 25 ppm of nitrate require your sanitation to be very stringent.

## Phosphate

Phosphate plays several very important roles in mashing, but is neutral in terms of flavor and should not be a problem in beer nor should you worry about adding any to the brewing water.

## Potassium

Potassium is necessary for yeast growth[215], but can interfere with some enzymatic reactions and lend a salty flavor to the finished beer. There is no need to add it to brewing water. Some British ales can contain up to 1100 ppm[65].

## Silicate

Silicate can contribute to haze and scale, but is flavor neutral and rarely a problem in brewing.

## Sodium

Sodium accentuates flavor, but can be unpleasant in high concentrations[176] and can even be harmful to yeast when excessive. Levels of 75 to 150 ppm are reasonable in brewing water, but some British ales can have as much as 230 ppm[65]. If you have an ion-exchange water softener (which replaces calcium ions with sodium), you should bypass it for brewing water. You would much rather have high levels of calcium than sodium in your brewing water.

## Sulfate

Sulfate accentuates hop bitterness and lends a long, dry finish to beer[176,177,178]. Miller claims that together with high sodium levels it is said to give a harsh flavor[66] but many British ales have very high levels of both ions[64] and are not unpleasant, so I tend to question this assertion. Sulfate is one of the primary ions

**Figure 9-3**: *Burton Bridge Brewery, Burton-upon-Trent, England.*

responsible for permanent hardness. If your water is high in sulfate and you want to brew beers that require low sulfate levels (e.g. Pilsner) your only options are to buy bottled water, purchase a Reverse Osmosis water treatment system, or buy distilled water and blend your tap water with the distilled (the ion concentration changes will all be linear – i.e. if you mix your water with distilled water 50/50, you will cut the sulfate concentration in half). In my experience, as little as 20 ppm of sulfate is too much for very hoppy Bohemian Pilsners.

## Tin

High levels of tin levels promote gushing[61] and levels exceeding 0.5 ppm can cause a haze in the beer[67].

## Zinc

Zinc is a yeast nutrient, crucial to many enzymatic processes, but can promote yeast autolysis and impede enzymatic reactions at high concentrations[69].

# What are pH, Alkalinity and Hardness?

The term "pH" stands for the "power of hydrogen" and is a measure of the acidity of a liquid. It ranges from 1 (very acidic) to 14 (very alkaline). Typically, you would like your mash pH to be in the mid to low 5's. This will drop in the boil, ferment, and conditioning, reaching a range of about 3.9 to 4.6 in most finished beers. Some sour styles like Lambiek/Lambic, Berliner Weiss, and Flanders Brown can reach well down into the low 3's. Note that if your wort pH is too low (below 5.0) it will reduce the amount of break that forms during the boil[25] and can result in problems with chill haze and shelf life.

The alkalinity of your water tells you how it will react to the addition of acid. Alkalinity can be mathematically defined as the concentration of bicarbonate ($HCO_3^-$), plus two times the concentration of carbonate (because carbonate ions, $CO_3^{-2}$, have twice the ability to react with acids), plus the concentration of hydroxide ($OH^-$), minus the concentration of hydrogen ions ($H^+$). Water having high alkalinity is difficult to brew with (especially for all-grain) because all those carbonate and bicarbonate ions keep the pH high when what we really want is for the pH to be in the range of 5.0 to 5.5. A high pH affects enzymatic reactions, polyphenol extraction from grain and hops, bitterness extraction from the hops, hot and cold break formation, and yeast performance. If your water's alkalinity is high, in most cases you can simply precipitate carbonate as calcium carbonate by boiling and then decanting the water off the white flakes.

A number of authors have written that alkaline water is inherently bad for brewing because it promotes the formation of harsh flavor components from hop compounds. However, I suspect that this is primarily due to the high pH extracting polyphenols (a.k.a. tannins) from the malt in the mash and hops in the boil, and would not be a problem if the mash and boil pH were lowered (with phosphoric acid, for example).

Hardness is primarily a measure of calcium and magnesium in your water. On a water analysis, the hardness is a calculated value which is a linear function of calcium, magnesium, iron, and manganese concentrations. Sometimes an analysis will say: "total hardness;" and "non-carbonate hardness." Total hardness is the sum of carbonate and non-carbonate hardness. From a brewer's perspective, hard water is usually a blessing. I say usually because for some styles, like Pilsner, you need soft water. Also note that the ion concentrations in the brewing water are far more important to all-grain brewers than to extract brewers. As extract brewers, we care mostly about the ions that affect flavor.

There are two types of hardness: temporary and permanent. The temporary hardness is that fraction of your total hardness that can be lowered by boiling. Sound familiar? Permanent hardness is that fraction which cannot. Think of water as being a sort of ion soup. There are calcium ions, carbonate ions, sulfate ions, and many other ions, all swimming around. When you aerate then boil this water, you boil out the dissolved carbon dioxide, the water can no longer support the levels of dissolved carbonate so it precipitates out as calcium carbonate, thus lowering both the hardness and the alkalinity. Calcium sulfate is far more soluble in water and won't react in this way. Therefore, water that has a high level of sulfate ions will always have quite a bit of calcium in it and thus will be permanently hard.

In water reports, hardness and alkalinity are often expressed as "ppm as calcium carbonate." What this means is that the water appears as if this many ppm of calcium carbonate were in it although some of the hardness or alkalinity may be due to other minerals.

## Matching Waters to Styles

Why should a brewer want to change perfectly good brewing water? Because certain ions have a big effect on the flavor of the finishcd beer and some styles (see Famous Brewing Waters, below, for some classic examples) require high levels of particular ions to taste authentic.

Many books will say that Bohemian Pilsners require very soft water. This is true, but "soft water" does not mean the water has no ions in it. Remember hardness is primarily based on the calcium and magnesium ion concentrations. If you took distilled water and added sodium bicarbonate (baking soda) or sodium carbonate (washing soda) to it, you could make the pH very high and, frankly, unsuitable for brewing. It would still be incredibly soft (no calcium or magnesium) but it would be terrible for brewing a Bohemian Pilsner. Furthermore, if you took distilled water and added calcium chloride to it, you could make it quite hard and still brew an excellent Bohemian Pilsner with it. What you really want for Bohemian Pilsner is water that is low in sulfate and carbonate/bicarbonate ions.

In table 9-1, we are assuming that you have determined that your water is acceptable for brewing (e.g. doesn't taste like iron or smell like fish) and that you know approximately what your water is like. The best way to tell what kind of water you have is by getting a water analysis (available free from your water supplier), but there are simpler ways that, for extract brewing, will do just as well. If, when you boil your tapwater, you get a powdery white precipitate, then your water is high in carbonates. If you don't get a white precipitate after boiling, but you have hard water (soap just doesn't want to lather) your water is probably high in sulfates. Another way to tell that you have high-sulfate water is if beers you make with plain tapwater (no salt additions) have a long, dry, lingering bitterness. You will have to get a water analysis to find out if your water is high in both carbonates and sulfates.

These guidelines are very general and will not produce a mineral profile that exactly imitates the water of a particular style. While it is sometimes possible to make very close approximations of some waters with very precise additions of various salts and acids, this table is meant to get the general characteristics needed to make a particular style of beer. This method also cannot account for the mineral content of various manufacturer's extracts.

In the following table, "Almost ion-free" means low levels of sulfate (less than 25 ppm) and carbonate/bicarbonate (less than 50 ppm). "Medium" means average levels (around 50 ppm of sulfate and around 100 ppm of carbonate/bicarbonate). "High $SO_4$" means 100 or more ppm of sulfate. "High $CO_3$" means 175 ppm or more of carbonate/bicarbonate.

**Table 9-1: Matching waters to beer styles.**

| STYLE | YOUR WATER | | | | |
|---|---|---|---|---|---|
| | Almost ion-free | Medium | High $SO_4$ | High $CO_3$ | High $SO_4$ and $CO_3$ |
| Pilsner (Bohemian) | **A or B** | **B** | **B** | **B** | **B** |
| Bière Blanche, Cream Ale/Lager, Dry Beer, Fruit Beer, Ice Beer, Pilsner (all except Bohemian), Tripel, Wheat (American), White, Witbier | **A** | **A or C** | **C** | **C** | **C** |
| 60/-, 70/-, 80/-, 90/-, Altbier (Düsseldorf-style), Altbier (Münster-style), Barleywine, Bavarian Weizen, Belgian Ale, Belgian Golden Strong Ale, Belgian Strong Ale, Berliner Weiss, Bière de Garde, Blonde Ale/Lager, Brown Ale (American or Northern English), California Common Beer, Continental Dark, Dark (American), Doppelbock (Helles), Dubbel, Eisbock, Export (Scottish), Flanders Brown Ale, Flanders Red Ale, Heavy, Helles Bock, India Pale Ale (American-style), Kölsch, Light (Scottish), Märzen, Mild (pale), Munich Helles, Oktoberfest, Pale Ale (American), Rauchbier, Red Beer, Rye Beer, Saison, Smoked Beer, Steinbier, Sticke, Trappist/Abbey Ales, Vienna, Weizenbock | **G** | **A** | **D** | **E** | **P** |
| Altbier (Dortmund-style), Dortmunder/Export | **H** | **H** | **A** | **I** | **J** |
| Bitters (all types), India Pale Ale (Traditional English-style), Old Ale | **K** | **K** | **H** | **I** | **J** |
| Black Beer, Bock (Traditional), Brown Ale (Southern English), Doppelbock (Traditional), Dunkelweizen, Mild (dark), Munich Dunkel, Porter | **L** | **M** | **F** | **A** | **F** |
| Stout (all types) Faro, Lambiek/Lambic | **N** | **L** | **O** | **L** | **O** |

## How to treat your water

Perform the following treatments based upon the style you are brewing and the water you have. Add the chalk along with the extracts! This is important because chalk will not fully dissolve in plain water, but will dissolve when added to the acidic wort in the kettle.

A - use tapwater

B - use distilled water

C - use low-ion bottled water (read the label – you want it low in sulfate and carbonate)

D - use 50% tapwater, 50% low-ion bottled water

E - aerate, boil, pour the water off the precipitate and add 3/4 level teaspoon of food-grade gypsum per 5 gallons

F - use low-ion bottled water and add 3 level teaspoons of food-grade chalk, along with the extracts, per 5 gallons

G - use tapwater, adding 2 level teaspoons of food-grade chalk and 1/3 level teaspoon of food-grade gypsum, along with the extracts, per 5 gallons

H - use tapwater, adding 1 level teaspoon of food-grade gypsum per 5 gallons

I - use tapwater, adding 3 level teaspoons of food-grade gypsum per 5 gallons

J - use tapwater, adding 2 level teaspoons of food-grade gypsum per 5 gallons

K - use tapwater, adding 4 level teaspoons of food-grade gypsum per 5 gallons

L - use tapwater, adding 3 level teaspoons of food-grade chalk, along with the extracts, per 5 gallons

M - use tapwater, adding 1 level teaspoon of food-grade chalk, along with the extracts, per 5 gallons

N - use tapwater, adding 5 level teaspoons of food-grade chalk, along with the extracts, per 5 gallons

O - use low-ion bottled water, adding 5 level teaspoons of food-grade chalk, along with the extracts, per 5 gallons

P - dilute tapwater 50/50 with distilled water

# Famous Brewing Waters

Some cities are associated with certain styles of beer. The obvious ones are Pilsen with Pilsner, Munich with Munich Dunkel and Dortmund with Dortmunder. Burton-on-Trent is famous for its Pale Ales and Dublin for its Stout. Have you ever wondered why? It's because of the water! If not for the extremely low-ion water of Pilsen, the brewers there would never have been able to brew those pale, highly-hopped lagers. Dublin water is very high in carbonates and thus pale beers were impossible to brew before brewing science figured out how ions affect brewing and how to change the ion profile of water.

You will notice that there are considerable ranges in some of the ion concentrations. One possible reason is that samples may have been taken at different times of the year (ion concentrations can vary greatly throughout the year). Another reason is that perhaps the samples were taken from various wells. Bear in mind that the ion concentrations in all waters vary from month-to-month, and there can be considerable variation in a particular area, so don't necessarily take these figures as "law." Note also, that it doesn't account for any processing the brewers may perform to alter the ion concentrations. The following table gives the ion concentrations in ppm (or mg/l).

### Table 9-2: Famous brewing waters.

| SOURCE | $Ca^{+2}$ | $Mg^{+2}$ | $Na^+$ | $CO_3^{-2}$ | $SO_4^{-2}$ | $Cl^-$ |
|---|---|---|---|---|---|---|
| Antwerp (De Konick) | 90 | 11 | 37 | 76 | 84 | 57 |
| Beerse region (Westmalle) | 41 | 8 | 16 | 91 | 62 | 26 |
| Brugge (Brugs Tarwbier) | 132 | 13 | 20 | 326 | 99 | 38 |
| Brussels region | 100 | 11 | 18 | 250 | 70 | 41 |
| Burton-upon-Trent | 260-300 | 45-65 | 30-55 | 200-300 | 630-725 | 25-40 |
| Dortmund | 225-250 | 25-40 | 60-70 | 180-550 | 120-280 | 60-100 |
| Dublin | 110-120 | 4 | 12 | 150-320 | 50-55 | 19 |
| Düsseldorf | 40 | n/a | 25 | n/a | 80 | 45 |
| Edinburgh | 100-140 | 18-60 | 20-80 | 140-225 | 96-140 | 20-45 |
| Köln (Cologne) | 104 | 15 | 52 | 152 | 86 | 109 |
| London | 50-55 | 20-35 | 80-100 | 100-160 | 30-80 | 30-60 |
| Munich | 75-110 | 18-21 | 2 | 150-175 | 10-80 | 2-35 |
| Pilsen | 7 | 2 | 2 | 15 | 5 | 5 |
| San Francisco | 24 | 15 | 28 | 104 | 39 | 39 |
| Vienna | 200 | 60 | 8 | 120 | 125 | 12 |
| Willebroek/Rumst region (Duvel) | 68 | 8 | 33 | 143 | 70 | 60 |

Sources: city water analyses, DeClerck, Hough, et. al, and Homebrew Digest posts from Bob Bloodworth, A.J. deLange, and Dave Draper.

## Adjusting Your Water

From the following tables, you can determine how many ppm of a particular ion is increased when you add a teaspoon or gram of the commonly used brewing salts. It works very simply: if you need 350 ppm of sulfate and your water analysis says you have 50, from the following tables you can determine how many

**Figure 9-4**: *Paulaner's Brewpub in Munich, Germany.*

grams or teaspoons of gypsum or Epsom Salts you need to add to get 300 additional ppm of sulfate. You will soon notice that adding gypsum to boost sulfate levels also adds calcium. Don't panic if you cannot get your water adjusted perfectly.

The primary ions of interest from an extract brewing perspective are sulfates and carbonates. For pale ales such as Bitters and India Pale Ales, make sure that you have enough sulfate and chloride in your water and don't be too concerned if the other ions are a little high or low. For dark beers, make sure that your carbonate levels are close. If you have an option (like calcium chloride), don't use gypsum (calcium sulfate) to boost calcium levels unless you need the additional sulfate ions too. For all Pilsners make sure that sulfate levels are low, especially for Bohemian Pilsners. You may even have to blend your water with distilled to reduce them.

## Adjusting Water with Salts

It is important to note that calcium chloride is very hygroscopic (it absorbs water) and must be kept in a well-sealed container. You will note that there are two types of calcium chloride listed: anhydrous (no water) and dihydrate (two molecules of water per molecule of $CaCl_2$). If you leave the anhydrous type out exposed to air, it will absorb water and quickly become the dihydrate. The dihydrate will absorb even more water (eventually, it will turn into a white soup!) and the data in the table below will no longer be valid. Therefore, you have to be very careful with all forms of calcium chloride and store them in screw-top containers that has a good seal in the lid.

The number of grams of each of these salts in a teaspoon can vary significantly depending on how finely they are ground. For the most accurate water adjustments, weigh out your additions rather than relying on a teaspoon for measurement.

Calcium Sulfate (Gypsum)

| $CaSO_4 \cdot 2H_2O$ | ppm $Ca^{+2}$ | ppm $SO_4^{-2}$ |
|---|---|---|
| 1g/liter | 232.88 | 557.77 |
| 1g/gallon | 61.58 | 147.36 |
| 1g/5 gallons | 12.31 | 29.47 |
| 1tsp/liter | 1117.82 | 2677.30 |
| 1tsp/gallon | 295.33 | 707.34 |
| 1tsp/5 gallons | 59.07 | 141.47 |

Magnesium Sulfate (Epsom Salts)

| $MgSO4 \cdot 7H2O$ | ppm $Mg^{-2}$ | ppm $SO_4^{-2}$ |
|---|---|---|
| 1g/liter | 98.64 | 389.58 |
| 1g/gallon | 26.06 | 102.93 |
| 1g/5 gallons | 5.21 | 20.59 |
| 1tsp/liter | 335.38 | 1324.57 |
| 1tsp/gallon | 88.61 | 349.95 |
| 1tsp/5 gallons | 17.72 | 69.99 |

Calcium Carbonate (Chalk)

| $CaCO_3$ | ppm $Ca^{+2}$ | ppm $CO_3^{-2}$ |
|---|---|---|
| 1g/liter | 400.44 | 599.55 |
| 1g/gallon | 105.80 | 158.40 |
| 1g/5 gallons | 21.16 | 31.68 |
| 1tsp/liter | 720.79 | 1079.19 |
| 1tsp/gallon | 190.43 | 285.12 |
| 1tsp/5 gallons | 38.09 | 57.02 |

Soldium Chloride (Table Salt)

| NaCl | ppm $Na^+$ | ppm $Cl^-$ |
|---|---|---|
| 1g/liter | 3393.37 | 606.62 |
| 1g/gallon | 103.93 | 160.27 |
| 1g/5 gallons | 20.79 | 32.05 |
| 1tsp/liter | 2084.86 | 3215.09 |
| 1tsp/gallon | 550.82 | 849.43 |
| 1tsp/5 gallons | 110.16 | 169.89 |

Calcium Chloride (anhydrous)

| $CaCl_2$ | ppm $Ca^{+2}$ | ppm $Cl^-$ |
|---|---|---|
| 1g/liter | 361.13 | 638.87 |
| 1g/gallon | 95.41 | 168.79 |
| 1g/5 gallons | 19.08 | 33.76 |
| 1tsp/liter | 3791.87 | 6708.14 |
| 1tsp/gallon | 1001.81 | 1772.29 |
| 1tsp/5 gallons | 200.36 | 354.46 |

Calcium Chloride (dihydrate)

| $CaCl_2 \cdot 2H_2O$ | ppm $Ca^{+2}$ | ppm $Cl^-$ |
|---|---|---|
| 1g/liter | 272.62 | 482.3 |
| 1g/gallon | 72.03 | 127.42 |
| 1g/5 gallons | 14.41 | 25.48 |
| 1tsp/liter | 1150.46 | 2035.31 |
| 1tsp/gallon | 303.95 | 537.73 |
| 1tsp/5 gallons | 60.79 | 107.55 |

# Further Reading

DeClerck, J., *A Textbook of Brewing*, Vol. 1 (Chapman and Hall, London, 1957). Hough, J. S., *The Biotechnology of Malting and Brewing*, (Cambridge University Press, Cambridge, 1985).

deLange, A. J., a series of posts on Classic Brewing Waters, *Homebrew Digests* #1761 to #1813.

Fix, G. J., *Principles of Brewing Science* (Brewers Publications, Boulder, 1989).

Hough, J. S., D. E. Briggs, R. Stevens, and T.W. Young, *Malting and Brewing Science*, Vol. 1 and 2 (Chapman and Hall, London, 1982).

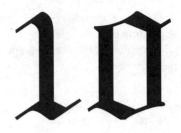

# YEAST

**W**hich ingredient affects the beer the most? The extract brand you use? The hop variety? The level of sulfate in the water? No. It's the yeast strain that you use. Yes, it's true and it's a crime that many homebrewers, even book authors, neglect the importance of yeast in recipes. After specifying a particular brand of extract and insisting that you should use 2 1/4 ounce of a particular hop variety and giving the sulfate level of the water in parts per million, there it is – on the very last line of the recipe: "Ale Yeast." No strain specified, sometimes not even a brand name! It's a crime…

Back in the early 1980's, when homebrewers usually had only two or three dry yeasts to choose from and no liquid yeasts available, that's when these attitudes about yeast were formed. But now, we have so many choices of yeasts: Wyeast Laboratories, The Yeast Culture Kit Company, Brewer's Resource, and Head Start Brewing Cultures, just to name a few. So, there's no excuse to limit your choices of yeast. Furthermore, once you have smelled and tasted the amazing diversity of aromas and flavors available, you will understand why I place so much importance on yeast.

Brewer's yeast is usually of the *Saccharomyces* genus. In a few styles, such as Lambieks/Lambics, the *Kloeckera* and *Brettanomyces* genera play important roles. There are many (myself included) who speculate that *Brettanomyces* yeasts were important to original 1720's-style Porters, 1830's-style India Pale Ales, and even modern, cask-conditioned strong ales. There are a number of species of the *Saccharomyces* genus that are important to brewing (for example *S. diastaticus* and *S. bayanus*) but the one that is most commonly used by beer brewers is *S. cerevisiae*. Formerly, top-fermenting or ale yeasts were classified as *S. cerevisiae*, whereas bottom-fermenting or lager yeasts were classified as *S. uvarum* (formerly called *S. carlsbergensis*). Recently, lager yeasts have been reclassified by yeast taxonomists to be a variant of *S. cerevisiae*, so now lager yeasts are officially known as *S. cerevisiae var. uvarum*[72]. There are many other genera and species of yeast, but usually their contributions to beer are unwelcome – they can give the beer off flavors and aromas or ferment all the sugars away leaving a very dry beer.

# The Language of Yeast

There are a number of words that need to be defined before talking about yeast.

## Attenuation

There are many different sugars present in wort. Not all of them are fermentable by all strains of yeast. Some yeast strains will eat virtually everything in sight, whereas others are more selective and only eat the simpler sugars. Attenuation is the measure of how much of the sugars in an average wort a particular yeast strain will eat. A yeast that is said to be a "good attenuator" or has "high attenuation" is one that will eat more types of sugar than one that is a "poor attenuator" or has "low attenuation." Neither type of yeast is better than the other – it's important to have both types at your disposal. If you want a maltier, sweeter beer, use a low attenuation yeast. A high attenuation yeast should be used when you want to make a drier beer. Some wild yeasts are known as "super attenuators." These yeasts make extremely dry and unpleasant beer.

## Autolysis

Autolysis sometimes occurs when yeast are starved for food. They excrete an enzyme that breaks down the cell walls of their neighboring yeasts. The resulting effect on the beer is a sulfury or rubbery aroma and flavor. Personally, I feel that the risk of autolysis has been overemphasized by some authors. My suspicion is that this is because back when these authors started brewing:

- liquid yeasts were unavailable,
- rehydration of dry yeast was not usually done, and
- most stores did not refrigerate their dry yeast.

I feel that with healthy, properly maintained yeasts (rehydration of dry yeasts and not letting liquid yeasts starve), and avoiding letting the fermenter get too warm, autolysis should not pose a problem for at least four weeks. I won a 1st place in the AHA Nationals 1st round with a Barleywine that spent 9 months in the primary at cellar temperatures! Granted, Barleywines have a lot more intensity to cover up off-flavors, so I wouldn't want to try this on an American Pilsner, but none of my homebrewed beers have ever showed any signs of autolysis and many have spent months in the primary.

## Bottom-fermenting

Bottom-fermenting yeast, unlike top-fermenting yeast, do not have the tendency to rise to the top of the fermenting beer. It used to be that lager yeasts (*Saccharomyces cerevisiae var. uvarum*) were bottom-fermenting and ale yeasts (*Saccharomyces cerevisiae*) were top-fermenting, but these days there are many yeasts that break these rules.

## Cropping

Cropping is the brewer's term for harvesting yeast. "Top-cropping yeast" is another name for "top-fermenting yeast" because the yeast can be harvested from the top of the fermenter. Similarly "bottom-cropping yeast" is another name for "bottom-fermenting yeast."

## Flocculation

Flocculation is the rate at which the yeast cells clump together during and after fermentation and is typically related to attenuation. A "good flocculator" or "strong flocculator" is one that quickly either forms a thick yeast cake that floats on the top of the beer like a large tan sponge (top-fermenting) or crashes to the bottom of the fermenter (bottom-fermenting). This type of yeast is likely to be a poor attenuator and leave a relatively sweet beer. A "weak flocculator" or "low flocculator" is a yeast that lingers in suspension – one that takes its time to sediment in the fermenter, keg or bottle. Some yeasts are such poor flocculators that you need to use some kind of finings or the yeast will continue to cloud the beer. If you reuse yeast and have a culture that used to flocculate well, but is beginning to flocculate poorly, you may have one of two problems: 1) mutation or 2) wild yeast infection. It's difficult to tell which is the cause of the problem, but whichever cause it is, the solution is to get a fresh culture.

## Pitching

Pitching is the brewer's term for adding yeast to the wort.

## Plate

A plate is what brewers and biologists commonly call a Petri Dish with some kind of media in it. Plate can also be a verb – see plating.

## Plating

Plating is a method of isolating yeast. Basically, it involves "pouring a plate" (pouring molten solid media into a Petri Dish), letting it cool and solidify, taking a sterilized loop of wire, dipping it into a yeast sample or a sample of beer containing yeast, streaking (dragging the wire across the media) the yeast out onto the plate, letting it grow, and then selecting a single colony to use either on another plate, to store on a slant or stab, or to inoculate a starter. If you streak the yeast well, you will be able to identify individual colonies. Each colony is very likely to have started from a single yeast cell. In this way, you can isolate yeast from mixed strain cultures or contaminated cultures. Volume II of this series covers plating as well as other yeast culturing techniques in detail.

**Figure 10-1**: *Petri dish.*

## Powdery

A powdery yeast is one that, after it settles in the bottom of the fermenter, keg or bottle, is easily disturbed. Poorly flocculating yeasts are more likely to be powdery (if they ever flocculate at all) and they tend to attenuate more highly than strongly-flocculating yeasts.

## Rehydration

Rehydration is the process by which dry (dried) yeast reabsorbs water. It is the first step in using dry yeast in a beer and is highly recommended. Yeast should be rehydrated for 15 to 30 minutes in water (not wort) that has been boiled to sanitize it and then cooled to between 90 and 110° F (32 and 43° C)[73]. See "Rehydrating Dry Yeast" below for more details on rehydration.

## Rousing

Rousing is the mixing of settled yeast back into suspension in fermenting beer. Some yeast strains are so eager to flocculate that they quit fermenting early. To get reasonable attenuation levels with these yeasts they must be roused. In commercial breweries this is a rather difficult job. At the Tadcaster Brewery (Samuel Smith's) they use pumps and sprayers to rouse the yeast. This not only resuspends the yeast but also aerates the fermenting beer increasing diacetyl production. For homebrewers, rousing can be done simply by carefully rocking the fermenter back and forth until the yeast is stirred up. Since the airlock prevents air from getting in and the headspace of the fermenter is all $CO_2$, aeration can be avoided. I usually rouse the highly flocculent yeasts after two or three days of fermentation and then every other day for a week. If you are fermenting on the cold end of the yeast's preferred temperature range, you may want to rouse every other day for two weeks.

**Figure 10-2**: *Fishtails rousing the yeast in the Yorkshire Stone Squares at Tadcaster Brewery (Samuel Smith's).*

## Single-Cell Yeast

A "single-cell yeast" is actually a misnomer. When someone says they use a single-cell yeast, that means that they have made up a batch using a single *strain* culture that started out as a single yeast cell (see Plating).

## Slant

A slant is a method for storing yeast. It consists of some solid media that has been molten, sterilized, and then allowed to solidify with the container (usually a tall, narrow, screw-top, glass tube) at an angle. The reason for this angle is because you get more surface area that way. Once the slant is prepared, a wire loop of yeast is usually dragged across the surface of the media. Slants are much better for storing yeast for longer periods of time (6 months to 1 year is usually the recommended length of time) than is liquid media.

**Figure 10-3**: *A yeast slant.*

Eventually, the yeast will starve, even on a slant, so you should prepare a new slant every 6 to 12 months and throw out the old one. Volume II of this series covers making and using slants as well as other yeast culturing techniques in detail.

## Slurry

Yeast slurry is the thick cake of yeast at the bottom of the fermenter (or starter). Note that in a fermenter, there will be two layers of sediment: a lighter tan sediment (the yeast) and a darker tan sediment (the hot and cold break).

**Figure 10-4**: *Yeast slurry at the bottom of a starter.*

## Stab

A stab is like a slant, but instead of dragging the yeast sample across the media, the sample is stabbed into the media. A stab is reported to protect a yeast sample longer than a slant.

## Starter

When we pitch the yeast, we want it to out-compete other microorganisms for food, oxygen and nutrients. If we pitch the yeast package into a small volume of wort first and then, pitch that into a larger volume, we are giving the yeast a significant advantage over its competitors. These intermediate, "mini-batches" of beer are called starters. In addition to building up a larger yeast mass, we have the option of pouring off much of the spent wort and pitching only the yeast.

## Top-fermenting

Top-fermenting yeast, unlike bottom-fermenting yeast, have the tendency to rise to the top of the fermenting beer. It used to be that lager yeasts (*Saccharomyces cerevisiae var. uvarum*) were bottom-fermenting and ale yeasts (*Saccharomyces cerevisiae*) were top-fermenting, but these days there are many yeasts that break these rules.

## Viable

Viability is the measure of what percentage of a yeast culture is still alive and able to reproduce.

## Wild Yeast

Let's face it... all yeasts used to be wild. Once yeast was identified as the cause of fermentation, techniques soon followed for isolating single yeasts from mixtures of many yeasts. In nature, there are many strains of yeast, all mixed together, floating around in the air, growing on the surface of fruits (that white powder on the skin of grapes is yeast!). Brewers isolated yeasts from these mixtures. They selected them primarily on the basis of flavor (how good is the beer they make), fermentation characteristics (fast-starting, fast-finishing), byproducts (actually, lack of unwanted ones), and flocculation. When a random yeast floats into your fermenter and multiplies up to significant numbers, you can usually tell because: 1) the beer turns out much too dry, 2) the beer becomes overcarbonated 3) the yeast used to flocculate well, but now it does not, and/or 4) the beer changes in flavor (clove aroma is very common).

# Yeast Phases

Various authors have described the phases through which the yeast pass in different ways. There are a number of authors that have incorrectly equated the term "respiration" with the phase in which yeast uptake oxygen. The term "respiration" means something very specific to microbiologists – it is a state in which the yeast are actually using the oxygen to gain energy from the sugars[218]. Because of a phenomenon called the Crabtree effect, where respiration is suppressed and instead the yeast continue fermentation, the yeast actually spend almost none of their time respiring. The Crabtree effect takes place when there is sugar available to the yeast, so you can see that in wort, which is loaded with sugars, the yeast will forgo respiration and go right to fermentation[74,83,218].

Now, this does not mean that the yeast don't have a use for the oxygen. On the contrary, the yeast use the oxygen not for energy, but for making compounds called unsaturated fatty acids and sterols which are then used by the yeast to build cell membranes[75,218]. In place of dissolved oxygen, the yeast are also able to utilize cold break for the unsaturated fatty acids it contains and use them for sterol synthesis[218]. If you have both insufficient oxygen and no cold break you may have weak yeast cell membranes and subsequently low alcohol tolerance[76].

There are many ways to separate the phases that yeast go through, but for the sake of this discussion, I'll break up the yeast's life cycle in to three phases: 1) the lag phase, 2) the log phase, and 3) the stationary phase. It is important to note that these phases (in the context of this discussion) represent the general yeast population and that at any given moment after you pitch the yeast, some individual cells within that population are in the physiological state defined by each of the three phases.

During the lag phase the yeast prepare their cell walls, consume amino acids, elementary peptides, other "nutrients," sugars, and oxygen. This initial period is also a period of acclimatization for the yeast when they get used to their new surroundings. The temperature, osmotic pressure (related to the wort gravity), and pH may be very different in the fermenter than they were in the starter (note that for dry yeast the rehydration would be prior to this discussion – the lag phase would start when the rehydrated dry yeast were pitched into the wort). If there is a sudden change in temperature or osmotic pressure, many yeast may die and the remaining ones could take days to finish the acclimatization.

**Figure 10-5**: *High kräusen (the log phase).*

The log phase is the next stage and during it, the yeast continue to consume nutrients and sugars and perform the majority of their yeast growth, i.e. cell division. During this phase considerable $CO_2$ is produced. Actually, the yeast bud/reproduce throughout their entire life cycle, but reproduction is most rapid during this phase. Some authors suggest that most of the ester production takes place during reproduction[16,78] which means that the more yeast mass you pitch, the less estery the beer will be. Two authors have even suggested reducing the amount of dissolved oxygen in the cooled wort to minimize yeast reproduction and therefore ester production[16,218]. I'm not sure this is such a good idea, but several commercial breweries actually do this, so it can be a viable procedure. The overwhelming majority of the research in this area indicates that reduced initial oxygen levels result in *increased* ester levels[87,88,90,91].

Different strains of yeast can have very different oxygen requirements. In one study, initial dissolved oxygen levels above 20% of saturation did not significantly increase growth or fermentation rate[80]. Other yeasts can have initial dissolved oxygen requirements approaching 100% of saturation[75]. It has been suggested that overoxygenation is a possibility[218], but I feel that this may be an exaggeration. Very little research has been done regarding this subject. On November 11, 1996, A. J. deLange reported in the Homebrew Digest that he periodically oxygenated pitched wort for several days to maintain a dissolved oxygen level of 30 to 35 ppm and the yeast continued to flourish. Mind you, this was an uncontrolled experiment on one yeast strain, but it does seem to indicate that overoxygenation may not be as big a problem as some authors have implied.

Finally the yeast enter the stationary phase when they have fulfilled their energy and growth requirements, and the growth rate has leveled-off. It is during the stationary phase that the yeast consume sugars and produce $CO_2$, ethanol, other compounds (in smaller amounts), e.g. higher alcohols, esters (which give ales their fruity aromas and flavors), acetaldehyde, *a-* acetolactic acid (the precursor of diacetyl), and many others. Research has indicated that the best time to pitch a starter is when it is in this stationary phase because this is when glycogen levels are highest.[84]

## Dry Versus Liquid Yeast

It used to be that dry yeast was the only form available to homebrewers and dry yeasts were made by the same companies that made bread yeast. Subsequently, the purity of those yeasts was not good enough to make consistent, clean beer that had a long shelf life. The advent of liquid yeasts changed the face of homebrewing. The yeasts are not actually liquid, but rather the media on which they are delivered is a liquid or a gel. Not only were liquid yeasts much purer and bacteria-free than those old dry yeasts, but they forced the dry yeast manufacturers to "clean up their act." Most dry yeasts available these days are very clean and can produce excellent beer with a long shelf life. The advantage of liquid yeasts is now simply a matter of variety. Only some yeasts can survive the process of drying, but all yeasts can be distributed in a liquid form.

# Rehydrating Dry Yeast

Before you use dry yeast, you should rehydrate it. This is done by sprinkling the dried yeast onto the surface of some sanitized water. Dried yeast should not be rehydrated in wort – it is far easier for the yeast cells to absorb water when there are no sugars in the rehydrating media. Despite the fact that many books and articles say that you should add malt extract, sugar, or nutrients to the water used for rehydration, the proper procedure is to boil some plain water (I microwave a cup of water in a Pyrex measuring cup, put a sanitized thermometer into it and cover with plastic wrap), let it cool to between 90 and 110° F (32 and 43° C), sprinkle the yeast onto the surface of the water (do not stir), and let the yeast rehydrate for 15 to 30 minutes. During the rehydration, the yeast may or may not should show a little activity at the surface. This is no indication as to the health of the yeast[81].

You should not simply pour the rehydrated yeast into your wort if it is more than 10° F cooler. Instead, for ale temperatures, you should slowly (taking 30 to 60 seconds) add cooled wort to the rehydrated yeast suspension until you double the volume (make sure to maintain proper sanitation). If the wort into which you are going to pitch the yeast is at lager temperatures, you should repeat the procedure once again. You must not simply allow the yeast suspension to cool naturally because it will take too long and the many of the yeast cells will die in the process[81].

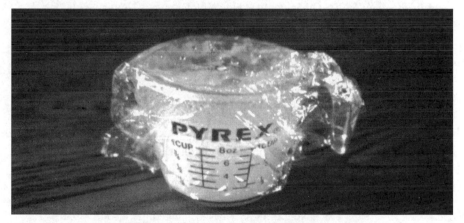

**Figure 10-6**: *Dry yeast rehydrating.*

You can, if you wish, pitch the rehydrated yeast into a starter (see below), but it doesn't help as much as you might think. Most liquid yeasts come in quantities that are so much smaller than the proper pitching rate, that to get good yeast performance (and the expected level of attenuation) you really should use a starter. The amount of yeast in a package of dry yeast (5 to 14 grams, usually) is not that far from the correct pitching rate if the yeast package has been maintained properly (refrigerated), is not too old, and has a reasonable percentage of viable cells.

# Attenuation

Attenuation is important to understand, especially when determining if your beer has reached a reasonable final gravity (FG) or is there a problem with the fermentation. There are a number of factors that affect attenuation. First of all, the mash temperature. Higher mash temperatures result in less of the wort's sugars being fermentable and more of the wort's sugars being unfermentable carbohydrates called dextrins. Lower mash temperatures result in more fermentable sugars and less dextrins. While extract brewers don't have direct control over mash temperatures, they can choose extracts that are more or less dextrinous (have more or less dextrins). Laaglander, "Hollander," "Dutch," and Northwestern's "European" Dried Malt Extracts are high in dextrins and therefore are not very fermentable.

Secondly, the addition of crystal malts, unfermentable sugars like lactose, or body-building additions of malto-dextrin will decrease the fermentability of the wort and result in lower attenuation. Finally, different strains of yeast will have different abilities when it comes to eating sugars. Some, will eat every sugar in sight (high attenuation). Others, only eat the simpler sugars (low attenuation). Appendices C and E provide the attenuation levels for many of the yeasts currently available to the homebrewer.

How do we calculate attenuation? Well, actually, calculating the actual attenuation is difficult because the alcohol that the yeast make is lighter than water so that throws off our measurements. What we typically mean when we are talking about attenuation is "apparent attenuation" which is what's listed in the appendices and is much easier to measure. To calculate the apparent attenuation, all we have to do is measure the original gravity (OG) and final gravity (FG) and plug them into the following formula:

apparent attenuation (in percent) = ( 1 - (FG - 1)/(OG - 1)) x 100

Therefore, if the original gravity was 1.072 and the final gravity was 1.018:

$$
\begin{aligned}
\text{apparent attenuation (in percent)} &= ( 1 - ( 1.018 - 1 )/( 1.072 - 1 )) \times 100 \\
&= ( 1 - 0.018/0.072) \times 100 \\
&= ( 1 - 0.25) \times 100 \\
&= 0.75 \times 100 \\
\text{apparent attenuation} &= 75\%
\end{aligned}
$$

# Starters

Now, before we begin this discussion, let us remember that in a commercial environment, brewers usually use a much smaller number of yeast strains than homebrewers. Therefore, most commercial brewers simply save the yeast from a previous batch and use it in a subsequent batch. Since most homebrewers use a much wider variety of yeast strains, most do not brew with the same yeast often enough to make such reuse practical. Therefore, yeast starters are used to build up a sufficient amount of yeast so that the cultured yeast dominates the wort and overruns any unwanted competing organisms. A large, healthy yeast population can be as important as good sanitation to ensuring that wild yeasts and bacteria don't spoil your beer.

The key to a healthy fermentation is pitching a sufficient number of viable yeast cells. A yeast starter is like a miniature batch of beer. Instead of pouring one to two ounces of yeast starter (typically what you get from a liquid yeast package) into 5 gallons of wort, you are pouring it into 500 ml of wort. It is much easier for two ounces of yeast starter to dominate 500 ml of wort than to dominate 5 gallons of wort. Then after the 500 ml starter gets going, you have a much larger yeast population which to pitch into the 5 gallons of wort.

**Figure 10-7**: *Active starter (ready to pitch or step-up).*

The most common way that homebrewers make starters is in 22-ounce beer bottles. Another alternative is to use a Champagne bottle. In both cases, what you need is a #2 drilled stopper and an airlock. I like to use an Erlenmeyer flask (don't fill it more than half-way) and a glass airlock (don't try this with a plastic airlock – it will melt). I boil up the starter in the flask and the steam produced not only sanitizes the stopper and airlock, but condenses to fill the airlock with sanitized water. Good sanitation is imperative because an infection in your starter not only means that your beer will be infected, but it could very well be undrinkable. It's a good idea to get into the habit of smelling and tasting (in a sanitary fashion) the starter before pitching. If it is sour or medicinal, you are better off using rehydrated dry yeast than an infected starter.

One option is to make your starter directly in your fermenter. The advantages are that you have one less thing to sanitize and one less transfer of yeast. The disadvantages are that it's much harder to sanitize a carboy or plastic pail than a bottle or flask and as I just mentioned, a few stray bacteria in your starter are much worse than a few stray bacteria in the main batch.

Ideally, you would like to step up no more than 5- to 10-fold at one time, but this is a guideline that is very often ignored and still the beer turns out just fine. If you really want to follow the rules, the 50 ml (about 1.75 fluid ounces) yeast culture you purchased should be pitched into a 500 ml starter. This starter, when finished, should be pitched into 5-liter starter. The 5 liter starter can be then pitched into a 50-liter batch of beer (about 13.2 gallons). None of the homebrewers I know go through these extreme-sounding measures. Personally, for ales I usually make a 1.5-liter starter from a 50 ml package of liquid yeast and then pitch that into a 5-gallon batch of beer (18.9 liters). This is a 30-fold step-up followed by about a 12-fold step up. For lagers or high-gravity ales, I recommend making a 500 ml starter, followed by a 4-liter starter.

There is some debate as to whether the starter gravity should be 1.020 (5 Plato) or closer to the gravity of the beer into which the starter will be pitched. The argument for the former method is that the higher gravity starter is more stressful on the yeast and that it is better to traumatize them less early on and then pitch into a higher gravity wort later. A progressive gravity method might be the most favorable to the yeast, i.e. begin with a small starter of 1.020 wort, stepped up to a larger starter of 1.040 wort (10 P) and then that pitched into a 1.060+ wort (15+ P). Sometimes, I will do just that with my starters, especially for high gravity beers, but most of the time, I simply make a 1.040 (10 P) starter wort.

Some homebrewers use dextrose or sucrose in place of malt extract in their starters. While this has shown to result in much higher yeast mass, the subsequent yeast can have difficulty fermenting some common wort sugars[82,83]. A starter solution that has a similar sugar distribution as wort is highly recommended.

A little yeast nutrient or energizer in your starter wort is a worthwhile precaution to supplement the nutritional requirements of your yeast, especially if you choose to use lower-gravity starter worts. I recommend 2.5 grams per liter (about a quart).

Here's a table that lists the weights (in ounces) to make approximate-gravity starter worts from dry malt extract. The reason I've listed 1.060 and 1.080 in the table is not because I suggest making starters of this gravity, however, you may want to use higher gravity worts for feeding starters. For example, I'll make a 1 liter 1.030 OG starter in a 2 liter flask. Then, 8 to 12 hours after high kräusen, I'll add 1 liter of 1.080 OG wort which is similar to starting the yeast in a 1.040 or 1.050 wort, but not as stressful. Note: that one ounce (weight) of dry malt extract is about 28 grams or three level tablespoons.

| Starter | 1.020 | 1.030 | 1.040 | 1.050 | 1.060 | 1.080 |
|---------|-------|-------|-------|-------|-------|-------|
| 250 ml | 1/2 oz. | 3/4 oz. | 1 oz. | 1 1/4 oz. | 1 1/2 oz. | 2 oz. |
| 500 ml | 1 oz. | 1 1/2 oz. | 2 oz. | 2 1/2 oz. | 3 oz. | 4 oz. |
| 750 ml | 1 1/2 oz. | 2 1/4 oz. | 3 oz. | 3 3/4 oz. | 4 1/2 oz. | 6 oz. |
| 1 L | 2 oz. | 3 oz. | 4 oz. | 5 oz. | 6 oz. | 8 oz. |
| 1.5 L | 3 oz. | 4 1/2 oz. | 6 oz. | 7 1/2 oz. | 9 oz. | 12 oz |
| 2 L | 4 oz. | 6 oz. | 8 oz. | 10 oz. | 12 oz. | 16 oz. |
| 4 L | 8 oz. | 12 oz. | 16 oz. | 20 oz. | 24 oz. | 32 oz. |

Another point that is often debated among homebrewers is whether starters should be hopped or not. Hops do have some anti-bacterial properties, so there can be some merit to this procedure, but I, personally, leave my starters out in the open in the kitchen where they are exposed to light, so I choose to not use hops to avoid the skunkiness of light-struck beer.

Virtually every homebrewing book and article in the past has said that the yeast should be pitched at high kräusen. There is research data suggesting that high kräusen is a bit too early to pitch. Yeast's primary method of storing energy is in the form of a carbohydrate called glycogen. When the yeast are introduced into a sugary environment, the first thing they do is use their glycogen reserves for food during the initial phase of life. As fermentation progresses the yeast again begin to store up glycogen. The fact is, that the very lowest level of glycogen in the yeast cells is at high kräusen. One study has shown that pitching yeast when it is low in glycogen increases the production of undesirable byproducts (such as acetaldehyde, sulfur dioxide, and diacetyl) and can result in high final gravities[84].

While it may be true that shorter lag times are a result of pitching the yeast at high kräusen, the true measure of the ferment quality should be its vigor, attenuation, the speed with which it finishes fermenting, and the level of byproducts. Although there have been studies that have found little or no correlation between glycogen levels and the quality of the ferment, more than one study has found that pitching the yeast when their glycogen levels are high results in superior ferments. The differing results of the studies could be due to differences between various strains of yeast or variations in fermentation conditions. Glycogen levels in the yeast are highest shortly after high kräusen. In my opinion, the ideal time to pitch the starter is from perhaps 8 to 12 hours after high kräusen.

One option is to wait until the starter has fermented-out completely and then pour-off the spent wort in the starter flask before pitching the yeast slurry. This is advantageous especially when using large starters: who would want to pour 2 liters of unhopped, amber starter wort fermented at 65° F (18° C) into 4 1/2 gallons of well-crafted, very pale, American Pilsner wort? The color, bitterness, and flavor of the finished beer can be compromised. The problem is, that waiting too long after fermentation can also result in low glycogen levels since the yeast use the glycogen for food when there's no wort sugar around. Within 24 to 48 hours after fermentation, the yeast's glycogen levels will have dropped considerably. Yeast that you intend to store for a long period of time (more than several days) should therefore be kept refrigerated (to slow metabolic activity) and fed occasionally with wort (which includes not only a variety of sugars but also amino acids and peptides).

To get the best of both worlds (high glycogen levels and a minimal amount of spent starter wort), you can repeatedly pour off the spent wort and add fresh wort. Each feeding will result in yeast growth and in the end you can pitch the equivalent yeast mass of a large starter while only adding the wort of a small starter. For example, with four decantings/feedings of 500 ml each, you would end up pitching almost the equivalent of a 2-liter starter, but only add 500 ml of starter wort to your beer and pitch just after high kräusen. Remember that you can increase the OG of the feed wort, which can help acclimate the yeast destined for a high-gravity batch.

One final consideration regarding starters is "selection." Any large yeast population will have a certain amount of variety, even among yeasts of the same strain. The characteristics most important in this discussion are flocculation and attenuation. These, in this context, are somewhat inversely proportional. More flocculent yeasts will be less attenuative and less flocculent yeasts will be more attenuative. If you make a starter and pour off the wort after some of the yeast settles (but while there is still some yeast in suspension), you are selecting the more flocculent yeasts (the ones that flocculated early). Alternatively, you can reculture from suspended yeast (after most have flocculated) and thus select the less flocculent yeasts.

Incidentally, the same is true if you are cropping (collecting yeast) in the primary or the secondary fermenter. Yeast in the bottom of the primary will tend to be those yeasts that flocculated early (less attenuative) and those in the secondary (or in bottles) will tend to be those yeasts that flocculated late (more attenuative).

## Starting From Slants

Some yeast cultures are only available as slants. It is possible to get several uses from a slant and to propagate it (theoretically) forever, but the methods to do this are beyond the scope of this book. What I do need to tell you is a "quick and easy" way to make up a starter from a yeast slant. You can get much better and more reliable directions from the yeast laboratories, but often that information doesn't trickle down to the homebrewer, so here's a very simple method for a single-use of a slant:

1.  - take the slant out of the refrigerator
    - make up 50 ml of 1.040 wort and boil it to sanitize
    - cool this wort to room temperature, since the slant will have warmed to this temperature
    - pour the wort into a sanitized bottle or flask
    - pour some of this wort into the vial that contains the slant
    - put the cap back onto the vial
    - shake the slant for 10 seconds
    - pour the liquid part from the slant vial into the rest of the 50 ml of wort
    - it is recommended that you NOT reuse the slant using this procedure (risk of infection is high)
    - aerate the starter
    - put an airlock onto this starter
    - place this into a warm place (65-70° F / 18-21° C) for ales or a cool place (55-60° F / 13-16° C) for lagers

2.  - three days later, make up 500 ml more sanitized wort
    - cool this to about the same temperature as the 50 ml starter
    - pour it and the 50 ml starter in to a sanitized bottle or flask
    - aerate the starter
    - put an airlock onto this starter
    - place this into a warm place (65-70° F / 18-21° C) for ales or a cool place (55-60° F / 13-16° C) for lagers

3.  - after three more days, you can use this in a low gravity ale or you can step it up again to 2 liters for an average-gravity ale or up to 4 liters for a high-gravity ale or lager.

# Reuse

There are several ways to re-use or stretch your yeast. Many brewers make a big starter for a package of liquid yeast, ferment it out and then split it into a half-dozen or so well-sanitized beer bottles. These can be stored in the refrigerator for several weeks and then stepped-up with starter wort when needed. The disadvantage of this method is that unless you use a pressure cooker for preparing your starter and bottles there will always be some amount of bacteria and wild yeasts in the starters. These can multiply while you have them stored away only to spoil your batch when you unknowingly pitch an infected starter. Also, storing yeast for an extended period of time (even in the refrigerator) can lead to the yeast using up all their glycogen and possibly even beginning autolysis.

Another way to get more out of your yeast is to do what the professionals do: repitch slurry from one batch to another. You should be very sure that the beer from which you cropped (harvested) the yeast tastes good and shows no signs of infection. There is some debate as to whether it is better to crop the yeast from the primary fermenter or the secondary (if you are using one). The advantage of using yeast from the secondary is that there is less hot and cold break in the slurry. Using yeast from the primary has the advantage of selecting for better flocculators and reducing the chance of infection (one less transfer). Personally, I prefer to use the yeast from the bottom of the primary. If you are planning to dryhop and you want to re-use the yeast from the bottom of the fermenter, I recommend that you use a secondary for the dryhopping and crop the yeast from the primary immediately after racking. Otherwise, you will have all these hops to wrestle with in your slurry.

# Yeast Washing

A procedure called "yeast washing" is done by some brewers, commercial and amateur, to reduce bacteria counts in cropped yeast. This is usually done by adding phosphoric, tartaric, or sulfuric acids until the pH of the water in which the yeast is being washed is just above 2.5. At this pH, most of the bacteria in the culture will be killed and the ratio of yeast to bacteria will (hopefully) be back to levels at which the bacteria do not produce noticeable amounts of their unwanted products. However, since wild yeasts are yeasts, they will be largely unaffected by the acid wash. Another problem is that even the cultured yeast performance will be affected by the washing, for example, flocculation can be reduced in the first batch fermented after washing. I recommend you hold off on this procedure and if you suspect your yeast culture, just buy another one. Yeast washing will be covered in detail in volume II of this book series.

## Dry Yeasts

As I noted earlier, dry yeasts have improved dramatically over the course of the last ten years. I still brew quite a few beers with dry yeast and I'm very happy with the results. In appendix C I've tried my best to describe the character of the most popular dry yeasts used for brewing beer.

## Liquid Yeasts

Liquid yeasts have given the homebrewer more variability than we could have ever imagined. There are literally hundreds of different yeast strains available commercially and many in private yeast banks (usually maintained by homebrew clubs). You can buy a culture of a yeast strain that is used by your favorite brewery and, conceivably (after several tries at the recipe), get very close to duplicating their beer. With so many yeast cultures available to the homebrewer, how do you pick a yeast? Appendices D and E will help you choose a liquid yeast for the particular style of beer you are brewing. This list of yeasts, and yeast suppliers is constantly growing, so it is impossible to be 100% up-to-date.

## Yeast at Bottling

Among Belgian commercial brewers, it is common to add more yeast at bottling time[78]. This is a good idea if the beer is very strong (let's say over 1.080 OG) and you are relying on the yeast and priming sugar to carbonate the beer. Some homebrewers add more yeast at bottling after a long lagering period. Personally, I have had no problems getting natural carbonation in beers lagered for four months *without* adding yeast at bottling.

There are two important considerations when adding yeast at bottling. If your yeast pooped-out prematurely due to the alcohol level and there is still a lot of fermentable sugar in the beer, adding more yeast and priming normally will give you two cases of gushers. Also, if you use a more attenuative or more alcohol tolerant yeast at bottling than you did in the primary fermentation, you can have the same problem. These two reasons are why you should take specific gravity readings for strong beers and know what your expected attenuations should be for various yeasts. If the FG is higher than expected, add more yeast (make a big starter, let it ferment out completely, pour off the spent wort, and pitch) and wait a week or two.

## Sulfury Aroma Production

Some yeasts, especially lager yeasts, have a tendency to create some sulfury aromas in the finished beer. These are a combination of hydrogen sulfide ($H_2S$), dimethyl sulfide (DMS), and other related sulfides (dimethyl disulfide, dimethyl trisulfide, and diethylsulfide)[85]. Their levels in the finished beer can vary considerably. A number of factors relating to sulfury aromas appear to be true:

- the sulfury aromas are created early in the fermentation,
- higher initial fermentation temperatures tend to increase their production,
- higher temperatures in the middle and end of the fermentation tend to decrease their levels in the finished beer[85].

Several researchers have experimented with varying the fermentation temperature in an effort to reduce sulfury aromas in lagers. Their research seems to indicate that a staggered fermentation temperature schedule (3 days at 43° F/6° C, 3 days at 50° F/10° C, and 3 days at 65° F/18° C) resulted in considerably lower sulfury aroma levels and a "more drinkable" beer than the same wort fermented at a constant 58° F (14.5° C) [85]. Note that these fermentation times *require* you to pitch the proper amount of yeast (ideally, about 1/5 of the entire yeast cake from a previous batch). There is no way that the beer will ferment in such a short time when typical homebrewers' pitching rates are used (a 1- or 2- liter starter).

## Wort Canning

A number of homebrewing books say that you can make wort in advance, can it in canning jars or bottles by simple boiling the wort in your kettle, and then store it for months till you need it. *This is an extremely dangerous procedure!* The pH of wort is not low enough to protect it from botulism (which can kill). Regardless of what other books tell you, *never* store unpitched wort for any length of time unless you have pressure-cooked it at 15 psi for at least 30 minutes to kill botulism *spores* or taken other precautions against botulism. Personally, I prefer to play it safe and make up starter wort from dried malt extract as I need it.

## Further Reading

"Jim's Fermentation Hints," *Lallemand Website*, http://www.lallemand.com/
"The Secret of Success," *Lallemand Website*, http://www.lallemand.com/
Aquilla, T., "The Biochemistry of Yeast: Debunking the Myth of Yeast Respiration and Putting Oxygen in Its Proper Place," *Brewing Techniques*, 5 (1) 50-57 (Jan/Feb 1997).
DeClerck, J., *A Textbook of Brewing*, Vol. 1 (Chapman and Hall, London, 1957).
Fix, G. J., "Sulfur Flavors in Beer," *Zymurgy*, 15 (3), 40-44 (Fall 1992).
Fix, G. J., "Wild Yeast," *Zymurgy*, 12 (4) 21-24 (Special 1989).
Fix, G. J., *Principles of Brewing Science*, (Brewers Publications, Boulder, 1989).
Hough, J. S., D. E. Briggs, R. Stevens, and T.W. *Young, Malting and Brewing Science*, Vol. 2 (Chapman and Hall, London, 1982).
Hough, J. S., *The Biotechnology of Malting and Brewing*, (Cambridge University Press, Cambridge, 1985).
Monk, P., "Yeast Nutrients in Brewing," *Zymurgy*, 12 (4) 25-27 (Special 1989).
Pickerell, A. T. W., A. Hwang, and B. C. Axcell, "Impact of Yeast-Handling Procedures on Beer Flavor Development During Fermentation," *ASBC Journal*, 49 (2), 1991, 87-92.
Rajotte, P., *First Steps in Yeast Culture - Part One*, (Alliage Éditeur, Montreal, Canada, 1994).
Rajotte, P., presentation at The Spirit of Belgium, Washington, D. C., November 1994.

# 11

# OTHER INGREDIENTS

In addition to the standard four ingredients, there are a great many others that are often used in the production of beer. There are many sources of sugars besides barley malt and other starches. Many ingredients add more than just sugar, take fruits for example. In recent years, spiced beers have grown in popularity.

In this chapter, the ingredients less-commonly used for making beer will be described. Try to resist the temptation to overdo these additions because they can easily get you into trouble. Too much refined sugar can give your beer a cidery flavor. Too much spice can make your beer downright unpleasant to drink (but don't give up on those over-spiced beers – let them age for a year or two and you may be pleasantly surprised).

## Other Sources of Fermentables

Barley malts are the most common source of fermentables in modern beer. As mentioned earlier, wheat malts and raw wheat are also widely used in beer. However, anything that contains starch or sugar can be used as a source of fermentables. If you want to get fermentables from starchy ingredients (such as potatoes, pumpkins, corn, or rice) you will have to mash them with some malt to convert the starches to sugars. This is beyond the scope of this text and will be covered in volume II of this series. There are many other sources of fermentables that don't have to be mashed and therefore are available for extract brewers. These include sugars of all types, fruits, juices, honey, maple syrup, and molasses.

## Nutrition

Yeasts need more than just sugar to lead healthy and happy lives – they also need nutrients such as amino acids, vitamins, and minerals. None of the other sources of fermentables described below have significant amounts of these nutrients. Therefore, if you begin to approach 20% of the fermentables in the wort from any of the sources below, you should think about adding some yeast energizer or you may have a sluggish fermentation or excessive levels of unwanted byproducts such as acetaldehyde. See "Yeast Nutrient and Yeast Energizer" later in this chapter for more information.

## White and Brown Sugars

Common table sugar is sucrose. Brewer's sugar, dextrose, and corn sugar are all names for glucose. Both can be used to increase the alcohol level of the beer without increasing the malt flavor or body. Many styles of beer require the use of these sugars (or the mashing of adjuncts that add lots of simple sugars) such as American Pilsner and Belgian Strong Ale. While perfectly good beer can be made with all-malt worts, they will generally either be too low in alcohol or too heavy-bodied for style.

Brown sugar in the US is simply white sucrose (table sugar) with a little bit of molasses added, but it does have its place in beer. I recommend adding no more than 10% by weight. I suggest using even less in paler beers, but who knows... it could be very interesting.

Glucose, fructose and sucrose are 100% fermentable. Brown sugar is pretty close to 100% fermentable, but can vary depending on the brand.

Adding too much of cane, corn or beet sugar can make your beer taste cidery. The general rule is to keep these sugars to below 25% of your fermentables. I've fermented pure corn sugar (glucose), cane sugar (sucrose) and invert sugar syrup ("inverted" sucrose, a mixture of sucrose, glucose, and fructose – see "Sugar Syrups" below) and found that all have a cidery flavor, but that the glucose was the most neutral, followed by the invert sugar. The fermented sucrose was the most cidery of the three.

Yeast can eat glucose and fructose directly. Each molecule of sucrose is a molecule of glucose and a molecule of fructose bonded together and the yeast cannot eat it whole. They must produce invertase (an enzyme) to break sucrose into its component glucose and fructose molecules *outside* their cell walls[82]. Because the invert sugar (the way that I made it) was only partly inverted, this implies that perhaps it is the invertase that causes that cidery flavor. On the other hand, I have a theory that perhaps at least part of the cidery flavor is due to the fact that worts with high percentages of these sugars simply don't have enough of the nutrients that yeast need for proper health. Further experimentation is necessary to determine if this is indeed the case.

## Rice Syrup and Rice Syrup Solids

Rice will lighten the body, reduce the malt flavor, result in a slightly drier beer, and make the beer paler when substituted for some of the malt. Rice adds a slightly different flavor than does using corn. If you are not mashing, you can still add rice, but in the form of rice syrup or rice solids. Rice syrup solids are a powder, the equivalent of dried malt extract, but made from rice. Note that while most American Pilsners are made with corn, Budweiser is made with rice. To make a beer approaching the character of Budweiser, unless you are mashing, the use of rice syrup or solids is essential. In some American Pilsners 40 to 50% rice may be used[86], but I suggest that you begin with about 35% rice syrup or solids and then adjust up or down from there. Rice syrup and solids are virtually 100% fermentable.

**Figure 11-1**: *Rice syrup solids.*

## Fruit

Fruit can be a tricky source of sugars, but a very rewarding one also. The reason that they are tricky is because 1) they are an abundant source of bacteria and wild yeast, 2) they can easily clog your airlock or even your blowoff tube, and 3) if you heat them too much you will set their pectin and have permanently cloudy beer. Another issue is when to add the fruit to the wort – in the boil, in the primary or in the secondary?

First, let's discuss sanitation. Because the skins of fruits are a breeding ground for wild yeasts and bacteria, sanitation is very important. You can, if you wish, simply accept the fact that you will be adding these to your beer and resign yourself to the fact that your beer will develop some lactic and/or acetic sourness. While there are many ways to sanitize the fruit, I'll just cover three: metabisulfites, pasteurization, and blanching.

Winemakers use sodium or potassium metabisulfite (a.k.a. Campden tablets) for sanitation of their fruit. Metabisulfites will kill some of the yeast and bacteria, but do not actually sterilize the wort. The survivors are inhibited (for a while – not permanently) by the metabisulfites so that the cultured yeast can out-compete the wild yeasts and bacteria for the sugars and nutrients. Metabisulfites work by producing sulfur dioxide ($SO_2$) gas when in an acidic solution. You then wait for the sulfur dioxide to dissipate somewhat (about 24 hours) and then add your fruit to the beer. You must crush the fruit and add the metabisulfites to the juice – you cannot simply soak the fruit in metabisulfite and water (you need the acidity of the juice to make the metabisulfites work). The idea is that you want to give your cultured yeast such a head start over the wild yeasts and bacteria that the aroma and flavor are not altered by these unwanted guests. You can use metabisulfites, but I prefer either pasteurization or blanching instead. I've talked to one brewer[92] who says that a beer he made with metabisulfites ended up producing a lot of $H_2S$ (hydrogen sulfide – "rotten egg smell"). Note: Some people have reactions to sulfites.

In pasteurization, you put the fruit into some water (as little as possible), heat it to 140 to 150° F (60 to 66° C) for 10 to 15 minutes and then cool it down as quickly as you can while maintaining good sanitation. If you let the temperature get too high, you will set the pectin in the fruit and will have cloudy beer. This is why the recipes that call for adding fruit in the last minute of the boil or even just after the boil will undoubtedly give your beer a haze. An alternative to adding the fruit to water is to squeeze the juice out of it and then pasteurize that.

**Figure 11-2**: *Macerating fruit in preparation for heating to pasteurization temperatures.*

I've had some success with blanching frozen fruit. I've done it with cherries, blueberries, raspberries, and peaches. What I did was freeze the fruit, then boil some water, and dip the fruit (using a sieve) into the boiling water for five seconds. My reasoning was that on unblemished fruit, all the wild yeasts and bacteria will be on the outsides of the skins.

Freezing the fruit first serves two purposes, one based upon science the other intuition. Freezing breaks open the sacks of juice in certain fruits (e.g. raspberries) and I theorized that working with frozen fruit would keep the majority of the fruit cold during the blanching and therefore perhaps only an insignificant portion of the pectin would be set. I was right about this, and the raspberry and cherry beers I made had neither haze nor sanitation problems. With the peaches I was not so lucky: no haze, but after a few months the beer began to develop a lactic sourness. It was still very tasty, though. One additional word of warning: cherries, blueberries, peaches, plums hold together during the dip in boiling water. Berries such as raspberries, blackberries, or boysenberries, release their juice when they hit the boiling water so you should expect to add the blanching water along with the fruit (make sure there's room for it in the fermenter).

**Figure 11-3**: *Blanching frozen fruit.*

Note that canned fruit (I recommend fruit canned in water, not heavy syrup) will be sanitary, but you should flame the lid with a butane lighter and sanitize the opener to kill any bacteria or wild yeast that are likely to live on these surfaces.

The next issue is blowoff. When you add fruit, you can expect to have the pulp ride up on the kräusen and can easily clog an airlock or even a smaller-diameter blowoff tube. For fruit, I recommend using only a large (1$^1$/$_4$" outside diameter) blowoff hose – the kind that you stick right into the neck of the carboy without a stopper. This is virtually impossible to clog (but it would still be prudent to check on it daily). After the really foamy part of fermentation is over, I switch to an airlock because it takes up less space and requires less maintenance. Be sure to check on the airlock every few days and refill it as necessary.

The next question is when to add the fruit. Raw fruit has aromas/flavors and sweetness. When you take away the sweetness, many fruits don't have much else to contribute. Fermentation will take away virtually all the sweetness, so you have to rely on the aroma/flavor of the fruit to lend something to your beer. Consider blueberries – mush some up and smell them. Do they have a characteristic aroma? Perhaps, but it is very subtle. The same goes for strawberries. Raspberries are the other extreme – very intense and unmistakable aroma. Cherries are somewhere in the middle. If you add the fruit at the beginning of fermentation, the $CO_2$ evolving from the beer will scrub much of the fruit aromatics right out of the beer. This is why I recommend that you wait until after the primary fermentation is over to add the fruit. Yes, it's true that there will be renewed yeast activity from the fruit sugars and some $CO_2$ will be released, but what's important is that it is but a fraction of the $CO_2$ that was produced during the main ferment, and therefore much more of the fruit's aromatics will have been preserved.

How long should the beer be kept on the fruit? It takes some time for the aromas, flavors and sugars to come out of the fruit. I recommend at least four weeks and you can easily extend this to eight or twelve. This is another reason why I like to rack the beer into a secondary when adding fruit – there probably will not be any problems with yeast autolysis, but it's better to be safe than sorry.

Don't forget that the fruit will actually take up space in the secondary and also that 5 gallons (18.9 liters) of beer with fruit in the fermenter is not 5 gallons of beer in the bottles. When I want 5 gallons with fruit in the secondary, I usually make about 4$^3$/$_4$ gallons (18 liters) of base beer in the primary. 1 quart (about 1 liter) of this will be lost to yeast and break left in the bottom of the primary and I usually count on about $^1$/$_2$ gallon (about 2 liters) or so of space for the fruit. If you are using a lot of fruit, you may want to start with only 4 gallons (15.1 liters) of wort in the primary. When bottling, remember to scale-down the priming sugar because once you rack the beer off the fruit, you will have quite a bit less than 5 gallons of beer. I usually assume that I will lose as much liquid as I gain from the fruit, so if I started with 4 gallons of wort, I'll prime as if I have 4 gallons of finished beer.

How much fruit to add?  Well, that depends on how much aroma/flavor you want and on the type of fruit.  Mind you, more is not always better.  If you are brewing just for your tastes and like a *lot* of fruit aroma/flavor, then pile them in there, but if you are brewing to do well in a competition, one very important factor is *balance*.  The judges will be asking themselves: does this still taste like beer?  It is supposed to be fruit *beer,* after all, not wine.  Remember, some fruits are much more intense than others.  Also consider that the stronger or darker the beer is the more fruit you will need to add.  Hop bitterness should be kept low because fruit flavors don't blend well with bitterness.

The following table gives some starting points for various fruits in pale, medium-gravity (around 1.050) beers.  You can double these rates for a Brown Ale, Porter or a 1.080 pale beer and even triple them for, say, an Imperial Stout.  I had an outstanding Sour Cherry English Brown Ale at the 1994 Home Wine and Beer Trade Association (HWBTA) National Competition that had an original gravity of 1.045 and was made with 15 pounds of sour cherries added for six weeks in the secondary. Another great fruit beer I've had was one that I tasted at a Brewers of South Suburbia meeting.  It was a 1.077 OG Imperial Stout and was made by Steve Kamp with $9^1/_2$ pounds of raspberries and $^1/_2$ pound of blueberries.

**Table 11-1: Suggested amounts of various fruits.**

| FRUIT | SUGGESTED AMOUNT TO MAKE *5 GALLONS* OF BEER |
|---|---|
| raspberries, apricots, boysenberries | 4 to 7 pounds ($1^3/_4$ to 3 kg) |
| peaches, apples, plums, cranberries, grapes, blackberries, currants (red or black) | 5 to 10 pounds ($2^1/_2$ to $4^3/_4$ kg) |
| cherries, blueberries, gooseberries, strawberries, kiwis | 7 to 15 pounds ($3^1/_4$ to $6^3/_4$ kg) |

Finally, you may be wondering how much sugar will the fruit add.  In Homebrew Digest #2190, Ken Schwartz pointed out that cherries, since they only contain about 14% sugar by weight, don't really contribute that much to the original gravity.  For example, adding 6 pounds of cherries is equivalent to adding only about 0.84 pounds of sugar.  Various fruits contain varying amounts of sugar.  Limes, lemons, tomatoes (technically, if it has seeds, it is a fruit), and cranberries contain only 1 to 4% sugar.  Red currants, grapefruits, guavas, cantaloupes, strawberries, raspberries, blackberries, papayas, apricots, watermelons, and peaches contain 6 to 9%.  Black currants, pears, honeydew melons, oranges, plums, blueberries, gooseberries, passion fruits, prickly pear cactus fruits, mangos, pineapples, pomegranates, and apples have 10 to 13% sugar.  Cherries, kiwis, persimmons, figs, grapes, bananas, and litchis contain 14 to 17%[93]. The types of sugars in various fruits vary, but in general, they are virtually 100% fermentable. This means that you should not expect any residual sweetness from the addition of fruit (unless, of course, it is a very, very strong base beer and you expect the yeast to poop-out from the alcohol made from the fruit).

## Fruit Extracts

An alternative to using real fruit is fruit extract. I've tried a number of fruit extracts with unpleasant results. Some varieties may be better, but the extracts I used were labeled "100% fruit" and I ran into a problem while trying to make a reasonable fruit beer from them. The problem was that when I added enough to the beer to get a decent fruit aroma and flavor the extract began to impart a slight medicinal aroma and added an unpleasant bitterness. If you do choose to try one of these extracts don't commit an entire batch – pour yourself a half glass of a similar finished beer and try adding the extract, drop-by-drop, with an eyedropper. Because these extracts are said to contain no sugars (double check with your supplier), you can add them at bottling time. Therefore, you can add fruit to just a six-pack if you wish.

## Juices

Commercially-made juices are a handy way to add fruit. They are already bacteria-free and (in most cases) they are crystal clear, so you've already solved two problems. There are three things that are important when considering fruit juices for addition to your beer (and all involve reading the label): 1) make sure the first ingredient is not "high fructose corn syrup" or some other refined sugars, 2) make sure they don't have any preservatives (such as sodium benzoate, potassium sorbate, or sorbic acid) – these can kill your yeast, and 3) check what kind of juices are really in there (most cherry juices are only partly cherry juice, the balance being white grape juice). If you do use fresh-squeezed juice that has not been sanitized in any way you can either try to sanitize it by pasteurizing (see above), add metabisulfite to give your cultured yeast an advantage (wait 24 hours after adding the metabisulfite before adding the juice to the beer) or simply use the juice raw and expect a bacterial infection. Odds are very good that you'll have one but there are several styles in which this is welcome.

I have had success with *Cherefresh 100% pure Cherry Juice from concentrate*. I added 48 fluid ounces of the juice to 1 gallon of a light American Wheat in the secondary and it turned out quite well. Again, had it been a Porter or a Doppelbock, I would have needed two or even three times the juice. I have also tried making a fruit beer from *Dole Mountain Cherry 100% juice frozen concentrate*. This didn't turn out as well as planned. While the label says "100% juice" the juices are: apple, grape, cherry, lemon, and clarified pineapple. As expected, the beer didn't smell or taste like cherries – it smelled faintly of watermelon. As with whole fruit, the sugars are virtually 100% fermentable, so you should not expect any residual sweetness from the juice.

## Honey

The use of honey in fermented beverages probably pre-dates beer. Honey is almost 100% fermentable and therefore will tend to lighten the body and increase the alcohol content of the beer. Honey does lend a little of its characteristic flavor to the beer. How much depends on the percentage of honey that you use. You can use any percentage, but as you begin to approach 50% the beer tends to taste less like beer and more like mead.

Light-flavored honeys, such as clover, have been said to be better suited for adding to beer, but I can't see why a darker honey, such as buckwheat, wouldn't be welcome in a beer. Perhaps the more robust honeys would be better in more robust beers, for example in a brown ale or a stout. Raw honey is full of wild yeasts and possibly even bacteria so you should at least pasteurize it (see under "Fruits," above). Boiling for a few minutes is also okay, but the longer you boil the more of the subtle aromatics you can get from honey will be lost. Inevitably during the heating of the honey you will see a scum form. This is mostly waxes which should be skimmed off and discarded. One last point about adding honey is that it is very low in yeast nutrients. Therefore, as the percentage of honey that you add to the beer increases, the more important it is to add some yeast energizer or you will have a very slow, weak fermentation.

## Maple Syrup

Maple syrup is an interesting addition to some styles of beer. It tends to work better with the less-hopped styles. There are two grades of maple syrup available: Grade A and Grade B. Grade B is quite a bit more intensely flavored and actually is better for brewing. I recommend that you seek out pure, 100% maple syrup and skip the grocery store "pancake syrup" which is mostly corn syrup with only a small amount of Grade B syrup added for flavor. Maple syrup is quite fermentable so it will only add a slight sweetness, some alcohol and, of course, that classic maple flavor. You can boil the syrup for a *few minutes* if you want to be very sure that it is sanitary, but if the syrup came in a can and is labeled "refrigerate after opening," I'm willing to bet that the can was filled with boiling hot syrup and there is no need to sanitize it. One-half gallon (about 2 liters) of Grade B syrup will add a very, very subtle flavor in a 5 gallon batch, which will be noticeable in only the very lightest, mildest beers. For a more pronounced flavor, 3 to 4 quarts (about 3 to 4 liters) are needed. In a very flavorful beer such as a Stout, you can safely add 4 quarts or more. As with fruits, the majority of the aroma/flavor of the maple syrup comes from its aromatics, which can be scrubbed-out by evolving $CO_2$. Therefore, I would recommend letting the primary fermentation subside before adding the syrup for the secondary fermentation.

I had the great pleasure of being selected a Best of Show judge at the First National Maple Brew-Off. I tasted a number of outstanding beers made with maple syrup as well as a few fermented beverages that were made entirely of maple syrup and water. They were outstanding! Maple syrup may be expensive, but the resulting beers are well worth the cost.

## Candi Sugar

Belgian candi sugar is an important ingredient in many Belgian styles. It comes in two basic types: white and several shades of dark, both of which are effectively 100% fermentable. White candi sugar is virtually all sucrose so you can safely substitute plain, white, table sugar for white candi sugar. Based upon tasting, I believe that dark candi sugar is simply slightly caramelized sucrose. If you cannot find dark candi sugar for a recipe, I would suggest heating a rather thick mixture of table sugar and water until it turns brown – be careful: stir constantly and don't burn the syrup. Russell Mast reported in the Homebrew Digest that a friend of his made amber candi sugar in this way and used 30 pounds of it in 10 barrels of a Belgian Strong Ale that won a gold medal in the 1994 Great American Beer Festival. Don't pour molten sugar into water or wort (or vice versa) – it *will* splatter! Pour the molten sugar onto a beer-clean (don't wash with soap – use detergent) disposable aluminum pie pan. Don't use wax paper – the wax will affect your beer's head retention. Brown sugar in the US is simply plain white sugar with some molasses added to it and is not a substitute for Belgian candi sugar.

**Figure 11-4**: *Dark candi sugar.*

## Sugar Syrups

I would be suspicious of anything simply labeled "sugar syrup." It can be any number of things, none of them bad, but you can't tell what proportion of which sugar they are or what proportion of water they are. "Glucose syrup" can be just dextrose and water but more than likely it is one of the other syrups described here, just misnamed. High-glucose corn syrup and high-maltose corn syrup are also rather ambiguous terms, but they appear to have specific meanings if produced specifically for brewing. High-glucose corn syrup is 43% glucose, 37% maltose and maltotriose, and 20% unfermentable sugars. High-maltose corn syrup is 72% maltose and maltotriose, 3% glucose, and 25% unfermentable sugars[94,95]. Ask your supplier for details on whatever you purchase and make sure that you know what the actual sugar profile is.

Invert sugar syrup also has some meaning. When you heat sucrose (table sugar made from either cane or beets) in a slightly acidic solution, some of it breaks down into its component glucose and fructose. Each sucrose molecule is one glucose and one fructose molecule bonded together. From a short boil at this acidity, only a small portion of the sucrose is broken down[96]. The reason that people would make invert sugar syrup is because breaking even a small amount of the sucrose into glucose and fructose keeps the sucrose from crystalizing. From the yeast's perspective, I feel that the small amount of inversion that you would perform is immaterial – just use sucrose (my guess is to use 20% less sucrose by weight to account for the water in the invert sugar syrup).

In general, I would avoid the use of these syrups in all but high-gravity Belgian Ales which would be sickeningly sweet if they were 100% malt-based.

## DE 62

DE 62 is a corn syrup with a specific distribution of various sugars[95]. It has a sugar distribution that resembles wort, which is why it is often called "wort similar sugar." Frankly, all-malt is much better for your yeast because despite the fact that their sugar profile is similar, they lack the amino acids and peptides that are essential nutrients for the yeast. However, in high-gravity Belgian Ales, that already have a lot of malt in them, DE 62 may be a good substitute for light candi sugar. Despite the fact that the sugar profile of DE 62 is similar to wort, its nutritional value to the yeast (nitrogen/amino acids) is not, so if you add more than 20% or so, you should think about adding some yeast energizer also.

## Golden Syrup

Golden syrup is a British product and is nothing more than invert sugar syrup. You can make it yourself (see "Sugar Syrups," above) or you can simply substitute sucrose (table sugar). In small amounts, I don't think it will taste much different.  I don't know the water percentage in Golden Syrup, but my guess would be about 20%, so use 20% less sucrose when you substitute.

## Black Treacle

Black Treacle is another British product.  It resembles molasses, but is a bit different.  Although Roger Protz does not list it as an ingredient in Theakston's Old Peculier, there are those who swear you cannot make a similar-tasting ale without Black Treacle.  How much you add has a lot to do with the intensity of the flavor of the base beer to which you plan to add the syrup.  I suggest that you begin with about 1 cup in a 5-gallon batch on darker beers and adjust to taste.  The flavor can be quite intense so be careful, especially on the lighter-colored beers.  I feel that it should be added to the boil (turn off the heat and stir well) to kill off any wild yeasts or bacteria that might be in the syrup.  But if the can is not bulging, then it must be all right, no?  Well, when the water content gets very low, many yeasts and bacteria simply cannot flourish, but they aren't dead.  When you add water, they can come to life and spoil your beer.

## Molasses

Molasses is basically the leftovers when they refine cane sugar and is available in light (or mild), dark (or robust), and blackstrap (in increasing intensity).  It has a slightly different flavor than Black Treacle, although there can be similar differences between manufacturers of molasses too.  As with Black Treacle, start with 1 cup in a 5-gallon batch for darker beers and add it to the boil to sanitize.  It is possible to increase the aromatics you get from the molasses by adding it after the main fermentation is over (just like with fruit or honey), but then you should dilute it with a few cups of water and bring it to a simmer for 15 minutes to sanitize it.  Let it cool before adding it to the fermenting beer.

## Vegetables

There are basically two types of vegetables to be considered for brewing: those that contain starch and those that don't.  I'll just briefly mention the type that contain starch here because you will have to mash them or you will get a starch haze in your beer.  Typical vegetables from which you can get fermentables are potatoes and yams.  The other type of "vegetable" that is most commonly used (for its flavoring capabilities and not for starch) is the pepper.  Actually, peppers are fruits because they have seeds, but since most people would look for peppers in the vegetable section of this book, I'll put them here.

There are more than 200 varieties of peppers and they vary in strength from 0 to more than 300,000 Scoville units.  Rather than try to cover all these peppers here, let me give you a starting point and suggest that you refer to the Special Ingredients issue of Zymurgy for more information[97].  The best pepper beer I've had was made with Serrano peppers. I recommend starting with 1/4 pound of de-stemmed, diced Serranos added to 5 gallons of beer, in the fermenter for a week, but steam the peppers first for 5 minutes to kill any wild yeasts or bacteria. A good pepper beer should not burn at the start, but should taste first like beer and then the heat of the peppers should creep up in the finish.

## Enzymes

There are three types of enzymes that are available to homebrewers for use in beer. They come labeled as amylase, papain, and pectic enzyme. Amylase enzyme is used primarily in the mash when using a lot of adjuncts that don't have any enzymes and is what converts the starches to sugars. Malt has amylase enzymes naturally, so you shouldn't have to use any in an all-malt mash, under normal circumstances. I've heard of adding it to the fermenter to lower the final gravity of beers that just happened to be too dextrinous, but I advise against using it in that way. The problem is that you have absolutely no control over how much of the dextrins the enzyme converts to fermentables. What you can end up with is a very watery beer with no mouthfeel or body. The "yeast with special enzymes" in some Pilsner kits contains amylase enzymes, therefore, I recommend against using it.

Papain contains enzymes that break down proteins. It can be used to reduce chill haze which is due to large proteins complexing with polyphenols (a.k.a. tannins), but similar to amylase, we have no control of how much of the protein in the beer is broken down. In addition to removing all the haze it can also ruin the head retention and body. Pectic enzyme is used to clear wines and fruit beers in which you have a haze due to pectin. I've heard it works miracles. Follow the directions on the label and keep it refrigerated because heat ruins pectic enzymes.

## Finings

Finings are covered under "Clarity and Finings" in chapter 6, Other Brewing Considerations.

## Spices, Herbs and Flavoring Extracts

If a spice or herb is edible, you can brew with it. The best source for information on brewing with spices and herbs is the Special Ingredients issue of Zymurgy[97]. Volume II of this series will have a whole chapter on herbs and spices, so I'm going to cover just the most popular ones here and offer two pieces of advice: 1) watch out for oils and 2) fresh spices can vary greatly in strength relative to dried. Oils ruin head retention and can give you an odd scum in the neck of the bottle, but only affect the beer's esthetics. Be careful when you substitute freshly-ground spices for a recipe that calls for grocery store variety spices and vice versa.

When you write down your recipe, make sure you are very specific on whether you used fresh or brand-name spices and whether they were pre-ground or you ground them yourself.

Various spices fade at different rates so that the character of beers flavored with several spices will change with time. After a week or two one spice may be dominant. After two months a different one may be more noticeable. After six months or a year a third spice may be at the forefront. When I make spiced beers, I always try to keep a few bottles for a few years and see how the aromas and flavors change with time. Spices are an interesting addition to fruit beers too.

Note that some spices available to homebrewers (e.g. wormwood and sweet gale, a.k.a. bog myrtle) are dangerous should be avoided.

## Cinnamon

Cinnamon is a common spice used in Holiday beers. It can be added to the boil or dry into the fermenter. As with hops, dry-spicing will add more aroma. For a 5-gallon batch, between 1 and 2 inches of cinnamon stick or 1 to 2 teaspoons may be added to the boil. For adding to the fermenter, I recommend you begin with no more than 1/4 of an ounce, and wait till fermentation has subsided.

## Coriander

Coriander was used in beer long before hops became popular. The Belgian Witbier style is characterized by its coriander aroma and flavor. One half ounce (about 15 grams) of pre-ground, grocery store variety coriander, boiled for the last five minutes of a 5 gallon batch adds a light coriander aroma and flavor. This amount is a bit too light for a Witbier, but can be a nice amount, along with other spices, for a spiced beer. For a Witbier, I recommend 1 to 1 1/2 ounces in the last five minutes of the boil or one ounce in the boil and another 1/2 ounce added in the fermenter. If you can, grind your own fresh coriander, but use only about 1/2 as much as the weaker, pre-ground variety.

## Curaçao Orange

Curaçao orange peels also called bitter orange peels, are really neither very orange-tasting or bitter. Curaçao orange peels are not even orange colored! They are grayish-green. They have an herbal character, similar perhaps to chamomile[100]. They come in chips or quarter-of-an-orange slices. About 1/2 to 3/4 ounce per 5 gallons is a good starting point for Witbiers. Regular navel orange peels are not a substitute (they lend a "ham-like" aroma to the beer). Add them in the last 5 minutes of the boil.

## *Ginger*

Another popular spice in holiday beers is ginger. Note that dried ginger is quite a bit more powerful than freshly-sliced, which is not what you would expect, so beware. Start with one ounce of fresh thinly-sliced ginger in the last 5 minutes of the boil for a 5-gallon batch. I've heard of brewers using as much as 6 ounces in a 5 gallon batch, but I would imagine that you would have to be some kind of fanatic to like that much. Thinly-sliced ginger is better than grated because it is easier to remove. Ginger mellows with time so you can use quite a bit more if you plan to let the beer age before drinking.

**Figure 11-5**: *Ginger root.*

## *Hazelnut Extract*

Hazelnuts are some of my favorites and their extract is my favorite to use in beer. I've used it in an English Brown Ale, although it should go well with any style of beer that is not too bitter. Every brand will have a different strength, but I recommend 40 ml (about 1 1/4 fluid ounces) in 5 gallons as a starting point.

## *Licorice*

Licorice adds an interesting touch to stouts and might be nice in a very small amount to other styles such as maybe a Trappist Dubbel style or maybe even a Barleywine. "Brewer's Licorice" is made from the extract of the licorice root and typically used in amounts varying from 2 to 6 inches for a 5-gallon batch. It should be added in the boil to dissolve and sanitize it.

## *Spruce*

Spruce is a nice addition to holiday beers. You can use spruce needles or spruce essence. I've never used it personally, so I can only go by what I've read. Additions for a 5-gallon batch range from a pint jar loosely filled to a cup tightly packed of new-growth spruce tips. 2 to 5 of teaspoons spruce extract are said to be the proper amounts for a 5 gallon batch[98,99]. I suggest adding the spruce with 5 minutes left in the boil, but I've also read that they should be boiled for 60 minutes.

# Miscellaneous Ingredients

## Lactose

Lactose is milk sugar and is not fermentable by yeast so it can be used to sweeten beer. It is not very sweet, so you will have to use a lot to get a significant amount of sweetness. 8 ounces (about 250 grams) in a 5-gallon batch adds a slight sweetness. One pound (about 500 grams) in 5-gallons adds a marked sweetness. To emulate a very sweet beer such as Mackeson's XXX or Dragon Stout, I would imagine that you may have to add more than two pounds. Note that while most yeasts cannot eat lactose[144], many bacteria can (such as **Lacto**bacillus), so you have to be very sure that your sanitation is very good or you will have gushers at the least and maybe worse. You can add it in the boil or at bottling time if you boil it up in a cup or two of water. Adding it at bottling time allows you to add it to-taste, but you run the risk of gushers if there are significant numbers of bacteria or yeast that can eat lactose. Adding it in the boil is slightly safer because any microbiota that can ferment lactose, will tend to do it in the fermenter.

## Malto-Dextrin

Malto-dextrin, another almost unfermentable carbohydrate, adds virtually no sweetness but adds body and mouthfeel. 1 pound (about 500 grams) is a typical addition to a 5-gallon batch. You should add it to the boil (at the end is fine). It has some fermentable sugar in it, so the apparent attenuation you can expect from it is about 16%. 1 pound in 5 gallons will add about 11 points (0.011) to your original gravity and about 9.3 points (0.0093) to your final gravity (so expect a higher FG and don't think you have a stuck fermentation).

## Heading Agents

I have no experience with heading agents and prefer to combat head retention problems by other means such as adding crystal malts. There are various types of heading agents available. All I can advise is to follow label directions.

## Foam-reducing Agents

The purpose of foam-reducing agents (e.g. Fermcap™ or Anti-foam) is to reduce the amount of foaming that occurs during fermentation and therefore, minimize the amount of beer that is lost to blowoff. For commercial brewers this is a more important factor than for homebrewers because for a professional, it is very costly to have to purchase a 15 barrel fermenter, yet only be able to put 12 barrels of beer in it. I have not used any of them yet, but I've read that they do perform as advertised and do not affect the head retention of the finished beer, because the foam-reducing agent adheres to the sides of the fermenter, settles with the yeast, and is removed during filtration[154,155]. It has been reported that these foam-reducing agents improve head retention because head-retaining substances are not lost in the blowoff. However, my research has shown that the loss of protein via blowoff is negligible and that there was no noticeable decrease in head retention from using the blowoff method[33]. If indeed the head retention is improved by foam-reducing agents, I suspect that it is by some means other than the reduction of protein loss (for example, settling of foam-negative lipids).

Note, that the amount used is extremely small, so that a gram scale is essential to The rate of use may vary from one manufacturer to another, so you should follow the package instructions, but if there are no instructions supplied, I suggest the following for a 5-gallon (18.9-liter) batch (based upon the Fermcap[TM] suggested rate of a minimum of 40 $g/m^2$ of fermenter exposed surface area):

- store in the refrigerator (unopened shelf-life is 6 months at room temperature – after blending with water, it should be used within 8 hours),
- shake well to mix the liquid,
- mix 2 grams of the liquid with an ounce (30 ml) of sanitized water (the commercial rate is quite a bit higher, but a smaller quantity of water is just impractical),
- blend well till a uniform "milky" appearance is achieved, and
- add to fermenter after the addition of yeast.

## Yeast Nutrient and Yeast Energizer

There is quite a bit of confusion about "yeast nutrient" and "yeast energizer." In an effort to clear it up, I contacted all the major homebrew supply distributors in the US and a couple of retailers that make their own yeast nutrition additives and discussed what it is that they call "nutrient" and "energizer."

The first thing that is important to note is that neither nutrient nor energizer are recommended for all-malt beers in which yeast nutrition is not suspect (there are some extracts that are labeled "malt extract" but may contain lots of corn sugar or glucose syrup). These additives are just simply are not needed for most batches and some can even give you off flavors.

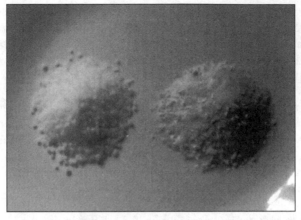

**Figure 11-6**: *Notice that the yeast nutrient (l) is white and pretty much all one size, whereas the yeast energizer is tan and is obviously made up of several different compounds.*

Except for three exceptions, "yeast nutrient" is pretty much all diammonium phosphate and should only be used for winemaking. One exception is BrewTek Yeast Nutrient which contains amino acids, peptones, and vitamins and is meant for use only in yeast starters, slants, and plates. Two other exceptions are "Fermax Yeast Nutrient" from Crosby and Baker and "Yeast Nutrient" from William's Brewery. They are a blend of various vitamins and other nutrients in addition to diammonium phosphate. They are what most other suppliers call Yeast Energizer (see below).

Yeast energizers vary in composition, but all contain some subset of the following ingredients: vitamins, amino acids, yeast hulls, autolysed yeast, and diammonium phosphate. Because honey (the primary ingredient in mead) has virtually no yeast nutrients, often the package will say something like "1 teaspoon per gallon of mead." Scale the recommended amount of energizer based upon the amount of nutrient-less sugar sources you have in the wort. If you have used, for example, 20% corn sugar, then use 20% of the amount of energizer recommended for mead. If the package doesn't give a recommended usage, I would rather be conservative and assume $1/2$ teaspoon per gallon for mead.

## Oak chips

Many brewers believe that India Pale Ales are supposed to have an oaky character. This is incorrect. Firstly, European oak was used for the casks and imparts far less oak character than American oak. Secondly, even American oak loses much of its oakiness after a few uses. If you were shipping beer to India with little hope of getting the cask back, would you use new casks or old, well-used ones? Finally, some casks were pitch-lined. It's a pretty good bet that there was little oak character in those original IPAs. Lambics have some oaky character, but I have a strong suspicion that it is created by the microbes and not the casks themselves.

Ballentine's IPA was aged in American oak casks for a short time (see... even professional brewers believed that IPAs were oaky) so if you were trying to duplicate this unique beer, oak chips would be in order. Rodenbach Grand Cru and similar beers definitely require some oak character. 1 ounce of American oak chips in 5 gallons of beer should take about 1 to 2 weeks to impart a noticeable oak aroma. Sanitize the chips by steaming or blanching, or boil them in water for a few minutes and add the water along with the chips. Don't use iodophor or bleach as sanitizers on oak chips: the chips would absorb the sanitizer and then later release it to the beer.

## Smoke

Smoked beers are great. Usually they are made from smoked malts, but if you are not brewing all-grain, you can still make your own smoked crystal malt on a smoker (see "Smoked Malts" in chapter 7). Don't use too much! $1/2$ pound of smoked grain will give a definite smoky character. Liquid smoke is also an alternative, but read the label and make sure you don't buy the stuff that has vinegar in it (like I did). One teaspoon in 5 gallons (18.9 liters) is a good starting point.

## Lactic Acid

Some styles (Lambic/Lambiek, Berliner Weiss, Witbier, and Flanders Brown/Red Ale) require a lactic sourness. The traditional way to achieve this is to inoculate the wort with a lactic bacteria. An alternative is to add food-grade lactic acid directly, although it does take a few months for the lactic acid to blend with the flavors of the beer. The amount to add depends a lot on the sweetness and strength of the beer, but here are some general guidelines for using 88% lactic acid.

**Table 11-2: Lactic acid suggested use.**

| Style | Suggested amount per bottle | Suggested amount per gallon |
|-------|------------------------------|------------------------------|
| Witbier | 0.2 to 1 ml | 2 to 10 ml |
| Flanders Brown/Red | 0. 5 to 1.5 ml | 5 to 15 ml |
| Berliner Weiss | 1 to 2.5 ml | 10 to 25 ml |
| Lambiek/Lambic | 3 to 5 ml | 30 to 50 ml |

## *Coffee*

Coffee Stout seems to be a very common use for coffee in beer. You don't have to limit yourself to Stouts or plain coffee, by the way – you can use flavored coffees too. I recommend steeping between $1/2$ pound and 1 pound of freshly-ground coffee beans in a few cups of boiling water (don't boil the beans) for 15 minutes or so and then run the liquid through a coffee filter. Then, get another fresh coffee filter and run it through again. You can even do that again a third time. The reason for all this extra filtering is to remove the oils that you are going to get from the beans. If left in the coffee, these oils will ruin your head retention. Add the cooled coffee into the primary at the end of fermentation.

## *Chocolate*

Last, but not least, chocolate. I've tasted some very good and some very bad beers made with chocolate. Although I've never made a beer with chocolate, I've read that the proper amount is between 1 and 6 ounces of bittersweet baker's chocolate added at the end of the boil on a 5-gallon batch[98]. As with coffee, oils are a problem. Cocoa powder has less oil, but it still has some, so it will affect head retention. George De Piro has reported in the Homebrew Digest that 8 ounces of cocoa powder in a 5-gallon batch will give a subtle but noticeable chocolate flavor. I have seen cocoa powders and syrups that are fat-free, but many of these contain aspartame (which some people should avoid, myself included), so read the label. Note also that both chocolate and cocoa are bitter so you want to back-off on the bitterness of the beer. We are used to chocolate being sweet so, as with fruit, you may want to make the beer on the sweet side with extra caramel malts and perhaps even lactose.

# Further Reading

Busch, J., "*Man Does Not Live by Hops Alone - Spice up Your Brewing with Ancient Ingredients*," 4 (6) 32-35 (Nov/Dec 1996). [Note: sweet gale and wormwood are mentioned in the sidebar on gruit and are available to homebrewers, but should be avoided because they are dangerous.]

Zymurgy Special Issue 1994 "*Special Ingredients and Indigenous Beers*," 17 (4), (Special 1994).

# RECIPES

**R**ecipes are just guidelines. Your kettle, stove, water and scales are different than mine. Also, no two fermentations are exactly the same. Therefore, although virtually every one of these recipes has won its share of competition awards, chances are they will come out just a bit different for you than they did for me. Fear not… the differences will be minor. These are all original recipes that I formulated by trial and error, making changes based upon feedback from judges at competitions.

Specific extracts have been listed, but you may substitute any quality extract of similar color. The resulting beer will be close to that which you would get if you used the extracts specified. The one exception is Laaglander Dried Malt Extract – this extract is very different from most and you should only substitute "Hollander Dried Malt Extract," "Northwestern European Dried Malt Extract," or "Dutch Dried Malt Extract" in its place. Specific yeasts have been suggested, but you may substitute another liquid yeast or you may even use dry yeast instead. The beer will taste different, but still quite good.

When you brew from these recipes, if the hops you buy are considerably lower or higher in %AA, divide the AAUs that I have listed by the %AA printed on the package of hops you've bought and that will give you the number of ounces you should use. For example, if the recipe calls for 2.5 ounces of 4.0%AA Fuggle hops (i.e.10AAU), but the Fuggle hops you get at the store are 5.0%AA, divide the 10AAUs listed in the recipe by 5.0%AA and use 2 ounces of hops. All these recipes call for hop pellets in the boil and whole hops for dryhopping. Use 10% more whole hops if you substitute them for pellets and vice versa. If you must make substitutions, see appendix B for which varieties to use in place of those listed in these recipes. For metric conversion, multiply ounces by 28.4 to get grams and divide pounds by 2.2 to get kilograms. All of these are 5 gallon batches (18.9 liters) and the recipes are for use with a 1.5 gallon (5.76 liter) partial boil. In the text following each recipe are the hop weights to be used if you choose to do a full boil.

Finally, the recipes assume that you are using a large enough fermenter so that the kräusen falls back into the fermenting beer (in other words, they are formulated assuming that you are *not* using the blowoff method). If you do choose to use the blowoff method, you will lose about 15% of the hop bitterness, so you should multiply the recipe hop weights by 1.18 to compensate for the loss due to blowoff (i.e. if the recipe says to use 1 ounce of hops, use 1.18 ounces).

# *ALES*

# Back-to-Basics Blonde Ale

### *Blonde Ale*

This recipe is for a beer that is very mild, mellow and drinkable. The Laaglander Light DME is used to give the beer a little higher final gravity and a creaminess that keeps this beer from being bland. It is low in original gravity, alcohol and bitterness. This is what you might call "lawnmower beer," but it has quite a bit of flavor despite being very light.

5 gallons (1.5-gallon partial boil)

3.3 pounds Munton & Fison Unhopped Light malt extract syrup
1.5 pounds Laaglander Light Dried Malt Extract (unhopped)
1.6 ounces Cascade pellets (5% AA; 8 AAU) boiled 60 minutes for bittering
1/4 teaspoon rehydrated Irish Moss (optional)
1 package Cooper's dry yeast  OR  Wyeast German Ale (#1007)
1/2 cup corn sugar (dextrose) for priming (at bottling time)
50 bottlecaps and bottles

OG: 1.038-1.040 (9.5-10P)
FG: 1.010-1.014 (2.5-3.5P)
approximate ABV: 3.6%
estimated IBUs: 20

Bring water to boil. Remove from heat and add extract, stirring to dissolve. Bring back to boil. Boil 10 minutes. Add bittering hops in a hop bag. Boil 45 minutes. Add rehydrated Irish Moss. Boil 15 minutes. Chill and mix with 4 gallons of boiled and chilled water. Aerate wort and pitch yeast. Ferment between 65 and 70° F (18 and 21° C).

If you do happen to use a full boil, use only 1 ounce of Cascade pellets (5 AAU) for bittering.

# Münchner Mond

### *Bavarian Weizen*

While it is admittedly difficult to get that creamy character from extract and even more difficult to get that "wheaty" flavor, this is a decent representation and allows the extract brewer to venture beyond barley. I've tried several wheat extracts and have been disappointed with two of them. One of them is 100% wheat and has a smoky almost "burnt" character. The other, tastes fine, but the manufacturer seems to have been  so concerned with the protein in the wheat that they held the mash at a low-temperature protein rest for too long. The result is a thin beer and very low head retention. Since wheat beers tend to have the best head retention of all the styles, I feel this is an unacceptable flaw. There may be other brands that are very good, but I've found that Munton & Fison and Alexander's are two manufacturers that make good wheat extracts.

5 gallons (1.5-gallon partial boil)

6.6 pounds Munton & Fison Wheat malt extract syrup (unhopped)
1 pound DeWolf-Cosyns Carapils crystal malt (8 Lovibond)
1.5 ounces Mount Hood pellets (4.1% AA; 6 AAU) boiled 60 minutes for
    bittering
Yeast Culture Kit Co. A85 or A50 yeasts, Wyeast Weihenstephan Wheat
    (#3068), OR Head Start "Weizen 68"
$7/8$ cup corn sugar (dextrose) for priming (at bottling time)
50 bottlecaps and bottles

OG: 1.050-1.054 (12.5-13.5P)
FG: 1.010-1.014 (2.5-3.5P)
approximate ABV: 5%
estimated IBUs: 15

Steep crushed malt in 1.5 gallons 170° F (77° C) water using a grain bag for 30 minutes. Remove the grain bag. Add extracts stirring well to dissolve. Bring to boil. Boil 10 minutes. Add bittering hops in a hop bag. Boil 60 minutes. Chill and mix with 4 gallons of boiled and chilled water. Aerate wort and pitch yeast. Ferment between 65 and 70° F (18 and 21° C).

If you do happen to use a full boil, use only 0.9 ounces of Mount Hood pellets (3.76 AAU) for bittering.

# San Francisco Gold

## California Common

A toasted malt flavor, an assertive bitterness, and a very familiar hop flavor are the hallmarks of this beer. While it is much easier to get that toasty flavor in a partial-mash or all-grain recipe, the DeWolf-Cosyns Caravienne lends a little of this toasty flavor. While you may be tempted to add toasted malt to this recipe and there are some authors who suggest adding toasted malt to extract batches, I advise against it. Toasted malt needs to be mashed and läutered properly or you will get a permanent starch haze in the finished beer.

5 gallons (1.5-gallon partial boil)

6 pounds Northwestern Gold malt extract syrup (unhopped)
1 1/2 pounds DeWolf-Cosyns Caravienne crystal malt (20 Lovibond)
1.7 ounces US Northern Brewer pellets (9.5% AA; 15.7 AAU) boiled 60
    minutes for bittering
0.8 ounces US Northern Brewer pellets (9.5% AA; 7.37 AAU) boiled 15
    minutes for flavor
1/4 teaspoon rehydrated Irish Moss (optional)
Wyeast California Lager (#2112) OR Yeast Lab L35 "California Lager"
1/2 cup corn sugar (dextrose) for priming (at bottling time)
50 bottlecaps and bottles

OG: 1.050-1.054 (12.5-13.5P)
FG: 1.010-1.014 (2.5-3.5P)
approximate ABV: 5%
estimated IBUs: 45

Steep crushed malt in 1.5 gallons 170° F (77° C) water using a grain bag for 30 minutes. Remove the grain bag. Add extract. Bring to boil. Boil 10 minutes. Add bittering hops using a hop bag. Boil 45 minutes. Add flavor hops in a second hop bag and rehydrated Irish Moss. Boil 15 minutes. Chill and mix with 4 gallons of boiled and chilled water. Aerate and pitch yeast. Ferment between 60 and 65°F (16 and 18° C). Bottle when the airlock slows to 1 bubble every two minutes.

If you do happen to use a full boil, use only 1 ounce of US Northern Brewer pellets (9.93 AAU) for bittering and 0.5 ounces of US Northern Brewer pellets (4.65 AAU) for flavor.

# Wolverhampton Mild

### Dark Mild

Mild used to be a very popular style of beer in England. Currently, its popularity has declined considerably and it is difficult to find anywhere except in Central England. Its a shame too, since these wonderful session beers are made for enjoying in quantity. I love beer and especially beer that is designed to be consumed in large amounts, is full of flavor, yet won't knock you out. Wolverhampton Mild is just such a beer. Flavorful, yet gentle... full-bodied, but not heavy. This is what Light Beers should be!

5 gallons (1.5-gallon partial boil)

3.3 pounds Northwestern Gold malt extract syrup (unhopped)
1.5 pounds European Light Dried Malt extract (unhopped)
1/4 pound Munton & Fison crystal malt (60 Lovibond)
1/4 pound DeWolf-Cosyns Chocolate malt (550 Lovibond)
1.75 ounces Fuggle pellets (4.9% AA; 8.6 AAU) boiled 60 minutes for bittering
Yeast Culture Kit Company A20 or A65 OR Wyeast London ESB (#1968)
1/2 cup corn sugar (dextrose) for priming (at bottling time)
50 bottlecaps and bottles

OG: 1.036-1.040 (9-10P)
FG: 1.010-1.014 (2.5-3.5P)
approximate ABV: 3%
estimated IBUs: 25

Steep crushed malt in 1.5 gallons 170° F (77° C) water using a grain bag for 30 minutes. Remove the grain bag. Add extract. Bring to boil. Boil 10 minutes.

Add bittering hops using a hop bag. Boil 60 minutes. Chill and mix with 4 gallons of boiled and chilled water. Aerate and pitch yeast. Ferment between 65 and 70°F (18 and 21° C). Bottle when the airlock slows to 1 bubble every two minutes.

If you do happen to use a full boil, use only 1.2 ounces of Fuggle pellets (5.8 AAU) for bittering.

# Old Reekie 70/-

## *Scottish Heavy*

Auld Reekie is what they used to call Edinburgh, Scotland. Thankfully, they've cleaned up the air quality problems – it's a beautiful city filled with friendly people who are more than willing to talk about life, love, and beer. Traditional Scottish Ales are not as plentiful as one might expect, but with the help of the CAMRA Good Beer Guide, there are many great Scottish beers on handpump and even a few on air dispense to be found. This recipe is a sort of blend of influences from various Scottish Ales throughout Lothian. Most Scottish Ales from Lothian have hop aromas, but in an effort to keep within AHA guidelines, this beer will be in the minority and will not have one.

5 gallons (1.5-gallon partial boil)

3.3  pounds Northwestern Gold malt extract syrup (unhopped)
1 pound Laaglander Light Dried Malt Extract (unhopped)
$1/2$ pound Munton & Fison Crystal malt (60  Lovibond)
2 ounces  DeWolf-Cosyns Roasted Barley (550  Lovibond)
$1/4$ teaspoon rehydrated Irish Moss (optional)
1.6  ounces East Kent Goldings pellets (4.65% AA; 7.4 AAU) boiled 60 minutes
     for bittering
Yeast Culture Kit Company A43 or A44  OR  Wyeast Scottish Ale (#1728)
$1/2$ cup corn sugar (dextrose) for priming (at bottling time)
50 bottlecaps and bottles

OG: 1.034-1.038 (8.5-9.5P)
FG: 1.010-1.014 (2.5-3.5P)
approximate ABV: 3%
estimated IBUs: 22

Steep crushed malt and roasted barley in 1.5 gallons 170° F (77° C) water using a grain bag for 30 minutes. Remove the grain bag. Add extracts stirring well to dissolve. Bring to boil. Boil 10 minutes. Add bittering hops in a hop bag. Boil

45 minutes. Add rehydrated Irish Moss. Boil 15 more minutes. Caramel flavor is an important part of many Scottish Ales – optionally, you may want to boil 1 hour before adding the hops to caramelize the wort more, but monitor the volume of the wort and add water so that you begin with 1 3/4 gallons of wort when you add the hops. Chill and mix with 4 gallons of boiled and chilled water. Aerate wort and pitch yeast. Ferment between 62 and 66°F (17 and 19° C).

If you do happen to use a full boil, use only 1.1 ounces of East Kent Goldings pellets (5 AAU) for bittering.

# New Guinea Extra Stout

### Foreign-style Stout

There are two distinct versions of Guinness Stout: the draft version and the version labeled "Extra Stout." The Guinness in cans is very much like the draft version. What we get here in the US in bottles is the Foreign-style version. The draft version is much lower in original gravity and alcohol than the "Extra." There is also an even stronger, slightly sweeter version brewed under contract at several breweries in the Caribbean. This recipe tries to imitate the bottled version we get in the U.S. You can get even closer with an allgrain recipe and by souring, pasteurizing, and then blending back 3% of the finished beer, but even simple recipe gets pretty close.

5 gallons (1.5-gallon partial boil)

3.3 pounds Northwestern Dark malt extract syrup (unhopped)
2.5 pounds Munton & Fison Light Dried Malt Extract (unhopped)
3/8 pound Roasted (unmalted) Barley
1/4 pound Black Patent Malt or Roasted Malt
2 teaspoons calcium carbonate (chalk) unless you know you have a lot of carbonate in your water
1.75 ounces Nugget pellets (11% AA; 18.9 AAU) boiled 60 minutes for bittering
1/4 teaspoon rehydrated Irish Moss (optional)
Wyeast Irish Ale (#1084), Yeast Culture Kit Company A13 "Irish Ale" OR Yeast Lab A05 "Irish Ale"
1/2 cup corn sugar (dextrose) for priming (at bottling time)
50 bottlecaps and bottles

OG: 1.048-1.052 (12-13P)
FG: 1.010-1.014 (2.5-3.5P)
approximate ABV: 5%
estimated IBUs: 48

Steep crushed malt and roasted barley in 1.5 gallons 170° F (77° C) water using a grain bag for 30 minutes. Remove the grain bag. Add extracts and chalk stirring well to dissolve (you may omit the chalk if your water has a lot of carbonates already). Bring to boil. Boil 10 minutes. Add bittering hops in a hop bag. Boil 45 minutes. Add rehydrated Irish Moss. Boil 15 minutes. Chill and mix with 4 gallons of boiled and chilled water. Aerate wort and pitch yeast. Ferment between 65 and 70° F (18 and 21° C).

If you do happen to use a full boil, use only 1.1 ounces of Nugget pellets (12 AAU) for bittering.

# Kensington Special

## Special Bitter

This recipe is meant to approximate Young's Special Bitter, best enjoyed on handpump, but available in the U.S. as Young's Ram Rod (in a slightly fizzier form). Young's actually uses 5% brewing sugar and 4% torrified (puffed) barley, but this beer is a little heavier (and to use the torrified barley, we would have to mash). The name actually comes from the fact that on our last trip to London, our local was a Young's pub just off Kensington High Street. Note that the table salt addition is based upon what I did to get my Chicago water (37 ppm Ca, 11 ppm Mg, 5 ppm Na, 25 ppm $SO_4$, 10 ppm Cl, 100 ppm $CO_3$) to more closely approximate London water (52 ppm, 32 ppm, 86 ppm, 32 ppm, 34 ppm, and 104 ppm, respectively). See the water chapter on how to modify your water.

5 gallons (1.5-gallon partial boil)

6 pounds Northwestern Gold malt extract syrup (unhopped)
1/2 pound DeWolf-Cosyns Caramunich crystal malt (80 Lovibond)
1.25 grams table salt
2.2 ounces Fuggle pellets (4.9% AA; 10.5 AAU) boiled 60 minutes for bittering
1.2 ounces East Kent Goldings pellets (4.65% AA; 5.6 AAU) boiled 15 minutes for flavor
1/4 teaspoon rehydrated Irish Moss (optional)
Yeast Culture Kit Company A17 "Pale Ale" OR Wyeast London Ale III (#1318)
1.5 ounces Target OR East Kent Goldings whole hops for dryhopping
1/2 cup corn sugar (dextrose) for priming (at bottling time)
50 bottlecaps and bottles

OG: 1.045-1.047 (11.25-11.75P)
FG: 1.009-1.013 (2.25-3.25P)

approximate ABV: 4.8%
estimated IBUs: 32

Steep crushed malt in 1.5 gallons 170° F (77° C) water using a grain bag for 30
minutes. Remove the grain bag. Add extracts and salt. Bring to boil. Boil 10
minutes. Add bittering hops using a hop bag. Boil 45 minutes. Add flavor hops
in a second hop bag and rehydrated Irish Moss. Boil 15 minutes. Chill and mix
with 4 gallons of boiled and chilled water. Aerate and pitch yeast. Ferment
between 68 and 72°F (20 and 22° C). Add dryhops when the airlock has slowed
to 1 bubble per minute. Bottle after two weeks. Even better, put it on
handpump!

If you do happen to use a full boil, use only 1.4 ounces of Fuggle pellets (6.8
AAU) for bittering and 0.8 ounces of East Kent Goldings pellets (3.65 AAU) for
flavor. Do not change the dryhopping for a full boil.

# Zum Urheber

### *Düsseldorfer Altbier*

If you haven't been to Düsseldorf or
Portland, chances are you have
misconceptions about the
Düsseldorf-style Altbier. The 1996
AHA guidelines are misleading, no
brewpub or microbrewery that I'm
aware of (except for Widmer) is
making anything remotely close to
the traditional version, and most
people who think they know the
style are thinking of something
completely different. Why?

*Duesseldorfer-typ Altbier*

Sheaf und Vine Braurei - Palos Hills, Illinois

Because there are three distinct styles of Altbier in Germany, all three are very
different and of those three, none of the classic examples of the Düsseldorf
version are exported. The three styles are: Düsseldorf-style, Münster-style and
what has been called "Dortmunder-style". Even in Düsseldorf, the most popular
Altbiers are modernized versions which are (in my opinion) underhopped.

The Münster-style is characterized by a single commercial example (Pinkus
Münster Alt) and is pale, contains a significant amount of wheat and an
intentional lactic sourness. The Northern German-style or Dortmunder-style
(because there are several breweries in Dortmund making this style) is basically
a brown, hoppy lager. An example of this style is DAB Dark. The Düsseldorf-

style version is extremely malty, slightly fruity, slightly sweet, and (most importantly) exceedingly bitter. Zum Uerige is the Jolt™ of German beer and the archetypal Düsseldorfer Altbier. This recipe attempts to approximate this jewel of the beer world.

Please, brew this beer. Tell your friends about the three different types of Altbiers and that you have to either brew it at home or go to a brewpub (in Düsseldorf or currently, only Widmer in Portland, Oregon) to taste the Düsseldorf-version. Teach them that it is supposed to be so bitter it knocks your socks off. Write to the AHA and tell that traditional Düsseldorfer Altbiers have 45 to 55 IBUs and than only modern interpretations have 30 to 40 IBUs. Help me educate beer lovers about this noble style and help make it as popular in the U.S. as it is in Düsseldorf.

5 gallons (1.5-gallon partial boil)

6.6 pounds Ireks Amber malt extract syrup (unhopped)
$^1/_4$ pound DeWolf-Cosyns Chocolate malt (550 Lovibond)
6.2 ounces German Spalt pellets (3.5% AA; 21.5 AAU) boiled 60 minutes for
    bittering
Wyeast European Ale (#1338) OR Yeast Culture Kit Company A37 "W 165 Alt"
    or A49 "Alt #2"
$^1/_2$ cup corn sugar (dextrose) for priming (at bottling time)
50 bottlecaps and bottles

OG: 1.048-1.052 (12.25-13.25P)
FG: 1.014-1.018 (3.5-4.5P)
approximate ABV: 4%
estimated IBUs: 55

Steep crushed malt in 1.5 gallons 170° F (77° C) water using a grain bag for 30 minutes. Remove the grain bag. Add extract. Bring to boil. Boil 10 minutes. Add bittering hops using a hop bag. Boil 60 minutes. Chill and mix with 4 gallons of boiled and chilled water. Aerate and pitch yeast. Ferment between 60 and 65° F (16 and 18° C). Bottle when the airlock slows to 1 bubble every two minutes.

If you do happen to use a full boil, use only 3.9 ounce of German Spalt pellets (13.6 AAU) for bittering.

# Southampton Dark

## Southern-style English Brown Ale

No, not Texas Brown, but a Brown Ale in the style of southern England. These beers are darker, sweeter and less hoppy than their northern cousins. This beer is not modeled after any particular beer, but is actually a sort of high-test Dark Mild. Karen and I have mixed feelings for the town of Southampton (the clear leader in confusing motorway signage, if there was a competition for such a thing). Some of our best and worst memories of England hail from there. Brown Ales are not nearly as popular in England as are Bitters. It's a shame though, since the rich creamy maltiness of this style is a nice departure from the bitterness that dominates most Bitters. Incidentally, probably the finest English Brown Ale I've ever had is from Chicago: Golden Prairie Nut Brown Ale.

5 gallons (1.5-gallon partial boil)

6 pounds Northwestern Gold malt extract syrup (unhopped)
1/2 pound DeWolf-Cosyns Caramunich crystal malt (70 Lovibond)
1/2 pound Munton & Fison Chocolate malt (325 Lovibond)
1.75 ounces Fuggle pellets (4.9% AA; 8.55 AAU) boiled 60 minutes for bittering
0.9 ounces Fuggle pellets (4.9% AA; 4.37 AAU) boiled 15 minutes for flavor
1/4 teaspoon rehydrated Irish Moss (optional)
Wyeast London ESB Ale (#1968) OR Yeast Culture Kit Company A20 yeast
1/2 cup corn sugar (dextrose) for priming (at bottling time)
50 bottlecaps and bottles

OG: 1.047-1.051 (11.75-12.75P)
FG: 1.011-1.015 (2.75-3.75P)
approximate ABV: 4.8%
estimated IBUs: 25

Steep crushed grain in 1.5 gallons 170° F (77° C) water using a grain bag for 30 minutes. Remove the grain bag. Add extracts. Bring to boil. Boil 10 minutes. Add bittering hops using a hop bag. Boil 45 minutes. Add flavor hops in a second hop bag and rehydrated Irish Moss. Boil 15 minutes. Chill and mix with 4 gallons of boiled and chilled water. Aerate and pitch yeast. Ferment between 68 and 72° F (20 and 22° C). Bottle when the airlock has slowed to 1 bubble every two minutes.

If you do happen to use a full boil, use only 1.1 ounces of Fuggle pellets (5.43 AAU) for bittering and 0.6 ounces of Fuggle pellets (2.8 AAU) for flavor.

# Mahogany Mirror Ale

## *American Brown Ale*

American Brown Ale is one of the most recent additions to the list of the world's beer styles. Originally called "Texas Brown" in the homebrewing world, it is a cross between the American Pale Ale style and the English Brown Ale style. It has the assertive bitterness and aggressive American hop flavor of an American Pale Ale and the maltiness of an English Brown Ale.

5 gallons (1.5-gallon partial boil)

6 pounds Northwestern Gold malt extract syrup (unhopped)
1 pound Munton & Fison Wheat Malt extract (unhopped)
$^1/_2$ pound DeWolf-Cosyns Caramunich crystal malt (20 Lovibond)
$^1/_2$ pound DeWolf-Cosyns Chocolate malt (550 Lovibond)
3.7 ounces Cascade pellets (5.1% AA; 18.6 AAU) boiled 60 minutes for bittering
1.5 ounces Cascade pellets (5.1% AA; 7.76 AAU) boiled 15 minutes for flavor
$^1/_4$ teaspoon rehydrated Irish Moss (optional)
Wyeast American Ale (#1056) OR Yeast Culture Kit Company A01 "American Ale"
1 ounce Cascade whole hops for dryhopping
$^1/_2$ cup corn sugar (dextrose) for priming (at bottling time)
50 bottlecaps and bottles

OG: 1.053-1.057 (13.25-14.25P)
FG: 1.013-1.017 (3.25-4.25P)
approximate ABV: 5%
estimated IBUs: 50

Steep crushed malt in 1.5 gallons 170° F (77° C) water using a grain bag for 30 minutes. Remove the grain bag. Add extracts. Bring to boil. Boil 10 minutes. Add bittering hops using a hop bag. Boil 45 minutes. Add flavor hops in a second hop bag and rehydrated Irish Moss. Boil 15 minutes. Chill and mix with 4 gallons of boiled and chilled water. Aerate and pitch yeast. Ferment between 65 and 70° F (18 and 21° C). Add dryhops when the airlock has slowed to 1 bubble per minute. Bottle after two weeks.

If you do happen to use a full boil, use only 2.25 ounces of Cascade pellets (11.4 AAU) for bittering and 0.9 ounces of Cascade pellets (4.8 AAU) for flavor. Use the same amount of dryhops.

# Caribbean Tonic Sweet Stout

## *Sweet Stout*

In the Islands, they believe that dark, sweet beers have "medicinal" properties. Next time you are down there, ask one of the locals about Dragon Stout and I'm sure they will give you all the details. Meanwhile you can give this recipe a try and see what it does for you. It is not quite as sweet as some stouts from the Caribbean, but you can always increase the sweetness by adding more lactose. The ESB yeasts were chosen because they lend a fruity complexity to the aroma which lends a nice touch to this beer. Any fruity ale yeast would be appropriate, even Coopers Dry yeast.

5 gallons (1.5-gallon partial boil)

3.3 pounds Northwestern Dark malt extract syrup (unhopped)
3 pounds  Laaglander Light Dried Malt Extract (unhopped)
1/2 pound DeWolf-Cosyns Special B crystal malt
1/2 pound DeWolf-Cosyns Caramunich crystal malt
1/4 pound Roasted (unmalted) Barley
1/4 pound Black Patent Malt or Roasted Malt
4 teaspoons calcium carbonate (chalk) unless you know your water is high in
   carbonate
1.5 ounces Galena pellets (12% AA; 17.5 AAU) boiled 60 minutes for bittering
1/4 teaspoon rehydrated Irish Moss (optional)
Wyeast London ESB Ale (#1968) OR Head Start Brewing Cultures "ESB"
1/2 cup corn sugar (dextrose) for priming (at bottling time)
50 bottlecaps and bottles

OG: 1.054-1.058 (13.5-14.5P)
FG: 1.013-1.017 (3.25-4.25P)
approximate ABV: 5%
estimated IBUs: 42

Steep crushed malt and roasted barley in 1.5 gallons 170° F (77° C) water using a grain bag for 30 minutes. Remove the grain bag. Add extracts and chalk, stirring well to dissolve. Bring to boil. Boil 10 minutes. Add bittering hops in a hop bag. Boil 45 minutes. Add rehydrated Irish Moss. Boil 15 minutes. Chill and mix with 4 gallons of boiled and chilled water. Aerate wort and pitch yeast. Ferment between 65 and 70° F (18 and 21° C).

If you do happen to use a full boil, use only 0.9 ounces of Galena pellets (10.7 AAU) for bittering.

# Sacred Heart Abbey Tripel

## Belgian Tripel

The Tripel style of beer was originated by the Trappist monks at Abdij Westmalle and has been copied by many secular breweries. This version is a little darker than the original because it is difficult to achieve such pale color when using extract. Westmalle Tripel does have live yeast in the bottle, but because of the very high gravity, few have been successful in reviving them. A large starter is required whichever yeast you use.

5 gallons (1.5-gallon partial boil)

8 pounds Alexander's Sun Country Pale malt extract syrup (unhopped)
3 pounds White Candi Sugar OR sucrose (table sugar)
1/4 pound Munton & Fison Light Dried Malt Extract (unhopped)
1.9  ounces Styrian Goldings pellets (5.4% AA; 10.3 AAU) boiled 60 minutes for bittering
0.9  ounces Hallertauer pellets (4.5% AA; 4.14 AAU) boiled 30 minutes for bittering and flavor
1.8 ounces Saaz pellets (3.2% AA; 5.82 AAU) boiled 15 minutes for flavor
1/2 teaspoon rehydrated Irish Moss (optional)
Wyeast Trappist High Gravity (#3787) OR Head Start "Two Monks" or "Trappist" yeast
7/8 cup corn sugar (dextrose) for priming (at bottling time)
50 bottlecaps and bottles

OG: 1.078-1.082 (19.5-20.5P)
FG: 1.012-1.016 (3-4P)
approximate ABV: 9%
estimated IBUs: 27

Heat water to about 170° F (77° C). Add extracts (we'll add the sugar later). Bring to a boil. Boil 10 minutes. Add Styrian Goldings hops using a hop bag. Boil 30 minutes. Add Hallertauer hops in a second hop bag. Boil 15 minutes.

Add Saaz hops in a third hop bag, sugar and rehydrated Irish Moss. Boil 15 minutes. Chill and mix with 4 gallons of boiled and chilled water. Aerate well and pitch a big yeast starter. Ferment between 65 and 70° F (18 and 21° C). Bottle when the airlock has slowed to 1 bubble every two minutes.

If you do happen to use a full boil, use only 1.1 ounces of Styrian Goldings pellets (5.71 AAU) for 60 minutes, 0.5 ounces of Hallertauer pellets (2.28 AAU) for 30 minutes and 1 ounce of Saaz pellets (3.2 AAU) for 15 minutes.

# Neumantinus Weizenbock

## *Bavarian Weizenbock*

Weizenbocks are particularly interesting beers. While most German styles are marked by subtlety, Doppelbocks and Weizenbocks give the Bavarian Braumeisters the opportunity to crank-up the gravity and the flavor. Of all the beers I tasted in Munich on my latest trip, Schneider Aventinus was clearly the most memorable. I guess it would technically be a Dunkelweizenbock (dark, strong wheat beer). I'm not exactly sure which yeast the Schneider brewery uses, but unlike most Weizen brewers, Schneider's beers are bottle conditioned with the fermentation yeast, so you can actually culture it yourself - right from the bottle. Also, despite the AHA style guidelines saying that Dunkelweizens have chocolaty and roasted malt character, only one of the many that I had in Munich actually had a chocolaty character (which was very slight) and none had any roasted malt character at all. Aventinus had virtually no dark malt nose or flavor. Put some of this beer away in the cellar – it will improve with age. I'd also like to point out that this recipe calls for slightly less priming sugar than might be expected for a Weizen. This is partly because the Aventinus is less carbonated than a typical Weizen and because it's common for beers to get slightly more carbonated as they age.

5 gallons (1.5-gallon partial boil)

9.9 pounds Munton & Fison Wheat malt extract syrup (unhopped)
3/4 pound DeWolf-Cosyns Caramunich crystal malt (70 Lovibond)
3 ounces Liberty pellets (4.0% AA; 12.3 AAU) boiled 60 minutes for bittering
Yeast Culture Kit Company A50 yeast, Head Start "Weizen 66" OR Yeast Lab
    W51 "Bavarian Weizen"
3/4 cup corn sugar (dextrose) for priming (at bottling time)
50 bottlecaps and bottles

OG: 1.072-1.076 (18-19P)
FG: 1.014-1.018 (3.5-4.5P)

approximate ABV: 7%
estimated IBUs: 25

Steep crushed malt in 1.5 gallons 170° F (77° C) water using a grain bag for 30 minutes. Remove the grain bag. Add extracts stirring well to dissolve. Bring to boil. Boil 10 minutes. Add bittering hops in a hop bag. Boil 60 minutes. Chill and mix with 4 gallons of boiled and chilled water. Aerate wort and pitch yeast. A large starter (2 liters) is recommended due to the high gravity of this beer. Ferment between 65 and 70° F (18 and 21° C).

If you do happen to use a full boil, use only 1.75 ounces of Liberty pellets (6.95 AAU) for bittering.

# Near a Savanna Pale Ale

### American Pale Ale

This recipe results in a beer that is very similar to Sierra Nevada Pale Ale. Ideally, we would like it to be a little drier, but that can be difficult with extract. One thing that you can do to make sure you get the maximum attenuation is to use a large starter (at least the equivalent of 2 liters). The signature character of this style is the flavor and aroma of Cascade hops.

5 gallons (1.5-gallon partial boil)

6.6  pounds Munton & Fison Unhopped Light malt extract syrup
1/2 pound DeWolf-Cosyns Caravienne crystal malt (20  Lovibond)
2.75 ounces Cascade pellets (5.1% AA; 14 AAU) boiled 60 minutes for bittering
1.5 ounces Cascade pellets (5.1% AA; 7.5 AAU) boiled 15 minutes for flavor
1/4 teaspoon rehydrated Irish Moss (optional)
Wyeast American Ale (#1056)  OR Yeast Culture Kit Company A01 "American Ale"
1 ounce Cascade whole hops for dryhopping
1/2 cup corn sugar (dextrose) for priming (at bottling time)
50 bottlecaps and bottles

OG: 1.048-1.052 (12.25-13.25P)
FG: 1.013-1.017 (3.25-4.25P)
approximate ABV: 5%
estimated IBUs: 40

Steep crushed malt in 1.5 gallons 170° F (77° C) water using a grain bag for 30 minutes. Remove the grain bag. Add extract. Bring to boil. Boil 10 minutes.

Add bittering hops using a hop bag. Boil 45 minutes. Add flavor hops in a second hop bag and rehydrated Irish Moss. Boil 15 minutes. Chill and mix with 4 gallons of boiled and chilled water. Aerate and pitch yeast. Ferment between 65 and 70° F (18 and 21° C). Add dryhops when the airlock has slowed to 1 bubble per minute. Bottle after two weeks.

If you do happen to use a full boil, use only 1.7 ounces of Cascade pellets (8.7 AAU) for bittering and 0.9 ounces of Cascade pellets (4.7 AAU) for flavor. Use the same amount of dryhops.

# Full Gale ESB

## *Extra Special Bitter*

This recipe results in a beer that is rather similar to Fuller's ESB. Several books say that Fuller's actually uses flaked corn (maize) and caramel in their ESB and I've heard that they have used 7% dark candi sugar (perhaps in place of the caramel they used to use – although most recently, I've heard that they no longer use sugars of any kind), but this recipe relies on two varieties of crystal malt to lend that caramelly flavor. This beer is a bit heavier in body, sweeter and lower in alcohol than Fuller's. Substituting 1/2 pound of dark candi sugar for the Caramunich and cutting back the Caravienne to 3/4 pound perhaps would be a bit closer to emulating the archetypal ESB.

5 gallons (1.5-gallon partial boil)

6 pounds Munton & Fison Unhopped Light malt extract syrup
1 pound DeWolf-Cosyns Caravienne crystal malt (20 Lovibond)
1/2 pound DeWolf-Cosyns Caramunich crystal malt (70 Lovibond)
5 grams Burton Water Salts unless you know your water is high in sulfate
2.5 ounces Fuggle pellets (4.9% AA; 12.4 AAU) boiled 60 minutes for bittering
1.7 ounces East Kent Goldings pellets (4.65% AA; 7.8 AAU) boiled 15 minutes
   for flavor
1/4 teaspoon rehydrated Irish Moss (optional)
Wyeast London ESB Ale (#1968)  OR  Yeast Culture Kit Company A20
1.5 ounces Challenger OR East Kent Goldings whole hops for dryhopping
1/2 cup corn sugar (dextrose) for priming (at bottling time)
50 bottlecaps and bottles

OG: 1.053-1.057 (13.25-14.25P)
FG: 1.010-1.014 (2.5-3.5P)
approximate ABV: 5%
estimated IBUs: 35

Steep crushed malt in 1.5 gallons 170° F (77° C) water using a grain bag for 30 minutes. Remove the grain bag. Add extracts and Burton Water Salts. Bring to boil. Boil 10 minutes. Add bittering hops using a hop bag. Boil 45 minutes. Add flavor hops in a second hop bag and rehydrated Irish Moss. Boil 15 minutes. Chill and mix with 4 gallons of boiled and chilled water. Aerate and pitch yeast. Ferment between 68 and 72° F (21 and 22° C). (These yeasts really dislike temperatures below 68° F and will slow down to a crawl if it gets too cold.) Add dryhops when the airlock has slowed to 1 bubble per minute. Bottle after two weeks.

If you do happen to use a full boil, use only 1.6 ounces of Fuggle pellets (7.6 AAU) for bittering and 1ounce of East Kent Goldings pellets (4.8 AAU) for flavor.

# Al's Special London Ale

## *Strong Export Bitter*

This recipe results in a beer that is very similar to Young's Special London Ale. The Laaglander DME gives it the high finishing gravity that balances well with the strong bitterness and chewy East Kent Goldings hop flavor. The East Kent Goldings dryhopping lend the signature nose of this noble ale. A very satisfying and warming beer.

5 gallons (1.5-gallon partial boil)

6.6  pounds Munton & Fison Unhopped Light malt extract syrup
1.75 pounds Laaglander Light Dried Malt Extract (unhopped)
1 pound English crystal malt (40  Lovibond)
10 grams Burton Water Salts unless you know your water is high in sulfate
3.7  ounces Northern Brewer pellets (6.2% AA; 22.7 AAU) boiled 60 minutes for
      bittering
2.2  ounces East Kent Goldings pellets (4.65% AA; 10.2 AAU) boiled 15 minutes
      for flavor
$1/3$ teaspoon rehydrated Irish Moss (optional)
Wyeast London Ale (#1028)  OR Wyeast London Ale III (#1318)
2 ounces East Kent Goldings whole hops for dryhopping
$1/2$ cup corn sugar (dextrose) for priming (at bottling time)
50 bottlecaps and bottles

OG: 1.064-1.066 (16-16.5P)
FG: 1.018-1.020 (4.5-5P)

approximate ABV: 6%
estimated IBUs: 56

Steep crushed malt in 1.5 gallons 170° F (77° C) water using a grain bag for 30 minutes. Remove the grain bag. Add extracts and Burton Water Salts. Bring to boil. Boil 10 minutes. Add bittering hops using a hop bag. Boil 45 minutes. Add flavor hops in a second hop bag and rehydrated Irish Moss. Boil 15 minutes. Chill and mix with 4 gallons of boiled and chilled water. Aerate and pitch yeast. Ferment between 65 and 70° F (18 and 21° C). Add dryhops when the airlock has slowed to 1 bubble per minute. Bottle after two weeks.

If you do happen to use a full boil, use only 2.2 ounces of Northern Brewer pellets (13 AAU) for bittering and 1.3 ounce of East Kent Goldings pellets (6 AAU) for flavor.

# K&A's Nuptial Ale

## *Raspberry/Cherry Ale*

This recipe is based upon the beer that I made for our wedding (actually, I've only adjusted the proportions of fruit to give a little more cherry and a little less raspberry aroma/flavor). At the time, my wife Karen was not very interested in beer... well, actually she hated it. She did like this beer however, as I had predicted. Everyone at the reception liked it also.

5 gallons (1.5-gallon partial boil)

3.3 pounds Northwestern Gold malt extract syrup (unhopped)
1.1 pounds Munton & Fison Light Dried Malt Extract (unhopped)
1 pound DeWolf-Cosyns Carapils crystal malt (8 Lovibond)
1.2 ounces East Kent Goldings pellets (4.65% AA; 5.4 AAU) boiled 60 minutes
   for bittering
1.7 ounces East Kent Goldings pellets (4.65% AA; 7.8 AAU) boiled 15 minutes
   for flavor
1/4 teaspoon rehydrated Irish Moss (optional)
Yeast Culture Kit Company A01 "American Ale"  OR  Wyeast American
   Ale(#1056)
3 pounds frozen raspberries
7 pounds frozen cherries (no stems)
3/4 cup corn sugar (dextrose) for priming (at bottling time)
50 bottlecaps and bottles

OG: 1.055-1.057 (13.75-14.25P)
FG: 1.013-1.015 (3.25-3.75P)
approximate ABV: 5%
estimated IBUs: 18

Steep crushed malt in 1.5 gallons 170° F (77° C) water using a grain bag for 30
minutes. Remove the grain bag. Add extracts, stirring well to dissolve. Bring to
boil. Boil 10 minutes. Add bittering hops in a hop bag. Boil 45 minutes. Add
flavor hops in a second hop bag and rehydrated Irish Moss. Boil 15 minutes.
Chill and mix with 2.5 gallons of boiled and chilled water. Aerate wort and pitch
yeast. Ferment between 65 and 70° F (18 and 21° C). After airlock has slowed
to one bubble per minute, prepare fruit as described in the Fruit section of chapter
11 and add the fruit to a sanitized secondary fermenter (don't use more than 1/2
gallon of water for blanching the raspberries since you will be adding it to the
fermenter). Siphon the beer onto the fruit and let it ferment. If you use a carboy
*definitely* use a 1 1/4 inch blowoff hose (no smaller – I did and have been finding
bits of raspberry pulp on the ceiling joists for more than four years now). Bottle
after the bubbles in the blowoff bucket slow to one bubble every two minutes.

If you do happen to use a full boil, use only 0.7 ounces of East Kent Goldings
pellets (3.3 AAU) for bittering and 1 ounce of East Kent Goldings pellets (4.79
AAU) for flavor.

# Old Bulldog

### Barleywine

The key to making a good
Barleywine is giving the yeast every
opportunity to finish the job. A big
starter is a must (at least 2 liters) but
what would be even better would be
to use the entire yeast cake (the
sedimented yeast in the bottom of the
fermenter) from a previous medium-
gravity batch. Barleywines
inevitably have a lot of higher
alcohols which take some time to
mellow out. This is why they

improve so much with age and why old bottles of Barleywine are so cherished.
Nine months to one year is the expected aging time, but you can shorten that by
keeping the fermentation temperature from getting too high (try to keep it
between 64 and 66° F / 18 and 19° C).

5 gallons (1.5-gallon partial boil)

8 pounds Alexander's Sun Country Pale malt extract syrup (unhopped)
3 pounds Munton & Fison Light Dried Malt Extract (unhopped)
1 1/2 pounds Laaglander Light Dried Malt Extract (unhopped)
1 1/2 pounds DeWolf-Cosyns Caravienne crystal malt (20 Lovibond)
9.4 ounces Cascade pellets (5.1% AA; 48 AAU) boiled 60 minutes for bittering
4.4 ounces Cascade pellets (5.1% AA; 22.5 AAU) boiled 15 minutes for flavor
1/2 teaspoon rehydrated Irish Moss (optional)
Wyeast American Ale (#1056) OR Yeast Culture Kit Company A01 "American
    Ale"
1/2 cup corn sugar (dextrose) for priming (at bottling time)
50 bottlecaps and bottles

OG: 1.100-1.104 (25-26P)
FG: 1.026-1.030 (6.5-7.5P)
approximate ABV: 9.7%
estimated IBUs: 90

Steep crushed malt in 1.5 gallons 170° F (77° C) water using a grain bag for 30
minutes. Remove the grain bag. Add extract. Bring to boil. Boil 10 minutes.
Add bittering hops using a hop bag. Boil 45 minutes. Add flavor hops in a
second hop bag and rehydrated Irish Moss. Boil 15 minutes. Chill and mix with
4 gallons of boiled and chilled water. Aerate wort *well* and pitch yeast. Ferment
between 64 and 68° F (18 and 20° C). Given all the sugars in this wort and the
alcohol that will be produced, this batch could take a month or more to ferment
out and another year to mellow.

If you do happen to use a full boil, use only 4.9 ounces of Cascade pellets (24.8
AAU) for bittering and 2.3 ounces of Cascade pellets (11.6 AAU) for flavor.

Note that the best way to make this beer is to first brew a batch of 1.050 original
gravity beer, rack that beer off into a secondary (or bottle it) and then pour this
batch's cooled wort right on top of the entire yeast cake of the previous batch. If
you do this, a blowoff tube is mandatory and you can expect up to 1/2 gallon of
blowoff. Empty the blowoff bucket often and refill with fresh water.

If you used a starter and it gets stuck at 1.070, for example, and there is no
change for a week, then your yeast was too weak. Take the entire yeast cake
from another batch and siphon this batch on top of that. Alternatively, you can
pitch three or four packages of rehydrated dry yeast. In either of these cases,
avoid aerating the wort at this point. While oxygen would be good for the yeast,

it would not be good for the beer, so we'll just pitch so much yeast that it doesn't need oxygen or to multiply.

When the time comes to bottle, the yeast will undoubtedly be pretty tired from all that alcohol so I recommend that you make up another 2-liter yeast starter and add it along with the priming sugar so you have fresh yeast for carbonation.

# Joteikiu Porteris

## *Original Baltic Porter/Imperial Stout*

Long before the Russian Imperial Court, Lithuania was an empire. Back in the 15th century, Lithuania was the largest country in all of Europe, stretching from the Baltic Sea to the Black Sea. Alas, Lithuanian Imperial Stout isn't a recognized style. Nonetheless, this is a rich, hearty Baltic Porter/Imperial Stout with a warming character that is perfect for those cold Lithuanian winters. The name comes from the Korzonas

family's ancestral village in Lithuania and the beer label includes the family crest. Since this beer is so sweet and high in alcohol, you may want to bottle it in small bottles like a Barleywine. It will keep and improve with time. I wouldn't be surprised if this beer continued to improve for 25 years!

Since the alcohol level is so high, it is imperative that you make up a huge starter (a gallon would not be too big) or (even better) use the entire yeast cake from a medium-gravity (1.050 or so) beer. This second method is really the recommended way to get the most from this recipe. Time this beer so that you are just racking a 1.050 beer off it's yeast cake on brewing day. Cool the wort down to pitching temperature and pour it on top of the whole yeast cake from the previous batch, aerating well. You must use a blowoff hose on this batch unless you put the 5 gallons into a 10 gallon fermenter. Considering the thickness of the kräusen on this beer, even 5 gallons of headspace may not be enough.

5 gallons (1.5-gallon partial boil; assuming blowoff)

6.6 pounds Northwestern Gold malt extract syrup (unhopped)
3.3 pounds Northwestern Amber malt extract syrup (unhopped)
3.3 pounds Northwestern Dark malt extract syrup (unhopped)
1 pound DeWolf-Cosyns Special B crystal malt
1 pound DeWolf-Cosyns Caramunich crystal malt
1/2 pound Roasted (unmalted) Barley
1 pound Black Patent Malt or Roasted Malt
1 pound DeWolf-Cosyns Chocolate Malt
1 cup Grandma's Robust Flavor Molasses
4 teaspoons calcium carbonate (chalk) unless you know than your water is high
    in carbonate
9.9 ounces Nugget pellets (11.1% AA; 110 AAU) boiled 60 minutes for bittering
5 ounces Brewer's Gold pellets (8% AA; 40 AAU) boiled 15 minutes for flavor
3/4 teaspoons rehydrated Irish Moss (optional)
No less than a 1/2 gallon (2 liter) starter from Wyeast London Ale (#1028) OR
    Yeast Lab A03 "London Ale"
1/2 cup corn sugar (dextrose) for priming (at bottling time)
50 bottlecaps and bottles (or more if you use smaller bottles)

OG: 1.120-1.124 (30-31P)
FG: 1.040-1.050 (10-12.5P)
approximate ABV: 11-12%
estimated IBUs: 150 (although, given the extreme gravity, this is a wild guess)

Steep crushed malt and roasted barley in 1.5 gallons 170° F (77° C) water using
two grain bags for 30 minutes. Remove the grain bags. Add extracts and chalk,
stirring well to dissolve. Bring to boil. Boil 10 minutes. Add bittering hops in
two hop bags. Boil 45 minutes. Add flavor hops in a third hop bag and the
rehydrated Irish Moss. Boil 15 minutes. Chill and mix with 4 gallons of boiled
and chilled water. Aerate wort well and pitch yeast. Ferment between 65 and 70°
F (18 and 21° C). Given all the sugars in this wort and the alcohol that will be
produced, this batch could take a month or more to ferment out and another year
to mellow.

If you do happen to use a full boil, use only 4.1 ounces of Nugget pellets (46
AAU) for bittering and 2.4 ounces of Brewer's Gold pellets (19 AAU) for flavor.

Note that the best way to make this beer is to first brew a batch of 1.050 original
gravity beer, rack that beer off into a secondary (or bottle it) and then pour this
batch's cooled wort right on top of the entire yeast cake of the previous batch. A

blowoff tube is mandatory and you can expect at least $1/2$ gallon of blowoff. Empty the blowoff bucket often and refill with fresh water. When I made this batch even the blowoff bucket blew off!

If you used a starter and it gets stuck at 1.070, for example, and there is no change for a week, then your yeast was too weak. Take the entire yeast cake from another batch and siphon this batch on top of that. Alternatively, you can pitch three or four packages of rehydrated dry yeast. In either of these cases, avoid aerating the wort at this point. While oxygen would be good for the yeast, it would not be good for the beer, so we'll just pitch so much yeast that it doesn't need to multiply.

When the time comes to bottle, the yeast will undoubtedly be pretty tired from all that alcohol so I recommend that you make up another 2-liter yeast starter and add it along with the priming sugar so you have fresh yeast for carbonation.

# Al's pLambic/pLambiek

## *Lambic/Lambiek-style*

First, I'll explain the name: true Lambic/Lambiek can only be made via spontaneous fermentation, which means that no yeast or bacteria is added to the wort. In true beers of this style, the wort is slowly cooled in a wide, shallow, open tub in the attic of the brewery (see "Coolships" in chapter 4). Yeast and bacteria float in through openings in the sides of the attic and inoculate the wort. If you are daring, you can try this at home, but chances are the beer will be undrinkable. Very few places in the world are suitable for making beer this way. In this recipe, instead of using spontaneous fermentation, we will be pitching cultures and/or bottle dregs, so, in deference to the brewers of the real Lambics/Lambieks, I add a "p" to designate that this is merely a pseudo-version of the style.

Why does this beer have two names? Well, because one is French and the other Flemish. If I just wrote pLambic, Armand and Guido DeBelder (Drie Fonteinen, Beersel, Belgium) may not be as gracious to me as they were on my last visit. If I just wrote pLambiek, then Jean-Pierre and Claude Van Roy (Cantillon, Anderlecht, Bruxelles, Belgium) might be angry with me. No... of course they wouldn't, but trying to walk the "middle ground" does make things a bit more complicated sometimes.

I've made a few compromises regarding this recipe. First of all, it should be made with unmalted wheat, but that's impossible unless we mash, so we will have to substitute malted wheat extract. It doesn't have the same flavor, but it's the best we can do. Next, traditionally, these beers are made with 3-year-old hops –

hops so old that they have lost virtually all their bittering potential. I've experimented with several varieties of very old hops and I believe that all but Cascade and Centennial varieties can be used. These two varieties seem to retain some character that I don't think is appropriate – chances are that this is just superstition on my part. If you don't have 3-year-old hops, you can make some by baking fresh hops in a 250° F (120° C) oven for 20 minutes. Incidentally, those hops should be aged exposed to the air (3 years in oxygen-barrier bags won't work!). Also, this is one case where I recommend that you use whole hops in the boil as opposed to pellets. Pellets age much too slowly.

The last problem are the yeasts. The yeasts and bacteria are up to you. There is no guarantee, no matter how little or how much you spend on cultures that what you make will turn out tasty. Some homebrewed examples are made with a wide variety of microbes. Others succeed with just a few cultures. One very successful batch I made was pitched with only one *Brettanomyces* culture and the dregs from a bottle of Cantillon Gueuze.

At a minimum, I suggest you pitch at least one ale yeast, one *Brettanomyces* yeast and one lactic acid bacteria. All the Cantillon beers and the Boon Marriage Parfait are unfiltered and unpasteurized, so you can pitch their dregs too if you wish. The more the merrier! Head Start Brewing Cultures and the Yeast Culture Kit Company are experts in these specialized yeast and bacterial cultures and will be happy to help you (they both have ads in the homebrewing magazines listed at the end of chapter 17).

These beers will take a long time to mature. The lactic character (assuming your lactic bacteria didn't expire) should take about six months to become evident. The horsey character made by the *Brettanomyces* will take at least eight months to begin to appear. One batch I made took three years to develop a strong horsy character and that may actually have floated in randomly when the airlock dried out (that has happened at least five times over the last three years).

I'd like to make one final note regarding this recipe. If you are blessed, the beer that results will be very traditional in flavor. The majority of Lambieks/Lambics that are imported into the US are very untraditional. They are very sweet, made with fruit syrups, do not have nearly enough sourness and are really more like sparkling fruit wines than Lambics/Lambieks. If this is the type of beverage you're expecting from this recipe, then don't bother with all the expensive cultures. There is little point in spending three years to make a beer only to overwhelm all of its subtle aromatic complexity with a gallon of fruit syrup. Check out K&A's Nuptial Ale and the section on making fruit beers in chapter 11.

5 gallons (1.5-gallon partial boil)

6.6 pounds Munton & Fison Unhopped Wheat malt extract syrup
5.1 ounces aged or baked whole hops (~0.75% AA; ~3.8 AAU) boiled 60
   minutes, mostly for tradition
At least one neutral ale yeast (like Wyeast American Ale (#1056))
At least one *Brettanomyces* yeast (like Head Start Brettanomyces Bruxellensis or
   Lambicus)
At least one lactic acid bacteria (like Yeast Culture Kit Company M3200
   *"Pediococcus damnosus"*)
3/4 cup corn sugar (dextrose) for priming (at bottling time)
50 bottlecaps and bottles

OG: 1.046-1.050 (11.5-12.5P)
FG: 1.004-1.010 (1.0-2.5P)
approximate ABV: 5%
estimated IBUs: 10

Heat water to about 170° F (77° C). Add extract. Bring to a boil. Boil 10
minutes. Add bittering hops using a hop bag. Boil 60 minutes. Chill and mix
with 4 gallons of boiled and chilled water. Aerate and pitch yeasts and bacteria.
Ferment between 65 and 70° F (18 and 21° C). There is evidence to indicate that
fermentation in European oak or plastic is better for this style than in glass. I
recommend wood or plastic for the first three months and then rack to glass for
the remainder of the year. Wait at least one year to bottle (keep refilling the
airlock to make sure it doesn't dry out). This beer will get more sour for two
years then start to get less sour and more fruity as the yeast convert the acids and
alcohols in the beer to esters.

If you do happen to use a full boil, use only 3.25 ounces of aged or baked whole
hops (2.46 AAU).

Once you've made this pLambiek/pLambic you have several options. You can
make another batch two years later and then blend the one-year-old and the three-
year-old and bottle that as a pseudoGueuze (French) or pseudoGeuze (Flemish).
You can prime it and bottle as you would a normal ale (incidentally, I've done
this with a two-year-old batch and it carbonated fine without a dosage of new
yeast). You can take all or part of it and add it to some raspberries to make a
pFramboise or to some cherries and make a pKriek. What I did was to make a 15
gallon batch of pLambic/Lambiek and then split it into four carboys (3.75 gal in
each): one contained 15 pounds of raspberries, the second contained 13 pounds of

whole cherries the third contained 12 pounds of pitted cherries and the last was empty.

## LAGERS

Lagers are far more difficult to make than ales. Yeast are living creatures and they don't like sudden temperature shocks any more than you or me. A 10° F drop is enough to cause some strains to shut down and go dormant. The difficult parts of making a Lager are pitching enough yeast, keeping the fermenter cool so the yeast don't produce noticeable levels of esters, and not shocking the yeast. See the section on making lagers in Chapter 6 for more details.

# Not Older, But Wiser American Pilsner

### American Pilsner

This recipe results in a beer that bears a slight similarity to Budweiser. Ideally, we would like it to be a little paler and drier, but that can be difficult with extract. You can reduce the darkening during the boil by doing a full boil, but the production of the extract has already darkened it considerably. One thing that you can do to make sure you get the maximum attenuation is to use a large starter (at least 2 liters). You can substitute corn sugar in place of the rice syrup solids to make something similar to Miller or Coors. The yeast suggested bears a remarkable resemblance to that actually used by Anheuser-Busch to make Bud. It creates a lot of acetaldehyde which gives Budweiser its characteristic "green apple" aroma. Use a different lager yeast, perhaps Wyeast North American Lager (#2272), if you want to make something more like Miller or Coors. Incidentally, the Beechwood aging of Budweiser is important because the yeast used has a tendency to drop out of suspension. The wood slats stacked loosely in the bottom of the lagering tanks give the yeast more surface area to settle upon thereby resulting in more exposed yeast to complete the fermentation of the beer. The recommended yeasts for this recipe have that same problem, therefore agitation of the fermenter (without the introduction of air) to resuspend the yeast may be necessary to help the yeast reabsorb diacetyl and acetaldehyde.

5 gallons (1.5-gallon partial boil)

4 pounds Alexander's Sun Country Pale malt extract syrup (unhopped)
3 pounds rice syrup solids
0.9 oz Tettnanger pellets (5.1% AA; 4.42 AAU) boiled 60 min for bittering
1/4 teaspoon yeast energizer
1/4 teaspoon rehydrated Irish Moss (optional)
Yeast Lab L34 "St. Louis Lager" yeast OR Wyeast Pilsen Lager (#2007)

$^3/_4$ cup corn sugar (dextrose) for priming (at bottling time)
50 bottlecaps and bottles

OG: 1.042-1.046 (10.5-11.5P)
FG: 1.006-1.010 (1.5-2.5P)
approximate ABV: 4%
estimated IBUs: 12

Heat water to about 170° F (77° C). Add extract and rice syrup solids. Bring to a boil. Boil 10 minutes. Add bittering hops using a hop bag. Boil 60 minutes adding the rehydrated Irish Moss when 15 minutes are left in the boil. Chill and mix with 4 gallons of boiled and chilled water. Aerate and pitch yeast. Ferment between 50 and 55° F (10 and 13° C). Lager for at least two weeks. See the Lagers section in chapter 6 for more details on brewing lagers.

If you do happen to use a full boil, use only 0.6 ounces of Tettnanger pellets (2.89 AAU) for bittering.

# Rheinstein Pils

### German Pilsner

The German Pilsner style of beer is somewhere between an American Pilsner and a Bohemian Pilsner. It tends to be lighter in body and color than the Bohemian (Czech) Pilsner and lower in hop rate. The actual bitterness perceived is perhaps similar to a Bohemian Pils because of the sulfates in the water, but in terms of actual IBUs, the German Pils is lower. As with

the American Premium Lager, it is difficult to get the color light enough when using extracts, but doing a full boil will minimize darkening during the boil. If you have high sulfate water (let's say over 70 PPM), you either have to lower the hop rate or mix your water with distilled. For example, if your sulfate level is 140 PPM and you mix it 50/50 with distilled, the resulting sulfate level will be 70 PPM. It's a little more complicated when you are brewing from all grain, but for extract brewing, ignoring the other ions and just concentrating on sulfate for this recipe works fine.

5 gallons (1.5-gallon partial boil)

8 pounds Alexander's Sun Country Pale malt extract syrup (unhopped)
1/3 pound Munton & Fison Extra Light Dried Malt Extract (unhopped)
2.1 ounces Hallertauer pellets (4.5% AA; 9.62 AAU) boiled 60 minutes for
    bittering
1.8 ounces Saaz pellets (3.2% AA, 5.77 AAU) boiled 15 minutes for flavor
1/4 teaspoon rehydrated Irish Moss (optional)
0.75 ounces Saaz pellets (3.2% AA, 2.4 AAU) boiled 1 minute for aroma
Yeast Culture Kit Company L09 "German Lager" yeast OR Wyeast Bavarian
    Lager (#2206)
2/3 cup corn sugar (dextrose) for priming (at bottling time)
50 bottlecaps and bottles

OG: 1.046-1.050 (11.5-12.5P)
FG: 1.010-1.014 (2.5-3.5P)
approximate ABV: 4.5%
estimated IBUs: 29

Heat water to about 170° F (77° C). Add extract. Bring to a boil. Boil 10
minutes. Add bittering hops using a hop bag. Boil 45 minutes. Add flavor hops
in a second hop bag and rehydrated Irish Moss. Boil 14 more minutes. Add
aroma hops in a third hop bag. Boil 1 minute. Chill and mix with 4 gallons of
boiled and chilled water. Aerate and pitch yeast. Ferment between 50 and 55° F
(10 and 13° C). Lager for at least 8 weeks – 12 weeks is even better. See the
Lagers section in chapter 6 for more details on brewing lagers.

If you do happen to use a full boil, use only 1.4 ounces of Hallertauer pellets
(6.14 AAU) for bittering and 1.2 ounces of Saaz pellets (3.69 AAU) for flavor.
You should still use 0.75 ounces of Saaz pellets (2.4 AAU) for aroma.

# Kirby's Pilsner

## Bohemian Pilsner

Bohemian Pilsner is the original crystal-clear, golden-colored beer. It is darker
and heavier-bodied than its American or German descendants and has more
toasty aromas and flavors. If you have significant levels of sulfate in your water
(let's say over 20 PPM), you either have to lower the hop rate or mix your water
with distilled till the level drops below 20. Why not just use all distilled water?
For extract brewing, we probably could since the extracts themselves will

probably add enough of the minerals that the yeast require. However, if your sulfate level is not too high, you can save yourself some money by using as much tapwater as possible. The suggested yeasts require two warnings: 1) they may require some kind of finings to help settle them and 2) they have a tendency to create a strong sulfury odor during fermentation (don't worry, it will fade during lagering).

5 gallons (1.5-gallon partial boil)

6 pounds Northwestern Gold malt extract syrup (unhopped)
$1/3$ pound Munton & Fison Extra Light Dried Malt Extract (unhopped)
$3/4$ pound DeWolf-Cosyns Carapils crystal malt (8 Lovibond)
4.3 ounces Saaz pellets (3.2% AA; 13.8 AAU) boiled 60 minutes for bittering
2.3 ounces Saaz pellets (3.2% AA, 7.37 AAU) boiled 15 minutes for flavor
$1/4$ teaspoon rehydrated Irish Moss (optional)
2 ounces Saaz pellets (3.2% AA, 6.4 AAU) boiled 1 minute for aroma
Head Start "Ur-Pils" yeast, Wyeast Czech Pils (#2278), OR Yeast Culture Kit
    Company L17 "Pilsen Lager"
$1/2$ cup corn sugar (dextrose) for priming (at bottling time)
50 bottlecaps and bottles

OG: 1.048-1.052 (12-13P)
FG: 1.012-1.016 (3-4P)
approximate ABV: 4.5%
estimated IBUs: 40

Steep crushed malt in 1.5 gallons 170° F (77° C) water using a grain bag for 30 minutes. Remove the grain bag. Add extract. Bring to a boil. Boil 10 minutes. Add bittering hops using a hop bag. Boil 45 minutes. Add flavor hops in a second hop bag and rehydrated Irish Moss. Boil 14 more minutes. Add aroma hops in a third hop bag. Boil 1 minute. Chill and mix with 4 gallons of boiled and chilled water. Aerate and pitch yeast. Ferment between 45 and 50° F (7 and 10° C). Lager for at least 8 weeks – 12 weeks is even better. Traditionally, Bohemian Pilsners are lagered at nearly 32° F (0° C). See the Lagers section in chapter 6 for more details on brewing lagers.

If you do happen to use a full boil, use only 2.75 ounces of Saaz pellets (8.68 AAU) for bittering and 1.45 ounces of Saaz pellets (4.65 AAU) for flavor. You should still use 2 ounces of Saaz pellets (6.4 AAU) for aroma.

# Helles Hath No Fury...

## *Munich Helles*

Whereas hop bitterness dominates in the Pilsner styles, malt takes center-stage in the Munich styles, both the Helles (Pale) and the Dunkel (Dark). Munich Helles should be creamy and soft with no harsh edges.

5 gallons (1.5-gallon partial boil)

6 pounds Northwestern Gold malt extract syrup (unhopped)
1/2 pound European Light Dried Malt Extract (unhopped)
3/4 pound German Light Crystal Malt (20 Lovibond)
2.1 ounces Hallertauer pellets (4.5% AA; 9.63 AAU) boiled 60 minutes for bittering
1/4 teaspoon rehydrated Irish Moss (optional)
0.5 ounces Hallertauer pellets (4.5% AA, 2.25 AAU) boiled 1 minute for aroma
Wyeast Bavarian Lager (#2206) OR Yeast Culture Kit Company L09 "German Lager" yeast
2/3 cup corn sugar (dextrose) for priming (at bottling time)
50 bottlecaps and bottles

OG: 1.050-1.054 (12.5-13.5P)
FG: 1.012-1.016 (3-4P)
approximate ABV: 4.5%
estimated IBUs: 24

Steep crushed malt in 1.5 gallons 170° F (77° C) water using a grain bag for 30 minutes. Remove the grain bag. Add extract. Bring to a boil. Boil 10 minutes. Add bittering hops using a hop bag. Boil 45 minutes. Add rehydrated Irish Moss. Boil 14 more minutes. Add aroma hops in a second hop bag. Boil 1 minute. Chill and mix with 4 gallons of boiled and chilled water. Aerate and pitch yeast. Ferment between 50 and 55° F (10 and 13° C). Lager for at least 8 weeks – 12 weeks is even better. See the Lagers section in chapter 6 for more details on brewing lagers.

If you do happen to use a full boil, use only 1.3 ounces of Hallertauer pellets (6 AAU) for bittering. You should still use 0. 5 ounces of Hallertauer pellets (2.25 AAU) for aroma.

# Theresienwiese Oktoberfest

## *Oktoberfest/Märzen*

Oktoberfest/Märzen is a difficult style to do well without all-grain brewing. Traditionally, it gains it's rich amber color and characteristic flavor from Munich and Vienna malts and not strictly from crystal malts. If you cannot get the Ireks extract, there are two other extract made from Munich malt, namely Marie's™ Munich Extract and William's Brewing German Gold. In fact these extracts may be preferred, but I've chosen to base this recipe on the more widely available extract. Most amber extracts are made simply with pale malts with small amounts of crystal and/or roasted malts for color. These will not give the right flavor profile for this style. This recipe is a little higher in original gravity than current commercial Oktoberfests and Märzens and not quite as high as traditional ones. Consider it an attempt to "turn back the clock" a few decades to when Oktoberfest beers were a little higher in gravity.

5 gallons (1.5-gallon partial boil)

6.6 pounds Ireks Amber malt extract syrup (unhopped)
1 pound Munton & Fison Light Dried Malt Extract (unhopped)
1/4 pound German light crystal malt (20 Lovibond)
1/4 pound German dark crystal malt (80 Lovibond)
2.5 ounces Hallertauer pellets (4.5% AA; 11.3 AAU) boiled 60 minutes for
    bittering
1/4 teaspoon rehydrated Irish Moss (optional)
Wyeast Bavarian Lager (#2206) or Munich Lager (#2308) OR Yeast Culture Kit
    Co. L09 "German Lager"
2/3 cup corn sugar (dextrose) for priming (at bottling time)
50 bottlecaps and bottles

OG: 1.056-1.060 (14-15P)
FG: 1.012-1.016 (3-4P)
approximate ABV: 5.8%
estimated IBUs: 26

Steep crushed malt in 1.5 gallons 170° F (77° C) water using a grain bag for 30 minutes. Remove the grain bag. Add extracts. Bring to a boil. Boil 10 minutes. Add bittering hops using a hop bag. Boil 45 minutes. Add rehydrated Irish Moss. Boil 15 more minutes. Chill and mix with 4 gallons of boiled and chilled water. Aerate and pitch yeast. Ferment between 50 and 55° F (10 and 13° C). Lager for at least 8 weeks – 12 weeks is even better. See the Lagers section in chapter 6 for more details on brewing lagers. Note that if you use the Wyeast

Munich Lager yeast, you may have to lager for 16 weeks until the sulfury aroma disappears.

If you do happen to use a full boil, use only 1.5 ounces of Hallertauer pellets (6.78 AAU) for bittering

# König Neumanstein

## *Münchner Dunkel*

This recipe is my attempt at reproducing Kaltenberg Brewery's König Ludwig Dunkel, one of the finest Münchner Dunkels I tasted while visiting Bavaria in the summer of 1995. I vividly recall sipping this wonderfully malty, slightly chocolaty, very rich lager at a little outdoor café in the town of Schwangau, literally in the shadow of Schloss Neuschwanstein. Traditionally this beer was made with all Munich malt which is why, like the Oktoberfest, I recommend that you use the Ireks, William's Brewing German Gold, or Marie's™ Munich extracts.

5 gallons (1.5-gallon partial boil)

6.6  pounds Ireks Amber malt extract syrup (unhopped)
1/4 pound DeWolf-Cosyns Chocolate malt (550  Lovibond)
1/2 pound German dark crystal malt (80  Lovibond)
2.1  ounces Hallertauer pellets (4.5% AA; 9.73 AAU) boiled 60 minutes for bittering
1/4 teaspoon rehydrated Irish Moss (optional)
Wyeast Bavarian Lager (#2206) or Munich Lager (#2308) OR Yeast Culture Kit Co. L09 "German Lager"
2/3 cup corn sugar (dextrose) for priming (at bottling time)
50 bottlecaps and bottles

OG: 1.051-1.055 (12.75-13.75P)
FG: 1.012-1.016 (3-4P)
approximate ABV: 5.1%
estimated IBUs: 24

Steep crushed malt in 1.5 gallons 170° F (77° C) water using a grain bag for 30 minutes. Remove the grain bag. Add extracts. Bring to a boil. Boil 10 minutes. Add bittering hops using a hop bag. Boil 45 minutes. Add rehydrated Irish Moss. Boil 15 more minutes. Chill and mix with 4 gallons of boiled and chilled water. Aerate and pitch yeast. Ferment between 50 and 55° F (10 and 13° C). Lager for at least 8 weeks – 12 weeks is even better. See the Lagers section in chapter 6 for more details on brewing lagers. Note that if you use the Wyeast Munich Lager yeast, you may have to lager for 16 weeks until the sulfury aroma disappears.

If you do happen to use a full boil, use only 1.3 ounces of Hallertauer pellets (6 AAU) for bittering

# Perlach Bock II

## Helles Bock

Helles Bock is a high-powered version of Münchner Helles. Both styles share a smooth and creamy malt quality, the Bock also having a touch of warming alcohol and a slightly higher hop rate to balance the sweetness of the added gravity. With this recipe, I am trying to duplicate what I feel is the best Helles Bock in Bavaria: St. Jakobus Blonder Bock from Forschungsbrauerei. Actually, the gravity and alcohol level of this beer land it in the low end of the Doppelbock style. Also, to ensure that the yeast don't poop-out trying to ferment this massive beer, make sure you use a very large starter (at least the equivalent of 3 liters).

5 gallons (1.5-gallon partial boil)

12 pounds Alexander's Sun Country Pale malt extract syrup (unhopped)
1.25 pounds German Light Crystal Malt (20 Lovibond)
4 ounces Hallertauer pellets (4.5% AA; 17.5 AAU) boiled 60 minutes for
    bittering
1/3 teaspoon rehydrated Irish Moss (optional)
0.75 ounces Hallertauer pellets (4.5% AA, 3.4 AAU) boiled 1 minute for aroma
A big starter of Wyeast Bavarian Lager (#2206) OR Yeast Culture Kit Company
    L09 "German Lager" yeast
2/3 cup corn sugar (dextrose) for priming (at bottling time)
50 bottlecaps and bottles

OG: 1.074-1.078 (18.5-19.5P)
FG: 1.019-1.023 (4.75-5.75P)
approximate ABV: 7.2%
estimated IBUs: 35

Steep crushed malt in 1.5 gallons 170° F (77° C) water using a grain bag for 30 minutes. Remove the grain bag. Add extract. Bring to a boil. Boil 10 minutes. Add bittering hops using a hop bag. Boil 45 minutes. Add rehydrated Irish Moss. Boil 14 more minutes. Add aroma hops in a second hop bag. Boil 1 minute. Chill and mix with 4 gallons of boiled and chilled water. Aerate and pitch a large yeast starter. Ferment between 50 and 55° F (10 and 13° C). Lager for at least 12 weeks. See the Lagers section in chapter 6 for more details on brewing lagers.

If you do happen to use a full boil, use only 2.2 ounces of Hallertauer pellets (9.8 AAU) for bittering. You should still use 0. 75 ounces of Hallertauer pellets (3.4 AAU) for aroma.

# Überdunkel

## *Traditional Bock*

The Traditional Bock is to the Münchner Dunkel what the Helles Bock is to the Münchner Helles. This is another style that is difficult to make using extracts. I've chosen to limit the crystal malt and avoid the use of chocolate malt because they really don't add the right flavors for this style. If you can get Marie's™ Munich Malt Extract or William's Brewing German Gold, I think that they may actually be better suited for this beer and you should replace both the Ireks and Alexander's extracts with one of them. Aerate the cooled wort well and use a big starter so you are not left with too-sweet a beer.

5 gallons (1.5-gallon partial boil)

6.6  pounds Ireks Amber malt extract syrup (unhopped)
4 pounds Alexander's Sun Country Pale malt extract syrup (unhopped)
1/3 pound German Dark crystal malt (80  Lovibond)
3.25 ounces Hallertauer pellets (4.5% AA; 14.5 AAU) boiled 60 minutes for
    bittering
0.75 ounces Hallertauer pellets (4.5% AA, 3.4 AAU) boiled 1 minute for aroma
1/3 teaspoon rehydrated Irish Moss (optional)
Wyeast Bavarian Lager (#2206) or Munich Lager (#2308) OR Yeast Culture Kit
    Co. L09 "German Lager"
2/3 cup corn sugar (dextrose) for priming (at bottling time)
50 bottlecaps and bottles

OG: 1.070-1.074 (17.5-18.5P)
FG: 1.018-1.022 (4.5-5.5P)
approximate ABV: 7%
estimated IBUs: 30

Steep crushed malt in 1.5 gallons 170° F (77° C) water using a grain bag for 30 minutes. Remove the grain bag. Add extract. Bring to a boil. Boil 10 minutes. Add bittering hops using a hop bag. Boil 45 minutes. Add rehydrated Irish

Moss. Boil 14 more minutes. Add aroma hops in a second hop bag. Boil 1 minute. Chill and mix with 4 gallons of boiled and chilled water. Aerate well and pitch a large yeast starter (at least the equivalent of 2 liters). Ferment between 50 and 55° F (10 and 13° C). Lager for at least 12 weeks. See the Lagers section in chapter 6 for more details on brewing lagers. Note that if you use the Wyeast Munich Lager yeast, you may have to lager for 16 weeks until the sulfury aroma disappears.

If you do happen to use a full boil, use only 1.8 ounces of Hallertauer pellets (8.26 AAU) for bittering. Use the same amount of aroma hops. You should still use 0. 75 ounces of Hallertauer pellets (3.4 AAU) for aroma.

# Alligator

## *Doppelbock*

In my opinion, the finest Doppelbock is Paulaner's Salvator. It is the originator of this style and as a result, virtually every Doppelbock since then has "-ator" in its name. Note that the current version of Salvator has an original gravity of 1.076 and a final gravity of 1.013, which is virtually impossible to do with an all-malt wort. Back in 1887, Paulaner Salvator started with an original gravity of 1.077 and ended with a  final gravity of 1.031, which is a much more reasonable attenuation. Since we don't have control of the mashing schedule, we would have to add some corn sugar to get close to the current version. Another alternative would be to simply try to duplicate the 1887 recipe. However, since judges are accustomed to the warming alcohol and lighter body of the current version, I think it would be a mistake to leave the final gravity so high. I've chosen to boost the original gravity a little and add some corn sugar to lighten the body while adding the expected alcohol. The result is a huge beer with tasty raisiny notes added by the DeWolf-Cosyns Special B crystal malt. To ensure that the yeast don't expire trying to ferment this extremely high-gravity beer, make sure you use a very large starter (at least the equivalent of 4 liters).

5 gallons (1.5-gallon partial boil)

9.9 pounds Munton & Fison Unhopped Light malt extract syrup
2 pounds corn sugar
1/2 pound DeWolf-Cosyns Special B crystal malt (200 Lovibond)
4.6 ounces Hallertauer pellets (4.5% AA; 20.5 AAU) boiled 60 minutes for
    bittering
1/2 teaspoon rehydrated Irish Moss (optional)
A big starter of Wyeast Bavarian Lager (#2206) OR Yeast Culture Kit Company
    L09 "German Lager" yeast
1/2 cup corn sugar (dextrose) for priming (at bottling time)
50 bottlecaps and bottles

OG: 1.087-1.091 (21.75-22.75P)
FG: 1.016-1.020 (4-5P)
approximate ABV: 9.3%
estimated IBUs: 37

Steep crushed malt in 1.5 gallons 170° F (77° C) water using a grain bag for 30
minutes. Remove the grain bag. Add extract and corn sugar. Bring to a boil.
Boil 10 minutes. Add bittering hops using a hop bag. Boil 45 minutes. Add
rehydrated Irish Moss. Boil 15 more minutes. Chill and mix with 4 gallons of
boiled and chilled water. Aerate and pitch a large yeast starter (at least the
equivalent of 4 liters). Ferment between 50 and 55° F (10 and 13° C). Lager for
at least 12 weeks. See the Lagers section in chapter 6 for more details on
brewing lagers.

If you do happen to use a full boil, use only 2.4 ounces of Hallertauer pellets (11
AAU) for bittering.

## Further Reading

Every issue of Zymurgy and Brewing Techniques contains recipes, but be aware
of the fact that the procedures used by the individual brewers vary considerably
and many things (like boil volume) are not included in the recipes so it can be
very difficult to get duplicate results. This is true of any recipe you will find in a
book. Furthermore, simply because a recipe has won a competition does not
mean that it is a good example of the style. Remarkably often, the winner is the
beer with the least flaws (always check the judges' comments, if available).
Sometimes the best recipes do not win because of procedural problems like
oxidation or infection. In my opinion, best-of-show recipes are a safe bet. Even
at the smallest homebrew competitions, I've yet to taste a beer that has won 1st,
2nd, or 3rd best-of-show and was not an outstanding example of the style.

# 13

# BEER TASTING

asting beer is more than just smelling it and gulping it down. This chapter will describe the techniques used by beer judges to assess beers in a competition. There is a certification program for beer judging which helps provide guidance, education, and accreditation for judges. The various levels you can achieve in this program helps competition organizers ensure that every group of beers is judged by at least one experienced judge.

Standard judging procedure involves six areas: the bottle, aroma, appearance, flavor, body & mouthfeel, and drinkability & overall impression. I will address both the positive and negative characteristics that are possible in each of the six areas. Note that it is important to remember that what is correct for one style may be wrong for another. What is considered thin body in an Imperial Stout will be heavy body for an American Pilsner. What is considered too bitter for a Scottish Ale may be not bitter enough for an India Pale Ale. In most styles, sourness is a flaw, whereas for some it is a requirement.

What is most important is to never just think "hey… it's just beer."

To judge well you need to look for flaws but be cautious that you don't talk yourself into tasting or smelling something that's not really there. Furthermore, you must look beyond malt sweetness and hop bitterness. You must consider all the aromas and flavors you have ever tasted and not limit your aroma and flavor descriptors to typical beer sources. If you smell sweat socks, that's valid. If you smell bananas or raspberries, then write that down. If you taste something that reminds you of plastic bandages, that's possible too. Whatever you taste or smell, write it down and if you're not sure where it might have come from, check the Troubleshooting chapter (chapter 14) for some possible sources.

Consider each of the following areas in the order listed. There is a reason for this order. Once you have poured the beer, you cannot properly assess the fill level, for example. Some aromas only last a minute and it is important to not delay this very important part of the tasting. The rest of the tasting areas can be done in pretty much any order, but the order given here is the one that you would most likely encounter if you were to judge at a sanctioned competition (one that has been recognized by a judging or homebrewing organization).

## Glassware

Ideally, you would like to use "beer clean" glassware to taste beer, but even at medium-sized competitions, anything but plastic cups are impractical. "Beer clean" means that it has been washed with detergent (not soap) and then rinsed well. Soap leaves a film which will ruin head retention. A good rule of thumb is: "if it makes suds, don't use it on beer glassware." I use either unscented dishwashing machine detergent (without special drying agents which also leave a film) or plain Washing Soda (sodium carbonate). These rinse clean and don't leave a film as long as you don't soak the glassware in them. When it comes to plastic cups, not all are created equal. The best kind are made from clear polystyrene (not styrofoam) and will have a "PS" molded into the bottom. More common are high-density and low-density polyethylene (HDPE and LDPE). These have a slight plastic smell and are not crystal clear unlike the clear polystyrene.

## Environment and Preparation

The ideal environment for beer tasting is smoke-free, brightly lit, and quiet. Once, I had to judge beer not far from a bar-b-cue grill… it was not easy. You should avoid using cologne and scented deodorant when you expect to judge beer. Brush your teeth and tongue well and floss. Avoid spicy or very hot foods before judging (and during breaks). Most competitions that are large enough to have multiple sessions will serve lunch to the judges and stewards (judges' assistants), but I can't recall a lunch during a judging intermission that didn't include onions and/or mustard (and I've seen many judges eating both during the break). Several have even had jalapeño peppers!

## Learning Aromas and Flavors

You may not yet be familiar with all the aromas and flavors that are being discussed here. Sure, we've all smelled cooked corn, but talking about the smell of dimethyl sulfide (DMS) and actually smelling it are two different things. I will provide the names of a few widely-available commercial beers that have one or another distinguishing aromas or flavors. By smelling and tasting these beers with the particular aroma or flavor in mind, you will be able to learn what exactly

it is we are looking for. For some smells I won't be able to give you a
commercial example either because there are none commonly available or
because it would be embarrassing to the brewer to have their beer suggested as a
classic example of a flaw. In every case I give below, the aromas and flavors are
appropriate for the style. What is appropriate in one style could be inappropriate
in another. Therefore, by learning the aroma of diacetyl from an English Bitter,
we can learn the aroma that would be a flaw in an American Pilsner. Whenever I
could, I chose two beers that were similar in other characteristics so that there
would be a minimal amount of distraction. You should rinse your mouth with
cool, unchlorinated (boiled and chilled or carbon-filtered) water between
tastings.

**Table 13-1 (sheet 1 of 2): Learning aromas and flavors.**

| Aroma / Flavor | Commercial example(s) high in this character | Commercial example(s) low in this character |
|---|---|---|
| Acetaldehyde/ green apple | Budweiser | Coors |
| Alcohol | Sierra Nevada Bigfoot, Duvel | Sierra Nevada Pale Ale, Bass Ale |
| Aldehydes | take any pale commercial lager pour it back and forth between two glasses to aerate well, pour it back into the bottle, recap, let it sit at room temperature for three days and then refrigerate two hours before serving | |
| Astringent | chew on grape skins or dark red apple peel | |
| Bitter | Ayinger Jahrhundert, Anchor Liberty Ale, Goose Island IPA | Coors |
| Clovey/ Phenolic | Tucher Weizen | Pyramid Wheaton Ale, Anchor Wheat Beer, Heartland Weiss |
| Cooked Corn/ DMS | Heileman's Old Style, Hacker-Pschorr Pils, Paulaner Premium Lager | Bass Ale |
| Diacetyl/ Butterscotch | Samuel Smith's Nut Brown Ale, Perry's Majestic | Dos Equis |

**Table 13-1 (sheet 2 of 2): Learning aromas and flavors.**

| Aroma / Flavor | Commercial example(s) high in this character | Commercial example(s) low in this character |
|---|---|---|
| Fruity/ Estery | Orval (bananas & bubble gum), Chimay Grand Reserve (plums and raisins) | Coors, Dos Equis |
| Lactic/ Sour | Cantillon Gueuze, Boon Geuze (please note that both of these beers have many other aromas and flavors other than lactic acid, but there are few beers in the world with as much sourness as these) | Coors |
| Malty | Ayinger Altbairisch Dunkel, Oregon Nut Brown Ale, Golden Prairie Nut Brown Ale | Beck's Dark, St. Pauli Girl Dark, Heineken Dark |
| Melanoidins | Spaten Oktoberfest, Ayinger Oktober Fest-Märzen, Paulaner Oktoberfest | Beck's Dark, St. Pauli Girl Dark, Heineken Dark |
| Oaky | Rodenbach Grand Cru | Liefmans Goudenband |
| Peaty/Smoky | Adelscott, Adelscott Noir | Bass Ale |
| Skunky | To get a beer to have this aroma, take any beer (except Miller products which are made such that they cannot turn skunky) and set it under fluorescent lights or in the sun for two days. Chill for an hour and serve. Several days at 50° F (10° C) in the dark seems to reverse the process. | Take a bottle of the same beer from a sealed case (where it has been in the dark), chill for an hour and serve. |
| Sulfate | Samuel Smiths Old Brewery Pale Ale (this beer has about 25 IBUs but is high in sulfate - note the dry finish and lingering bitterness) | Pilsner Urquell (this beer has about 41 IBUs, but is low in sulfate - note it has about the same *perceived* bitterness as the Samuel Smiths, but a soft finish and an abrupt end to the bitterness) |
| Sweet | Mackeson's XXX | Sierra Nevada Porter |

# Bottle Inspection

Bottle inspection really does not count actually towards the quality of a beer, but there are important factors that can later help you determine the cause of some problems. The most common factor assessed during bottle inspection is the fill level. A low fill level can be a source of oxidation, but more importantly it can be a source of doubt in a judge's mind. I recommend a normal fill level primarily so that some less-experienced judges don't imagine oxidation that is not really there.

Another thing that judges look for is what's called "ring around the collar." This is a ring of scum that is stuck to the inside walls of the bottle neck, just at the level of the beer. Many immediately assume that this is due to an infection, but although it is a possible source, I believe that it is just as likely to be protein from your priming solution if you used Dried Malt Extract or wort to prime your beer.

The final thing that judges look at is the bottom of the bottle. Is there yeast or is this a filtered beer? Is the yeast cake compact and firm or is it loose and powdery? If it is loose an powdery pouring will have to be done more carefully than if it was a filtered beer or if the yeast cake was compact and firm.

When you open the bottle, don't be fooled by the "ffffft" you hear – the sound is dependent mostly on the headspace and is not an indication of over- or under-carbonation.

# Aroma

Probably borrowed from wine tasting, the expressions "nose" and "bouquet" are often used to mean the same as "aroma." As I said in the introductory paragraphs, it is important to not limit yourself to malt- and hop-related aromas. Remember that the yeast produces all kinds of aromatic compounds. Problems with your beer are often only noticeable in the smell and other times the aroma indicates problems long before they become apparent in the flavor.

Don't smell the beer constantly. Your nose will get accustomed to many of the aromas and be blind to them. Take a few, short, strong sniffs and write down your impressions. Strong sniffs are better than gentle ones because they get more of the aroma compounds up into the olfactory cleft where you sense smells. I like to cover the glass with my hand and swirl the beer to bring out more of the aroma compounds. I then make a small opening between my hand and the glass, just big enough for my nose, and sniff the beer.

The first aromas to look for are the most fleeting. They are those associated with oxidation. Look for "wet cardboard" or "wet paper" smells. From there, consider fruity aromas: bananas, plums, raspberries, currants, lemons, limes, mixed-fruit, grapefruit, orange or any other fruit, even exotic ones like passionfruit. Many strong dark ales have "ripe fruit" aromas. "Raisins" are a common smell in many amber beers especially in Dubbels.

Malt is a natural thing to expect in the aroma of a beer. Actually, part of what we often call a "malty" nose is actually due to a compound called dimethyl sulfide or DMS. It indeed usually comes from malt and in small amounts is pleasant and an important part of pale-colored lagers and especially the Kölsch style of ale. When it gets too strong DMS can smell like cooked corn (maize) or parsnips.

Another part of what we call "malt aroma" is from melanoidins. It is difficult to describe the smell of these compounds, so the easiest way for me to convey to you how to identify them is to suggest that you smell a few beers that are high in them. I feel high-melanoidin beers can have a slight "grape-like" aroma which can be misjudged as esters, so you should be careful. Oktoberfest beers are high in melanoidins and, personally, I believe that they are one of the defining factors in a good example of the style. Spaten, Ayinger, Paulaner, Hofbräuhaus, and Hacker-Pschorr are some of the best. Paulaner Salvator Doppelbock is also very high in melanoidins.

Hops are also common, but are not welcome in many styles. Some fruity aromas such as grapefruit and citrus can come from certain hop varieties. "Piney," "cheesy," "floral," "woody," and "resiny" aromas often are imparted by certain varieties. I've even smelled "minty" and "buttery" aromas in some varieties.

Are there any off aromas? Common problem smells are associated with vegetables (cabbages, celery, onions, etc.). Other problem aromas are "plastic bandages," "medicine mouthwash," "electrical fire," "rubbery," "nail polish remover," and "rubbing alcohol."

Then there are those odd aromas for which there are no clear names. They can be welcome in some styles and problems in others. One that my cousin Linas and I had labeled "Belgian aroma" is actually due to higher alcohols. It is a common aroma in so many Belgian Ales that it is not surprising that we labeled it as such. This aroma, in general, tends to have a slight clove-like character, some alcohol-like pepperyness, often a blend of fruit aromas. It is better to take the extra time and note the component aromas rather than simply use a canned phrase such as "Belgian aroma" or "Brettanomyces aroma" since it forces you to be more critical and improves your perceptiveness.

Other aromas include "goaty," "skunky," "sweaty," "turpentine," "horsey," "leathery," "smoky," "peaty," "garbage," "fecal," and every judge's nightmare: "baby diaper." Believe it or not, I've smelled every one of these in commercial or homebrewed beers and have tasted all but the baby diaper beer.

# Appearance

There are three main beer attributes when it comes to appearance: color, clarity, and head retention. The color that is appropriate for a particular style is defined as a range. Frankly, except for a few styles, the acceptable color range is quite wide. The styles in which the color is usually scrutinized more are Witbier, Berliner Weiss, Kölsch, American Lagers, Stouts, and Schwarzbier. Did you notice what all these styles have in common? Yes, they are at the extremes of the color scale. While it is difficult to say confidently that an English Bitter is too light or too dark, it is easy to notice an amber Witbier or a brown Stout. Usually, if the brewer has selected the right ingredients for the style, chances are the color will come automatically.

The color can influence judges, however. If there are two Bitters with exactly the same flavor and aroma, but one is noticeably deeper in color, that beer may be perceived as having a deeper flavor. While judges try to avoid such biases, human nature is difficult to suppress.

Clarity is next on the list and is again dependent on the style. It is easier to simply consider the styles which have acceptable haze: Witbier, Rye beer, Lambiek/Lambic, and the German Wheat beers. For all the other styles, the more clarity, the better. Clarity is a minor point, I believe, and technically worth only 1 or 2 out of 50 points on most beer judging forms. I feel its a crime to filter all the body out of a beer in the interest of clarity. I would score a rich, medium-bodied, hazy Brown Ale much higher than a thin, watery, crystal-clear one. Overfiltering strips a beer of all its body – it's an insult to the beer.

The final attribute associated with appearance is head retention. Lacing is also a factor here and is related to head retention (lacing, also called "Brussels Lace," is the lace-like or web-like pattern of foam that remains on the sides of the glass as you drink it). While a reasonable amount of head retention is desirable in most styles, some are simply expected to have good head retention (the wheat beers) and others are excused for not having it (Lambics/Lambieks and the very high alcohol beers).

# Flavor

Flavor is intimately connected with aroma. Our tongues can only discern four tastes (sweet, salty, sour, and bitter), but our noses can distinguish hundreds! Therefore, what we smell as we drink determines a lot of the flavor we perceive. Much of what was said regarding beer aromas applies to beer flavors. There are several taste perceptions that are (for the most part) independent of the aroma. One of them is astringency, which is caused by polyphenols from malt and hops. It is a dry, puckering flavor – like chewing on a red apple peel or a grape skin.

Another flavor that is semi-independent of aroma is sourness. I say "semi-independent" because experienced judges can distinguish between several different acids based upon aroma. Acetic acid (vinegar) has a characteristic aroma, for example. Usually unwelcome, there are several styles in which some acidity is required: Witbier, Lambiek/Lambik, Berliner Weiss, Flanders Red Ale, and Flanders Brown Ale.

Saltiness is from minerals in the water. High levels of chloride are usually the source of saltiness (not surprisingly, since sodium chloride is table salt and potassium chloride is "salt substitute"). There was only one time that I noticed saltiness in a commercial beer. It was during a blind tasting of seven commercial beers in which Samuel Smith's Old Brewery Pale Ale was served immediately following Budweiser. This brings up an important point: that lingering flavors from one beer can affect the perception of a subsequent beer. I tasted the same beers in a different order and did not notice saltiness in the Old Brewery Pale Ale. You can see how rinsing with unchlorinated water would be important during a tasting, especially when including a variety of beer styles.

Sweetness is obvious, but maybe not. I've read in several books where Düsseldorf Altbiers are said to be dry. I tried nearly a dozen while I was there this last summer, paying close attention to the level of bitterness and the alleged dryness. When you concentrate on the sweetness alone and ignore the bitterness (no small feat for a beer with more than 45 IBUs!), you notice that there is a gentle sweetness throughout the beer. It's just that there is so much bitterness, the beer can be mistaken for being dry overall. Some were drier than others, true, but none were devoid of sweetness.

Bitterness can come from more than just hops. Dark grains add some bitterness. Again, experienced judges can discern between hop and dark grain bitterness. You should try and see if you can't learn to tell the difference.

Part of judging the flavor is evaluating the balance of the beer. Depending on the style, various flavors should either be evenly balanced or one should dominate. The most basic balance is bitterness versus sweetness. An India Pale Ale's flavor should be dominated by bitterness whereas the balance of an English Brown Ale should be slightly towards malty sweetness. In fruit beers, the fruit must be in balance with the "beer flavors." The same is true for spiced and specialty beers.

When you take a sip of the beer, you should swish it around your entire mouth before swallowing. On your first sip, concentrate on the initial flavors and the flavors shortly after that. I find that some beers will have spikes of flavor in the mid-palate, whereas others change very little throughout the tasting. On your second sip, concentrate on how the balance changes throughout the palate – does it slowly increase in bitterness? Incidentally, sulfates in the beer will cause this. Does it start sweet and dry out into the finish? Is it round and malty throughout?

## Body & Mouthfeel

Body is a measure of how thick a beer feels on the palate. Some say that mouthfeel is the same thing. I, personally, believe that mouthfeel is the general term and that body is but a part the total mouthfeel in a beer. Other attributes that are part of mouthfeel are carbonation (low, medium, high, effervescent) and the "feel" of the beer (oily, silky, creamy, chewy, etc.). Note that, currently, on most judging forms "conditioning" (carbonation) is included in the flavor portion of the scoring. Incidentally, work is underway at the Beer Judge Certification Program to create BJCP beer scoresheets (currently most competitions use the AHA beer scoresheets) and it is likely that this section will be renamed simply "Mouthfeel" and will include body, astringency, carbonation, warmth, and any other mouth sensations that are not associated with the four basic tastes.

## Drinkability & Overall Impression

This is clearly the most subjective part of the beer juding. This is where the judge can boost the score of a beer that he/she "likes" or give a low score to a beer that is uncategorizeably unpleasant. Most beer judging is based upon a 50-point scale. In the new BJCP scoresheets that are being currently developed, the score guidelines are a bit more fine-grained than the AHA guidelines. An "outstanding" category has been added to identify the best of the best. I have always resevered the upper part of the 40's range for truly memorable beers. Few commercial beers would score in the "outstanding" range. In my opinion, where the beer scores in this range depends on how much "wonderfulness" the beer has. Yes, this is not very quantifiable or scientific, but you will know it when you taste it – a certain charisma that makes this beer stand out from the rest. Some are only slightly outstanding, others captivate. The highest score I've ever awarded in a homebrewing competition was a "47." This was at the first round of the AHA Nationals in 1994. That beer ended up not only winning 1st place in the Lambic category, but also wound up taking best of show. It was truly a wonderfuly beer.

## Further Reading

Hardy, F. and A. R. Korzonas, "Judging Your Brew," *Zymurgy,* 17 (5), 70-72 (Winter 1994).
Papazian, C. and G. Noonan, "Aroma Identification," *Beer and Brewing, Vol.8,* (Brewers
      Publications, Boulder, Colorado, 1988).
Papazian, C., "Testing Yourself," *Zymurgy,* 9 (1), (Spring 1986).

# 14

# TROUBLESHOOTING

𝕴 feel that this chapter contains perhaps the most important information in this book. Nothing can be more frustrating than a nagging problem with one or (even worse) all of your beers. Some problems can be just irritating like haze or a beer being too dark. Other problems can make your beer unpleasant to drink. In many books, the troubleshooting section consists of pointers to other parts of the book. Perhaps unique to this book, a lot of new material is presented here that is not covered in the other chapters.

## "Review Sanitation Procedures"

Sanitation problems are such a common cause of trouble that I've compiled the following list that you should review when sanitation is suspect. When a problem solution includes the phrase "Review Sanitation Procedures," that means that you should step back and consider all the techniques that you use regarding sanitation.

- Are you sanitizing every piece of equipment that comes in contact with cooled wort?
- Are you using the recommended concentrations of sanitizers (see chapter 5)?
- Are you maintaining the proper contact times for the sanitizers (these vary from 10 to 15 minutes – I recommend you stick with 15 minutes)?
- Are you avoiding rinsing with infected tapwater? Perhaps you should be rinsing with boiled water instead?
- Are you avoiding placing sanitized equipment (like racking canes) onto unsanitized surfaces?

- Are you avoiding using old, scratched plastic equipment?
- Perhaps it's time to replace those racking canes, fillers and siphon hoses (yearly is recommended)?
- Are you avoiding topping-up your fermenter with unsanitized tapwater?
- Are you starting with 4 gallons of boiled/chilled tapwater or did you just use it from the faucet?
- Are you cooling the hot wort quickly?
- Are you pitching a large-enough yeast starter to minimize lag time?
- Are you aerating sufficiently to minimize lag time?
- Are you using filtered air (or oxygen) for aeration during the summer months or just using room air for aeration when there's lots of wild yeast and bacteria in the air?
- Is there beerstone (a brown crust) built up in the fermenter (beerstone gives bacteria and wild yeast a place to hide from sanitizers – see "There's a white film or brown crust on the inside of my carboy." in chapter 16).

# Boiling and cooling

## Boilover

**Cause:** Boilover is caused by a thick head of foam being created by proteins in the boiling wort trapping the escaping water vapor.
**Solution:** One way to minimize your chances of a boilover is to stand by with a sieve as the wort is coming to a boil and to skim the hot break scum that forms on the top of the wort. Other ways to fight-off an impending boilover are to blow on the foam, stir, lower the heat, and splash a little cold water on the foam – a spray bottle would be ideal. Depending on the vigor of the boil and the amount of protein in the wort, some of these techniques may not work, but together they are certain to stop boilover.

## Break formation (hot and cold)

Break formation is dependent on various factors. Hot and cold break are mostly protein, but they also contain hop resins, other organic matter, and ash. It is not mandatory to remove the hot and cold break from your beer, but removing it may improve the clarity and stability of the finished beer. Also, break material is believed to interfere with the yeast's uptake of nutrients[101]. Removing the break is said to be important[101], but removing all the cold break can result in sluggish and incomplete fermentations, especially if the cooled wort is under-aerated[41].

**Cause:** Insufficient boil vigor. The more vigorous and hotter the boil, the better the hot break formation will be (boiling at higher altitudes, where the boiling temperature is lower, can result in poorer break formation).

**Solution:** Partially covering the kettle will reduce the heat loss and increase the boil vigor.

**Cause:** A pH below 5 can significantly reduce break formation[102].
**Solution:** Add a little calcium carbonate to the boil to raise the pH into the range of 5.0 to 5.5.

**Cause:** Boiling too long can redissolve the hot break[103].
**Solution:** Under normal conditions (pH, altitude, and mineral content), the best break is achieved in a one-hour boil[104].

**Cause:** Slow cooling results in smaller break particles which settle more slowly.
**Solution:** Cool the wort rapidly, using some kind of wort chiller.

## Cannot get a rolling boil

**Cause:** While you are heating the kettle from the bottom, heat is also escaping from the kettle sides and top and in the evaporating water vapor.
**Solution:** One solution, although an expensive one, is to increase the size of your burner. Another solution is to cover your pot partly – do not cover it completely (see "Cooked corn aroma"). A third solution is to insulate your kettle, or at least the lid of the kettle, but be sure to use flameproof and heat-resistant insulation and don't use insulation (like fiberglass) whose fibers can accidentally fall into the wort.

## Carbon monoxide

**Cause:** Combustion produces colorless, odorless, and poisonous carbon monoxide as a byproduct.
**Solution:** When you use a gas burner in an enclosed space you must provide a way for carbon monoxide to be vented outdoors. A range hood is perfect for this. A carbon monoxide detector is also a good idea, but mount it 10 or 20 feet from your burner to minimize false alarms. You also need to provide for a source of fresh air or both you and your burner will run out of it. A blue flame means more complete combustion (less soot and carbon monoxide production) than a yellow one. Adjust the air intake of your burner to minimize the yellowing of the flames.

## Lower than expected Original Gravity

**Cause:** You didn't mix the wort well with the pre-boiled water.
**Solution:** The wort is heavy and will sink straight to the bottom of the fermenter. Unless you stir well, only a small part of the wort will have mixed with the water and you'll get a low hydrometer reading. The solution is to mix the wort well. It is also important to mix well so that the temperature evens out. Since we are not using a wort chiller, we are relying on the cool pre-boiled water to cool the wort

down so it doesn't kill the yeast. If you don't mix well, the yeast will hit 65° F water and may be shocked.

**Cause:** You are using a 2.5-gallon recipe, but accidentally making 5 gallons.
**Solution:** Check the recipe – is it for 3 gallons or maybe only 2.5 gallons? Not all recipes are for 5 gallons.

**Cause:** You forgot to compensate for the temperature of the wort when reading the hydrometer.
**Solution:** Hot wort is thinner than cooled wort. Therefore, you need to compensate for the temperature if you are not taking a reading at 60° F (15.5° C). Note that some hydrometers are calibrated for use at 68° F (20° C). See the tables under Hydrometers in chapter 4 for hydrometer temperature compensation.

**Cause:** You measured water incorrectly and accidentally made 6 gallons instead of 5.
**Solution:** It is easy to overshoot your target volume if you guess instead of measuring. Commonly, we use 7.5-gallon fermenters and they should only be 2/3 full when making a 5-gallon batch. You can pre-measure 1-gallon increments in your fermenter and mark the outside with graduations, but there are two things to take into consideration: 1) hot liquids shrink when they cool and 2) if the fermenter is on a slant your graduations are not accurate. You can solve #1 by making two scales: one for boiling water and the other for 80° F (27° C) because this is about the temperature at which your wort will be when you mix the hot wort with the cool water. First, put a gallon of cold water into the fermenter. Mark this "1gal cold." Then, add 5 ounces of cold water and mark this "1 gal hot." Remove 5 ounces and repeat for 2, 3, 4, and 5 gallons. Make sure you are on a level plane when you make the permanent 1-gallon graduations.

### Steam

**Cause:** Floors can get slippery and walls can stain from condensing steam.
**Solution:** You need to provide a way to vent it outdoors. Again, the range hood is perfect.

# Fermentation

## Egg-drop soup

**Cause:** Sometimes, during fermentation you will see white blobs rising and diving inside the fermenter. This is cold break which is made up of proteins. Fermenting on cold break increases higher alcohol (fusel alcohol) production[123], but other factors (such as temperature) are more important. It has been shown that excessive hot and cold break can inhibit yeast activity and later reduce beer clarity[101].

**Solution:** The easiest thing to do is ignore the cold break. If you insist on removing it, you can cool your wort, pitch your yeast, let your wort sit for 2 or 3 hours until the cold break settles and then siphon off the beer into another sanitized container for fermentation. The risk is that you may leave a significant amount of the yeast in the first container along with the cold break. Personally, I don't worry about the cold break.

## Fermentation didn't start

The most common problem reported by beginners is "two days have passed and I haven't seen any activity in the airlock."

**Cause:** The vigorous portion of the fermentation occurred during the first night and the brewer simply missed the fireworks.
**Solution:** Do nothing. There was no problem. If there is a brown ring around the fermenter, just above the level of the beer, then the vigorous part of the fermentation has already occurred and all that is left is to wait for the yeast to settle and you can bottle.

**Cause:** There is a $CO_2$ leak between the lid and the fermenter or between the airlock and the lid.
**Solution:** A small leak is nothing to worry about, but if you really want to be meticulous about counting airlock bubbles, you should buy yourself a glass fermenter. The seal between the rubber stopper and glass carboy or between the blowoff hose and glass carboy will always be a better seal than the lid of a plastic fermenter unless you get one that has a gasketted lid. Personally, I think that moving to glass is a good idea after a few batches simply because it's easier to sanitize.

**Cause:** The dry yeast was not rehydrated.
**Solution:** Next time, rehydrate the yeast. This time, you can cross your fingers and wait or you can hydrate some more yeast and pitch again.

**Cause:** The liquid yeast was used without a starter.
**Solution:** Next time, use a starter. This time, being patient is probably all you need to do – the yeast will eventually start.

**Cause:** You pitched some very weak yeast (sometimes only 10% of old, mishandled yeast is alive).
**Solution:** Only buy refrigerated yeast that is marked with an expiration date. Again, this time, you probably only need to wait a little longer.

**Cause:** The yeast was pitched when the wort was too hot (above 120° F, 49° C), or yeast was forgotten.
**Solution:** Pitch more yeast.

## Fermentation doesn't stop

**Cause:** You may have insufficiently aerated the wort.
**Solution:** *Don't* aerate the fermenting wort. Aerating after fermentation has begun will increase diacetyl and ester levels in the finished beer. What you *should* do is rehydrate some more dry yeast and add that or make up a big starter from well-aerated wort, let the wort ferment out, pour-off the spent wort and then add the slurry.

**Cause:** You could be trying to ferment at too cool a temperature for your chosen yeast.
**Solution:** Try raising the fermentation temperature above 65° F (18° C) for ales and above 50° F (10° C) for lagers. You may also need to add fresh yeast because yeast that has been temperature-shocked can ferment sluggishly even when the temperature is raised.

**Cause:** Poor nutrition can be a cause of long, weak fermentation.
**Solution:** Adding 1/4 teaspoon of yeast energizer may help.

**Cause:** The yeast may be weak.
**Solution:** Pitch more yeast.

**Cause:** A long, lingering fermentation can be from a wild yeast or bacterial infection, however some cultured yeast strains (especially *Brettanomyces*) are very slow fermenters. Wild yeasts, particularly *Saccharomyces diastaticus* can eat sugars and dextrins that are inedible by cultured yeasts. Bacteria don't usually produce $CO_2$, it's true, but the bacteria can cut large dextrins into smaller sugars that are fermentable by the cultured yeast.
**Solution:** Review Sanitation Procedures unless you know that you are using a very slow-moving yeast.

## Fermentation restarted after racking or dryhopping

**Cause:** Most often, this is not fermentation, but rather $CO_2$ simply coming out of solution. Racking the beer agitates it and the pressure differences in the hose can cause some of the $CO_2$ that is dissolved in the beer to bubble out. Dryhopping introduces some agitation as well as millions of nucleation sites for bubbles to form. After racking or dryhopping, the airlock may start to move again for a day or two. This may be just $CO_2$ coming out of solution, but it can also be restarted fermentation (See "There is too much dissolved $CO_2$" under "Fermentation weak.")
**Solution:** In 99% of the cases, the solution is: don't worry.

## Fermentation weak

**Cause:** The yeast count is too low. If you did not rehydrate your dry yeast in 90 to 110° F (32 to 43° C) water, the yeast are just not as healthy (and you may have

even killed a significant percentage) if you just sprinkled the dry yeast into the wort. If you didn't use a starter for your liquid yeast, your yeast count is likely to be low, especially if you used an older package of yeast. If you dumped your 90° F (32° C) rehydrated yeast or 70° F (21° C) starter into 50° F (10° C) wort, you may have killed many of them and certainly temperature-shocked the rest.
**Solution:** Add more yeast, but treat them more carefully this time: rehydrate dry yeasts and make starters for liquid yeasts.

**Cause:** The fermentation temperature is too cold.
**Solution:** Raise the fermentation temperature. However, you may also have to add fresh yeast too. It depends on the yeast strain whether or not the yeast will rebound from a chilly vacation.

**Cause:** You had insufficient aeration and/or yeast nutrition.
**Solution:** It's too late to aerate this batch, but you can make up a big starter of yeast, pour off the spent starter wort and add this to the fermenter. In subsequent batches, aerate better and if you go to great lengths to remove all the cold break, you may want to simplify them to leave a little of the cold break behind. Cold break has many compounds that are important for good yeast health.

**Cause:** There is too much dissolved $CO_2$. $CO_2$ impedes fermentation and if you have too high a level dissolved in the beer, it can slow the yeast activity[40]. It has been suggested that too-thorough removal of cold break can rob the beer of nucleation sites and result in a buildup of $CO_2$ [41].
**Solution:** Swirling the fermenter will cause some of the dissolved $CO_2$ to bubble out of solution and this may restart fermentation for a while. You may have to keep repeating this procedure up to several times per day. Raising the temperature may help. If you suspect that cold break removal is the cause, consider modifying your break removal methods so that not all the cold break is removed in future batches.

**Cause:** Poor nutrition can cause sluggish fermentation, but is unlikely unless you have used a large percentage of refined sugar or your malt extract happens to be made with a lot of refined sugars.
**Solution:** Rule out all other causes of sluggish fermentation before adding yeast energizer. Follow the usage recommendations on the package. If the labeling only refers to mead (honey "wine"), try using 20% of the recommended dosage.

## Film floating on top

**Cause:** If it's at the beginning of fermentation, it could very well be yeast. If it's at the end of fermentation and you let your airlock dry out or your fermenter lid does not fit well, it is probably mold or aerobic bacteria (the type that require some air).
**Solution:** If it's yeast, then it's not a problem. If it's mold or aerobic bacteria, your beer may still be fine. Molds and aerobic bacteria can be avoided by ensuring that air is excluded from the fermenter once fermentation has begun. If

this is a pLambic/pLambiek-style beer and you pitched the dregs from a commercial Lambiek/Lambic, chances are it is probably not mold but rather a pellicle-forming yeast. If it is indeed a mold, your beer will probably smell moldy and there is nothing you can do to rescue this batch. Go ahead and try bottling it anyway – it may still be drinkable, but probably won't win any awards. If it's an aerobic bacteria it could be an acetic acid bacteria in which case the beer will smell like vinegar and taste sour (eventually). Several commercial Belgian styles of beer have mild vinegary notes. Whether you accept the vinegary character in a beer or not is a matter of personal preference. Finally, I should mention that there are many harmless aerobic microbes that will only affect the appearance (ring around the neck) of your beer.

## Green foam during fermentation

**Cause:** You probably allowed a significant amount of hop pellets into the fermenter.

**Solution:** Take care that the pellets don't clog a narrow blowoff tube (you should really be using a BIG blowoff hose) or airlock. If there is no chance of clogging, then there's nothing to worry about.

## Ropey appearance

**Cause:** "Rope" is a term used for the jelly-like, material that is formed by some bacteria, including *Pediococcus,* and floats just below the surface of the fermenting beer.

**Solution:** Unless you intentionally pitched *Pediococcus,* I recommend you Review Sanitation Procedures for future batches and consider turning this batch into a pLambic/pLambiek.

## Rotten-egg aroma

**Cause:** It is not uncommon for yeast to produce hydrogen sulfide ($H_2S$) during fermentation. It smells exactly like rotten eggs. Lager yeasts are more likely to produce it than ale yeasts.

**Solution:** In most cases, the aroma will decrease either by the end of fermentation or after a few weeks of aging. Some yeast strains can require you to lager for four months before the sulfury smells go away. One batch I made with Wyeast Munich Lager #2308 took four months for a bad odor to fade in the beer - it smelled just like home perm solution. After the sulfury smell went away, the beer won several ribbons. Note that the yeast play an important role in the removal of the hydrogen sulfide[109] so separating the beer from most of the yeast can slow the removal of $H_2S$ and filtering would pretty much stop it completely.

**Cause:** Hydrogen sulfide can be caused by bacterial infection.

**Solution:** Review Sanitation Procedures.

## Stuck fermentation (higher than expected Final Gravity)

**Cause:** You have a very unfermentable wort. Usually this is caused by using a malt extract such as Laaglander, "Dutch," "Hollander," or "European" Dried Malt Extract. With these four extracts, I have known brewers to experience apparent attenuations of only 55%. Overuse of crystal malt or malto-dextrin also increases unfermentablity.

**Solution:** All you can do is make another batch that is very fermentable (very fermentable extract (such as Coopers), no crystal malt, no malto-dextrin) ferment it with a yeast that is very attenuative (like Wyeast #3787 Trappist Ale) and then blend those two batches together into two secondary fermenters.

**Cause:** You have reached the typical attenuation level of the yeast you used. Measure the specific gravity and calculate the Apparent Attenuation and compare it to what is expected for your yeast in appendix E. If the Apparent Attenuation is not listed for your yeast, you'll have to assume that it should be between 70 and 75%.

**Solution:** Wait for the beer to clear and bottle – there's nothing wrong after all.

**Cause:** You have temperature-shocked the yeast. Sudden temperature changes can cause yeast to go dormant. Some strains of yeast can tolerate 10° F (6° C) drop in temperature, others will be affected somewhat if they are cooled more than 2° F (1° C) in an hour.

**Solution:** Add more yeast and be more gentle this time.

**Cause:** You are trying to ferment at too cold a temperature. While most of the yeast is in suspension and actively fermenting, the temperature of the wort is considerably higher (fermentation generates heat). When the yeast begin to run out of sugar and start to slow down, the temperature drops. If the ambient temperature is too cold, the yeast will become dormant and leave a higher than expected finishing gravity. Also, colder temperatures mean that more $CO_2$ will stay in solution and the yeast can also be inhibited by high levels of dissolved $CO_2$.

**Solution:** Move the fermenter to a warmer place. Note that if your fermenter is in direct contact with a cold cement floor, the bottom of the carboy may be much, much colder than the room air temperature. It can help to resuspend the yeast by swirling, but don't allow air into the fermenter or you will have oxidation problems. In some cases, you may have to add more yeast because the yeast simply refuse to wake up even after warming. Swirling will also drive off dissolved $CO_2$, so if $CO_2$ toxicity is the problem, this will help that also.

**Cause:** You have created a beer with a high alcohol level but you did not aerate the wort enough or you used too-small a starter. Under-aerating the wort and starter will result in yeast that has low alcohol tolerance[76].

**Solution:** Make up another big starter (taking special care to aerate the starter wort well), let that ferment out and add the yeast slurry to the fermenter.

Especially if you are making a high-alcohol beer, you should use at least a 2 liter starter and a 4 liter starter would not be too big. Ideally, if you have another fermenter, you can brew another batch of medium-gravity beer, let that finish fermenting, rack it off the yeast and then rack your stuck, high-alcohol beer on top of the entire yeast cake from the medium-gravity beer.

**Cause:** You didn't aerate enough and pitched too little yeast. In an oxygen-free environment, where there is some glucose present, the yeast don't make certain enzymes[74]. I suspect that the yeast inherit some of these enzymes from their parent, but if you start with too little oxygen or too little yeast, several generations down the line, the yeast simply don't have the right enzymes to ferment the wort completely.

**Solution:** Add more yeast from an all-malt starter that has been aerated well.

**Cause:** You added too much glucose in the form of corn sugar or honey, for example, and you did not pitch enough yeast. In a high-glucose environment, the yeast don't make certain enzymes[74]. The yeast simply don't have the right enzymes to ferment the more complex sugars in the wort.

**Solution:** Next time, don't add so much glucose. To save this batch, add more yeast from an all-malt starter that has been aerated well.

**Cause:** You have made an extremely high gravity wort and therefore have made a beer with very high alcohol levels (although you did aerate well and used a big starter initially).

**Solution:** You can try adding a more alcohol-tolerant yeast such as Pasteur Champagne yeast, but in most cases, you have simply made a very strong beer that will not carbonate naturally and will always be sweet.

**Cause:** The yeast has settled while there is still lots of sugar in the beer because you used an highly-flocculent yeast such as Wyeast "London ESB" (#1968) or Yeast Culture Kit Company's A42 or A20.

**Solution:** Without removing the airlock (so the headspace is all still $CO_2$), swirl the fermenter to resuspend the yeast. This is called "rousing" the yeast.

**Cause:** You added malto-dextrin to the wort.

**Solution:** Malto-dextrin has an apparent attenuation of only about 16% so 1 pound in 5 gallons will add about 9.3 points (0.0093) to your final gravity.

**Cause:** You used a yeast that was built-up in an all-glucose or all-sucrose starter. In a high-glucose environment, the yeast don't make certain enzymes[74]. The yeast simply don't have the right enzymes to ferment the more complex sugars in the wort.

**Solution:** Next time, make your starter from malt extract. To save this batch, add more yeast from an all-malt starter that has been aerated well.

**Cause:** You removed all the hot and cold break from your wort. As the concentration of dissolved $CO_2$ increases in the fermenting beer, it inhibits the yeast[40]. There are some brewing researchers who believe that completely trub-

free wort does not provide nucleation sites for $CO_2$ to form bubbles which causes the $CO_2$ concentration to exceed the normal solubility (supersaturation)[41].
**Solution:** In the long term, if you determine that this is indeed the source of your problem, you may want to consider modifying your cold break removal methods to allow some of the cold break to remain in the wort. There is general agreement that hot break should be removed as much as possible, but that cold break not only provides $CO_2$ nucleation sites but also nutrition for the yeast. To save this batch, without removing the airlock, can swirl the fermenter twice per day to help outgas some of the dissolved $CO_2$.

**Cause:** The yeast and break have yet to settle out. Suspended hot and cold break and yeast will cause the specific gravity to read higher than it really is.
**Solution:** Wait till the yeast and break settle before you decide if the FG is too high.

**Cause:** You have provided insufficient nutrition for the yeast.
**Solution:** This is only likely if you used a lot of refined sugar, cider, or honey in the wort. If you suspect that this is the case, try adding $1/4$ teaspoon of yeast energizer.

**Cause:** You have used a tall, narrow fermenter. Some yeast strains (e.g. Whitbread Ale or Weihenstephan 34/70) simply don't like to ferment in tall, narrow fermenters[34,233].
**Solution:** Don't use tall, narrow fermenters when using yeasts that don't perform well in them.


# Siphon keeps stopping

**Cause:** You have insufficient height difference between the source and destination.
**Solution:** Insufficient height difference is a problem because the flow is too slow. When you siphon, some of the $CO_2$ that is dissolved in the beer will come out of solution mostly due to the pressure differences in the hose during siphoning. When the flow is fast, any $CO_2$ bubbles that form are pushed out before they get a chance to join forces and make a big, problematic bubble. The solution is to increase the height difference between the level of the beer/wort in the supply container and the level of the beer/wort in the receiving container (note that sometimes the height difference is big enough at first, but after a while the level in the supply container has dropped and the level in the receiving container has risen and you have a problem). Sometimes you will have to get a longer hose to make the difference bigger.

**Cause:** You have a sudden change in diameter from the racking cane to the hose.
**Solution:** A sudden increase in the inside diameter (ID) of the siphon setup (going from a large ID of the cane to a small ID of the hose or vice versa) can

cause too much turbulence and too much bubble formation. I don't believe that a sudden decrease would cause as many problems, but it might. The solution is to match the diameters of the cane and hose more closely.

**Cause:** You are using too large a diameter hose. Too large an inside diameter siphon hose means the flow will be slow and can mean there won't be enough flow rate to push the little bubbles that always form out of the siphon before they can combine to make a big bubble and big problems for you.
**Solution:** use a smaller diameter hose – I use all $5/16$" inside diameter hoses for my siphon setup.

**Cause:** You are waiting too long between bottles.
**Solution:** A small amount of bubbles is common. Unless you have a hole in the middle of your siphon setup, those aren't air bubbles forming – they are $CO_2$ and unless your siphon is breaking down, they are nothing to worry about. If you wait too long between bottles (I'm assuming you are bottling here) the bubbles can combine and give you problems. If you cannot bottle fast enough yourself, try getting a brewing partner – usually, they will work for homebrew. When my wife Karen or cousin Linas help me bottle, they rinse a sanitized bottle and hand it to me to fill. Meanwhile I give them a filled bottle to cap. While I'm filling, they are capping and rinsing the next sanitized bottle.

**Cause:** You have too much fermentation activity.
**Solution:** If the beer is still fermenting actively, this can also be your problem. It is possible to rack fermenting beer, but you need to keep all the above in mind, especially the small diameter hose and keeping a large height difference between source and receiving containers.

**Cause:** You have an air leak in your siphon setup.
**Solution:** Fix the leak.


# Bottles and pouring

## Overcarbonated

**Cause:** You bottled before the fermentation was complete.
**Solution:** You can remedy the problem on your next batch by waiting until your airlock has slowed to one bubble every two minutes for ales – one bubble every four minutes for lagers. To save this batch, you can open and re-cap each bottle.

**Cause:** You overprimed the beer.
**Solution:** If you realize (after consulting chapters 5 and 6) that you have overprimed, you may be able to save this batch by opening and re-capping each bottle.

**Cause:** You have a wild yeast infection.

**Solution:** Wild yeast infections often cause overcarbonation because there are many wild yeasts that can eat more complex sugars than typical cultured yeasts. Many of these yeasts also lend a strong phenolic (clovey, medicinal, plastic-like) aroma to the beer. If you have both overcarbonation and phenolic aroma, you can almost be assured that the cause is a wild yeast infection. The solution would be to Review Sanitation Procedures.

**Cause:** You have a bacterial infection.
**Solution:** Bacteria usually don't create $CO_2$, so they are not the direct cause of the overcarbonation, but they can break-up larger sugars (which your cultured yeast can subsequently eat and convert into $CO_2$). If you have overcarbonation with no phenolic aroma, but a distinct sourness, then your problem is probably bacterial. A slight sourness can be simply caused by the overcarbonation itself, so don't blame bacteria until the sourness gets intense. Again, Review Sanitation Procedures.

**Cause:** You have a poor distribution of priming sugar (only if some of the bottles are undercarbonated).
**Solution:** It's very difficult to save this batch. Chilling the beer to very cold temperatures will reduce gushing, but what if you have one of the bottles that was undercarbonated. The key is to mix the priming sugar with water and boil it for a few minutes (to sanitize) since this sugar syrup mixes much better with the beer than simply pouring granulated sugar into the priming vessel.

**Cause:** You are serving the beer too warm.
**Solution:** The colder the beer, the more $CO_2$ it will hold in solution. If the beer is being served too warm, too much $CO_2$ will bubble out when you pour and not enough will stay in solution. Try serving it cooler (within reason: lagers shouldn't have to be served any colder than 45° F / 7° C and ales no colder than 50° F / 10° C).

## Ring around the neck

**Cause:** My research indicates that priming with dried malt extract or wort can be as common a cause for this phenomenon as infection. Dried malt extract and wort contain protein and therefore can create a mini kräusen to be formed during conditioning.
**Solution:** If switching to corn sugar priming solves the problem, then protein in the primings was indeed the cause. If you insist on using DME or wort for priming, you can minimize the chances of developing a ring by boiling the primings well, chilling rapidly and making sure to exclude the hot and cold break when adding the primings to the beer.

**Cause:** The beer is infected with an aerobic bacteria or mold.
**Solution:** Some homebrewing books say that a ring of material at the fill level of the bottle is a sure sign of infection. This kind of misinformation does a great

disservice to homebrewers since many competition judges dismiss perfectly good beers on the grounds that the ring around the neck is a sign of infection. If it turns out that an infection was indeed the cause of the problem, Review Sanitation Procedures. You may find that you must use filtered air or oxygen to aerate/oxygenate your wort to avoid rings in the neck of the bottles.

## Undercarbonated

**Cause:** You have not conditioned the beer long enough.

**Cause:** You have been storing the beer too cold (during conditioning, while the carbonation is created).
**Solution:** These two causes are often related. If you are conditioning at 65° F (18° C), you should not expect proper carbonation for at least 10 days. Two weeks are usually recommended. (It has been suggested by one author that all the $CO_2$ is produced quickly and that most of the conditioning time is simply the $CO_2$ dissolving into the beer. This is incorrect, since if it were true, bottles opened three days after bottling would give a big hiss, but in fact, they don't.) If you are trying to condition an ale at 50° F (10° C), you may wait forever (depending on the yeast) for proper carbonation – that's just far too cold for most ale yeasts. A common cause for slow conditioning is the storage of bottles on a cold, concrete cellar floor. The direct contact heat transfer to the cold floor is much more efficient than heat transfer to the bottles from the warm air and the bottles end up being too cold for the yeast.

**Cause:** You underprimed the beer.
**Solution:** Many brewers expect American Pilsner-like carbonation, but are only priming at an English Bitter rate. English Bitters can have less than half the carbonation level of an American Pilsner. If you want more carbonation, then add more priming sugar next time. To save this batch, you can re-prime each bottle, but personally, I feel the hassle and risk of infection outweigh the benefits.

**Cause:** You overfilled the bottles. Leaving little or no headspace will slow the rate of carbonation and may even reduce the final carbonation level.
**Solution:** There's little that can be done to save this batch. Just remember to not overfill on the next batch.

**Cause:** You have a capper problem.
**Solution:** Capper problems can range from improper adjustment, to using the wrong diameter bell, to a cheap capper simply wearing-out. Also, make sure you are not trying to put on 1-inch (US) caps on with a 29mm capper bell (some European bottles, such as those from Cantillon take these, larger, caps).

**Cause:** You have deformed bottlecap liners (some bottle cap liners can be boiled to sanitize, others are ruined). Often this problem is characterized by some bottles being correctly carbonated while others are totally flat.

**Solution:** In all my correspondence with bottlecap manufacturers, never has boiling been mentioned as a recommended method of sanitation. In fact, if you boil oxygen-absorbing bottlecaps, you will ruin their absorbing capabilities. Bottom line: don't boil your bottlecaps – use sanitizers instead.

**Cause:** You had poor distribution of priming sugar (only if some bottles are overcarbonated).

**Solution:** It's very difficult to save this batch. Chilling the beer to very cold temperatures will reduce gushing on the overcarbonated bottles, but what if you have one of the bottles that was undercarbonated? On the next batch mix the priming sugar with water and boil it for a few minutes (to sanitize) since this sugar syrup mixes much better with the beer than simply pouring granulated sugar into the priming vessel. This symptom can also be caused by underpriming or deformed caps and an infection, but that is much less likely.

**Cause:** The alcohol level has exceeded the yeast's tolerance. Perhaps you underaerated at pitching time – this will result in yeast that has a low alcohol tolerance. Perhaps you have made too big (too high an OG) beer for your yeast to handle. Most healthy yeasts can handle 8, 9 or even 10% ABV providing that you aerated the cooled wort enough at pitching time and pitched enough yeast (i.e. used a big starter). This corresponds (roughly) to OGs of 1.080, 1.090 or 1.100.

**Solution:** Now is certainly too late to aerate. A possible (but risky) solution is to make up a healthy yeast starter and add a few drops of healthy yeast to each bottle. Some books recommend adding a few grains of dry yeast to each bottle. I feel you really should rehydrate the yeast in warm water first (it's bad enough when you add yeast to cool wort – imagine the yeast's surprise when you toss them into a highly alcoholic beer!). See chapter 10 for more on yeast rehydration. Note that you should probably use the same yeast that you used for fermentation. If you use a more attenuative yeast or one that is naturally more alcohol tolerant like Red Star Pasteur Champagne yeast, you can have gushers because the new yeast is eating not only the priming sugar but also the yeast left behind by the main fermentation yeast.

**Cause:** You are serving the beer too cold.

**Solution:** The colder the beer, the more $CO_2$ it will hold in solution. If the beer is being served too cold, too much $CO_2$ will stay in solution and not enough will bubble out. Try serving it warmer.


## Uneven carbonation

**Cause:** You had poor distribution of priming sugar.

**Solution:** On the next batch mix the priming sugar with water and boil it for a few minutes (to sanitize) since this sugar syrup mixes much better with the beer than simply pouring granulated sugar into the priming vessel.

**Cause:** You overfilled some bottles and underfilled others. Leaving little or no headspace will slow the rate of carbonation and may even reduce the final carbonation level.
**Solution:** Next time, try to keep the fill level between 3/4" and 1$^1$/$_2$" (2 and 4 cm).

**Cause:** You have a capper problem.
**Solution:** Capper problems can range from improper adjustment, to using the wrong diameter bell, to a cheap capper simply wearing-out. Also, make sure you are not trying to put on 1-inch (US) caps on with a 29mm capper bell (some European bottles, such as those from Cantillon take these, larger, caps).

**Cause:** You have deformed bottlecap liners (some bottle cap liners can be boiled to sanitize, others are ruined). Often this problem is characterized by some bottles being correctly carbonated while others are totally flat
**Solution:** In all my correspondence with bottlecap manufacturers, boiling never been mentioned as a recommended method of sanitation. In fact, if you boil oxygen-absorbing bottlecaps, you will ruin their absorbing capabilities. Bottom line: don't boil your bottlecaps – use sanitizers instead.


# Aroma

## *Acetaldehyde aroma*

**Cause:** Acetaldehyde is an intermediate product in ethyl alcohol production and has a familiar green-apple aroma. Under normal circumstances, the yeast releases some acetaldehyde into the beer, but then reabsorbs it later. Some yeast strains (particularly Wyeast Pilsen Lager #2007) leave more of it in the finished beer than others. Filtering or fining the beer before the yeast have had a chance to reabsorb the acetaldehyde increases the amount that you will have in the finished beer. Young beer or beer that has not been lagered long enough is often high in acetaldehyde.
**Solution:** Allow the beer to continue conditioning/lagering on the yeast longer.

**Cause:** You temperature shocked the yeast (which causes the yeast to settle prematurely).
**Solution:** If you smell acetaldehyde in the beer, let it lager longer. Rousing may help (See chapter 10). You may even want to consider pitching more yeast.

**Cause:** Insufficient oxygen can be a cause for elevated acetaldehyde levels (as much as an 8-fold increase)[106,107]. Elevated acetaldehyde levels can also be a result of pitching yeast with low glycogen levels[84].
**Solution:** If either of these two factors are suspected, proper aeration and pitch timing should be stressed on subsequent batches (see chapter 10).

**Cause:** Poor yeast nutrition can increase acetaldehyde levels[142].

**Solution:** I theorize that part of the cidery aroma that comes from brewing beers with 40 or 50% corn or cane sugar may be from acetaldehyde due to poor yeast nutrition. Clearly, these huge percentages of non-malt sugars are not recommended, but if for some reason you must use them, I suggest adding some yeast energizer (in a pinch you can even toss a package of dried yeast into the boil for yeast nutrition). The proper solution to this problem is to increase the malt percentage.

**Cause:** High pitching rates tend to increase acetaldehyde production, but they also help reduce the acetaldehyde produced[142] (assuming you give the yeast enough conditioning time to reabsorb what they have produced).

**Solution:** If you pitch a large starter, you will want to make sure that you condition the beer long enough before fining, filtering, or (in the case of highly-flocculent yeast) racking.

**Cause:** Lagers fermented above 46° F (8° C) may show increased acetaldehyde levels[109]. This is highly strain dependent and may not be a factor with many yeasts. Another study found that although 54° F (12° C) fermentations increased acetaldehyde production, they also reduced the acetaldehyde faster, so the net level was lower in the finished beer[142]. Two other studies show how strain-dependent this can really be: one found no difference in acetaldehyde levels in fermentations done at 54°, 60°, and 68° F (12°, 16° and 20° C), whereas another found a huge increase in acetaldehyde levels when the fermentation temperature was increased from 50° to 68° F (from 10° to 20° C)[142].

**Solution:** If you do have acetaldehyde problems with a particular yeast, try fermenting cooler or plan an extended lagering time.

**Cause:** It has been suggested that bottle conditioning with weakened yeasts (especially beers that have been in the secondary for a long time) can create acetaldehyde which the yeast are too weak to reabsorb[110].

**Solution:** If this is indeed the problem (if the beer did not have an acetaldehyde aroma at bottling time, but does after bottle conditioning) you will want to add fresh yeast at bottling time the next time you make this recipe.

**Cause:** Enteric bacteria can cause elevated acetaldehyde levels[108].
**Solution:** Review Sanitation Procedures.

## Acetic acid aroma

**Cause:** Acetic acid (vinegar) can be created by yeast, but when it is, it is usually at such low levels that it is below the flavor threshold. When acetic acid becomes readily identifiable by smell and taste, the cause is usually bacterial. Acetic acid bacteria are either aerobes or micro-aerophilic, meaning that they either need or prefer air[108].

**Solution:** In addition to looking at "Review Sanitation Procedures," it is also a good idea to consider if you are properly isolating the beer from air. There is nothing that can be done to save beer that has been overwhelmed by acetic acid bacteria other than to expose it to air and let the bacteria finish the job – call the result not beer, but malt vinegar.

## Alcohol aroma

**Cause:** You might think that ethanol is the source of most alcohol aroma in beer. Actually, other, more complex alcohols (higher alcohols, a.k.a. fusel alcohols or fusel oils) have far more of that familiar "alcohol aroma." Therefore, it only takes a small amount of these higher alcohols to impart a rather strong alcohol aroma to your beer.

**Solution:** During aging, these higher alcohols will esterify in the presence of yeast and acids and create mostly fruity flavors. The solution therefore, is further conditioning on the yeast. Some esterification may occur without the presence of yeast, but a small fraction of that done by yeast.

**Cause:** Higher fermentation temperatures increase higher alcohol production[142].
**Solution:** Use cooler fermentation temperatures, especially for high-gravity beers.

**Cause:** Certain yeasts are more prone to produce higher alcohols.
**Solution:** Changing your yeast strain may help.

**Cause:** Underpitching can increase higher alcohol production. One study found that increasing the pitching rate decreased the higher alcohol content, however in subsequent repitchings, the difference leveled-out[142].
**Solution:** Pitch more yeast.

**Cause:** Wort nutrient imbalances can increase higher alcohol production. Both excesses and deficiencies in amino acids have been found to increase higher alcohol production[105,142].
**Solution:** If you are adding lots of sugar (such as corn sugar, honey, or table sugar) your wort may be deficient in amino acids – try backing-off on the simple sugars. If you are a lot of yeast energizer, you may want to try decreasing the quantity used.

**Cause:** Excessive sugar additions may be the problem. Several studies have found that additions of glucose or sucrose increase higher alcohol production[142]. However, other studies have found just the opposite[142,143]. Some researchers believe that the reason for these differing results is that this phenomenon is highly strain-dependent[142].
**Solution:** This is example of the importance of being familiar with your yeast. If indeed you used a lot of sugar, try reducing the amount used.

**Cause:** You have a high gravity wort. High gravity worts tend to increase higher alcohol production[142].

**Solution:** Suggesting a reduction in gravity would be silly – of course you wanted a high-gravity beer – however, remember that aging on the yeast will convert some of the alcohols to esters. Just be prepared to age strong beers for months or even a year.

**Cause:** High initial dissolved oxygen levels have shown to increase higher alcohol production in some studies, but underaeration also has found to increase them[142, 215].

**Solution:** Know your yeasts' oxygen requirements and neither over-oxygenate nor under-oxygenate.

**Cause:** If the yeast you are using is not prone to higher alcohol production, it could be a sanitation problem: many wild yeasts are strong producers of higher alcohols and some enteric bacteria have been found to influence higher alcohol production in cultured yeast[108]. (See also "Fruity Aroma" below.)

**Solution:** Review Sanitation Procedures.

**Cause:** Fermentation on hot and cold break increases the production of higher alcohols[123]. Increased amino acid levels can increase higher alcohol production[142] and there have been studies that found significant amounts of amino acids in cold break[39].

**Solution:** More rigorous hot and cold break removal may help reduce the production of higher alcohols.

## Apple aroma

**Cause:** Most often, apple aroma is caused by acetaldehyde (see "Acetaldehyde aroma"), but can also be from the ester ethyl hexanoate[111].

**Solution:** If you get this aroma and can rule out acetaldehyde as the cause, then reducing this ester can be done by fermenting at a cooler temperature or changing to a different yeast. (See also "Fruity aroma" below.)

## Baby diaper aroma

**Cause:** Yes, believe it or not, you can get this smell in a beer. It's caused by a bacterial infection and the only thing you can do is dump the batch and start over. Even if you can ignore the smell, I would avoid drinking the beer – it won't kill you, but it can give you a nasty stomach ache and a case of diarrhea. Solution: Nothing can be done to save this batch, but to avoid it in future batches, Review Sanitation Procedures, especially paying attention to fast cooling and pitching enough healthy yeast. The bacteria that cause odors like this take hold between the time that the wort begins cooling and the time that the yeast make it an inhospitable environment for these types of (wort spoiling) bacteria (consuming all the oxygen and nutrients, lowering the pH and eating up the sugars in the wort).

## Banana aroma

**Cause:** Banana aroma is caused by an ester (see "Yeast Phases" in chapter 10), specifically, isoamyl acetate.

**Solution:** Reducing the fermentation temperature, increasing starter size, and/or changing to a different yeast strain. Note that Wyeast Weihenstephan Wheat (#3068) and Belgian Ale (#1214) are known for their isoamyl acetate production. There seem to be other factors than temperature involved in the latter strain's production of the banana ester - I've corresponded with more than two dozen brewers all over the US regarding Wyeast #1214 and there appear to be many inconsistencies with this yeast. Some brewers report lots of banana aroma with cool fermentation, others with warm. Some report no banana aroma with cool fermentation, others with warm. There was a slight correlation with glucose content (i.e. the addition of corn sugar), but there were also several contradictions in this respect. This kind of data is very unscientific, especially since the result (the amount of banana ester) was measured by over two dozen different noses! More research is clearly needed. (See also "Fruity aroma" below.)

## Butterscotch aroma

**Cause:** Butterscotch, buttery, or toffee aromas are caused by a chemical compound called diacetyl. Given the opportunity, normal yeast will absorb and convert the diacetyl to less noticeable compounds. Some yeast strains are more prone to diacetyl production than others. Wyeast Irish Ale (#1084) and The Yeast Culture Kit Company's A42 are well known as strong diacetyl producers.
**Solution:** Change yeast.

**Cause:** The yeast sedimented too quickly or was filtered out of the beer too early.
**Solution:** Keep the yeast in contact with the beer and give them the opportunity to convert the diacetyl.

**Cause:** You used too-short a lagering time at too-cold a temperature.
**Solution:** Either you can lager longer or you can use what is called a "diacetyl rest." A diacetyl rest is a method in which the temperature of the finished lager is raised from typical lager fermentation temperatures up into the range of 55 to 65° F (13 to 18° C) for two to ten days[112].

**Cause:** Your beer has a *Pediococcus* bacteria infection.
**Solution:** Review Sanitation Procedures.

**Cause:** Air was introduced during fermentation[142].
**Solution:** Minimize the introduction of air during fermentation. One of the reasons that Samuel Smith's beers have such high levels of diacetyl is because their yeast requires them to use a brewing system which results in a lot of air being introduced during fermentation.

**Cause:** Air was introduced after fermentation, e.g. during bottling[113].
**Solution:** Be careful to not introduce air after fermentation is complete.

**Cause:** Increased fermentation temperature increases diacetyl production, but it also increases diacetyl reduction[142].
**Solution:** Clearly the worst thing to do is to ferment warm and condition cold. For the absolute minimum diacetyl levels, ferment cool or cold and condition warm for at least a few days before cold conditioning (in the case of lagers).

**Cause:** Increased pitching rates increases diacetyl production, but it also increases diacetyl reduction[142].
**Solution:** This shouldn't be a problem provided you give the yeast enough time in contact with the beer to reduce the diacetyl they have created.

**Cause:** Insufficient initial dissolved oxygen can increase diacetyl levels in the finished beer[114]. This is highly strain-dependent. The Ringwood yeast strain is notorious for producing lots of diacetyl unless the wort is nearly saturated with oxygen.
**Solution:** Make sure you have sufficient initial dissolved oxygen (note that this is highly strain-dependent).

**Cause:** Overaeration can increase diacetyl production[142].
**Solution:** Know your yeasts' oxygen requirements and don't over- or under-aerate.

**Cause:** Insufficient yeast nutrition, specifically the amino acid valine, can increase diacetyl production[142]. An all-malt wort should have sufficient valine, but if you've used a lot of adjuncts or refined sugars, you may have a deficiency. Increased percentages of corn grits in all-grain mashes (which would, in the case of yeast nutrition, be similar to increased levels of refined sugars in an extract beer) have been shown to result in beers with increased diacetyl levels[214].
**Solution:** Don't add too much refined sugar (more than 20% begins to have a profound effect).

**Cause:** Respiratory-deficient, "petite mutant" yeast has difficulty reducing diacetyl. Yeast reuse increases the likelihood of problems from mutations.
**Solution:** While the brewer has little direct over yeast mutations, you can limit the number of generations that you reuse the yeast and discard yeast from batches that begin to show a marked increase in diacetyl. Some strains of yeast can have a four-fold increase in diacetyl in as little as four generations[115].

**Cause:** Hallertauer and related hops as finishing or dry hops can give a buttery aroma. While not exactly like butterscotch, Hallertauer hop aroma can be mistaken for diacetyl even by experienced beer judges.
**Solution:** Don't overdo additions of Hallertauer and related varieties for finishing and/or dry hopping.

## *Buttery aroma*

See "Butterscotch aroma."

## *Cardboard aroma*

**Cause:** Cardboard, "wet cardboard" or papery aromas are usually the result of oxidation of the finished beer.
**Solution:** Avoid introducing air at any point after the beer has started fermenting.

**Cause:** It is also possible that oxygen which is introduced while steeping crystal malts and/or dark grains binds with melanoidins only to be released later during storage of the finished beer[142]. Aeration of boiled wort while it is still hot (called Hot Side Aeration) has a similar effect. Aeration this early in the process usually first becomes apparent as sherry-like aromas, but it is possible that these are masked by other aromas or perhaps they are thought to be acceptable by some tasters. Nonetheless, air introduced at any time in the process except in cooled wort prior to fermentation, can eventually impart a cardboard aroma.
**Solution:** Careful handling of hot wort is how to avoid this defect. It is important to note that un-oxidized melanoidins can slow the formation of staling compounds in beer[212]. Furthermore, some researchers have found that isohumulones inhibit the oxidation of alcohols and the autoxidation of fatty acids[212]. This would indicate that high hop rates would not only improve the storageability of beer from a bacterial perspective, but also would help reduce staling.

## *Celery aroma*

**Cause:** Celery aroma, along with many other vegetive smells, are most often the result of a bacterial infection. Coliform bacteria infections can give celery-like aromas and is one of two common "wort-spoiling bacterias" (along with *Hafnia protea* which lends an intense cooked-corn aroma). They are called wort-spoiling bacteria because they are sensitive to low pH and alcohol and therefore cause their damage between the time that the wort has cooled and the time that the yeast have started vigorous fermentation. These bacteria usually impart no flavor, but their effect on the aroma is unmistakable.
**Solution:** Review Sanitation Procedures, especially reducing chilling time and making sure that enough viable yeast is pitched.

## *Cheese aroma*

**Cause:** Some hop varieties, most notably Fuggle, can take on cheesy aroma as they age in the presence of air. Dryhopping with such hops can impart a cheesy aroma to the beer.

**Solution:** Always check the aroma of any hops you plan to use for finishing or dryhopping and don't use any hops that smell questionable.

**Cause:** Another possible source of a cheesy aroma are certain fatty acids produced by certain strains of *Kloeckera* and/or *Saccharomyces* yeast[116]. Unless you are making a pLambic/pLambiek, these aromas are clearly unwelcome and sanitation is to blame.
**Solution:** Review Sanitation Procedures.

**Cause:** Butyric acid has been described as having a cheesy aroma and I've heard from one chemist that it is produced by the fermentation of starch (*Saccharomyces diastaticus* can ferment starch[151]), therefore unconverted starch in the wort may cause a cheesy aroma.
**Solution:** Avoid the introduction of unconverted starch into the wort. Don't simply steep malts (such as Pilsner, Pale Ale, Toasted, or Aromatic malts) or unmalted grains (like oatmeal or flaked barley) that should instead be mashed (see "Grain Bags" in chapter 4).

## Cidery aroma

**Cause:** The use of refined sugars such as glucose (corn sugar or dextrose), fructose, sucrose (table sugar or Candi Sugar), invert sugar (Golden Syrup), brown sugar, demerara, raw sugar, Sucanat™, or turbinado, have long been associated with cidery aromas. I have personally tasted very cidery homebrew which, upon further investigation, proved to have been brewed with 50% table sugar. In an effort to determine if the type of sugar made a difference, I made "beer" from three types of white sugar: brewer's corn sugar, table sugar and invert sugar (which I made by boiling table sugar in water for 10 minutes with a few drops of lemon juice – it can be made more "golden" by boiling a bit longer). The resulting hop-less "beers" were tasted double-blind. The results were that the invert sugar tasted the most cidery, the table sugar a little less cidery and the corn sugar tasted very neutral, like vodka and seltzer water. Now, this informal experiment is not conclusive, but it did prove that the flavors of various simple sugars produce various flavors when fermented. One possibility is that what we call a cidery aroma could be nothing more than elevated acetaldehyde levels and that the precautions listed above under "Acetaldehyde aroma" should instead be followed. Perhaps the decreased amount of nutrients in a wort made with high levels of corn, beet, or cane sugars is the cause of the increase in acetaldehyde. Further experimentation is needed.
**Solution:** Aging the beer may help: if the cidery character is due to acetaldehyde, the yeast will reabsorb it, given time. Reduce the amount of nutrient-less sugar sources or add yeast energizer in subsequent batches.

## Clovey aroma

**Cause:** Clove-like aromas are unwelcome in most styles, but are expected in Bavarian Weizens and many Belgian Ales. They are produced by the yeast. Sometimes these aromas can also be called "smoky," "medicinal," "phenolic," or "plastic." Some yeast strains are more likely to produce clovey aromas, for example Wyeast Bavarian Wheat (#3056) and Weihenstephan Wheat (#3068) or Yeast Culture Kit Company's A85.
**Solution:** Use a different yeast strain. If you want a more fruity than clovey than fruity character in your weizen, try a warmer fermentation temperature. Cooler fermentation tends to favor clovey character whereas warmer tends to favor a fruity character in weizen yeasts.

**Cause:** Warmer fermentation temperatures increase the production of clovey aromas in yeasts (such as many Belgian yeasts) that are prone to this character.
**Solution:** Ferment cooler.

**Cause:** Some wild yeasts, especially *Saccharomyces diastaticus*, are strong producers of clovey aromas.
**Solution:** Review Sanitation Procedures.

**Cause:** Certain compounds in wort have been reported to increase the 4-vinyl guaiacol production and wheat malt is said to increase the content of these compounds in wort[117].
**Solution:** If you are not trying to make a Bavarian Weizen, but are using a lot of wheat, try reducing the wheat content or changing yeast strains because some are more prone to 4-vinyl guaiacol production.

**Cause:** Small amounts of chlorine (e.g. residue from using chlorine bleach for sanitation or adding chlorinated municipal tapwater into the fermenter) can react with compounds in the wort to create chlorophenols which have medicinal aromas and flavors. These have very strong aromas and flavors – they have a taste threshold on the order of parts-per-trillion!
**Solution:** Make sure to rinse well after sanitizing with chlorine bleach and boil all brewing water if your municipal water contains chlorine. If your municipal water works rely on chloramines for sanitation, you will have to use an activated charcoal filter to get these compounds out of your water – boiling will not remove them. Don't use bleach water in airlocks if there is risk of suckback.

## Coffee aroma

**Cause:** Unless you added coffee to your beer, coffee aromas are most likely to have originated from Roasted (unmalted) Barley and Roasted (black) Malt.
**Solution:** If the coffee aroma is excessive, reduce coffee, Roasted Barley and/or Roasted Malt additions.

# Cooked cabbage aroma

**Cause:** Cooked cabbage aroma is caused by "wort spoiling bacteria."
**Solution:** See "Celery aroma."

# Cooked corn aroma

One of the most common aromas in beer is the cooked corn aroma. It is caused by a chemical called dimethyl sulfide (DMS). In small amounts, it is welcome in pale lagers an is part of their character. It is also a common aroma in many Kölsch beers, despite the fact that they are ales. DMS is considered a defect in most other ales and at high levels is a flaw in all styles. DMS is rapidly created from S-methyl methionine (SMM) when the wort is above 158° F (70° C)[118].

**Cause:** When boiling the wort with the kettle uncovered, most of the DMS that is created boils away. If you boil with the kettle covered or if the boil is not very vigorous (i.e. if it is just a simmer), excessive DMS can remain in the wort and carry through to the finished beer.
**Solution:** Boil vigorously and never completely cover the kettle with the lid.

**Cause:** Once the kettle is removed from the heat, but while the wort is still above 158° F (70° C), lots of DMS is still being created from SMM. Therefore, slow cooling will increase the DMS in the finished beer.
**Solution:** Cool the hot wort quickly (ideally in less than 30 minutes).

**Cause:** The temperature of the fermentation also has an effect on how much DMS is in the beer. A significant portion of the DMS in the wort is oxidized to dimethyl sulfoxide (DMSO). During fermentation, yeast will reduce DMSO to DMS. At lower fermentation temperatures, more DMSO will be reduced than at higher temperatures[119]. Furthermore, some DMS is scrubbed out of the beer by evolving $CO_2$ – how much is dependent on yeast strain and fermentation temperature (more is scrubbed out at higher fermentation temperatures)[118].
**Solution:** Ferment warmer if practical, however, this is a minor source of DMS and therefore other, more likely sources should first be investigated.

**Cause:** If the DMS level is extremely powerful, the most likely source is bacterial. Many bacteria can reduce DMSO to DMS, most notably *Hafnia protea* (formerly called *Obesumbacterium proteus*) and some enteric bacteria[118,119].
**Solution:** Review Sanitation Procedures.

**Cause:** Allgrain brewers have control over their malt selection so that they can choose malts that are low in SMM. North American 6-row malts can have ten times the SMM of English or Belgian 2-row Pale Ale malts[118]. German 2-row Pilsner and North American 2-row malts fall somewhere between these two extremes. In general, the darker the malt, the less SMM it has. To extract brewers, the malt used to make the extract (if it is properly made) should not make a difference. My guess is that the dehydration process removes DMS and therefore the quality of the extract and not the type of malt used is of much greater importance. I have made many award-winning Pale Ales with Northwestern Gold extract and it is made from North American 6-row malt. **Solution:** After you have ruled out the other, more likely causes of excessive DMS, should you try using a different brand of malt extract.

## Diacetyl aroma

See "Butterscotch aroma."

## Dimethyl Sulfide (DMS) aroma

See "Cooked corn aroma."

## Electrical fire aroma

**Cause:** At intense levels, the same phenolic chemicals that give beer clovey aromas can give beer a smell that resembles an electrical fire or a toasted printed circuit board. Usually, cultured yeasts don't produce extreme amounts of these phenolic aromas – very high levels are probably due to wild yeast.
**Solution:** See "Clovey aroma."

## Fecal aroma

See "Baby diaper aroma."

## Floral aroma

**Cause:** Floral aromas are usually caused by certain strains of yeast (certain higher alcohols).
**Solution:** If the floral aroma is excessive, first try changing yeast or fermenting at a slightly cooler temperature. (See also "Alcohol aroma" above.)

**Cause:** Certain varieties of hops can add a floral note to the beer.
**Solution:** The most floral hops are probably Willamette, but other hop varieties that have a floral note are Oregon Goldings, Washington Goldings, East Kent Goldings, German Northern Brewer, Nugget, Perle, Styrian Goldings and British Columbian Goldings. Try changing hop varieties.

## Fruity aroma

**Cause:** Beer gets fruity aromas from chemical compounds called esters. Esters are created by the yeast from alcohols and acids. Different yeast strains produce different combinations of esters. Some yeast strains produce quite a bit more of one ester than another, for example Wyeast Weihenstephan Wheat (#3068) and Yeast Culture Kit Company's A85 produce predominantly isoamyl acetate (the

banana ester). At warmer temperatures (i.e. not at lager temperatures), Wyeast American Lager (#2035) makes raspberry esters. Some yeast strains produce a number of esters in nearly the same amounts, resulting in a mixed-fruit aroma. In addition to other, unique aromas, *Brettanomyces* yeasts produce incredibly high levels of esters, very commonly "bubble gum" and banana esters.
**Solution:** Try a different yeast.

**Cause:** Higher temperature fermentations increase ester production[142].
Solution: To increase ester levels, raise fermentation temperature. Conversely, to lower ester levels, ferment cooler. Temperature is the greatest factor influencing ester formation.

**Cause:** Aeration during fermentation raises ester levels[79,120].
**Solution:** Aeration during fermentation also increases diacetyl so it is not a recommended method for increasing fruitiness. If you are trying to decrease ester production, you may want to consider where in your process you may be adding air to the beer during fermentation (e.g. during transfer from primary to secondary fermenters).

**Cause:** Underpitching (not pitching enough yeast) increases ester production[77,78,142].
**Solution:** Use a larger starter. Another possible solution is to reduce aeration/oxygenation of the cooled wort. Although it can cause other problems (such as poor alcohol tolerance), reducing the amount of dissolved oxygen in the cooled wort can reduce ester production, by decreasing yeast reproduction. I've also read where some yeasts produce more esters when they have insufficient oxygen[121], so this highlights the importance of being familiar with your yeast strains and what their individual oxygen demands are.

**Cause:** Yeast growth can result in higher ester levels. There is conflicting data on this point. Actually, more studies have found that a decrease in yeast growth will increase ester production[87], whereas others have found that factors which increase yeast growth (such as increased aeration and increased nutrients) have increased ester levels in the finished beer[142].
**Solution:** There is general agreement that a larger starter will decrease ester production.

**Cause:** Underaeration increases ester production, especially in high-gravity worts[87,88,89,90,91,142].
**Solution:** Know your yeast strain's oxygen requirements and make sure you aerate/oxygenate enough.

**Cause:** Some strains of enteric bacteria create esters[108].
Solution: Review Sanitation Procedures.

**Cause:** Increased levels of sucrose (via table sugar additions) have been found to slightly increase ester production[142].
**Solution:** Don't overdo additions of sucrose.

**Cause:** After fermentation is complete, if the beer is not separated from the yeast, further ester formation can continue as the yeast converts alcohols and acids into esters. This is called "esterification" and is especially true for high-alcohol styles such as Barleywine and Doppelbock.

**Solution:** Other than by removing the yeast via filtering (see Volume II of this series) there is no way to stop the effects of esterification, but refrigeration can slow it's progress.

**Cause:** Increased unsaturated, long-chain fatty acid content in wort has shown to decrease ester production[87,123,142].

**Solution:** The only way for extract brewers to control this factor is to try another brand of extract, however, this is such an unlikely cause of excessive ester production, you should rule out other causes first.

**Cause:** Factors that increase higher alcohol production will generally increase ester production[142].

**Solution:** See "Alcohol aroma" above.

**Cause:** Low levels of lipids (from barley strain or excessive recirculation during mashing) can increase ester production[122]. It is important to note, however, that a lot of the lipids that do make it into the kettle end up in the hot and cold break[123]. It has been found that worts with higher levels of hot and cold break tend to have lower ester levels[87].

**Solution:** Recirculation is done for extract brewers by the extract manufacturer, so the only option would be to change brands of extract, but this is so unlikely you should rule out the other causes first. Hot and cold break carryover to the fermenter, however, is under the control of the extract brewer. So, if you are experiencing excessive levels of esters and you are going to great lengths to remove all traces of hot and cold break from the fermenter, you may want to allow some of the cold break to pass into the fermenter and see if that doesn't reduce ester production.

## Garbage aroma

**Cause:** Although caused by different bacteria, a garbage-like aroma should be treated similarly to Baby diaper aroma.

**Solution:** See "Baby diaper aroma."

## Goaty aroma

**Cause:** Goaty aromas are caused by a class of fatty acids which have been named from the Latin word for goat. These include caproic acid, caprylic acid, and capric acid. The production of these compounds is only welcome in pLambiek/pLambic beers and is produced by certain strains of *Kloeckera* and *Saccharomyces yeast*.

**Solution:** Unless you are making a pLambic/pLambiek, change yeast or Review Sanitation Procedures. Increased fermentation temperatures, increased pitching rate and increased aeration have a tendency to slightly reduce free fatty acids[142]. Note that these factors may be used to your advantage in making pLambics/pLambieks.

## Grainy aroma

**Cause:** There are many interpretations for a grainy aroma and often they are lumped together with husky aromas. I believe that the two should be covered separately and that grainy is a positive attribute whereas husky is a negative one. To me, a grainy aroma is that of fresh grain. The difference between grainy and malty is blurred. Rarely is there much fresh grain aroma in finished beer. Simply boiling the wort drives off many of the delicate aromatics. Nonetheless, I believe that the process of making extract eliminates far more grain aromatics than boiling and that adding a little light crystal malt to an extract batch adds back some of that grain aroma. Dark grain aroma is clearly a different issue altogether.
**Solution:** Start with pale extracts and add dark crystal, chocolate, and roasted malts, as well as roasted barley to add a fresher, more complex aroma than simply starting from dark extracts.

## Grapefruit aroma

**Cause:** The most common source of grapefruit aroma is from Cascade, Columbus, or Centennial hops. Using these hops for either flavor or aroma (finishing and especially dryhopping) adds this character to a varying extent.
**Solution:** Use a different hop variety.

**Cause:** Some yeasts, especially English yeasts, add a citrusy note that could be perceived as a grapefruit aroma, but this is less likely.
**Solution:** Use a different yeast strain.

## Grassy aroma

**Cause:** Some hops can give this character, especially if they have been insufficiently dried.
**Solution:** Smell the hops before you use them and if they smell grassy, avoid them.

**Cause:** Various compounds produced during fermentation can give grassy aromas[109].
**Solution:** If these are indeed the source of the grassy aroma, they will be reduced during aging.

**Cause:** Grassy aromas can be caused by poor malt storage[117].

**Solution:** If you rule out hops and insufficient aging as a cause of this character, consider trying a different brand of extract.

## Green apple aroma

See "Acetaldehyde aroma."

## Ham aroma

**Cause:** Orange peel is an ingredient used in Witbiers. Actually, there are two types of orange peel used in Witbiers: "Curaçao orange" and "sweet orange." Neither of these is the common orange we find at the grocery store. Using the common "grocery store" orange in a beer gives it a ham-like aroma, possibly in cooperation with coriander.
**Solution:** Don't use the common "grocery store" oranges in Witbiers. Curaçao and sweet orange are available from some homebrew supply shops.

## Honey aroma

**Cause:** Most beers with a honey aroma get it from the yeast. The compound responsible for this aroma is similar to diacetyl and is called 2,3-pentanedione.
**Solution:** There is very little written about it, but given its similarity to diacetyl (it is produced similarly to diacetyl except that it is associated with leucine instead of valine), except for the bacterial and hop sources, I suggest looking in "Butterscotch aroma" for suggestions regarding the increase or reduction of 2,3-pentanedione.

**Cause:** When used in massive amounts (approaching 50% of the fermentables), honey can lend a honey-like note to your beer.
**Solution:** Limit the use of honey unless that is the character you are seeking.

## Hop aroma missing

**Cause:** Assuming there was a hop aroma to begin with (if not, see chapter 8 on how to add hop aroma), a diminishing hop aroma is caused by oxidation. This can be due to molecular oxygen in the headspace or dissolved into the finished beer as a result of careless handling during racking or bottling. However, this is not the only source of oxidation – other oxidized compounds in the beer, such as melanoidins, can release their oxygen during storage and cause the loss of hop aroma.
**Solution:** Avoid introducing air into hot wort and into the beer after fermentation has begun, especially during racking and bottling.

## Horsey aroma

**Cause:** The production of horsey aromas is not yet clearly understood, but it has been traced to *Brettanomyces* yeasts. Initially, many *Brettanomyces* yeasts produce tremendous amounts of esters, but after six or eight months, they can, under the proper conditions, produce tetrahydropyridines which are responsible for the horsey aroma[124]. Ethyl alcohol and the amino acid lysine are required for the production of the horsey character.
**Solution:** If you get horsey aromas, but are not making a pLambic/pLambiek, then your sanitation should be suspect. Review Sanitation Procedures.

## Lactic aroma

**Cause:** A lactic aroma is actually a misnomer (lactic acid itself smells very slightly like white glue) because the smell we associate with a lactic bacteria infection is completely different. Except for beers in the Berliner Weiss, Lambiek/Lambic, or Flanders Red/Brown Ale styles, it is a flaw. In beer, bacteria from primarily the *Lactobacillus* and *Pediococcus* genera produce lactic acid and this aroma. Usually the majority of the lactic acid and this characteristic aroma are produced in the finished beer as opposed to being made during fermentation. In pLambic/pLambiek beers, significant sourness takes no less than three months and can take up to eight months to become prominent.
**Solution:** If you had not intended a lactic fermentation, sanitation is the culprit. Review Sanitation Procedures.

## Leathery aroma

**Cause:** A leathery aroma is unwelcome in all but the Lambic/Lambiek and some historical styles of beer. The compounds responsible for it are tetrahydropyridines, the same ones that are responsible for horsey aromas[124].
**Solution:** See "Horsey aroma."

## Lightstruck aroma

**Cause:** "Lightstruck aroma" is another name for "skunky aroma."
**Solution:** See "Skunky aroma."

## Malt aroma missing

**Cause:** What we call a malt aroma can often be low levels of dimethyl sulfide (DMS).
**Solution:** See "Cooked corn aroma" but be careful to not overdo the factors that increase DMS – they are considered faults in all ales except for Kölsch.

**Cause:** Another group of compounds responsible for what we call malt aroma are called melanoidins. Crystal malts have some melanoidins, but the true source of melanoidins in beers are high-kilned malts such as Vienna, Munich, DeWolf-Cosysns' Aromatic, and (of course) Weyermann's Melanoidin malts.
**Solution:** In addition, adding crystal malts and/or roasted malts can add-back some of the grain character lost during the malt extract production process. If you are trying to add melanoidins to your beer, some malt extracts are made from a significant portion of Munich malt (Marie's™ Munich Malt Extract, William's Brewing German Gold, and Ireks Amber) so these would be your first choice for styles that require a lot of melanoidins (such as Munich Dunkel, Traditional Bock, and Altbier). Note: don't add high-kilned malts without mashing.

## Meaty aroma

**Cause:** One source of a meat-like aroma is the excessive use of coriander.
**Solution:** Don't overdo the coriander additions.

**Cause:** Some wort-spoiling bacteria can produce meaty aromas.
**Solution:** Review Sanitation Procedures. Try to shorten cooling times and pitch larger yeast starters to minimize lag time.

## Medicinal aroma

**Cause:** A medicinal aroma is due to phenolic compounds.
**Solution:** See "Clovey aroma."

## Medicine mouthwash aroma

See "Clovey aroma."

## Moldy aroma

**Cause:** A moldy aroma is obviously due to mold. The mold can add its aroma not only after fermentation but also from moldy grains or hops. Note that molds cannot live without air so you cannot have mold living in your beer during fermentation while the yeast are actively producing $CO_2$ purging the oxygen from the headspace. Also, the chances of having problems with molds are quite a bit higher during the summer when the humidity in the air is higher.
**Solution:** If you have problems with molds in your fermenter, be careful with sanitation before the yeast begin to ferment the wort, exclude air from the fermenter after fermentation has completed, bottle as soon as it is reasonable and consider getting a dehumidifier for your brewing area. Don't use old grains or hops that have been kept in damp conditions. If your supplier doesn't take care of their grains and hops, tell them you are taking your business elsewhere until they clean up their act.

## Mousy aroma

See "Horsey aroma."

## Musty aroma

See "Moldy aroma."

## Nail polish remover aroma

**Cause:** Nail polish remover aroma is most likely to be caused by the ester ethyl acetate. As with all esters, higher-temperature fermentations result in more ester production. Solvent-like aromas can also come from higher alcohols. Higher alcohol production also increases with fermentation temperature.
**Solution:** Limit fermentation temperatures to below 70° F (21° C) if possible.

**Cause:** The amount of esters and higher alcohols produced is dependent on the yeast strain.
**Solution:** Consider changing the yeast strain that you are using.

**Cause:** Some wild yeasts are capable of producing large amounts of ethyl acetate.
**Solution:** You may want to Review Sanitation Procedures.

**Cause:** The use of non-food grade plastic fermenters or hoses can give a solvent-like aroma.
**Solution:** Use only food-grade plastic fermenters and hoses.

**Cause:** Underpitching (not pitching enough yeast) increases ester production[77,78].
**Solution:** Use a larger starter.

## Nutty aroma

**Cause:** There are various nutty aromas, some positive, others negative. The positive nutty aromas can come from toasted malts and from some strains of yeast (Lallemand Nottingham yeast can lend a slight nutty aroma). The negative nutty aromas are usually the result of oxidation, especially Hot-Side Aeration (HSA).
**Solution:** Be careful to avoid aeration of hot wort (above 80° F, 27° C) and after fermentation is complete.

## Oaky aroma

**Cause:** While fermenting in oak or the addition of oak chips to the beer are the obvious sources of oak aroma, it is not quite that simple. American oak and European oak are quite different. Also, if using American oak, only white oak should be used. European oak lends virtually no oaky aroma. A few weeks in contact with new American oak will impart more oak aroma than three years in contact with European oak. I believe that an oaky character may be imparted to a Lambic/Lambiek by *Brettanomyces* yeast or some other microbiota in the fermentation. I judged Jim Liddil's 1994 AHA National Competition Best of Show pGueuze in the first round and remember that it had a significant oaky character. However, it was extract-based (which rules out husk character) and was fermented in plastic with no oak chips added.

**Solution:** If you are getting an unwanted oaky aroma and are not using oak chips or fermenters, then Review Sanitation Procedures.

## Onion aroma

**Cause:** The most common cause of this aroma is wort spoiling bacteria.
**Solution:** See "Celery aroma."

**Cause:** I have noticed an onion-like aroma in several different beers that were reportedly dryhopped with East Kent or Styrian Goldings, however, I'm not sure if this was perhaps due to mishandling and oxidation or whether there are clonal selections that have this characteristic.
**Solution:** If the hops you used were of questionable quality, the solution would be to get fresh hops.

## Orange aroma

**Cause:** You must be careful the way you select your orange peels when trying to impart an orange aroma. There are three primary types of oranges whose peels might be considered for brewing: Curaçao orange, "grocery-store" orange and Sweet orange. Curaçao orange peel (also called bitter orange peel, although it is not very bitter) imparts an herbal aroma similar perhaps to chamomile and grocery-store orange lends a ham-like aroma to beer. Sweet orange peel does indeed impart an orange aroma, similar to Cointreau or Grand Marnier[100]. A very orange-like aroma can be produced by certain yeast strains. Wyeast Belgian White Ale (#3944) yeast fermented at 68° F (20° C), for example, adds a little orange aroma to the beer. Finally, coriander can add an orange-like aroma to beer.
**Solution:** If you are getting an undesirable orange aroma in your beer, but are not adding coriander, orange peels, or orange extracts, I suggest you try changing to a different yeast.

## Papery aroma

See "Cardboard aroma."

## Parsnip aroma

See "Celery aroma."

## Peaty aroma

**Cause:** Peaty aroma (a peat-smoked aroma, actually) can be imparted by using peat-smoked grain, either homemade or commercially made.
**Solution:** Only a very small amount of smoked grain is required to add a lot of aroma.

## Peppery aroma

**Cause:** Other than the obvious (peppers), alcohols lend a peppery aroma to beer. Ethyl alcohol has much less "alcohol aroma" as compared to the higher alcohols. Higher alcohols (sometimes called fusel alcohols) have much more intense "alcohol aromas."
**Solution:** To reduce the production of higher alcohols, ferment at a cooler temperature or change the yeast strain you are using. See also "Alcohol aroma" above.
**Cause:** Some hop varieties can lend a peppery aroma.
**Solution:** See appendix B for a listing of hop varieties that have a "black pepper" aroma.

## Phenolic aroma

See "Clovey aroma."

## Pine aroma

**Cause:** Some varieties of hops have a pine-like aroma when fresh and others have a pine-like aroma when stale.
**Solution:** If you don't like that pine-like aroma, avoid the use of old hops that have it (see appendix B).

**Cause:** I've heard of using spruce needles in the boil to impart a spruce-like aroma, but have never heard of using pine.
**Solution:** I would recommend against using any part of the pine in your beer unless you can verify elsewhere that it is safe to do so.

## Plastic aroma

See "Clovey aroma."

## Plastic bandage aroma

See "Clovey aroma."

## Playdough™ aroma

**Cause:** This aroma is quite distinct and comes from certain aldehydes in the beer. These aldehydes are oxidized alcohols. This aroma, therefore, comes from exposing completed beer (beer that already has alcohol) to air. Note that oxygen most often enters a plastic fermenter through a poorly-fitting lid (I prefer gasketted lids), but in rare cases of very long aging times, enough oxygen can pass directly through the walls of the fermenter. HDPE (high-density polyethylene, the plastic from which most food grade pails are made) is slightly permeable to oxygen. LDPE (low-density polyethylene) and polycarbonate (the clear plastic often used for plastic water-cooler bottles) are even more permeable to oxygen than HDPE.
**Solution:** Do not allow finished beer to become oxidized, either by aeration during bottling or via an ill-fitting lid or stopper on your fermenter.

**Cause:** Letting your airlock dry out is a sure way to expose your beer not only to oxygen, but also to allow bugs to fly into your fermenter.
**Solution:** Keep your airlocks filled – check them often, especially when the humidity is low. S-shaped airlocks are much less likely to dry out than the 3-piece style.

## Raisin aroma

**Cause:** Some yeasts can impart a raisin-like aroma to beer, but the most likely source for a raisin aroma is from dark crystal malts such as DeWolf-Cosyns Special B. Even 1/4 pound of this crystal malt added to a 5-gallon batch can add a noticeable raisin-like aroma.
**Solution:** Don't overdo the dark crystal malt additions.

## Resiny aroma

**Cause:** Many hop varieties have very resiny aromas which are imparted to beer when they are used as finishing or dry hops. Some of the most resiny hops are East Kent Goldings, Styrian Goldings, and Nugget. See appendix B for more varieties.
**Solution:** If you want this aroma, use these hops – if you don't, avoid them.

## Rotten egg odor

See "Sulfur aroma."

## Rotten vegetable odor

See "Celery aroma."

## Rubbery aroma

**Cause:** Rubbery aromas can be imparted by yeast that have undergone autolysis. Autolysis is a condition in which starved yeast release an enzyme that causes neighboring yeast to break down.

**Solution:** Once the fermentation is complete, only a minimal amount of yeast is required for conditioning. Minimize the amount of yeast in contact with the beer to reduce the effects of autolysis and keep the beer cold. Healthy yeast is much less likely to autolyse so only pitch healthy yeast.

**Cause:** Underoxygenated wort can result in yeast that has a higher tendency to autolyse[215].

**Solution:** Make sure you aerate or oxygenate your wort well.

**Cause:** Zinc increases the likelihood of autolysis[69].

**Solution:** Do not add excessive amounts of zinc.

**Cause:** Skunky aromas can sometimes be characterized as rubbery.

**Solution:** See "Skunky aroma."

**Cause:** Butyric acid has been described as having a rubbery aroma and I've heard that it can be produced by the fermentation of starch (*Saccharomyces diastaticus* can ferment starch[151]), therefore unconverted starch in the wort may cause a rubbery aroma.

**Solution:** Unconverted starch can be introduced into the wort by simply steeping malts (such as Pilsner, Pale Ale, Toasted, or Aromatic malts) or unmalted grains (like oatmeal or flaked barley) that should instead be mashed (see "Grain Bags" in chapter 4). Minimize the likelihood of introducing unconverted starch into your wort.


## Sherry aroma

**Cause:** Sherry-like aromas are the result of Hot-Side Aeration (HSA) which is quite simply the aeration of the wort while it is hot. The cooler the temperature, the less oxidation that takes place. Note that there is a difference between oxygenation and oxidation. Oxygenation is the dissolving of oxygen in a liquid. Oxidation is a chemical reaction between oxygen (or an electron acceptor) and another compound.

**Solution:** Cooling the wort to below about 80° F (27° C) before aeration minimizes the amount of oxygenation to a level that is not noticeable in the finished beer.

**Cause:** Oxygen in the finished beer can also sometimes give sherry-like aromas.

**Solution:** Minimize aeration of finished beer.

## Skunky aroma

**Cause:** When hopped wort or beer are exposed to light, chemical reactions take place in certain hop compounds (isohumulones) forming chemicals called mercaptans. Mercaptans are the actual compounds that gives skunks their aroma. This aroma is also called "lightstruck." The energy of the light effects the rate of the reaction, sunlight taking as little as five minutes through clear glass, fluorescent light taking a few hours, and incandescent light taking quite a bit longer. The color of the glass does reduce the rate of the reaction, dark brown glass being the best at protecting the beer. Green and clear glass provide virtually no protection. There is a large American brewery that uses clear glass for their bottles, but their beer does not get skunky. Why? Because they use specially modified hop extracts that are not sensitive to light. You may read that only ultraviolet light will affect the hop components. This is false. By a process called non-radiative energy transfer, light of blue wavelength and below is absorbed by other molecules and then transferred to the isohumulones. In beer, it is believed that the primary absorber (the sensitizer) is riboflavin[125].
**Solution:** Minimize exposure to light from the time the boil is started, through fermentation, to serving time.

**Cause:** Canned beer has been reported to have developed skunky aromas. Certainly light is not at fault here, so there must be another source. It is believed that heat and possibly agitation can cause skunky aromas.
**Solution:** Protect your finished beer from extreme heat and agitation.

## Smoky aroma

**Cause:** Unless it is from smoked malt (or malt that has been kilned using peat- or wood-fired kilns), the most common source of smoky aroma is yeast.
**Solution:** See "Clovey aroma."

## Solvent-like aroma

See "Nail polish remover aroma."

## Sour milk aroma

See "Lactic aroma."

## Spicy aroma

**Cause:** Some yeasts can impart a spicy aroma. The yeast used by the Abbey Notre Dame de Scourmont (the makers of Chimay Trappist Ales) is one such yeast.
**Solution:** Change yeast variety.

**Cause:** Higher temperatures cause more of all yeast byproducts to be made.
**Solution:** Ferment cooler.

**Cause:** Some hop varieties lend a spicy aroma including Crystal, Saaz, and Tettnanger. See appendix B for more spicy hop varieties.
**Solution:** If you want spicy character, consider these hop varieties – if you don't, avoid them.

**Cause:** Obviously, spices give spicy aromas. Cinnamon, nutmeg and allspice are just some of the spices that might be used in beer.
**Solution:** See chapter 11 for more on spices.

## Spruce aroma

**Cause:** Spruce needles are used by some brewers to add spruce aroma to beer. It is also possible to buy spruce essence. I have recently tasted a Holiday Spiced Ale from a commercial brewer that lists cinnamon, orange peel, and nutmeg on the label (no spruce), but there is a definite spruce character in both the nose and flavor. Perhaps this brewer is trying to be secretive or maybe the combination of yeast, spices and aroma hops gives this beer a spruce aroma.

## Stale aroma

**Cause:** Stale aromas are most likely the result of oxidation. This can be caused by the introduction of air during racking or bottling or can be from Hot-Side Aeration (see "Sherry aroma"). Staling takes time, but can be accelerated by heat and/or agitation.
**Solution:** See "Cardboard aroma."

## Sulfur aroma

**Cause:** Sulfur aromas are usually from yeast. Yeast autolysis can impart sulfur aromas.
**Solution:** See "Rubbery aroma."

**Cause:** It is not uncommon for yeast to produce hydrogen sulfide ($H_2S$) during fermentation. It smells exactly like rotten eggs. Lager yeasts are more likely to produce it than ale yeasts.
**Solution:** In most cases, the aroma will dissipate either by the end of fermentation or after a few weeks of aging. Some yeast strains can require you to lager for four months before the sulfury smells go away. One batch I made with Wyeast Munich Lager #2308 took four months for a bad odor to fade in a beer – it smelled just like home perm solution. After the sulfury smell went away, the beer won several ribbons. Note that altering the fermentation temperature to a staggered schedule can reduce the sulfury aroma (see "Sulfury Aroma Production" in chapter 10).

**Cause:** Various bacteria, including *Zymomonas* and *Pectinatus* produce hydrogen sulfide.
**Solution:** Review Sanitation Procedures.

**Cause:** In rare cases, pantothenate or pyroxidine vitamin-deficient wort can increase hydrogen sulfide production to levels that spill over into the finished beer[117, 215].
**Solution:** Reduce non-malt sources of fermentables (i.e. increase malt) or add Yeast Energizer.

**Cause:** Sulfur dioxide above 20 PPM is noticeable in aroma and taste. The uncommon (and not recommended) practice of adding sulfites (e.g. via Campden tablets or potassium metabisulfite) to force-carbonated beer at packaging time can increase sulfur dioxide levels above the flavor threshold[92].
**Solution:** Do not add sulfites to beer.

## Sweaty aroma

**Cause:** Isobutyric acid and caproic acid have been associated with sweaty aromas[126,127].
**Solution:** The only references to isobutyric acid that I could find was regarding their content in hops. For more on caproic acid, see "Goaty aroma."

## Toffee aroma

**Cause:** Toffee aroma can be the result of scorching the wort at the bottom of the kettle.
**Solution:** Do not try to use too much heat in bringing the wort to a boil, turn off the heat (or remove the kettle from the heat if you are using an electric stove) before you pour the malt extract into the hot water. Make sure the extract is well dissolved before putting the kettle back onto the heat.

**Cause:** Some crystal malts can add toffee aromas.
**Solution:** After ruling out scorching, consider trying a different maltster's crystal malt.

## Tomato plant aroma

**Cause:** Tomato plant aroma is caused by oxidation.
**Solution:** See "Cardboard aroma."

## Vinegar aroma

See "Acetic acid aroma."

## Wet cardboard aroma

See "Cardboard aroma."

## Winey aroma

**Cause:** Wine-like aromas can be caused by higher alcohols[117].
**Solution:** See "Alcohol aroma."

## Woody aroma

**Cause:** Besides the obvious (direct contact with wood), woody aromas can be created by some strains of yeast, oxidation, and some varieties of hops.
**Solution:** Consider trying a different strain of yeast, watch aeration of hot wort and finished beer and consider trying a different strain of yeast.

## Yeasty aroma

**Cause:** In moderate amounts, yeasty aromas are usually pleasant and accepted in most styles. When levels get high, yeasty aromas become a flaw. Unflocculent yeast can impart a yeasty aroma. If a normally well-behaved yeast upon repitching begins to have flocculation problems, this is a common sign that a mutation has occurred in a significant portion of the yeast population or that a wild yeast has established itself among the cultured yeast. Yeast autolysis (see "Rubbery aroma") can also impart a yeasty aroma.
**Solution:** You can remove some of an unflocculent yeast with the use of finings or all of it with filtering. If you suspect problems with your yeast culture, discard it and purchase new yeast (i.e. don't repitch it again).

# Appearance

## Chill haze (cloudy only when cold)

**Cause:** Chill haze is a cloudiness that appears only when the finished beer is cooled. Chill haze is a result of polyphenols (a.k.a. tannins, extracted from the grain and hops) combining with large-sized proteins (from the malt and protein-containing adjuncts). The resulting compounds are soluble when the beer is warm (room temperature), but become insoluble when the beer is chilled. Also, there is research that indicates that only polymerized polyphenols react with proteins to form haze and therefore oxidation (which contributes to the polymerization) is required to cause haze[228].

**Solution:** There are five main ways to reduce or eliminate it:
- reduce the amount of polyphenols that are extracted from the malt and hops,
- reduce the amount of large proteins that go into the wort,
- remove some of the polyphenols that have made it into the finished beer,
- break down the large proteins in the beer into smaller proteins,
- lager the beer in bulk and rack the beer off the settled haze, and
- filter the chill haze out of the beer.

See "Chill haze" in chapter 6 for details on all these methods.

**Cause:** There is evidence that only oxidized polyphenols lead to chill haze[228].
**Solution:** Minimize splashing and other sources of aeration during transfer, especially after fermentation is complete.

## Permanent haze

**Cause:** Permanent hazes fall into two general categories: chemical hazes (such as those from iron or tin in the water) and biological hazes (such as unflocculent yeasts and bacterial haze).
**Solution:** See "Chemical haze" and "Biological haze" in chapter 6.

**Cause:** There is evidence that oxidized polyphenols lead to permanent haze[227,228].
**Solution:** Minimize splashing and other sources of aeration during transfer, especially after fermentation is complete.

**Cause:** Starch can also give you a permanent haze.
**Solution:** Don't use malts that require mashing (like Pilsner, Pale Ale, toasted, or Biscuit) in extract beers.

## Poor head retention

**Cause:** Head retention is mostly dependent on the amount of small- and medium-sized proteins in the beer.
**Solution:** The primary control of the small- and medium-sized protein content in an extract brewer's wort has been decided by the extract manufacturer, but you still have the choice of which brand of extract you use. Some result in beer that has much better head retention than others. However, there are still ways that you can add additional head retention. Crystal malts improve head retention. Even $1/2$ to 1 pound of crystal malt added to a 5-gallon extract batch will make a sizable difference. Wheat improves head retention, so you might try substituting one or two pounds of wheat extract for barley malt extract. Although I've never used it, I've read that brewer's licorice improves head retention, but I would limit its use to dark beers such as Porters and Stouts.

**Cause:** Glassware that is not very clean or that has a thin film of soap on it can ruin the beer's head retention. If the first beer you pour has poor head retention, but the second glass of the same beer has better head retention, then this is probably the source of your problem. Oils, fats, lipstick, lip balm, and wax can all ruin head retention. Often the bubbles end up much larger than the usual tight, creamy head, eventually popping and collapsing. Rinsing agents (either included in dishwashing powder or added to a special reservoir in the dishwasher) can also reduce head retention. Note that soap or oil in the kettle, fermenters, or on other brewing equipment (like your wooden spoon) can get into the beer and ruin the head retention weeks later when the beer is finished.
**Solution:** Clean glassware not with dishwashing soap (the kind that makes suds) but with plain old washing soda or dishwashing machine detergent. Avoid rinsing agents. Washing soda is my first choice for cleaning all brewing equipment. Don't use brewing equipment for cooking (i.e. don't use your wooden brewing spoon for making shrimp scampi).

**Cause:** Overuse of adsorbents such as bentonite can reduce head retention.
**Solution:** Don't overdo additions of adsorbents.

**Cause:** Hops can improve head retention.
**Solution:** Add more hops. Note that even dryhops can help.

**Cause:** Proteolytic enzymes such as papain can reduce head retention.
**Solution:** I would recommend against the use of proteolytic enzymes such as papain since they are not at all selective on the type of proteins they break down: large, haze-forming proteins or smaller, head-retaining proteins.

**Cause:** Alcohols can reduce head retention.
**Solution:** Make sure there are plenty of medium-sized proteins in your beer if you are making a high-alcohol beer. This shouldn't be a problem for all-malt beers but can be if you are adding a lot of low-protein sources of fermentables like refined sugars.

**Cause:** Some lipids (fat-like substances) in the wort can reduce head retention.
**Solution:** The lipid content in extracts is decided by the manufacturer. It is very unlikely that a commercially made extract would have a lipid content high enough to affect head retention. Nonetheless, isinglass removes some lipids and can increase head retention (see chapter 6).

**Cause:** The products of yeast autolysis can decrease head retention.
**Solution:** Next time, pitch only healthy yeast, aerate well, and do not allow the finished beer to sit on the settled yeast longer than necessary.

## Too dark

**Cause:** You used dark extracts.
**Solution:** Use only pale or extra-pale extracts if you are trying to make a pale beer. Also, remember that not all extracts are created equal. Some labeled "Pale," "Gold" or "Light" are much darker than others. Those labeled "Extra Light" tend to be some of the palest.

**Cause:** Dark crystal malts.
Solution: Use only the lightest crystal malts if you feel your beer is too dark.

**Cause:** As extract ages, it darkens due to melanoidin-forming reactions called Browning Reactions.
**Solution:** Use fresh extract. Dried malt extracts are less prone to darkening via Browning Reactions. If you must store extract for a long time, cold storage will slow these reactions.

**Cause:** Wort darkens during the boil, especially in concentrated boils.
Solution: Boiling all five gallons (a full boil) instead of just 1 1/2 or 2 gallons (a partial boil) will reduce wort darkening.

**Cause:** Wort oxidation increases color.
**Solution:** Avoid aerating hot wort (wait until it cools to aerate) and to minimize the aeration during racking and bottling.

**Cause:** Polyphenols (a.k.a. tannins) extracted from the malt can darken the wort.
**Solution:** Keep the pH of the steeping grain and the boil to be below 5.5 to minimize the extraction of polyphenols. You can lighten the color of the beer if a significant part of the darkness is from polyphenols by fining the beer with PVPP, a.k.a. Polyclar (see "Chill haze" in chapter 6).

**Cause:** Copper catalyses browning reactions[128].
**Solution:** This is an unlikely source of darkening, but if you have ruled out all other sources of wort darkening, you may want to consider sources of copper (water, kettles, chillers, plumbing) in your brewing. Note that deionized water (from a reverse-osmosis water system, for example) can be very reactive with copper plumbing.

## Too light

**Cause:** Insufficient dark malts.
**Solution:** You can add darker crystal malts (if a chocolate or roasted malt flavor is inappropriate for the style) or small amounts of chocolate or roasted malts or roasted barley (although roasted barley adds a reddish tone). One final note: don't judge the color of the beer in the fermenter – it will darken quite a bit as the yeast settles.

# Flavor

You'll notice that for many flavors, I simply refer you to the corresponding aroma. This is because the aroma and flavor are so closely tied and because the same compounds that create the aroma are also responsible for the flavor.

## Alcohol flavor

**Cause:** Ethyl alcohol, the main alcohol produced by the yeast, may be the most abundant, but it is also not nearly as flavorful or aromatic as higher alcohols (a.k.a. fusel alcohols). When you have a strong alcohol flavor it is most likely due to higher alcohols.
**Solution:** See "Alcohol aroma" for suggestions on how to reduce higher alcohols.

## Burning flavor

**Cause:** Higher alcohols can impart a burning sensation in the mouth.
**Solution:** See "Alcohol aroma" on how to reduce higher alcohol production.

## Burnt flavor

**Cause:** The most likely source of a burnt flavor is scorching the malt.
**Solution:** Always remove the kettle from the heat before adding the extract and make sure it is well dissolved before restarting the heat.

**Cause:** One wheat extract that I've used has a strong burnt flavor. The first time I used it, I blamed my technique. The second time, I realized that it was the malt – it smells burnt right from the can. This extract does make an interesting Rauchweizen however…
**Solution:** Don't use brands of extract that you have found you don't like.

## Butterscotch flavor

See "Butterscotch aroma."

## Buttery flavor

See "Butterscotch aroma."

## Cidery flavor

See "Cidery aroma."

## Clinging bitterness

**Cause:** A long, dry, lingering bitterness is caused by high levels of sulfate ions in the water. If you are adding gypsum or magnesium sulfate to your wort, this could be the source of the problem. If not, then check with your water supplier – ask for a copy of the most recent water analysis. If the sulfate levels are above, say 50 PPM, they begin to have a significant effect on the perceived bitterness, especially in the finish. If you are trying to make a Bohemian Pilsner, sulfate levels over 15 PPM can be too high.

**Solution:** If you are adding gypsum or magnesium sulfate, use less. If your tapwater is naturally high sulfates, you may need to blend it with distilled water (I use 1/2 distilled water when I make Bohemian Pilsners – you may have to use a larger or smaller percentage of distilled water, depending on your tapwater's sulfate concentration).

## Clovey flavor

**Cause:** A clovey flavor is usually a byproduct of the yeast.
**Solution:** See "Clovey aroma."

**Cause:** Old grain can develop a clovey flavor. More specifically, I've found a plastic bandage kind of aftertaste develops in very pale crystal malts, like Carapils® and Dextrin malts if they are stored for long periods of time.
**Solution:** I've successfully eliminated this problem by storing my Carapils® with a desiccant in a food grade bucket with a tightly-sealed, gasketted lid. Zipper-lock freezer bags are okay, but Tupperware® or head-sealed bags are best for smaller quantities.

## "Extract twang"

**Cause:** "Extract twang" is a tartness I believe is caused by old, stale extract.
**Solution:** Use only fresh malt extract.

**Cause:** I believe that "extract twang" can be caused by too much refined sugar. Solution: Avoid extracts that are not all-malt (ones that contain large amounts of refined sugars) and don't add too much refined sugar to your wort. For most worts under 1.050 or so, don't use more than 10 or 15% refined sugar and don't exceed 40% in any recipe.

## Harsh flavor

Harshness in a beer can come from a variety of sources. Although tasting carefully can suggest the most likely sources, it is impossible to teach these skills without tasting together in person. I can only give you recommendations as to where the harshness can come from and you will have to assess your recipe and techniques when trying to eliminate the problem.

**Cause:** Higher alcohols are the most likely source of harshness, and will mellow with aging, if and only if the yeast is not separated from the beer.
**Solution:** See "Alcohol aroma" for suggestions on how to reduce higher alcohols.

**Cause:** Oxidized polyphenols add astringent and harsh character to beer[213].
**Solution:** Avoid the introduction of oxygen to hot wort or to beer any time after fermentation has begun.

**Cause:** Some hops can be harsher than others, but don't immediately assume that high-alpha hops are more harsh than low- or medium-alpha hops. Some high-alpha hops can lend just as smooth a bitterness as some low-alpha hops.
**Solution:** Try changing hop varieties.

**Cause:** High carbonate water (bicarbonate, actually) has been blamed for harshness, but test batches I have made indicate otherwise – 500 PPM of carbonate/bicarbonate was no more harsh than 50 PPM of carbonate/bicarbonate as long as you compensate for the pH. Astringency adds harshness to beer and since high carbonate/bicarbonate water increases the pH of the mash and when steeping crystal malts, astringent polyphenols are extracted from grain and hops when the pH is high.
**Solution:** If you have high-carbonate/bicarbonate water, adjust the pH so it is around 5.5 with a few drops of lactic or phosphoric acid. Note that polyphenol (a.k.a. tannin) astringency will mellow with aging.

**Cause:** A high-pH boil extracts harsh components from the hops[104,157].
**Solution:** Check your boil pH. If it is higher than 5.5, you may want to add phosphoric, lactic, or some other food-grade acid (1 drop at a time) till the pH is below 5.5. Don't overdo it or you can decrease the amount of break that forms. Note also that a lower pH will decrease hop utilization, so you may have to add more hops to get the same amount of bitterness[104,157].

**Cause:** An excessively long boil can extract harsh components from the hops[104].
**Solution:** For reasonable hop utilization, you should boil the hops in the wort for at least an hour, but to minimize the extraction of unpleasant flavors, you should not boil longer than 2 hours[104].

**Cause:** Even if the carbonate/bicarbonate content of your water is not exceedingly high, you can still extract a lot of polyphenols from your crystal malt if you steep the crystal malt in the entire 5 1/2 to 6 1/2 gallons of brewing water. 1 pound of pale crystal malt in 5 gallons of water can easily result in a pH over 6.5 (this depends on your water, but with my moderate-carbonate/bicarbonate water one pound of 20L crystal in 6 gallons of water yields a pH of 6.8 which is high enough to extract significant polyphenols).
**Solution:** Don't steep crystal malts in the entire 5 1/2 to 6 gallons of brewing water – just steep it in 1 1/2 or 2 gallons of water and then add the rest of the water after removing the grain bag (full boils).

**Cause:** Excessive sodium in the presence of sulfate has been suggested as a source of harshness[66].
**Solution:** If you are using an ion-exchange water softener (the kind to which you add salt blocks or crystals) bypass it for brewing. If your water is naturally high in sodium, you will have to use bottled water for all or part of your brewing water or you can buy a reverse-osmosis water system.

## Metallic flavor

**Cause:** High iron or other metal content in the water is a common source of metallic flavor.
**Solution:** Get a water analysis and check the iron content. Some water filters will remove iron.

**Cause:** The use of mild steel (the kind that rusts) kettles, fermenters, or utensils can give the beer a metallic taste.
**Solution:** Use only stainless steel, aluminum, copper, or plastic utensils.

**Cause:** Over-scrubbing aluminum or stainless steel kettles removes the protective oxide layer and exposes fresh, reactive metal to the wort adding a metallic flavor.
**Solution:** Don't over-scrub – just leave that grayish protective layer. If you must scrub the kettle, don' t use it for a week to allow the oxide layer to reform.

**Cause:** Hydrolysis of grain lipids and then the subsequent oxidation of unsaturated fatty acids can lend a metallic flavor[117].
**Solution:** You should store malt and other grains in a dry environment, ideally in sealed containers or polyethylene bags.

## Not bitter enough

**Cause:** You have poor hop utilization. The most common source of underhopping is forgetting to compensate for wort gravity during the boil. Thick worts extract less bitterness from the hops than thinner worts. If you take a recipe that was designed for a full 5-gallon boil and make it using a partial boil, you will undoubtedly have beer that is not bitter enough.
**Solution:** You need to compensate for the lower hop utilization rate that you get when you boil high gravity wort. See "Hops" in chapter 15.

**Cause:** You didn't add enough hops.
**Solution:** Add more hops next time (or you can add bitterness as late as bottling time with the use of isomerized hop extracts).

**Cause:** You made an IPA from a recipe in *Zymurgy,* but it comes out tasting malty and not bitter. What happened? You followed the recipe to the letter, but the beer comes out under-bittered. Chances are that the water that the recipe author used was high in sulfates and your water is low in sulfates. Sulfate ions dramatically increase the perception of bitterness.
**Solution:** Add sulfates to your water. See chapter 9.

**Cause:** You have too many unfermentables in the wort. A recipe was formulated using, for example, Munton & Fison Dried Malt Extract, but you substituted "Dutch," "Hollander," Northwestern "European," or Laaglander Dried Malt Extract. These last four extracts are not very fermentable and leave a high level of residual sweetness. This residual sweetness overpowers the hop bitterness and it appears that the beer is not bitter enough.
**Solution:** Don't substitute dried malt extracts which are high in unfermentable carbohydrates for dried malt extracts which have average levels of unfermentable carbohydrates.

**Cause:** You added the hops too early in the boil. It has been speculated that the hot break that forms at the beginning of the boil coats the hops and interferes with their utilization. My experiments with First Wort Hopping (a method of imparting hop character to the beer, in which some of the hops are added to warm wort, before it comes to a boil) indicated that the utilization of the "First Wort" hops is significantly lower than a similar amount of hops added after the wort has been boiling for 10 minutes, despite a similar total boiling time.
**Solution:** Let the wort boil for 10 minutes before adding the bittering hops.

**Cause:** You have incomplete fermentation. When the beer comes out too sweet, the bitterness will appear to be insufficient.
**Solution:** See "Too sweet" below.

**Cause:** Your boil pH is too low. If the boil pH is lower than 5.0, the solubility of humulone (the major bittering agent in hops) is severely decreased[104]. There is, however, still some bitterness imparted by the hops (from other bittering compounds in the hops), but not nearly as much as in higher pH boils.
**Solution:** Add calcium carbonate to the boil (a little bit at a time) till the pH is above 5.0.

**Cause:** The use of PVPP (Polyclar AT) removes a small amount of the bitterness[129].
**Solution:** I have not sent samples to the lab to be analyzed, but blind tasting of beer that has been fined with PVPP versus the same beer unfined indicates that the difference is extremely small. I believe that less than 5% of the bitterness will be removed by the use of PVPP.

## Peppery flavor

**Cause:** Alcohol lends a peppery flavor to beer. Higher alcohols add more aroma and flavor than ethyl alcohol.
**Solution:** For suggestions on how to reduce higher alcohol production, see "Alcohol aroma."

**Cause:** Some hop varieties can lend a peppery flavor.
**Solution:** See appendix B for a listing of hop varieties that have a "black pepper" character.

## Raisin flavor

**Cause:** Some dark crystal malts (for example, DeWolf-Cosyns Special B) add a strong raisin-like aroma and flavor to your beer, even at rates of 1/4 pound per 5 gallon batch.
**Solution:** Use dark crystal malts sparingly unless you want a highly raisin/plum aroma and flavor in your beer.

## Salty flavor

**Cause:** High levels of brewing salts can add a salty flavor. Especially sodium and potassium chlorides can add salty flavors.
**Solution:** Take a look at your water analysis and use the right water (diluting with distilled if you must) for each style of beer. See chapter 9.

## Sharp flavor

**Cause:** An overly sharp flavor is most often the result of too much roasted malt or roasted barley in the recipe. Also, acidity can contribute to sharpness. These two sources are related since dark malts add acidity to the beer. If the amount of dark malts is not excessive (let's say not more than 1 pound in a medium-gravity beer) and bacterial sources of acidity are ruled out, perhaps your water has insufficient carbonate. Carbonate ions balance the acidity of the dark malts – it is because of the high levels of naturally occurring carbonates in Dublin water that this city has become world famous for its stouts. In fact, other styles of beer were virtually impossible to brew there until water chemistry was understood by brewers.
**Solution:** Check your boil pH and add calcium carbonate (chalk) to raise the pH to around 5.5 if it is too low.

**Cause:** Bacterial infections can create acidity.
**Solution:** Review Sanitation Procedure.

## Soapy taste

**Cause:** In an experiment done by the First Draft Brewclub in Madison, Wisconsin, a split batch of beer was brewed where one half of the wort was essentially without hot and cold break and the other half included most of the break from the batch. The half that included the break had a shorter lag time, was slightly darker and included a mild "fatty-soapy" taste[153]. Better separation of break from wort has been found to lower fatty acid levels in the finished beer[174].

**Solution:** Try to remove more of the hot and cold break before fermentation.

**Cause:** Weak or too-short a boil. Fatty acids are said to contribute to a soapy taste. Malt is the primary source of free fatty acids in wort. Fatty acid levels are reduced during the boil[174].

**Solution:** Make sure you have a rolling boil for at least an hour.

**Cause:** Weak fermentation can cause increased levels of fatty acids in the finished beer. During fermentation, the concentration of higher (larger) fatty acids drops, whereas the concentration of lower (smaller) fatty acids rises.[174] Factors that accelerate fermentation (higher pitching rates, better oxygenation, higher temperature) result in decreased levels of fatty acids in the finished beer[174].

**Solution:** Pitch more yeast, aerate/oxygenate the cooled wort better, and consider a slightly higher fermentation temperature if reasonable.

**Cause:** Some yeast strains result in increased levels of fatty acids in the finished beer[174].

**Solution:** Try a different yeast strain.

**Cause:** Ginger can add a soapy flavor to beer.

**Solution:** Don't overdo ginger additions. Also note, that aging a few months will mellow-out the ginger character and the "dishwashing soap" taste.

## Sour

**Cause:** Bacterial infections can cause sour flavors.

**Solution:** Review Sanitation Procedures.

**Cause:** Dark grains can add sourness.

**Solution:** See "Sharp flavor" above.

**Cause:** The addition of acids such as lactic, phosphoric or "acid blend" can cause sourness.

**Solution:** Acids, such as lactic and phosphoric, are quite powerful and it does not take much of them to add significant sourness. Add them very carefully, one drop at a time. You may even need to dilute a few drops in cup of water for more control.

## Stale flavor

See "Stale aroma" above.

## Too bitter

**Cause:** You miscalculated your hop utilization. The specific gravity of the boil has a major effect on the hop utilization. Thick worts get a lot less bitterness out of the hops than thin worts. If you take a recipe that was formulated for a 1 1/2-gallon boil, but you make it with a full 5-gallon boil, the beer will be much too bitter.
**Solution:** You must compensate for varying hop utilization when changing the amount of water you are using in the boil. See "Hops" in chapter 15.

**Cause:** You overhopped the beer.
Solution: Don't just guess regarding hop additions. Use a trusted recipe or calculate an estimated bitterness using the formulas in the "Hops" section of chapter 15.

**Cause:** Sulfate increases the perception of bitterness[176,177,178], so the recipe your friend in Pilsen made will taste far too bitter when you make it in Burton-upon-Trent. Recipes rarely give information about the water used, but they should. All the recipes in this book are designed around relatively soft water that is low in sulfate.
**Solution:** If you have high-sulfate water, you will have to either lower the hop rate or dilute your water with distilled.

**Cause:** Sanitation can affect bitterness. It does not affect bitterness directly, but because the residual sweetness in the beer balances the bitterness, if your beer gets infected and all the residual sweetness disappears, the beer will taste too bitter.
**Solution:** Review Sanitation Procedures if you suspect this problem (it often goes hand-in-hand with overcarbonation).

## Too dry

**Cause:** The usual reason that a beer is too dry is a bacterial or wild yeast infection. Most cultured yeasts are only roughly 75% attenuative, leaving a significant sweetness. *Lactobacillus* and *Pediococcus* bacteria, *Saccharomyces diastaticus* and yeasts of the *Brettanomyces* genus can ferment sugars that cultured yeasts cannot. The resulting beer is much too dry, usually overcarbonated and often tastes too bitter.
**Solution:** Review Sanitation Procedures.

**Cause:** Adding amylase enzymes (sometimes labeled "special Pilsner enzyme") at fermentation time can cause too much of the unfermentable sugars and dextrins to be broken down into fermentable ones and leaving the beer too dry.

**Solution:** I recommend against the use of enzymes in the fermenter.

**Cause:** not enough unfermentables in the wort: A recipe was formulated using a pound or two of "Hollander," "Dutch," Laaglander, or Northwestern "European" Dried Malt Extract but you substituted, for example, Munton & Fison Dried Malt Extract. The four former extracts are not very fermentable and leave a high level of residual sweetness. You may also have substituted refined sugar for malt extract – corn, cane, beet, and candi sugar are 100% fermentable and will lead to a drier beer.

**Solution:** Don't substitute dried malt extracts which have *average* levels of unfermentable carbohydrates for dried malt extracts which have *high* levels of unfermentable carbohydrates. Also, don't add too much corn, cane, beet, or candi sugar.

**Cause:** You used a highly attenuative yeast.

**Solution:** Next time, use a low-attenuation yeast (see appendices C, D, and E).

**Cause:** You didn't add enough crystal malt.

**Solution:** If they style of beer allows for a little more caramel flavor, add a bit more crystal malt to the recipe next time.

## Too sweet

**Cause:** Crystal malts add unfermentable sugars and subsequently increase the sweetness of the beer.

**Solution:** Unless you are experimenting with weird flavors, anything more than 2 pounds of crystal malt in a medium-gravity beer would be considered excessive (you can use more in high-gravity beers).

**Cause:** You have incomplete fermentation.

**Solution:** See "Stuck fermentation."

**Cause:** You substituted unfermentable dried malt extracts for normal ones.

**Solution:** There is little you can do other than to add additional bitterness via isomerized hop extract or brew a beer that's too well-attenuated and blend the two into the secondaries.

**Cause:** You tried to imitate a beer that has a lot of non-malt sugars in it, but you made it all-malt. Note that some beers, like Belgian Strong Ales (for example, Duvel) would be much too sweet if they were all malt.

**Solution:** In high-alcohol beers that you do not want to be thick and sweet, you must use some corn, cane, or candi sugar. Upwards of 20% refined sugar may be required to duplicate the original gravity and alcohol level of these beers without being sickeningly sweet and heavy.

**Cause:** Your beer is not bitter enough. Hops balance the sweetness in the beer and a lack of bitterness can make the beer taste too sweet.

**Solution:** See "Not bitter enough" above.

### Yeast bite

**Cause:** Yeast bite is a bitterness due to yeast autolysis (where starving yeast release enzymes that break down the walls of their neighbors). Pitching very weak yeast or severely underoxygenating the wort would probably the only ways you would experience autolysis these days. In my experience, modern dry and liquid yeasts are quite hardy and I've yet to experience the effects of autolysis with them.

**Solution:** There's no way to fix this batch, but in the future, aerate/oxygenate your wort better and don't abuse your yeast: rehydrate dry yeast, don't starve your yeast starters (never let them sit for more than a week at room temperature without feeding) and if all else fails, switch to a different yeast strain.

### Yeasty flavor

**Cause:** A yeasty flavor can come from unflocculent yeast or yeast autolysis.
**Solution:** See "Yeasty aroma."

# Body and mouthfeel

## Astringent

**Cause:** Astringency is a mouth-drying flavor that is felt mostly on the roof and back of the mouth and, underside of the tongue, on the insides of the cheeks. It is caused by polyphenols (a.k.a. tannins) in the beer. Polyphenols come from the grain and hops.

**Solution:** See "Chill haze" in chapter 6 for how to reduce polyphenol extraction. If you are still experiencing astringency, you can try reducing the polyphenols by fining with PVPP (a.k.a. Polyclar) after fermentation. See "Chill haze" in chapter 6 for how to use PVPP. Note that tannic astringency will mellow with aging. One of the reasons that some homebrewing books say that homebrewed beer tastes best after some aging is because the procedures defined in some of these books can extract excessive polyphenols (a.k.a. tannins) and aging will soften the astringency these polyphenols provide. If you minimize polyphenol extraction, most ales will taste best as soon as the beer carbonates and the yeast settles (strong beers benefit from aging as the higher alcohols go through a process called esterification).

**Cause:** Oxidized polyphenols (a.k.a. tannoids) are strong sources of astringency in the beer[230].
**Solution:** Avoid introducing air into the beer after fermentation has started.

## Body too heavy

**Cause:** You have incomplete fermentation.
**Solution:** See "Stuck fermentation."

**Cause:** You used too much crystal malt.
**Solution:** Don't exceed 2 pounds of crystal malt in medium-gravity beers.

**Cause:** Too much malt when making high-alcohol beers that are not meant to be heavy. A typical example is Duvel. A beer with the original gravity and alcohol level of Duvel made from all malt would be excessively sweet and heavy.
**Solution:** You may have to use upwards of 20% cane, corn or candi sugar to make a high-alcohol beer that is not very heavy in body. This is also true for lower alcohol beers that are light-bodied such as American Pilsners. For these beers the non-malt part of the fermentables can be as high as 40%!

## Body too thin

**Cause:** Especially if it is also overcarbonated, bacterial or wild yeast infections are usually to blame for a beer being too thin.
**Solution:** Review Sanitation Procedures.

**Cause:** The use of refined sugars such as cane, corn, or candi sugars reduces body.
**Solution:** Replacing refined sugars with dried malt extract will increase the body.

**Cause:** Your beer has insufficient dextrins.
**Solution:** Add malto-dextrin powder. 8 ounces (weight) in a 5-gallon batch is a typical amount.

**Cause:** You overfiltered the beer.
**Solution:** If you must filter, use a pore size such as 3 microns which will not affect the body too much.

**Cause:** use: The use of proteolytic enzymes (such as papain) can cause the body of the beer to be too thin.
**Solution:** I advise against the use of enzymes in the fermenter.

## Chewy mouthfeel

**Cause:** A chewy mouthfeel is the result of high amounts of small- and medium-sized proteins and, to a lesser extent, dextrins. The amounts of protein in the extract you use has been determined for you by the manufacturer – generally speaking the extracts that give better head retention will also be the ones that give a more chewy mouthfeel.
**Solution:** Select the extract you use based upon the characteristics you want. Familiarize yourself with several different brands – some will be more fermentable and make a drier, thinner beer, others will be less fermentable and will make a sweeter, chewier beer.

**Cause:** You added too much malt. A high-gravity, all-malt beer will be chewy.
**Solution:** If you want to make a high-alcohol beer that is not chewy, you will have to add some sources of fermentables that do not add dextrins or proteins, for example, cane, corn, or candi sugar. DE 62 may be a good choice because its sugar profile is similar to that of all-grain wort, but it doesn't have the proteins that make the beer chewy.

**Cause:** You added excessive crystal malt.
**Solution:** If your beer is too chewy, try cutting back on the crystal malts next time you make this recipe.

**Cause:** Malto-dextrin powder adds a chewy mouthfeel.
**Solution:** Don't overuse malto-dextrin powder.

## Oily mouthfeel

**Cause:** Oats, rye and heather[97] give beer an oily mouthfeel.
**Solution:** While it is impossible to add oats or rye without mashing, one homebrew supplier sells an "Oatmeal Stout" extract. I would not be surprised if more extracts became available with grains such as oats or unmalted barley.

**Cause:** You have a bacterial infection.
**Solution:** Review Sanitation Procedures.

## Silky mouthfeel

**Cause:** Dispensing the beer with a handpump (also called a beer engine) adds a creamy, silky mouthfeel. Goose Island Brewing Company in Chicago often has the same beer available on handpump or via $CO_2$ pressure. The difference is stunning!
**Solution:** Buy a beer engine. An inexpensive trick to imitate a beer engine is to use a 10cc oral syringe you can buy from a drugstore[130]. Pour your beer into a glass as you usually do, but leave 2 additional ounces of space for the head that will be formed. Draw 10cc of the beer into the syringe. Holding the tip just above the surface of the beer in the glass, squirt the contents of the syringe into the glass. This will cause excess carbonation from the beer to be expelled and the beer will have a silkier mouthfeel.

**Cause:** Another way to get a silky mouthfeel is to dispense the beer using a blend of $CO_2$ and nitrogen. This is how draft (and canned) Guinness gets part of its silky mouthfeel. The key is dispensing the beer at high pressure, but with a mixture of $CO_2$ and another gas (like nitrogen) which is not very soluble in beer.
**Solution:** The details of this method is beyond the scope of this book. Kegging systems (including mixed-gas dispensing) are covered in Volume II of this series.

## Warming

**Cause:** Alcohol adds a warming feel to beer. Higher alcohols add more than plain ethyl alcohol.
**Solution:** See "Alcohol aroma."

# Further Reading

DeClerck, J., *A Textbook of Brewing*, Vol. 1 (Chapman and Hall, London, 1957).
Ensminger, P. A., "Light and Beer," *Zymurgy,* 19 (3) 38-43 (Fall 1996).
Fix, G. J., "Diacetyl: Formation, Reduction, and Control," *Brewing Techniques*, 1 (2) 20-25 (Jul/Aug 1993).
Fix, G. J., "Fusel Alcohols," *Zymurgy,* 16 (3) 32-37 (Fall 1993).
Fix, G. J., "Sulfur Flavors in Beer," *Zymurgy,* 15 (3) 40-44 (Fall 1992).
Fix, G. J., "The Detriments of Hot-Side Aeration," *Zymurgy,* 15 (5) 34-40 (Winter 1992).
Fix, G. J., *Principles of Brewing Science* (Brewers Publications, Boulder, 1989).
Foster, T., "Clear Beer Please," *Beer and Brewing Vol. 9* (Brewers Publications, Boulder, Colorado, 1989), 60.
Hough, J. S., D. E. Briggs, R. Stevens, and T.W. Young, *Malting and Brewing Science,* Vol. 1 and 2 (Chapman and Hall, London, 1982).
Hough, J. S., *The Biotechnology of Malting and Brewing*, (Cambridge University Press, Cambridge, 1985).
Korzonas, A. R., "When Fermentation Rears Its Dirty Head," *Brewing Techniques*, 4 (3), 50-54, (May/Jun 1996).
Raines, M., "Methods of Sanitization and Sterilization," *Brewing Techniques*, 1 (2) 30-33 (Jul/Aug 1993).
*Zymurgy Special Issue 1987* "Troubleshooting" 10 (4) (Special 1987).

# 15

# RECIPE FORMULATION

Inevitably, most homebrewers depart from using other brewer's recipes or those printed in books and want to begin formulating their own recipes. To really become a master recipe formulator, you need lots of experience with each component of the recipe: malt, hops, yeast, water, spices, fruits, vegetables, etc. Even with lots of experience, however, rarely is a recipe perfect on the first try. Using the techniques and guidelines in this chapter will help you get close on the first try and reduce the time that it takes you to perfect your recipe.

## Brewing for Competition

In the past, most homebrew judges had the tendency to favor the bigger beers. Even at the American Homebrewers Association National Competition, beers of much higher original gravity and alcohol level for a particular style have been judged as the top beers in their category. Personally, I am against brewing beers intentionally big for style simply to win competitions. Furthermore, judges are becoming more and more sensitive to the overstepping of this style guideline. Nonetheless, currently, targeting the original gravity of your recipe to be at the high end of the range for the style is probably still the wisest course. As judges gain more experience this will diminish in importance and smaller beers will be on equal footing with bigger beers.

One other word of advice: make sure your beer fits the guidelines for the style in all respects. If the guideline says "medium to high hop aroma," make sure that your beer has some kind of hop aroma. Many times I've judged in competitions where none of the entries met *all* of the guidelines. I am quite confident that a beer with one or two minor technical flaws that meets all the guidelines would be judged superior to a technically flawless beer that is missing some defining style characteristics.

Finally, there is a fine line that needs to be walked by judges and brewers alike: the issue of commercial examples versus competition guidelines. Many competitions are based upon guidelines that don't account for the finest commercial examples. Therein lies the problem. What if a brewer presents a perfect copy of the classic commercial version of the style, but it is outside the guidelines set forth for the competition? A very tricky situation, no?

I have faced this dilemma as a brewer and a judge. As a brewer, I have chosen only to stretch the guidelines a bit (55 IBUs are not that far from 48, are they... especially for a style described as "high hop bitterness?"). As a judge, I have chosen to be more lenient when the beer oversteps the guidelines if it is in the direction of a well-known commercial example. However, if another beer in that competition was to be perfect in every way and within the guidelines, I would have to judge that beer superior. Please note that it is not original gravity here that is being debated... no, rather it is the bitterness of Düsseldorf Altbiers and roasted (unmalted) barley in Porters. It would be so much better for both judges and brewers if the authors of the competition style guidelines were more receptive to the advice of experienced judges.

## Learning From Others

The first step in recipe formulation, at least the way that I started formulating my own recipes, is to look at other brewers recipes. Look at as many recipes (especially prize-winning recipes) as you can for the style of beer you would like to brew. When looking at *Zymurgy* Winner's Circle recipes, pay close attention to the judges' comments. If the judges said: "too bitter for style" or "too fruity for a lager" you don't have to discard the recipe, but rather learn from the brewer's mistakes. Look up the problems in chapter 14 and figure out what the brewer did wrong. Then, by comparing the various recipes, you can begin to find similarities and differences.

Your recipe should probably have most of the similarities (if most of the recipes use East Kent Goldings for dryhopping, then you probably want to do the same). Study the differences. Are there any patterns? You may want to include one of the differences especially if the judges' comments reflect this as a positive. For example, if the judges said that a particular Imperial Stout had a nice licorice flavor and the recipe contains a 4-inch stick of brewer's licorice, then you may consider adding that to your recipe. Remember, however, that deviations from the norm are a double-edged sword when it comes to brewing for competitions. What one judge feels is a great innovation, another could consider a fault.

Let's look at an example. Here, side-by-side, are three different recipes for American Brown Ale for a 1.5 gallon boil (remember the boil gravity makes a difference in the hop utilization):

| Recipe 1 | Recipe 2 |
|---|---|
| 6 lb. dark malt extract syrup | 6.6 lb. amber malt extract syrup |
| 6 oz. 40° L crystal malt | 8 oz. 60° L crystal malt |
| 2 oz. 500° L chocolate malt | 4 oz. 550° L chocolate malt |
| 4 oz. 4% AA Mt. Hood pellets (60 min) | 3 oz. 5% AA Cascade pellets (60 min) |
| 2 oz. 4% AA Cascade pellets (15 min) | 1 oz. 5% AA Cascade pellets (15 min) |
| 1 oz. Cascade whole hops (dryhopping) | 3/4 oz. Cascade whole hops (dryhoping) |
| Wyeast American Ale #1056 | BrewTek Calif. Pub Brewery CL-50 |
| 1/2 cup corn sugar for priming | 1/2 cup corn sugar for priming |

### Recipe 3

5 lb. Amber dried malt extract
8 oz. 40° L crystal malt
6 oz. 550° L chocolate malt
4 oz. 4.2% AA Fuggle pellets (60min)
1 oz. 4% Willamette pellets (15min)
1 oz. Cascade whole hops (dryhopping)
Wyeast Irish Ale #1084
1/2 cup corn sugar for priming

So, what can we learn from studying these three recipes? Well, it appears that our recipe should contain either amber or dark malt extract, although in these three recipes, amber is used more often. About 6 to 8 ounces of crystal malt and 2 to 6 ounces of chocolate malt should be used. Bittering hops are quite varied, suggesting that any of the three varieties listed here could be used (actually, many more varieties would be appropriate, but let's focus on these three recipes). Bittering hops vary in AAUs from 15 to 18 (one AAU is one ounce of 1% alpha acids – simply multiply ounces times % alpha acids to get AAUs). Cascade pellets are used for flavor on two of the three recipes, but note that across the three recipes, the flavor hops vary from 4 to 8 AAU. All three recipes agree on whole Cascades for dryhopping and 1/2 cup of corn sugar for priming, but they can't agree on the yeast strain.

For our recipe then, we would probably use 6 pounds of amber or dark malt extract, 8 ounces of 40° L crystal malt and 4 ounces of chocolate malt. For bittering, we would use perhaps 16 AAU of one of the three varieties used in the recipes and 6 AAU of Cascades for flavor and 1 ounce of Cascades for dryhopping. Any one of the three yeasts could be our choice and we would use ¹/₂ cup corn sugar for priming.

# Converting Full-boil to Partial-boil Recipes

A common problem with recipes is when you use a full-boil (all 5 gallons boiled) recipe, but make it using a partial boil or vice versa. Hop utilization is the main concern. If you have a full-boil recipe and you want to make it using a 1.5-gallon boil, you simply need to increase the bittering and flavoring hops by 75% (in other words, multiply the bittering and flavoring hops by 1.75). The aromatic effects of the finishing hops would not be affected by the gravity as much as the boiling or flavor hops so I would either use the weight given in the recipe or perhaps multiply their weight by only 1.25. The dryhops would still be added to the full 5 gallons, so we would not change the amount of dryhops used.

# Converting Partial-boil to Full-boil Recipes

Since the volume boiled in other brewers' partial-boil recipes can vary, I won't give you specific factors by which to multiply the hop quantities. In stead, I recommend that you use the hop utilization formulas under "Hops" in the "Starting From Scratch" section below. First, you calculate the IBUs for each addition in the partial boil recipe. Then use the AAU or MAAU formulas to calculate the amount of hops needed to get the same level of bitterness for a full boil. If the author has not told us their boil volume, all we can do is calculate the hop additions based upon the typical IBUs for the particular style (see appendix A).

# Converting All-grain Recipes

It seems that the majority of prize-winning recipes are all-grain or partial mash recipes these days. Does this mean that we need to brew from grain to win awards? No, of course not. With the high-quality extracts available to homebrewers these days, there is no reason why virtually any recipe could not be converted to an extract recipe and do just as well in competition. I believe that part of the reason that all-grain and partial mash recipes dominate the awards is because by the time that a homebrewer has learned how to formulate recipes, he/she has probably advanced to using grain. This chapter may help extract brewers advance more quickly so they can brew blue-ribbon beers before they advance to grain brewing. Therefore, since there are so many all-grain and partial mash recipes published, we will need a way to convert them to extract batches. Note that if it is an all-grain recipe, it was obviously a full 5-gallon boil and we must compensate for the lower hop utilization if we only do a 1.5 gallon boil.

## The Simple Method

The simplest way to convert from all-grain or partial mash recipes is to multiply the weight of the base malts (Pilsner, Pale Ale, Munich, etc.) by a factor and use the resulting weight in light extract. The reason that this is not very accurate is described in "The Better Method."

When using the Simple Method of converting grain recipes to extract, all you need to do is add up the weight of all the grains that need to be mashed (Pilsner, Pale Ale, Wheat, Vienna, Munich, Toasted, Aromatic, Biscuit and any unmalted grains such as flaked barley or oats) and divide it by 1.3. Therefore, if the recipe calls for 8 pounds of Pale Ale malt, you should use 8.0/1.3 or 6.15 pounds of light extract syrup. You can round this down to 6 pounds.

If you plan to use dried malt extract (which has more sugars per pound because it has less water) you need to use a factor of 1.64 instead. So, if the recipe calls for 8 pounds of Pale Ale malt, you should use 8.0/1.64 or 4.87 pounds of light dried malt extract. You can round this up to 5 pounds.

For the hops, since we are only doing a 1.5-gallon boil, we would need to use approximately 75% more hops. Therefore, we would multiply the weights of the boiling and flavor hops by 1.75 and use those amounts. The aromatic effects of the finishing hops would not be affected by the gravity as much as the boiling or flavor hops so I would either use the weight given in the recipe or perhaps multiply their weight by only 1.25. The dryhops would still be added to the full 5 gallons, so we would not change the amount of dryhops used.

## The Better Method

One problem with the Simple Method is that while any brewer can mix a pound of malt extract with a gallon of water and get the same original gravity, there can be large differences between the original gravities when two brewers mash a pound of grain and make a gallon of wort. Varying equipment, varying temperatures, varying amounts of runnings all contribute to these differences.

To eliminate this problem, first we need to talk about "points" and pounds and points-per-pound-per-gallon. Points are quite simply the original gravity if you take away the 1 to the left of the decimal point and the decimal point itself. These are also called "brewers' degrees" or "excess gravity" (G). Therefore, a

1.057 original gravity wort has 57 points (or 57 brewers' degrees or 57 G). If you take a pound of most malt extract syrups and dissolve it into a gallon of water you will get between 35 and 37 points, or a wort that is between 1.035 and 1.037. Therefore, we speak of extracts (or grains, for that matter) as giving a certain number of points-per-pound-per-gallon or pts/lb/gal. One notable exception is Alexander's Sun Country Pale Malt Extract which only gives 33 pts/lb/gal (but it comes in 4 pound cans).

When it comes to all-grain or partial mashing, one brewer might get 25 pts/lb/gal whereas another may get 32 pts/lb/gal. So, to be more accurate, we need to work backwards from the brewer's original gravity and then figure out how we can get there. I will be covering this technique in great detail in the next section so I'll just outline it here.

First, we take the original gravity (OG) of the recipe and subtract the gravity points contributed by the crystal and dark malts. The points that are left need to be provided by the extract. Perhaps a rough example will illustrate this better. Suppose the OG of the recipe is 1.050 and is made with 11 pounds of Pale Ale malt and 1 pound of crystal malt. We will still use the pound of crystal malt, so we need to subtract its contribution from the OG. Let's assume that the pound of crystal will provide 25 pts/lb/gal. But we're making 5 gallons so we need to divide the 25 by 5 to determine how many points the crystal malt will contribute to the entire 5 gallons. The 1 pound of crystal malt will contribute about 5 points to the OG.

Subtracting 5 from 50 leaves 45 gravity points to get from extracts. If you know exactly how many pts/lb/gal you get from a particular extract, you can use that value, but on the average, syrups give 36 and dried malt extracts give 45. Next, multiply the gravity points you want times the gallons you are brewing. 45 times 5 gallons gives 225 points. Let's say we are using all dried malt extract. If we divide 225 by the 45 pts/lb/gal we get from most dried malt extracts, we find that we need 5 pounds of dried malt extract.

Note that if we would have used the Simple Method, we would have used 6.7 pounds of dried malt extract. The reason for the difference is because the brewer of the recipe got relatively few pts/lb/gal from their grain. Conversely, if the author of the recipe had gotten a lot of pts/lb/gal from their grain, the Better Method would account for that too.

This method should work quite well as long as the grain used in the original recipe is Pilsner or Pale Ale malts. We introduce another deviation from the original recipe when we substitute light extract for Vienna, Munich, Aromatic or other types of high-kilned malts. You can correct for these deviations slightly, by adding a little more crystal malt for the darker base malts, but the flavors will not be exact. If you can get Munich malt extract (for example Marie's™ Munich Malt Extract or William's Brewing German Gold) it will substitute adequately for the Munich malt (these two extracts are made with $1/2$ Munich malt and $1/2$ pale malt).

For the hops (just as in the Simple Method) since we are only doing a 1.5-gallon boil, we would need to use approximately 75% more hops. Therefore, we would multiply the weights of the bittering and flavor hops by 1.75 and use those amounts. Since the aromatic effects of the finishing hops would not be affected by gravity as much as the bittering or flavor hops, I recommend multiplying the finishing hops (if the recipe calls for them) by 1.25. The dryhops would still be added to the full 5 gallons, so we would not change the amount of dryhops used.

## Style Guidelines

After a while, you will be able to judge the proper amount of each ingredient to use for a given style. When you are just starting out, you may have a little difficulty. So, to give you a starting point, I'll suggest some guidelines. These guidelines assume 5-gallon batches, malt extract syrups are used, that *only 1 1/2 gallons of wort are boiled* (if you do a full boil, you will have to use less hops), that hop pellets are used in hop bags and that the non-blowoff method of fermentation is used. When "light/amber/dark extract" is specified, it means that any of the three are acceptable. Regarding hop varieties, the suggested hops are based upon character and not necessarily the country of origin. Therefore, "American" hops include Cascade, Centennial, Columbus, and Willamette. "English" hops include East Kent Goldings, Fuggles, Target, Styrian Goldings and other Goldings. "German" hops include Hallertauer, Hersbrucker, Mount Hood and Liberty. "Czech" hops include Saaz and Ultra. See appendix D for yeast suggestions.

# Ales (Table 15-1)

| Style | Malts & Sugars | Hops | Other Important Factors |
|---|---|---|---|
| **American Brown Ale** | 1 - 4 oz chocolate malt<br>0 - 1# light crystal<br>OR 0 - 1/2# dark crystal<br>5 - 6# light/amber extract | American<br>7-17 AAU (60 min)<br>2 - 5 AAU (15 min)<br>0 - 1 oz dryhopping | wide range of bittering AAUs reflects the wide range of OGs – use more hops for higher OGs; |
| **American Pale Ale** | 0 - 1# light crystal<br>5 - 7# light extract | American<br>5 - 17 AAU (60 min)<br>2 - 5 AAU (15 min)<br>0 - 1 oz dryhopping | wide range of bittering AAUs reflects the wide range of OGs – use more hops for higher OGs; |
| **Barleywine** | | | |
| American Barleywine | 0 - 1/2 oz chocolate malt<br>0 - 2# crystal<br>12 1/2 - 16# light extract | American<br>20 - 50 AAU (60 min)<br>0-10 AAU (15 min)<br>0 - 1 oz dryhopping | because of the high gravity, you must use a 2.5 gallon boil (I've accounted for it in the hop additions already); use a very large starter and aerate well; |
| English Barleywine | 0 - 1/2 oz chocolate malt<br>1 - 2# crystal<br>9 - 16# light extract<br>0 - 1# corn sugar | English<br>20 - 50 AAU (60 min)<br>0 - 10 AAU (15 min) | because of the high gravity, you must use a 2.5 gallon boil (I've accounted for it in the hop additions already); use a very large starter and aerate well; |
| **Belgian Ale** | 0 - 1 oz chocolate malt<br>0 - 1# light crystal<br>OR 0 - 1/2# dark crystal<br>5 - 6# light/amber extract | German/Czech<br>5 - 15 AAU (60 min)<br>0 - 2 AAU (15 min) | often spiced with coriander, grains of paradise and other spices; |
| **Belgian Strong Ale** | | | |
| **Belgian Strong Golden Ale** | 0 - 1# very light crystal<br>7 - 9# light extract<br>1 - 2# corn or cane sugar | German/Czech<br>5 - 17 AAU (60 min)<br>0 - 4 AAU (15 min)<br>0 - 1 oz dryhopping | use a very big starter; sometimes spiced; |

| | | | |
|---|---|---|---|
| **Other Belgian Strong Ales** | 0 - 1# crystal<br>7 - 11# light/amber extract<br>1 - 2# corn or cane sugar | German/Czech<br>5 - 20+ AAU (60 min)<br>0 - 4 AAU (15 min)<br>0 - 1 oz dryhopping | use a very big starter; sometimes spiced; |
| **Biére de Garde** | 0 - 1 oz chocolate malt<br>0 - 1# light crystal<br>7 - 9# light extract | German/Czech<br>5 - 17 AAU (60 min)<br>0 - 4 AAU (15 min) | yeast selection very important – check appendix D; use a big starter; |
| **Bitter** | | | |
| Ordinary Bitter | 0 - $^1/_2$ oz chocolate malt<br>$^1/_2$ - 1# crystal<br>3.3 - 5# light/amber extract | English<br>5 - 12 AAU (60 min)<br>1 - 4 AAU (15 min)<br>0 - $^1/_2$ oz dryhopping | high-sulfate water is important; |
| Special or Best Bitter | 0 - $^1/_2$ oz chocolate malt<br>$^1/_2$ - 1# crystal<br>$4^1/_2$ - 6# light/amber extract | English<br>10 - 15 AAU (60 min)<br>1 - 4 AAU (15 min)<br>0 - 1 oz dryhopping | high-sulfate water is important; |
| Extra Special Bitter | 0 - $^1/_2$ chocolate malt<br>$^1/_2$ - $1^1/_2$# crystal<br>$5^1/_2$ - 8# light/amber extract<br>0 - $^1/_2$# corn sugar | English<br>12 - 24 AAU (60 min)<br>2 - 5 AAU (15 min)<br>0 - 1 oz dryhopping | high-sulfate water is important; |
| Strong Export Bitter | 1 - $1^1/_2$# crystal<br>7 - $8^1/_2$# light/amber extract<br>0 - 1# corn sugar | English<br>22 - 32 AAU (60 min)<br>2 - 5 AAU (15 min)<br>0 - 1 oz dryhopping | high-sulfate water is important; |
| **English Brown Ale** | | | |
| Northern-style English Brown Ale | $^1/_2$ - 1# light crystal<br>5 - 7# light/amber extract | English<br>5 - 12 AAU (60 min)<br>0 - 2 AAU (15 min) | use crystal malt no darker than 20 L; |
| Southern-style English Brown Ale | $^1/_4$ - $^1/_2$# chocolate malt<br>$^1/_4$ - 1# light crystal<br>OR $^1/_4$ - $^1/_2$# dark crystal<br>$4^1/_2$ - 6# light/amber/dark extract | English<br>$3^1/_2$ - 9 AAU (60 min)<br>0 - 2 AAU (15 min) | don't overdo the chocolate malt; |
| English Dark Mild | $^1/_4$ - $^1/_2$# chocolate malt<br>$^1/_4$ - 1# light crystal<br>OR $^1/_4$ - $^1/_2$# dark crystal<br>3.3 - 5# light/amber/dark extract | English<br>$3^1/_2$ - 9 AAU (60 min)<br>0 - 2 AAU (15 min) | be careful to not overdo the chocolate; |

| | | | |
|---|---|---|---|
| **English**<br>**Old**<br>**Ale** | 0 - 2 oz chocolate malt<br>1 - 2# crystal<br>6 - 10# light extract<br>0 - 1# corn sugar<br>0 - $^1/_2$ cup molasses | English<br>13 - 32 AAU (60 min)<br>2 - 4 AAU (15 min)<br>0 - 1 oz dryhopping | wide range of bittering AAUs reflects the wide range of OGs – use more hops for higher OGs; |
| **Flanders**<br>**Brown Ale** | 0 - 1 oz chocolate malt<br>$^1/_4$ - $^3/_4$# dark crystal<br>6 - 8$^1/_2$# light extract | German/Czech<br>6 - 14 AAU (60 min) | ferment with Flanders Brown Ale yeast and bacteria; if you can get Munich malt extract, use it in place of the light extract and don't add any chocolate malt; |
| **Flanders**<br>**Red Ale** | $^1/_4$ - $^1/_2$# medium crystal<br>0 - 1 oz chocolate malt<br>5 - 7$^1/_2$# light crystal<br>$^1/_2$ - 1# corn sugar | German/Czech<br>6 - 14 AAU (60 min) | ferment with Flanders Red Ale yeast and bacteria; if you can get Munich malt extract, use $^1/_2$ light extract and $^1/_2$ Munich malt extract; aging in oak or with oak chips would add an additional authenticity; |
| **India Pale Ale** | | | |
| Traditional English-Style India Pale Ale | 0 - $^1/_2$# very light crystal<br>8 - 12# light extract | English<br>32 - 60 AAU (60 min) | because of the high gravity, you must use a 2.5 gallon boil (I've accounted for it in the hop additions already), use a very large starter; |
| American-style India Pale Ale | 0 - 1# very light crystal<br>6$^1/_2$ - 10# light extract | American<br>12 - 32 AAU (60 min) | because of the high gravity, you must use a 2.5 gallon boil (I've accounted for it in the hop additions already), use a very large starter; |
| **Kölsch** | 0 - 1# very light crystal<br>5 - 7# light extract | German/Czech<br>5 - 13 AAU (60 min)<br>0 - 2 AAU (15 min) | ferment at the cool end of the ale range and then larger cold; |
| **Lambiek/Lambic** | | | |
| Lambiek /Lambic | 0 - 1# very light crystal<br>6 - 7$^1/_2$# wheat extract | 3 oz of three-year old whole hops (or fresh whole hops that have been baked for 20 min in a 250° F oven) | yeast and bacteria are crucial to this style – see appendix D; |

| Geuze /Gueuze | 0 - 1# very light crystal<br>6 - 7$\frac{1}{2}$# wheat extract | 3 oz of three-year old whole hops (or fresh whole hops that have been baked for 20 min in a 250° F oven) | yeast and bacteria are crucial to this style – see appendix D; made by blending old (2-3 years) and young (1 year) Lambiek/Lambic and then bottling the mixture; |
|---|---|---|---|
| Faro | 0 - 1# very light crystal<br>6 - 7$\frac{1}{2}$# wheat extract | 3 oz of three-year old whole hops (or fresh whole hops that have been baked for 20 min in a 250° F oven) | yeast and bacteria are crucial to this style – see appendix D; see appendix A for more on this style; |
| Fruit Lambieks /Lambics | 0 - 1# very light crystal<br>6 - 7$\frac{1}{2}$ wheat extract<br>3 - 7# fruit | 3 oz of three-year old whole hops (or fresh whole hops that have been baked for 20 min a 250° F oven) | yeast and bacteria are crucial this style – see appendix D; |
| **Porter** | | | |
| Original 1722-style Porter or Entire | 2 - 4 oz black malt<br>$\frac{1}{4}$ - $\frac{1}{2}$# smoked crystal<br>7$\frac{1}{2}$ - 12# light/amber extract | English<br>20 - 50+ AAU (60 min)<br>2 - 4 AAU (15 min) | the use of black malts is not at all authentic, but the proper malts must be mashed; probably had a lactic sourness so it would require use of lactic bacteria or lactic acid in addition to the various yeasts including *Brettanomyces*); |
| Porter (Modern) | $\frac{1}{4}$ - 1# chocolate malt OR $\frac{1}{4}$ - $\frac{3}{4}$# black malt<br>$\frac{1}{4}$ - 1# crystal<br>5 - 8# light/amber/dark extract | English<br>9 - 24 AAU (60 min)<br>2 - 4 AAU (15 min) | this is a great style to begin with because the dark malts can cover many mistakes; |
| **Saison** | 0 - 1# light or medium crystal<br>6 - 10# light extract<br>1 - 2# corn or cane sugar | German Czech<br>5 - 17 AAU (60 min)<br>0 - 4 AAU (15 min)<br>0 - 1 oz dryhopping | yeast important – see appendix D; can be spiced with spices such as star anise or dried sweet orange peel (Belgian, not navel oranges); |

| Scottish Ale | | | |
|---|---|---|---|
| Light or 60/- | 0 - 4 oz roasted barley<br>$1/2$ - 1# crystal<br>3 - 5# light/amber extract | English<br>4 - 10 AAU (60 min)<br>0 - 2AAU (15 min)<br>0 - $1/2$ oz dryhopping | ferment on the cool end of the ale range and use a big starter; |
| Heavy or 70/- | 0 - 4 oz roasted barley<br>$1/2$ - 1# crystal<br>5 - 6# light/amber extract | English<br>6 - 12 AAU (60 min)<br>0 - 2 AAU (15 min)<br>0 - $1/2$ oz dryhopping | ferment on the cool end of the ale range and use a big starter; |
| Export or 80/- | 0 - 4 oz roasted barley<br>$1/2$ - 1# crystal<br>6 - 7# light/amber extract | English<br>6 - 20 AAU (60 min)<br>0 - 2 AAU (15 min)<br>0 - $1/2$ oz dryhopping | ferment on the cool end of the ale range and use a big starter; |
| 90/- and Strong Scottish Ale | 0 - $1/2$ roasted barley<br>$1/2$ - 2# crystal<br>7 -13# light amber extract | English<br>11 - 40+ AAU (60 min)<br>0 - 2 AAU (15 min) | wide range of bittering AAUs reflects the wide range of OGs – use more hops for higher OGs; ferment on the cool end of the ale range and use a big starter; |
| Stout | | | |
| Dry Stout | $1/4$ - $1/2$# roasted barley<br>0 - $1/4$# black malt<br>4 - $61/2$# light/amber/dark extract | English<br>9 - 14 AAU (60 min)<br>0 - 2 AAU (15 min) | use a big starter of some alternative yeast; make sure to aerate well; |
| Foreign style Stout | $1/4$ - $1/2$# roasted barley<br>0 - $1/4$# black malt<br>6 - 10# light/amber/dark extract | English<br>14 - 30 AAU (60 min)<br>0 - 2 AAU (15 min) | wide range of bittering AAUs relfects the wide range of OGs use more hops for higher OGs; |
| Imperial Stout / Original Baltic Porter | 0 - 1# roasted barley<br>$1/4$ - 1# black malt<br>9 - 14# light/amber/dark extract | English<br>25 - 50+ AAU (60 min) | because of the high gravity, you must use a 2.5 gallon boil (I've accounted for it in the hop additions already); use a very large starter and aerate well; |
| Oatmeal Stout | 0 -$1/2$# roasted barley<br>0 -$1/4$#black malt<br>$41/2$ - 8# oatmeal stout extract | English<br>14 - 30 AAU (60 min)<br>0 - 2 AAU (15 min) | do *not* use raw oatmeal – it will only make the beer cloudy; |

| | | | |
|---|---|---|---|
| Sweet Stout | 0 - $1/2$# roasted barley<br>2 - 4 oz black malt<br>$1/2$ - 1# crystal malt<br>$41/2$ - 8# light/amber/dark extract<br>0 - 1# lactose | English<br>14 - 30 AAU (60 min)<br>0 - 2 AAU (15 min) | don't use more than $1/2$# of dark crystal; lactose can be added at bottling time to taste; espcially watch sanitation if you use lactose; |

**Trappist/Abbey Ales**

| | | | |
|---|---|---|---|
| Dubbel | $1/2$ - 4 oz chocolate malt<br>0 - 4 oz Special B crystal<br>$41/2$ - 10# light crystal<br>1 - $11/2$# dark candi or carmelized cane sugar | German/Czech<br>5 - 17 AAU (60 min) | if you can get Munich malt extract, use that in place of the light extract and omit the chocolate malt; yeast selection important – see appendix D; |
| Tripel | 0 - 1# very light crystal<br>7 - 10# light extract<br>1 - 2# corn or cane sugar | German/Czech<br>5 - 17 AAU (60 min)<br>0 - 4 AAU (15 min)<br>0 - 1 oz dryhopping | ferment on the cool end of the ale range and use a big starter; |

**Wheat Beers**

| | | | |
|---|---|---|---|
| American Wheat | 0 - 1# light crystal<br>5 - $71/2$# wheat extract | American/German<br>4 - 12 AAU (60 min) | this is a tough style – there is little to cover up any mistakes; |
| Bavarian Weizen | 0 - 1# light crystal<br>5 - $71/2$# wheat extract | German/Czech<br>4 - 8 AAU (60 min) | yeast selection very important – see appendix D; |
| Berliner Weiss | 0 - $1/2$# light crystal<br>3.3. - $51/2$# wheat extract | German/Czech<br>2 - 3 AAU (60 min) | use the light crystal only for the low-end original gravities; add lactic acid or a lactic acid bacterial culture; |
| Dunkelweizen | $1/2$ - 2 oz chocolate malt<br>0 - 1# crystal<br>5 - $71/2$# wheat extract | German/Czech<br>4 - 8 AAU (60 min) | yeast selection very important – see appendix D; the chocolate malt is not quite right for the style, but it is the only alternative; |
| Weizenbock | 0 - 1# cyrstal<br>$81/2$ - 11# wheat extract | German/Czech<br>12 - 30 AAU (60 min) | yeast selection very important – see appendix D; |

| White, Witbier or Bière Blanche | $3/4$ - 1# very light crystal<br>5 - 7# wheat extract | German/Czech<br>6 - 12 AAU (60 min) | requires $1^1/4$ oz ground coriander (last 5 min of boil); if available, $^1/_2$ oz of Curaçao orange peel (not navel orange); yeast and lactic bacteria selection very important – see appendix D; see appendix A for more information; |
|---|---|---|---|

## Lagers (Table 15-2)

| Style | Malts & Sugars | Hops | Other Important Factors |
|---|---|---|---|
| **American Lager** | | | |
| American Pilsner | 3 - $5^1/_2$# extra light extract<br>1 - 2# corn sugar<br>OR 1 - 2# rice syrup solids | German/Czech<br>4 - 8 AAU (60 min) | use a large starter; |
| American Dark | 1 - 2 oz black malt<br>3 - $5^1/_2$# extra light extract<br>1 - 2# corn sugar<br>OR 1 - 2# rice syrup solids | German/Czech<br>4 - 8 AAU (60 min) | use a large starter; |
| Malt Liquor | 4 - 5# extra light extract<br>2 - 3# corn sugar<br>OR 2 - 3# rice syrup solids | American/Czech<br>6 - 10 AAU (60 min) | use a large starter; |
| Pre-Prohibition American Lager | 4 - 6# extra light extract<br>1 - 2# corn sugar<br>OR 1 - 2# rice syrup solids | American/German<br>12 - 25 AAU (60 Min) | use a large starter; |
| Post-Prohibition American Lager | 3 - $5^1/_2$# extra light extract<br>1 -2# corn sugar<br>OR 1 - 2# rice syrup solids | American/German<br>6 - 16 AAU (60 min) | use a large starter; |
| Robust American Lager | 0 - 1 oz chocolate malt<br>$^1/_2$ - 1# crystal<br>6 - 7# light/amber extract | German/Czech<br>6 - 17 AAU (60 min)<br>0 - 4 AAU (15 min)<br>0 - 1 oz dryhopping | use a large starter; |

| Bock | | | |
|---|---|---|---|
| Traditional German Bock | $1/4$ - $1/2$# chocolate malt<br>$1/4$ - $1/2$# crystal<br>8 - 10# light/amber extract | German/Czech<br>6 - 22 AAU (60 min)<br>0 - 2 AAU (15 min) | use a large starter; chocolate malt is not quite appropriate, but it's the best we can do unless you can get Munich malt extract (in which case you should not use any chocolate malt; |
| Helles Bock | $1/4$ - $1/2$# light crystal<br>8 - 10# light/amber extract | German/Czech<br>6 - 22 AAU (60 min)<br>0 - 2 AAU (15 min) | use a large starter; |
| Doppelbock | $1/4$ - $1/2$# crystal<br>10 - 14# light/amber extract | German/Czech<br>15 - 33 AAU (60 min)<br>0 - 2 AAU (15 min) | use a very large starter or; ideally, use the dregs from a previous batch; |
| Eisbock | $1/4$ - $1/2$# crystal<br>10 - 14# light/amber extract | German/Czech<br>15 - 33 AAU (60 min)<br>0 - 2 AAU (15 min) | use a very large starter traditionally, once the beer has finished fermenting, it is frozen and ice is removed; since the yeast has probably been killed by freezing, the resulting beer must be force-carbonated; |
| **Continental Dark** | 1 - 2 oz chocolate malt<br>$1/4$ - $1/2$# crystal<br>5 - 7# light/amber extract<br>$1/2$ - 1# corn sugar | German/Czech<br>6 - 10 AAU (60 min) | use a large starter; |

| | | | |
|---|---|---|---|
| **Dortmunder / Export** | 7 - 8# light extract | German/Czech<br>9 - 15 AAU (60 min) | use a large starter; this style requires relatively high sulfate levels; |
| **Dortmund-style Altbier** | 1 - 2 oz chocolate malt<br>5 - 7# light/amber extract | German/Czech<br>9 - 20 AAU (60 min) | use a large starter, this style requires relatively high sulfate levels; |
| **Munich Helles** | $^1/_4$ - $^1/_2$# light crystal<br>6 - 7$^1/_2$# light extract | German/Czech<br>7 - 12 AAU (60 min)<br>0 - 2 AAU (15 min) | use a large starter; |
| **Munich Dunkel** | $^1/_4$ - $^1/_2$# chocolate malt<br>$^1/_4$ - $^1/_2$# light crystal<br>6 - 7$^1/_2$# light/amber extract | German/Czech<br>5 - 14 AAU (60 min)<br>0 - 2 AAU (15 min) | use a large starter; chocolate malt is not quite appropriate, but it's the best we can do unless you can get Munich malt extract (in which case you should not use any chocolate malt); |
| **Oktoberfest / Märzen** | $^1/_4$ - $^1/_2$# light crystal<br>2 - 4 oz dark crystal<br>7 - 9# light extract | German/Czech<br>7 - 15 AAU (60 min) | use a large starter; lots of crystal malt is not quite right for this style (nor is chocolate malt), but it's the best we can do without Munich malt extract; if you can get Munich malt extrract, use half light half Munich malt extract and don't use any of the dark crystal malt; |

| Pilsner | | | |
|---|---|---|---|
| Bohemian Pilsner | 1/4 - 1/2# light crystal<br>6 - 71/2# light extract | Saaz<br>13 - 17 AAU (60 min)<br>2 - 4 AAU (15 min)<br>1 - 2 oz (1 min) | unless your water extremely soft, use distilled water for this beer; use a large starter; |
| German Pilsner | 1/4 - 1/2# very light crystal<br>6 - 7# light extract | German/Czech<br>10 - 15 AAU (60 min)<br>0 - 2 AAU (15 min)<br>0 - 1/2 oz (1 min) | use a large starter; |
| Dutch Pilsner | 1/4 - 1/2# very light crystal<br>5 - 7# light extract | German<br>4 - 9 AAU (60 min)<br>0 - 1/2 oz (1 min) | use a large starter; |
| **Rauchbier** | 0 - 1/2# light smoked crystal<br>2 - 4 oz dark smoked crystal<br>61/2 - 10# light extract | German<br>5 - 20 AAU (60 min) | you can't buy smoked crystal malt, but you can make it in a smoker (see "Smoked Malt" later in this chapter); wide range of bittering AAUs reflects the wide range of OGs - use more hops for higher OGs; |
| **Schwarzbier and Black Beer** | | | |
| Schwarzbier | 1/2 - 11/2# black malt<br>1/2 - 1# crystal<br>21/2 - 41/2# amber/dark extract<br>2# Laaglander, "Dutch" or Northwestern "European" dried malt extract | German<br>11 - 16 AAU (60 min) | the dried malt extracts suggested are not very fermentable and are used to leave a high final gravity and signficant sweetness; |
| Black Beer | 1/4 - 1/2# black malt<br>41/2 - 6# light extract<br>1# corn sugar | German<br>6 - 11 AAU (60 min) | use a large starter; |
| **Vienna** | 1/4 - 1/2# light crystal<br>2 - 4 oz dark crystal | German/Czech<br>7 - 14 AAU (60 min) | use a large starter; |

# Mixed Styles (Table 15-3)

| Style | Malts and Sugars | Hops | Other Important Factors |
|-------|------------------|------|-------------------------|
| **Altbier** | | | |
| Düsseldorf-style Altbier | $1/4$ - $1/2$# chocolate malt<br>6 - 7# light/amber extract | German<br>16 - 22 AAU (60 min) | the chocolate malt is not quite authentic, but using the proper malts would require mashing; ferment at 55 to 60° F and then cold condition at 40 to 45° F; if you can get Munich malt extract, use it in place of the light or amber extract; |
| Sticke | $1/4$ - $1/2$# chocolate malt<br>7 - 8# light/amber extract | German<br>16 - 22 AAU (60 min)<br>$1/2$ -1 oz dryhopping | ferment at 55 to 60° F and then cold condition at 40 to 45° F; if you can get Munich malt extract, use it in place of the light or amber extract; |
| Münster-style Altbier | $1/4$ - $1/2$# very light crystal<br>$51/2$ - 6# wheat extract | German<br>5 - 8 AAU (60 min) | ferment with ale yeast and then condition at 60 to 65° F for 6 months with a lactic bacteria; |

| **Blonde Ale/Lager** | 5 - 7# light extract<br>0 - 1# corn sugar | American/German<br>5 - 12 AAU (60 min)<br>0 - 2 AAU (15 min)<br>0 - 1/2 oz (1 min) | Range of bittering AAUs reflects the range of OGs – use more hops for use more hopps for higher OGs; |
|---|---|---|---|
| **California Common Beer** | 1/4 - 1/2# light crystal<br>1 - 3 oz dark crystal<br>6 - 7# light extract | US Northern Brewer<br>4 - 5 AAU (60 min) | ferment at temperatures juice (without with lager yeast and then cold-condition; |
| **Fruit** Beer | 1/2 - 1# light crystal<br>51/2 - 6# light/wheat extract | Any type<br>4 - 5 AAU (60 min) | add some sanitized fruit or juice (without preservatives) in the secondary; |

# Starting From Scratch

Now that we have a basic idea of how we formulate recipes, let's begin with the details. The steps below are listed in order that they should be performed. Note that we will be working on duplicating a commercial beer. If you are trying to brew an original beer, you must envision the beer you want to create. Note that in the rest of this chapter, we will be assuming that we're making a 5-gallon batch of the target beer.

## Assessing the Target Beer

The first step is usually assessing the target beer. I suppose you could try to brew a beer you have never tasted (and this has been done, with Düsseldorf Altbiers, for example), but this is rare. Consider all aspects of the beer using the methods described in chapter 13. Take notes – you will refer back to them often. Next, read the rest of this chapter with a glass of the target beer in your hand, assessing each component of the flavor and determining the ingredients you need to add to gain each particular aspect of the beer.

## Reading and Researching

You can make your job much easier if you read about and research your target beer. The first place I usually look is in Fred Eckhardt's *The Essentials of Beer Style*. This book lists hundreds of commercial beers along with their original and final gravities as well as their alcohol content, bitterness (in International Bittering Units or IBUs) and color. Other books that I frequently use are Michael Jackson's *Pocket Guide to Beer*, *The New World Guide to Beer*, *Beer Companion*, and *The Great Beers of Belgium*. For British beers, I refer to The

*Real Ale Drinker's Almanac* by Roger Protz and *Brewing Real Ale at Home* by Graham Wheeler and Roger Protz. Note that this last book assumes very low extraction rates for mashing and very low hop utilization – my advice is to adjust the values listed in the recipes to more closely match your own extractions and utilizations.

Also, there is a lot of information to be gained from the Classic Beer Style Series from Brewers Publications, however I would put more weight in the main text of the book than in the recipes in back since the authors often don't use their own good advice in their recipes. Every issue of Brewing Techniques contains an article on one of the classic beer styles. Other than the one on Altbiers, they tend to be quite accurate. Finally, there are a number of excellent articles on world-famous breweries in current and back issues of Zymurgy. For example, there has been an article by Darryl Richman on the brewers of Pilsner Urquell, Martin Lodahl and Phil Seitz have both written articles on brewing various Belgian styles and there is an article by Roger Deschner on Düsseldorfer Altbiers.

This research can turn up things like (and these are *real* examples) the lagering time and temperature of Pilsner Urquell, the hop varieties used in Orval or that Rodenbach contains flaked corn (maize). Every little bit of information you can extract from books is a step closer to duplicating a commercial beer. You can even gain valuable knowledge on brewery tours. Usually, the tour guide doesn't know much about brewing, but 9 times out of 10 the brewmaster will take you aside and answer your questions when they find out you're a homebrewer.

## Crystal Malts

Crystal malts have their primary flavors, which are common to all crystal malts, and flavor overtones, which differ from one malt to another. The primary flavors are caramel and a little sweetness. Darker crystal malts have more intense caramel flavors and the very dark crystal malts can have a little roasted malt bite too. For example, some of the lighter Briess crystal malts have wonderful "milk chocolate" overtones. Durst Dunkel Crystal has definite apricot overtones. See chapter 7 for details on the flavor overtones of many crystal malts available to homebrewers.

When you taste the target beer, does it have a light caramel flavor and aroma or a rich caramel flavor and aroma or no caramel flavor or aroma at all? If it has no caramel at all, you can still use 1/2 pound or so of a light crystal (e.g. Caramel Pils) malt to get a little sweetness, body and improve head retention, but be careful — some of the very light crystal malts require mashing (see chapter 7). For a light caramel flavor, use 1/2 to 1 pound of 10 to 20° Lovibond crystal malt. Medium caramel flavor requires 1/2 to 1 pound of 20 to 40° Lovibond crystal malt or about 1/4 to 1/2 pound of a darker, 50 to 80° Lovibond crystal malt.

Be careful when adding the medium or dark crystal malts in excess of 1/2 pound because they can add a dark, sharp or burnt flavor that you may not have expected. Small amounts (1 to 4 ounces) of dark crystal malts add a nice complexity to amber and even to pale beers. Very dark crystal malts can add a rich caramel flavor along with other intriguing flavors and aromas to amber and dark beers. You should use no more than 1/2 pound of very dark crystal malt unless you're making something very big like an Imperial Stout. The darkest crystal malts can be used in place of some or all of the black malt in a dark beer when you want to add less sharpness than you get with chocolate and black malts, but remember that you may also be adding sweetness and other flavors such as raisin or ripe fruit which may be out-of-place.

Sometimes, you will need to use the overtones provided by the crystal malts as a primary flavor component. For example, when trying to duplicate Chimay Grande Reserve, you will need to use from 1/4 to 1/2 pound of DeWolf-Cosyns Special B crystal malt to get this beer's distinctive raisin-like aroma and flavor.

Finally, because crystal malts are so different in flavor and aroma, adding smaller amounts of different crystal malts adds depth of character and complexity to beers. For example, if you are having problems with a Special Bitter having a one-dimensional character, try replacing that 1 pound of 20° Lovibond crystal in the recipe with 1/2 pound of Mich. Weyermann Carahell®, plus 1/4 pound of Briess 20° Lovibond crystal, plus two ounces each of Durst Cara-Munich and DeWolf-Cosyns Caramunich.

## Dark Grains

Dark grains include chocolate malt, black malt (a.k.a. roasted malt, a.k.a. black patent malt) and roasted (unmalted) barley. Chocolate malt, in my opinion, does lend a slight chocolaty flavor. It adds a rich, dark malt flavor with much less sharpness than black malt. Dark malts impart an aroma similar to the crust of a dark bread such as pumpernickel or dark rye. Of course dark grains add color. Note that a small amount of roasted (unmalted) barley adds a reddish tint to beer, so if you insist on making a "red animal" beer, about 1 ounce of roasted barley should do the trick.

For a small amount of dark malt character in an amber beer, 1 to 4 ounces of chocolate or 1 to 2 ounces of black malt is about right. Some commercial brewers use what would be equivalent to about 1/10 to 1/16 ounce of black malt in pale beers to add some color without adding virtually any dark malt flavor. For color and flavor in a Southern-style English Brown Ale, use 1/4 to 1/2 pound of chocolate malt along with some medium or dark crystal malts. For an extract Munich Dunkel (which should, technically, get its color from Munich Malt in an all-grain recipe) try 1/4 to 1/2 pound of chocolate malt, and 1/4 to 1/2 pound of medium to dark crystal malt. Mich. Weyermann has a variety of dark malts called "Carafa®" that range from a chocolate malt color to a black malt color. The lightest, Carafa® I, has a color in the range of 300 - 340° Lovibond and is a very smooth chocolate malt.

Don't use more than 4 ounces of black malt in anything other than a Porter, Stout, or a very big (high-gravity) brown beer because it will add too much sharpness. I would recommend avoiding black malt in any beer that is supposed to have a smooth malt flavor (like a Munich Dunkel).

For Porters and Stouts, you can use 1/2 to 1 pound of chocolate malt or you can substitute black malt for some of the chocolate, but I would not exceed 1/2 pound of black malt in anything but a very big Porter or an Imperial Stout. Roasted barley is required in Dry and Foreign-style Stouts – use about 1/4 to 1/2 pound. You can also use smaller amounts in other Stouts for some coffee-like aroma and a "drying" character in the flavor. In Imperial Stouts I tend to use 1/2 to 1 pound of roasted barley, but depending on how big it is, you can use more that that. When it comes to Imperial Stouts, it is difficult to overdo the dark malts as long as you balance their acidity with carbonates (see chapter 9). In my last two Imperial Stouts, I used 1 1/2 pounds of black malt which was just about right. I used only 1/2 pound of roasted barley, but feel that 1 pound would not have been too much. However, these were 1.098 and 1.120 beers!

## High-Kilned Malt Extracts

Certain beer styles get their characteristic malt flavors from high-kilned malts such as Vienna and Munich. These malts require mashing, so we cannot use them in extract beers directly. To the best of my knowledge, there are only three malt extracts that are made from Munich malt: Marie's™ Munich Malt Extract, William's Brewing German Gold, and Ireks Amber Extract. If you cannot get one of these extracts, you will have to make-do by using some crystal and/or chocolate malts to approximate the flavor of high-kilned malts, but it's impossible to get it perfect. The caramelly flavors of crystal malts as well as the roasty flavors of chocolate malt are out-of-place in these beers. The styles that are difficult to get right without high-kilned malts as the base flavor are: Flanders Brown and Red Ales, Trappist/Abbey Dubbel, Munich Dunkel, Traditional Bock, Altbier, Oktoberfest/Märzen, Vienna, Doppelbock, Dunkelweizen, Eisbock, and Bamberger Rauchbier.

Incidentally, I'm not sure about Ireks Amber, but I know that the Marie's and William's extracts are made from 1/2 Munich malt and 1/2 pale malt. Perhaps some day an extract manufacturer may start making extract from 100% Munich malt. That would be perfect for Munich Dunkel and Altbier styles.

## Smoked Malt

You may think that smoked malt is out of the question for an extract brewer because it has to be mashed. This is true, but there is no law that prohibits you from making your own smoked crystal or dark malts, which do not need to be mashed. This is a far better way to get a smoky flavor into Smoked Porters or Rauchbiers than the use of liquid smoke extracts (which usually contain vinegar). Be very careful how much you use. Naturally, the more you smoke the grain, the less you will need to use. Start out light or make a 1-gallon test batch. I recommend a starting point of smoking no more than 1/2 pound of your crystal malt for a medium-gravity beer and then increase that if you feel it is necessary. Smoke aromas and flavors in the best beers are very subtle and should be in the background, not clunk you on the head.

I've never personally smoked grain, so I corresponded with Ed Westemeier, who has quite a bit of experience with it, and the procedures that follow are based on Ed's wisdom[131]. To make the smoked grain, use a smoker or barbecue. Electric smokers are best. Soak the grains and the smoking wood overnight so they don't burn when they are heated. Beech and fruit tree woods are a good choice – hickory chips will give you the strongest smoke flavor and will remind you of bacon and cheese. Once you have coals, add the wood, put the grill back on and spread the grain on a fine metal screen on top of the grill. Smoke the grain for 1 hour. Let the grain dry thoroughly if you plan to use a mill to crush the grain – otherwise it will gum it up.

## Refined Sugars and Rice Extracts

Some high-alcohol styles are heavy in body (Barleywine, Old Ale, Scottish Strong, Doppelbock, Eisbock) and others are lighter in body than they would be if they were all-malt (Belgian Blonde Strong Ale, Trappist Strong Ale, Tripel). Note again, that even some normal-alcohol styles are lighter in body than they could be if they were all-malt (American Pilsner, Blonde Ale/Lager, American Dark Lager). Taste the target beer and consider whether it could be that the beer was made lighter by the addition of corn (maize) or rice or even by the use of refined sugars. We won't be able to use corn or rice in our extract version, because they need to be mashed, but you can add corn, cane or candi sugars. 10% will lighten the body a bit, 20% noticeably and 30 or 40% will lighten the body significantly. I would recommend only using corn sugar for higher percentages because my experiments have shown that it imparts slightly less of a cidery flavor than cane or candi sugars, which are sucrose. All these sugars add about 41 pts/lb/gal, in other words, 1 pound of corn sugar dissolved in 1 gallon of water will give you a specific gravity of about 1.041.

Brown sugar adds not only the alcohol and body-slimming of white sugars, but also a molasses flavor. I would experiment cautiously with brown sugar, turbinado, raw sugar, and Sucanat™, since their flavors can be quite pronounced and may be unwelcome in some styles when used in larger amounts. I recommend using them only in darker styles of beer. These sugars will give you around 39 pts/lb/gal.

Rice Syrup or Rice Syrup Solids are also options for lightening the body of a beer, but not as much as pure sugars. The amount of gravity points that rice syrup adds is dependent on the amount of water in the syrup, but I suggest assuming about 30 pts/lb/gal as a starting point. Rice Syrup Solids are to rice what Dry Malt Extract is to malt – they are dehydrated to a powder form. Rice Syrup Solids give about 45 pts/lb/gal.

## Honey, Molasses and Treacle

Small amounts of honey don't really add a noticeable amount of honey flavor. Only when the honey begins to approach half of the fermentables does a honey-like flavor start to show through. Honey is almost entirely fermentable and therefore it will lighten the body of the beer, but remember that it does not have the nutrients necessary for good yeast health so if the amount that you add exceeds 20% of the fermentables, you had better add some yeast nutrient or you may have a sluggish fermentation. Honey adds about 35 to 37 pts/lb/gal.

Molasses and treacle add a sharp, resinous, sometimes buttery flavor to beer and therefore should probably only be used on darker, sweeter beers. There are those who say that it is impossible to duplicate Theakston's Old Peculier without treacle, but Roger Protz's *The Real Ale Drinker's Almanac* makes no mention of it in the ingredient list for this beer. The brands of molasses and treacle that I've tasted all have slightly different flavors, so while it may be true that molasses and treacle do taste different, the differences are not necessarily greater than the differences between various brands of molasses. If your target beer has a sort of resiny flavor like molasses or brown sugar or even Boston-style baked beans, you will want to add between 1/2 and 1 cup of molasses, added in the last 5 minutes of the boil (stir well so it doesn't scorch – the molasses will immediately sink to the bottom of the kettle).

## Extracts

Once we have determined all the other fermentables for our recipe, we need to make up the rest of the original gravity (OG) with extracts. These days, I usually use gold or light extract for all colors of beer and use crystal malts and dark grains for color. I find that it gives me more control over the color of the beer since the light malt extracts tend to be more consistent in color (when fresh).

Also, I like to add crystal malts and grains to add-back some of the malt flavors and aromas which are lost during the extract-making process and adding these on top of an amber or dark malt extract makes the beer too dark.

First, we need to determine how much OG we already have from the crystal malts, dark grains and other fermentables. Estimating exactly how much gravity you get from crystal malts and dark grains is a tricky problem because there are several variables. Firstly, there is the fact that there is some variation in the efficiency of extraction from one homebrewer's setup to another's. Secondly, as grains age they can gain or lose water which will decrease or increase their extract potential. Luckily, the variations are usually only one or two pts/lb/gal and rarely are more than two or three pounds of these grains used in a 5-gallon batch. Therefore, you can usually get within one or two points of your target gravity. Actually, measurement error (in both weights and liquid volumes) is probably a larger source of error.

Another thing that I usually do is use one whole package of extract syrup and then make up the difference with dry malt extract because it is easier to store a partially used package of dried malt extract than a half of a can of extract syrup.

Let's say, for example, that we have determined that we want to use 8 ounces of DeWolf-Cosyns Cara-Munich crystal malt, 4 ounces of DeWolf-Cosyns Chocolate malt and that we want our original gravity to be 1.055 (i.e. 55 points). Here's how the math would look:

| | | |
|---|---|---|
| DeWolf-Cosyns Cara-Munich: | ($1/2$ lb x 26 pts/lb/gal)/5 gallons | = 2.6 pts |
| DeWolf-Cosyns Chocolate Malt: | ($1/4$ lb x 26 pts/lb/gal)/5 gallons | = 1.3 pts |
| Northwestern Gold Extract Syrup: | (6 lbs x 36 pts/lb/gal)/5 gallons | = 43.2 pts |

Subtotal   47.1 pts

What's left is to subtract the 47.1 points from the 55 target points, leaving 7.9 points to add via dried malt extract. But remember that you need 7.9 points in each gallon, so we must multiply the 7.9 by 5 gallons and then divide by the number of pts/lb/gal in the dried malt extract (45). The math looks like this:

$$\frac{7.9 \text{ points } \times \text{ 5 gallons}}{45 \text{ pts/lb/gal}} = 0.9 \text{ pounds of dried malt extract}$$

## Color

Some brewers place a great deal of importance on the color of the beer. Personally, I try my best to match the color to the style, but I don't lose any sleep over it. Since both beers and malts have Lovibond numbers associated with them, it is a natural inclination to try to use mathematics to predict the color of the finished beer. Alas, it is not so simple. For light-colored beers it is pretty close, but as soon as we start to approach even light amber beers, the relationships are no longer linear and the whole process breaks down[132]. Furthermore, oxidation throughout the brewing process and caramelization during the boil further darken the beer. Therefore, I feel that you should simply use your common sense when it comes to choosing which color grains you use and you should get the color pretty close. What I mean is, I'm sure you know better than to use a pound of 80 Lovibond crystal malt when attempting to make a pale amber beer - you should probably use 20 Lovibond crystal malt or even $1/2$ pound 20 Lovibond and $1/2$ pound 8 Lovibond.

There are several scales used for color. The old scale, still used by homebrewers and maltsters, is in degrees Lovibond. The American Society of Brewing Chemists uses SRM or "Standard Research Method" degrees. European brewers use degrees EBC (European Brewing Congress). The Lovibond and SRM degrees are roughly the same. You can convert EBC to SRM by first adding 1.2 to the EBC degrees and then dividing by 2.65. To convert back the other way, first multiply SRM degrees by 2.65 and then subtract 1.2. This formula only works for pale colors.

It does help to have some visual reference for what various colors look like. The easiest way to do this is to give you a number of commercial examples, so you can see them for yourself. Here's a table of some widely available beers and their color in degrees Lovibond[132].

| beer | degrees Lovibond |
|------|------------------|
| Budweiser | 2 |
| Molson Export Ale | 4 |
| Bass Ale | 9.8 |
| Michelob Classic Dark | 17 |

For those who want to accurately check the color of their beer, Dennis Davison has developed The Homebrew Color Guide which is available through homebrew supply shops nationwide. Its 9 cells range from 3 to 19 degrees Lovibond/SRM and it has been checked on a spectrophotometer and found to be very accurate.

If you would like to read more about the subject of beer color and predicting it more accurately, I recommend Ray Daniels' three part article, *Beer Color Demystified* in Brewing Techniques[133] and appendix B of George and Laurie Fix's *Vienna, Märzen, Oktoberfest* (see Further Reading at the end of this chapter).

## Water

For extract brewers, the main concerns should be sulfates and carbonates. Sulfate ions accentuate hop bitterness and cause the bitterness to linger in the finish[176,177,178]. You should use low sulfate water (ideally, less than 10 PPM) for Bohemian and American Pilsners. For Burton Ales (IPAs and Burton-style Bitters) you should make sure that your sulfate levels are between 500 and 700 PPM. Dortmunders and Viennas also require relatively high sulfate levels. For all other styles, keep the sulfate levels moderate (below 50 PPM). If your target beer has a long, lingering dry, bitter finish, you need at least 200 PPM of sulfate in your water. Remember to account for any sulfates in your brewing water before making any additions.

Carbonates can give all-grain brewers headaches, but the only concern for extract brewers is that there should be sufficient carbonates to balance the acidity of the dark grains in Porters, Stouts, and Schwarzbiers. Typically, for these styles you would like to have the carbonate level be between 150 and 350 PPM, remembering to account for any carbonates in your brewing water. See chapter 9 for more details on matching water to styles.

## Hops

Appendix B discusses the differences of various hops and suggests varieties for particular styles. If your target beer has a hop aroma, compare it to the aromatic descriptions in appendix B and see which varieties match the intended character. Hops are an area where reading and research about your target beer can make your recipe formulation much easier.

What appendix B doesn't tell you is how many ounces of hops to use for a particular amount of finishing aroma, flavor or bitterness. There are a great many variables associated with the amount of bitterness that is extracted from the hops. Complicated formulas have been proposed to account for such things as altitude, filtration, and how full the hop bags are stuffed with the hops. Alas, these complicated formulas appear to have been conjured up from speculation and guesses with little or no experimental data. I have personally tried these formulas and have found them to suggest hop rates as much as double the correct hop rate[134]. Experiments are currently underway to try to develop proper formulas which include the most important factors, such as boil gravity, hop rate, and boil time. In the meantime, we do have some simple formulas that account for boil gravity and time, have stood the test of time and, while not accounting for every possible variable, have proven to give quite accurate estimations for the desired bitterness.

First of all, we need to discuss International Bittering Units (IBUs). In the recipes of chapter 12, the hop rates were given in ounces and the Alpha Acid percentage of the hops used were listed. In parentheses, the Alpha Acid Units (AAUs) are given. This is merely the weight in ounces of the hops times the percentage Alpha Acid of the hops used. The problem with using AAUs is that they are volume-dependent (you need to specify the number of gallons in the recipe along with the AAUs) and because they do not account for varying utilizations. Commercial brewers talk about bitterness in IBUs – when you look in Fred Eckhardt's *The Essentials of Beer Style* or Roger Protz's *The Real Ale Drinker's Almanac* (Third Edition and later), the bitterness units listed are, in fact, International Bittering Units. IBUs are measured using light transmittance, but are approximately the isomerized alpha acids in the beer in milligrams per liter. So, you can see that armed with the IBUs for our favorite beer and a relatively accurate set of formulas, we can get pretty close to our favorite beer's bitterness level. I'll present the formulas and then I'll show you how to use them with an example.

The formulas below are based upon those first published by Jackie Rager in *Calculating Hop Bitterness in Beer*[135]. Glenn Tinseth, in his World Wide Web page on Hop Utilization, incorporates the boil gravity into the utilization table, making it two-dimensional. I will provide similar tables but there will be six of them accounting for three additional factors. The utilization factors listed in the tables below are based upon my experience with and adjustments to Rager's utilization rates and upon test batches I had analyzed at The Siebel Institute of Technology in Chicago.

One important utilization factor that has yet to be included in any IBU estimation formulas is blowoff. I performed several experiments to determine the effect of the blowoff method of fermentation on bitterness, protein, and higher alcohols[33]. What the data showed was that while protein and higher alcohol levels were only slightly different using the blowoff method versus non-blowoff, there was a significant loss of bitterness using the blowoff method.

The other utilization factors are the use of whole versus pelletized hops and not using hop bags. Therefore, I present six utilization tables:

1.   pelletized hops in hop bags using the blowoff method,
2.   pelletized hops in hop bags using the non-blowoff method,
3.   whole hops in hop bags using the blowoff method,
4.   whole hops in hop bags using the non-blowoff method,
5.   whole hops without hop bags using the blowoff method, and
6.   whole hops without hop bags using the non-blowoff method.

By now, you should know what the original gravity of you beer will be. Based upon you original gravity and the boil volume in gallons or liters, determine the boil gravity from the boil gravity table.

The following table is used to estimate the final specific gravity of the boil (the specific gravity at the end of the boil). Select the intended original gravity of the finished beer and the number of gallons you are boiling. The estimated boil gravity can then be read at the intersection between the row and column. Note that boil gravities over 1.200 are not recommended (indicated by N/R).

### Table 15-4: Boil Gravity

| 5gal OG | boil gallons | | | | | | |
|---|---|---|---|---|---|---|---|
|  | 1.5 | 2.0 | 2.5 | 3.0 | 3.5 | 4.0 | 4.5 |
| 1.030 | 1.100 | 1.075 | 1.060 | 1.050 | 1.043 | 1.038 | 1.033 |
| 1.035 | 1.117 | 1.088 | 1.070 | 1.058 | 1.050 | 1.044 | 1.039 |
| 1.040 | 1.133 | 1.100 | 1.080 | 1.067 | 1.057 | 1.050 | 1.044 |
| 1.045 | 1.150 | 1.113 | 1.090 | 1.075 | 1.064 | 1.056 | 1.050 |
| 1.050 | 1.167 | 1.125 | 1.100 | 1.083 | 1.071 | 1.063 | 1.056 |
| 1.055 | 1.183 | 1.138 | 1.110 | 1.092 | 1.079 | 1.069 | 1.061 |
| 1.060 | 1.200 | 1.150 | 1.120 | 1.100 | 1.086 | 1.075 | 1.067 |
| 1.065 | N/R | 1.163 | 1.130 | 1.108 | 1.093 | 1.081 | 1.072 |
| 1.070 | N/R | 1.170 | 1.140 | 1.117 | 1.100 | 1.088 | 1.078 |
| 1.075 | N/R | 1.188 | 1.150 | 1.125 | 1.107 | 1.094 | 1.083 |
| 1.080 | N/R | 1.200 | 1.160 | 1.133 | 1.114 | 1.100 | 1.089 |
| 1.085 | N/R | N/R | 1.170 | 1.142 | 1.121 | 1.106 | 1.094 |
| 1.090 | N/R | N/R | 1.180 | 1.150 | 1.129 | 1.113 | 1.100 |
| 1.095 | N/R | N/R | 1.190 | 1.158 | 1.136 | 1.119 | 1.106 |
| 1.100 | N/R | N/R | 1.200 | 1.167 | 1.143 | 1.125 | 1.111 |
| 1.105 | N/R | N/R | N/R | 1.175 | 1.150 | 1.131 | 1.117 |
| 1.115 | N/R | N/R | N/R | 1.183 | 1.157 | 1.138 | 1.122 |
| 1.110 | N/R | N/R | N/R | 1.192 | 1.164 | 1.144 | 1.128 |
| 1.120 | N/R | N/R | N/R | 1.200 | 1.171 | 1.150 | 1.133 |

The following six tables give values for utilization (U) to be used in the formulas on page 355. If you wish to use these tables for Dr. Bob Technical's Hop-Go-Round, multiply the values in these tables by 100 and use them for "HOP UTILIZATION RATE – %."

**Table 15-5: Pelet hop utilization using the Blowoff Method and Hop Bags.**

| FINAL boil gravity | BOIL TIME IN MINUTES | | | | | | |
|---|---|---|---|---|---|---|---|
| | 5 | 10 | 15 | 20 | 30 | 45 | 60 |
| 1.030 | 0.021 | 0.042 | 0.064 | 0.085 | 0.126 | 0.188 | 0.249 |
| 1.040 | 0.020 | 0.041 | 0.061 | 0.081 | 0.120 | 0.179 | 0.237 |
| 1.050 | 0.019 | 0.039 | 0.058 | 0.077 | 0.115 | 0.171 | 0.226 |
| 1.060 | 0.019 | 0.037 | 0.055 | 0.073 | 0.110 | 0.163 | 0.216 |
| 1.070 | 0.018 | 0.035 | 0.053 | 0.070 | 0.105 | 0.156 | 0.206 |
| 1.080 | 0.017 | 0.034 | 0.050 | 0.067 | 0.100 | 0.149 | 0.197 |
| 1.090 | 0.016 | 0.032 | 0.048 | 0.064 | 0.095 | 0.142 | 0.188 |
| 1.100 | 0.015 | 0.031 | 0.046 | 0.061 | 0.091 | 0.136 | 0.179 |
| 1.110 | 0.015 | 0.029 | 0.044 | 0.058 | 0.087 | 0.129 | 0.171 |
| 1.120 | 0.014 | 0.028 | 0.042 | 0.056 | 0.083 | 0.124 | 0.163 |
| 1.130 | 0.013 | 0.027 | 0.040 | 0.053 | 0.079 | 0.118 | 0.156 |
| 1.140 | 0.013 | 0.025 | 0.038 | 0.051 | 0.076 | 0.113 | 0.149 |
| 1.150 | 0.012 | 0.024 | 0.036 | 0.048 | 0.072 | 0.107 | 0.142 |
| 1.160 | 0.012 | 0.023 | 0.035 | 0.046 | 0.069 | 0.103 | 0.136 |
| 1.170 | 0.011 | 0.022 | 0.033 | 0.044 | 0.066 | 0.098 | 0.130 |
| 1.180 | 0.011 | 0.021 | 0.032 | 0.042 | 0.063 | 0.093 | 0.124 |
| 1.190 | 0.010 | 0.020 | 0.030 | 0.040 | 0.060 | 0.089 | 0.118 |
| 1.200 | 0.10 | 0.019 | 0.029 | 0.038 | 0.057 | 0.085 | 0.113 |

## Table 15-6: Pellet hop utilization using the
## Non-blowoff Method and Hop Bags.

| FINAL | BOIL TIME IN MINUTES | | | | | | |
|---|---|---|---|---|---|---|---|
| boil gravity | 5 | 10 | 15 | 20 | 30 | 45 | 60 |
| 1.030 | 0.025 | 0.051 | 0.065 | 0.101 | 0.150 | 0.224 | 0.296 |
| 1.040 | 0.024 | 0.048 | 0.072 | 0.096 | 0.143 | 0.213 | 0.282 |
| 1.050 | 0.023 | 0.046 | 0.069 | 0.092 | 0.137 | 0.204 | 0.270 |
| 1.060 | 0.022 | 0.044 | 0.066 | 0.087 | 0.131 | 0.194 | 0.257 |
| 1.070 | 0.021 | 0.042 | 0.063 | 0.084 | 0.125 | 0.186 | 0.246 |
| 1.080 | 0.020 | 0.040 | 0.060 | 0.080 | 0.119 | 0.177 | 0.234 |
| 1.090 | 0.019 | 0.038 | 0.057 | 0.076 | 0.114 | 0.169 | 0.224 |
| 1.100 | 0.018 | 0.036 | 0.055 | 0.073 | 0.108 | 0.161 | 0.214 |
| 1.110 | 0.017 | 0.035 | 0.052 | 0.069 | 0.103 | 0.154 | 0.204 |
| 1.120 | 0.017 | 0.033 | 0.050 | 0.066 | 0.099 | 0.147 | 0.195 |
| 1.130 | 0.016 | 0.032 | 0.047 | 0.063 | 0.094 | 0.140 | 0.186 |
| 1.140 | 0.015 | 0.030 | 0.045 | 0.060 | 0.090 | 0.134 | 0.177 |
| 1.150 | 0.014 | 0.029 | 0.043 | 0.058 | 0.086 | 0.128 | 0.169 |
| 1.160 | 0.014 | 0.028 | 0.041 | 0.055 | 0.082 | 0.122 | 0.162 |
| 1.170 | 0.013 | 0.026 | 0.039 | 0.052 | 0.078 | 0.116 | 0.154 |
| 1.180 | 0.013 | 0.025 | 0.038 | 0.050 | 0.075 | 0.111 | 0.147 |
| 1.190 | 0.012 | 0.024 | 0.036 | 0.048 | 0.071 | 0.106 | 0.140 |
| 1.200 | 0.011 | 0.023 | 0.034 | 0.046 | 0.068 | 0.101 | 0.134 |

**Table 15-7: Whole hop utilization using the Blowoff Method and Hop Bags.**

| FINAL | BOIL TIME IN MINUTES | | | | | | |
|---|---|---|---|---|---|---|---|
| boil gravity | 5 | 10 | 15 | 20 | 30 | 45 | 60 |
| 1.030 | 0.019 | 0.038 | 0.057 | 0.076 | 0.114 | 0.169 | 0.224 |
| 1.040 | 0.018 | 0.036 | 0.055 | 0.073 | 0.108 | 0.161 | 0.214 |
| 1.050 | 0.017 | 0.035 | 0.052 | 0.069 | 0.103 | 0.154 | 0.204 |
| 1.060 | 0.017 | 0.033 | 0.050 | 0.066 | 0.099 | 0.147 | 0.195 |
| 1.070 | 0.016 | 0.032 | 0.047 | 0.063 | 0.094 | 0.140 | 0.186 |
| 1.080 | 0.015 | 0.030 | 0.045 | 0.060 | 0.090 | 0.134 | 0.177 |
| 1.090 | 0.014 | 0.029 | 0.043 | 0.058 | 0.086 | 0.128 | 0.169 |
| 1.100 | 0.014 | 0.028 | 0.041 | 0.055 | 0.082 | 0.122 | 0.161 |
| 1.110 | 0.013 | 0.026 | 0.039 | 0.052 | 0.078 | 0.116 | 0.154 |
| 1.120 | 0.013 | 0.025 | 0.038 | 0.050 | 0.075 | 0.111 | 0.147 |
| 1.130 | 0.012 | 0.024 | 0.036 | 0.048 | 0.071 | 0.106 | 0.140 |
| 1.140 | 0.011 | 0.023 | 0.034 | 0.046 | 0.068 | 0.101 | 0.134 |
| 1.150 | 0.011 | 0.022 | 0.033 | 0.043 | 0.065 | 0.097 | 0.128 |
| 1.160 | 0.010 | 0.020 | 0.030 | 0.042 | 0.062 | 0.092 | 0.122 |
| 1.170 | 0.010 | 0.020 | 0.030 | 0.040 | 0.059 | 0.088 | 0.117 |
| 1.180 | 0.010 | 0.019 | 0.028 | 0.038 | 0.056 | 0.084 | 0.111 |
| 1.190 | 0.009 | 0.018 | 0.027 | 0.036 | 0.054 | 0.080 | 0.106 |
| 1.200 | 0.009 | 0.017 | 0.026 | 0.034 | 0.051 | 0.077 | 0.101 |

### Table 15-8: Whole hop utilization using the
### Non-blowoff Method and Hop Bags.

| FINAL | BOIL TIME IN MINUTES | | | | | | |
|---|---|---|---|---|---|---|---|
| boil gravity | 5 | 10 | 15 | 20 | 30 | 45 | 60 |
| 1.030 | 0.023 | 0.045 | 0.068 | 0.091 | 0.135 | 0.201 | 0.266 |
| 1.040 | 0.022 | 0.043 | 0.065 | 0.086 | 0.129 | 0.192 | 0.254 |
| 1.050 | 0.021 | 0.041 | 0.062 | 0.082 | 0.123 | 0.183 | 0.243 |
| 1.060 | 0.020 | 0.040 | 0.059 | 0.079 | 0.118 | 0.175 | 0.232 |
| 1.070 | 0.019 | 0.038 | 0.057 | 0.075 | 0.112 | 0.167 | 0.221 |
| 1.080 | 0.018 | 0.036 | 0.054 | 0.072 | 0.107 | 0.159 | 0.211 |
| 1.090 | 0.017 | 0.034 | 0.051 | 0.068 | 0.102 | 0.152 | 0.201 |
| 1.100 | 0.016 | 0.033 | 0.049 | 0.065 | 0.098 | 0.145 | 0.192 |
| 1.110 | 0.016 | 0.031 | 0.047 | 0.062 | 0.093 | 0.139 | 0.183 |
| 1.120 | 0.015 | 0.030 | 0.045 | 0.060 | 0.089 | 0.132 | 0.175 |
| 1.130 | 0.014 | 0.029 | 0.043 | 0.047 | 0.085 | 0.126 | 0.167 |
| 1.140 | 0.014 | 0.027 | 0.041 | 0.054 | 0.081 | 0.121 | 0.160 |
| 1.150 | 0.013 | 0.026 | 0.039 | 0.052 | 0.077 | 0.115 | 0.152 |
| 1.160 | 0.012 | 0.025 | 0.037 | 0.049 | 0.074 | 0.110 | 0.145 |
| 1.170 | 0.012 | 0.024 | 0.035 | 0.047 | 0.070 | 0.105 | 0.139 |
| 1.180 | 0.011 | 0.023 | 0.034 | 0.045 | 0.067 | 0.100 | 0.132 |
| 1.190 | 0.011 | 0.022 | 0.032 | 0.043 | 0.064 | 0.096 | 0.126 |
| 1.200 | 0.010 | 0.021 | 0.031 | 0.041 | 0.061 | 0.091 | 0.121 |

## Table 15-9: Whole hop utilization using the
## Blowoff Method *without* Hop Bags.

| FINAL | BOIL TIME IN MINUTES | | | | | | |
|---|---|---|---|---|---|---|---|
| boil gravity | 5 | 10 | 15 | 20 | 30 | 45 | 60 |
| 1.030 | 0.020 | 0.040 | 0.060 | 0.079 | 0.118 | 0.176 | 0.233 |
| 1.040 | 0.019 | 0.038 | 0.057 | 0.076 | 0.113 | 0.168 | 0.223 |
| 1.050 | 0.018 | 0.036 | 0.054 | 0.072 | 0.108 | 0.161 | 0.213 |
| 1.060 | 0.017 | 0.035 | 0.052 | 0.069 | 0.103 | 0.153 | 0.203 |
| 1.070 | 0.017 | 0.033 | 0.050 | 0.066 | 0.098 | 0.146 | 0.194 |
| 1.080 | 0.016 | 0.032 | 0.047 | 0.063 | 0.094 | 0.140 | 0.185 |
| 1.090 | 0.015 | 0.030 | 0.045 | 0.060 | 0.090 | 0.133 | 0.177 |
| 1.100 | 0.014 | 0.029 | 0.043 | 0.057 | 0.086 | 0.127 | 0.168 |
| 1.110 | 0.014 | 0.027 | 0.041 | 0.055 | 0.082 | 0.122 | 0.161 |
| 1.120 | 0.013 | 0.026 | 0.039 | 0.052 | 0.078 | 0.116 | 0.154 |
| 1.130 | 0.013 | 0.025 | 0.037 | 0.050 | 0.074 | 0.111 | 0.140 |
| 1.140 | 0.012 | 0.024 | 0.036 | 0.048 | 0.071 | 0.106 | 0.140 |
| 1.150 | 0.011 | 0.023 | 0.034 | 0.045 | 0.068 | 0.101 | 0.133 |
| 1.160 | 0.011 | 0.022 | 0.033 | 0.043 | 0.065 | 0.096 | 0.127 |
| 1.170 | 0.010 | 0.021 | 0.031 | 0.041 | 0.062 | 0.092 | 0.122 |
| 1.180 | 0.010 | 0.020 | 0.030 | 0.039 | 0.059 | 0.088 | 0.116 |
| 1.190 | 0.009 | 0.019 | 0.028 | 0.038 | 0.056 | 0.084 | 0.111 |
| 1.200 | 0.009 | 0.018 | 0.027 | 0.036 | 0.054 | 0.080 | 0.106 |

## Table 15-10: Whole hop utilization using the
## Non-blowoff Method *without* Hop Bags.

| FINAL boil gravity | BOIL TIME IN MINUTES | | | | | | |
|---|---|---|---|---|---|---|---|
| | 5 | 10 | 15 | 20 | 30 | 45 | 60 |
| 1.030 | 0.024 | 0.047 | 0.071 | 0.094 | 0.141 | 0.210 | 0.278 |
| 1.040 | 0.023 | 0.045 | 0.068 | 0.090 | 0.135 | 0.200 | 0.265 |
| 1.050 | 0.022 | 0.043 | 0.065 | 0.086 | 0.128 | 0.191 | 0.253 |
| 1.060 | 0.021 | 0.041 | 0.062 | 0.082 | 0.123 | 0.183 | 0.242 |
| 1.070 | 0.020 | 0.039 | 0.059 | 0.078 | 0.117 | 0.174 | 0.231 |
| 1.080 | 0.019 | 0.038 | 0.056 | 0.075 | 0.112 | 0.166 | 0.220 |
| 1.090 | 0.018 | 0.036 | 0.054 | 0.071 | 0.107 | 0.159 | 0.210 |
| 1.100 | 0.017 | 0.034 | 0.051 | 0.068 | 0.102 | 0.152 | 0.201 |
| 1.110 | 0.016 | 0.033 | 0.049 | 0.065 | 0.097 | 0.145 | 0.191 |
| 1.120 | 0.016 | 0.031 | 0.047 | 0.062 | 0.093 | 0.138 | 0.183 |
| 1.130 | 0.015 | 0.030 | 0.045 | 0.059 | 0.089 | 0.132 | 0.174 |
| 1.140 | 0.014 | 0.028 | 0.043 | 0.057 | 0.084 | 0.126 | 0.166 |
| 1.150 | 0.014 | 0.027 | 0.041 | 0.054 | 0.081 | 0.120 | 0.159 |
| 1.160 | 0.013 | 0.026 | 0.039 | 0.052 | 0.077 | 0.115 | 0.152 |
| 1.170 | 0.012 | 0.025 | 0.037 | 0.049 | 0.073 | 0.109 | 0.145 |
| 1.180 | 0.012 | 0.024 | 0.035 | 0.047 | 0.070 | 0.104 | 0.138 |
| 1.190 | 0.011 | 0.023 | 0.034 | 0.045 | 0.067 | 0.100 | 0.132 |
| 1.200 | 0.011 | 0.022 | 0.032 | 0.043 | 0.064 | 0.095 | 0.126 |

In the following "IBU" formulas the one on the left is if you choose to use ounces and gallons and the one on the right is if you choose to use grams and liters. AAUs (alpha acid units) are simply the number of ounces of hops times their alpha acid percentage (e.g. 2 ounces of 7% alpha acid hops are 14 AAUs). MAAUs (*metric* alpha acid units) are grams of hops times their alpha acid percentage (e.g. 60 grams of 7% alpha acid hops are 420 MAAUs). "Gal" is the number of gallons of beer that you are making, *not* the boil volume. Similarly, if you are using the metric IBU formula, L is the number of liters of beer that you are making, *not* the boil volume.

The last variable is S... the "system factor." Because every brewer's system is slightly different, you may get slightly higher or lower utilizations. You may have to adjust these formulas or use slightly different utilization percentages if you find that you are consistently getting too much or too little bitterness. I suggest that you start with S = 1 and then, if you find you are getting more bitterness than expected, increase S to 1.01, 1.05, or more (if necessary). Conversely, if you find you are getting less bitterness than expected, decrease S to 0.99, 0.95, or even less (if necessary). *Pencil* in your value for S below and fine-tune it for your brewing system.

In both formulas, U is the utilization from one of the six tables above, depending on the type of hops you are using, the method of fermentation, and if you used a hop bag. These formulas will tell you how many IBUs you will get from a particular amount of hops. An alternative to using these formulas is to simply use Dr. Bob Technical's Hop-Go-Round (see Using the Hop-Go-Round below).

$$\text{System Factor:} \quad \boxed{S =}$$

$$IBUs = \frac{AAUs \times U \times 74.62 \times S}{Gal} \qquad IBUs = \frac{MAAUs \times U \times 9.962 \times S}{L}$$

The following "AAU" and "MAAU" formulas will estimate how many alpha acid units of hops you need to get a particular number of IBUs.

$$AAUs = \frac{Gal \times IBUs}{U \times 74.62 \times S} \qquad MAAUs = \frac{L \times IBUs}{U \times 9.962 \times S}$$

Other factors which you may want to consider, but are beyond the scope of this book are filtration, bitterness lost to hot and cold break, the ratio of humulone to cohumulone in the hop variety used, hop rate (higher hop rates result in lower utilization), wort carbohydrate composition, and yeast flocculation characteristics (slowly flocculating yeast can reduce utilization by as much as 4% relative to normally flocculant yeast)[136]. Far more research is needed before the quantitative effects of these factors can be incorporated into reliable bitterness estimation formulae.

## Using the Hop-Go-Round

Rather than using the formulae on the previous page, you can use Dr. Bob Technical's Hop-Go-Round. As I've mentioned before, for my system, the utilization rates on the back are a bit optimistic (especially for shorter boils and higher boil gravities), so I use tables 15-5 through 15-10. Simply match up the % Alpha Acid of the hops you are going to use with the "HOP UTILIZATION RATE – %." To calculate the weight of hops you need for a given IBU level, hold the two inner wheels together while either matching up the "OUNCES" or "GRAMS" arrows with the IBUs you want and read the weight of hops required where it intersects with the batch size in gallons on the outer ring.

To calculate the IBU contribution from a particular hop addition, after matching up the % Alpha Acid of the hops you are going to use with the "HOP UTILIZATION RATE – %," hold the inner two wheels together, match up the weight of the hops with the batch size in gallons and read the IBUs pointed at by the "GRAMS" or "OUNCES" arrows.

## Calculating Hop Additions

We will use the IBU and AAU formulas together to estimate the total amount of hops needed in the boil. First, we will choose the total number of IBUs we want for the beer (based upon the style guidelines or our imagination), but we will not use that value until later. Next, we will choose the weight of the finishing hops from Table 15-11 below. Now, we can calculate the estimated IBUs that the finishing hops will contribute using the IBU formula. Next, we will choose the weight of the flavor hops from Table 15-12 and again, using the IBU formula, calculate the estimated IBUs contributed by the flavor hops. Then, we will subtract the IBUs contributed by the finishing and flavor hops from the total IBUs we want for the beer. The result is how many IBUs are required from the boiling hops. Finally, we use the AAU (or MAAU) formula to calculate how many alpha acid units we need for the bittering addition (60 minute boil).

## Flavor and Finishing Hop Amounts

The following two tables will help you choose the correct amount of finishing and flavor hops you should use for your beer. The aromatic qualities added by dryhops and finishing hops are slightly different so you can, if you like, use both. Remember that dryhops add quite a bit more aroma and can easily overpower finishing hops if you are not careful.

**Table 15-11: Fishing hops.**

| Finishing Hop Aroma | Amount |
|---|---|
| Mild | 1 to 1¹/₂ ounces  OR  30 to 60 grams |
| Medium | 2 to 2¹/₂ ounces  OR  60 to 90 grams |
| Strong | 3 to 3¹/₂ ounces  OR  90 to 120 grams |

**Table 15-12: Flavor hops.**

| Hop Flavor | Amount |
|---|---|
| Mild | ¹/₄ to ¹/₂ ounce  OR  7 to 15 grams |
| Medium | ¹/₂ to 1 ounce  OR  15 to 30 grams |
| Strong | 1 to 2 ounces  OR  30 to 60 grams |

The range on the finishing hop amounts depends on the hop variety (some are more aromatic than others – you can tell just by smelling them) and on how fresh they are. My experience has shown that the boil gravity has an influence on how much hop flavor you get from the hops. It is not an exact science and the correct amount of flavor hops and finishing hops are two areas in which there is no substitute for experience. The range on the flavor hops is partly dependent on the hop variety and partly on the boil gravity (higher gravity boils require more hops than lower gravity boils). Note that too much of some hop flavors can make the beer sickeningly sweet, so take it easy at first and don't overdo it. Also, note that these amounts of both finishing and flavor hops are for low- or medium-strength beers. If you are making an a Barleywine, for example, you may need a bit more than 1 ounce of hops for a medium hop flavor.

Resist the temptation of trying to reduce polyphenol (a.k.a. tannin) extraction by increasing the flavor and aroma hops. Leave the bittering to the bittering hops and keep within the guidelines above. Finishing hops add very little bitterness to begin with and exceeding the suggested amounts of flavor hops will produce an unbalanced beer.

## Hop Calculation Example

An example will show how easy all of these formulas and tables are to use. Suppose we were going to make 5 gallons of 1.050 original gravity beer in which we wanted a medium hop nose (but were not going to dryhop), medium hop flavor and 35 IBUs of total bitterness. We are going to boil only 2.5 gallons of wort (losing about 1/2 gallon to steam) and then add it to 3 gallons of boiled, chilled water in a 7.5 gallon fermenter (so there will be no blowoff). We'll use a system factor of 1.

To calculate the estimated bitterness contribution from the finishing hops, which we plan to boil 5 minutes, we first need to know the ending boil gravity. From Table 15-4, we determine that the ending boil gravity will be 1.100. Table 15-11 says that we should use between 2 and 2 1/2 ounces of hops for a medium finishing hop aroma. We'll use 2 ounces of 5% alpha acid Willamette pellets, which amounts to 10 AAUs. From Table 15-6 we can see that a 5 minute boil in 1.100 gravity wort will give a 0.018 utilization factor if we use the non-blowoff method of fermentation. Plugging these values into the IBU formula, we have:

$$\text{IBUs} = \frac{10 \text{ AAUs} \times 0.018 \times 74.62 \times 1}{5 \text{ gal}} = \frac{13.43}{5} = 2.69 \text{ IBUs from the finishing hops}$$

Next, we calculate the bitterness contribution from the flavor hops, which we plan to boil 15 minutes. From Table 15-12, we determine that we should use between 1/2 and 1 ounce of hops for a medium hop flavor. We'll use 1 ounce of 6% alpha acid Cascade pellets, which amounts to 6 AAUs. From Table 15-6 we can see that a 15 minute boil in 1.100 gravity wort will give a 0.055 utilization factor if we use the non-blowoff method of fermentation. Plugging these values into the IBU formula gives us:

$$\text{IBUs} = \frac{6 \text{ AAUs} \times 0.055 \times 74.62 \times 1}{5 \text{ gal}} = \frac{24.62}{5} = 4.92 \text{ IBUs from the flavor hops}$$

Finally, we subtract the flavor and finishing hop IBUs from our target of 35:

$$35 - (2.69 + 4.92) = 35 - 7.61 = 27.39 \text{ IBUs needed from the bittering hops}$$

We'll be boiling our bittering hop pellets 60 minutes, so from Table 15-6 we find that we will be getting a 0.214 utilization factor from a 60 minute boil in a 1.100

gravity boil if we use the non-blowoff method of fermentation. Plugging these values into the AAU formula, we get:

$$AAUs = \frac{5 \text{ gal} \times 27.39 \text{ IBUs}}{0.214 \times 74.62 \times 1} = \frac{136.95}{15.97} = 8.58 \text{ AAUs needed from the bittering hops}$$

We will be using 6% alpha acid Cascade pellets so, to find out how many ounces to use, we'll divide the 8.58 AAUs needed by the alpha acid percent:

8.58 AAUs / 6% alpha acid = 1.43 ounces of boiling hops needed

So, to sum up our hop additions, we will be using:

1.43 ounces of 6% AA Cascade pellets, boiled 60 minutes for bittering,
1 ounce of 6% AA Cascade pellets, boiled 15 minutes for flavor, and
2 ounces of 5% AA Willamette pellets, boiled 5 minutes for finishing.

Finally, let's not forget that we used Table 15-6 for our utilizations so we should ensure we won't have blowoff during the fermentation or our beer will be less hoppy than expected.

## Yeast

When trying to duplicate a commercial beer, the yeast is often the most important factor and most difficult to get right. This is especially true for ales and is crucial when the yeast character is a dominant feature of the beer as it is in many Belgian Ales. Luckily, the number of yeast strains available to homebrewers is ever increasing.

Appendices C, D, and E contain tables of most of the dry and liquid yeast strains currently available to homebrewers. If you are not trying to duplicate a particular commercial beer, you should choose your yeast by the character you would like it to have. The appendices will give you some idea of the attenuation and character of the yeast. When looking for an ale yeast, don't ignore the lager yeasts - some lager yeasts have wonderful fruity aromas when allowed to ferment at ale temperatures. Also, if you are trying to make something like a lager, but do not have the facilities to keep the beer at 40 to 50° F (4 to 10° C), you may be able to get pretty close by using an ale yeast that produces low levels of esters. Appendices D and E will give you some suggestions.

## *Adjusting Original Gravity*

What if you finished the boil, added the wort to the cold water in the fermenter, stirred well and still the original gravity (OG) is not what you had expected? Before we discuss this, I must stress the importance of stirring well before measuring the gravity. The thick, heavy wort will tend to sink to the bottom of the fermenter and unless you stir well, you may think that your OG is lower than it really is. This is really the most common mistake made when measuring OG.

But what if you stirred very well and still the OG is lower or higher than expected? One problem could be that you boiled away more or less water from the boil than you had planned. This is why it's a good idea to have gallon (or liter) graduations marked on your fermenter. If you were shooting for 5 gallons, but made $4^1/_2$, your OG will be 10% higher than you had expected. Similarly, if you had expected 5 gallons, but ended up with $5^1/_2$, your OG will be 9% lower than you wanted.

If the OG is too high and you have room in the fermenter (including space for the kräusen), you can simply add water. You should boil the water first so you sanitize it (and evaporate chlorine if your water is chlorinated). If you are pressed for space (i.e. you don't think you'll have enough room for the kräusen if you add the water), you can wait till the main part of the fermentation has subsided and then add the boiling water. You will want to cool the water first if it is more than about 15% of the beer volume, otherwise, it will raise the temperature of the beer too much and possibly kill the yeast. Important: adding oxygen to fermenting wort will increase diacetyl and ester levels in the finished beer; adding oxygen to finished beer will give stale (most often cardboard-like) aromas. Therefore, if you are adding cooled water to the fermenter after fermentation has started, you should:

1.  cool the boiled water quickly (don't just let it sit at room temperature) so it does not absorb oxygen from the air, and
2.  minimize splashing because that will also introduce oxygen into the fermenting beer.

If the OG is too low, your best bet is to just accept it, and make a note in your logbook to add more malt next time you make this recipe. How much more? The values in the following table give the specific gravity and Plato degree increases for various additions of syrup and dry malt extract and are based on the average points-per-pound-per-gallon added by various manufacturers' extracts.

**Table 15-13: Increasing the original gravity by increasing the weight of the malt extract.**

| to raise OG by 0.001 | ounces per gallon | grams per liter |
|---|---|---|
| malt extract syrup | 0.44 | 3.35 |
| dry malt extract | 0.36 | 2.68 |

Another way to look at it is "How much will an ounce of malt extract add to my original gravity?" Again, this table is based upon average malt extract contributions.

**Table 15-14: Another perspective on increasing original gravity by adding more malt extract.**

| Addition | malt extract syrup | dry malt extract |
|---|---|---|
| 1 ounce (wt) / gallon | 0.00225 (0.5625 P) | 0.0028 (0.703 P) |
| 1 pound / 1 gallon | 0.036 (9 P) | 0.045 (11.25 P) |
| 1 pound / 5 gallons | 0.0072 (1.8 P) | 0.009 (2.25 P) |
| 1 gram / liter | 0.0003 (0.75 P) | 0.00037 (0.93 P) |

If you insist on raising the OG of *this* batch, you will have to boil the extract in water to sanitize it. Ideally, you would like to boil it for an hour to get a good hot break, but with small additions you can get by with a 15-minute boil. You will also want to chill it quickly to get a good cold break. You can use the tables above, but don't forget that you have to account for the water you are adding too. I feel the easiest way to make this adjustment is to figure out how many gravity points you want, how many you already have and the difference is how much you need to add. Perhaps an example is the easiest way to demonstrate this procedure:

Let's say we miscalculated something in our recipe and we now have 5 gallons of 1.048 wort, but we wanted 1.054 wort. Let's also assume that our fermenter has room for 1/2 gallon of additional wort while still having enough room for the kräusen that will be produced. Our final volume will be 51/2 gallons and they will be at a specific gravity of 1.054. First we need to figure out how many total gravity "points" we will need in the fermenter (1.054 is 54 "points"):

51/2 gallons  x  54 points/gallon  =  297 points

Next, we calculate how many points we already have in the fermenter:

5 gallons  x  48 points/gallon  =  240 points

What we need to add is 57 points (297 - 240 = 57). We'll be using dried malt extract which (from table 15-4) increases the specific gravity by 0.045. In other words, it adds 45 points per pound per gallon, so we calculate the number of pounds we need by dividing the points needed by 45:

$$\frac{57}{45} = 1.27 \text{ pounds}$$

So what we need to do is boil 1 1/4 pounds of dried malt extract in 1/2 gallon of water for 15 minutes, chill it and then add it to the fermenter. The resulting OG of the 5 1/2 gallons of wort will be 1.054. There is a limit to how many points you can add this way – if the gravity adjustment wort is too thick, it will scorch and affect the flavor of the finished beer. You should probably limit yourself to no more than about 3 pounds per gallon (which would be a whopping 1.135 boil gravity!).

On the other hand, if you want to lower the OG of the wort or you want to lower the *effective* OG of the finished beer, you can use this same method to calculate how much water you need to add to get a given OG. Again, an example is probably the easiest way to demonstrate.

Let's say we are trying to make an ESB and the style guidelines for a competition we are going to enter say that the maximum gravity for an ESB is 1.055. We have 4 1/2 gallons of wort at 1.064 so we need to lower it to 1.055. First, we multiply the gallons we have times the gravity points we have to determine the total number of points we have in the fermenter:

$$4 3/4 \text{ gallons } \times \quad 64 \text{ points } = \quad 304 \text{ points}$$

Now, we divide those 304 points by 55 points to calculate the volume required:

$$\frac{304}{55} = 5.53 \text{ gallons}$$

Subtracting 4 3/4 from 5 1/2 gallons leaves 3/4 gallon or 3 quarts. So, to lower the OG (or effective OG) of this batch, you need to add 3 quarts of boiled water. As before, if you are adding the water to fermenting or finished beer, it is important that you add the water without splashing and boil it to sanitize, remove chlorine, and (most importantly) remove dissolved oxygen which would increase diacetyl and esters in fermenting beer or oxidize finished beer.

## *Fermentation, Conditioning and Lagering*

If you are trying to duplicate a particular commercial beer, it helps to know the fermentation temperature and the conditioning/lagering temperature/schedule that the brewer uses. This information is not as impossible to get as you might think. If you go on a tour of the brewery, it is rare that you can't find someone who will at least tell you the hops they use and the fermentation temperature. Sometimes you can even find out which yeast strain, the percentage of each grain they use and any number of other useful pieces of information.

Even if you can't visit the brewery, you can often find out the fermentation schedule by reading and researching. Check Michael Jackson's books. He often has information about the fermentation and lagering or conditioning temperatures. For example, in his *Pocket Guide to Beer*, he notes that Orval undergoes a secondary fermentation at around 60° F for five to seven weeks and then is bottle conditioned for an additional two months at relatively warm temperatures.

# Further Reading

Daniels, R., "Beer Color Demystified," *Brewing Techniques*, 3 (4,5,6), (Jul/Aug, Sep/Oct, Nov/Dec 1995).

Fix, G.J. and L. Fix, *Vienna, Oktoberfest, Märezn*, (Brewers Publications, Boulder, CO, 1991).

Nummer, Dr. Brian A, "Brewing with Lactic Acid Bacteria," *Brewing Techniques,* p.56-63, May/June 1996, Vol. 4, No. 3.

See also "Further Reading" following Appendix A.

# FREQUENTLY ASKED QUESTIONS

These are the questions most often asked that pertain to beginning and intermediate brewing. Advanced frequently asked questions will be covered in volume II of this series.

## Sanitation

**My friend uses his mouth to start siphons, never sanitizes anything and his beer still tastes good. Why do I have to go through all that trouble?**

Your friend is brewing infected beer. We all are brewing infected beer, frankly. We cannot make 100% sterile wort in our homes. Minimizing the amount of bacteria and wild yeasts that get into the wort, onto equipment, and into the bottles means that you will have a better chance of making consistently good beer that has a good shelf life. If you consume all the beer you make within two weeks of making it, you can use very sloppy sanitation techniques and never notice an off flavor or aroma. But, if you plan on putting aside a bottle for tasting six months or a year from now, the quality of your sanitation techniques will be tested.

## Can I sanitize my mouth with whiskey before using it to start a siphon?

Probably not. The contact time for sanitation with alcohol is 15 minutes. You will probably get buzzed long before your mouth is sanitary enough to start a siphon. Bottom line: don't use your mouth to start siphons.

## What's the difference between sterilization and sanitation?

When you sterilize, you kill *all* microbes, *including* their spores. Sterilization is virtually impossible in the home brewery. Your only hope for sterilizing wort or utensils is in a pressure cooker. Regular boiling, bleach, iodophor, oxygen-based sanitizers, and alcohol are only *sanitizers* – they don't kill spores. It is a misuse of the term "sterilization" to use it in association with "sanitation" although many authors do. Incidentally, metabisulfites (a.k.a. Campden tablets) are not even sanitizers – while they do kill some yeasts and bacteria, their primary use is to inhibit the growth of microbes till your cultured yeast can establish itself[137]. Metabisulfites work by creating sulfur dioxide, but only in an *acidic* solution. Therefore, the brewers out there who think they are sanitizing equipment by soaking it in a solution of potassium metabisulfite and water might as well be using plain water.

## Can I use alcohol to sanitize?

Yes, but 70% alcohol is a better sanitizer than 100% alcohol and the contact time is 15 minutes, so you cannot simply spray on the alcohol/water mixture and use the piece of equipment immediately[138]. Be careful – the alcohol is very flammable.

# Malts, Sugars and Extracts

## I've read that you have to mash crystal malts. Should I?

I've read that in some homebrewing books too. Perhaps crystal malts available to homebrewers 15 years ago were poorly made and therefore required mashing. Modern crystal malts are very low in unconverted starch and most can safely be used in extract recipes without mashing. The exceptions to this rule are the very pale crystal malts such as Dextrine and some Cara-Pils malts (see chapter 7).

## Which malts require mashing?

There are a great many names for various malts and new malts coming out all the time, so it's easier to list which malts don't require mashing. Except for a few very pale varieties (see chapter 7) there is no need to mash crystal malts (Caravienne, Caramunich, Crystal 60, Special B, for example), Chocolate Malt,

Roasted Barley and black malts (such as Black Patent, Roasted Malt, and Carafa®). All the rest of the malts (Pilsner, Pale Ale, Biscuit,Toasted, Munich, Vienna, etc.) require mashing. Incidentally, all the flaked and unmalted grains (oats, barley, corn, etc.) also must be mashed. If you don't mash these malts and grains they will give your beer a permanent starch haze.

## Can I mash grain in a mesh grain bag?

Yes, but you run the risk of permanently cloudy and/or astringent beer. Once you hear how easy it is to convert Pale Ale malt, you will be tempted to simply dump the crushed grain into your grain bag, steep it in a gallon and a half of 158° F water for an hour and then pull the bag out. It's true that you have converted the starches to sugars, but there are many other factors that are not considered. One is pH. When you mash, you rarely use more than 1.5 quarts per pound of grain. When you steep you use about a gallon per pound. The water/grain ratio in steeping is all wrong for getting the pH in the right range for conversion and for minimizing polyphenol (a.k.a. tannin) extraction. Another factor is clarifying the sweet wort. When you mash, you use a lauter tun to recirculate the sweet wort until it runs clear. When you steep you simply pull out the grain bag and let it drip dry. This "tea bag" method of mashing will allow starches, lipids (fat-like substances), and other undesirable particles to get into your wort. You see that the two are not equivalent. If you insist on doing a partial mash, make yourself a small lauter tun and don't just try to use a grain bag.

## What's the difference between "steeping " and "mashing?"

Steeping is simply the process of soaking malts and grains their sugars, dextrins, and flavors into the steeping water. No conversion of starches takes place. It is only to be done with malts and grains (such as roasted barley) that don't require mashing. Mashing, on the other hand, involves the conversion of starches to sugars and dextrins, and (in more complicated mashing schedules) breaking large proteins into smaller proteins and amino acids. Mashing also implies that läutering will be done, whereas steeping can be done simply be soaking a mesh grain bag full of crushed malts and grains in some hot water (see "Can I mash in a mesh grain bag? above).

## I've read that dried malt extract is inferior to malt extract syrup. Why?

It's not. I suspect that the person who wrote this had tried using one of the very unfermentable extracts (see chapter 7) and, as a result, got a very sweet beer. As long as you are aware that some dried malt extracts (DMEs) are less fermentable than others and select the brand you use based on whether you want a sweeter or drier beer, there really isn't any difference in quality or the flavor of the finished beer. In fact, if your only supplier has very old extracts, you may want to use

DME because old DME (as long as it was stored dry) is usually in better condition than old malt extract syrup.

## Can I use a coffee grinder to crush my grains?

It is not recommended. A coffee grinder will damage the husks too much if you run it long enough so that most of the grains are broken. If you damage the husks too much, you will extract excessive polyphenols from them which will lead to astringent beer.

## I've heard to never add corn sugar to a recipe. Why not?

Excessive use of corn, candi, invert, or table sugar can give your beer cidery aromas and flavors. See "Other Sources of Fermentables" in chapter 11 and "I've heard to ignore the directions on the can of extract" below. Some styles of beer cannot be made without these sugars – don't get obsessive when it comes to avoiding refined sugars.

## What are specialty grains?

Some brewers use the term "specialty grains" for the grains that do no have to be mashed and can therefore be used in extract brewing: crystal malt, chocolate malt, black malt and roasted barley. Other brewers call all non-pale malts "specialty grains."

## I've read that crystal malts give "crisper and cleaner" tastes than caramel malts. Is this correct?

I've read that too and also that historically there was a difference, but what we buy at the store are modern crystal and caramel malts. Among modern malts, there is no distinction: they are two different names for the same type of malt.

## I've seen recipes that contain saccharine. Should I really be putting this in my beer?

Saccharine was listed as an ingredient in some older recipes for sweeter beers. Back when those recipes were written, yeasts were not very pure so that bacterial and super-attenuative yeast infections resulted in very dry beers. Since saccharine is unfermentable, it could be used to sweeten these beers. These days, we have many pure yeast strains to choose from, including many that have low attenuation. I suggest leaving off the saccharine and using a low-attenuation yeast (see appendices C, D, and E). You can also add sweetness by substituting a pound of Laaglander, "Dutch," "Hollander," or Northwestern's "European" dried malt extract. These three DMEs contain a lot of unfermentable sugars and the resulting beer comes out sweet. Finally, you can add lactose (see chapter 11) which is an unfermentable sugar to increase the sweetness of the finished beer, but be extra careful with sanitation because, while most yeasts can't eat lactose[144], many bacteria can.

## Should I store grains in the freezer?

You are probably better off not storing them in the freezer. When you take the cold grains out and open the container, they will quickly attract moisture from the air in the room. Store grains in vapor-barrier plastic bags or buckets with good seals and they will keep for years.

## How should I store a partially-used package of malt extract?

If I know that I'm not going to use up a complete package of malt extract, I will use dried malt extract because it is easier to measure and store the partially-used DME than malt extract syrup. If you have some syrup left over (or you purchased it in bulk), I recommend storing it in airtight food-storage containers in the refrigerator if only for a few days or in the freezer if for a few weeks. Dried malt extract will keep for a very long time even at room temperature, provided that you are careful to protect it from the moisture in the air. Airtight food storage containers are ideal for storing DME. Unless you live in a very dry climate, DME will turn into something resembling amber glass if exposed to air for as little as a few days.

## Is it true that you should not crush dark malts/grains or they will give your beer an astringent flavor?

No. You should crush all your malts/grains. In fact it's ironic that anyone should blame dark grains for astringency. Astringency comes from polyphenols (a.k.a. tannins). It is true that polyphenol extraction from the grain increases if you *overcrush* your grain, but it is far more important that you watch the pH of the water in which you are steeping the grains. A high pH (over 5.8 or so) will extract far more polyphenols than a lower pH. Dark grains (and here's where the irony comes into play) actually *decrease* the pH, thereby *decreasing* the likelihood of astringency! You have to make special efforts (like adding lots of calcium carbonate, which increases pH) to get an astringent dark beer.

## My homebrew supplier has some old extract on sale. Is it still usable?

Old extract tends to be dark and can give your beer a slight tartness some judges describe as "extract twang." The beer made with this extract will probably not win any competitions, but it will certainly be drinkable.

## Judges say my beer has "extract twang." What's that?

I believe that "extract twang" is the fault of old, stale extract. It may also be caused by using brands of extract that are not all-malt – extracts that are made with large percentages of various refined sugar syrups. Stick to fresh extract from manufacturers you trust and don't overdo additions of refined sugars.

## I have a bulging can of extract. Is it still usable?

I would avoid it. As long as you boil it, it won't kill you, but it's not going to make very tasty beer and I'd rather throw away the can of extract than waste 4 hours making lousy beer.

## Can I use Malto-Dextrin powder without mashing?

Yes. It will dissolve completely in your wort and add only a tiny bit of sweetness and some body. Remember that malto-dextrin is only partially fermentable (about 16%) so it will add a lot to your final gravity (FG).

# Hops

## Is it true that larger hop cones are not as fine quality as smaller cones?

No. Cone size is much more a factor of genetics and variety than anything else. Seeded cones (ones that were pollinated) are significantly larger and have slightly lower alpha acid percentages than unseeded ones[139]. Most modern hops are not seeded, but a few English varieties still are. Hop seeds pose problems for some commercial brewing systems and hop pellet manufacturers, but should be of no concern to homebrewers.

## Is it true that I shouldn't buy whole hops in which a large number of cones are broken?

No. The growers compress the hops into bales of approximately 200 pounds and wrap them in burlap. Only the biggest homebrew supply shops buy 200 pounds of hops at a time so there will be another intermediary hop broker who will break the bales down into smaller quantities. By the time you get the hops they will have been packaged and repackaged several times. It is not surprising that a lot of the cones will be broken. The color of the hops should also not be a major factor in determining quality. Brown patches on some of the hops are acceptable, but certainly the majority of the hops (say, 90%) should be somewhere between yellow-green and medium-green. I judge the quality of the hops primarily by their aroma. If the hops smell cheesy, moldy, like turpentine, or otherwise unpleasant, I reject them.

## Is it true that hops should be stored in the dark?

No. Some say that light causes hops to turn skunky. Nonsense. They spent a good part of the summer in sunlight. Light affects alpha acids only after they are isomerized. Light will cause the hops to turn slightly paler, but will not affect their brewing properties[49].

## I've read that only in lightly hopped beers should all the hops be added at the beginning of the boil and not divided into bittering, flavoring, and aromatic additions. Is that right?

No. Düsseldorfer Altbiers are an example of a very highly-hopped beer in which all the hops are added as a single addition, strictly for bittering. Whether you add all the hops as a single addition or in several additions (bittering, flavor, aroma), should depend on whether hop flavor and aroma are appropriate for the style.

## Is it true that you can balance malt sweetness with hop flavor?

No. As a matter of fact, some hop varieties (like East Kent Goldings and similar hops) actually *increase* the perceived sweetness of the beer! Some hop varieties (like Saaz, Crystal, and Tettnanger) add spicy flavors which don't necessarily increase sweetness, but their flavors certainly don't balance malt sweetness. In beer, bitterness and acidity are what balances the malt sweetness.

## Is it true that using only bittering hops (and not flavor or aroma hops) will result in a less-pleasant and coarse bitterness?

No. Coarse or unpleasant bitterness is more likely the cause of oxidized polyphenols[141]. Some hop varieties do have a more coarse bitterness than others, and it's important to note that they are not necessarily the high-alpha ones (see chapter 8).

## I've read that dryhopping can add harsh astringent flavors to my beer if left too long. Is this true?

No. Astringency in beer comes from polyphenols. The extraction of polyphenols into beer is dependent on time, temperature, and (most importantly) on the pH. The pH of finished most beers is below 4.2 and presumably you are storing the beer at room temperature or cooler. It is my belief that the polyphenol extraction under these conditions is so slow that even months on dryhops will not impart noticeable levels of astringency. My own brewing experiments have supported this. If you are experiencing astringency, look elsewhere in your procedures for the source (see chapter 14).

### I grow hops in my yard. Can I use undried hops in my beer?

I recommend against it. Drying the hops drives off many aromatic compounds which you don't want in your beer. Undried hops are likely to give your beer grassy aromas.

# Yeast

### How long can you keep a package of liquid yeast?

I have made great beer with two-year-old liquid yeast. It took a long time to start going, but the resulting beer was great. A starter is recommended for all liquid yeasts, but I would say it is mandatory for liquid yeast packages older than six months. It also depends on whether the yeast was always stored at cool temperatures or if it got hot during shipping. If you make a starter and the starter is not sluggish, smells normal, and tastes good, you should have no problems.

### I accidentally froze my yeast. Should I still use it?

Warm it up, make a starter and see how the starter behaves. If it is sluggish, toss it and get fresh yeast. If it seems to perform like a normal starter, go ahead and use it.

### Can I use honey, corn sugar, or table sugar for a yeast starter?

You really should use wort for starters. I use dried malt extract because it's convenient and you can store a partially-used package in a well-sealed plastic container. Using non-malt sugars for starters is bad for two reasons: 1) the yeast may have difficulty with more complex sugars when is sees them in the wort and 2) these non-malt sugars don't have the nutrients that yeast need for proper health. Beer made with a refined sugar starter (even with nutrients added) can result in much higher diacetyl levels[115].

### I've read that lagers should have diacetyl and therefore you should select a lager yeast that produces a lot of diacetyl. Is that right?

No. Diacetyl is considered a fault in most lagers (Bohemian Pilsners being a notable exception). In a lager that has been properly lagered, the yeast will have reabsorbed the diacetyl they have created. Some lager yeasts do create quite a bit of diacetyl and these strains require the beer to be lagered longer than the yeasts that create less diacetyl.

## My friend makes great beer without using starters. Are starters really necessary?

You can make great beer without starters, but your chances of infection are much lower if you minimize lag time. A starter can cut lag times from 3 days down to 12 hours or less. Also, starters can help you get lower final gravities, especially in higher-alcohol beers.

## I've read that overpitching (adding too much yeast) increases the risk of autolysis. Is that right?

Homebrewers are so likely to underpitch, adding ten or twenty times the typical amount of yeast that a homebrewer pitches would still not be overpitching. Furthermore, even if you use the entire yeast cake from a previous batch, if the wort is all-malt and you aerate or oxygenate well, your yeast will have more than enough nutrients and oxygen for complete fermentation and are no more likely to autolyse than if you would have pitched a smaller amount. The keys to avoiding autolysis are to never let the yeast starve and make sure that as the expected alcohol level of the beer increases, you increase the level of dissolved oxygen in the cooled wort.

## What should I do if my yeast starter is ready, but I'm not ready to brew?

If you are going to brew within a week, let it ferment out completely (so the yeast settles). Two days before brewing, pour-off half of the spent wort and pour some fresh starter wort onto the dregs. Your yeast will be just past high kräusen right when you need it. If it will be more than a week before you brew, let it ferment out completely and then put it into the refrigerator. It can stay there for a month with no problems (just keep the airlock filled). Three or four days before brewing, let it warm back up for a day, pour-off the spent wort and add some fresh starter wort onto the dregs. It will be ready just in time for brewing day.

## I've read that when dry yeast is rehydrated, if it doesn't produce a frothy head, it's defective and should be thrown out. Is that right?

No. During rehydration, the yeast may or may not show a little activity at the surface. This is no indication as to the health of the yeast[73].

## I've read that excessive glucose can cause yeast mutation Is this correct?

Excessive glucose in the wort can result in the yeast not producing various enzymes (permeases) that are necessary for more complex sugars to be fermented[82]. I suppose this can be thought of as a sort of mutation, however, in most cases it is reversible.

## Some books say that liquid yeast only needs one day of preparation. Is this correct?

In most cases, no. If you happen to get a Wyeast liquid yeast package that is only two days old, it may indeed puff-up in one day, but you really should use a starter which will take at least one additional day. If the Wyeast package is three months old, it will take about three or four days to be ready. Good beer can be made from a Wyeast package without a starter, but a starter makes a big difference (especially with lager yeasts) in lag time and attenuation.

## I've read that insufficient oxygen can result in formation of petite mutants. Is this right?

Nowhere in my reading have I found anything that induces the formation of petite mutants (a.k.a. "respiratory deficient" yeast) other than acridine orange or ethidium bromide[74]. It is true that under anaerobic conditions (without oxygen) when there are high levels of glucose in the wort, yeast cells fail to develop fully-functioning mitochondria[74]. However, these yeast cells will develop normal mitochondria in 6 to 8 hours in a low-glucose, aerobic environment[74]. Conversely, petite mutation is irreversible and occurs spontaneously at frequencies of 0.5% or higher[74] although this is highly strain dependent.

## Can I salvage yeast from the bottoms of bottle-conditioned beers?

Yes. Flame the lip of the bottle with a butane lighter to kill off any bacteria or wild yeast that may have settled on it, pour off the beer and treat the dregs like liquid yeast. You must use a starter and if the beer is imported and may be very old, there may be little live yeast left in the bottle. Smell and taste a sample of the starter and discard it if it does not smell or taste right.

## I've read that most brewers' yeasts need some hops in the wort so that they behave normally. Is this true?

Indirectly, but it is certainly not that the yeast have some sort of affinity towards hopped wort. It is true, that hops do play a role in the formation of hot and cold break[104,157,159] and that uncoagulated break material can adhere to the yeast cells and interfere with fermentation[104]. If you must boil wort without hops, you should definitely use Irish Moss and possibly even Bentonite (see chapter 6).

# Water

### Is it true that permanently hard water is best for brewing?

Not exactly. Before brewers understood water chemistry and when local water dictated the styles of beer that they could brew, yes, permanently hard water (water that is high in calcium from calcium sulfate) made it easy to brew pale beers. We do understand water chemistry now and we aren't limited by the local water to brewing any one particular style of beer. Permanently hard water makes it difficult to brew a Bohemian Pilsner to style, without somehow removing all those sulfate ions. The sulfate ions will accentuate the bop bitterness and give a long, lingering dry bitterness in the finish. This is great for Bitters and India Pale Ales, but is the wrong flavor profile for Bohemian Pilsners.

### Is it true that sulfate adds bitterness to the finished beer?

No, not directly. Sulfate itself is very mildly bitter (taste some gypsum) and certainly won't add any noticeable bitterness from a few teaspoons in 5 gallons of water. Actually, the sulfate ion affects the *perceived* bitterness in the beer by accentuating what bitterness is in the beer from isomerized alpha acids[176,177,178]. 30 IBUs and 500 ppm of sulfate is far more bitter than 40 IBUs and 5 ppm of sulfate.

### I've read that adding acids to your brewing water will cause carbonates to precipitate. Is this correct?

No, in the kettle or mashtun, adding acids will lower the pH, cause the balance of $CO_3^-$, $HCO_3^-$, and $H_2CO_3$ to shift towards $H_2CO_3$ and the excess carbonates will evolve as $CO_2$ gas[160]. Unfortunately, calcium will also be lost in the reaction (e.g. calcium lactate will be created if you use lactic acid for acidification)[161].

### Is it true that bicarbonate and carbonate add a harsh bitterness to the finished beer?

No, not directly. Many authors confuse astringency with bitterness, but the two are very different (see chapter 13). High-carbonate/bicarbonate waters affect all-grain brewing much more significantly than they do extract brewing, but their affect can be minimized by monitoring pH and making sure that whenever you steep (or mash) malts, that the pH is below about 5.8. High pH water extracts polyphenols (a.k.a. tannins) from the malts and hops, and lends a harshness to the beer as astringency.

## Doesn't soft water have a low pH?

No. While it is true that chalky water has a high pH, a high pH does not necessarily mean that the water is hard or vice versa. Remember that hardness is primarily based on the calcium and magnesium ion concentrations in the water. If you took distilled water (which has a pH of 7.0, neutral) and added sodium carbonate to it (washing soda) it would still be extremely soft (no calcium or magnesium, right?) but it would have a much higher pH. On the other hand, if you added calcium chloride to distilled water, you could make it quite hard without significantly raising the pH.

## My water stains the sink blue. Is it safe to brew with this water?

Yes. What you have is called "aggressive water" running through copper pipes. The science behind this is rather complicated, but generally speaking, the softer the water, the more likely it is to be aggressive and dissolve copper from your pipes. You can safely brew with this water, but:
- you will probably need to add minerals for most styles (see chapter 9), and
- you may want to consider switching to plastic pipe because the copper pipes will, in time, spring leaks[162].

# Boiling

## Why boil?

Boiling sanitizes the wort, removes chlorine from your water, coagulates proteins so you have less hazy beer, isomerizes hop alpha acids for bittering, and boils off unwanted compounds such as DMS. There are kits that say that you don't have to boil (just add the extract to hot water then add cool water and add yeast) and they will make tasty beer, but they can often be hazier than if they were actually boiled and are more likely to be infected.

## If I choose to boil a pre-hopped kit extract, what boil volume should I use?

Since there is no concern over hop utilization in a pre-hopped kit, you can boil any volume that fits in your kettle. However, the less-concentrated the boil (i.e. the more water you use) the less the wort will darken during the boil. Then again, if you boil 2.5 gallons and then add that to 2.5 gallons of cold water in the fermenter, the water in the fermenter had better be very cold, otherwise the resulting wort (after mixing) will be too hot for the yeast.

### Won't a rolling boil cause hot-side-aeration (HSA)?

No. The steam evolving from the wort will purge any oxygen out of the kettle headspace, so no matter how vigorous the boil, the wort will not get oxidized.

### Can I use an electric stove?

The average electric stove produces less heat than the average gas stove which makes it a little more difficult to bring the wort to a boil, but most will work just fine (see "Stoves" in chapter 4).

# Cooling, Racking, and Aeration

### Is it okay to allow hops from the boil to carry over into the fermenter?

Since the wort is cool, no further isomerization is going on and therefore, there is virtually no further bitterness being imparted to the finished beer. The main concern would be the added risk of clogging the airlock or blowoff hose. If you can do it without aerating hot wort, I recommend that you should try to prevent hops (especially whole hops) from passing into the fermenter. Some brewers have been shocked by the scary green foam you get if pellets carry into the fermenter. Unless clogging of the blowoff tube or airlock is likely, there is no need to be scared.

### I've read that it's a good idea to allow the yeast to sit on the break for a while and then rack the beer off the break. Isn't there a risk of losing a lot of the yeast by doing this?

Hot and cold break contain compounds that the yeast can (and like to) eat. Several authors have suggested pitching the yeast a couple of hours before racking the beer off the break. Depending on your yeast, it is true that you can leave a lot of your yeast behind in the "settling tank" along with your break. Personally, I don't go through any great lengths to eliminate all of the break and therefore I don't have to worry about this problem. If you pitch a yeast starter of sufficient size and aerate/oxygenate your wort enough for the gravity and strain of yeast you are using, you really don't need the added nutrition of the break. See also "I've read that leaving the cold break in the wort results in cloudy and astringent beer. Is that right?" below.

### I've read that leaving the cold break in the wort results in cloudy and astringent beer. Is that right?

Not exactly. Cold break is primarily proteins and protein-polyphenol complexes. The cold break can be utilized by the yeast for some important compounds, so leaving it in the wort does have some benefit (especially in underoxygenated worts). However, there are a number of reasons to remove as much of the break from the wort as is reasonable. I do not believe that astringency is one of them, but certainly studies have shown that clarity of the finished beer is increased when the cold break is removed[39]. Furthermore, some researchers believe that uncoagulated cold break can coat yeast cells and impair fermentation[39]. Fermenting on the break material can lead to increased levels of higher (fusel) alcohols[123], but I have not noticed any overabundance of higher alcohols in any of the beers in which I fermented on most of the hot and cold break. Some informal research has implicated fermenting on break material as the cause for some soapy flavors in the beer. Again, I have not noticed this in my experience. Note however, that in extract brewing much of the break has already been removed during the extract production and you get only a fraction of the break that you can get in some all-grain batches. My advice: don't worry *too* much about the break.

### Does it matter if I aerate before or after pitching the yeast?

No – just make sure you cool the wort first.

### Can I use ice to chill my hot wort?

Sure, as long as you are sure there are no bacteria or wild yeasts in it. I used to use ice water to chill my wort before I built a wort chiller, but I used to pour boiling water into clean plastic jugs, close them up, let them cool in the cellar overnight (so I don't overwork my refrigerator) and then chill the water to about 33° F in the freezer. Some of this water I added to the kettle and the rest I poured into the fermenter. At this time, I was boiling about 3 gallons of wort down to 2 1/2 and then adding 1 1/2 gallons of ice water to the kettle and another gallon of ice water to the fermenter. Note that ice usually contains air bubbles and can contain quite a bit of dissolved oxygen. If you are using this method of cooling and are experiencing the effects of Hot-Side Aeration (sherrylike aromas, cardboard-like aromas) this may be the source. Overall, using ice directly in the wort is not a very good method of chilling hot wort and you really should consider some of the more efficient and advanced methods (see "Boiling and Cooling" in chapter 4).

### Can I use dry ice to chill my hot wort?

I recommend against it. There is no telling what kinds of bacteria or wild yeast may be frozen into the ice. The freezing will not necessarily kill these microbes.

# Fermentation

## Doesn't blowoff remove nasty fusel alcohols?

Yes, but only a very small percentage of them. Experiments that I've done and described in my article "When Fermentation Rears Its Dirty Head" in *Brewing Techniques*[33] show that the difference in higher (fusel) alcohols is not significant between the blowoff and non-blowoff methods of brewing. The main difference is in the loss of bitterness (see "Hops" in chapter 15).

## I've read all kinds of different fermentation temperatures for Berliner Weissbiers from 59° F (15° C) to 113° F (45° C). What's the right temperature?

Well, it certainly isn't 59° F (15° C) because the Lactobacillus bacteria will be dormant at that temperature[163]. Although it is the preferred temperature of many lactic acid bacteria, you also don't want to ferment at 113° F (45° C) because your yeast will produce far too many higher alcohols. I recommend you simply ferment at the warm end of normal fermentation, around 70° to 75° F (21° to 24° C) and give beer several months in a glass secondary for the sourness to develop.
Alternatively, you could make a gallon of unhopped wort, ferment with just lactic acid bacteria for a day or two at 113° F (45° C) and then boil this wort along with the rest of the extract and the hops – this will boil off most of the DMS that would be produced at that high fermentation temperature[163].

## I've read that if the scum on the top of the fermenting wort falls back into the ferment, the resulting beer will have harsh flavors. Is that right?

No. This is a very common misconception. The main effect of allowing the dirty head, as it's called, to fall back into the ferment is that the beer will be slightly more bitter than if you skim or blow it off. This bitterness is no more or less harsh. See "Doesn't blowoff remove nasty fusel alcohols?" above.

## What's "too hot" for fermentation?

Every yeast strain is different. Some will make fine beer even at 80° F or more. Remember that the actual beer may be 10° F higher than the room temperature in a high-gravity beer. Try a small batch if you are afraid to commit 5 gallons. Note that if your question is "Can I brew in the summertime?" then the answer depends not only on temperature, but also on how much life there is in your air during the summer. In my house, in the summertime, there is a slightly phenolic wild yeast that lives in the air. In the wintertime, I'm sure it's here too, but probably in much smaller numbers because of the temperature, air circulation, and humidity. In any event, in the summertime, the beers I brew have a faint clovey/phenolic aroma and flavor. It's not bad, but it doesn't fit in all styles. I've successfully gotten that wild yeast under control by purchasing a filtered-air aeration system. I don't have to go to all these lengths during the winter, but if I want to brew in the summertime, I have to take this extra step.

### I've read that a tall, narrow fermenter results in a better fermentation than a wide, squat one. Is that right?

Not necessarily. For some yeasts, exactly the opposite is true. See "Can I ferment in 5-gallon stainless steel soda kegs?" below. Even if your yeast is happy in a tall, narrow fermenter, settling time is directly proportional to fermenter depth.

### Should I keep my fermenter in the dark?

Yes. Once the hop alpha acids have been isomerized, they can cause a beer to smell skunky if exposed to light. Strong sunlight can skunk a beer in 5 minutes whereas incandescent lights may take weeks or months (depending on the wattage, distance, and color of the beer – dark beers are less susceptible).

### My airlock clogged and blew right off my fermenter! The fermenter sat around without an airlock for more than 8 hours. Is my beer ruined?

Unlikely. Many brewers, including commercial brewers like Young's, Samuel Smith's, and Liefmans, use open fermenters. During the time that your beer was exposed to the air, it was producing a lot of $CO_2$ which would have kept any dust from falling in, especially since your fermenter had such a small opening exposed. Even fruit flies are unlikely to get into the fermenter. If the risk of kräusen fouling your airlock is still high, I would switch to a blowoff tube. If the kräusen has begun to subside, clean out the airlock, resanitize it, and put it back on the fermenter.

### Why does my Fermometer™ show warmer than the room temperature?

Fermentation is exothermic, which means that it produces heat. In a high-gravity wort, your yeast can generate so much heat that the beer is 10° F higher than the room temperature. All you can do is try to cool the fermenter down so that it doesn't get too hot (try to keep fermentation below 75 or 80° F (24 or 27° C)). One trick is to put the fermenter into a tub of water and slip a tee-shirt over it. The shirt will wick water over the fermenter and the evaporating water will cool the fermenter.

## Should I replace the beer lost to blowoff or left behind after racking?

You have two options: yes and no. Let's consider them. If you add water to replace the beer that was "blown-off" or left behind after racking into the secondary, you will be diluting your beer. If you overshot your target original gravity and instead of 1.050 you got 1.055, then perhaps you wouldn't mind adding some boiled water to top-up the fermenter. On the other hand, if you worked very hard to reach that 1.120 original gravity for your Barleywine, you certainly don't want to dilute it, do you? If your concern is oxidation, don't worry about it – the headspace in the fermenter is all $CO_2$ – all the oxygen has been pushed out through the airlock. If you use a secondary, even if there is a large headspace after racking, this is not really a problem: racking the beer will release some dissolved $CO_2$ which will purge the air out of the secondary's headspace. If you do choose to add water make sure you boil and cool it first. Boiling will drive-off all the dissolved oxygen (which you don't want at this point in the process), remove much of the chlorine and kill any wild yeasts or bacteria that might be hanging around. Cool it as quickly as you can or oxygen from the air will re-oxygenate the water leading to oxidized beer when you add it to the fermenter. Rack gently – don't splash while adding the water.

## Why does my beer *start* to ferment again after racking to the secondary?

There are there possible causes for this phenomenon where a batch of beer that appeared to have been done begins moving the airlock again. First, if you have a very flocculent yeast strain, racking will resuspend it again and this may cause fermentation to restart for a day or two. The other two causes have to do with $CO_2$ saturation, so I need to give a little background on that first. When the beer begins to ferment, the $CO_2$ produced by the yeast first dissolves into the beer. Once the saturation limit is reached, the $CO_2$ will *usually* bubble out of the beer and move the airlock. The second (and most common) cause for this "restarted fermentation" is that racking has caused some of the $CO_2$ to bubble out of solution (due to pressure changes during racking, warming, and agitation) and this causes the airlock to move again (for perhaps an hour or two). The third cause is related to the fact that $CO_2$ concentration in solution can cause yeast to slow or even stop fermenting. The extent to which yeast are affected by this is strain dependent. You may have noticed that I said "usually bubble out of the beer" earlier. It has been suggested that in some cases (excessive trub removal is one theory) too much $CO_2$ will dissolve into the beer and impede fermentation. If this is the case, racking (or swirling) the carboy will cause the beer to start fermenting again for a day or two. Fermenting at a warmer temperature can help because the cooler the beer, the more $CO_2$ will dissolve into it.

## Why does my beer *stop* fermenting after racking to the secondary?

In the previous question, I explained how when the yeast begin fermenting, the $CO_2$ produced first dissolves into the beer and only then begins to bubble out. I also explained why racking causes some $CO_2$ to come out of solution. That question was about beer that had already finished fermenting. This one is the case where fermentation is still actively fermenting. Racking can cause enough $CO_2$ to bubble out of solution that it will take a few hours for the yeast to re-saturate the beer with $CO_2$. Only after the beer is re-saturated with $CO_2$ will the airlock begin to move again.

## What's wrong with adding chlorinated tapwater to my fermenter?

While the amount of chlorine in municipal tapwater is usually not very high, the chlorine can react with compounds in the wort to create chlorophenols which have particularly strong smells. They give beer a plastic-like or medicinal aroma. Besides sanitation, boiling-off chlorine is an important reason for boiling all your brewing water before use.

## There's a white, powdery film floating in my fermenter. Is my beer ruined?

Maybe. Maybe not. The film can be yeast, mold, or an aerobic bacteria (one that requires some air). Whether your beer is ruined or not depends on which microbe it is. If it's at the beginning of the fermentation, it's probably yeast. Many ale yeasts form small floating colonies at first which later grow to cover the whole of the fermenting beer. If it is indeed yeast, leave it alone... it's fine. If it's at the end of your fermentation, you probably let your airlock run dry or you have a big air leak in your lid. It could still be okay. Rack the beer into another container, trying to avoid siphoning up some of that film (i.e. leave a little more in the fermenter than usual). Smell and taste the beer. Don't worry... nothing dangerous can live in beer. If smells and tastes fine or only slightly odd, you can still let it finish fermenting and then bottle – some very odd-looking fermentations have made spectacular beer. If it really smells bad, then you might as well dump it. In the future, make sure your fermenter lid fits better and that your airlock doesn't dry out.

## Can I use Clinitest™ or one of the other sugar test kits to determine when I should bottle?

I'm not yet convinced these tests are useful for determining when fermentation is complete. At issue is exactly which sugars cause a reaction in these tests. For the tests to be useful, they should react to *all* fermentable sugars and *only* to fermentable sugars. I suspect that none of the tests meet these requirements. If, however, you can find a test that meets these requirements, it could be useful in determining when fermentation is complete. There are said to be "glucose specific" tests available, but these are completely useless. Glucose is the sugar most easily usable by yeast and therefore will be consumed first, so even in a half-complete normal fermentation, there should be no glucose remaining.

## There's a white film or brown crust on the inside of my carboy. Is it still safe to use it?

If the film was on the carboy when you got it, I'm not sure if I'd use it, but if the carboy was clear initially and became cloudy after use, it's one of two things: beerstone or calcium carbonate. Beerstone is a brown crust which forms slowly during fermentation (or during the boil in your kettle) and will build up after many batches. It is said to be a good hiding place for bacteria and wild yeasts. Beerstone is mostly calcium oxalate and can be removed by filling the carboy with a cup (about 250 ml) of muriatic acid (hydrochloric acid – available in hardware stores – follow the safety precautions listed on the bottle) in 5 gallons (18.9 liters) of water and letting it sit for a week. Rinse well. Don't let muriatic acid contact stainless steel! If you have beerstone on stainless steel, use phosphoric or nitric acid and be very careful. I simply used a paper towel, rubber gloves, eye protection, and scrubbed the inside of my kettle with 10% phosphoric acid.

Calcium carbonate film is white and can form slowly if your water has significant levels of carbonate/bicarbonate or it can form overnight if you leave your fermenter filled with a solution of washing soda (sodium carbonate) or sanitizers such as B-Brite or One-Step. Calcium carbonate can be removed by filling the fermenter with a mild acid solution (a cup of vinegar or lemon juice in 5 gallons / 18.9 liters of water) for a few days and then rinsing well with water.

## What is a diacetyl rest?

At warmer temperatures (55 or 60° F and above) most yeast strains will reabsorb most of the diacetyl they produce during the earlier part of fermentation. When making a lager, since the fermentation is done at a colder temperature, some yeasts have trouble re-absorbing the diacetyl. A diacetyl rest is used in such cases. One of the reasons for lagering is to allow the yeast to reabsorb the diacetyl. Performing a diacetyl rest may reduce the amount of time you need to lager the beer. Wait until fermentation is 2/3 complete (when your specific gravity has dropped 2/3 of the way to the expected FG). Slowly raise the temperature of the beer until it is between 55 and 65° F (13 and 18° C) and hold it there for one to two days. Then, slowly cool the beer back down to between 33 and 45° F (1 and 7° C) for lagering. Commercial breweries usually raise and lower the temperature of the beer only 2 to 3° F (1 to 2° C) per day, but I think that 5° F (3° C) per day is sufficiently slow to avoid shocking the yeast.

## Can I ferment in 5-gallon stainless steel soda-pop kegs?

I recommend against using soda-pop kegs as primary fermenters, but they acceptable as secondaries. There are a number of reasons I don't like soda kegs as primaries. First of all, unless you simply leave the lid off and cover the top with plastic, you have only the two connectors to vent $CO_2$ during fermentation. To use the liquid fitting as a vent, you will have to remove the connector and dip tube. Even if you remove both the liquid and gas connectors and dip tubes, the openings are very small. They can clog with blowoff material and pressure can build up in the tank. Although these tanks are rated to 130 psi (about 9 kg/cm$^2$) and the chances of explosion are low, if both vents clog and pressure builds up, the beer will carbonate and when the clogs are blown out, you can lose half your batch to foam! A second reason for not using soda kegs as primaries is because they are tall and thin. Tall, narrow (height greater than 5 times the width) fermenters have been found to result in slow and/or incomplete fermentations with some yeasts[164,233]. Tall commercial fermenters are often fitted with stirring devices for this reason[165]. Two yeasts that are known to be problematic with tall, narrow fermenters are Weihenstephan 34/70 and the Whitbread single-strain ale yeast[233]. Do not sanitize stainless steel with chlorine bleach– use iodophor or a percarbonate-based sanitizer like B-Brite or One-Step.

## Should I lager in a secondary or in bottles?

You can do either or both. Lagering in a secondary will reduce the amount of yeast you have in the bottom of each bottle. I recommend lagering in a secondary for a month and then in bottles for one to three more. Different yeasts require different amounts of lagering.

## Can I use dry ice to expel air from my fermenter?

I recommend against it. There is no telling what kinds of bacteria or wild yeast may be frozen into the ice. The freezing will not necessarily kill these microbes.

## What is beechwood aging and should I do it?

You may have heard that Budweiser is "beechwood aged." Some books have suggested that this is used to clarify the beer, but in fact, it's just the opposite. The yeast that Anheuser-Busch uses to make Budweiser is highly flocculent. It is so flocculent that if not for beechwood aging the yeast would settle to the bottom of the aging tanks and only the top layer of yeast would be interacting with the beer. As a result, the beer would require a very long lagering time. By loosely stacking sanitized beechwood "chips" (about 4 inches wide, 1/4 inch thick, and two feet long) to the conditioning tanks, the yeast have many more times the surface area on which to settle and thus far more yeast is exposed to the beer during the lagering process[166]. This reduces the amount of lagering time needed for the yeast to reduce acetaldehyde and diacetyl. The beechwood chips add no flavor to the beer and are not part of the "kräusen tradition." Since sanitation is extremely difficult and since homebrewers have the option of simply swirling the fermenter to resuspend flocculent yeasts, beechwood aging is not recommended for homebrewing.

# Bottling

## Do I need to add yeast at bottling time?

This is a common practice among Belgian brewers, especially those making very strong beers. You don't really need to add yeast (I've had no problems with carbonation without adding yeast at bottling time even with a beer that sat in the secondary for a year!), but it will certainly help strong beers carbonate faster.

## I've read that you can reduce oxygen in the headspace by putting the bottlecaps loosely on the filled bottles and waiting 15 minutes to crimp the caps on. Does this work?

I believe that it would work but I don't think that you have to wait 15 minutes. What you have read assumes that the yeast will begin eating the priming sugar and producing $CO_2$ which purges the oxygen out of the headspace. The turbulence associated with filling the bottle will cause quite a bit of the $CO_2$ that is in solution to bubble out of the beer. That will purge the oxygen out of the headspace in 5 minutes or less if you put the cap on quickly (while the $CO_2$ is still bubbling out of the beer). Some commercial bottling systems shoot a stream of water or tap the bottom of the bottle to cause the beer to foam just before capping. All of these procedures can increase the shelf life of your beer, but recall that since your beer has yeast in the bottle and yeast is a very strong oxygen scavenger, you don't have to be as concerned as the commercial brewers who are bottling filtered beer.

## Can I use a dishwasher to sanitize my bottles?

I've heard some homebrewers successfully use their dishwasher's "sanitize" cycle for sanitizing bottles. Others run their bottles through the dishwasher with some bleach in the wash cycle with good results. The only problem is when some inside surfaces of the bottles evade the spray of the machine. Unless you only put sparkling clean bottles into the dishwasher or are 100% sure that the entire inside surface of every bottle is touched by the spray, you can have infections. The heat from the "sanitize" cycle is probably more reliable than relying on bleach.

## Can I bake my bottles to sanitize them?

Yes – 250° F (120° C) for 30 minutes should be good, but let them cool slowly overnight. Quickly cooling them is a sure way to shatter bottles. I've read that repeated baking and cooling weakens the glass, but then I've read about homebrewers who have baked bottles dozens of times with no problems. I think that slow cooling (with the oven door closed) is the key to not weakening the glass.

## If I rinse my bottles after use, should I still sanitize them?

Yes. Absolutely.

## Do I have to sanitize my bottlecaps?

It is strongly recommended. While the heat involved during the manufacturing of bottlecap linings probably sanitizes them, remember that someone probably used their hands to repackage the bottlecaps into the bag which you purchased. It's a safe bet that they didn't wear sterile surgical gloves.

## I've read that introducing air at bottling time will cause the yeast to reproduce excessively and get caught in some kind of "transitionary phase" due to lack of nutrients. Is this true?

I seriously doubt it. Yeast growth is not simply a factor of oxygen supply as this implies. There are many reasons for not introducing air after fermentation has completed (oxidation of alcohols to aldehydes, oxidation of polyphenols, etc.) because they lead to stale and unpleasant flavors, but I don't think that excessive reproduction or abnormal metabolism are a concern.

## Can I prime my beer by just adding a teaspoon of sugar into each bottle?

This is an old technique. It is neither sanitary nor is it very accurate. I recommend against it and suggest that you prime the beer as described earlier in this book.

## Is it true that you should always weigh priming sugar?

Weighing priming sugar (especially corn sugar) is slightly more accurate than measuring it by volume (because the volume varies with how firmly you pack the sugar), but it's not absolutely necessary.

## Doesn't corn sugar absorb a lot of water? Doesn't that mean that volume measurements should be more accurate than weight measurements?

Corn sugar does absorb a little water, but it's not as much as you might think (just over 1%)[167]. It's unlikely that most homebrewers' scales or measuring cups are even close to 1% precision. Weight measurements will be slightly more precise because how firmly you pack the sugar can have a significant effect on the volume. Table sugar (sucrose) will absorb even less water than corn sugar, but Dried Malt Extract will absorb far more (you really must store Dried Malt Extract in a well-sealed container).

## Corn sugar priming adds a noticeable flavor to finished beer, doesn't it?

Corn sugar is glucose (a.k.a. dextrose) and is a part of all worts. Glucose and fructose together are typically 8.9% of the wort and sucrose is another 5.5%[168]. I mention sucrose because, although the yeast can't eat sucrose directly, they release an enzyme called invertase into the wort which breaks each molecule of sucrose into a molecule of glucose and a molecule of fructose. If you add, for example, $1/2$ cup of corn sugar to 5 gallons of 1.050 wort, that only increases the gravity by 3%. Clearly this is an insignificant increase in the amount of glucose in the wort and will not change the flavor noticeably.

## I've read that priming with dried malt extract gives finer bubbles than priming with corn sugar. Is that true?

No. $CO_2$ is $CO_2$ and regarding carbonation, it doesn't matter which sugars were fermented to produce it. In the main ferment, you will get a healthier fermentation if your wort does not have too much corn sugar or sucrose in it, but at priming time, there is absolutely no difference in the quality of the carbonation.

## Can I use plastic 1-liter and 2-liter soda bottles for bottling beer?

Yes, but you had better consume the beer within a month or so. These bottles are made of a plastic that is oxygen-permeable and therefore the beer will show noticeable oxidation within a month or two (how soon, depends on storage temperature). The $CO_2$ pressure inside the bottles will *not* keep oxygen out – that is not how gasses work.

## Can I use glass juice bottles or canning jars for bottling beer?

It is not recommended. They are not made to hold pressure and can even explode.

## Should I vary the amount of priming sugar based on the final gravity?

If the beer is not fully fermented (i.e. there is still a small amount of fermentable sugar remaining), it is possible to bottle the beer using a smaller than normal amount of priming sugar, but this method is not recommended. If you miscalculate and there is more fermentable sugar remaining than you had expected, you will have overcarbonated beer at best and possibly even bursting bottles. Also, because there is still going to be a lot of suspended yeast in the beer, you will have more than the usual amount of yeast in the bottom of each bottle. I recommend that you wait till the beer is fully fermented before bottling. As long as you wait till the fermentation is complete, the priming sugar amount should be the same regardless of the final gravity.

## There's a white film on my bottles. Is it safe to use them?

It's most likely that you soaked the bottles in washing soda (sodium carbonate), B-Brite, or One-Step solution too long (overnight is too long). I believe it's safe to use them, but if you would really rather remove the film, soak the bottles in a mild acid solution (a cup of vinegar or lemon juice in 5 gallons / 18.9 liters of water) for a few days and then rinse well with water.

## Can I use twist-off bottles?

I would recommend against it. Firstly, they are much thinner glass than pry-off bottles. Secondly, they are made to be capped by a completely different type of capper which I've never seen available to homebrewers. The concern is that some of the bottles may not seal and the beer will be flat. Depending on the type of capper you have, one in 100 may be flat or one in 3 may be flat. I would only use twist-off bottles in an emergency.

## Can I use twist-off bottlecaps for capping non-twist-off bottles?

The main difference between twist-off bottlecaps and pry-off bottlecaps is that they are made of thinner metal. I have run across twist-off caps in many homebrew competitions and haven't noticed any correlation between this type of cap and undercarbonation. Therefore, I think it's fine to use them.

### When I push the bottle filler into the bottom of the bottle, beer sprays in. Isn't this a source of oxidation?

You're absolutely right. If the beer is spraying into the bottle, you have too much pressure (the bigger the height difference between the top of the beer in the bottling bucket/carboy and the level of the beer in the bottle, the higher the pressure). I recommend that you raise the bottle and filler so that the bottom of the filler is only a few inches below the level of the beer in the bottling bucket/carboy. Now the beer will run slowly and gently into the bottle when you push down on the valve. Once the tip is submerged, you can lower the bottle and filler together to increase the pressure and speed up the flow.

### Can I use a bucket with a spigot instead of siphoning?

Sure. I've tried one of these and was not happy with it. The spigot on the particular bucket I used allowed a little air to be sucked into the stream of beer. There are spigots which don't have this problem, but even if you do find one of those, you should still do everything you can to avoid aerating fermenting wort and finished beer. Attach a hose to the spigot so that the wort or beer does not splash into the receiving container.

## Troubleshooting

### How do I clean this burnt-on crud off the stove?

Brewing can take a toll on your stovetop. Usually, we brewers get blamed for the burnt-on crud that appears on the stovetop when we finish our boil and remove the kettle. Unless you had a boilover, the source of this crud is not the brewing, but actually spillage that occurred before we brewed and our long boil simply baked-on the existing spills. There are three keys to easy cleanup after the boil. Firstly, before you begin brewing, clean the stove so it sparkles – this will ensure that there is nothing to bake-on. Secondly, rub a light coat of soap onto the stovetop under where the kettle will sit – this is an old camping trick to make cleanup easier. Finally, lay out some aluminum foil around the burner (be careful, it does burn!). If you do get some burnt-on crud that you have to remove, the best way I've found to get rid of it is to spray some Fantastic™ or Formula 409™ onto the cooled stovetop, let it sit for 15 minutes and then scrape the crud off with a razor blade (be careful!).

### Why, after five good batches, did I suddenly have three bad ones?

The two most likely answers are: 1) the good ones were made in the winter and the bad ones in the summer, or 2) you have a scratch in your plastic fermenter (or a hairline crack in your glass fermenter) and some nasty wild yeast has taken up residence there. If the problem is not seasonal (see What's "too hot" for fermentation?), check all your equipment and replace the old, scratched, stained plastic parts.

# Miscellaneous

## Can I brew 5 gallons of strong beer and dilute it into 10 gallons of normal beer?

Yes. This is called high-gravity brewing and is done by some large commercial breweries. What you have to remember is that any oxygen you add after fermentation will give you off aromas/flavors. Boiling the water will remove all the oxygen and you should let it cool before adding it, but if you let it sit around it will reabsorb more oxygen (so cool the water quickly and use it right away). Don't splash when adding the water to minimize oxidation.

## I've heard to ignore the directions on the can of extract. Why?

Extract producers want to make sure that nobody is intimidated by brewing, so they put the simplest possible instructions on the can of extract. You can usually make drinkable beer using the instructions on the can, you will probably make better-tasting, less-hazy beer if you follow the instructions in this book. Many kits say that you should add corn sugar. Corn sugar adds alcohol to the beer without adding body or flavor. Most homebrewers, many of whom are rebelling against years of limited choices in terms of beer styles, are seeking dark, thick, flavorful beers. It is this "dark, thick beer is good – pale, thin beer is bad" mentality that started the rumor that adding corn sugar (or any refined sugar) is evil and should be avoided at all cost. There is nothing wrong with adding refined sugars to beers if the style dictates that it is necessary. You could not make a beer like Duvel without refined sugar. If it was all-malt, it would be thick and chewy and not refreshing. Let's not overreact: let's use refined sugars when appropriate.

## I've read about plastic fermenters and 2-liter bottles that are "UV coated" to protect the beer from skunking. Why do I still have to store the fermenter and bottles in the dark?

It is true that ultraviolet light does cause a hop compound called isohumulone to undergo chemical changes which result in the formation of prenyl-mercaptan, the compound that gives skunks their characteristic smell. "UV coatings," however, do not prevent beer from getting skunky. Via a process called non-radiative energy transfer[169], blue light will also cause beer to turn skunky – it does not require ultraviolet light[170]. Clear and green glass and plastic let these blue wavelengths through quite easily. Brown glass offers some protection, but not enough so you can simply let your beer sit out in the light. Incidentally, sunlight and fluorescent lights take much less time to cause skunking than incandescent lights.

## I've just spent all this time and money to make 2 gallons of very strong Barleywine. If I take a hydrometer reading before pitching and then several more to determine when it is done, I'll be throwing out more than 10 percent of my precious beer! Is there some way I can return my hydrometer samples to the fermenter?

Pre-fermentation you can simply boil the sample in the microwave or on the stove for a minute or two (to re-sanitize it) and return it to the fermenter. After fermentation, it's probably best to not try this. In general, I think it's safest to discard post-fermentation hydrometer samples. You can, however, reduce the amount of beer you need for the sample: rather than taking a 200 ml sample, you can take a 50 ml sample, dilute it with 150 ml of water and then multiply the points of the reading by 4. For example, if the diluted beer reads 1.008, the actual gravity is 1.032. Don't rely on kitchen-grade measuring cups for this dilution – you really need a graduated cylinder.

## I have no way of fermenting at lager temperatures. Can I still make something that tastes like a lager?

Some ale yeasts are not very fruity. See appendix D for some recommendations. The cooler you ferment the beer, the more lager-like it will be. Even if you cannot ferment at 45 or 50° F, doesn't mean that you cannot try fermenting a lager yeast at 60°. It may be a little fruitier than a lager fermented at 45° F, but it will still taste good. Please note that some yeasts can give extremely sulfury aromas when fermented warm. Usually, these aromas will fade with time.

## Is it possible to can excess wort for use later (for starters, kräusening, etc.)?

Yes, it's possible and many brewers do it. However, since the pH of most worts is well above 4.6, you should take all the standard precautions against Botulism. Pressure-canning (in a pressure-cooker) for 15 minutes at 250 F (120 C) is the safest bet. The absence of a bulging lid is *not* a guarantee of safety (although a bulging top does indicate an infection of some sort – throw the wort out). To be extra safe, I recommend that you boil the canned wort *again* for 15 minutes, just before use, to denature any Botulism toxin that may have been produced during storage. Personally, I prefer to make up starter or kräusening wort *as needed* and not mess with the risks of long-term wort storage.

## What's w/v?

This represents an *approximation* of w/w, which is the weight percentage of a solution. It is commonly *misused* where w/w is actually meant. If you send a bottle of beer to a laboratory for analysis, they will give you the alcohol content, for example, either as alcohol percentage by weight (w/w) or alcohol percentage by volume (v/v). Weight/volume measurements are only an approximation which makes *creating* solutions (5 grams of calcium sulfate in 100 ml of water is 5% w/v) easier and is only reasonably accurate when the solvent is water. No beer label, lab analysis, or style guideline should use the units "alcohol percentage w/v."

## Is it legal to ship beer?

It is illegal to send beer via the US Postal Service. It is illegal to send beer across state lines without the proper legal paperwork *except* for analytical purposes. Since homebrewing competitions are primarily for getting your beer's aroma and flavor analyzed by a certified judge, sending beer to homebrewing competitions is within the law, even if you are shipping across state lines. Private shipping companies (UPS, FedEx, etc.) can and do ship alcoholic beverages but many clerks are not aware of this and will refuse to accept a package if you tell them that you are shipping beer.

## Does the beer have to be below 50° F (10° C) for finings to work?

No. When using gelatin, virtually any temperature is acceptable. When fining with isinglass, it is recommended that you keep the beer below about 68° F (20° C), simply because isinglass breaks down and becomes useless quite quickly above that temperature. It is true, however, that clarification is more effective at cooler temperatures because protein-polyphenol complexes are less soluble and the thus gelatin and isinglass finings not only remove yeast, but also more of the chill haze[70].

## How should I use oak in my beers?

While fermenting in oak or the addition of oak chips to the beer are the obvious sources of oak aroma, it is not quite that simple. American oak and European oak are quite different. Also, if using American oak, only white oak should be used. European oak lends virtually no oaky aroma. A few days in contact with American oak will impart more oak aroma than three years in contact with European oak. Many brewers are under the impression that India Pale Ales are supposed to have an oaky character. Nothing could be further from the truth. Firstly, the brewers of the original IPAs used European oak for their casks. Secondly, after a few uses even American oak loses much of its oakiness. If you were shipping beer to India, not expecting to have the cask returned, would you use your newest casks or your oldest? Finally, some brewers used pitch-lined casks.

Some styles do actually have an oaky aroma as part of their character. These are Flanders Brown Ales (more specifically, Rodenbach Grand Cru) and Lambics/Lambieks. However, I believe that an oaky character may be imparted to a Lambic/Lambiek by *Brettanomyces* or some other microbiota in the fermentation. I judged Jim Liddil's 1994 AHA National Competition Best of Show pGueuze in the first round and remember that it had a significant oaky character. However, it was extract-based (which rules out husk character) and was fermented in plastic with no oak chips added.

Using oak casks for fermentation is beyond the scope of this book. If you want to use oak chips, I recommend that you should sanitize them either by steaming for a few minutes or by dipping the chips in boiling water for a few seconds. Anything more than a few seconds will quickly remove much of the flavor you are seeking. Alternatively, you can boil the chips in water for a few minutes and then add the water along with the chips. Do not use sanitizers (especially bleach and iodophor) on the chips since they will absorb the sanitizer and can then ruin the beer flavor. Note that yeast and bacteria will penetrate deep into the wood and that they will be impossible to sanitize completely. One ounce of American oak chips kept in the fermenter for a week or two will give you a noticeable oak aroma.

## Can extract beers compete with all-grain beers in competition?

Not only can they compete, but they can win! Using fresh, high-quality ingredients, there are very few styles than cannot be brewed from extract. Old, oxidized extracts and cheap extracts which contain a significant percentage of glucose syrup are two sources of the misconception that extract beers are inherently inferior to all-grain beers. Furthermore, historically, most beginners started with extract and most experienced brewers have progressed to all-grain brewing. Naturally, more experienced brewers' beers are more likely to be closer to the intended style and less likely to have procedural errors in formulation, boiling, cooling, aeration, fermentation, and bottling. These are some of the reasons that, historically, all-grain beers have gained more than their share of ribbons.

# SUMMARY

So there you have it. Hopefully the information I've presented here will help you enjoy this hobby as much as I do. If you've listened to my advice and brewed your first beer before continuing your reading, you may even be enjoying one of your own beers as you read this.

There are three things that helped me improve my homebrewing more than all the book reading I've done:
- joining a homebrewing club,
- subscribing to the Homebrew Digest electronic newsletter, and
- joining the Beer Judge Certification Program.

Join or form a homebrewing club. That's how I got started in brewing – a handful of homebrewers and a dozen or so others who were interested in starting to brew formed a club at work. Our second meeting was at a homebrew supply store at which we tasted homebrewed beer and I was hooked. I bought a book, all the equipment, and enough ingredients to brew two beers. I now know that the hops were stale, the yeast was almost dead, the crystal malt should not have come in a paper bag and I paid about twice the price I would pay at a typical homebrew supply store these days. We couldn't bring beer onto company premises, so that club fizzled out in a year or two.

Luckily, I stumbled upon the Homebrew Digest electronic "newsletter" and have been a participant ever since 1987. I've learned more from the Homebrew Digest and the other electronic digests (see Further Reading at the end of this chapter) than from all the beer and brewing books in my personal library.

Over the course of the next several years, I've joined four more clubs and try to make it to as many meetings as I can. Each club has it's own character. The first I joined (Headhunters) is mostly social. The second is not just a homebrew club, but also has many non-brewing members. This club, The Chicago Beer Society (1996 AHA Homebrew Club of the Year, incidentally), holds many commercial beer tastings throughout the year and has a formidable newsletter that caters to both brewers and non-brewers. The third and fourth clubs I joined (Brewers of South Suburbia and The Urban Knaves of Grain) are primarily homebrewing-oriented with style meetings, informal judgings, and "What's wrong with this beer?" sessions.

At all these club meetings, members bring in their homebrewed beers and share them with fellow members. Sometimes they need advice, other times they are just sharing a prize-winner from a recent competition. It is interesting to note that the members of these clubs span several generations, races, socioeconomic groups, and genders. Three of the clubs hold yearly homebrew competitions which attract entries from coast to coast. This brings me to my next piece of advice.

Next to the Homebrew Digest, there is no better source of learning than judging at a homebrew competition. Not only do you get to sample a wide variety of beer flavors and aromas, but also you get to hear what other judges think about this beer. You learn what it takes to be a prize-winner and what certain flaws taste like. As soon as you have read about all-grain brewing, whether it is from the second volume of this series or whether it is from another source, I encourage you to go take the Beer Judge Certification Program exam and become a BJCP judge (see Further Reading below). You won't regret it.

## Entering competitions

Speaking of judging, the benefit of entering competitions is much greater than simply winning ribbons. You can get unbiased opinions of your beer. The judging at a competition should be far more objective than asking a fellow club member because they may not want to hurt your feelings and because the environment for beer tasting is hopefully better at a competition than at a noisy club meeting. Whether it is better to enter a large competition to which you have to ship beer or a smaller, local competition depends on the local judge pool. If you have a lot of good, experienced local judges, the local competition may be better because your beer will always suffer somewhat during shipment.

Shipping beer is a pretty complicated subject itself. It is illegal to send beer via the US mail. It is perfectly legal to ship via private carriers such as UPS and FedEx. I've read where shipping clerks have said that sending beer across state lines requires a license, but competitions are primarily for *analysis* and you are not getting paid for the beer (in fact you are *paying* to have it analyzed) so you need not have a license. Many clerks at these private carriers are not aware of these rules and therefore will not accept a package if they are told it contains beer.

Most competitions require that you only use 12-ounce brown or green bottles without labels or raised brand lettering, so if you plan to enter a competition, make sure that you have at least several beers from each batch in these types of bottles. Brown bottles are recommended because while you may keep your beer in the dark, you can never be sure if the competition organizer will.

**Figure 17-1**: *Packing beer for shipment.*

Packing beer for competition is a chore, but not as big a chore as *unpacking* beers that have been packaged poorly! Styrofoam peanuts are a definitely bad idea. The preferred cushioning materials are solid styrofoam, bubble wrap, and crumpled newspaper. Probably the best method for shipping beer is to reuse those boxes used by beer-of-the-month clubs. Alternatively, I've put bottles in alternating holes in a case of beer and filled the empty six-pack holes with crumpled newspaper. I've then put that beer box into a larger cardboard box and filled the space between the boxes (on all six sides) with crumpled newspaper and sheets of styrofoam (see figure 17-1).

## But other books say differently...

You may find that other books suggest different procedures than I describe in this book. Some are simply a matter of choice and others are downright bad brewing practice. When it comes to the debatable ones, I've tried to present both sides of the argument (such as blowoff versus non-blowoff, the use of secondaries, or various ways to brew lagers) and leave the decision up to you. I've tried my best to discourage the bad methods (such as starting siphons with your mouth, aerating hot wort, canning wort without pressure-cooking it, and not rehydrating dry yeast) despite the fact that other books may say that these are acceptable procedures.

## Where do we go from here?

In the second volume of this series, I cover the basics of brewing from grain: partial mashing and all-grain brewing. Many partial mash and all-grain recipes are provided to get you started. Then, I go into recipe formulation for all-grain brewing. Later chapters cover topics such as yeast culturing, building and tuning a draft beer system, counter-pressure bottling, and troubleshooting all-grain brewing problems.

## Final Thoughts

As much as I've tried to make this book 100% accurate, I'm sure that I've slipped-up in a few places. If you have any corrections or if you have some questions that weren't answered anywhere in this book, please contact me via my website, http://www.brewinfo.com/brewinfo/ or send me email at korz@brewinfo.com. Due to the volume of email I receive, I apologize in advance if I can't give you a personal reply.

## Further Reading

See the Further Reading sections at the end of each chapter.

Brewing Techniques, PO Box 3222, Eugene, Oregon, 97403; 503-687-2993; btcirc@aol.com

The New Brewer (professionally oriented), Institute for Brewing Studies, PO Box 1679, Boulder, Colorado, 80306; 303-447-0816

Zymurgy, Association of Brewers, PO Box 1679, Boulder, Colorado, 80306, 303-447-0816

The Beer Judge Certification Program (BJCP), c/o Celebrator Beer News - PO Box 375, Hayward, California, 94543; http://www.bjcp.org

The Homebrew Digest: homebrew-request@hbd.org or http://hbd.org

The Lambic Digest (an electronic newsletter about homebrewed and commercial Lambics/Lambieks and other Belgian beers): *The Lambic Digest is in the process of moving – please see my website for its new location.*

JudgeNet (a daily electronic newsletter for homebrewers and beer-lovers interested in judging beer on a serious, but non-professional level): judge-request@synchro.com

NetNews: rec.crafts.brewing

There are also literally hundreds of beer- and homebrewing-related World Wide Web pages, but they often have a tendency to move, so since they are all interconnected via hyperlinks, you should be able to surf your way through them by starting at my website: http://www.brewinfo.com/brewinfo/

Appendix A

# BEER STYLES

## The Basics

eer? Ale? Lager? What's the difference? In modern terms, beer is the general term, whereas ale and lager are more specific descriptions. Both ales and lagers are beer. First of all, let me tell you what the differences are not. Neither ales nor lagers are inherently stronger, more bitter, darker, or thicker. There is incredible diversity among both ales and lagers. The difference actually is that ales are fermented at warmer temperatures (usually 60 to 70° F) and lagers are fermented cooler (usually 40 to 55° F). In terms of flavor and aroma, ales have fruity flavors and aromas whereas lagers are generally not fruity. Many pale lagers have a slight cooked-corn aroma which is acceptable in pale lagers, but considered a defect in most ales. Many ales have a butterscotch or buttery aroma/flavor which is acceptable in most ales, but considered a defect in most lagers.

Why have styles? From a beer drinker's perspective, putting a style on the label or faucet handle helps indicate what the beer is generally going to taste like. Virtually all brewers agree that Sweet Stouts should be sweet, dark ales with some amount of dark malt character. If you are not in the mood for a sweet dark ale, you probably would not order (or purchase in a store) a beer labeled "Sweet Stout." From a homebrewer's perspective, styles are important so we can shoot for a target and then find out (from competition or from other beer-lovers tasting our results) how close we came to that target. Finally, from a beer judge's perspective, styles make it possible to judge beers objectively. If we did not have styles, we could only judge beer on how much we like them. On a hot, humid day, I would score an IPA higher on the "preference scale" than a Scottish Strong

Ale. The same two beers' scores would be reversed on a cold, snowy evening. Judging each against a set of guidelines allows us to tell how "good" the beer is in a far more objective way.

## Some Terminology

There are a great many words used in association with beer tasting. It's important to know these if you hope to communicate with other brewers and/or with beer judges. "Nose," "bouquet," "aroma," and "fragrance," are all terms which refer to how the beer smells. "Clarity" refers to whether the beer is crystal clear or hazy. Incidentally, in some styles haziness is acceptable. Color can vary from almost clear to black. I once made a beer so dark that you could not see an automobile headlight through it! "Head retention" is how long the head stays well-formed on top of the beer and is related to "lacing" or "Brussels Lace" which are the webs of very fine bubbles that cling to the sides of the glass as you drink it.

"Taste" and "flavor" are usually used interchangeably, regardless of whether this is technically proper or not. "Character" is a rather nebulous word which can refer to anything from aroma to flavor to the way the beer feels in your mouth. Sometimes it is a combination of perceptions. You can only tell from context what the taster means. For example "strong dark malt character" probably refers to both the aroma and flavor that dark malts impart on the beer. Flavor and aroma are tied much more closely than you might think.

Unless otherwise noted, "balance" refers to the relative levels of hop bitterness and malt sweetness. "Evenly balanced" means that neither the bitterness nor maltiness dominate. Depending on the style, the balance can swing from decided bitterness to dominating maltiness. Incidentally, on a commercial beer label, "bottle-conditioned" means that the beer is bottled with some yeast – this means that the beer can change slightly (particularly the balance) with age especially in stronger beers.

"Dry" means not sweet and it is important to not mistake hop bitterness for dryness. You can balance the sweetness of a beer by the use of bitterness, but if you consider it's sweetness independently, you will realize that it is still sweet. Sulfate ions in the water can impart a dryness in the finish (the aftertaste) which does, indeed, dry-out what might otherwise be a sweet beer in the fore-taste (the initial flavor of the beer) and mid-palate (the flavor between the fore-taste and finish).

Diacetyl is a chemical produced by yeast and then reabsorbed by it if given the proper conditions. It lends a butterscotch aroma and flavor to the beer. Diacetyl is acceptable in most ales but is considered a flaw in most lagers.

"Body" and "mouthfeel" can mean different things to different people. To some, they are synonymous. To others, body is strictly how thick the beer feels in your mouth — from thin to heavy. These people usually consider mouthfeel to be a combination of body, carbonation and other tactile factors such as "creaminess" or "oiliness" or "warmth" (from the alcohol in the beer). I tend to take this latter approach.

"OG" stands for Original Gravity and it is the specific gravity of the "beer" before yeast is added. It is a measure of how much malt and other sugars are dissolved in the beer and plays a major part (along with how much of the sugars are converted to alcohol by the particular yeast used) in the alcoholic strength of the beer. "AA" (as used in this appendix) stands for Apparent Attenuation which is the percentage of the Original Gravity that was lost during the fermentation. A higher Apparent Attenuation means the beer will be drier and have more alcohol. A lower Apparent Attenuation means the beer will be sweeter and have less alcohol.

"ABV" stands for Alcohol by Volume and is simply the percentage of alcohol in the beer measured as a ratio of volumes (volume of alcohol divided by the volume of the entire beer). It is different from Alcohol by Weight (ABW) which is about 0.8 times the ABV because alcohol weighs less than water. Most of the world uses ABV.

"IBUs" stands for International Bitterness Units and is a measure of how much bitterness there is in a beer. Note, that it is not necessarily a measure of how bitter a beer is – a beer that has a lot residual sweetness (a beer in which the yeast has eaten relatively little of the sugars in the wort) can have a lot of IBUs, but still not taste very bitter. "SRM" stands for Standard Research Method and is a measure of the color of the beer. Lovibond degrees, another method for measuring beer color, are effectively equivalent to SRM degrees.

# Ales

Ales are as old as time. People have been making ales (by the modern definition) probably since before written language. A written recipe for something that we would now consider an ale has been discovered to be at least 4000 years old. Over the last 50 years, except for Belgium and Britain, ales had almost become extinct, but lately, especially in the United States and Canada, they are experiencing a rebirth in popularity.

Among English-speaking brewers, originally, "Ale" was a strong, unhopped malt beverage. "Beer," at that time (around 1400 to 1700 in England), was a weaker malt beverage which contained hops. In modern terms, however, "Ale" is a warm-fermented, hopped, malt beverage and "Lager" is a cool-fermented, hopped, lagered malt beverage. "Beers" are either "Ales" or "Lagers."

Oddly enough (or perhaps reverting back to 15th-century nomenclature?), some states have misused the modern term "ale" to mean a strong malt beverage. Therefore, some lagers (especially imported ones which don't want to have separate labels for every state) will have "ale" printed somewhere on the label to comply with this law. On such example is Hacker-Pschorr Alt Munich Dark. In the US, I've seen "ALE" printed sideways on the label. Combined with the word "Alt" in the name, this beer can be mistaken for an Altbier, but in fact this is a Munich Dunkel Lager. "Alt" means "old" in German and so the name simply translates to "Old Munich Dark." Even more bizarre, some ales cannot be labeled as such because their alcohol level is too low. Celis Pale Bock is actually an ale, but since it only has 4.0% ABW, it cannot be sold in Texas with "ale" anywhere on the label.

## American Amber Ale

This category was inspired by the article "West Coast Amber Ales" by David Brockington in Brewing Techniques[171]. For quite some time, beers in this category have been included in the American Pale Ale category. American Amber Ales still have some things in common with the new (narrower) American Pale Ale style description: they are generally medium- to well-hopped in bitterness, flavor, and often aroma, and the hop character is often citrusy or floral. They differ from beers in the new American Pale Ale category in that they typically have a medium to medium-heavy caramel character, are usually a bit sweeter, the additional caramel and sweetness tends to swing the malt/bitterness balance more towards the middle and sometimes even to the malt side. Low to medium diacetyl is acceptable. Fruitiness is low to medium and body is usually medium. Commercial examples: Big Time Atlas Amber, Mendocino Red Tail Ale, St. Rogue Red Ale, Bell's Amber, Rhino Chasers American Amber Ale. OG: 1.045 - 1.063; AA: 69 - 79%; ABV: 4.4 - 6.5; IBUs: 20 - 45; SRM: 7 - 14.

## American Brown Ale

American Brown Ale is a relatively new style. It has the bitterness, hop flavor and often the hop aroma of an American Pale Ale, but it also has the color and maltiness of an English Brown Ale. It does not have the dominating crystal malt character of an American Amber Ale. Their color ranges from dark copper to brown. Low to medium diacetyl is acceptable. Commercial examples: Brooklyn Brown Dark Ale, Pete's Wicked Ale, Full Sail Brown Ale. OG: 1.040 - 1.056; AA: 69 - 80%; ABV: 4 - 6.0; IBUs: 25 - 50; SRM: 15 - 24.

## American Pale Ale

The American Pale Ale style is characterized by American (citrusy or floral) hop flavor and (usually) hop aroma. Cascade and Willamette hops are very often the varieties of choice in this style. Pale golden to copper colored, the balance of American Pale Ales should be decidedly towards bitterness. American Pale Ales are generally on the dry side. Caramel character from crystal malt and diacetyl are typically very low to low. Fruitiness can be low to medium and body is usually medium. Commercial examples: Sierra Nevada Pale Ale, Summit Extra Pale Ale. OG: 1.042 - 1.056; AA: 75 - 84%; ABV: 4.5 - 6.0; IBUs: 20 - 45; SRM: 4 - 8.

## Barleywine

### American-style Barleywine

American-style Barleywines differ from their English counterparts as having American hop character (some even having a hop nose), being considerably stronger and usually drier. They always have a warming alcohol note in the flavor and often can be quite harsh until they are aged for a few months. Balance is usually even between bitterness and maltiness, with some versions being slightly dominated by hop bitterness. Body is medium-heavy to heavy. Esters are usually medium-high to high and diacetyl is usually low. Bottle-conditioned Barleywines increase in ester levels and can improve for decades. Commercial examples: Anchor Old Foghorn, Sierra Nevada Bigfoot. OG: 1.090+; AA: 69 - 82%; ABV: 8+; IBUs: 50+; SRM: 12 - 22;

### English-style Barleywine

English-style Barleywines are usually quite a bit maltier than their American cousins and most are not nearly as strong. Alcohol is always apparent in the flavor. Balance can be even or slightly towards either bitterness or maltiness. Caramel flavor is often more pronounced than in American versions. Diacetyl, hop flavor and aroma are low to medium. The stronger bottle-conditioned versions can be sweetish when young, by then becoming decidedly drier over the next several years. Commercial examples: Thomas Hardy's Ale (the brewery calls this an Old Ale, but it has the character of a Barleywine, especially after a few years of aging), Bell's Old Ale (yes, but it tastes much more like an English Barleywine), Young's Old Nick, and Fuller's Golden Pride (two rather low-alcohol examples). OG: 1.084+; AA: 45 - 77%; ABV: 7.2+; IBUs: 50+; SRM: 16-26;

402

## Belgian Ale

Belgian Ale is perhaps a misnomer, since all the Belgian styles presented here are ales, however, this is also a distinct style of beer, although in Belgium, the title is rarely used for these beers. They resemble pale English bottled ales in some ways, but are usually much more aromatic, fruity, slightly less bitter and many are spiced with coriander, grains of paradise, and other spices. Some have a mild phenolic/clovey character which would be considered a serious defect in all other styles except Bavarian Weizens or Rye beers. Their balance runs from malty to slightly bitter. Yeast character is usually an important part of their character although spices can dominate some examples. Commercial examples: De Koninck, Rubens Gold, Palm, Ginder Ale, Horse Ale. OG: 1.040 - 1.055; AA: 70 - 85%; ABV: 4 - 6; IBUs: 20 - 35; SRM: 3 - 14.

## Belgian 19th-Century Ales

A number of intriguing beer styles that were made in Belgium during the 19th century have since become extinct. I have very little information on them, but would like to at least mention them for completeness. For example, there was a style of beer called "Liège Saison," a low-gravity (1.020-1.025 OG), highly-hopped beer with 10 to 15% spelt in the grist. Other styles included La Blonde van Vlaanderen, Uytzet des Flandres, l'Orge d'Anvers, Diest, Hoegaerd, Zoeg, Louvain Blanche, and Louvain Peeterman[216].

## Belgian Strong Ale

### Belgian Golden Strong Ale

Basically, there is one beer which is the originator of this style and many subsequent beers with similar characteristics. Duvel is the originator of this style, but oddly, in its first formulation, it was dark beer. Medium golden in color, it is highly carbonated, lightly fruity with a slightly nutty, very slightly phenolic/clovey flavor. The beer is deceptively strong with a sweetish fore-taste and a dryish finish. Other beers of this style can often be quite a bit more phenolic/clovey and fruity. This is one of those styles that cannot be made without some portion of refined sugar. Commercial examples: Duvel, Deugniet, Satan. OG: 1.065 - 1.080; AA: 77 - 85%; ABV: 7 - 9; IBUs: 25 - 35; SRM: 3.5 - 5.5.

### Other Belgian Strong Ales

Belgium is the land of strong beers. This is actually quite unfortunate in a way, since it limits the amount that one can sample at a sitting. The other (non-Duvel-like) strong ales from Belgium can vary in color, sweetness, maltiness and alcoholic strength. Balance is usually dominated by alcohol and malt, bitterness taking a back seat. Typically, these beers are very low in diacetyl. Many are spiced. Almost a sub-style of Belgian Strong Ales is typified by Celis Grand Cru and Hoegaarden Grand Cru – these are beers spiced like Witbiers, but are all-barley malt. Some Belgian Strong Ales, like Bush (marketed as Scaldis in the US, for obvious reasons) can pass as Barleywines. Commercial examples: De Dolle Brouwers Stille Nacht, De Dolle Brouwers Oerbier, Brigand, Celis Grand Cru, Hoegaarden Grand Cru, Gouden Carolus, Bush (the strongest beer in Belgium, marketed as Scaldis in the US - the Christmas version, "Noel," is dryhopped). OG: 1.065 - 1.098+; AA: 65 - 85%; ABV: 7 - 12+; IBUs: 25 - 40+; SRM: 7 - 20.

## Bière de Garde

Bière de Garde means "beer to keep" implying that it is meant to be stored. This dates back to the days when summer brewing was impractical and a stronger beer was brewed in the spring to be stored for summer consumption. They are medium-strong in alcohol, have expressive yeast character (often slightly phenolic/clovey/spicy), quite fruity and complex, although rather light in body for their alcohol level (indicating that there is probably some candi sugar added) and their balance is usually towards the malty side. Many have a slight woody, musty, cellar-like aroma which can be considered a fault by some judges. Most are medium amber, dryish and highly carbonated, but some are quite sweet and have toffee/caramel notes. Color does vary from blonde to dark amber in some examples. Commercial examples: 3 Monts, Lutèce, Pot Flamand, Castelain (Ch'ti), La Choulette, Jenlain, Bière des Sans Culottes. OG: 1.060 - 1.080; AA: 72 - 85%; ABV: 4.5 - 8; IBUs: 20 - 35; SRM: 5 - 18

## Cask-Conditioned Real Ale

"Cask-Conditioned Real Ale," or simply "Real Ale," is not a style of beer but rather it is a method of packaging and serving. "Cask-Conditioned" literally means that the beer is unfiltered and has undergone a small amount of fermentation in the cask which gives the beer its carbonation (condition). In the US, we might call a "cask" a "keg," but I think it's best that we don't use the word "keg" because in Britain, "Keg Beer" is the opposite of Cask-Conditioned beer – it's what they call filtered, force-carbonated beer that is served via $CO_2$ pressure. This last point is more important that you might think. There are four traditional ways to dispense Cask-Conditioned Real Ale: gravity, handpump, electric pump, and air pressure. $CO_2$-pressure is not an acceptable method of dispense for Real Ale.

Cask-Conditioned Real Ale is more difficult to handle than Keg Beer for both commercial brewers and for publicans (barkeepers). Real Ale requires priming (or timing the casking of the beer) and fining (because otherwise the yeast will take too long to settle), and is at its peak for a shorter time than Keg Beer especially after broaching (starting to remove beer) because as beer is drawn out, air is allowed into the headspace. Real Ale oxidizes within a few days of when it is first served, unlike Keg Beer, therefore Real Ale is available in many different sizes of cask so that if a pub is taking more than a day or two to finish a cask, they can order a smaller size next time.

Another (non-traditional) method of dispense is "mixed-gas" or "Nitrokeg." Mixed-gas beer is filtered, force-carbonated, and served by a mixture of nitrogen and $CO_2$ pressure. Since nitrogen is almost insoluble in beer, nitrogen dispense does not add fizz. $CO_2$ is included in the mix because the beer would eventually go flat without it. Guinness is one beer that is usually served this way, but the large commercial brewers in Britain are beginning to serve Bitters and other ales like this. It may result in a glass of beer that looks like a traditionally-dispensed beer, but since the beer is filtered it's not the real thing.

One of the most controversial methods of dispense is the "cask breather." A cask breather is a device that is attached to the top of a Cask-Conditioned cask of beer and allows $CO_2$ (rather than air) into the headspace as beer is drawn off by traditional means (gravity or handpump). The $CO_2$ is effectively at atmospheric pressure and is not used to push the beer to the faucet. The Campaign for Real Ale (CAMRA) officially does not approve of the use of cask breathers, however, some individual CAMRA members (such as myself) are supportive of them. I feel that their use prevents slow-moving Real Ales from spoiling for weeks and therefore encourages publicans to stock a wider variety of beers.

There are two styles of serving beer with a handpump: the northern style and the southern style. In the north, they prefer a rich, creamy head on the handpumped beers. In the south, they prefer a more gentle pour in which the $CO_2$ is not released as a frothy head. Therefore, in the north, they use handpumps with "swan neck" faucets and "sparklers." Sparklers are small caps on the end of the faucet which have several small holes in them. When the beer is forced through the sparkler, much of the $CO_2$ comes out of solution and beer develops a frothy head. Contrary to what I've seen done in most US pubs that have handpumps, in the UK the glass is held up as high as possible so that the sparkler is quickly submerged. In the US, I usually see the staff spraying the beer into the glass which knocks out virtually all the $CO_2$ and makes the beer foam all over the outside of the glass.

Finally, a quick note about Draughtflow® cans is in order. These tall cans were designed to imitate the northern style of handpumped beers. They contain a small plastic device called a "widget" and are charged with nitrogen at high pressure. When the can is opened, beer is forced out of the widget through a small hole – this stream of beer results in a sparkler-like cascade of beer and tight creamy head. A 20-ounce (US) glass is necessary to hold the entire beer. It is important to note that the beers in these cans is pasteurized and therefore not "Real Ale." CAMRA and most true Real Ale lovers in the UK look down upon these cans, but I can tell you that the mouthfeel of these Draughtflow beers is not that different from true handpumped beers. Until every town in the US has pubs serving true Cask-Conditioned beers, Draughtflow cans may be the only way for many of us to experience something resembling the smoothness of handpumped Real Ales.

## *English Bitter*

Note that in Britain, there are no rules as to how a beer is named and these designations are primarily for homebrewing competition categorizations.

### Ordinary Bitter

Ordinary Bitters are the lightest in body and alcohol of the bitters. Of primary importance in this style is drinkability. Bitterness dominates in the balance, some examples being quite bitter. Sulfate levels can vary, so these beers may or may not have a long, lingering bitter finish. Usually, there is quite a bit of caramel flavor and although attenuation is low, the low original gravity ensures that residual sweetness is also quite low. Yeasts used tend to be lightly fruity, often with citrusy character, but some examples are strongly fruity. Bitters traditionally have low carbonation, but some bottled varieties have medium carbonation. Hop flavor and aroma can be present (may be dryhopped), but should be of British varieties, especially East Kent Goldings, Fuggle and Target. Diacetyl can vary from low to high. Commercial examples: Young's Bitter, Boddington's Bitter, Fuller's Chiswick Bitter. OG: 1.030 - 1.038; AA: 65 - 79%; ABV: 3 - 3.8; IBUs: 20 - 35; SRM: 5 - 12;

### Special or Best Bitter

Special or Best Bitter is the next higher designation for Bitters. Characteristics are similar to Ordinary Bitters except that residual sweetness can be a little higher thanks to the higher original gravity (there is more gravity to begin with so there can be more left behind). Commercial examples: Young's Special, Brakspear Henley Ale, Fuller's London Pride, Samuel Smith's Museum Ale (marketed as Old Brewery Pale Ale in the US), Timothy Taylor Landlord, Goose Island Best Bitter, Wellington County Arkell Best Bitter, Shepherd Neame Masterbrew Bitter, Spanish Peaks Black Dog Ale, Nor'Wester Best Bitter, Flowers Original. OG: 1.039 - 1.045; AA: 65 - 80%; ABV: 3.7 - 4.8; IBUs: 23 - 45; SRM: 5 - 14;

### Extra Special Bitter

The next higher designation for Bitters is Extra Special Bitter, although there are

only a handful that use this name.  Characteristics are similar to Ordinary and
Special Bitters except that residual sweetness can be even higher (often not very
noticeable due to the high bitterness) and caramel character tends to be even
higher.  Bitterness perhaps not as dominant in some examples (but balance is still
at least slightly on the bitter side).  Commercial examples include Fuller's ESB,
Oasis ESB, Big Time ESB, Shepherd Neame Bishop's Finger, Wynkoop ESB,
Gale's HSB.  OG: 1.046 - 1.060;  AA: 65 - 80%;  ABV: 4.4 - 6.0;  IBUs: 30 - 55;
SRM: 8 - 14;

## Strong Export Bitter

When I decided to add this subsection, I knew of but one commercial example of
this style, but it is such a fine beer that it is a crime to not have a style in which to
include it.  Since then, I've tasted another that appears to fit the category
description I've come up with and I'm sure there are other strong British-style
ales that aren't quite Old Ales.  Bitterness dominates slightly and I would say that
dryhopping with British varieties is mandatory.  Fruity complexity and a very
round softness typify this style.  Body is medium to full.  Bitterness is
aggressive, but the intense maltiness tends to hide it well.  Diacetyl is medium to
high.  Commercial examples: Young's Strong Export Bitter (marketed in the US
as Young's Special London Ale), Ushers 1824 Particular Ale.  OG: 1.060 - 1.070
AA: 67 - 79%;  ABV: 5.8 - 7;  IBUs: 45 - 65;  SRM: 8 - 14;

## *English Brown*

### Northern-style English Brown

Northern-style English Brown Ales are not as dark, malty or sweet as their
southern counterparts.  Popularized in northern England, beers of this style tend
to be very lightly fruity and more carbonated than the southern-style.  Balance is
either very slightly towards bitterness or slightly towards maltiness - never too
far from even balance.  These beers can range in sweetness from dryish to
slightly sweet.  Bitterness is subdued but is more apparent in the northern
version.  Diacetyl is low to medium.  Hop flavor and aroma are very low.  Some
examples have a decidedly nutty flavor, others a hint of chocolate.  Body is
medium to medium-light.  Commercial examples: Newcastle Brown Ale, Samuel
Smith's Strong Brown Ale (marketed in the US as Nut Brown Ale), Vaux Double
Maxim.  OG: 1.040 - 1.055  AA: 73 - 85%;  ABV: 3.7 - 5.2;  IBUs: 20 - 35;
SRM: 10 - 14;

### Southern-style English Brown

Southern-style English Brown Ales are much darker, maltier, sweeter and
(usually) slightly less alcoholic than their northern cousins.  They also tend to be
fruitier, often taking on hints of ripe fruit.  Carbonation is usually very low as in

most ales from southern England. Balance is decidedly towards malt and diacetyl can be low to medium. Hop bitterness, flavor and aroma are very low. These beers are smoothly dark – never having any sharpness from black malts. Body tends to be medium. Commercial examples: Golden Prairie Nut Brown Ale, Oregon Nut Brown Ale, Mann's Brown Ale. OG: 1.034 - 1.052; AA: 65 - 75%; ABV: 3.3 - 4.8; IBUs: 18 - 30; SRM: 15 - 25;

## English Mild

### 19th-Century Mild

"Mild" has been used to identify many different types of beer over the years. In the 1820's, newly brewed (young) Porter was called "Mild." These style guidelines are based on bits and pieces of information on 1800's Mild Ales that I've pieced together into a purely speculative description. Included among the many sources are *Old British Beers and How to Make Them* by Dr. John Harrison and members of the Durden Park Beer Circle and Terry Foster's *Porter*. I speculate that this was (by today's standards) a strong, smoky (from brown malt, which was kilned over hardwood fires), brown to dark brown ale. Hop bitterness and flavor would probably have been medium to high. Fruitiness was probably low to medium-high. Commercial examples: none. OG: 1.060 - 1.090; AA: 65 - 80%; ABV: 5.6 - 9.0; IBUs: 40 - 100+; SRM: 12 - 20;

### Mild (Modern)

As you can see from 19th-Century Mild above, Mild has changed quite a bit in character over the years. Around 1913 it was a 1.050 beer, more highly hopped than the Porter of those days, in which 20% of the grain was replaced by sugar[172]. In modern terms, Mild has come to be thought of as a dark, low-alcohol, low-bitterness beer meant for restoring necessary fluids after a long day's work in the coal mines. In Wales and in some English counties, Mild is known as "Dark" although both historically and currently, pale Milds exist. It is a richly malty beer, full of flavor, but still light to medium-light in body. Chocolaty notes are popular in the dark versions. Hop bitterness, flavor and aroma are very low. Fruitiness can be low to medium-high. Commercial examples: Banks's Mild, Highgate Mild (known as Dark in some counties), Brains Dark, Pacific Coast's Mariner's Mild, Goose Island PMD Mild, Fuller's Hock, McMullen's AK, Ansell's Mild, Robinson's Best Mild (a rare, pale version). OG: 1.030 - 1.040; AA: 65 - 81%; ABV: 2.8 - 3.8; IBUs: 12 - 25; SRM: 8 - 40;

## *English Old Ale*

### 19th-Century Old Ale

19th-century English Old Ales, also known as Strong or Stock Ales, were very high-gravity, high-alcohol beers.  Not only were *Saccharomyces* yeasts involved in the fermentation, but also lactic acid bacteria and *Brettanomyces* yeasts.  They varied from dry to sweet and from slightly sour to very sour.  Lactic acid levels ranged from about 0.162% to 0.63%[173] which translates to approximately 7 ml to 27 ml of 88% lactic acid per gallon (similar in sourness to traditional Lambieks/Lambics!).  Some brown malt may have used which means that there may have been a smoky character.  These beers were highly hopped, but given that some were very malty, the balance could range from quite bitter[173] (for a dry example) to decidedly more malty than bitter.  Often they were dryhopped at a rate of about 1/2 ounce per gallon[173].  Some brewers used quite a bit of refined sugar in the kettle (my guess would be 10 to 20% for the English versions – North American versions were of lower gravity and could contain 25% adjuncts or refined sugar[211]).  Many of these ales were aged in barrels for several years before serving.  Commercial examples: none.  OG: 1.085 - 1.100;  AA: 60 - 90%;  ABV: 6.5 - 7.8;  IBUs: 40 - 90;  SRM: 8 - 17;

### Old Ale (Modern)

Modern Old Ales are dark, sweetish, fruity ales, often with a warming character from rather high alcohol levels.  They often have a molasses/brown sugar character, some with toffee notes.  Color can vary widely from copper to dark brown.  Diacetyl also varies from low to high.  Bitterness can be rather high, but usually the balance is dominated by malt.  A high percentage of unfermentables is common.  The bottle-conditioned versions do tend to dry out with age and can continue to improve for decades.  Most have low hop flavor and aroma, but they can be noticeable in some examples.  Caramel flavor is often quite prominent.  Commercial examples: Gale's Prize Old Ale, Greene King Winter Ale, Marston's Owd Roger, Hardington Brewery's Old Ale, Theakston's Old Peculier.  OG: 1.052 - 1.080;  AA: 55 - 80%;  ABV: 5.0 - 7.8;  IBUs: 20 - 70;  SRM: 10 - 35;

## *English Pale Ale*

The term "Pale Ale" is used interchangeably with "Bitter" in England.  There are no rules or guidelines as to what separates these two names in what is apparently the same style of beer.  Some have suggested that Pale Ales are bottled Bitters or that they are distinguished by carbonation.  I'm afraid that, in my opinion, this is simply not enough justification for a separate style.  See English Bitter.

## Flanders Brown Ale

The flavor profile of Flanders Brown Ales dates back to the days when beers were spontaneously fermented as it has a lactic sourness as part of its character. They are sometimes called "Oud Bruin" (Flemish for Old Brown). Hop bitterness is low. These beers are dominated by malt, often have mild toasty notes and they have no hop aroma or flavor. Sourness is usually subdued, but is clearly noticeable, sometimes even in the aroma. These beers can have wonderfully sweet and malty aromas resembling French pastry. Liefmans, the one of the most respected brewers of this style, had up until recently, made a basic beer called Goudenband and also a blended basic beer, a Kriek and a Frambozen, the latter are fruit beers (cherry and raspberry, respectively) made from a base of Goudenband. Alas, the Liefmans brewery has been purchased by the Riva Group and the recipe for Goudenband has been changed. It is now a strong beer, which, itself is very tasty. Hopefully, public outcry will convince them to continue production of the old recipe. Commercial examples: Liefmans Goudenband, Felix, Roman, Crombé. OG: 1.042 - 1.060; AA: 68 - 78%; ABV: 4.0 - 5.8; IBUs: 15 - 25; SRM: 10 - 20.

## Flanders Red Ale

Actually, Flanders Red Ales are a sub-type of the Flanders Brown Ale style. It's just that there are a group of these beers that are distinctly different from the "more brown" beers of this type. These beers are more sour than the other type, but they are still low in hop bitterness and virtually without hop aroma or flavor. They can have mild toasty notes and a decidedly oaky aroma and flavor. The classic producer of this style, Rodenbach, brews primarily two varieties: one simply called Rodenbach and the other, Rodenbach Grand Cru (there is also a version called Alexander which is like the Grand Cru but with a secondary fermentation on cherries). Both beers are reddish in color and are decidedly sour, have an oak aroma (although it is quite a bit stronger in the Grand Cru). The difference in the two beers is that after primary fermentation in modern tanks at 71 F (21.5 C) and lagering at 59 F (15 C) for 7 to 8 weeks, the Grand Cru is aged in huge oak vats for 1 1/2 to 2 years[179]. The "regular" or "classic" version spends a slightly shorter time lagering (4 - 5 weeks) and then is blended with 30% Grand Cru[179]. Every two batches or so, a layer of wood is scraped-off the insides of the oak tuns to expose fresh wood. This is done to remove beerstone (calcium oxalate - which blocks oxygen permeation)[179], but also has the effect of giving the beer more oak flavor. Thanks to the three types of malts, the yeast and the oak, both of these Rodenbach beers develop a cherry-like flavor. Commercial examples: Rodenbach, Rodenbach Grand Cru, Paulus, Bacchus, Vichtenaar, Bourgogne de Flandres/Vlaamse Bourgogne. OG: 1.042 - 1.060; AA: 65 - 78%; ABV: 4.0 - 5.8; IBUs: 14 - 25; SRM: 10 - 16.

## Grand Cru

While many believe that Grand Cru is a style, it is not. Brewers often add the title "Grand Cru" to a special beer that is more rare or costly to produce than their regular beer. It means little more than "Special Vintage" or "Deluxe." For example, Celis Grand Cru is an all-malt version of Celis White and Rodenbach Grand Cru is aged almost two years in oak vats.

## *India Pale Ale*

### Traditional English-style India Pale Ale

India Pale Ales (IPAs) originated back when India was under British Colonial Rule and special beers had to be brewed to survive the long journey by ship. We can really only speculate as to how they tasted, but certain things we can learn from breweries' old brewing logs and deduce from what history we do know. For example, the sloshing of the beer during the long journey and likelihood of *Brettanomyces* yeast being present ensured that it was well attenuated (i.e. there was little residual sugar left – the beer was surely quite dry). Dr. John Harrison and the Durden Park Beer Circle (a homebrew club in England) have published a book called *Old British Beers and How to Make Them*. In this book, they give recipes for classic British beers, but the recipes have been scaled-down and are designed to work with modern ingredients (or provide instructions on how to make something similar with ingredients that are no longer made). It is from this book and quite a few recent articles that I base these style guidelines.

First of all, we know that the base beer was an amber-colored ale, but was brewed to a higher strength and more highly hopped to protect it from spoiling during the long journey. The original brewers of this style were in Burton-on-Trent where the water is exceedingly high in calcium and sulfate. The calcium ensures that the water will be easy with which to brew pale beers, but the sulfate intensified the hop bitterness and gave beers made with it a long, lingering, dry, bitter finish. This, combined with the high hop rate means these beers were incredibly bitter. Surely there must have also been a spillover of hop flavor. Hops would be British varieties (most likely Goldings), and the casks were dryhopped (between 6 ounces and 1 pound per UK barrel or between 0.7 and 1.8 ounces per 5 gallon batch)[180]. However, four months at sea in a cask that's relatively oxygen-permeable would certainly reduce the dryhop character.

Refined sugar was a significant part of the wort in some IPA recipes. I could not find exact numbers in any book on Pale Ales, but I did find a reference in Greg Noonan's Scotch Ale. Because of their popularity, India Pale Ales began to be brewed in Scotland and there the sugar additions varied from 4 to 10 1/2 %[181]. It is important to note that there is no refined sugar mentioned in any of the IPA recipes listed in *Old British Beers and How to Make Them*.

Due to the long time spent in wooden casks, it is quite likely that these ales had a horsey character imparted by yeasts of the *Brettanomyces* genus, similar to that of modern Lambics/Lambieks. Finally, although it is a common belief that the oak casks used imparted a oaky flavor and aroma, this is not correct. European oak imparts far less flavor than American oak and I've read several British books in which American oak is said to be unsuitable for cask manufacture because it imparts a flavor to the beer, unlike European oak. Commercial examples: White Horse India Pale Ale (there are many beers in Britain *labeled* IPA or India Pale Ale, but only the White Horse is higher than 1.055 original gravity or has the requisite bitterness – alas, this beer was a "special" batch), Fuller's India Pale Ale (bitterness seems less than 80 IBUs, but this beer comes close, I believe). OG: 1.060 - 1.080; AA: 77 - 85%; ABV: 6.2 - 8.5; IBUs: 80 - 100+ (it is difficult to judge what the actual IBUs were on these beers – it is known that they used hops at a rate of up to 10 ounces per 5 gallons, but what is unknown is the effect of such high rates on utilization; it is known, however, that due to the limits of isohumulone solubility[182] and losses during fermentation, the bitterness can never be too much higher than 100 IBUs); SRM: 8 - 14;

## American-style India Pale Ale

I've included American-style IPAs here for three reasons: 1) although there is no mention of hop variety in the American Homebrewers Association for the IPA style, many judges have criticized IPAs which have a noticeable American hop character, 2) the brewers of Ballentine's IPA intentionally (perhaps assuming, incorrectly, that the Traditional British version had one) imparted an oaky character to their interpretation by storing the beer in American oak casks for secondary fermentation, and 3) there are a number of very good commercial examples which I wanted to highlight. Firstly, I'd like to note that modern American interpretations of the IPA style are (on average) slightly lower in gravity, alcohol and bitterness than what we deduce the Traditional British versions had. Nonetheless, bitterness is still very dominant, strength evident, hop flavor high and many have a strong hop aroma. They are also not quite as dry as what we believe the Originals were. Commercial examples: Sierra Nevada Celebration Ale, Tupper's Hop Pocket (Old Dominion), HopDevil IPA (Victory), Anchor Liberty Ale, Renegade Red (High Country), Steelhead IPA, Commodore Perry IPA (Great Lakes), Grant's India Pale Ale (although the gravity is on the low side, the relative bitterness of this beer is exceptionally high). OG: 1.050 - 1.075; AA: 70 - 80%; ABV: 5.0 - 7.8; IBUs: 45 - 100; SRM: 4 - 14;

## Kölsch

Kölsch is a style of beer that technically can only be brewed in Köln (there are a few exceptions for breweries nearby that had already been brewing a Kölsch when the Kölsch Convention went into effect). It is a light-bodied, pale, clean, soft, all-malt ale with assertive bitterness, a restrained fruitiness and a rather high level of carbonation. Sweetness varies from dry to slightly sweet. Some examples have a light hop nose (Saaz or other spicier varieties). Kölsch may contain up to 20% wheat malt, the balance being Pils and Vienna malts. Commercially, it is fermented at 64 to 72° F (18 - 22° C) with a secondary fermentation at 57 to 64° F (14 - 18° C)[183] and then cold-conditioned at 32 - 39° F (0 - 4° C) for two to six weeks[184]. Several of the best commercial examples have a moderate DMS component in the aroma, usually considered a flaw in all other ales. Commercial examples: Gaffel, Peters, Reissdorf, Gilden, Mühlen (from Malzmühle Brewery), Päffgen, St. Severin's Kölsch, Pyramid Kälsch, Broad Ripple Kölsch. OG: 1.044 - 1.049; AA: 78 - 86%; ABV: 4.4 - 5.0; IBUs: 16 -34; SRM: 3 - 7;

## Lambiek/Lambic

### Lambiek/Lambic

Several hundred years ago, all beers were spontaneously fermented, in other words, the brewer would set out the wort and whatever wild yeasts (and, inevitably, bacteria) that floated in, fermented the wort into beer. Brewing technology advanced and all but the traditional lambic/lambiek brewers adopted the modern methods. Personally, I know that if I set out wort without adding yeast, 9 times out of 10 it results in a very clovey beer, not at all like these wonderful beers. The Zenne/Senne valley, which surrounds Bruxelles/Brussels, Belgium has been blessed with a unique combination of wild yeasts and bacteria such that spontaneously fermented beer made there is one of the most complex and flavorful beverages made in the world.

Lambic in French, Lambiek in Flemish, this is the base beer for all the rest in this category and is sometimes served unblended (but only in very specialized cafés of the region). These beers are brewed from malted barley and unmalted wheat (30 - 40% of the mash), boiled up to 3 hours with intentionally aged hops (aged 3 years until virtually all their bitterness is gone) strictly for their bacteriostatic properties, and spontaneously fermented in chestnut or European oak barrels for up to 3 years. Not all beers labeled Lambiek or Lambic are 100% spontaneously fermented, live beers. Some are filtered, mixed with ordinary ales or pasteurized (in the commercial examples, I'll note which are traditional and which are not).

These beers can be extremely sour with complex fruity aromas. Lactic and acetic acids provide the sourness. Some believe that strong acetic (vinegar) character is a flaw, others find it an acceptable variation. Lambieks/Lambics with a strong acetic component are called "hard." There is virtually no bitterness whatsoever. The best examples of the style also have a "horse blanket" aroma sometimes called "horsey." Traditional versions tend to be very dry and have a medium-thin body. Many of these beers also have an oaky character, but I believe that it may be imparted by the yeasts and bacteria rather than the barrels (I've tasted homebrewed versions that were fermented in plastic, yet still had an oaky character). Lambic/Lambiek (like English Bitter) is low in carbonation and usually served either by gravity or handpump. Cantillon occasionally bottles a particularly good single cask and labels it "Grand Cru Cantillon Bruocsella 1900." Cloudiness is acceptable as is a slight musty aroma. Commercial examples (if you can find unblended Lambic/Lambiek, it is definitely traditional): Cantillon, Boon, De Neve, Girardin, Vander Linden, De Keersmaeker, Vandervelden (Oud Beersel), Timmermans. OG: 1.044 - 1.056; AA: 82 - 98%; ABV: 4.7 - 6; IBUs: 10 - 15; SRM: 4 - 15;

## Geuze/Gueuze

Gueuze (French) or Geuze (Flemish) is made by blending old (2 or 3 years old) and young (1 year old) Lambiek/Lambic and then bottling the mixture. Traditionally, no sugar is added at bottling and the carbonation comes strictly from the sugars remaining in the young beer. Traditional versions of Geuze/Gueuze are effervescent but have all the other characteristics of Lambics/Lambieks (intense sourness, fruity complexity, cloudiness, horsey aroma, etc.). Although not strong, these beers age extremely well. During aging, some of the acids are joined to the alcohols to form esters, increasing the fruitiness and decreasing the sourness. Some beers of this style are harshly sour, but mellow to a soft and very pleasant sourness after a few years aging. Commercial examples (traditional unless otherwise noted): Drie Fonteinen Geuze, Cantillon Gueuze, Boon Geuze, Girardin Geuze, Hanssens Geuze, De Troch Geuze, Geuze Fond Tradition, Lindemans (the Cuveé René Gueuze is traditional, the regular Gueuze is filtered and sweetened), St. Louis Gueuze (untraditional, filtered, sweetened), Chapeau Gueuze (untraditional, filtered, sweetened – very sweet), Belle-Vue Gueuze (untraditional, filtered, sweetened, perfumy). OG: 1.044 - 1.056; AA: 82 - 98%; ABV: 4.7 - 6; IBUs: 10 - 15; SRM: 4 - 15;

## Faro

Although there are some pasteurized, bottled examples, but traditional Faro is made from mixing young Lambic/Lambiek with sugar syrup and caramel. It was meant to be a sweetish, light, refreshing everyday drink, but is just about extinct.

Cantillon's Jean-Pierre Van Roy told me that he makes a Faro for one or two cafés by blending 10 liters of young Lambic/Lambiek with 1 liter of sugar syrup and a spoonful of caramel. Draft Faro should be virtually uncarbonated, but it is a live product and therefore will dry out as time passes (this is why it is made in very small batches). Despite what some books may say, Faro is not sweetened Gueuze/Geuze; Gueuze/Geuze by definition is Lambic/Lambiek that carbonates via refermentation in the bottle, whereas Faro traditionally was a cask product. Commercial examples: Cantillon, Boon, Lindemans. OG: 1.044 - 1.056; AA: 70 - 89%; ABV: 4 - 5.5; IBUs: 10 - 15; SRM: 8 - 18;

## Fruit Lambieks/Lambics

Fruit Lambics/Lambieks include Kriek (cherries), Framboise (raspberries), Pêche (peaches), Vigneronne or Muscat (grapes). They are made from adding fruits (or, in "fake" versions, syrups) to old Lambieks/Lambics for a secondary fermentation. Later, this is usually mixed with young Lambic/Lambiek and bottled, but some brewers still make a draft version. The majority of these beers that make it to the US are filtered, sweetened and made with syrups – very untraditional procedures and flavors. Traditional fruit Lambieks/Lambics are not sweet, but dry and the fruit flavor/aroma ranges from very faint to moderate. Commercial examples: Cantillon Rosé de Gambrinus (25% cherries, 75% raspberries), Hanssens Kriek (probably the best Kriek), Drie Fonteinen Kriek (available in bottles or draft at the Beersel café of the same name), Cantillon Kriek, Boon Kriek, De Troch Kriek, Boon Framboise, Cantillon Gueuze Vigneronne, Timmermans Kriek (untraditional, filtered sweetened), Lindemans Kriek (untraditional, filtered, sweetened), Timmermans Framboise (untraditional, filtered, sweetened), Lindemans Kriek (untraditional, filtered, sweetened), Chapeau (brewed by De Troch, all are extremely untraditional and excessively sweet). OG: 1.044 - 1.056 (plus the fruit); AA: 70 - 95%; ABV: 5 - 6.8; IBUs: 7 - 12; SRM: *not applicable;*

# Porter

## Original 1720's-style Porter, Entire Butt, or Entire

Porter originated in London in the 1720's. The most popular story regarding its invention associates it with Ralph Harwood of the Bell Brewhouse in Shoreditch[185]. Although this attribution has been written in many books, all the authors seem to have gotten it from the same source: John Bickerdyke's *Curiosities of Ale and Beer*, published 150 years after the creation of Porter. Several modern writers speculate that, for various reasons, it is unlikely that Ralph Harwood was indeed the originator of Porter[186]. I've read conflicting accounts on the making of this style. It is entirely possible that several varieties of Porter were made. One account suggests that fermentation took place in 24 to

48 hours, then was casked for one day and distributed[221]. Foster suggests that Porter was aged for several months in wooden vats (which are impossible to sanitize completely), so we can be pretty sure that this variety had a slight lactic sourness from lactic acid bacteria and some "horse-blanket" aroma and acidity from *Brettanomyces*[186]. Another account of this variety is not specific regarding the aging time of the Porter, but says:

> On this footing stood the Trade until about the Year 1722 ; when the Brewers conceived that there was a Mean to be found preferable to any of these Extremes; which was, that Beer should be well brewed, and, from being kept its proper Time, becoming Mellower (i.e. neither New nor Stale), it would recommend itself to the Public[222].

In the quote above, "Stale" beer was aged considerably (no, it was still good; it has nothing to do with the modern meaning of "stale") and many patrons were in the habit of ordering blends of new and stale. These original Porters were brewed mostly from brown malt[185,187] although one account says "two Bushels of pale Malt with six of brown[223]." Just previous to the advent of black malt (even now sometimes called "Patent Malt," referring to the 1817 patent on the barrel roaster) one 1815 account said that Porter was made from "very high dried brown malt" (kilned at around 185 or 190° F), made from a mix of pale and porter malt (where 1/4 to 2/3 was pale malt), and a mash temperature between 154 and 160° F[231]. The use of brown malt implies that these beers were at least slightly smoky (because the malt was kilned under hardwood fires) and dark, but not opaque (unlike modern interpretations). Regarding the second variety of Porter, given their relatively long maturation and lactic and *Brettanomyces* fermentation, I would suspect that they were quite dry, whereas the first variety would probably have been sweet and lively.

I'm inclined to believe that the second variety (the type that was aged several months) would be more representative of this style. I base this primarily on the fact that the brewers of mid- to late-1700's were building huge wooden vessels for making Porter[186]. In vessels of this depth, beer will neither ferment in two days nor will the yeast settle in a reasonable amount of time, i.e. the size of the fermenters implies a long fermentation. Note that there is a sentence in reference 221 that could be interpreted such that Porter was a sort of "continuously brewed" beer: where several casks of beer were drawn off from a large vat and then an equal amount of fresh wort added back to the vat. This would be a possible explanation for the widely varying process descriptions. Commercial examples: none. OG: 1.060 - 1.090; AA: 70 - 90%; ABV: 6.2 - 9.2; IBUs: 40 - 100+; SRM: 14 - 20;

## Late 19th-century Porter

In 1817, the barrel roaster was invented and dark beers changed considerably. In stead of being made up of various proportions of brown, amber, and pale malts, dark beers began to be made from mostly pale malt (which brewers realized was more *economical* than brown malt, despite being more expensive) and a small percentage of extremely dark malt. After Black Patent Malt became common in Porters, I believe that the flavor of the beer changed considerably and late-1800's Porters had a dark-roasted malt flavor similar to modern Porter. I do believe, however, that they were more bitter, slightly higher in gravity, and perhaps still retaining the lactic sourness of their brown malt-based cousins (based upon the lactic sourness of Old Ales during this period[173]). Commercial examples: none. OG: 1.060 - 1.090; AA: 70 - 90%; ABV: 6.2 - 9.2; IBUs: 40 - 100+; SRM: 16 - 35;

## Pre-Prohibition Porter

American brewers in the 1750's (who were primarily of Anglo-Saxon background) brewed Porter the east as did Midwestern brewers in the 1830's to 1860's[211]. By the 1880's, lager brewers of German heritage had pretty much replaced the ale brewers in the United States, but many still brewed a Porter[211]. For example, we know that in the 1890's, Schlitz made a top-fermenting Porter[211]. By the early 1900's, Porter was brewed by at least 22 breweries west of the Mississippi[220]. Up until the 1830's or so, brown malt was the primary source of fermentables in Porter, although adjuncts are said to have been used when malt was scarce[220]. Since the middle of the 19th century, a mixture of black and pale malts has been the norm and adjuncts have been used by American brewers to compensate for high-protein malts rather than for reasons of economy. These Porters were typically higher OG than modern Porters and were hopped heavily (from a rate of 5 ounces of hops per 5-gallon batch in Colonial Porters to around 2$^1/_2$ ounces by the 19th century)[220]. The guidelines below are purely speculative, drawn from bits and pieces of the references noted above. Commercial examples: none. OG: 1.055 - 1.080; AA: 65 - 80%; ABV: 5.5 - 8.0; IBUs: 50+; SRM: 18 - 35;

## Baltic Porter (Modern)

The last time I visited Lithuania was in 1976 when it was still under soviet rule. You could get beer but it was Pilsner Urquell on the black market. The soviet-made "beer" was called Zigulinis and tasted like 50% Old Frothingslosh and 50% flat orange soda-pop. My dad visited again in 1991 and reported that breweries were springing up all over and many were making Porter (Porteris in Lithuanian) again. From what I can gather, "Porter" is what Eastern Europeans (especially Latvians, Lithuanians, Estonians, Poles, and Russians) used to call

Imperial Stout (see "Imperial Stout" below) which is why I make it a point to mention "Modern" in the title of this subsection. My dad described Utenos Porteris as "dark brown, thick, malty, sweetish, and *strong*." I gave him a Courage Imperial Russian Stout to taste and he said the two were clearly related styles. In general, I'm told that Baltic Porters tend to be sweeter than Imperial Stouts and that many are bottom-fermenting[219]. Please bear in mind that the guidelines below are speculations, based on my assumption that Baltic Porter is closely related to Imperial Stout and email discussions with my (non-brewing) relatives in Lithuania. Commercial examples: Utenos Porteris, Vilniaus Porteris, Svyturio Porteris, Zywiek Porter, Carnegie Porter, Koff Porter (Saku Estonian Porter is an incredible beer, bursting with melanoidins, but at only 6.6% ABV and an OG well below 1.080, it is really more of a high-alcohol Modern Porter). OG: 1.080 - 1.100; AA: 65 - 80%; ABV: 6.8 - 11+; IBUs: 70 - 100+; SRM: 30+;

## Porter (Modern)

Modern Porter is principally a lighter version of Stout. In fact, originally, Stout was called "Stout Porter." This version of Porter is dark, balanced evenly between bitterness and malt, can be fruity and can vary in sweetness from dry to medium-sweet. Some bottom-fermenting versions are brewed, which do not have a fruity aroma. Although it is made with dark malts (sometimes with a little roasted unmalted barley too, although this is against the current AHA guidelines) it should not be excessively sharp-flavored from too much black malt. Some versions include slight licorice or coffee notes. Commercial examples: Samuel Smith's Taddy Porter, Young's London Porter, Burton Bridge Porter, Pimlico Porter, Boulder Porter, Yuengling's Pottsville Porter, Sierra Nevada Porter, Saku Estonian Porter, Whitbread Porter, Flag Porter. (I feel Anchor Porter is actually more of Pre-Prohibition-style Porter or even a Sweet Stout, and with an OG of 1.066 and AA of 73%, not surprisingly). OG: 1.040 - 1.065; AA: 71 - 82%; ABV: 3.8 - 6.5; IBUs: 30 - 50; SRM: 16 - 35;

## *Real Ale*

See "Cask-Conditioned Real Ale" above.

## *Sahti*

Sahti is a traditional fermented beverage of Estonian and Finnish origin and is sometimes called sörö. It is made primarily of malted barley, but usually contains a significant percentage of rye and/or oats. Sahti is flavored with juniper berries, but can also contain hops. Fruity, citrusy and clovey flavors and aromas are common, some varieties also are slightly sour or can have chocolaty highlights. Usually, it is fermented with bread yeast. It may be pale or dark, clear or cloudy.  Commercial examples: Lammin, Finlandia, Joutsa, Honkajoki, Mafia, Sysma.  OG: 1.080 - 1.100;  ABV: 7.0 - 9.0;  IBUs: 0 - 30;  SRM: 5 - 20.

## Saison

"Saison" means "season" and the season is summer.  These beers were brewed for summer consumption.  They came in a variety of strengths but most of the current commercial versions are of the stronger type.  Saisons are pale to amber in color, effervescent, tart and very aromatic (fruity and clove-like aromas from the yeast).  Many have a hoppy aroma – some brewers choose to dryhop with British hops such as Goldings, whereas others use Saaz and German varieties.  Some commercial versions are spiced with spices such as star anise and dried sweet orange peel (the Belgian variety, not navel oranges).  Alcoholic strength is evident and often the beers will have a sweetish mid-palate, but a dry finish.  Commercial examples: Saison Dupont, Sezoens, Moinette, Saison Silly, Saison de Pipaix.  OG: 1.045 - 1.080;  AA: 75 - 88%;  ABV: 4.3 - 7.8;  IBUs: 20 - 45;  SRM: 6 - 12;

## Sake

Sake is often called rice wine, but it is not.  It is a beer because it is made from grain: rice.  There are many different kinds of Sake – it can be sweet or dry, filtered or unfiltered, almost clear to yellow.  Since making Sake is outside the scope of this book, I won't spend much more time on it.  For more information about Sake and making it at home, I recommend you get *Sake U. S. A.* by Fred Eckhardt.

## Scottish Ale

Scottish Ales are similar to English Bitters, except that they are fermented cooler (which means they will be less fruity), are hopped a little less (less bitter and only low hop flavor or aroma), often have a touch of roasted malt or barley, and sometimes have mild smoky notes (as often from yeast as from peat-kilned malts).  Despite what some books say about Scottish Ales, many of them *do* have some hop aroma and flavor and they are not completely without bitterness.  They are often quite a bit darker than Bitters of similar gravity.  As with Bitters, the brewers don't really keep to any consistent naming convention other than if a brewery makes a 60/- and a 70/-, the 70/- will be higher in OG and alcohol.  Note: the /- represents shillings, so that "60/-" is read as "60 shilling."

### Light or 60/-

These are the lightest of the Scottish Ales, ranging from copper to dark brown in color.  Malt usually dominates, but they are light in body and alcohol.  Hop bitterness is medium to low.  Hop flavor and aroma are medium to none and carbonation is low on these beers.  Commercial examples: Caledonian 60/-,

Maclay 60/-, Belhaven 60/-.  OG: 1.030 - 1.036;  AA: 65 - 78%;  ABV: 2.5 - 3.5; IBU: 15 - 30;  SRM: 10 - 25;

## Heavy or 70/-

These beers are slightly bigger than the 60/- ales, also ranging from copper to dark brown in color. Malt usually dominates, but they are still relatively light in body and alcohol. Hop bitterness is medium to low. Hop flavor and aroma are medium to none and carbonation is low on these beers. Commercial examples: Caledonian 70/-, Maclay 70/-, Borve Ale, Greenmantle Ale, Belhaven 70/-. OG: 1.035 - 1.040;  AA: 65 - 78%;  ABV: 3.3 - 4.0;  IBU: 15 - 35;  SRM: 10 - 25;

## Export or 80/-

These beers are slightly bigger than the 70/- ales, also ranging from copper to dark brown in color. Malt usually dominates, but they are medium-light to medium in body and alcohol. Hop bitterness is medium to low. Hop flavor and aroma are medium to none and carbonation is low on these beers. Commercial examples: Caledonian 80/-, Younger No. 3, Dark Island, Golden Promise, Maclay 80/-, St. Andrew's Ale, Ptarmigan, Belhaven 80/-, Bear Ale. OG: 1.040 - 1.050;  AA: 65 - 80%;  ABV: 3.8 - 5.0;  IBU: 20 - 50;  SRM: 10 - 25;

## 90/- and Scottish Strong Ale

This is rather wide category, but the problem is that strong ales in Scotland do cover a very wide range and that there is no consistent naming convention. Note that this category covers the beers commonly called 90/- and beers called Strong Ales (not to imply that these two are equivalent). There is so much overlap among commercial beers that delineation is difficult. Ranging from copper to dark brown in color, malt dominates in these ales. They can be medium to heavy in body and are medium-high to high in alcohol. Hop bitterness is medium to low. Some can be quite sweet. A noticeable alcohol warmth is required in the stronger examples. Hop flavor and aroma are medium to none and carbonation is low on these beers. Commercial examples: Belhaven 90/-, Old Jock, Merman XXX, Caledonian Strong Ale (marketed in the US as MacAndrew's Scotch Ale), Wee Heavy (Vermont Pub and Brewery), Odell's 90 Shilling, Skullsplitter, Traquair House Ale, McEwan's Scotch Ale. OG: 1.050 - 1.100+;  AA: 60 - 85%; ABV: 5 - 10+;  IBU: 30 - 70+;  SRM: 10 - 35;

## 19-century Scottish Ales

In the 1800's, Scottish Ales (just as ales throughout the brewing world) were typically much higher gravity than they are these days. Based on John Harrison's *Old British Beers and How to Make Them*, W. H. Roberts' *The Scottish Ale Brewer and Practical Maltster* (published in 1847), and Greg Noonan's *Scotch Ale*, I've pieced-together some guidelines on what these beers were (or may have been) like. One thing that set these beers apart from other high-gravity beers of the time was the relatively low attenuation, partly due to high mashing temperatures and partly due to the use of highly-flocculant yeast. Balance would be decidedly towards malt and hop bitterness would be used simply to prevent the ale from being cloyingly sweet. Relatively cool fermentation temperatures would keep the esters and higher alcohols low and diacetyl would probably be rather high given the tendency of the yeast to flocculate early. Ales of a wide range of gravities were produced: for example in 1872, Younger made a 60/- (1.060-1.062), an 80/- (1.070), a 100/- (1.080), a 120/- (1.092-1.094), a 140/- (1.104), a 160/- (1.126), and in 1910, a 200/- (1.126)[187]. Commercial (modern) examples: none. Please remember that these guidelines are based upon speculation, especially the bitterness. OG: 1.060-1.126; AA: 55 - 70%; ABV: 5.0 - 9.5; IBU: 40 - 70; SRM: 12 - 35;

## Stout

### Dry Stout

Dry Stout is the national drink of Ireland. Bottled Guinness is not a Dry Stout (it is a Foreign-style Stout), but Draft Guinness and the Guinness in cans are. Dry Stouts are lightly fruity, have a coffee-like nose and palate. They must be smooth, drinkable and refreshing – not heavy. Bitterness is medium-high and comes from both hops and from dark grains. Some dark malt aroma is inevitable. Hop flavor and aroma is low to none. Commercial examples: Draught Guinness, Guinness Pub Draught (in cans), Beamish Genuine Stout, Murphy's Irish Stout. OG: 1.035 - 1.050; AA: 77 - 85%; ABV: 3 - 5.5; IBUs: 30 - 50; SRM: 35+;

### Foreign-Style Stout

This is a high-gravity version of Dry Stout, but inevitably the increase in gravity means a slight increase in sweetness. Sierra Nevada Stout, New Glarus Coffee Stout, Guinness Extra Stout (in the Caribbean, an even stronger and sweeter version is brewed), Sheaf Stout. OG: 1.050 - 1.075; AA: 74 - 82%; ABV: 5 - 7.5; IBUs: 35 - 70; SRM 35+;

### Imperial Stout

Back in the 18th century, a very strong stout was donated to Russian military hospitals which led to a request by the empress to have the beer supplied to the Russian imperial court (hence the "Imperial" or sometimes even "Imperial Russian" designation). This style is the biggest and thickest of all beers. Imperial Stouts are massively fruity with raisins, currants and ripe fruit in the nose. Rich chocolaty aromas and flavors abound. Body is heavy and the beer is decidedly alcoholic in aroma and flavor. There should be a lot of dark malt aroma but a burnt character should not be too dominant. Imperial Stouts have to be hopped to incredible levels, but it is only to balance the incredible weight of the malt in them. The hop/malt balance is nearly even, but don't forget that alcohol and dark malts add bitterness too. From what I can gather, this style was called "Porter" in Eastern Europe and is predecessor of the "Baltic Porter" style. Publicity material for A Le Coq Imperial Extra Double Stout was written in both English and Russian, the word "ПOPTEPІb" contained in the latter text[217] which, in Russian, would be pronounced "Porter." Commercial examples: Courage Imperial Russian Stout, Samuel Smith's Imperial Stout, Bell's Expedition Stout, Grant's Imperial Stout. OG: 1.070 - 1.100+; AA: 65 - 82%; ABV: 7 - 11+; IBUs: 50 - 100; SRM: 35+;

## Oatmeal Stout

Oatmeal Stouts are usually semi-sweet, sort of half-way between Foreign-style and Sweet Stouts in sweetness and an oily silkiness from the oats. It is, in fact, possible for extract brewers to make this style since the introduction of Oatmeal Stout extract. Oats must be mashed, so you cannot simply add them to your extract recipe. Malt/hop balance is about even and hop flavor and aroma are low to none. Commercial examples: Samuel Smith's Oatmeal Stout, Young's Oatmeal Stout, Anderson Valley Barney Flats Oatmeal Stout, Oasis Zoser Stout. OG: 1.035 - 1.060; AA: 65 - 78%; ABV: 3.3 - 6; IBUs: 20 - 50; SRM: 35+;

## Sweet Stout

Sweet Stouts are just that: sweet. Actually, their sweetness can range from slightly sweet to extremely sweet. They are sometimes called "Milk Stouts" because of the milk sugar (lactose, which is not fermentable by yeast) that is added to give them their sweetness. Even light-gravity versions are medium to heavy bodied. Bitterness is low to medium, but balance is always towards malt. Hop flavor and aroma are low to none. Commercial examples: Mackeson's XXX, Dragon Stout, Tennent's Milk Stout, Stoudt's Fat Dog Stout. OG: 1.035 - 1.066; AA: 60 - 75%; ABV: 3.2 - 5.6; IBUs: 20 - 40; SRM: 35+;

## *Trappist/Abbey Ales*

The designation "Trappist Ale" is actually a legal term designating origin and not style. There are five Trappist breweries in Belgium (the makers of Orval, Chimay, Westmalle, Rochefort, and St. Sixtus) and one in The Netherlands (the makers of La Trappe). Secular breweries making similar beers may only call them Abbey beers, although there is rarely an abbey associated with the brewery. There are two styles that have become popular among the Trappist and "Abbey" breweries: Dubbel and Tripel. Since the other Trappist Ales are basically singular, unique beers, it would be silly to create a style for a single beer which is why I've grouped them all under the "Other Trappist/Abbey Ales" category.

## Dubbel

Dubbels are dark amber to dark brown in color, their balance is towards malt. The best examples are malty, yet dry (a very unique and beguiling trait), smooth with no rough edges. Body is medium thanks to the addition of dark candi sugar and although they are strong, alcohol should not be strongly evident. A faint clovey aroma is noticeable in some and the spicy aroma of higher alcohols is found in others. Commercial examples: Westmalle Dubbel, Rochefort 6, Celis Dubbel, Rochefort 8, Tilburg Dubbel (marketed as Koningshoeven in Holland and La Trappe Dubbel in the US), Westvleteren 4 Dubbel, Steenbrugge Dubbel, Chimay Première, Grimbergen Dubbel, Affligem Dubbel. OG: 1.040 - 1.080; AA: 75 - 87%; ABV: 3.2 - 7.8; IBUs: 20 - 35; SRM: 10 - 20;

## Tripel

Tripels are pale strong, effervescent beers with a solid hop bitterness, although balance is still slightly towards the malt. They are light-bodied for their size, owing to the addition of white candi sugar. Commercial examples: Westmalle Tripel, Grimbergen Tripel, Tilburg Tripel (marketed as Koningshoeven in Holland and La Trappe Tripel in the US – it is light copper colored), Affligem Tripel, Brugse Tripel, Steenbrugge Tripel, Chimay Cinq Cents (white cap). OG: 1.065 - 1.095; AA: 75 - 87%; ABV: 6.3 - 10; IBUs: 20 - 35; SRM: 3.5 - 8;

## Other Trappist/Abbey Ales

The other Trappist Ales are really one-of-a-kind beers. Some can fit into other broad categories like Belgian Strong Ale, but each has distinct qualities that set it apart from other beers. For quite some time, I have been lobbying for a subcategory in homebrewing competitions that would provide a subcategory called "Trappist Other, specify" that would give homebrewers the opportunity to get feedback on their attempts to brew beers similar to these world-classics. The brewer would specify the commercial example he/she tried to emulate. Chimay Grand Reserve ("capsule bleu" or "blue cap" in the 33 cl form) is one of those beers that would fit the Belgian Strong Ale category, but it also has a unique spicy character and a peppery/raisiny flavor. Orval is a unique beer in every respect. A *Brettanomyces* yeast added during conditioning adding not only horsey, leathery and bubblegum aromas, but also a light refreshing sourness. Besides Hallertauer and Golding hops in the boil, Orval also is dryhopped with Goldings – rare among Belgian brews.

Rochefort 10 is another unique beer with a spicy, chocolaty, warming character and a flavor reminiscent of ripe fruit. It has such deep flavors that this alone makes it stand apart from other strong ales. In addition to it's Dubbel and Tripel, the Schaapskooi brewery also makes an Enkel (single) and a Quadrupel which are both unique beers. In addition to Westvleteren's Dubbel (the smallest of all the Dubbels) they also brew a 6 (Special), an 8 (Extra) and 12 (Abt/Abbot), the last being the highest gravity beer in Belgium with an original gravity of 12 Belgian degrees or 1.120. An excellent and interesting beer in the Abbey "style" is brewed by New Belgium Brewing Company and called "Abbey Ale."

## Wheat Beers

### American Wheat

American Wheat is basically a low-bitterness pale-colored ale with a significant portion of wheat. It should have some wheat flavor and possibly aroma also, but is different from Bavarian Weizen in that it simply has a basic, fruity nose (no clovey phenolics). The wheat should also lend a creaminess to the palate. Bitterness is low, hop flavor and aroma are very low or none. Body can be light to medium. Commercial examples: Heartland Weiss, Pyramid Wheaten Ale, August Schell Weiss. OG: 1.040 - 1.055; AA: 70 - 85%; ABV: 4.3 - 5.5; IBUs: 10 - 30; SRM: 2 - 9;

### Bavarian Weizen

Bavarian Weizen (or, sometimes, Weiss) is characterized by a clovey/banana aroma, a creamy body and a wheaty flavor. Bitterness is low, hop flavor and aroma are very low to none. The yeast used is the main difference between an American and a Bavarian wheat beer. Clove-like/phenolic aromas are usually considered a flaw in most beers, but they are an expected character in Bavarian Weizens. If the label says "Hefe" that means the bottle contains yeast (usually not the fermentation yeast), whereas "Kristall" means the beer has been filtered. Commercial examples: Pschorr-Bräu Weizen, Franziskaner Hefe-Weissbier, Great Lakes Hefe-Weizen, Weihenstephan Altbayerisches Hefe-Weizen, Paulaner Altbayerische Weissbier, Schneider Weisse, Tucher Weizen (without yeast) and Hefe-Weizen (with yeast). OG: 1.040 - 1.056; AA: 73 - 82%; ABV: 4.3 - 5.6; IBUs: 10 - 20; SRM: 2 - 9;

### Berliner Weiss

Berliner Weiss, as the name implies, is a style from Berlin. It is a very low-gravity, light, refreshing wheat beer, but its most unique character is the intentional lactic bacteria that is part of the fermentation. Horsey notes from *Brettanomyces* are acceptable. The tart sourness of the lactic acid defines this style. These are some of the lowest-gravity beers in the world, but also they are some of the most refreshing. Those people who call American Pilsners "lawnmower beers" (i.e. great after mowing the lawn) have never tasted a Berliner Weiss. Personally, I find no beer more refreshing on a hot day than a Berliner Weiss. Commercial examples: Schultheiss Berliner Weiss, Berliner Kindl Weisse. OG: 1.028 - 1.036; ABV: 2.6 - 3.6; AA: 77 - 85%; IBUs: 3 - 8; SRM: 2 - 4.

## Dunkelweizen

Dunkelweizen is the dark version of Bavarian Weizen. Some books say that these beers are very chocolaty. None of the Dunkelweizens I tasted in Bavaria last summer had significant chocolaty aromas or flavors. The darkness appears to come from either Munich malts or from very small additions of very dark malts. Most did have a very slight dark malt aroma, but chocolaty is definitely not an adjective that came to mind. Some had the characteristic clove/banana aroma, others smelled cleanly fruity. Commercial examples: Schneider Dunkel Weiss, Pschorr-Bräu Dunkel Weiss, Dachsbräu Hefe-Weizen, Hopf Dunkelweizen. OG: 1.040 - 1.055; AA: 70 - 81%; ABV: 4.3 - 5.3; IBUs: 10 - 20; SRM: 10 - 23;

## Weizenbock

Weizenbock is a high-gravity Bavarian Weizen or American Wheat beer. Obviously, the clove/banana character is optional. These beers should definitely have a creamy body and warming alcohol notes. They are very soft and smooth, often deceptively strong. Some varieties may be dark in color, but do not have any dark malt character. Commercial examples: Schneider Aventinus, Pyramid Weizenbock, Dominion Wheat Bock, Erdinger Pinkatus. OG: 1.066 - 1.080+; AA: 65 - 80%; ABV: 6.5 - 7.8+; IBUs: 15 - 30+; SRM: 7 - 25;

## *White, Witbier or Bière Blanche*

These beers are a Belgian style of beer that dates back to the days before hops were used in most beers. Back then, brewers used many spices in beer, coriander being quite common. While some other Belgian beers in other styles contain coriander, Witbiers are typified by it. Witbiers are made from a large portion of unmalted wheat in addition to malted barley and possibly a small amount of oats. In addition to the coriander, they are also spiced with Curaçao (bitter) orange peel and some also contain some Sweet orange peel (no, this is nothing like the grocery-variety navel orange peels). Witbiers have an orange-like character, but it is not imparted by the orange peels. Curaçao orange peels are mostly bitter with a slight chamomile-like aroma. Sweet orange peel adds another, different aroma. Most of the orange-like character in these beers actually comes from the coriander, but the yeasts used in this style are very fruity and can add a citrusy note. These beers have a significant lactic component (another historical remnant) which blends well with the citrusy character of the yeast. Commercial examples: Celis White, Hoegaarden Wit, Steendonk Wit, Brugs Tarwebier (a.k.a. Blanche de Bruges), Dentergems, Blanche des Neiges. OG: 1.042 - 1.055; AA: 75 - 89%; ABV: 4 - 6; IBUs: 15 - 22; SRM: 2 - 4.

# Lagers

Lagers, relative to ales, are quite a new development. Integral to their production is storage at cold temperatures ("lagern" is a German word meaning "to store"). Lagering technique dates back 500 years[188], but serious commercial production of lager started only about 150 years ago. Another thing that these beers have in common are that they are fermented with "lager" or "bottom-fermenting" yeasts, typically at temperatures between 40 and 55° F (4 and 13° C). After the primary fermentation, the beer goes through a secondary fermentation (the lagering) usually at even colder temperatures. Pale lagers, because of the grains that they are made from and several other factors, can have a noticeable amount of dimethyl sulfide (DMS) in their aroma – at low levels, this cooked-corn aroma is a pleasant addition to the beer and is often thought of as a significant component of malt aroma – at higher levels, however, it is considered a defect. Some pronunciation notes: "Märzen" should sound like MARE-tsen, "bräu" is BROY, "Spaten" is SHPA-ten, "Spezial" is SHPE-tsial, and "Sticke" is SHTEEK.

## *American Lager*

### American Pilsner

American Pilsners are very pale, light-bodied, refreshing lagers which are usually made with a significant proportion of their barley replaced with corn or rice (up to 40%). This lightens their body by reducing the amount of protein in the beer. Typically, American Pilsners are very highly filtered which also contributes to their light body. Bitterness levels are low as are hop flavors and aromas. Balance can be slightly towards malt or bitterness, the latter being more common. There should be no detectable diacetyl. A mild DMS aroma is acceptable. While acetaldehyde is considered a fault in every other beer style, the most popular example of this style has quite a bit of it in the aroma and flavor, therefore acetaldehyde becomes an acceptable characteristic in American Pilsners. Commercial examples: Miller Beer, Budweiser, Miller High Life, Coors, Michelob, Miller Genuine Draft, Coors Extra Gold, Stroh's, Foster's, Henry Weinhardt's, Red Dog, Corona. OG: 1.040 - 1.048; AA: 72 - 85%; ABV: 4.0 - 5.2; IBUs: 10 - 20; SRM: 2 - 5;

### American Dark

Originally, all beers were no lighter than brown. Eventually, malt making and brewing techniques improved to where pale beers were possible. Most of the remaining dark lagers, such as Munich Dunkel or Oktoberfest, are dark because their base malt is slightly darker. American Dark is basically American Pilsner with a very small amount of very dark grain or caramel color added. The difference is that in the case of Munich Dunkels, the large amount of slightly darker malt adds a significant amount of flavor, whereas in American Dark lagers, there is virtually no flavor contribution. Commercial examples: Michelob Classic Dark, Capital Dark, Berghoff Dark. OG: 1.040 - 1.048; AA: 70 - 82%; ABV: 4.0 - 5.2; IBUs: 10 - 20; SRM: 14 - 20;

## Light Beer

Light Beers are very pale, very light-bodied, refreshing lagers which are made with a significant proportion of their barley replaced with corn or rice (up to 40%). This lightens their body by reducing the amount of protein in the beer. Typically, Light Beers are very highly filtered which also contributes to their light body. Bitterness levels are low as are hop flavors and aromas. Balance can be slightly towards malt or bitterness, the latter being more common. There should be no diacetyl detectable. A mild DMS aroma is acceptable. Commercial examples: Miller Lite, Bud Light, Coors Light, Michelob Light, Miller Genuine Draft Light, Labatt's Light, Löwenbräu Light, Stroh's Light, Henry Weinhardt's Special Reserve Light, Corona Light. OG: 1.031 - 1.038; AA: 69 - 102%; ABV: 3.0 - 4.4; IBUs: 9 - 20; SRM: 2 - 4;

## Cream Ale/Lager

Cream Ale has mysterious beginnings. The history of this style is spotty and there have been suggestions that it is brewed with a blend of ale and lager yeasts. Rumor has it that one "Cream Ale" is nothing more than that brewery's Pilsner blended with their Ale. Frankly, I don't believe there is enough difference between these beers and American Pilsners to make a distinction in aroma or flavor.

## Dry Beer

Originated by Japanese brewers, Dry Beer is made with enzymes that break virtually all the larger sugars in the malt to fermentable sugars which results in a beer that has almost no flavor. Apparent attenuation often was above 90%! In the US, this was just another fad.

## Ice Beer

Made by freezing finished beer and removing the ice, thereby raising the alcohol level, many of these beers have water added back in to lower the alcohol level. Another fad beer with virtually no noticeable difference in flavor or aroma from American Pilsener.

## Malt Liquor

Actually a legal designation in some states, Malt Liquor, as a style, is nothing more than a high-alcohol version of American Pilsner. Commercial examples: Colt 45, Mickey's Malt Liquor, Labatt's Extra Stock, Old English 800, Molson Brador. OG: 1.048 - 1.070; AA: 70 - 92%; ABV: 4.8 - 8.4; IBUs: 14 - 24; SRM: 2 - 7;

## Red Beer

Another fad beer. Usually nothing more than American Pilsner with a little reddish color added. On the other hand, some brewers, in the process of making a Red Beer have actually added some additional malt flavor and aroma and a little more bitterness and have made respectable Vienna-style lagers. Others, haven't.

## Pre-Prohibition American Lager

Before Prohibition, American lagers were quite different from what they are today. They had much higher original gravities, higher hop rates and used less adjuncts, typically, 20 to 25%. Corn was preferred by some brewers[189,190] although others preferred rice[211]. These were more flavorful beers and bear little resemblance to modern American Pilsners. In an old tavern in downtown New Buffalo, Michigan called Casey's Pub, there is a photograph on the wall dated 1885. The interior of the pub in the photo is decorated with dozens of Schlitz signs and the beer in the hands of every patron is clearly dark brown! I discussed this with Peter Blum, Archivist and Historian at The Stroh Brewery Company (which purchased the Schlitz brewery), and he said that most breweries around the turn of the 20th century brewed four styles and some brewed more. It was not uncommon for half of a brewer's brands to be dark lagers. Typically a brewery might have an amber "Vienna" and a pale "Bohemian-style" (also called "Budweiser" by several breweries) which were more golden than current Pilsners, and perhaps a "Würtzburger" and a "Tivoli" or maybe a "Bavarian," which were decidedly dark. Many brewers made brown Bock beers in the spring. These were undeniably American adaptations of European styles and therefore distinctly different beers. It is important to note that adjuncts were used to compensate for the high protein levels in American barley malts rather than for reasons of economy[211]. Finally, the apparent attenuation of these beers was low by today's standards[211]. Commercial examples: none. OG: 1.050 - 1.060; AA: 65 - 70%; ABV: 5.1 - 6.2; IBUs: 30 - 45; SRM: 2 - 15

## Post-Prohibition American Lager

After Prohibition, the standard lagers were quite a bit lower OG and less hoppy than Pre-Prohibition Lagers but certainly more bitter and fuller-bodied than today's American Pilsners. They would have come close to Robust American Lagers except that they were lighter-bodied due to the additions of 20 to 35% adjuncts (some brewers preferring corn, others rice)[190,191,211]. At this time many breweries began to cut down on the number of styles they brewed. Note that during World War II, original gravities took their steepest drop, many dipping below 1.040. Commercial examples: none. OG: 1.044 - 1.050; AA: 70 - 82%; ABV: 4.4 - 5.2; IBUs: 20 - 35; SRM: 2 - 15;

## Robust American Lager

Robust American Lagers are somewhat of a return to Pre-Prohibition American Pilsners. They are all-malt, much fuller-bodied, darker, maltier, more bitter and have a lot more hop flavor and aroma than American Pilsners. Balance can be slightly towards bitterness or malt. Often they are dryhopped with German or Czech hops or their American cousins. Commercial examples: Samuel Adams Boston Lager, Brooklyn Lager, Lakefront Riverwest Stein, Hurricane Reef Lager (Miami Brewing Company). OG: 1.048 - 1.055; AA: 65 - 75%; ABV: 4.8 - 5.5; IBUs: 20 - 40; SRM: 2.5 - 9

# *Bock*

## American Bock

Everyone has heard the story that Bock beer is from the bottom of the barrels or tanks. Don't believe a word of it! Years ago, US brewers would make seasonal Bock beers similar to their German counterparts (see below). However, over the years, the OG and alcohol level of these beers dropped till what remained was usually the brewer's regular beer colored a bit with caramel (see American Dark). I don't think there's much point in including the modern "American Bock" beers (those caramel-added beers) in this style definition because when a microbrewery makes a Bock these days, it's in the German style. In the 19th century, there were American Bock beers of respectable gravity, but just as with American Pilsners, Porters, etc., they used a significant percentage (about 20%) of adjuncts such as corn or rice.

## Traditional German Bock

Bock beers were traditionally brewed for springtime or Christmas. These dark versions are similar in characteristics to Munich Dunkels except higher in gravity (and therefore alcohol) with a proportional increase in bitterness. "Traditional" in the name of this style refers to the fact that, only relatively recently have malting and brewing techniques progressed to the point where pale beers can be brewed. Prior to the 19th century, the palest beers possible were dark amber. Note that the color comes from Munich malts which are slightly darker base malts, not from the addition of chocolate or black malts. There should be no sharp edges in these beers and the alcohol should be noticeable without being harsh. Sweetness from malt and bitterness from hops should be about evenly balanced. Commercial examples: Aass Bock, Hacker-Pschorr Dunkeler Bock, Dunkel Ritter Bock (Kaltenburg Brewery), Klosterbock Dunkel. OG: 1.064 - 1.072; AA: 67 - 80%; ABV: 6 - 7.5; IBUs: 20 - 40; SRM: 14 - 30;

## Helles Bock

Just as Traditional German Bock is a high-alcohol version of Munich Dunkel, Helles Bock is a high-alcohol version of a pale lager. These beers should be soft and warming and their alcohol strength should be noticeable without being harsh. Sweetness from malt and bitterness from hops should be about evenly balanced. Most Maibocks (May Bocks) are Helles Bocks, although they tend to be at the dark end of the color range and have a touch more hops. The Bavarian Helles Bocks tend to be rather malt-dominated whereas pale Bocks from the Einbecker brewery (in the north of Germany) tend to have a little more bitterness as well as hop flavor and aroma. Commercial examples: Einbecker Ur-Bock Hell, Einbecker Maibock, St. Jakobus Blonder Bock (Forschungsbrauerei) [incidentally, at 1.076 OG, this beer is big enough to be labeled a Doppelbock], Hacker-Pschorr Heller Bock, Ayinger Maibock, Hofbräuhaus Maibock, Stoudt's Mai-Bock. OG: 1.064 - 1.072; AA: 68 - 82%; ABV: 6 - 7.5; IBUs: 20 - 40; SRM: 4 - 8;

## Doppelbock

First brewed by the Pauline monks to be consumed during lent, these are extra high-gravity Bock beers. The monks called their beer "Salvator" (savior) and virtually all Doppelbocks brewed since then have names that end in "-ator." Their Paulaner brewery has since been secularized and still brews Salvator, but the recipe has changed to have a higher attenuation (and therefore, more alcohol) than when the monks brewed it. The style name "Doppelbock" is relatively new and was certainly only adopted after the beer was made publicly available. By German law, they must have an original gravity of at least 1.072. Doppelbocks have extremely rich malt flavors, are slightly sweetish, have a warming touch of alcohol (which should never be so strong as to be harsh or rough) and are hopped such that the balance is decidedly malty, but not cloyingly sweet. The color usually comes from high-kilned malts (like Munich and perhaps Melanoidin or Aromatic malts) and not from dark roasted malts, however Spaten's Optimator has a good dose of dark roasted malt. There never should be any sharpness from roasted malts. Although the modern versions are lagers, Doppelbocks inevitably have some plum-like aromas. Their body is very full, hop flavor low and they have no hop aroma. Commercial examples: Salvator (Paulaner), Andechs Doppelbock Dunkel, Fortunator (Ayinger; marketed as Celebrator in the US), Maximator (Augustiner), Optimator (Spaten), EKU 28 Kulminator (not an Eisbock as many believe). OG: 1.072 - 1.080+; AA: 60 - 78%; ABV: 7 - 10+; IBUs: 15 - 28+; SRM: 12 - 30;

## Eisbock

"Eis" is the German word for "ice." These beers are the original ice beers. Alcohol freezes at a lower temperature than water so if you chill a beer until the water begins to freeze and remove some of it, the resulting beer will be stronger. There has been some question as to the legality of this process among homebrewers, but Dennis Davison's excellent article on Eisbocks in Zymurgy[192] has set the record straight: as long as you don't sell it, it's legal. Eisbocks are thick, rich and smooth. They should have noticeable alcohol, but should not be rough. Malt dominates the palate with just enough hops to prevent the beer from being cloying. There should be no diacetyl and DMS should be low. Commercial examples: Kulmbacher Reichelbräu Eisbock, Niagara Falls Eisbock. OG: 1.066 - 1.100+ (before ice removal); AA: 64 - 83% (before ice removal); ABV: 10 - 16+; IBUs: 25 - 50+ (before ice removal); SRM: 10 - 30;

## Cask-Conditioned Lager

Just as with Cask-Conditioned Real Ale, this is a method of packaging/serving rather than a style. I've even read Roger Protz refer to it as "Real Lager."[193] See Cask-Conditioned Real Ale, above.

## Continental Dark

These are beers that are simple, dark lagers that are not as malty or full-bodied as the Munich Dunkel style. They are slightly maltier and more bitter than the American Dark Lager style, but not significantly. Commercial examples: Beck's Dark, St. Pauli Girl Dark, Heineken Dark, Grolsch Dark. OG: 1.045 - 1.055; AA: 75 - 85%; ABV: 4.5 - 5.5; IBUs: 14 - 25; SRM: 15 - 23;

## Dortmunder/Export

Dortmunder-style lager, also called "Dort" or "Export" is similar in flavor to the popular German Pilsner style except that it is slightly higher in gravity (and, therefore, alcohol), darker gold in color, and it is made from very different water. The difference between German Pilsners and Dortmunders shows how much water can influence a beer's flavor. Dortmund's water is higher in sulfates than that used for most German Pilsners, which intensifies the bitterness of the hops and gives the beer a long, lingering dry finish. If you compare guidelines, you will notice that Dortmunders have less IBUs than German Pilsners, but when you taste them, they have similar apparent bitterness. The Dortmunder-style lager should have the lingering bitter and dry finish. Dortmunder Exports are light in body, golden in color, can have a low to medium hop nose and the balance is decidedly towards bitterness. Commercial examples (although I do not believe any of the German ones are imported to the US at this time): DAB (Dortmunder Actien Brauerei) Export, Dortmunder Union Export, Thier's Export, Ritter Export, Kronen Export, Yebisu (Sapporo), Gordon Biersch Export, Saratoga Lager, Stoutd Export Gold. OG: 1.048 - 1.060; AA: 75 - 85%; ABV: 4.8 - 6; IBUs: 23 - 30; SRM: 4 - 6;

## Dortmund-style Altbier

"Dortmund-style Altbier" is a name coined by Roger Deschner, author of *The Regal Altbiers of Düsseldorf* in Zymurgy magazine[194]. They are also sometimes called "Northern-German-style Altbiers." It is very important to distinguish between these beers and the Düsseldorf Altbier style. First of all, the Düsseldorf-style Altbiers are ales and these are lagers. You won't find "Dortmund-style Altbier" on any label, however, because nobody in Germany refers to them in this way. Breweries all over northern Germany brew a medium-brown lager and many simply call it an "Altbier" or, more commonly, an "Alt." The reason Dortmund was chosen for the name of this category is because of the number of breweries in this city making a beer of this style. You see, in addition to being rather high in sulfates, Dortmund's water is also quite high in carbonates, which means that it is much easier to brew beers with some dark malt in them to balance the alkalinity of the carbonates. In fact, if you order an Alt in any German city other than Düsseldorf (or possibly Köln), you will get one of these. They are medium- to dark-brown lagers, balanced slightly towards bitterness (but nowhere near the bitterness of a Düsseldorf Altbier) and, much of their apparent bitterness can come from the relatively high levels of sulfates in the water. Commercial examples: DAB Traditional "German Dark Beer," Alaskan Amber, Dortmunder Union Dark Beer, Kirin Alt, St. Stan's Amber. OG: 1.040 - 1.057; AA: 75 - 85%; ABV: 4 - 5.7; IBUs: 25 - 40; SRM: 10 - 25;

## Munich Helles

This style is the Munich brewers' pale version of the Munich Dunkel style. It actually has a lot in common with the Dunkel style – it is just made with Pilsner malt instead of the darker, Munich malt. Munich Helles ("Hell" means "light-colored") is dominated by malt, very soft, sweetish, with just enough hops to balance the malt and add a gentle bitterness in the finish. A good Munich Helles has a creamy, medium body and a noticeable, but not overpowering DMS aroma. There should be very little or no diacetyl. Commercial examples: Augustiner Hell, Hacker-Pschorr Edelhell, Hofbräuhaus Helles, Stoudt's Gold, Löwenbräu Hell (the version brewed in Munich, not the Swiss version which is a German Pils, nor the limp, corn-filled version brewed by Miller), Paulaner Original Münchner Hell, Spaten Münchner Hell, Weihenstephan Helles, Unionsbräu Hell. OG: 1.044 - 1.055; AA: 68 - 79%; ABV: 4.5 - 5.5; IBUs: 18 - 25; SRM: 3 - 5;

## Munich Dunkel

This is the original lager style from Munich. "Dunkel" means dark. Because of the rather high level of carbonates in Munich water, pale beers were difficult to brew and the acidity of dark malts balanced the alkalinity of the water, so towns that had high-carbonate water (Munich, London, Dublin) became famous for dark beers. Munich Dunkels are very malty – chocolaty even – and there is just enough hop bitterness to keep them from tasting cloyingly sweet. Some have toasted aromas and flavors, others just a rich chocolaty smoothness. DMS and diacetyl should be very low. There should be no sharpness from dark-roasted malts - in fact, no roasted flavors at all. Munich Dunkels should be dark amber to dark brown (not opaque) and should get their flavor and color from what are called high-kilned base malts (Munich and Vienna) and not from chocolate or black malts. Commercial examples: König Ludwig Dunkel, Ayinger Altbairisch Dunkel, Kloster Andechs Andechser Dunkel, Spaten Dunkel Export, Hacker-Pschorr Export Dunkel, Lakefront East Side Dark, Paulaner Alt-Münchner Dunkel, Erdinger Dunkel, Augustiner Edelstoff Dunkel, Augustiner Dunkel Export, Benediktiner Dunkel, Karneliten Bräu Girgl Dunkel Vollbier, Schmaltz Alt (despite the name – a respectable Dunkel). OG: 1.045 - 1.058; AA: 66 - 78%; ABV: 4.5 - 5.8; IBUs: 12 - 30; SRM: 15 - 30;

## Oktoberfest/Märzen

Originally this style was brewed by Gabriel Sedlmayr at his Spatenbräu (now just Spaten) brewery and associated with Oktoberfest back around 1810. It was inspired by the reddish-amber, Vienna-style lager brewed by Sedlmayr's contemporary Anton Dreher. Märzen means "March" and that's when this beer was traditionally brewed and then stored (lagered) in caves during the entire summer until it was ready for consumption for Oktoberfest (a celebration of the Crown Prince's engagement). Enough history, let's talk about the beer. Oktoberfest, also called Märzen, Wiesenmärzen or Wies'nmärzen, is slightly maltier and stronger than modern versions of Vienna-style lagers and has always been darker because of the higher carbonate content in Munich water (and therefore the need to use darker base malts). These beers are malt-dominated in the balance, especially in the nose. Their aroma and flavor should be from melanoidins (from Munich and Vienna malts) and not caramelly (i.e. from crystal malts). They can have a little alcohol warmth which can sometimes be noticeable in the aroma also. Bitterness is always quite low and there is little or no hop flavor or aroma. Body is medium to medium-full. Incidentally, Oktoberfest begins in September and ends 16 days later on the first Sunday in October. Commercial examples: Spaten Ur-Märzen Oktoberfest, Hacker-Pschorr Oktoberfest, Paulaner Münchner Märzen, Stoudt's Fest, Löwenbräu Oktoberfestbier (again, the German brewery), Zip City Märzen. OG: 1.050 - 1.065; AA: 70 - 79%; ABV: 4.5 - 6.5; IBUs: 20 - 30; SRM: 7 - 14;

## Pilsner

### Bohemian Pilsner

This is the original Pilsner. It originated in and got its name from the town of Pilsen in what is now the Czech Republic. It is only possible to make a beer like this with extremely low-sulfate water because the bitterness must be intense, but should not linger. It is made from all very pale Pilsner malt and gets its light amber color from the long mashing process used (the decoction method of mashing). Saaz hops should be obvious in the flavor and are desirable in the aroma. Body should be medium. While diacetyl is considered a fault in every other lager style, the finest example of this style has quite a bit of it in the aroma and flavor, therefore diacetyl becomes an acceptable (perhaps even a desirable) characteristic in Bohemian Pilsners. Commercial examples: Pilsner Urquell, Budweiser Budvar, Staropramen, Gambrinus. OG: 1.044 - 1.056; AA: 69 - 76%; ABV: 4.0 - 5.3; IBUs: 35 - 45; SRM: 2 - 5;

## German Pilsner

German Pilsners (often labeled "Pils") are usually hopped less than Bohemian Pilsners, but thanks to more sulfate in their water, they have a higher apparent bitterness. These beers are usually a little less malty, lighter-bodied and drier than Bohemian Pilsners. Hop flavor and aroma are usually low. Commercial examples: Bitburger, König Pilsner, Veltins Pils, Warsteiner, Jever (a beer with 42 to 44 IBUs and an extremely high apparent bitterness), Beck's, St. Pauli Girl (these last two are at the thin/low hop rate end of the style). OG: 1.045 - 1.050; AA: 73 - 83%; ABV: 4.2 - 5.0; IBUs: 23 - 45; SRM: 3 - 8;

## Dutch Pilsner

Dutch-style Pilsners are softer and less bitter than German Pilsners. Typically, they are very low in hop flavor and aroma and their balance may be slightly towards malt. Their body is light and they are typified by softness. When they do have a hop aroma it is usually floral as opposed to spicy as in the Bohemian Pilsners. They are pale yellow in color. Commercial examples: Heineken, Grolsch, Stella Artois (Belgian). OG: 1.040 - 1.050; AA: 73 - 80%; ABV: 4 - 5; IBUs: 14 - 25; SRM: 2 - 4;

## *Rauchbier*

Bamberg is the last remaining place where smoked beers are prevalent. "Rauch" means "smoke" in German and 200 years ago it would have been silly to call one of these beers a "smoked" beer since all beers from this region tasted of smoke. It is the way that they dried the malt, using beechwood-fired kilns. Other sources of heat have been employed for drying malt in most places, but at several maltsters in Bamberg, they still use the traditional methods which result in a smoky malt and subsequently a smoky beer. Naturally, any beer could be made from these malts, but in Bamberg, the center of the Rauchbier world, Vienna-style lagers are most common. Commercial examples: Aecht Schlenkerla Rauchbier, Braurei Spezial Lager, Braurei Spezial Märzen, Schlenkerla Ur-Bock (1.076), Kaiserdom Rauchbier (at the strong end of the smokiness scale, but not outside the bounds). OG: 1.045 - 1.076; AA: 68 - 79%; ABV: 4.5 - 7.4; IBUs: 15 - 40; SRM: 5 - 25;

## Schwarzbier and Black Beer

Schwarzbier means "Black Beer" in German. Although probably it was originally an ale, Schwarzbiers and Black Beers are now lagers. There appears to be some discrepancy as to what they should taste like. Jackson describes Köstritzer Schwarzbier as "sweet" and "malty," but then put it with the dry Asashi, Kirin, Sapporo and Suntory Black Beers. This is further complicated by the reunification of Germany and the subsequent changing of the recipe for the Köstritzer Schwarzbier from a 40 IBU, 1.048 beer made with 80% Munich malt and 20% roasted malt which was fermented down only to 3.5% ABV, to a 35 IBU, to a 1.050 beer made with 50% Pale Lager malt, 43% Munich malt and 7% roasted malt which is fermented down to 4.6% ABV195. Rather than trying to reconcile the two widely divergent interpretations, I will split the Black Beers into their own category.

### Schwarzbier

The difference between Schwarzbiers and Munich Dunkels is clear without even tasting them. Schwarzbiers are made with a significant proportion (7 to 20%) of very dark roasted malt (around 450 Lovibond) and traditionally were not fully attenuated, whereas Munich Dunkels were traditionally made with all Munich malt. The most recent version of Köstritzer Schwarzbier I tasted (it has a black label rather than the while label in Jackson's *Beer Companion*, but this may simply be the US label) had a little black malt aroma and a slight Munich Malt aroma. It was deep mahogany colored although not opaque. The dark malt flavor was mild, not at all sharp, the balance was slightly towards malt throughout the palate and the beer was rather dry – just a hint of sweetness. Very smooth and clean. It is clear that only a small percentage of the malt was roasted. Body was medium-light. Overall, the beer is dryish and refreshing with only a touch of dark malt character. Commercial examples: Köstritzer Schwarzbier (There is also a beer that may be similar in sweetness to the old version of Köstritzer, but since it is made without hops, it would be completely different in flavor: Mather's Black Beer from Leeds in West Yorkshire). OG: 1.045 - 1.056; AA: 60 - 78%; ABV: 3. 5 - 4.6; IBUs: 35 - 40; SRM: 25+;

### Black Beer

The Black Beers I'm referring to here are those represented by the Japanese brewers, not the Brazilian Xingu Black Beer which is somewhere between a Munich Dunkel and a Schwarzbier. These Japanese Black Beers are quite well attenuated resulting in a dry (not sweet) beer with a light to medium body. They are hopped to a moderate bitterness and have very low to no hop aroma or flavor.

Roasty character may be evident in the nose and flavor. Some brewers further lighten the body with the addition of small amounts of rice. It is really a sort of dryish Modern Porter made with lager yeast. One commercial version is only reddish-brown in color, the rest being decidedly black and virtually opaque with slight reddish hues. Commercial examples: Asashi Black Beer, Kirin Black Beer, Sapporo Black Beer (marketed as "Black Stout Draft" in the US, despite being a lager), Suntory Black Beer. OG: 1.044 - 1.052; AA: 74 - 85%; ABV: 4.7 - 5.2; IBUs: 20 - 28; SRM: 16 - 25;

## Vienna

Originally brewed by Vienna's Anton Dreher in the mid-1800's, this style has all but disappeared in Europe. The related Oktoberfest/Märzen style still remains, however. Modern Viennas are medium-bodied, amber lagers. Their balance is slightly towards malt and they are moderately hopped. Viennas usually have little or no hop flavor or aroma. Diacetyl and DMS should be very low. Commercial examples: Ambier, Abita Springs Amber Lager, Lakefront Steinbeer (no, sorry, not made with hot rocks), Sprecher Special Amber, Capital Märzen, Millstream Schild Brau, Negra Modelo, Noche Bueno, Dos Equis, Coors Winterfest, Red Wolf (although recent tastings indicate that they have decreased both the malt and hops). OG: 1.046 - 1.057; AA: 74 - 83%; ABV: 4.5 - 6; IBUs: 19 - 28; SRM: 6 - 12;

# Mixed Styles

These styles of beer either have mixed (both ale and lager) production methods or can be made as either an ale or a lager.

## Altbier

### Düsseldorf-style Altbier

Surely one of the most misunderstood and misrepresented styles in the world, the Düsseldorf-style Altbier has very distinct characteristics. "Alt" means "old" in German and is used in the name of this style to indicate that it is brewed in the old, pre-lager, brewing method. Despite being ales, these Altbiers (also referred to as "Alts") are cold-conditioned for three to eight weeks. Düsseldorf-style Altbiers are *very malty* and *intensely hoppy*. While other authors may disagree, my discussions with brewers and beer drinkers in Düsseldorf confirm that anything less is *not* a Düsseldorfer Altbier! I've narrowed the IBU guideline below such that it doesn't necessarily include all the Altbiers made in Düsseldorf, but I contend that not all the commercial Altbiers made in Düsseldorf are good examples of the style.

Their color ranges from medium amber to medium brown, which they gain from mostly Munich malts, but some brewers use a very small amount (less than 1%) of Black malt. Alts are low in diacetyl and have no DMS in the aroma. Some interpretations are not very fruity in the nose, but most are quite fruity (Zum Schlüssel has a soft, mixed-berry nose and Im Füchschen has an unmistakable Thompson's grape aroma) in both aroma and palate. Malt flavor and aroma are strong, but hop bitterness dominates the palate. There is some hop flavor and a touch of hop aroma, but I believe that it is simply spillover from the very high hopping rate – there should be a single hop addition: all bittering hops (Zum Uerige uses only Spalt or Spalter Select). All are medium-bodied, but are still refreshing. The bitterness ends abruptly and does not linger into the finish indicating low-sulfate water. These beers are gently malty-sweet throughout the palate (if you peek behind the bitterness which can make them seem dry). Commercial examples: Zum Uerige, Zum Schlüssel, Im Füchschen, Widmer Ur-Alt, Schlösser Alt, Schumacher Alt, Grolsch Amber Ale (although the last three are quite a bit less bitter than the other four). OG: 1.045 - 1.052; AA: 70 - 80%; ABV: 4.3 - 5; IBUs: 40 - 55; SRM: 13 - 19;

## Sticke

"Sticke" is local slang for "secret" in Düsseldorf. Sticke is a variety of Düsseldorfer Altbier that is brewed only a few times per year and is not advertised (that's the secret). This is done because the beer is meant as a reward for regular customers. The differences between it and regular Alt are that Sticke is slightly higher in original gravity, sometimes lagered longer and often dryhopped. OG: 1.050 - 1.055; AA: 64 - 76%; ABV: 4.5 - 5.2; IBUs: 45 - 65; SRM: 14 - 17;

### Münster-style Altbier

Although it is a one-of-a-kind beer, Pinkus Müller Alt deserves to have a category of its own. The beer is golden in color, made with 40% wheat malt, fermented with ale yeast and then lagered at cellar temperatures for six months. During the lagering, a resident lactic bacteria adds a refreshing sourness. While it is quite aggressively hopped, both the bitterness and maltiness are considerably lower than those of its cousins in Düsseldorf. OG: 1.044 - 1.047; AA: 72 - 79%; ABV: 4.9 - 5.1; IBUs: 16 - 20;

## *Altes Einbecker Bier*

The name for this style is adapted from Darryl Richman's *Bock* from the Classic Beer Styles Series. "Alt" means old, therefore this style description is meant to attempt to characterize the style of beer brewed in the city of Einbeck back in the 14th through 18th centuries. I really owe it to Darryl for making the risky (yet educated) first guess at what this style's guideline should look like. Because this period pre-dates the discovery of lager yeast, this beer would clearly be an ale, but due to the northern climate and the fact that brewing was only done during the late fall and winter, a period of cold storage, or what we now call lagering, is likely. We know for a fact that the beer was made from $1/3$ wheat malt and $2/3$ barley malt and that they used the palest malts they could (although malting techniques were well behind modern standards and therefore the malts would still yield a dark amber to dark brown beer)[226]. Since the malt back then was kilned under wood fires, it is quite certain that this beer would have a slight smoky character. To brew this beer with modern malts, I would use a blend of dark wheat malt, Munich malt, and smoked malt. The water there is quite soft, rivaling Pilsen. Richman suggests that both *Saccharomyces* and *Brettanomyces* yeasts probably played a role and that attenuation was low. *Brettanomyces* yeasts tend to be slow fermenters, but rather strong attenuators, so if they are indeed involved, I would suspect the beer would have been attenuated more on the order of modern beers (so I will extend Darryl's proposed attenuation range a little bit). It is known that the beer had a noticeable acidity[226], presumably from both the *Brettanomyces* and from lactic bacteria (not surprising since sanitation of wooden fermenters and casks is next to impossible) but since tastes have changed considerably since the Middle Ages, it's difficult to tell how sour the beer really would have been. Hop rates are suspected to be rather high (Darryl bases this on the presumption that the beer was not very attenuated and thus rather sweet) although further reasoning for a high hop rate is the fact that the beer was distributed over a wide portion of Germany and it was already known at this time that high hop rates helped protect the beer from spoiling. Strength was another method of ensuring that the beer traveled well and therefore it is likely that alcohol levels were high enough to lend a warming character to the beer. Commercial examples: none. OG: 1.060 - 1.070; AA: 65 -75%; ABV: 5 - 6.5; IBUs: 40 - 60; SRM: 10 - 14.

## *Ainpoeckisches Pier*

A related style to the Altes Einbecker Bier, this is the Munich brewers' adaptation of the Einbecker style of pre-lager Bock. Thanks to the chalky (high carbonate/bicarbonate) water of Munich, darker malts had to be used. As in the Altes Einbecker Bier, the hardwood-kilned malt would have lent a smoky character to the beer, so with modern malts, I would use a blend of Munich, dark wheat, and smoked malts, as well as adding some Biscuit, Aromatic, and/or Melanoidin malts. Hopping was not as aggressive as the Einbecker version. Again, these speculative guidelines are adapted from Darryl Richman's first guess in *Bock*[226]. Commercial examples: none. OG: 1.060 - 1.070; AA: 65 - 75%; ABV: 5 - 6.5; IBUs: 25 - 40; SRM: 15 - 25.

## Blonde Ale/Lager

Blonde Ales and Lagers have become so popular among brewpubs that it is necessary to include them as a style. They are usually brewed with the American Pilsner drinker in mind and are meant to provide an approachable selection for beer drinkers that are not yet accustomed to strong malt and/or hop flavors. These beers are generally golden in color, low to medium in malt flavor, light in body and low in bitterness. The ales are very mild in fruitiness and the lagers usually low in DMS. Slight diacetyl is common in both. This could be where the rare Cream Ales that happen to be fruity could be categorized. Commercial examples: Goose Island Blonde, Catamount Gold, Mill City Spring Fever Blonde Ale. OG: 1.040 - 1.060; AA: 71 - 83%; ABV: 4 - 6.5; IBUs: 15 - 33; SRM: 2 - 7.

## California Common Beer

California Common is another style that stems from (what was until recently) a single commercial example, but it is very popular among homebrewers. The beer is Anchor Steam™, but since the name is trademarked, the style has come to be known as California Common. The defining characteristics are a toasty maltiness in the aroma and flavor, assertive bitterness, very low fruitiness, medium hop flavor (Anchor uses US Northern Brewer) and medium body. The balance is just about even, perhaps just a shade towards hop bitterness. Slight diacetyl aroma and flavor are acceptable. No DMS aroma. Commercial examples: Anchor Steam, Rogue Dead Guy Ale (I don't know if they intentionally brewed to this style, but this beer definitely reminds me of the California Common style), Old Dominion Victory Amber. OG: 1.047 - 1.052; AA: 65 - 74%; ABV: 4.5 - 5.1; IBUs: 30 - 40; SRM: 8 - 14;

## Fruit Beer

Fruit beers are one of the fastest-growing styles among microbreweries/ brewpubs. Many are simply regular beers to which fruit extracts have been added. These tend to have medicinal and/or overly bitter flavors. The best examples are fermented on real fruit which is clearly much more difficult than adding a syrup. Another common fault among beers of this style is overdoing the fruit flavor/aroma, making the beer taste like a fruit wine. These are beers, let us not forget. Therefore, a good balance of fruit and beer flavor is essential for a good example of the style. Bitterness should be low so as to not compete with the fruit flavors. Any type of fruit can be used and the amount added depends very much on the intensity of the particular variety of fruit and on the intensity of the flavor in the beer style. Commercial examples: Blueberry Wheat (Brimstone), Raspberry Wheat (Oxford), Raspberry Wheat (Oaken Barrel), Rogue 'n' Berry, Rogue Cran-n-Cherry Ale, Spanish Peaks Honey Raspberry Ale. OG: 1.028 - 1.100+; AA: 65 - 80%; ABV: 2.8 - 10+; IBUs: 10+; SRM: 2+;

## Herb/Spice Beer

As with fruit beers, virtually any style of beer can have herbs or spices added to it. The herbs or spices should not overpower the beer flavors. Bitterness should usually be low so as to not compete with the herb or spice flavors. The herbs or spices can be added at the end of the boil, in the fermenter or can be soaked in vodka to make a "potion" and then this potion can be added at bottling time[196]. Commercial examples: Samuel Adams Old Fezziwig Ale, Anchor Our Special Ale (different recipe every year - often spiced), CooperSmith's Sigda's Chili Beer, Leann Fraoch (heather ale), Ed's Original Cave Creek Chili Beer (this beer has a pepper in every bottle and the pepper flavor keeps getting stronger as the beer ages - when young, it is well-balanced; as it ages, it becomes overpowering). OG: 1.028 - 1.100+; $\Lambda\Lambda$: 65 - 80%; ABV: 2.8 - 10+; IBUs: 10+; SRM: 2+;

## Malt Liquor

In some states, Malt Liquor is not a style but a legal designation that is required to be put on the label of beers that have more than a specified alcohol percentage. While it may be useful for consumers to know when they are purchasing a strong beer, if the brewing community were to agree upon what every style meant and labeled their beers accordingly, we would not have this problem. Having to add "Malt Liquor" to the label is one thing, but in some states the government has redefined the meaning of existing beer terminology (in Texas, if you label your beer an "Ale," it must be more than 4% alcohol by weight and if you label it "Beer" it must be more than 1/2% alcohol by volume, but not more than 4% alcohol by weight). As a style see "American Lager" above.

## Rye Beer

Although it is not possible to make without mashing, it should be noted that beers made with rye are possible and are growing in popularity. Rye adds more texture than flavor, lending an oily mouthfeel to the beer. If added in large amounts (more than 30%) it can add a mild spiciness - some have described it as minty. I feel it makes the beer taste "tangy." Rye can be added to virtually any style of beer, but the stronger-flavored styles may overpower any character that the rye would impart. It may be fermented with a yeast that gives the beer a Bavarian Weizen-like clovey aroma and flavor. Commercial examples: Red Hook Summer Rye, Schierlinger Roggenbier, Riley's Rye (Steelhead), Goldroggen (Schlägl). OG: 1.028 - 1.100+; 67 - 80%; ABV: 2.8 - 10+; IBUs: 10+; SRM: 2+;

## Smoked Beer

This category is meant to encompass all the smoked beers that are not specifically of the Rauchbier style or the lightly-smoky versions of Scottish Ales

(heavily-smoked ones should probably be in this category). It includes Smoked
Porters, Peated Beers (beers made with peat-kilned malt) and Polish Grodzisk
Beers. Commercial examples: Alaskan Smoked Porter, Adelscott Bière au Malt
à Whiskey (Peated, from Fischer Brewery), Adelscott Noir (Peated), Old Bawdy
(a Peated Barleywine, from Pike Place Brewery), Nessie (Peated, from
Eggenberg Brewery). OG: 1.028 - 1.100+; AA: 67 - 80%; ABV: 2.8 - 10+;
IBUs: 10+; SRM: 2+;

## Specialty Beer

Specialty Beers would be virtually anything that doesn't fit any one of the other
categories. They include beers made with a significant amount of honey, maple
syrup, potatoes, oats (but not in a stout - that would be an Oatmeal Stout) and
Jerusalem artichokes. This is where I would put beers that contain both fruit and
herbs/spices, for example, Raspberry-Ginger Brown Ale. Whatever the special
ingredient, it should be noticeable, but not overpowering (it should still taste like
beer). Commercial examples: Golden Prairie Maple Stout, Pumpkin Ale, Rogue
Hazelnut Brown Nectar. OG: 1.028 - 1.100+; AA: 60 - 85%; ABV: 2.8 - 10+;
IBUs: 10+; SRM: 2+;

## Steinbier

Steinbier is defined by process rather than ingredients, but there are only four
commercial breweries (that I know of) that use this very old process for making
beer. Therefore, although these four breweries' products define the style as we
know it today, there is no reason that any style of beer could not be made with
this process. "Stein" means "stone" in German and this is the key to this
interesting brewing method. Before metalwork advanced to the point where very
large metal kettles could be built, some brewers used heated stones to boil their
wort. One of the breweries is Rauchenfels which makes Rauchenfels Steinbier
from a 1.048 wort made from a 50/50 blend of pale barley and wheat malts,
hopped to 27 IBUs with Tettnanger and Hersbrucker hops[197]. They also make
Rauchenfels Steinweizen made from 60% wheat and less hops. The stones they
use are heated by beechwood fires so the beers take on a slightly smoky aroma
and flavor.

The second brewery is Boscos Pizza Kitchen and Brewery in Germantown,
Tennessee. Their Famous Flaming Stone Beer™ has an original gravity of 1.049
and a final gravity of 1.011. They use a wood-fired pizza oven to heat the
stones[197]. The third brewery is Brimstone Brewing Company in Baltimore,
Maryland, which makes Brimstone Stone Beer. They heat their stones with an
oak fire, so a slightly different smoke character is imparted. At Brimstone, their
Steinbier is an ale made from a 1.050 wort hopped to about 35 IBUs, made from
25% wheat and dryhopped with Cascades[198]. At both Rauchenfels and

Brimstone, some of the heating is done using the kettle's normal heating system and the cooled stones are later added to the fermenters where the yeast can eat the caramelized sugars off the surface of the stones. The fourth brewery is Copperhead Brewing in Ottawa, Canada. Alas, I don't have any information about their beer. So as you can see, there is little in common regarding the style (other than the original gravity) and it is the process that sets this style apart from the others.

It is important to note that not just any rocks can be used. The rocks you use must be able to withstand intense heating and then sudden cooling without shattering. Graywacke stones are used at Rauchenfels and Boscos uses Colorado pink granite[197]. At Brimstone, they use 150 pounds of diabase stones to boil 15 US barrels of wort (about 465 gallons)[198].

# Further Reading

Babinec, T. and S. Hamburg, "Confessions of Two Bitter Men," *Zymurgy,* 18 (2), 36-44 (Summer 1995).

Bergen, R., "A Stout Companion," *Brewing Techniques,* 1 (4) 18-21 (Nov/Dec 1993).

Bergen, R., "American Wheat Beers," *Brewing Techniques,* 1 (1) 14-17 (May/Jun 1993).

Bouckaert, P., "Brewery Rodenbach: Brewing Sour Ales," posted to Lambic Digest #846.

Brockington, D., "West Coast Amber Ale," *Brewing Techniques,* 3 (6), 36-44, (Nov/Dec 1995).

Cantwell, D., F. Allen, and K. Forhan, "Beer from the Stainless: Producing Traditional British Cask Beers in America," *Brewing Techniques,* 1 (4) 22-28 (Nov/Dec 1993).

Davison, D., "Eisbock: The Original Ice Beer," *Zymurgy,* 18 (5), 37-42 (Winter 1995).

Davison, D., "Inside Berlin's Own Beer," *Zymurgy,* 19 (5), 36-41 (Winter 1996).

Eckhardt, F., *The Essentials of Beer Style* (Fred Eckhardt Associates, Portland, Oregon, 1989).

Fix, G. J and L. Fix, *Vienna, Oktoberfest, Märzen,* (Brewers Publications, Boulder, Colorado, 1991).

Fix, G. J., "Explorations in Pre-Prohibition American Lagers," *Brewing Techniques,* 2 (3) 28-31 (May/Jun 1994).

Fix, G. J., "Explorations in Pre-Prohibition American Lagers," *Brewing Techniques,* 2 (3), 28-31, (1994).

Foster, T., *Pale Ale,* (Brewers Publications, Boulder, Colorado, 1990).

Foster, T., *Porter,* (Brewers Publications, Boulder, Colorado, 1992).

Guinard, J-X., *Lambic,* (Brewers Publications, Boulder, Colorado, 1990).

Harrison, J., *Old British Beers and How to Make Them* (Durden Park Beer Circle, London, 1991).

Jackson, M., "Be On Your Guard for Fine French Beers," *Zymurgy,* 18 (2) 25-26 (Summer 1995).

Jackson, M., "Russian Stout: It's a Coq and Bolshevik Story," *Zymurgy,* 13 (5) 20-21 (Winter 1990).

Jackson, M., *Beer Companion* (Running Press, Philadelphia, Pennsylvania, 1993).

Jackson, M., *The Great Beers of Belgium* (CODA, Antwerp, Belgium, 1992).

Jackson, M., *The New World Guide to Beer* (Running Press, Philadelphia, Pennsylvania, 1988).

Jankowski, B., "American Porters - Marching to Revolutionary Drummers," *Brewing Techniques,* 5 (2) 34-43 (May/Jun 1997).

Jankowski, B., "The Beers of Christmas," *Brewing Techniques,* 3 (6) 64-69 (Nov/Dec 1995).

Jankowski, B., "The Bushwick Pilsners," *Brewing Techniques,* 2 (1), 38-43, (Jan/Feb 1994).

Jankowski, B., "The Bushwick Pilsners: A Look at Hoppier Days," *Brewing Techniques,* 2 (1) 38-43 (Jan/Feb 1994).

Lewis, M., *Stout,* (Brewers Publications, Boulder, Colorado, 1995).

Lodahl, M., "Belgian Trappists and Abbey Beers," *Brewing Techniques,* 2 (6) 28-35 (Nov/Dec 1994).

Lodahl, M., "Belgium... A Land of Endless Riches," *Zymurgy,* 18 (1) 40-44 (Spring 1995).

Lodahl, M., "Lambic: Belgium's Unique Treasure," *Brewing Techniques,* 3 (4) 34-46 (Jul/Aug 1995).

Lodahl, M., "Old, Strong, and Stock Ales," *Brewing Techniques*, 2 (5) 22-29 (Sep/Oct 1994).

Lodahl, M., "Old, Strong, and Stock Ales," *Brewing Techniques*, 2 (5), 23, (Sep/Oct 1994).

Lodahl, M., "Witbier: Belgian White," *Brewing Techniques*, 2 (4) 24-27 (Jul/Aug 1994).

Maes, J., "Is Belgium's Brewing Culture at Risk?," *Zymurgy*, 18 (1) 46-49 (Spring 1995).

Miller, D., *Continental Pilsner*, (Brewers Publications, Boulder, Colorado, 1990).

Mosher, R., "A Turn-of-the-Century British Account of Selected 19th Century Belgian Brewing Methods," *Brewing Techniques*, 2 (6) 46-49 (Nov/Dec 1994).

Noonan, G. J., *Scotch Ale*, (Brewers Publications, Boulder, Colorado, 1993).

Nummer, B. A., "Brewing with Lactic Acid Bacteria," *Brewing Techniques*, 4 (3) 56-63 (May/Jun 1996).

Ostrum, J. W., "Weizen - An Old Style Finds New Life in Modern Craft Breweries," *Brewing Techniques*, 4 (2) 44-49 (Mar/Apr 1996).

Protz, R., "Straight up - it's real lager," *What's Brewing*, Feb 1997, 12.

Protz, R., *The Real Ale Drinker's Almanac* (Neil Wilson Publishing Ltd., Glasgow, Scotland, 1993).

Rahn, P. and C. Skypeck, "Traditional German Steinbier," *Zymurgy*, 17 (4), 16-18, (Special Issue 1994).

Rajotte, P., *Belgian Ale*, (Brewers Publications, Boulder, Colorado, 1992).

Renner, J., "Reviving the Classic American Pilsner - A Shamefully Neglected Style," *Brewing Techniques*, 3 (5) 70-71 (Sep/Oct 1995).

Renner, J., "Reviving the Classic American Pilsner," *Brewing Techniques*, 3 (5), 70-71, (Sep/Oct 1995).

Richman, D., "Bock and Doppelbock," *Brewing Techniques*, 3 (2) 36-41 (Mar/Apr 1995).

Richman, D., "Pilsner Urquell: The Brewery," *Zymurgy*, 14 (2) 30-36 (Summer 1991).

Richman, D., *Bock*, (Brewers Publications, Boulder, Colorado, 1994).

Seitz, P., "Brewing Better Belgian Ales," *Zymurgy*, 18 (1) 50-57 (Spring 1995).

Slosberg, P., "The Road to an American Brown Ale," *Brewing Techniques*, 3 (3) 32-37 (May/Jun 1995).

Thomlinson, T., "India Pale Ale," *Brewing Techniques*, 2 (2), 26, (Mar/Apr 1994).

Warner, E., *German Wheat*, (Brewers Publications, Boulder, Colorado, 1992).

*Zymurgy* Special Issue 1994 "Special Ingredients and Indigenous Beers" 17 (4), (Special 1994).

Appendix

# HOP VARIEITIES and USAGE

## Hop Varieties

Many of the hop varieties that I've described below are unavailable to homebrewers or completely discontinued. So why would I include them here? Well, what if you found an old recipe in a book or magazine or inherited one from your grandfather, and now you would like to reproduce the bitterness, flavor and aroma as accurately as possible? Knowing the approximate alpha acid percentage and/or lineage is a starting point in finding an appropriate substitute from among modern hop varieties. Please note that sometimes hops inherit some of their characteristics from their parents (Liberty's aroma is similar to Hallertauer Mittelfrüh) and other times there is no similarity (Cascade was an attempt to be similar to Fuggle). If you don't find the hop you are searching for in one of the main sections, check under "Other Hops" at the end. It is important to remember that when substituting hop varieties, you must compensate for varying alpha acid levels (see "Hop Varieties" in chapter 8 and "Hops" in chapter 15). Unless otherwise noted, most of the following information on hop aromas and flavors comes from my own personal experiments whereas the lineage, alpha acid, beta acid, and cohumulone data comes from multiple references listed in Further Reading or from personal communications with Ralph Olson and Dr. Greg Lewis at HopUnion, USA[201].

Aroma and flavor are the most distinctive attributes of hops and in suggesting substitutes below, I've been primarily concerned with matching these characteristics rather than the bittering character (some hops have a rougher bitterness than others). Note that although virtually all the hop oil evaporates from bittering hops, when high bittering hop rates are used, some of the flavor and aroma of the hops does slip through. For some varieties below, I have specified one set of varieties for bittering substitutes and another set for aroma/flavor. If you are using very high bittering hop rates, you may want to consider using the aroma/flavor substitutes even for bittering because of the aromatic/flavor "spill-over" that may occur.

## Admiral

This is a new hop from Wye College. Admiral is an extremely high-alpha variety, related to Target, Northdown and Challenger. Samples were unavailable for analysis. Substitutes: My guess would be Target, Northdown, or Challenger.

## Ahil

One of the so-called "Super Styrians," a group of Slovenian-bred high-alpha hops, Ahil is related to Brewer's Gold and certainly does not have Styrian Golding character. Substitutes: Apolon, Atlas, or Aurora.

## Alliance

Alliance is an offspring of Whitbread Golding Variety, which was bred as a Fuggle replacement. Substitutes: Whitbread Golding Variety, or Fuggle.

## Apolon

Another of the "Super Styrians, " Apolon is related to Northern Brewer and again, should not be used as a substitute for Styrian Goldings. Substitutes: Ahil, Atlas, or Aurora.

## Aquila

A mid-alpha variety, similar to Cluster which was introduced in 1988, but is being phased out[199]. I've never seen this hop listed with any hop distributors, so I've been unable to even get a sample for testing. Its alpha acid percentage is typically between 6% and 8%. Substitutes: If you do find a recipe that calls for it, I would imagine that Cluster would be a logical substitute, but given that another source says that Aquila is an aroma hop, I am suspicious of it's similarity to Cluster[200].

## Atlas

Another of the "Super Styrians, " Atlas is related to Northern Brewer and should not be used as a substitute for Styrian Goldings. Substitutes: Ahil, Apolon, or Aurora.

## Aurora

The last of the "Super Styrians, " Aurora is related to Northern Brewer and should not be used as a substitute for Styrian Goldings. Substitutes: Ahil, Apolon, or Atlas.

## Banner

Another mid-alpha variety, which (just like Aquila) is similar to Cluster, was introduced in 1988 and is being phased out[199]. Substitutes: This is another hop I've been unable to find. Its alpha acid percentage is typically between 9% and 11%. I'm more confident in recommending Cluster as a substitute because another source corroborates that Banner is a bittering hop. Don't forget to compensate for the fact that Banner has a higher alpha acid percentage than Cluster.

## Bianca

Bianca is an ornamental hop released in 1994 that is said to have Saaz-like aromatic qualities (it has Saaz in its lineage) and although it is not planned to be grown for commercial brewing use, it is said to have potential in the homebrewing market. Bianca and its half-sister Sunbeam are unique in that they have bright yellow leaves and reddish to bright red stems.

## Bohemian Red

Another name for Saaz.

## Bramling

Bramling is a parent of Bramling Cross and a clonal selection of an English Golding. Substitutes: it's difficult to say whether East Kent Goldings or Bramling Cross would be a better selection, although there's no proof that either of them would smell or taste like Bramling.

## Bramling Cross

An "aroma variety" from Britain. It is a grandparent of Saxon and Viking. Bramling Cross has a unique toasty, buttery, slightly resiny aroma with some woody notes. Substitutes: Fuggle, in my opinion, based on aroma.

## Brewer's Gold

Intensely resiny, this hop has black currant/fruity and slightly spicy aromas and flavors. It is good as an experimental aroma and flavor hop in American ales, but can be a bit overpowering in larger amounts. This hop was rejected by British brewers when it was introduced because of its intense "American"

aroma[202]. Brewer's Gold is the aroma hop used in Pete's Wicked Ale[203].
Substitutes: As a bittering hop, any of the low- to medium-alpha hops would
work. For aroma and flavor, ironically, Northdown would be a good choice.

## British Columbian Goldings

Related to Goldings from East Kent (the classic English ale hop) but grown in
British Columbia, Canada, it is quite resiny, slightly candy-like and sweet with a
hint of floral character. A reasonable substitute for East Kent Goldings. A good
choice for all British ales such as Bitter, Scottish Ale, IPA, Old Ale and
Barleywine. Sometimes you will see "B.C. Kent Goldings" which is a misnomer.
Kent is a county in England. The Goldings are either from Kent or they are from
somewhere else like British Columbia or Oregon. Substitutes: East Kent
Goldings or, in a pinch, Fuggles or Willamette would be different, but
appropriate for style.

## Bullion

Primarily used for bittering, this resiny, fruity, slightly earthy/woody/leathery
hop has a slight raspberry aroma/flavor. At higher bittering rates, it can show
some roughness. It can be used experimentally as an aroma/flavor hop in small
amounts. Substitutes: for bittering, any medium-high alpha hops such as Cluster,
Brewer's Gold, or Northern Brewer.

## Cascade

With its distinctive grapefruit aroma/flavor, Cascade is the classic American Ale
aroma/flavor hop. It adds a citrusy character even when used as a bittering hop.
This hop has such a strong character that it should really be reserved for
American Ales (although it has turned up in several commercial British Bitters –
none of which are imported, unfortunately). Commercial beers in which
Cascade is prominent: Sierra Nevada Pale Ale, Anchor Liberty Ale. Substitutes:
Centennial and Columbus have a similar aroma/flavor, but remember that they
are considerably more bitter.

## Centennial

Centennial (named CrJ-90 during development) has been called "Super
Cascade." A high-alpha version of Cascade, but slightly rougher, this hop can be
used for bittering anywhere you would use Cascade, but as an aroma/flavor hop,
it can be quite intense due to the high essential oil content (can be as much as
twice the typical oil content of Cascade). Commercial beers in which Centennial
is prominent: Sierra Nevada Celebration Ale, Sierra Nevada Bigfoot Barleywine-
style Ale[204]. Substitutes: Just as Cascade is very recognizable, so is Centennial –
Cascade would be the best substitute, but don't forget to compensate for its lower

alpha acid content. The citrusy character of Columbus make it a strong candidate for a Centennial substitute.

## Challenger

An aroma variety from Britain with a mild resiny character (not too unlike East Kent Goldings), Challenger is a granddaughter of Northern Brewer, a niece of Northdown and second cousin of Target. It is used as the aroma hop in Orkney's Dark Island and along with other hops in many English Bitters[205]. Substitutes: East Kent Goldings, Phoenix, Styrian Goldings, British Columbian Goldings.

## Chelan

A very high-alpha hop with an extremely high percentage of beta acids. A daughter of Galena, this variety is similar to Galena in terms of analytical data. Samples were not available in time for press.

## Chinook

Chinook is a very high alpha hop which, for some reason, has gained a reputation for having a rather rough character. My experience shows that its bitterness is just as smooth as many hops of much lower alpha acid. Chinook has a pleasant, but intense aroma: slightly spicy and very piney. They are like a cross between Saaz and a pine forest. Substitutes: For bittering, a high-alpha hop, such as Eroica, Galena, or Nugget. For aroma/flavor, the pine-like character is unlike any other hops, however Southern Cross has both spicy and piney character although in different proportions. Sticklebract is quite piney also. Saaz, Crystal and Tettnanger would give a similar type of spiciness as Chinook.

## Cluster

Cluster is used primarily as a bittering hop, but can give a nice black currant aroma and flavor. Substitutes: Brewer's Gold for flavor and aroma; for bittering, I would use Chinook, Galena, Eroica, or Olympic.

## Columbia

Columbia is an obsolete high-alpha U.S. hop that, was derived from Fuggle and another hop derived from Fuggle. The aroma is said to have been similar to Fuggle. Substitutes: Fuggle, Willamette.

## Columbus

Columbus is a U.S. high alpha hop that has a very low cohumulone level. It has an intense, citrusy hop aroma rather similar to Cascade and Centennial. It also has a slight woody character. Columbus is the only hop used in Anderson Valley

IPA.  Substitutes: For bittering, Nugget and Chinook would be reasonable.  For aroma/flavor, Cascade or Centennial.

## Comet

Another obsolete high-alpha U.S. hop with a high cohumulone percentage.  It is said to have had a "Wild American" aroma, which means that it had an aroma similar to the wild hops native to the United States.  Substitutes: Chinook, Eroica, Galena, Nugget, or Olympic.

## Crystal

Crystal is a very recent American-grown cousin of Hallertauer Mittelfrüh.  Much spicier than its German ancestors, the spiciness (cinnamon, black pepper and nutmeg) of this hop is its trademark.  Commercial beers in which Crystal is prominent: Goose Island's 1993 Christmas beer (it smelled like cinnamon although no spices were used – only Crystal dryhopping)[206].  Substitutes: Any of the Hallertauer varieties, Mount Hood, or Liberty, but they will be much less spicy.  Perhaps Tettnanger or Saaz, which are spicier might be a better substitute or would work well blended with Mount Hood or Liberty.

## East Kent Goldings

Goldings from East County Kent are the classic English ale hop.  They are the most common aroma and dryhop among British brewers of Real Ales.  What we refer to as East Kent Goldings can actually be one of several varieties that some refer to as the "East Kent Golding group" (Old Golding, Canterbury Golding, Whitebine)[207].  Other Golding clonal selections include Petham, Bramling, Rodmersham, Cobbs, Amos's Early Bird, Mathon, and Easwell[207].  Intensely resiny, candy-like, sweet and slightly floral, this hop is so smooth that you almost cannot over-bitter with it.  It can give beers a strange sugary sweetness when too much is used as a flavor hop (more than, say, 1 ounce in a 5 gallon batch).  I have noticed a slight onion-like aroma in several different beers reportedly dryhopped with Goldings, although I'm not certain if this was due to mishandling and oxidation or perhaps it is a characteristic of one of the clonal selections.  East Kent Goldings are used exclusively for aroma in R&D Deuchars IPA, Samuel Smith's Old Brewery Bitter and Museum Ale (labeled Old Brewery Pale Ale in the U.S.), Young's Special London Ale and Thomas Hardy Country Bitter[205].  Sometimes you will simply see East Kent Goldings labeled as "Kent Goldings" which are equivalent, but "B.C. Kent Goldings," "Oregon Kent Goldings" and "Washington Kent Goldings" are simply mis-named.  Substitutes: British Columbian Goldings, Styrian Goldings, Oregon Goldings, or Washington Goldings.

## Eroica

Primarily a bittering hop, Eroica is woody and chocolaty. It has a very neutral hop flavor and a smooth bitterness despite its high cohumulone percentage. In higher amounts as a flavoring hop, it adds a sweetness that is slightly unpleasant, not unlike a beer that has too much East Kent Goldings flavor. A good general-purpose bittering hop for all ales and lagers, but production of this hop is declining steeply[199]. Substitutes: Galena, Nugget, or Olympic.

## First Gold

This is a not only a new English hop variety, but a new type: a dwarf hop. This type of hop does not need to be grown on 15- to 20-foot-tall strings to give acceptable yield as do "tall" hops. It was bred from Whitbread Goldings Variety and a dwarf male. First Gold has a nice (Goldings-like) resiny and strong cinnamon aroma with hints of woody character and black pepper; It is like a spicy Goldings hop. Substitutes: Perhaps a mix of East Kent Goldings and Crystal (for the cinnamon character).

## Fuggle

Another classic English ale hop, Fuggle (pronounced with a short "u") is woody, earthy and slightly fruity. Whether to use Fuggle or Goldings for British ales is a matter of personal taste… Fuggle gives a more earthy, less sweet hop aroma/flavor than Goldings. It is a good choice for aroma/flavor in all British ale styles and is used exclusively for dryhopping Theakston's Best Bitter and XB and blended with Goldings for dryhopping literally hundreds of British Ales[205]. It is used exclusively (naturally) in Fuggles Imperial Special Ale. Substitutes: Willamette (a slightly floral cousin grown in the U.S.) or, for English ales, Goldings would be stylistically correct, but quite different in aroma and flavor.

## Galena

Primarily a bittering hop, Galena is fruity, candy-like, slightly citrusy and herbal. A good general-purpose bittering hop for all ales and lagers. More Galena is grown in the U.S. than any other hop (nearly 18 million pounds in 1992)[199]. Substitutes: Eroica, Nugget, or Olympic.

## Green Bullet

Green Bullet is a high-alpha, often organically-grown hop from New Zealand. It is a daughter of Smoothcone and was bred for high alpha acid level, not necessarily aroma. It has been used as an aroma hop in several Pilsners and other lagers that have won international awards. A dominant feature of Green

Bullet's aroma is a unique raisiny character. It also has resiny aroma/flavor and a slight floral note. Substitutes: perhaps some of the resiny varieties like the various Goldings hops.

## Hallertauer

Literally, it means "from Hallertau" and therefore hops labeled simply "Hallertauer" could be Hallertauer Hersbrucker, Hallertauer Tradition, Hallertauer Mittelfrüh, Hallertauer Hüller, or even Perle (which is far inferior to the other hops in this list). I've often seen hops labeled "U.S. Hallertauer," which, upon further investigation turned out to be Mount Hood. This makes sense from a marketing perspective, the name Hallertauer commanding far more respect at this time than Mount Hood, and indeed Mount Hood is a relative of the finest of the hops from this region, Hallertauer Mittelfrüh. Some hops labeled "U.S. Hallertauer" are actually Hallertauer Mittelfrüh grown in the U.S.. There has been an increase in U.S.-grown Hallertauer Mittelfrüh acreage over the last few years. Although these hops are very good, they are still a step below Hallertauer Mittelfrüh grown in the Hallertau region. If you see hops labeled simply "Hallertauer," ask your supplier for more information. Substitutes: Well, frankly, if a recipe calls for simply Hallertauer, you can use any of the German Hallertauer varieties with equal odds that you will have selected the correct one or you can go with one of their U.S.-grown cousins, Mount Hood, Liberty, or Crystal (although crystal might be overly spicy).

## Hallertauer Hüller

This is the same hop as Hüller Bitterer. It was the first hop developed specifically for bittering by Hüll Hop Research Institute, but never became very popular because it simply did not have a high enough alpha acid percentage.

## Hallertauer Magnum

This is a high-alpha hop developed at the Hop Research Institute in Hüll, typically 11 to 13% alpha acids. Substitutes: Yakima Magnum.

## Hallertauer Mittelfrüh

Hallertauer Mittelfrüh is one of the Noble hops (in one school of thought). It has a sweet aroma with a slight cinnamon-like spiciness. I have mistaken its aroma in beer for diacetyl – Hallertauer Mittelfrüh imparts a sort of pastry-like sweet bouquet with mild buttery notes. It is the ideal choice for all German lagers, but is virtually unavailable to homebrewers. More and more German growers have been planting this hop because its quality and rarity commands a high price. Hopefully, production will continue to increase to the point where Hallertauer Mittelfrüh will be easily available to homebrewers. Substitutes: Mount Hood,

Liberty, Hallertauer Tradition, Hersbrucker, Pacific Hallertauer, or New Zealand Hallertau Aroma.

## Hallertauer Tradition (German-grown)

Hallertauer Tradition is said to have aromatic and flavor characteristics very similar to Hallertauer Mittelfrüh, but is higher-yielding, more vigorous and much more disease-resistant. Substitutes: Hallertauer Mittelfrüh, U.S. Hallertauer Tradition, Mount Hood, Liberty, Hersbrucker, Pacific Hallertauer, or New Zealand Hallertau Aroma

## Hallertauer Tradition (U.S.-grown)

U.S.-grown Hallertauer Tradition has a rather mild character relative to other hops. It has some Hallertauer Mittelfrüh aroma and flavor (a sort of complex pastry-like/buttery character) and a very slight Saaz-like spiciness. Overall, it is a very elegant aroma and flavor. Substitutes: German Hallertauer Tradition, Hallertauer Mittelfrüh, Mount Hood, Liberty, Hersbrucker, Pacific Hallertauer, or New Zealand Hallertauer Aroma.

## Herald

Another new English dwarf hop which is a sister of Pioneer. Primarily bred as a high-alpha hop, according to The National Hop Association of England, it is said to have "very acceptable" flavor and is not expected to be used as a dryhop. Substitutes: Pioneer would be my only guess.

## Hersbrucker

Technically called "Hersbrucker Spät," which means "Late-harvest hop from Hersbruck." A fine German hop – not quite a Noble hop – but close. It has a red wine/tobacco-like aroma. A good choice for bittering, flavor and/or aroma in all German ales and lagers. Substitutes: Hersbrucker Pure, Hallertauer, Mount Hood, Liberty, or Spalt.

## Hersbrucker Pure

This is a new German "aroma" hop developed at Hüll Hop Research Institute. It is reported to have "outstanding aroma... of the type Hersbruck Spät."[208]

## Hüller Bitterer

See Hallertauer Hüller.

## Keyworth's Midseason

A daughter of Neomex and an aunt of Progress. This is about all the information I have about this hop other than the fact that British brewers failed to embrace it due to its "American" aroma.

## Kirin II

Kirin II is a Japanese hop variety with a high cohumulone percentage. This is all the information I have on this variety.

## Klon

All I can find on this hop is that it is grown in The Ukraine along with Saaz hops.

## Liberty

Liberty is a recently released American-grown cousin of Hallertauer Mittelfrüh. It is spicy (cinnamon), resiny, pastry-like and slightly sweet. It is recommended for any German or American lager. It is quite close to the Hallertauer Mittelfrüh in character, perhaps a little bit spicier. Substitutes: Mount Hood, Hallertauer Mittelfrüh, Crystal (even spicier), or other Hallertauer varieties.

## Lubelski/Lublin/Lubliner

These are Polish-grown Saaz hops (or a Polish-grown clonal selection of Saaz) with very respectable and Noble characteristics. They have a pastry-like aroma similar to Hallertauer Mittelfrüh, are slightly woody with a little buttery aroma. Nicely spicy, these hops have an interesting milk chocolate note in the aroma. Lublin hops are quite similar to Czech Saaz and can be used anywhere that Saaz would be acceptable. Substitutes: Czech Saaz; also Tettnanger or U.S. Saaz would be close.

## Midland Goldings

Midland Goldings are Goldings grown in the English Midlands. They have a rich, resiny aroma very similar to East Kent Goldings, but they have a slight grassy note. Substitutes: East Kent Goldings, Styrian Goldings, British Columbian Goldings.

## Mount Hood

Another recently released American-grown cousin of Hallertauer Mittelfrüh. It is spicy (cinnamon), resiny and slightly sweet. It is recommended for any German or American lager. It is quite close to the Hallertauer Mittelfrüh in character, perhaps a little bit spicier. I recommend against using this hop for beers in which you want dominant bitterness – in a recent experiment I found its bitterness to be slightly abrasive when used in a recipe where the bitterness strongly dominated the malt. Substitutes: Liberty, Hallertauer Mittelfrüh, Crystal (even spicier), or other Hallertauer varieties.

## New Zealand Hallertauer Aroma

New Zealand Hallertau Aroma is a triploid variety bred from German Hallertauer Mittelfrüh. They are slightly woodier and a little less spicy than true Hallertauer Mittelfrüh. These hops also have some nice resiny, pastry-like and slightly citrusy character. In terms of chemical analysis, New Zealand Hallertau Aroma are not very close to Hallertauer Mittelfrüh (alpha and beta acid levels being much higher, humulene and caryophyllene levels lower and a significantly lower H/C ratio), but their aroma and flavor have adequate similarity. Substitutes: Mount Hood, Liberty, Hallertauer Tradition, Hersbrucker, or Pacific Hallertauer.

## Northdown

A medium-alpha aroma hop from Britain, Northdown is low in cohumulone and a relative of Challenger and Target. Northdown has a very resiny nose with black currant notes. It also has just a hint of buttery, Hallertauer-like aroma. This hop is used, along with other aroma hops, for finishing in quite a few English Real Ales and is the exclusive aroma hop used in Tetley Dark Mild, Walker Dark Mild, Walker Best Bitter and Walker Winter Warmer (all of which are dry hopped with Northdown)[205]. Substitutes: Phoenix is very similar, but if that were not available, I would use a blend of one of the Golding hops (for the resiny character) and Brewers Gold (for the black currant aroma).

## Northern Brewer (Hallertau)

Northern Brewer grown in Hallertau is very German in character. It has some similarity to U.S.- or British-grown Northern Brewer, but is more floral and less rough. Recommended for bittering German lagers, but could be used experimentally for aroma/flavor in German or American lagers. Substitutes: any of the Hallertauer varieties or U.S. Northern Brewer (although this is quite a stretch).

## Northern Brewer (U.S.)

A very distinctive, earthy hop, U.S. Northern Brewer is the exclusive hop used in Anchor Steam™. This hop has a very woody, earthy, slightly fruity aroma/flavor. It is a bit rough, but not unpleasantly so. Substitutes: Hallertauer Northern Brewer, perhaps with a little Pride of Ringwood added for earthiness.

## Nugget

Floral, resiny, candy-like aroma/flavor, this hop has been used as an aroma hop by some brewers. In my opinion, Nugget has some aroma/flavor characteristics in common with East Kent Goldings! It is used primarily as a bittering hop, but it provides a very smooth bitterness despite its high alpha acid level. Substitutes: Galena or Olympic.

## Olympic

Slightly citrusy, minty, not as rough as Galena or Eroica, Olympic is primarily a bittering hop, but could be used experimentally as an aroma hop to capitalize on its interesting minty character. Substitutes: Nugget, Perle, Eroica, or Galena.

## Omega

Omega is a high-alpha variety grown in Britain. I found very little information about this hop variety, but despite its high alpha acid level, it apparently has good aromatic qualities because it is used as both a bittering and aroma hop in Borve Ale from Borve Brew House in Aberdeenshire, Scotland[205].

## Oregon Goldings

Oregon Goldings are Goldings grown in Oregon, and their aroma and flavor clearly show their resiny Goldings character, but oddly, they are woodier with some light citrusy notes. They are rather a unique hop with a distinctive character. Oregon Goldings are equivalent to "Washington Goldings" or "U.S. Goldings." Sometimes you will see "Oregon Kent Goldings" which is a misnomer. Kent is a county in England. The Goldings are either from Kent or they are from somewhere else like Oregon or British Columbia. Substitutes: I would use 90% of East Kent Goldings and 10% Cascade to add that citrusy character.

## Pacific Gem

Another very woody and rustic high-alpha hop from New Zealand. Alpha acid levels are consistently above 13%, sometimes as high as 14.4%! Pacific Gem is very fruity with distinct strawberry aroma along with its woody character. Substitutes: perhaps Fuggle because it is both woody and fruity.

## Pacific Hallertau

Unavailable for analysis, this is a new hop which is a triploid variety bred from and reported to have very similar character to Hallertauer Mittelfrüh. Chemical analysis shows many similarities to Hallertauer Mittelfrüh. Substitutes: Hallertauer varieties, such as Hallertauer Mittelfrüh, Liberty, Hallertauer Tradition, or Mount Hood.

## Perle

Perle is spicy, leathery, slightly floral and fruity. It was originally intended to be a Hallertauer Mittelfrüh substitute, but did not quite hit the target. It can be used as an aroma hop in German and American lagers, but some brewers feel it is a bit too rough for an aroma hop and use it just for bittering. Substitutes: Hallertauer varieties, Mount Hood, or Liberty.

## Phoenix

Phoenix is a seedling of Yeoman developed at Wye College in England. According to The National Hop Association of England, it is said to have "very attractive" aroma and may be a substitute for Challenger. In my opinion, it's aroma is resiny, buttery, and black currant-like with hints of cinnamon. Substitutes: Northdown (quite similar), East Kent Goldings, Challenger, other Goldings.

## Pioneer

A sister of Herald, this is another new dwarf hop bred at Wye College in England. Pioneer has primarily a resiny/candy-like (Goldings) aroma with a little black pepper-like spiciness. It's aroma is quite mild, however, which explains why The National Hop Association of England doesn't expect it to be used as a dryhop. You shouldn't let that discourage you from using Pioneer as an aroma hop, however. Substitutes: East Kent Goldings or possibly it's sister, Herald.

## Polnischer Lublin

See Lubelski/Lublin.

## Progress

Progress is an aroma variety grown in Britain. Slightly resiny and spicy with mild ripe-fruit, Thompson's grape aromas – Progress has some aromatic qualities in common with East Kent Goldings and Fuggle. It is a relative of Whitbread Golding Variety and Keyworth's Midseason. It is the exclusive aroma hop used in Golden Promise from Caledonian Brewing Company in Edinburgh, Scotland and used along with other hops in many other British ales[205]. Substitutes: I would recommend using a blend of East Kent Goldings and Fuggle.

## Pride of Ringwood

Intensely woody, very earthy, very herbal and slightly rough, this Australian hop is used in many Australian lagers and ales. Its woodiness comes through very clearly. Much of the Pride of Ringwood that comes to the U.S. is organically grown and if this is important to you, perhaps you should experiment with it. Substitutes: Super Alpha, Pacific Gem, Cluster, or U.S. Northern Brewer.

## Record

Record is an offspring of Northern Brewer originally developed in Belgium and planted widely in Germany, but lacking in the characteristic aroma of traditional German varieties. Substitutes: Having never worked with Record, I can only speculate that a logical substitute, given its lineage, would be Northern Brewer.

## Red Sell

This hop is reported, in one book, to be used along with East Kent Goldings by Traquair House Brewery in both their Bear Ale and Traquair House Ale. It appears that there is no such hop variety, however, one of the major Golding growers in East Kent England is Tony Redsell. Most likely, Traquair House Brewery uses East Kent Goldings grown by Tony Redsell.

## Saaz

One of the Noble hops (in both schools of though), it is the exclusive hop used in Pilsner Urquell. Very spicy, cinnamon-like, earthy, Saaz (pronounced ZAHTS) is recommended for Bohemian Pilsners and German and American lagers. U.S.-grown Saaz are not as refined as the Czech-grown, but more recent crop years have yielded very respectable results. Substitutes: Tettnanger and Ultra are the closest, but Crystal might be a decent substitute.

## Saazer

Another name for Saaz.

## Savinja Goldings

See Styrian Goldings.

## Savinski

Another name for Styrian Goldings.

## Saxon

A descendent of Bramling Cross, Saxon is a low-cohumulone hop with a rather high alpha-acid content (around 10.5% for the seedless type). It is a sibling of Viking. I have been unable to get a sample of this hop for brewing some test batches. Substitutes: It seems to me that Viking or Bramling Cross would be reasonable guesses.

## Serebrianka

The only facts I could find about this hop variety are that it is of Russian origin and that it was crossed with Fuggle to create Cascade, therefore if you come across it in a recipe, because Cascade has virtually nothing in common with Fuggle in terms of aroma or flavor, I would use Cascade as a substitute (although there is absolutely no guarantee that there is any similarity).

## Shinshuwase

The only information I have on this Japanese medium-alpha hop is that it has a very high cohumulone percentage.

## Southern Cross

Spicy and lemony character typifies this high-alpha variety from New Zealand. Southern Cross also has some slight piney and woody character. Although these are primarily bittering hops, I feel that their spiciness and interesting lemony character would make them useful aroma/flavor hops. Substitutes: perhaps Chinook (which has similar spicy and piney character, although in far different proportions) or maybe Strisselspalt (thanks to it's lemony aroma).

## Spalt

Spalt (pronounced SHPAWLT) is a German aroma hop from the hop growing region of the same name and is considered a Noble hop in one school of thought. It has a slight woody character and does have some aroma characteristics common with some "undisputed" Noble hops. Spalt has a cinnamon-like spiciness that is about halfway in intensity between Hallertauer Mittelfrüh and Crystal. The most common hop among Düsseldorfer Altbiers. In fact, Spalt and Spalter Select are the only two hop varieties used in Zum Uerige, the most highly regarded Düsseldorfer Altbier[209]. Substitutes: Spalter Select or one of the Hallertauer varieties.

## Spalter Select

Spalter Select (pronounced SHPAWL-ter se-LECT) is a new variety related to Spalt. As noted above, it is used in Zum Uerige when supplies of Spalt are scarce[209] so I would venture to guess that it has significant similarity to Spalt in aroma and flavor. Substitutes: Spalt.

## Sticklebract

Sticklebract is a high-alpha hop grown in New Zealand. It has a nice pine-like aroma with hints of citrus. Sticklebract also has a significant amount of that pastry-like aroma found in Hallertauer Mittelfrüh. It is interesting to note that the hops in New Zealand are grown virtually pesticide-free. Sticklebract is a daughter of First Choice. Substitutes: perhaps a blend of one of the Hallertauer varieties for the pastry-like character and some Chinook or Southern Cross for the piney aroma.

## Strisselspalt (French)

Strisselspalt is an old variety which is grown in the Alsace region of France. It is quite aromatic, has quite a bit of Hallertauer Mittelfrüh character with some floral aroma, a slight lemony character and some slight resiny/woody notes. Typical alpha acid levels are 3 to 5%. Substitutes: Hallertauer Mittelfrüh, Mount Hood, Liberty, Hersbrucker, Southern Cross (perhaps blended with one of the others, to take advantage of its lemony character).

## Strisselspalt (U.S.)

U.S.-grown Strisselspalt is very different in aroma from its French-grown cousins. It is slightly resiny, slightly citrusy, with a rather strong grassy character. Substitutes: This is a tough one. I would probably use French Strisselspalt, despite the differences.

## Styrian Goldings

Styrian Goldings (pronounced STEE-ree-en GOL-dings) are actually Fuggle hops grown in Slovenia, but has little in common with Fuggle when it comes to aroma and flavor. They are also called Savinja Goldings. They actually are remarkably similar to East Kent Goldings with their resiny, candy-like, sweet, slightly floral aroma. They are recommended for British Ales, anyplace you would used Goldings. Styrian Goldings are used in Whitbread Porter for dryhopping, following an 1850's recipe[205]. They are also used for dryhopping Burton Bridge's Summer Ale and Bridge Bitter, Ind Coope Draught Burton Ale, Thomas Hardy's Ale, and Castle Eden Ale. Substitutes: East Kent Goldings or British Columbian Goldings[205].

## Sunbeam

Sunbeam is an ornamental hop released in 1994 that is said to have Saaz-like aromatic qualities (it has Saaz in its lineage) and although it is not planned to be grown for commercial brewing use, it is said to have potential in the homebrewing market. Sunbeam and its half-sister Bianca are unique in that they have bright yellow leaves and reddish to bright red stems. Samples were unavailable for analysis.

## Super Alpha

Super Alpha is a high-alpha hop from New Zealand which is extremely woody and rustic. It also has some nice resiny character. It is a cross of English and German hop varieties. Substitutes: Pacific Gem and Pride of Ringwood are similarly woody although Pacific Gem is very fruity.

## Talisman

I could find very little about this hop variety other than that it was bred as an "improved Cluster"[207] has an extremely high cohumulone percentage and that it is virtually obsolete. It has a typical alpha acid percentage of 7 to 9%. Substitutes: Cluster, Nugget, or Olympic.

## Target

Target is a high-alpha variety, very popular among British hop growers. It also has a pleasant aroma and is widely used as an aroma hop. Its aroma has green apple, wood and a slight solvent-like character. I feel that it definitely has some Fuggle-like aromas. Target is used in John Smith's Cask Bitter and Magnet as both a bittering and aroma hop[205]. After a brewery tour in August of 1994, I was told by Ken Don, the head brewmaster at Young's Ram Brewery, that they had switched from East Kent Goldings to Target for dryhopping Young's Special London Ale. I believe that I noticed this change, but from recent tastings, I feel that they have changed back – or perhaps they are alternating between the two varieties. Substitutes: Fuggle, Willamette.

## Tettnanger

Originally marketed as a Saaz substitute, Tettnanger is one of the Noble hops (in both schools of thought). It is herbal, slightly woody, slightly spicy. Tettnanger is appropriate in German, Bohemian and American lagers (I've read that it is used quite a bit in Budweiser). Substitutes: Saaz or Crystal.

## Ultra

Ultra is another U.S.-grown hop derived from Hallertauer. It also contains some Saaz, which contributes to its low alpha acid level. Personally, I feel that its peppery, spicy, Saaz-like aroma dominates any Hallertauer character it may have. Substitutes: Crystal, Saaz, Tettnanger.

## Viking

A descendent of Bramling Cross and a sibling of Saxon, Viking has quite a low cohumulone percentage. Substitutes: Saxon would be my best guess.

## Washington Goldings

Washington Goldings are Goldings grown in Washington state, and their aroma and flavor clearly show their resiny Goldings character, but oddly, they are woodier with some light citrusy notes. They are rather a unique hop with a distinctive character. Washington Goldings are equivalent to "Oregon Goldings" or "U.S. Goldings." Sometimes you will see "Washington Kent Goldings" which is a misnomer. Kent is a county in England. The Goldings are either from Kent or they are from somewhere else like Washington or British Columbia. Substitutes: I would use 90% of East Kent Goldings and 10% Cascade to add that citrusy character.

## Whitbread Golding Variety (WGV)

Whitbread Golding Variety (also known as WGV or 1147) is ~~a daughter of Bates~~ Brewer and bred as a disease-resistant Golding-type hop. It is very similar to East Kent Goldings in aroma and flavor, but has a strong, fresh tobacco-like aroma with a little Fuggle-like woodyness. WGV is not considered to be a "true Golding." It is a very unique, very rugged-scented hop variety. It is used along with Challenger for dryhopping Highgate Mild Ale (also sold as Highgate Dark Ale)[205]. Substitutes: I would use a blend of Fuggle (for the woodyness) and either East Kent Goldings, Styrian Goldings, or British Columbian Goldings.

## Willamette

A U.S.-grown cousin of Fuggle, Willamette (pronounced wil-LAM-et) is very similar to Fuggle except it is more fruity and has a floral note. It is earthy, fruity, slightly woody and slightly floral. It can be used in British and American ales. It is used in Sierra Nevada Porter and Anderson Valley Boont Amber. Substitutes: Fuggle.

## Wye Target, Wye Challenger, Wye Northdown, Wye Saxon...

These hop names simply include where they were bred: Wye College in Kent, England. They are equivalent to Target, Challenger, Northdown, Saxon, etc.

## Yakima Magnum

A U.S.-grown version of Hallertauer Magnum (pronounced YAK-i-maw MAG-num), these hops has even higher alpha acid levels (often 14.0%) than the German-grown version. They have an intensely spicy (black pepper, cinnamon, nutmeg) and slightly citrusy aroma. Substitutes: Crystal or perhaps Hallertauer Magnum.

## Yeoman

Yeoman is an English high-alpha hop with acceptable English aroma. Its grandfather is a brother of Target.

## Zatec

Another name for Saaz.

## Zenith

Zenith is an English medium-alpha, aroma hop. Its grandmother was Keyworth's Early.

## Other hops

The following are hop varieties for which I had even less information - if I have the country of origin and some lineage information, I have put it in parentheses after the hop name: Janus (English; an attempt at a Fuggle replacement bred from WGV), First Choice (New Zealand; a parent of Sticklebract; bred from a California Cluster), Density (English; an attempt at a higher-alpha Fuggle replacement bred from Bullion), Smooth Cone (New Zealand; aroma hop bred from a California Cluster; parent of Green Bullet), Defender (English; an attempt at a higher-alpha Fuggle replacement bred from Bullion), Alliance (English; an attempt at a Fuggle replacement bred from WGV), CaliCross (New Zealand; quite high in cohumulone), Harley's Fulbright (New Zealand), Pride of Kent (England), Sunshine (England, parent of Comet and grandparent of Bianca and Sunbeam), Blisk, Columbia, Dunav, Neoplanta, Nordgard, Southern Brewer, Elsasser, Orion (German; midrange alpha), and BB1 (Canadian, obsolete, and parent of Brewer's Gold, Bullion, and Northern Brewer)[199,201,202,207,210].

### Hop Data (Table B-1)

| Variety | Alpha Acid % | Beta Acid % % of Alpha | Cohumulone Acid |
|---------|--------------|------------------------|-----------------|
| Admiral | 13.0 - 16.0 | n/a | 33 - 39 |
| Ahil | 8.0 - 10.0 | 3.5 - 4.5 | 26 - 28 |
| Alliance | 4.5 - 5.5 | 2.0 - 3.0 | 24 - 28 |
| Apolon | 8.0 - 10.0 | 3.0 - 4.0 | 26 - 33 |
| Aquila | 6.0 - 8.0 | 4.0 - 6.5 | 45 - 50 |
| Atlas | 8.0 - 10.0 | 2.8 - 3.8 | 28 - 34 |
| Aurora | 8.5 - 10.5 | 3.5 - 5.0 | 22 - 27 |
| Banner | 9.0 - 11.0 | 5.0 - 7.0 | 30 - 36 |
| Bianca | 7.0 - 8.0 | ~3.4 | 20 - 28 |

| Variety | Alpha Acid % | Beta Acid % % of Alpha | Cohumulone Acid |
|---|---|---|---|
| Bramling | 4.0 - 5.5 | 2.0 - 3.0 | 25 - 28 |
| Bramling Cross | 5.5 - 7.0 | 2.5 - 3.5 | ~34 |
| Brewer's Gold | 7.0 - 11.0 | 4.0 - 6.0 | 33 - 46 |
| British Columbian Goldings | 4.0 - 5.5 | 2.0 - 3.0 | 27 - 34 |
| Bullion | 6.0 - 13.5 | 4.5 - 5.5 | 41 - 46 |
| Cascade | 4.5 - 7.0 | 4.5 - 7.0 | 33 - 42 |
| Centennial | 9.5 - 11.5 | 3.5 - 4.5 | 29 - 30 |
| Challenger | 6.5 - 10.0 | 3.0 - 6.0 | 16 - 28 |
| Chelan | ~13.3 | ~9.5 | ~35 |
| Chinook | 12.0 - 14.0 | 3.0 - 4.0 | 29 - 34 |
| Cluster | 4.5 - 11.5 | 3.5 - 6.5 | 36 - 47 |
| Columbia | 5.0 - 10.5 | 3.5 - 4.5 | 32 - 43 |
| Columbus | 14.0 - 16.0 | 4.5 - 5.5 | 30 -35 |
| Comet | 6.5 - 14.0 | 3.5 - 5.5 | 37 - 47 |
| Crystal | 2.0 - 4.5 | 4.5 - 6.5 | 20 - 26 |
| East Kent Goldings | 4.0 - 5.5 | 2.0 - 3.0 | 25 - 28 |
| Eroica | 10.0 - 14.0 | 4.0 - 5.5 | 36 - 46 |
| First Gold | 6.5 - 8.5 | 3.0 - 4.1 | ~33 |
| Fuggle | 4.0 - 5.5 | 1.5 - 2.0 | 21 - 32 |
| Galena | 9.0 - 14.0 | 6.0 - 9.0 | 30 - 44 |
| Green Bullet | 12.5 - 13.5 | 6.5 - 7.5 | 40 - 45 |
| Hallertauer | 3.5 - 5.5 | 3.5 - 5.5 | 13 - 24 |
| Hallertauer Hüller | 4.5 - 7.0 | 4.5 - 5.5 | 26 - 28 |
| Hallertauer Magnum | 11.0 - 13.0 | 4.0 - 6.0 | 27 - 32 |
| Hallertauer Mittelfrüh | 3.0 - 6.0 | 3.5 - 5.5 | 16 - 17 |
| Hallertauer Tradition (German) | 4.5 - 7.0 | 4.0 - 5.0 | 26 - 29 |
| Hallertauer Tradition (USA) | 5.0 - 6.0 | 4.0 - 5.0 | 26 - 29 |
| Herald | 11.0 - 13.0 | 4.8 - 5.5 | ~37 |
| Hersbrucker (Hallertau) | 3.0 - 5.5 | 4.0 - 5.5 | 19 - 25 |
| Hersbrucker Pure | ~4.7 | ~2.4 | 25 - 27 |
| Hersbrucker (U.S.) | 3.5 - 5.5 | 5.5 - 7.0 | 20 - 30 |
| Hüller Bitterer | 4.5 - 7.0 | 4.5 - 5.5 | 26 - 31 |
| Keyworth's Midseason | 6.0 - 8.0 | 2.5 - 3.5 | ~ 47 |
| Kirin II | 6.0 - 8.0 | 5.5 - 6.5 | 42 - 46 |
| Klon | 3.0 - 4.5 | 6.0 - 7.2 | n/a |
| Liberty | 3.0 - 5.0 | 3.0 - 4.0 | 24 - 30 |
| Lubelski/Lublin/Lubliner | 3.0 - 4.5 | 2.5 - 3.5 | 25 - 30 |
| Midland Goldings | 4.0 - 5.5 | 2.0 - 3.0 | 25 - 30 |

| Variety | Alpha Acid % | Beta Acid % % of Alpha | Cohumulone Acid |
|---|---|---|---|
| Mount Hood | 5.0 - 8.0 | 5.0 - 7.5 | 20 - 25 |
| Northdown | 7.5 - 9.5 | 5.0 - 5.5 | 23 - 24 |
| Northern Brewer (Hallertau) | 7.0 - 10.0 | 3.5 - 5.0 | 28 - 33 |
| Northern Brewer (U.S.) | 8.0 - 10.0 | 3.0 - 5.0 | 20 - 30 |
| Nugget | 12.0 - 14.0 | 4.0 - 6.0 | 20 - 31 |
| Olympic | 9.0 - 14.5 | 4.0 - 7.0 | 22 - 35 |
| Omega | 9.0 - 11.0 | 3.0 - 3.5 | 25 - 30 |
| Oregon Goldings | 5.0 - 6.0 | 2.0 -2.5 | 37 - 43 |
| Perle | 7.0 - 9.5 | 4.0 - 5.0 | 27 - 33 |
| Phoenix | 8.5 - 11.5 | 4.2 - 5.5 | ~30 |
| Pioneer | 8.0 - 10.0 | 3.5 - 4.0 | ~37 |
| Polnischer Lublin | 3.0 - 4.5 | 2.5 - 3.5 | 25 - 30 |
| Progress | 5.0 - 7.5 | 2.0 - 2.5 | 25 - 30 |
| Pride of Ringwood | 7.0 - 10.0 | 4.0 - 6.0 | 33 - 39 |
| Record | 6.0 - 8.5 | 4.5 -5.5 | 21 - 30 |
| Saaz | 3.0 - 4.5 | 3.0 - 4.5 | 24 - 28 |
| Savinja Goldings | 3.5 - 5.5 | 3.0 - 4.0 | 22 - 33 |
| Savinski | 3.5 - 5.5 | 3.0 - 4.0 | 22 - 33 |
| Saxon | 7.0 - 9.0 | 4.0 - 5.0 | 17 - 22 |
| Serebrianka | ~ 2.4 | ~5.5 | 22 - 25 |
| Shinshuwase | 3.0 - 7.0 | 3.5 - 6.0 | 47 - 54 |
| Spalt (German) | 4.0 - 5.5 | 4.0 - 5.5 | 21 - 28 |
| Spalt (U.S.) | 3.0 - 6.0 | 3.0 - 5.0 | 20 - 25 |
| Spalter Select | 3.5 - 5.5 | 2.5 - 5.0 | 23 - 25 |
| Sticklebract | 13.5 - 14.5 | 8.0 - 8.5 | 35 - 40 |
| Strisselspalt (French) | 3.0 - 5.0 | 3.0 - 5.5 | 20 - 25 |
| Strisselspalt (U.S.) | 6.0 - 8.0 | 6.0 - 7.0 | 25 - 30 |
| Styrian Goldings | 4.5 - 6.0 | 2.0 - 3.0 | 22 - 33 |
| Sunbeam | ~4.5 | ~2.5 | ~36 |
| Talisman | 8.0 - 9.0 | ~ 6.0 | 45 - 54 |
| Target | 9.0 - 16.0 | 4.0 - 8.0 | 32 - 37 |
| Tettnanger (German) | 3.5 - 5.5 | 3.5 - 5.0 | 22 - 29 |
| Tettnanger (U.S.) | 4.0 - 5.0 | 3.0 - 4.0 | 20 - 25 |
| Ultra | 2.0 - 3.5 | 3.0 - 4.5 | 23 - 38 |
| Viking | 7.0 - 9.0 | 3.5 - 4.5 | 23 - 25 |
| Washington (State) Goldings | 5.0 - 6.0 | 2.0 - 2.5 | 37 - 43 |
| Whitbread Golding Variety (WGV) | 6.0 - 7.5 | 2.0 - 3.0 | 25 - 30 |

| Variety | Alpha Acid % | Beta Acid % % of Alpha | Cohumulone Acid |
|---|---|---|---|
| Willamette | 4.0 - 6.0 | 3.0 - 4.0 | 29 - 36 |
| Yakima Magnum | 12.0 - 14.0 | 4.0 - 7.0 | 27 - 32 |
| Yeoman | 10.0 - 11.5 | 5.0 - 5.5 | 24 - 28 |
| Zenith | 8.5 - 10.5 | 3.0 - 3.5 | 22 - 28 |

# Matching Varieties to Styles

In this section I suggest hop varieties that might be most appropriate for particular styles of beer. Please note that these are only suggestions and that you should not necessarily limit yourself to these relationships. However, when entering homebrew competitions, some categories specifically state hop varieties. The guidelines may say that only Noble hop aroma is appropriate or only English hop aroma is appropriate. In these cases, for the sake of doing well in the competition, you may want to stick with the standard hop varieties. In some other competition categories, there is no stipulation as to the type of hops used, but there are many judges who are biased towards or against a certain hop variety for that style. For example, in the American Homebrewer's Association guidelines, there are no rules regarding the type of hops used in India Pale Ales (IPAs). But, despite the fact that Anchor's Liberty Ale falls within the guidelines for an IPA and has lots of Cascade character, many judges feel that because IPA is an English style and will subsequently score down for the use of Cascades. This is wrong, but it happens. You may want to take that possibility into consideration when selecting hops for your IPAs.

**Table B-2 (sheet 1 of 2): Matching hop varieties to styles.**

| STYLE | HOP VARIETY |
|---|---|
| American Ales (Pale, Brown, Porter, Stout, Barleywine) | Cascade, Centennial, Columbus, Willamette |
| American Lagers (Light, Standard, Premium) | Tettnanger, Liberty, Hallertauer, Mount Hood, Saaz, Hersbrucker, Ultra, Crystal Crystal, Spalt |
| Australian Lagers/Ales | Pride of Ringwood, New Zealand Hallertau Aroma, Super Alpha, Pacific Gem |
| Belgian Ales (Trappist, Abbey, Saison, Oud Bruin, Witbier, others) | Goldings, Hallertauer, Mount Hood, Liberty, Hersbrucker |
| Bohemian Lagers (Pilsner) | Saaz, Tettnanger, Crystal, Ultra |

Table B-2 (sheet 2 of 2): Matching hop varieties to styles.

| STYLE | HOP VARIETY |
|---|---|
| British and Irish Ales (Bitter, IPA, Brown, Mild, Stout, Old Ale, Barleywine) | Goldings, Fuggle, First Gold, Northdown, Target, Challenger, Progress,Willamette, Pioneer |
| California Common (e.g. Anchor Steam™) | U.S. Northern Brewer |
| Düsseldorfer Altbier | Spalt, Spalter Select |
| General-purpose bittering | Olympic, Nugget, Galena, Cluster, any aroma hop can be used for bittering |
| German Lagers (Pils, Dortmunder, Helles, Bocks, Dunkel, Oktoberfest, Märzen) | the Hallertauer varieties, Hersbrucker, Mount Hood, Liberty, Saaz, Tettnanger, Spalt, Spalter Select, Pacific Hallertauer, Ultra |
| Kölsch | Saaz, Spalt, Crystal, Hallertauer, Tettnanger, Mount Hood, Liberty, Hersbrucker, Spalter Select, Ultra |
| Lambiek/Lambic (Geuze/Gueuze, Kriek, Framboise, Lambiek/Lambic, Faro) | Aged hops, preferably two- to three-year-old mild hops such as the Hallertauer varieties, Goldings, Tettnanger, or Saaz – if you don't have aged hops, you can make some by baking fresh whole hops in an oven for 30 minutes at 250° F (120° C). |
| Münster Altbier | Hallertauer, Saaz, Tettnanger |

# Selecting Hops by Aroma/Flavor

Sometimes you may want to select a hop variety by aroma or flavor rather than by what hops are traditionally used. The following table will help you choose a hop variety based upon the character that it will add to your beer.

Table B-3 (sheet 1 of 2): Aromas/flavors of hop varieties.

| Aroma/Flavor | Hop Varieties |
|---|---|
| "Noble" | Hallertauer Mittelfrüh, Hallertauer Tradition, Liberty, Mount Hood, Saaz, Spalt, Spalter Select, Tettnanger |
| black currant | Brewer's Gold, Cluster, Northdown, Phoenix |
| black peppery | Crystal, Ultra |
| buttery | Bramling Cross, Hallertauer Mittelfrüh, Hallertauer Tradition, Northdown, Phoenix |

**Table B-3 (sheet 2 of 2): Aromas/flavors of hop varieties.**

| Aroma/Flavor | Hop Varieties |
|---|---|
| candy-like | British Columbian Goldings, East Kent Goldings, Nugget, Oregon Goldings, Styrian Goldings, Washington Goldings |
| chocolaty | Eroica, Lubelski, Lublin, Polnischer Lublin |
| cinnamon | Crystal, First Gold, Hallertauer Mittelfrüh, Hallertauer Tradition, Liberty, Lubelski, Lublin, Mount Hood, Saaz, Spalt |
| citrusy | Cascade, Centennial, Columbus, Galena, Olympic |
| earthy | Bullion, Northern Brewer, Pride of Ringwood, Willamette |
| floral | East Kent Goldings, Green Bullet, Nugget, Oregon Goldings, Strisselspalt (French), Styrian Goldings, Washington Goldings, Willamette |
| fruity | Bullion, Fuggle, Galena, Northern Brewer, Pacific Gem, Progress, Willamette |
| grapefruity | Cascade, Centennial, Columbus |
| green apple | Target |
| herbal | Galena, Pride of Ringwood, Tettnanger |
| lemony | Southern Cross, Strisselspalt (French) |
| pastry-like | Hallertauer Mittelfrüh, Hallertauer Tradition, Liberty, Lubelski, Lublin, New Zealand Hallertau Aroma, Polnischer Lublin, Sticklebract |
| piney | Chinook, Sticklebract |
| raspberry | Bullion |
| red wine | Hallertauer Mittelfrüh, Hersbrucker |
| raisiny | Green Bullet |
| resiny | Bramling Cross, British Columbian Goldings, Bullion, Challenger, East Kent Goldings, First Gold, Green Bullet, Liberty, Midland Goldings, Mount Hood, Nugget, Oregon Goldings, Phoenix, Pioneer, Progress, Styrian Goldings, Washington Goldings, Whitbread Golding Variety (WGV) |
| spicy | Brewer's Gold, Chinook, Hallertauer Tradition, Liberty, Lubelski, Lublin, Perle, Polnischer Magnum, Progress, Saaz, Southern Cross, Tettnanger |
| strawberry | Pacific Gem |
| tobacco-like | Hersbrucker, Whitbread Golding Variety (WGV) |
| woody | Bramling Cross, Bullion, Columbus, Eroica, Fuggle, Northern Brewer, New Zealand Hallertau Aroma, Oregon Goldings, Pacific Gem, Pride of Ringwood, Southern Cross Spalt, Super Alpha, Target, Tettnanger, Ultra, Willamette |

# Further Reading

Haunold, A. and G. B. Nickerson, "Development of a Hop with European Aroma Characteristics," *ASBC Journal*, 45 (4) 146-151.

Haunold, A. and G. B. Nickerson, "Mt. Hood, a New American Noble Aroma Hop," *ASBC Journal*, 48 (3) 115-118.

Haunold, A., "Development of Hop Varieties," *Zymurgy,* 13 (4) 15-23 (Special 1990).

Haunold, A., et. al., "One-Half Century of Hop Research by the U.S. Department of Agriculture," *ASBC Journal*, 43 (3) 123-126.

*Hop Variety Specifications*, HopUnion, USA.

Hough, J. S., D. E. Briggs, R. Stevens, and T.W. Young, *Malting and Brewing Science*, Vol. 2 (Chapman and Hall, London, 1982).

Kenny, S.T., "Identification of U.S.-Grown Hop Cultivars by Hop Acid and Essential Oil Analyses," *ASBC Journal*, 48 (1) 3-8.

Laws, D. R. J., Shannon, P. V. R., John, G. D., "Correlation of Congener Distribution and Brewing Performance of Some New Varieties of Hops," *ASBC Journal*, 34 (4) 166-170.

Meilgaard, M., "Hop Analysis, Cohumulone Factor and the Bitterness of Beer: Review and Critical Evaluation," *Journal of the Institute of Brewing*, 66.

Nickerson, G. B. and P. A. Williams, "Varietal Differences in the Proportions of Cohumulone, Adhumulone and Humulone in Hops," *ASBC Journal*, 44 (2) 91-94.

Protz, R., *The Real Ale Drinker's Almanac*, (Lochar Publishing Ltd., Moffat, Scotland, 1990).

Protz, R., *Real Ale Almanac* (Neil Wilson Publishing Ltd., Glasgow, Scotland, 1993).

Smith, Q. B., "Matching Hops with Beer Styles," *Zymurgy,* 13 (4) 55-60 (Special 1990).

Van Valkenburg, D. "A Question of Pedigree - The Role of Genealogy in Hop Substitutions," *Brewing Techniques*, 3 (5), 56-57, (Sep/Oct 1995).

# DRY YEAST CHARACTERISTICS

ote that one producer of yeasts has stated in their literature that there currently does not exist a true dry lager yeast – that all so-called "lager" dry yeasts are merely ale yeasts that are able to perform at lager temperatures. They claim to be working on a true dry lager yeast, but it is not yet available for evaluation. I have not done tests that would verify whether or not the yeasts below that are labeled "lager" are indeed Saccharomyces cerevisiae var. uvarum. The attenuation, flocculation and characteristics are all based upon my own tests. Unless a yeast is specifically listed as "lager" below, it is labeled "ale" or "brewer's" yeast.

| Yeast | Attenuation | Flocculation | Characteristics |
|-------|-------------|--------------|-----------------|
| Coopers | low (62 - 67%) | good; | quite neutral; very light mixed-fruit aroma; very clean aroma during fermentation; very slight hazelnut aroma; leaves a slightly sweeter beer; note that this is not the yeast used by Cooper's Brewery; |
| Cordon Brew | low (61 - 66%) | fair; powderey | strong apple aroma; fruity; |
| Danstar London | medium-low (63 - 68%) | medium; | fast starter; very fruity – raisins, pears, apricots; a clean, flavorful, and distinctive yeast, slightly slower in settling; |
| Danstar Manchester | medium (68 - 73%) | high; | fast starter; powdery aroma, mild apple aroma (esters, not acetaldehyde); another clean and distinctive yeast; |
| Danstar Nottingham | medium (72 - 78%) | high; slightly powdery; | very fast starter, very neutral; light mixed-fruit aroma; very clean during fermentation; |

| Yeast | Attenuation | Flocculation | Characteristics |
|-------|-------------|--------------|-----------------|
| Danstar Windsor | medium-low (64 - 70%) | poor, quite powdery; | a little sulfury during fermentation; medium mixed-fruit aroma; slightly more acidity than most yeasts; |
| Doric | medium (70 - 75%) | poor; quite powdery; | slightly sulfury during fermentation (will dissipate); nutty; not very fruity – quite neutral; slightly citrusy but clean flavor; |
| Edme | medium-low (65 - 70%) | fair; powdery; | powdery, slightly woody aroma; slightly citrusy but clean flavor; |
| Glenbrew | high (82 - 87%) | good; slightly powdery; | contains a "special enzyme" for creating very dry ales with very low final gravities; slightly clovey aroma and flavor; |
| Morgan's Ale | medium (70 - 75%) | good | very fast starter, quite sulfury – takes quite some time to dissipate; quite neutral flavor; |
| Morgan's Lager | medium-high (78 - 82%) | good; | very fast starter; rather fruity strawberry nose even fermented at 45° F (7° C); bready/slightly citrusy flavor; some diacetyl; |
| Munton's | medium (70 - 75%) | fair; powdery; | slight apple and pear aromas; clean, fruity flavor; |
| Munton's Gold | high (82 - 87%) | good; | slightly woody aroma; quite neutral flavor; quite dry; moderate diacetyl; |
| Pasteur Champagne | medium (72 - 78%) | fair; slightly powdery; | fast starter; slight clovey aroma; slight sulfur aroma during fermentation; excellent alcohol tolerance; good for very high gravity ales (some brewers first pitch an ale yeast into very high gravity worts and then later pitch this yeast when the first yeast is overcome by alcohol); |
| Superior Lager | medium-high (73 - 78%) | good; compact; | compact; powdery nose; very clean otherwise; no fruitiness in aroma or flavor; ferments vigorously at 54° F (12° C); may perform well at even lower temperatures; |
| Unican | medium (68 - 73%) | good; slightly powdery; | some diacetyl; nice, light, mixed-fruit aroma; clean flavor; plain white package – no brand name; |
| Yeast Lab Australian Ale | low (59 - 64%) | high; compact; | nicely fruity; slightly sulfury (may dissipate with age); nice green grape flavor; |
| Yeast Lab Whitbread Ale | medium high (73 - 78%) | high; compact; | bready aroma; strong apricot aroma; tart, snappy, dryish, yet clean flavor; this yeast has been known to have difficulty fermenting in tall, narrow fermenters; |

| Yeast | Attenuation | Flocculation | Characteristics |
|---|---|---|---|
| Yeast Lab Amsterdam Lager | medium (71 - 76%) | high; compact; | nutty aroma; slight apple; very slightly fruity; nice, clean, neutral flavor; will ferment very slowly at 54° F (12° C), but does much better at 60° F (16° C); also ferments cleanly at 70° F (21° C), but much fruitier – more apple; |
| Yeast Lab European Lager | medium-low (68 - 73%) | medium; powdery; | strong acetaldehyde producer – would require rather long lagering; ferments smoothly and quickly at 54° F (12° C); also ferments cleanly at 70° F (21° C), but produces a lot of apple aroma (acetaldehyde); |

# SELECTING LIQUID YEAST

With well over 300 yeasts from at least seven different labs, the job of selecting a particular yeast for your recipe can be a daunting task. What most brewers do is get to know a half dozen or so yeasts and learn their characteristics well.

In this appendix, I've grouped the various yeast strains together by characteristics based upon the labs' recommendations and my own personal experience. Within each group, the strains are *not* in any particular order of preference. The differences between any two yeasts in a group may be small or large, but in most cases, making the same recipe with two different yeasts from a particular group will produce two distinctively different beers. Also note that there are no rules that say you cannot use a yeast from a different group to make a particular beer. The only yeasts that perhaps might give you stylistic problems are the phenolic ones (Bavarian Weizens, Belgian Ales and Witbiers). These yeasts are generally not appropriate for the other beer styles in which the clovey phenolics are usually considered a fault.

Since the list of labs and the strains they distribute is constantly changing, this appendix is merely a snapshot of the yeast market, but every effort has been made to be as up-to-date as possible.

# Styles

## American Ales (Pale, Brown, Porter, Stout, Barleywine)

*Advanced Brewers Scientific*: ABS001 Northwest Microbrewery Ale
*Brewers Resource*: BrewTek CL-10 American Microbrewery 1, BrewTek CL-20
    American Microbrewery 2, BrewTek CL-50 California Pub Brewery Ale
*Head Start Brewing Cultures*: Head Start #100 No.1 Ale, Head Start #101
    American Ale
*Saccharomyces Supply Company*: RTP Acme Ale, RTP U.S. Ale
*Wyeast Laboratories*: #1056 American Ale, #1272 American Ale II
*Yeast Culture Kit Company*: A01 American Ale, A58, A96
*Yeast Lab*: A02 American Ale

## American and Australian Lagers (all)

*Brewers Resource*: BrewTek CL-620 American Megabrewery, BrewTek CL-630
    American Microbrewery Lager
*Head Start Brewing Cultures*: Head Start #200 Americana, Head Start #201
    American Pils
*Wyeast Laboratories:* #2007 Pilsen Lager, #2035 American Lager, #2272 North
    American Lager
*Yeast Culture Kit Company*: L20 St. Louis Lager
*Yeast Lab*: L34 St. Louis Lager

## Bavarian Weizen

*Brewers Resource*: BrewTek CL-920 German Wheat, BrewTek CL-930 German
    Weiss
*Head Start Brewing Cultures*: Head Start #300 Weizen 66, Head Start #301
    Weizen 68
*Saccharomyces Supply Company*: RTP German Wheat
*Wyeast Laboratories*: #3056 Bavarian Wheat, #3068 Weihenstephan Wheat,
    #3333 German Wheat
*Yeast Culture Kit Company:* A50 Bavarian Weizen, A85
*Yeast Lab*: W51 Bavarian Weizen

## Belgian Ales (Trappist, Abbey, Saison, Belgian Ale, Belgian Strong)

*Advanced Brewers Scientific*: ABS003 La Chouffe Belgian Ale
*Brewers Resource*: BrewTek CL-300 Belgian Ale #1, BrewTek CL-320 Belgian
    Ale #2, BrewTek CL-340 Belgian Ale #3, BrewTek CL-380 Saison
*Head Start Brewing Cultures*: Head Start #141 Calais, Head Start #142 De
    Saison, Head Start #120 Two Monks, Head Start #121 Trappist, Head Start
    #370 Witbier, Head Start #371 Nit-Wit
*Saccharomyces Supply Company*: RTP Belgian Ale

*Wyeast Laboratories*: #1214 Belgian Ale, #1388 Belgian Strong Ale, #1762
  Belgian Abbey II, #3787 Trappist, #3942 Belgian Wheat
*Yeast Culture Kit Company*: A16 Trappe Ale, A35 Belgian Wit, A36 Belgian Ale,
  A18, A25, A26, A35, A36, A38, A48, A66, A67, A68, A69, A70, A71, A72,
  A73, A74, A75, A76, A78, A88, A107
*Yeast Lab*: A08 Trappist Ale

## Berliner Weiss

*Head Start Brewing Cultures*: Head Start #310 Berliner Weisse-B, Head Start
  #310B Berliner Weiss-B with Lacto-Capsules, Head Start #311 Berliner
  Weiss-S, Head Start #330 Lactobacillus delbrückii [bacteria]

## Bohemian Lagers (Pilsner)

*Advanced Brewers Scientific*: ABS005 Czech Lager
*Brewers Resource*: BrewTek CL-600
*Head Start Brewing Cultures*: Head Start #220 Ur-Pils, Head Start #221 Präger
*Saccharomyces Supply Company*: RTP Czech Pilsner Lager
*Wyeast Laboratories*: #2278 Czech Pils, #2124 Bohemian Lager
*Yeast Culture Kit Company*: L17 Pilsen Lager
*Yeast Lab*: L31 Pilsner Lager

## California Common

*Brewers Resource*: BrewTek CL-690 California Gold
*Head Start Brewing Cultures*: Head Start #230 California Common
*Wyeast Laboratories*: #2112 California Lager
*Yeast Culture Kit Company*: L21 California Lager
*Yeast Lab*: California Lager

## Düsseldorf Altbier

*Head Start Brewing Cultures*: Head Start #170 Düsseldorfer
*Saccharomyces Supply Company*: RTP German Alt Ale
*Wyeast Laboratories*: #1338 European Ale
*Yeast Culture Kit Company*: A37 Altbier, A49 Alt #2
*Yeast Lab*: A06 Düsseldorf Ale

## English Ales - Dryer (Bitter, Mild, Northern-style Brown, IPA, Porter, Barleywine)

*Brewers Resource*: BrewTek CL-110 British Microbrewery Ale,
  BrewTek CL-120 British Pale Ale 1, BrewTek CL-130 British Pale Ale 2,
  BrewTek CL-240 Irish Dry Stout, BrewTek CL-260 Canadian Ale
*Head Start Brewing Cultures*: Head Start #150 English Ale, Head Start #161 IPA

*Saccharomyces Supply Company*: RTP English Ale, RTP Irish Ale
*Wyeast Laboratories*: #1028 London Ale, #1098 British Ale, #1275 Thames Valley Ale, #1335 British Ale
*Yeast Culture Kit Company*: A17 Pale Ale, W06 Barleywine (Champagne Yeast), A18, A21, A53, A59, A62, A64, A65, A95
*Yeast Lab*: A03 London Ale, A04 British Ale

## English Ales - Sweeter (Bitter, Sweet Stout, Mild, Southern-style Brown, Porter)

*Brewers Resource*: BrewTek CL-150 British Real Ale, BrewTek CL-160 British Draft Ale, BrewTek CL-170 Classic British Ale
*Head Start Brewing Cultures*: Head Start #151 Best Bitter, Head Start #152 London Tap, Head Start #160 ESB, Head Start #190 SnP
*Saccharomyces Supply Company*: RTP London Special Bitter Ale, RTP Scotch Ale
*Wyeast Laboratories*: #1084 Irish Ale, #1318 London Ale III, #1968 Special London
*Yeast Culture Kit Company*: A06 Stout Ale, A15 English Ale, A20, A42, A60, A61, A90, A97

## Flanders Brown, Flanders Red

*Head Start Brewing Cultures*: Head Start #333 Lactobacillus "flanderii," Head Start #320 Flanders Red, Head Start #321 Flanders Brown
*Yeast Culture Kit Company*: A39

## Fruit Beers

*Brewers Resource*: BrewTek CL-150 British Real Ale
*Wyeast Laboratories*: #1338 European Ale
*Yeast Culture Kit Company*: A20, A39

## German and Austrian Lagers (all)

*Brewers Resource*: BrewTek CL-630 American Microbrewery Lager, BrewTek CL-650 Old Bavarian Lager, BrewTek CL-660 Northern German Lager
*Head Start Brewing Cultures*: Head Start #231 Dampfbier, Head Start #250 Festbier, Head Start #251 Weisenfest, Head Start #270 Leitpold, Head Start #271 Kellerbier/Rauchbier, Head Start #272 Nürnburger, Head Start #280 Hansen [alcohol tolerant]
*Saccharomyces Supply Company*: RTP German Lager
*Wyeast Laboratories*: #2206 Bavarian Lager, #2308 Munich Lager
*Yeast Culture Kit Company*: L02 Bavarian Lager, L05 Munich Lager, L09
*Yeast Lab*: L32 Bavarian Lager, L33 Munich Lager

## Irish (Dry) Stout

*Brewers Resource*: BrewTek CL-240 Irish Dry Stout
*Head Start Brewing Cultures*: Head Start #190 SnP
*Saccharomyces Supply Company*: RTP Irish Ale
*Wyeast Laboratories*: #1084 Irish Ale
*Yeast Culture Kit Company*: A13 Irish Ale
*Yeast Lab*: A05 Irish Ale

## Kölsch and Münster Altbier

*Brewers Resource*: BrewTek CL-400 Old German Ale, BrewTek CL-450 Kölsch
*Head Start Brewing Cultures*: Head Start #171 Kölsch
*Wyeast Laboratories*: #1007 German Ale, #2565 Kölsch
*Yeast Culture Kit Company*: A04 German Ale

## Lambieks/Lambics

*Brewers Resource*: BrewTek CL-5200 (*Brettanomyces lambicus*), BrewTek
   CL-5600 (*Pediococcus damnosus*) [bacteria]
*Head Start Brewing Cultures*: Head Start #350 *Brettanomyces bruxellensis*, Head
   Start #331 *Pediococcus damnosus* (a.k.a. *P. cerevisiae*) [bacteria], Head Start
   #340 Brettanomyces lambicus, Head Start #341 *Brettanomyces bruxellensis*,
   Head Start #342 *Kloeckera apiculata*, Head Start #343 *Brettanomyces
   anomala,* Head Start #344 *Candida lambicus*, Head Start #400
   *Saccharomyces diastaticus* [experienced brewers only]
*Wyeast Laboratories*: #3278B Belgian Lambic Blend [yeasts and bacteria]
*Yeast Culture Kit Company*: M3220 Brettanomyces [bacteria], M3200
   Pediococcus [bacteria]

## Miscellaneous Ales

*Brewers Resource*: BrewTek CL-980 American White Ale
*Head Start Brewing Cultures*: Head Start #140 Cambrai Nord [for French Ale],
   Head Start #141 Calais [for Biere de Garde], Head Start #302 Steinweizen,
   Head Start #303 *Torulaspora delbrückii*
*Wyeast Laboratories*: #1087 Wyeast Ale Blend, #1742 Swedish Ale
*Yeast Lab*: A01 Australian Ale, A07 Canadian Ale

## Miscellaneous Lagers

*Advanced Brewers Scientific*: ABS004 Swedish Lager
*Brewers Resource*: BrewTek CL-670 Swiss Lager
*Head Start Brewing Cultures*: Head Start #240 Continental Dry [Danish], Head
   Start #241 Viking [Swedish], Head Start #260 Strassbourger [French], Head
   Start #261 Continental Lager [French]

*Wyeast Laboratories*: #2042 Danish Lager, #2178 Wyeast Lager Blend, #2247
Danish Lager II

## Miscellaneous Cultures

*Head Start Brewing Cultures*: Head Start #351 *Brettanomyces dublinensis*
(anomala) [cask conditioning strain from Ireland], Head Start #334
*Lactobacillus delbrückii spp. lactis*, Head Start #335 *Lactobacillus* mixed
culture [bacteria]

## Scottish Ales

*Brewers Resource*: BrewTek CL-200 Scottish Ale, BrewTek CL-210 Scottish
Bitter
*Head Start Brewing Cultures*: Head Start #111 Scotch Ale, Head Start #112 Wee
Heavy
*Saccharomyces Supply Company*: RTP Scotch Ale
*Wyeast Laboratories*: #1728 Scottish Ale
*Yeast Culture Kit Company*: A34 Scotch Ale, A43, A44, A93, A94

## Witbier

*Brewers Resource*: BrewTek CL-900 Belgian Wheat
*Head Start Brewing Cultures*: Head Start #370 Witbier, Head Start #371 Nit-Wit,
Head Start #372 Sour-Wit [includes bacteria]
*Wyeast Laboratories*: #3944 Belgian White
*Yeast Culture Kit Company*: A35 Belgian Wit, A18, A35, A41, A79

# Characteristics

## More attenuative (drier beer)

*Brewers Resource*: BrewTek CL-130 British Pale Ale 2, BrewTek CL-240 Irish
Dry Stout, BrewTek CL-260 Canadian Ale, BrewTek CL-320 Belgian Ale
#2, BrewTek CL-400 Old German Ale, BrewTek CL-450 Kölsch
*Head Start Brewing Cultures*: Head Start #101 American Ale, Head Start #142
De Saison, Head Start #200 Americana [lager], Head Start #240 Continental
Dry [lager]
*Wyeast Laboratories*: #1007 German Ale, #3787 Trappist [clovey], #2042 Danish
Lager, #2247 Danish Lager II
*Yeast Culture Kit Company*: A68, A71, L09 German Lager, L20 St. Louis Lager
*Yeast Lab*: A03 London Ale, A04 British Ale, A05 Irish Ale, A07 Canadian Ale,
A08 Trappist Ale [clovey], L31 Pilsner Lager, L34 St. Louis Lager

## Less attenuative (sweeter beer)

*Brewers Resource*: BrewTek CL-150 British Real Ale, BrewTek CL-210 Scottish Bitter, BrewTek CL-680 East European Lager
*Head Start Brewing Cultures*: Head Start #160 ESB, Head Start #220 Ur-Pils [lager], Head Start #250 Festbier [lager]
*Saccharomyces Supply Company*: RTP London Special Bitter Ale, RTP Scotch Ale
*Wyeast Laboratories*: #1338 European Ale, #1742 Swedish Ale, #1968 Special London, #2112 California Lager, #2124 Bohemian Lager
*Yeast Culture Kit Company*: A08 Barleywine Ale, A20, A39, A42, A65, L21 California Lager
*Yeast Lab*: A06 Düsseldorf Ale

## More diacetyl

*Advanced Brewers Scientific*: ABS001 Northwest Microbrewery Ale
*Brewers Resource*: BrewTek CL-10 American Microbrewery 1, BrewTek CL-160 British Draft Ale
*Head Start Brewing Cultures*: Head Start #161 IPA, Head Start #190 SnP
*Saccharomyces Supply Company*: RTP English Ale
*Wyeast Laboratories*: #1028 London Ale, #1084 Irish Ale, #1968 Special London
*Yeast Culture Kit Company*: A06 Stout Ale, A42, A60
*Yeast Lab*: A05 Irish Ale

## More fruity

*Advanced Brewers Scientific*: ABS001 Northwest Microbrewery Ale, ABS002 Australian Ale
*Brewers Resource*: BrewTek CL-110 British Microbrewery Ale, BrewTek CL-150 British Real Ale, BrewTek CL-160 British Draft Ale, BrewTek CL-210 Scottish Bitter
*Head Start Brewing Cultures*: Head Start #142 De Saison, Head Start #190 SnP
*Saccharomyces Supply Company*: RTP U.S. Ale
*Wyeast Laboratories*: #1272 American Ale II, #3942 Belgian Wheat
*Yeast Culture Kit Company*: A36 Belgian Ale, A18, A48, A60, A74, A75, A76, A78, A90
*Yeast Lab*: A07 Canadian Ale

## Less fruity (good for making lager-like beers at ale temperatures)

*Brewers Resource*: BrewTek CL-10 American Microbrewery 1, BrewTek CL-270 Australian Ale, BrewTek CL-450 Kölsch

*Head Start Brewing Cultures*: Head Start #100 No. 1 Ale, Head Start #140 Cambrai Nord
*Saccharomyces Supply Company*: RTP Acme Ale
*Wyeast Laboratories*: #1056 American Ale, #1275 Thames Valley Ale
*Yeast Culture Kit Company*: A01 American Ale, A72, A107

## High alcohol tolerance

*Brewers Resource*: BrewTek CL-130 British Pale Ale 2, BrewTek CL-170 Classic British Ale
*Head Start Brewing Cultures*: Head Start #120 Two Monks, Head Start #121 Trappist
*Wyeast Laboratories*: #1388 Belgian Strong Ale, #1762 Belgian Abbey II
*Yeast Culture Kit Company*: W06 Barleywine (Champagne Yeast), A25, A36, A38, A48, A68, A69, A70
*Yeast Lab*: A08 Trappist Ale
*Head Start Brewing Cultures*: Head Start #280 Hansen [lager]

## High temperature tolerance

*Brewers Resource*: BrewTek CL-10 American Microbrewery 1, BrewTek CL-270 Australian Ale, BrewTek CL-450 Kölsch
*Head Start Brewing Cultures*: Head Start #100 No. 1 Ale, Head Start #140 Cambrai Nord
*Saccharomyces Supply Company*: RTP Acme Ale
*Wyeast Laboratories*: #1056 American Ale, #1275 Thames Valley Ale
*Yeast Culture Kit Company*: A01 American Ale, A72, A107

## Citrusy

*Brewers Resource*: BrewTek CL-120 British Pale Ale 1
*Wyeast Laboratories*: #1318 London Ale III, #1335 British Ale

## Woody

*Brewers Resource*: BrewTek CL-110 British Microbrewery Ale, BrewTek CL-150 British Real Ale, BrewTek CL-200 Scottish Ale
*Wyeast Laboratories*: #1028 London Ale
*Yeast Culture Kit Company*: A13 Irish Ale
*Yeast Lab*: A01 Australian Ale

Appendix

# LIQUID YEAST CHARACTERISTICS

The information presented here is copied, with permission, from sales literature or personal communications with the respective yeast laboratories. In some cases, I have some personal comments to add, in which case I've enclosed my opinions of the yeast in square brackets. I would like to thank the yeast laboratories for their help and permission to reprint their yeast"s descriptions here. A big thanks goes out to Advanced Brewers Scientific, Brewers Resource, Head Start Brewing Cultures, Saccharomyces Supply Company, Wyeast Laboratories, Yeast Culture Kit Company and Ycast Lab.

## *ALE YEASTS*

| Yeast | Attenuation | Flocculation | Characteristics and Notes |
|-------|-------------|--------------|---------------------------|
| **Advanced Brewers Scientific** | | | |
| ABS001 Northwest Ale | – | – | "This yeast is a fruity, top-fermenting strain with a signature diacetyl character. It is used in several breweries in the Pacific Northwest." |
| ABS002 Australian Ale | – | – | "Crisp, yet fruity character typifies this top-fermenter." |
| ABS003 La Chouffe Belgian Ale | – | – | "This yeast is a distinctive, estery, phenolic strain from the land of distinctive beers." [obviously, this would be the yeast of choice for emulating La Chouffe ales;] |

| Yeast | Attenuation | Flocculation | Characteristics and Notes |
|---|---|---|---|
| **Brewers Resource** | | | |
| BrewTek CL-10 American Microbrewery 1 | High | Medium | "A smooth, clean, strong-fermenting ale yeast that works well down to 56° (13° C); The neutral character of this yeast makes it ideal for cream ales and other beers in which you want to — maintain a clean malt flavor." [fruitiness is subdued; strong attenuation; a good choice for emulating Sierra Nevada Ales, Anchor Ales, or any other American Ales;] |
| BrewTek CL-20 American Microbrewery 2 | Medium | Medium | "Gives an accentuated, rich and creamy malt profile with detectable amounts or diacetyl. Use it in lower gravity beers where the malt character should not be missed or in Strong Ales for a robust character." |
| BrewTek CL-50 California Pub Brewery Ale | Medium | Medium | "This yeast is good for that classic U.S. small brewery flavor. This yeast produces terrific American Red and Pale Ale styles. While attenuation is normal, this yeast produces a big, soft, well-rounded malt flavor that really lets caramel malt flavors shine. Threshold diacetyl, and esters play only to support the silky-smooth profile, even in well-hopped beers." [in a private communication, Jeff Mellem from Brewer's Research told me that this yeast is more "sensitive to dextrins" than most strains; "attenuation and malt character varies far more with this strain than other yeasts"] |
| BrewTek CL-110 British Microbrewery Ale | Medium | Medium | "Provides a complex, oaky, fruity ester profile and slightly full-flavored finish suitable to low-and medium-gravity British ale styles. Very distinct, this classic, old fashioned yeast is great for traditional bitters and is a rare find for Mild Ale fans." |
| BrewTek CL-120 British Pale Ale 1 | Medium | High | "Produces a bold, citrusy character which accentuates mineral and hop flavors. The distinct character of this yeast makes it best suited for use in your classic British Ales or Bitters." [a good choice for emulating Bass, Boddington's, or Marston's Bitters;] |
| BrewTek CL-130 British Pale Ale 2 | High | Medium | "This is a smooth, full-flavored ale yeast. Mildly estery, this yeast is a strong fermenter and highly recommended for strong or spiced ales. This yeast is smooth, well-rounded and accentuates caramel and other malt nuances." |
| BrewTek CL-150 British Real Ale | Low | Medium | "This is the yeast for those longing for the character of a real pub bitter. This yeast has a complex, woody, almost musty ester profile that characterizes many real ales. Typically underattenuating, mild sweetness in the finish." [very fruity – berries, especially pears; complex, interesting flavor; despite its low attenuation, this yeast allows hop character through more than others;] |
| BrewTek CL-160 British Draft Ale | Medium to high | Medium | "One of our favorite ale yeasts, it gives a full-bodied, well-rounded flavor with a touch of diacetyl. This yeast has a way of emphasizing malt character like no other yeast we've used. Highly recommended for Porters and Bitters." [mixed-fruit aroma and flavor, good attenuation; this yeast has high oxygen needs; attenuation considerably higher with higher initial dissolved oxygen levels;] |

| Yeast | | | Description |
|---|---|---|---|
| BrewTek CL-170 Classic British Ale | Medium to high | Medium | "Like CL-160, this yeast produces a beautiful draft Bitter or Porter. This yeast leaves a complex ale with very British tones and fruity esters, it also produces a classic Scottish Heavy and plays well in high-gravity worts." |
| BrewTek CL-200 Scottish Ale | Medium | Medium | "This is a truly unique yeast for a classic Scottish Heavy, 90/- or strong ale. This yeast produces a soft, fruity malt profile with a subtle woody, oaky aroma reminiscent of malt whisky. A mild, mineral-like dryness in the finish makes this a very complex yeast strain." |
| BrewTek CL-210 Scottish Bitter | High | Medium | "This yeast will produce a bitter like you've never experienced. The soft, yeasty, fruity nose yields to a well-attenuated malt flavor and big ester complex of ripe fruit, apricots and rose petals. This yeast has a teasing finish with a dry and complex, yet smooth, fruity character." |
| BrewTek CL-240 Irish Dry Stout | High | Medium | "A true, old-fashioned, top-fermenting yeast which leaves a very recognizable character to Dry Stouts. Has a vinous, almost lactic character which blends exceptionally well with roasted malts. Highly attenuative." [vinous and lactic characters are unrelated]; |
| BrewTek CL-260 Canadian Ale | High | Medium | "A clean, strong-fermenting and well-attenuating ale yeast that leaves a pleasant, lightly fruity, complex finish. Well suited for light Canadian Ales as well as full-flavored Porters and British styles such as Bitter and Pale Ale." |
| BrewTek CL-270 | Medium | Medium | "This yeast produces a malty, bready, nutty character with a pleasant honey-like finish. This Australian Ale yeast emphasizes malt nuances and is very forgiving in warmer fermentations for those who cannot ferment under controlled conditions." |
| BrewTek CL-300 Belgian Ale #1 | Medium | Medium | "This yeast produces a truly classic Belgian Ale flavor – robust and estery with big notes of clove and fruit in the aroma and flavor." [a good choice for emulating De Koninck or Palm;] |
| BrewTek CL-320 Belgian Ale #2 | High | Medium | "This is a traditional Trappist strain that is particularly good in doubles and triples. This strong-fermenting yeast attenuated well and produces a complex, dry, fruity and estery malt [sic] sought after in fine imported Belgian Ales." |
| BrewTek CL-340 Belgian Ale #3 | Medium | Medium | "Slightly more refined that our CL-300, this yeast also produces a classic Trappist character, with notes of spice and fruit. Mildly phenolic, this is a strong fermenting yeast, well-suited to Trappist and other Belgian Ales." |
| BrewTek CL-380 Saison | Medium | Medium | "A pleasant yeast best used to recreate country French and Belgian Ales. This yeast leaves a smooth, full character to the malt with mild yet pleasant esters and flavors reminiscent of apple pie spices." |

| Yeast | Attenuation | Flocculation | Characteristics and Notes |
|---|---|---|---|
| BrewTek CL-400 Old German Ale | Medium | Medium | "For traditional Alt Biers, this yeast is a strong fermenter which leaves a smooth, attenuated, yet subtle ester profile. Use this yeast in your favorite German Ale recipes. This yeast also makes a slightly dry but clean, quenching wheat beer." [most Diesseldorfer Altbiers are not dry – they are slightly sweet; in my opinion, a less-attenuative yeast would be a better choice for this style;] |
| BrewTek CL-450 Kölsch | High | Medium | "This yeast produces an astonishingly clean, lager-like flavor at the temperatures which smoothes with time into a clean, well-attenuated flavor. Mineral and malt characters come through well, with a clean, lightly yeasty flavor and aroma in the finish." |
| BrewTek CL-900 Belgian Wheat | Medium | Medium | "A top-fermenting yeast which produces a soft, bread-like flavor and leaves a sweet, mildly estery finish. Although this yeast tends lends its delicious Belgian character to any beer, it is best when made with Belgian Pils [malt] and finished with coriander and orange peel." |
| BrewTek CL-920 German Wheat | High | High | "This is a true, top-fermenting Weizenbier yeast: intensely spicy, clovey and phenolic. This yeast is highly attenuative and flocs in large, loose clumps. Use this yeast for all Weizen recipes. This yeast is particularly good in Weizenbocks." |
| BrewTek CL-930 German Weiss | Medium | Medium | "Milder than our German Wheat above, our 930 strain, from a famous German yeast bank, still produces the sought-after clove and phenolic characters, but to a lesser degree, with a fuller, earthier character underneath." |
| BrewTek CL-980 American While Ale | Medium | Low | "This is a smooth, American-style wheat beer yeast with an exceptionally round, clean malt flavor. The poor flocculation of this yeast leaves a cloudy "Hefe-Weizen" appearance, yet its smooth flavor makes it an integral part of a true, unfiltered wheat beer." [Hefe-Weizen is a German style which is cloudy as a result of the yeast in the bottom of the bottle being intentionally stirred-up during pouring; in all but a few commercial examples, the top-fermenting yeast is filtered out and the beer is bottled with a lager yeast;] |
| **Head Start Brewing Cultures** | | | |
| Head Start #100. No. 1 Ale | – | High | "Origin: US; This yeast is used by many Micro- and Pub-breweries. It is an excellent, clean fermenter. It may finish slowly." |
| Head Start #101. American Ale | – | Medium-high | "Origin: US; Another popular strain used by several Pub-breweries in California, it is slightly sulfury and drier than #100." |

|  | | |  |
|---|---|---|---|
| Head Start #111. Scotch Ale | — | Medium | "Origin: Great Britain; Isolated from one of the classic Scottish Ale breweries, this yeast is neutral to somewhat dry in flavor." |
| Head Start #112. Wee Heavy | — | Medium | "Origin: Great Britain; This is a Scottish Ale strain from one of Scotland's finest ale breweries." |
| Head Start #140. Cambrai Nord | — | Low | "Origin: France; This is a French Ale pure culture, which is neutral in flavor." |
| Head Start #141. Calais | — | Low-medium | "Origin: France; This is a Biere de Garde mixed culture. It is vinous and slightly phenolic in flavor." |
| Head Start #142. De Saison | High | — | "Origin: Belgium; This yeast is from a small Belgian brewery. It is very fruity and an attenuative to balance the high mashing temperatures used for this style. This strain was formerly known as AB321." |
| Head Start #150. English Ale | High | Medium | "Origin: Great Britain; This yeast ferments dry and crisp with a slight fruitiness." |
| Head Start #151. Best Bitter | — | Medium | "Origin: US; This strain is from a Northwest Microbrewery brewing authentic, cask-conditioned ales." |
| Head Start #152. London Tap | — | Medium | "Origin: Great Britain; This is a cask-conditioned, Best Bitter strain from a London Microbrewery." |
| Head Start #160. ESB | — | Medium | "Origin: Great Britain; This yeast ferments malty and complex." |
| Head Start #161. IPA | — | Medium | "Origin: Great Britain; Producing slightly more diacetyl than most yeasts, this strain has a mildly sulfury note that will age away." |
| Head Start #170. Düsseldorfer | — | High | "Origin: Germany; This is a classic Alt strain which produces a beer with dry and clean flavor." [virtually all Düsseldorfer Altbiers are not dry – they are slightly sweet; a less attenuative yeast would be a better choice for this style;] |
| Head Start #171. Kölsch | — | Medium-high | "Origin: Germany; This strain is from a German Kölsch Microbrewery." |
| Head Start #190. SnP | — | Medium | "Origin: Ireland; This is a Stout and Porter strain from Ireland. It ferments fruity with some residual diacetyl." |
| Head Start #300. Weizen 66 | — | Medium | "Origin: Germany; This is the same strain used by many of Munich's Wheat Beer Breweries. To increase clove and phenolic flavors ferment at warmer temperatures 70 - 80° F (21 to 27° C)." |

| Yeast | Attenuation | Flocculation | Characteristics and Notes |
|---|---|---|---|
| Head Start #301. Weizen 68 | – | Medium | "Origin: Germany; Classic Weizen strain producing more clove and phenolic flavors as compared to #300. Ferment at 70° F (21° C) for best results." [this yeast has an explosive fermentation – make sure you can handle a lot of kräussen; this yeast produces a lot of banana esters along with the clove aromas; a good choice for beers similar to Schneider Weisse, Schneider Avertinus, Paulaner Altbayerische Weissbier, Pschorr-Bräu or Pschorr-Bräu Dunkel Weiss;] |
| Head Start #302. Steinweizen | – | Medium | "Origin: Germany; Top-fermenting yeast from a German Steinbier brewery. This yeast does not produce the Bavarian Weizen style's phenolics. This is the same yeast used by the brewery for their Steinbier as well as their Steinweizen." |
| Head Start #303. Torulaspora delbrückii [a.k.a. Saccharomyces delbrückii] | – | – | "Origin: Germany; This yeast was isolated from a German wheat beer." |
| Head Start #120. Two Monks | – | – | "Origin: Belgium; This is pair of yeast cultures. One is an ale yeast of Trappist origin [#120A] and the other is a mixture of bottling yeasts [#120B]. The yeasts are alcohol tolerant." |
| Head Start #121. Trappist | – | – | "Origin: Belgium; This is another pair of yeast cultures. The first is a mixture of ale yeasts of Trappist origin [#121A] and the other is a mixture of bottling yeasts [#121B]. These yeasts are alcohol tolerant." |
| Head Start #370. Witbier | – | Medium | "Origin: Belgium; This is a popular Wit culture from belgium. It produces tart and phenolic flavors. |
| Head Start #371. Nit-Wit | – | Medium | "Origin: Belgium; This is a Witbier yeast from Bruxelles. It is a mixed culture and results in a drier beer than with #370." |
| **Saacharomyces Supply Company [Note that these yeasts are also known as "RTP" or "Ready To Pitch" yeasts. They are provided at volumes that do not require you to make a starter, however, freshness is therefore a much more important factor with these yeasts.]** | | | |
| RTP Acme Ale | Medium [72 - 76%] | Low-medium | "Ferments dry and clean, well-balanced." [this is a very clean, very neutral yeast strain. I recommend fermenting it above 63° F (17° C) unless you pitch a very large starter, it can be so clean at ale temperatures that some brewers use it to emulate lagers; this yeast would be a good choice for emulating beers such as those from Sierra Nevada, Anchor, or many other American Microbreweries.] |

| | | | |
|---|---|---|---|
| RTP English Ale | Medium [72 - 76%] | Medium | "Ferments clean with mild fruitiness and slight diacetyl." [this yeast has a distinctively British signature and therefore would be suggested for brewing beers similar to Young's, Fuller's or perhaps even Samuel Smith's;] |
| RTP Irish Ale | Medium-low [70 - 75%] | Medium | "Fruity and clean, slight diacetyl, great for Stouts." [indeed this yeast is a good choice for Stouts – it leaves quite a bit more diacetyl than most of the other ale yeasts, which adds a nice roundness to all English styles; this strain is a good choice for emulating Irish Stouts such as Guinness, Murphy's, or Beamish;] |
| RTP Belgian Ale | Medium-low [70 - 75%] | Low medium | "Good for strong abbey-style ales, Dubbels, Tripels, or Barleywines. It lends a spicy character with a sweet finish." [this yeast has a tendency to lend a phenolic/clovey note, so I don't know how much good it would be for a Barleywine, but it would be my first choice for a beer such as La Chouffe;] |
| RTP German Alt Ale | Medium [72 - 76%] | High | "Dry and clean, well-balanced." [this is one of several Altbier strains that are used by various German breweries, its high flocculation suggests to me that it may be less-dry than the manufacturer's description suggests – I would consider this good, since I feel that most Traditional Altbiers are not very dry;] |
| RTP London Special Bitter Ale | Low [68 - 73%] | Very High | "Rich malty character with some fruitiness." [this is one of my favorite strains; it has a very English character and its strong flocculation characteristics make it a good choice for making Cask-Conditioned Real Ales; it may require some rousing to complete fermentation; this is a great yeast for brewing beers similar to Fuller's or Samuel Smith's Bitters;] |
| RTP U.S. Ale | Medium [72 - 77%] | Medium | "From a large American Microbrewery, this yeast is a fast fermenter, producing a fruity, clean, mildly estery ale. It is similar to the RTP Acme strain." [this yeast tends to be a little fruitier than the RTP Acme strain, but is a strong performer and a good choice for any number of American Microbrewed ales from Stouts to Scottish Ales to Stock Ales;] |
| RTP German Wheat | Medium [72 - 77%] | Low | "Ferments warm, producing a spicy Weizen with a nice balance of banana and clove flavors." [of the two general types of German Weizen yeasts (clove-only and banana-and-clove) this is one of the latter, it hails from an old, medium-sized brewery just west of Munich; this yeast has an almost explosive fermentation – make sure you can handle a lot of kräusen;] |

| Yeast | Attenuation | Flocculation | Characteristics and Notes |
|---|---|---|---|
| RTP Scotch Ale | Low [68 - 73%] | Medium-high | "Produces malty sweet ales. Good for Scottish styles, and high-gravity ales such as Barleywines." [this strain would be my choice for emulating beer such as McEwan's, Younger, or Traquair House ales;] |
| **Wyeast Laboratories [Note: the names of yeasts have been known to change, but number have always been constant]** | | | |
| Wyeast #1007 German Ale | Medium [73 - 77%] | Low | "This yeast ferments dry and crisp, leaving a complex yet mild flavor. It produces an extremely rocky head and ferments well down to 55° F (13° C). Recommended fermentation temperatures: 55 - 66° F (13 - 19° C)." [fruitier than the other two Wyeast German Ale yeasts, #1338 and #2565; has a tendency to subdue the malt flavors and allow hop bitterness to come through more; a good choice for a Kölsch, but only if fermented in the low 60's F;] |
| Wyeast #1028 London Ale | Medium [73 - 77%] | Medium | "This yeast has a rich, minerally profile, producing a beer that's bold and crisp with some residual diacetyl. Recommended fermentation temperature 60 - 72° F (16-22° C)." [produces a woody character, this is a very versatile yeast – it can be used for everything from a Bitter to an Old Ale and makes an outstanding Barleywine if a large-enough starter is used and the wort is well-aerated;] |
| Wyeast #1056 American Ale | Medium [73 - 77%] | Low-medium | "Used commercially for several classic American Ales, this strain ferments dry, finishes soft, smooth and clean, and is very well-balanced. Recommended fermentation temperatures: 60 - 72° F (16 - 22° C)." [very clean; very neutral; can be used to imitate lagers; it doesn't really like temperatures much below 63° F (17° C) – you must use a big starter if you wish to ferment below 63° F, a good choice for emulating Sierra Nevada Ales, Anchor Liberty Ale and many other American Microbrewed Ales; makes a good American Wheat;] |
| Wyeast #1084 Irish Ale | Medium-low [71 - 75%] | Medium | "This yeast leaves a slight residual diacetyl and fruitiness, and is great for Stouts. It makes clean, smooth, soft and full-bodied beers. Recommended fermentation temperature 62 - 72° F (17 - 22° C)." [this yeast does leave a noticeable level of diacetyl, which can be pleasant, especially in Stouts and Bitters;] |

| Yeast | Attenuation | Flocculation | Description |
|---|---|---|---|
| Wyeast #1087 Wyeast Ale Blend | Medium-low [71 - 75%] | Good | "These packages contain a higher volume of yeast [2.75 fl. oz - 80 ml] for larger batches. The blends have been selected to insure a quick start, good flavor and good flocculation. Recommended fermentation temperature 64 - 68° F (18 - 20° C)." [despite the larger volume, a starter is still highly recommended;] |
| Wyeast #1098 British Ale | Medium [73 - 75%] | Medium | "This yeast is from Whitbread. It ferments well down to 64° F (18° C). Recommended fermentation temperature: 64 - 72° F (18 - 22° C)." ["tart" is the best description of this yeast's character, a mixed-fruit aroma and flavor, with a hint of citrusy and bready character, a good choice for Bitters and Stronger English styles;] |
| Wyeast #1214 Belgian Ale | Medium [72 - 76%] | Medium | "Abbey-style top-fermenting yeast, suitable for high-gravity beers. Estery. Recommended fermentation temperature: 58 - 68° F (14 - 20° C)." [this yeast has a tendency to create lots of banana esters at warmer temperatures; this is especially true for higher-gravity worts which generate more heat during fermentation; I recommend a large starter and a fermentation temperature between 58 and 63° F (14 and 17° C); suggested for emulating beer such as Chimay Grand Reserve, Westvleteren Abt and Rochefort 10.] |
| Wyeast #1272 American Ale II | Medium [72 - 76%] | High | "Fruitier and more flocculant than 1056. Slightly nutty, this yeast produces a soft, clean beer with a slightly tart finish." |
| Wyeast #1275 Thames Valley Ale | Medium [72 - 76%] | Medium | "Produces classic British bitters, rich complex flavor profile with a clean, well-balanced, light malt character and low fruitiness." [quite clean and neutral aroma – low diacetyl; very mildly citrusy; slight tartness in flavor; very slight banana ester; fermented at 60° F (16° C); is very neutral with faint milk chocolate aroma, a good choice for beers such as Henley Brakspear Bitter or Young's Special Bitter;] |

| Yeast | Attenuation | Flocculation | Characteristics and Notes |
|---|---|---|---|
| Wyeast #1318 London Ale III | Medium-low [71 - 75%] | High | "From a traditional London brewery with great malt and hop profile. A true top-cropping strain [a strong tendency to flocculate to the top of the fermenter] this yeast is fruity with a very light, soft, balanced palate and finishes slightly sweet." [citrus dominates with some mixed-fruit overtones; clean, tart flavor, a good choice for various English Ales since many English brewers use yeasts that are citrusy;] |
| Wyeast #1335 British Ale II | Medium [73 - 76%] | High | "Typical of British ale fermentation profile with good flocculating and malty flavor characteristics. Crisp finish; fairly dry." [slightly citrusy, with a nice, mixed-fruit background; slightly floral overtones; very smooth, clean flavor, ferments well at 60° F (16° C), but produces a very neutral beer with just a hint of nutty character;] |
| Wyeast #1338 European Ale | Low [67 - 72%] | Medium | "From Wissenschaftliche in Munich. Full-bodied, complex strain finishing very malty. Produces a dense, rocky head during fermentation. Recommended fermentation temperature 60 - 72° F (16 - 22° C)." [slightly malty nose, very malty flavor; slightly sweet, slightly fruity; this is *definitely* the proper choice for Düsseldorfer Alts;] |
| Wyeast #1388 Belgian Strong Ale | Medium [73 - 77%] | Low | "Neutral flavor yeast with moderate to high alcohol tolerance. Fruity nose and palate – dry, tart finish." [this yeast does have a tendency to take a long time to settle; a good choice for emulating Belgian Strong Blond Ales such as Duvel or Lucifer;] |
| Wyeast #1728 Scottish Ale | Low [69 - 73%] | High | "Ideally suited for Scottish-style ales and high-gravity ales of all types. Recommended fermentation temperature 55 - 70° F (13 - 22° C)." [I've spoken with several homebrewers who have used this yeast; one reports a smoky character fermented at 60 - 65° F (16 - 18° C) and a concord grape ester fermented warmer; another homebrewer told me that he got a very strong smoky aroma from this yeast at 80 - 85° F (27 - 30° C); the other five homebrewers got no smoky aroma and feel this is one of the most neutral of Wyeast's strains; I've used it at 63° F (17° C), where it was not smoky and quite lager-like and at 70° F (22° C), where it was nicely fruity (mixed fruit); this variation could be related somehow to the makeup of the wort (e.g. the amount of ferulic acid;)] |

| | | | |
|---|---|---|---|
| Wyeast #1742 Swedish Ale [a.k.a. Swedish Porter] | Low [69 - 73%] | Medium | "Stark beer Nordic style yeast of unknown origin. This yeast lends a floral nose and malty finish." |
| Wyeast #1762 Belgian Abbey II | Medium [73 - 77%] | Medium | "High gravity yeast with distinct warming character from ethanol production. It results in a beer that is slightly fruity with a dry finish." [has a tendency to create a lot of higher alcohols and has good alcohol tolerance; a good choice for emulating beers from Rochefort or Chimay;] |
| Wyeast #1968 Special London [a.k.a. London ESB] | Low [67 - 71%] | High | "Highly flocculant top-fermenting strain with rich, malty character and balanced fruitiness. This strain is so flocculant that additional aeration and agitation is needed. An excellent strain for cask-conditioned ales. Recommended fermentation temperature: 64 - 72° F (18 - 22° C)." [slight citrusy note; I've found that aeration during fermentation is not *required* for this yeast to perform well, but rousing does help; it is true, however, this is one of a group of yeasts that responds well to aeration during fermentation – the result is increased diacetyl in the finished beer, a good choice for emulating beer such as those from Fuller's or Samuel Smith's]. |
| Wyeast #2565 Kölsch | Medium [73 - 77%] | Low | "With a hybrid of ale and lager characteristics, this strain develops excellent maltiness with subdued fruitiness and a crisp finish. Ferment well at moderate temperatures. Recommended fermentation temperatures: 56 - 64° F (13 - 18° C)." [less fruity than the other two Yeast German Ale yeasts – slightly softer/maltier profile than #1007 - drier, crisper, not as malty as #1338;] |
| Wyeast #3056 | Medium | Medium | "This yeast is a blend of top-fermenting strains producing malty estery and phenolic wheat beers. Recommended fermentation temperatures: 64 - 70° F (18 - 21° C)." [can be unpredictable - should be used fresh (within four months of packaging) to get any clove character, less fruity than Wyeast #3068. This yeast would be good choices for Bavarian Weizens in the style of Tucher;] |

| Yeast | Attenuation | Flocculation | Characteristics and Notes |
|---|---|---|---|
| Wyeast #3068 Weihenstephan Wheat | Medium [73 - 77%] | Low | "This is unique top-fermenting yeast which produces the unique and spicy Weizen character, rich with clove, vanilla and banana. Best results are achieved when fermentations are held around 68° F (20° C). Recommended fermentation temperatures: 64 - 70° F (18 - 21° C)." [this yeast has an almost explosive fermentation – make sure you can handle a lot of kräusen; you can control the balance of banana and clove by varying the fermentation temperature – warmer gives more banana, colder gives more clove; this is the yeast you would use for emulating beers like Schneider Weisse, Schneider Aventinus, Paulaner Altbayerische Weissbier, Pschorr-Bräu Weizen or Pschorr-Bräu Dunkel Weiss;] |
| Wyeast #3333 German Wheat | Medium-low [70 - 76%] | High | "This yeast strain has a subtle flavor profile for a German wheat yeast with the classic Weisse profile. It has a fruity, sharp, tart crispness. [less banana than the #3068; very mild banana/bubblegum fruitiness and a nice, mellow clovey/phenolic nose; clove just slightly stronger than fruit, but both subdued; fermented nicely (with similar aroma/flavor) at 62° F and at 70° F (17° and 21° C)]; |
| Wyeast #3787 Trappist [a.k.a. Trappist High Gravity] | High [75 - 80%] | Medium | "A robust top-cropping yeast [this means that the yeast has a strong tendency to flocculate on top of the fermenting beer] with a phenolic character, this strain can tolerate alcohol levels of up to 12%. It is ideal for Biere de Garde. This strain ferments dry with a rich ester profile and malty palate." [produces a lot of banana ester when fermented above 65° F (18° C); if you use a big starter, this yeast will ferment well at 50° F (10° C) but at this temperature, you will eventually get a stuck fermentation (possibly even due to CO₂ levels) so you must warm up the fermenter & resuspend the yeast to get normal attenuation; lends a malty yet dry palate; my first choice for imitating beers like Westmalle Dubbel, Westmalle Tripel, or Rochefort 6;] |
| Wyeast #3942 Belgian Wheat | Medium [72 - 76%] | Medium | "An estery, low phenol-producing yeast, this train is from a small Belgian brewery. It lends apple and plum notes and a dry finish." |

| | | | |
|---|---|---|---|
| Wyeast #3944 Belgian White Beer | Medium [72 - 76%] | Medium | "This yeast has a tart, slightly phenolic character and is capable of producing distinctive Witbiers and Belgian ales. This strain is quite alcohol tolerant. Recommended fermentation temperature: 60 - 68° F (16 - 20° C)." |

**Yeast Culture Kit Company**

| | | | |
|---|---|---|---|
| A01 American Ale | – | | "Recommended Styles: Barleywine, Brown Ale, IPA, Bitter. Origin: California, USA. Clean, crisp and neutral. Easy to use." |
| A04 German Ale | – | | "Styles: Kölsch, Cream Ale. Origin: Germany. Description: Clean and fruity; produces exquisitely flavorful light-bodied ales." |
| A06 Stout Ale | – | | "Styles: Brown Ale, Porter, Stout, Imperial Stout. Origin: Ireland. Description: low attenuation; slight diacetyl." |
| A08 Barleywine Ale | – | | "Styles: Barleywine, Old Ale. Origin: Dorchester, England. Description: tends to leave a high residual sweetness." |
| A13 Irish Ale | – | | "Styles: Stout, Imperial Stout. Origin: Dublin, Ireland. Description: The Real Thing from Ireland. Nutty, woody and complex." |
| A15 English Ale | – | | "Styles: Brown Ale, English Bitter, Mild, IPA. Origin: Ireland. Description: Complex with strong yeast flavors. [this is the Ringwood strain; it requires very high levels of dissolved oxygen; it has a strong tendency towards diacetyl; it is a volcanic fermenter;]" |
| A16 Trappe Ale | – | | "Styles: Trappist Ales. Origin: Belgian Monastery. Description: Typical Trappist esters and aroma." [a good choice for emulating Chimay or Rochefort;] |
| A17 Pale Ale | – | | "Styles: Brown Ale, English Bitter, Mild, IPA. Origin: London, England. Description: Very smooth and mellow with a distinct yeast signature." [a good choice for emulating beers from Young's, Fuller's, or Samuel Smith's;] |
| YCKC A18 | – | | [a rather fruity yeast of English origin; a good choice for emulating beer from Thompsons, Smiles, or St. Austel;] |
| YCKC A19 | – | | [a good yeast for Witbiers, my recommendation for emulating beers such as Dentergems, Hoegaarden, or Brugs Tarwebier;] |

| Yeast | Attenuation | Flocculation | Characteristics and Notes |
|---|---|---|---|
| YCKC A20 | — | — | [a classic English ale yeast, full of fruit with hints of citrus, my first choice emulating any of the Fuller's or Young's ales;] |
| YCKC A21 | — | — | [another classic English ale yeast, this one is less fruity than the others, but no less English in character; good for emulating Worthington White Shield or Draught Bass;] |
| YCKC A25 | — | — | [good alcohol tolerance and an estery, slightly peppery profile; good for duplicating beers from Rochefort or Chimay;] |
| YCKC A26 | — | — | [spicy and slightly nutty with a restrained fruitiness, a good choice for emulating beers such as Kwak Pauwel or Gouden Carolus;] |
| YCKC A34 Scotch Ale | — | — | "Styles: Barleywine, Scottish Ale, Scottish Bitter, Strong Ale. Origin: Edinburgh, Scotland. Description: Clean, ferments well at cool temperatures." [good for emulating beers from McEwan's, Younger, or Caledonia;] |
| YCKC A35 Belgian Wit | — | — | "Styles: Wit. Origin: Central Belgium. Description: Spicy, slight phenolic character compliments orange and coriander." [another good Witbier yeast; good for imitating Hoegaarden, Dentergems, or Brugs Tarwebier;] |
| YCKC A36 Belgian Ale | — | — | "Styles: Belgian Ales, Dubbel, Tripel. Origin: Houffalize, Belgium. Description: Distinct yeast signature. Very fruity." [ferments clean and soft but with a distinctively Belgian character, a good choice for duplicating beers from d'Achouffe;] |
| YCKC A37 Altbier | — | — | "Styles: Alt. Origin: Bavaria, Germany. Description: This strain is used by many Alt breweries. It has a distinct profile." |
| YCKC A38 | — | — | [good alcohol tolerance; a good choice for strong blond Belgian ales such as Duvel, Lucifer, or Deugniet;] |
| YCKC A39 | — | — | [ferments soft and malty; good for emulating Flemish Brown Ales sauch as Liefmans, Felix, or Roman Dobbelen] |
| YCKC A41 | — | — | [crisp and tart; a good choice for imitating Belgian Witbiers such as Brugs Tarwebier, Hoegaarden Wit, or Honnels Wit;] |

|  | | |  |
|---|---|---|---|
| YCKC A42 | — | High | [a strong flocculator and may need to be roused just to finish it's job; responds well to aeration during fermentation which gives the finished beer a strong diacetyl character in the nose and palate; my first choice for imitating the ales of Samuel Smith's or other high-diacetyl beers;] |
| YCKC A43 | — | — | [ferments well even at cooler temperatures; a good choice for emulating Scottish ales such as those from Caledonian or McEwan;] |
| YCKC A44 | — | — | [another ale yeast that tolerates cooler temperatures well and is another good choice for brewing beers similar to those from Caledonian or McEwan;] |
| YCKC A48 | — | — | [very fruity, with a tendency to produce high alcohols; good alcohol tolerance; a good choice for beers such as Brigand or Kasteel Bier;] |
| YCKC A49 | — | — | [this is an Altbier yeast of unknown origin; the lab refers to this as "Alt #2";] |
| YCKC A50 Bavarian Weizen | — | — | "Styles: Weizen, Weizenbock. Origin: Bavaria, Germany. Description: Clove and banana esters blend well with the sweet fruitiness of wheat malt to produce a classic Weizen. Recommended fermentation temperatures: 64 - 66° F (18 - 19° C)." |
| YCKC A51 | — | — | [rumor has it that this is the NCYC 1187 yeast; it is a relatively slow fermenter and has relatively high dissolved oxygen needs, it is used by quite a few microbreweries and brewpubs;] |
| YCKC A53 | — | — | [lightly-fruity English ale yeast; good choice for Draught Bass or Worthington White Shield;] |
| YCKC A58 | — | — | [used by several American Microbreweries and Brewpubs; it produces a clean ale with medium fruitiness and is very well-behaved;] |
| YCKC A59 | — | — | [another English ale yeast with subdued fruitiness; a good choice for emulating Marston's Pedigree and Bitter or Draught Bass;] |
| YCKC A60 | — | — | [wonderfully complex and fruity English ale yeast; produces more diacetyl than most; a good choice for imitating Gale's or Shepherd Neame's ales;] |

| Yeast | Attenuation | Flocculation | Characteristics and Notes |
|---|---|---|---|
| YCKC A61 | – | – | [lends a rose-like note and seems to have a tendency to produce more higher alcohols at warmer temperatures than most yeasts; good for emulating Royal Oak or maybe even Thomas Hardy's Ale;] |
| YCKC A62 | – | – | [a lightly-fruity British yeast from England's West Country; a good strain to use for imitating beers from St. Austel, Smiles, or Thompson's;] |
| YCKC A64 | – | – | [another fruity and complex English ale yeast with a slight nutty character; a good choice for emulating Shepherd Neame's or Gale's ales;] |
| YCKC A65 | – | – | [not as attenuative as some of the other yeasts and lends a pleasant licorice note to the beer; it is of Welsh origin, so it would by my first choice for brewing Welsh ales such as Brains SA, Brains Dark, or Bullmastiff Brewery Bitter;] |
| YCKC A67 | – | – | [lends a slightly spicy note, so it would be a good choice for emulating beers such as Nounou or Gulden Draak;] |
| YCKC A68 | – | – | [decent alcohol tolerance; good for strong blonde Belgian ales such as Pirat or Duvel;] |
| YCKC A70 | – | – | [good alcohol tolerance; a good choice for strong blonde Belgian ales such as Lucifer, Duvel, or Pirat.] |
| YCKC A71 | – | – | [a good attenuator; a good choice for emulating beer such as Monseigneur or Cuvee Chateau de Flandres;] |
| YCKC A72 | – | – | [a rather natural yeast; reportedly comes from Belgium; good for the less-wild Belgian Ales such as De Koninck or Palm;] |
| YCKA A73 | – | – | [a good yeast for Dubbels or Tripels; a good choice for emulating beers such as Affligem or Grimbergen;] |
| YCKC A74 | – | – | [quite fruity with hints of plums; good for imitating beers such as the La Trappe or Rochefort Trappist Ales;] |

| | | |
|---|---|---|
| YCKC A75 | – | [very fruity, complex and tart; this yeast is said to come from a Saison brewery, thus it would be a good choice for emulating Saison Silly, Saison Regal or perhaps Saison Dupont;] |
| YCKC A76 | – | [another yeast from a Saison brewery; this yeast might be good fror brewing something resembling Saison Dupont, Saison Silly, or Saison Regal;] |
| YCKC A78 | – | [this is an interesting yeast with lots of fruity complexity; a good choice for attempts at duplicating De Dolle Brouwers' or Rodenbach's beers;] |
| YCKC A79 | – | [another Witbier yeast; a good choice for emulating Honnels Wit or Hoegaarden Wit;] |
| YCKC A85 | – | [a Bavarian Weizen yeast which gives a banana/clove/vanilla character to the beer; you can control the balance of banana and clove by varying the fermentation temperature – warmer gives more banana, colder gives more clove, this is the yeast you would use for emulating beers like Schneider Weisse, Schneider Aventinus, Paulaner Altbayerische Weissbier, Pschorr-Bräu Weizen or Pschorr-Bräu Dunkel Weiss; this yeast has an almost explosive fermentation – make sure you can handle lots of kräusen;] |
| YCKC A88 | – | [this yeast would be a good choice for imitating a beer such as Cervoise;] |
| YCKC A90 | – | [a strong producer of fruitiness with hints of Cognac in the flavor, this yeast will work even at cooler fermentation temperatures, although it will create a beer that is more nutty than fruity; reportedly from Burton-on-Trent; good for emulating beers from Burton Bridge Brewery or Marston's;] |
| YCKC A93 | – | [a yeast of Scottish origin;] |
| YCKC A94 | – | [another yeast of Scottish origin;] |
| YCKC A95 | – | [from a brewery in Suffolk county England, so I would guess that it might be a decent choice if you were trying to emulate beers from Eastern England;] |

| Yeast | Attenuation | Flocculation | Characteristics and Notes |
|---|---|---|---|
| YCKC A96 | – | – | [a very versatile strain, this yeast can be used for anything from an American Pale ale to an Imperial Stout; this yeast is reportedly used by a Midwestern microbrewery;] |
| YCKC A97 | – | – | [a fruity English ale yeast which can lend a bit of licorice aroma; good for emulating Courage Director's Bitter or perhaps Samuel Smith's beers;] |
| YCKC A107 | – | – | [a yeast that the lab calls "Belgian high temp" because it behaves quite well even at high fermentation temperatures;] |
| W06 Barleywine [Champagne Yeast] | – | – | "Styles: Barleywine, Mead. Origin: Montreal, Canada. Description: Extremely clean, malty and full-bodied. Ferments well down to 48° F (9° C)." [very good alcohol tolerance; some brewers use this yeast after their primary yeast poops out;] |
| **Yeast Lab** | | | |
| A01 Australian Ale | Medium | Medium | "This all-purpose strain produces a very complex, woody and flavorful beer. It is of Australian origin. Great for Brown Ales and Porters." |
| A02 American Ale | Medium | Low | "This clean strain produces a very fruity aroma with a soft and smooth flavor when fermented cool. This is an all-purpose ale yeast." |
| A03 London Ale | Medium | Medium | "Classic Pale Ale strain, very dry. A powdery yeast with a hint of diacetyl and rich minerally profile, crisp and clean." |
| A04 British Ale | Medium | Medium | "This strain produces a great light-bodied ale, excellent for pale Ales and Brown Ales, with a complex estery flavor. Ferments dry with a sharp finish." [quite fruity with nice citrus and ripe fruit overtones;] |
| A05 Irish Ale | High | High | "This top-fermenting strain is ideal for Stouts and Porters. Slightly acidic, with a hint of butterscotch in the finish, soft and full-bodied." |
| A06 Düsseldorf Ale | Medium | High | "This German Altbier yeast strain finishes with full body, complex flavor and spicy sweetness." |
| A007 Canadian Ale | High | Medium | "This strain produces a light-bodied, clean and flavorful beer, very fruity when fermented cool. Good for light and cream ales." [nice grape esters make this a good choice for emulating alesa from Molson or Labatt's; fermentation temperatures over 70° F (21° C) tend to over-accentuate the grape esters;] |

| | | | |
|---|---|---|---|
| A08 Trappist Ale | High | High | "This is a typical Trappist strain, producing a malty flavor with a balance of fruity, phenolic overtones when fermented warm. This yeast is quite alcohol tolerant." |
| W 51 Bavarian Weizen | Medium | Moderate | "This strain produces a classic German-Style wheat beer, with moderately high, spicy phenolic overtones reminiscent of cloves." |

## LAGER YEASTS

| Yeast | Attenuation | Flocculation | Characteristics and Notes |
|---|---|---|---|
| **Advanced Brewers Scientific** | | | |
| ABS004 Swedish Lager | – | – | "This is a Swedish lager yeast for Nordic-style lager beers." |
| ABS005 Czech Lager | – | – | "Not one of the many 'pilsner' strains, this yeast is from the oldest brewery in Prague." |
| **Brewers Resource** | | | |
| BrewTek CL-600 Original Pilsner | Low-medium | Medium | "This yeast leaves a full-bodied lager with a sweet, mildly under-attenuated finish and subdued diacetyl character. Use this distinct, flavorful strain in classic Czechoslovakian Pilsners or any lager in which you would like to emphaize a big, malty palate." |
| BrewTek CL-620 American Microbrewery | Medium | Medium | "This is a smooth yeast with slightly fruity character when fresh which lagers into a smooth, clean- tasting beer. Use this strain for your lightest, cleanest lagers or those in which you want unobtrusive yeast character." |
| BrewTek CL-630 American Microbrewery Lager | Medium | Medium | "A strong fermenter, this yeast leaves a clean, full-flavored, malty finish despite its strong attenuation. This is a very old strain, commonly used by pre-prohibition American breweries.Being quite versatile, use CL-630 in all lager styles in which you wish to get a clean, full flavor." |
| BrewTek CL-650 Old Bavarian Lager | Medium-high | Medium | "Well-rounded and malty with a subtle ester complex and citrus undertones, this distinct, Southern German yeast strain is great for full-flavored, classic German lagers such as Bock, Dunkel and Helles styles." |

| Yeast | Attenuation | Flocculation | Characteristics and Notes |
|---|---|---|---|
| BrewTek CL-660 Northern German Lager | Medium | Medium | "This yeast exhibits the classic clean, crisp, traditional Northern German Lager character. Used in German Pilsners, Mexican and Canadian lagers, this strong-fermenting, forgiving lager yeast is an excellent strain for everything from general-purpose lagers to the finest European beers." |
| BrewTek CL-670 Swiss Lager | Medium | Medium | "A unique strain that has both a clean, crisp lager flavor and a soft, smooth maltiness, this yeast is perfect for European Pilsners. Like our CL-660 strain, this is an excellent all-purpose lager yeast for those wanting a fuller, rounder palate." |
| BrewTek CL-680 East European Lager | Medium | Medium | "From a very old European brewery, CL-680 imparts a smooth, rich, almost creamy character, emphasizing a big malt flavor and clean finish. This is our choice when brewing lagers in which the malt character should be full and smooth, such as Märzens, Oktoberfests and Dunkels." |
| BrewTek CL-690 California Gold | Medium-high | Medium | "Used to recreate 'California Common beers' this yeast leaves a slightly estery, well attenuated finish. The character of this yeast is quite distinct, try it in American or Robust Porters for a new and unique flavor profile." [personally, I feel that American Porters are not a distinct style;] |
| **Head Start Brewing Cultures** | | | |
| Head Start #200. Americana | – | Medium-high | "Origin: US. This strain ferments clean and is a good attenuator. It is very characteristic for this style of beer." |
| Head Start #201. American Pils | – | Medium | "Origin: US. This is a Pilsner lager strain used by a large American brewery." |
| Head Start #220. Ur-Pils | – | – | "Origin: Czech Republic. This is a famous Pils pure culture strain obtained in the Czech Republic. It ferments malty and clean. Optimum fermentation temperature: 50° F [10° C]." |
| Head Start #221. Präger | – | Medium | "Origin: Czech Republic. This is an old classic from Prague (a mixed culture containing two known strains). Expect minor sulfury flavors early in fermentation." |

| | | | |
|---|---|---|---|
| Head Start #230. California Common | – | Medium-High | "Origin: US. Warm-temperature lager strain. Optimum fermentation temperature: 50° F [10° C]. However, this yeast will ferment well up to 60° F [16° C] while still producing classic lager flavors." [I've used this yeast as warm as 65° F (18° C) with minimal fruitiness;] |
| Head Start #231. Dampfbier | – | | "Origin: Germany. This is a German steam beer yeast. Slightly fruity, but otherwise similar to #230." |
| Head Start #240. Continental Dry | – | Low-Medium | "Origin: Denmark. This is a Danish lager strain and it ferments dry and crisp." |
| Head Start #241. Viking | – | Medium | "Origin: Sweden. This strain is used by one of Sweden's largest breweries to make a Pils. It is a clean fermenter." |
| Head Start #250. Festbier | – | Low-Medium | "Origin: Germany. This yeast results in a rich and full-bodied beer." |
| Head Start #251. Weisenfest | – | Medium | "Origin: Germany. This strain from Munich makes a typical festbier. It can also be used for any lager style." |
| Head Start #260. Strassbourger | – | Medium | "Origin: France. This is a German-style lager yeast used in the Strassbourg region of France. It is slightly sulfury." |
| Head Start #261. Continental Lager | – | Medium | "Origin: France. This yeast is used in several small French lager breweries." |
| Head Start #270. Leitpold | – | Medium | "Origin: Germany. This is a classic Munich lager yeast that ferments clean. Optimal temperatures: 8° C [46° F] for fermentation and 4° C [40° F] for lagering." |
| Head Start #271. Kellerbier/ Rauchbier | – | High | "Origin: Bamberg, Germany. Used in this brewery's Kellerbier (an unfiltered hoppy lager) and also in their world-renown Rauchbier, this yeast is an exceptional flocculator." |
| Head Start #272. Nürnburger | – | Medium | "Origin: Germany. This is a German Pils and Kellerbier strain used by one of Nuremberg's largest breweries." |
| Head Start #280. Hansen | – | Medium | "Origin: Germany. This is an alcohol-tolerant lager strain. It withstands up to 13% alcohol." |

| Yeast | Attenuation | Flocculation | Characteristics and Notes |
|---|---|---|---|
| **Saccharomyces Supply Company** [Note that these yeasts are also known as "RTP" or "Ready To Pitch" yeasts. They are provided at volumes that do not require you to make a starter, however, freshness is therefore a much more important factor with these yeasts.] | | | |
| RTP German Lager | Medium (72 - 76%) | Medium | "Used by many German breweries and American Brewpubs. It gives a beer that is full-bodied and rich with a malty sweetness." [this is probably the most popular lager yeast used in Germany and among American Microbreweries;] |
| RTP Czech Pilsner Lager | Medium-low (70 - 75%) | Medium-high | "A classic Pilsner yeast, which produces malty and clean lagers. Moderate sulfur produced early in the fermentation." [in my experience, this yeast produces lots of sulfur aroma throughout fermentation, but this dissipates during lagering; a good choice for any of the Czech Pilsners such as Pilsner Urquell or Budweiser Budvar;]. |
| **Wyeast Laboratories** [Note: the names of yeasts have been known to change, but numbers have always been constant] | | | |
| Wyeast #2007 Pilsen Lager | Medium-low (70 - 75%) | Medium | "A classic American pilsner strain, it is sturdy and simple to use. It ferments dry and crisp. Recommended fermentation temperature: 48 - 56° F [9 - 13° C]." [tends to create more acetaldehyde than most; the recommended strain for emulating beers such as Budweiser or Bud Light;] |
| Wyeast #2035 American Lager | Medium (73 - 77%) | Medium | "Not a Pilsner strain, this yeast produces a bold, complex and woody beer with a slight diacetyl note. Recommended fermentation temperature: 48 - 58° F [9 - 14° C]." [this strain doesn't come from St. Louis (as many believe) but rather from a brewery much further north;] |
| Wyeast #2042 Danish Lager | Medium (73 - 77%) | Low | "This yeast produces beer that is rich, crisp and dry. Its soft profile accentuates hop characteristics. Recommended fermentation temperature: 46 - 56° F [8 - 13° C]." |
| Wyeast #2112 California Lager | Low (67 - 71%) | High | "This yeast is particularly well-suited for producing 19th-century-style West Coast beers. It retains lager characteristics at temperatures up to 65° F [18° C] and produces malty, brilliantly-clear beers." [a good yeast for California Common beers or for making lagers when you don't have the facilities to maintain lager temperatures; rumor has it that this yeast was used to make Anchor Porter several years ago, but now they use the Liberty Ale yeast for their Porter also;] |

| Yeast | Attenuation | Flocculation | Description |
|---|---|---|---|
| Wyeast #2124 Bohemian Lager | Low (69 - 73%) | Medium | "This is a Pilsner yeast From Weihenstephan. It ferments clean and malty and leaves a lot of residual sugars in higher-gravity beers. Recommended fermentation temperature: 46 - 54° F [8 - 12° C]." [this is reportedly the Weihenstephan 34/70 yeast; lightly sulfury nose during fermentation – this will fade away with aging; this strain produces relatively low levels of diacetyl; very clean and malty if fermented at around 50° F [10° C], but above 54° F [12° C] it gets quite fruity; it produces a nice mixed-fruit aroma/flavor when fermented at 70° F [22° C] – although an ale made with this yeast would still have to be lagered to eliminate the sulfury character; note that this yeast has been known to have difficulty fermenting in tall, narrow fermenters;] |
| Wyeast #2178 Wyeast Lager Blend | Medium-low (71 - 75%) | Good | "These packages contain a higher volume of yeast (2.75 fl. oz. - 80 ml) for larger batches. The blends have been selected to insure a quick start, good flavor and good flocculation. Recommended fermentation temperature: 46 - 56° F [8 -13° C]." [despite the larger volume, a starter is still highly recommended;] |
| Wyeast #2206 Bavarian Lager | Medium (73 - 77%) | Medium | "Used by many German breweries, this yeast produces beers that are rich, full-bodied and malty. Recommended fermentation temperature: 48 - 58° F [9 - 14° C]." [your safest bet for virtually any German lager style; this strain produces relatively low levels of diacetyl; it does tend to be a little fruity in high gravity worts – pitching a very large starter a will help reduce the fruitiness;] |
| Wyeast #2247 Danish Lager II | Medium (73 - 77%) | Low | "This yeast has a clean, dry flavor profile and is often used in aggressively-hopped Pilsners. It has a clean, very mild flavor, slight sulfur production during fermentation and a dry finish. Recommended fermentation temperature: 46 - 56° F [8 - 13° C]." |
| Wyeast #2272 North American Lager | Medium-low (70 - 76%) | High | "A traditional culture of North American Lagers (US and Canadian) and light Pilsners, this strain flocculates well. This yeast gives a malty finish. Recommended fermentation temperature: 48 - 56° F [9 - 13° C]." |
| Wyeast #2278 Czech Pils | Medium-low (70 - 74%) | Medium-high | "A classic Pilsner strain from the home of Pilsners which gives a dry but malty finish. It is the perfect choice for Pilsners and Bock beers. The sulfur aroma produced during fermentation dissipates with conditioning. Recommended fermentation temperature: 46 - 54° F [8 - 12° C]." |

| Yeast | Attenuation | Flocculation | Characteristics and Notes |
|---|---|---|---|
| Wyeast #2308 Munich Lager | Medium (73 - 77%) | Medium | "This is a demanding strain, but is capable of producing some of the finest lagers made. It produces a beer that is very smooth, well-rounded and full-bodied. Recommended fermentation temperature: 48 - 56° F [9 - 13° C]." [does indeed make for a very smooth beer and I've used it down to 45° F (7° C) with no problems; it does produce some sulfury aromas that can take some lagering to disappear; this is another yeast that has a tendency to be fruity in high-gravity worts – a very large starter will help reduce this fruitiness; tends to make more diacetyl than most of the other strains and could therefore benefit more from a diacetyl rest;] |
| **Yeast Culture Kit Company** | | | |
| L02 Bavarian Lager | Medium | Medium | "Use this classic strain for medium-bodied lagers and Bocks, as well as Vienna and Märzen styles. It will produce a beer that is rich in flavor with a clean, malty sweetness. Recommended fermentation temperature: 50 - 52° F [10 - 11° C]." |
| L05 Munich Lager | Medium | Medium | "This is a German brewing strain for medium-bodied lagers and Bocks. Its flavor profile is subtle yet complex, smooth and soft. It will produce a hint of sulfur during fermentation which will fade during lagering. Recommended fermentation temperature: 48 - 50° F [9 - 10° C]." |
| L09 German Lager | High | Medium | "Styles: German lagers, including Bocks, most other lager styles. Origin: Bavaria, Germany. This classic strain produces a light lager in both flavor and body, fermenting dry and clean. It is a common strain used in many German lager breweries. Recommended fermentation temperature: 48 - 52° F [9 - 11° C]." |
| L17 Pilsen Lager | – | – | "Styles: Bohemian Pilsner, American lagers. Origin: Pilsen. Description: This yeast produces beers that are extremely clean, malty and full-bodied. It ferments well down to 48° F [9° C]. Recomended fermentation temp: 48 - 50° F [9 - 10° C]." |

| | | | |
|---|---|---|---|
| L20 St. Louis Lager | High | Medium | "This strain produces a round, very crisp and clean fruity-flavored beer with medium body. It is recommended for American-style lagers. Recommended fermentation temperature: 50 - 52° F [10 - 11° C]." |
| L21 California Lager | Medium | High | "A California Common beer strain, this yeast produces a beer that is malty with a sweet, woody flavor and subtle fruitiness. Recommended fermentation temperature: 64 - 65° F [18° C]." |
| **Yeast Lab** | | | |
| L31 Pilsner Lager | High | Medium | "This classic strain produces a light lager in both flavor and body, fermenting dry and clean." |
| L32 Bavarian Lager | Medium | Medium | "Use this classic strain for medium-bodied lagers and Bocks, as well as Vienna and Märzen styles. It will produce a beer that is rich in flavor with a clean malty sweetness." |
| L33 Munich Lager | Medium | Medium | "This is a Wissenschaftliche strain for medium-bodied lagers and Bocks. It gives subtle but complex flavors, smooth and soft, with a hint of sulfur when fresh." |
| L34 St. Louis Lager | High | Medium | "This strain produces a round, very crisp and clean fruity flavor. It is a good choice for American-style lagers." |
| L35 California Lager | Medium | High | "A California Common beer strain, this yeast produces a beer that is malty with sweet woody flavor and subtle fruitiness [even at warmer fermentation temperatures]." |

## OTHER YEASTS AND BACTERIAL CULTURES

| Yeast | Attenuation | Flocculation | Characteristics and Notes |
|---|---|---|---|
| **Brewers Resource** | | | |
| BrewTek CL-5200 Brettanomyces lambicus & BrewTek CL-5600 Pediococcus damnosus | — | — | "The unique flavor profile associated with Belgium's Lambic beers is in large measure due to the unusual fermentation they undergo. In addition to *S. cerevisiae* [common ale yeast], other organisms are involved. The greatest contributors are *Brettanomyces lambicus* [or *Brettanomyces bruxellensis*] and *Pediococcus damnosus* Brettanomyces yeasts contribute a unique and complex flavor, often described as 'horsey' or 'old leather.' This flavor seems to be encouraged by the presence of wood. [I believe it is the slight porosity of wooden casks that encourages the development of *Brettanomyces* yeast contributions, not simply contact.] *Pediococcus damnosus* bacteria is the primary acid producer in Lambic fermentations." [although available separately, it is recommended that you use them together; both cultures can take six or eight months till their contributions reach proper levels in the beer; in a private communication, Jeff Mellem of Brewer's Resource said their research indicates that better sourness is achieved from the *Pediococcus* when added 2 to 3 weeks ahead of the *Brettanomyces*;] |
| **Head Start Brewing Cultures** | | | |
| Head Start #310 Berliner Weisse-B | — | — | "Origin: Germany. This is a Berliner ale strain (AB310) and a Lactobacillus bacteria (AB335). Includes a recipe for Berliner Kindl-style Weiss. Allow at least several weeks for acidity to develop. Split fermentations are recommended. Recipe and instructions provided." |
| Head Start #310B Berliner Weisse-B with Lacto-Capsules | — | — | "Origin: Germany. This is the same as #310 except that Lacto-Capsules are substituted for the *Lactobacillus* liquid culture. Lacto-Capsules require no starter and are very easy to use." |
| Head Start #311 Berliner Weiss-S | — | — | "Origin: Germany. This is a Berliner ale strain (AB310) along with AB333 *Lactobacillus* culture and AB341 *Brettanomyces bruxellensis*. Includes a recipe and instructions for a Schultheiss-style Weiss. Allow at least 3 weeks for acidity to develop and 3 months for *Brettanomyces* character to appear." |

| | | |
|---|---|---|
| Head Start #320<br>Flanders Red | – | "Origin: Belgium. This is a mixture of yeasts, some wild, (AB320) and *Lactobacillus flanderii* (AB333). It will produce the lactic and acetic tartness and unusual flavors characteristic of Flanders' styles. It's 'slow good.' Expect fermentation to last several weeks. Recipes and instructions are included." |
| Head Start #321<br>Flanders Brown | – | "Origin: Belgium. A clean, fruity yeast (AB321) and *Lactobacillus flanderii* (AB333), it will produce the lactic and acetic tartness and unusual flavors characteristic of Flanders' styles. It's 'slow good.' Expect fermentation to last several weeks. Recipes and instructions included." |
| Head Start #330<br>Lactobacillus<br>delbrückii | – | "Origin: US. This is a very fastidious bacterial culture [i.e. one that has very demanding nutritional needs], a slow acid producer and is homofermentative [i.e. it creates only one product – in this case lactic acid]. It ferments glucose and maltose, but not dextrin. Optimum fermentation is $37^\circ$ C [$99^\circ$ F] and it does not grow below $25^\circ$ C [$77^\circ$ F]. Use this culture to sour authentic Berliner Weiss beers." |
| Head Start #331<br>Pediococcus<br>damnosus<br>(a.k.a.<br>P. cerevisiae) | – | "Origin: US. This bacterial culture is a slow acid producer, is homofermentative and produces diacetyl. It ferments glucose and maltose quickly and dextrins only very slowly. Optimum fermentation temperature is $25^\circ$ C [$77^\circ$ F] and will not grow above $37^\circ$ C [$99^\circ$ F]. Use this culture to sour Lambics or in sour beers where some diacetyl is desired." |
| Head Start #333<br>Lactobacillus<br>"flanderii" | – | "Origin: the Flanders region of Belgium. This bacterial culture was isolated from AB320. It is a very hardy culture and will quickly sour beer or wort in 3 weeks. This culture is heterofermentative, producing lactic acid, acetic acid, ethanol and $CO_2$ from glucose and maltose, but not dextrin. It tolerates hop alpha acids. Optimum fermentation temperature: 25 - $37^\circ$ C [77 - $99^\circ$ F]. Use this culture to sour Lambics, Flanders [Brown Ales] or Berliner Schultheiss-style beers or in sour beers where both lactic and acetic acids are desired." |

| Yeast | Attenuation | Flocculation | Characteristics and Notes |
|---|---|---|---|
| Head Start #334 Lactobacillus delbrückii spp. lactis | — | — | "Origin: US. This bacterial culture is for experienced brewers. It is homofermentative and can be used for sour beers or for sour mashing. Optimum fermentation temperature: 37° C [99° F]. This bacteria will not grow below 25° C [77° F]." |
| Head Start #335 Lactobacillus mixed culture | — | — | "Origin: US. This is the same culture as the Lacto-Capsules. Optimum fermentation temperature: 25 - 37° C [77 - 99° F]. It is homofermentative. This culture ferments glucose, maltose, dextrins and lactose. Can be used post-fermentation to adjust lactic acid content with the use of lactose. Use this culture to sour wit beers or Berliner Kindl style Weisse. Do not use this culture in sour beers where lactose will be used to sweeten the beer." |
| Head Start #340 Brettanomyces lambicus | — | — | "Origin: US. This is the 'country' strain found more commonly in Lambic beers outside of Bruxelles." |
| Head Start #341 Brettanomyces bruxellensis | — | — | "Origin: US. This is the 'city' strain found originally in Lambic beers made in Bruxelles." |
| Head Start #342 Kloeckera apiculata | | | "Origin: US. This culture rapidly ferments glucose to acetic and lactic acids and produces a protease considered desirable in Lambic beers." |
| Head Start #343 Brettanomyces anomala | | | "Origin: Netherlands. Isolated from Lambic beer, it is another 'Brett' in the strain arsenal for Lambics." |
| Head Start #344 Candida lambicus | | | "Origin: US. Isolated from Lambic beer, this culture is an oxidative yeast that forms a protective pellicle on the surface of lambic beers during fermentation. It also contributes slightly to ester formation." |
| Head Start #350 Brettanomyces bruxellensis | | | "Origin: Great Britain. This is a cask conditioning strain isolated from English Ale in the early 1900's. ["bruxellensis" is probably a misnomer – perhaps it should be called something like "britannicus?"] |

|  | |  |
|---|---|---|
| Head Start #351 Brettanomyces dublinesis (anomala) | | "Origin: Ireland. This is a cask conditioning strain isolated from Dublin Stout in the late 1800's. This strain is very filamentous, growing like rubber on agar." |
| Head Start #372 Sour-Wit | | "Origin: Belgium. This is Wit yeast (AB370) and Lacto-Capsules for acidification. Instructions included." |
| Head Start #400 Saccharomyces diastaticus | | "Isolated from Lambic beer, this is a super-attenuative yeast. It will create strong phenolics and a pellicle. It is recommended only for experienced brewers." |
| **Wyeast Laboratories** | | |
| Wyeast #3278B Belgian Lambic Blend | Variable / Low-medium | "Belgian Lambic-style yeast blend with lactic bacteria. It lends a rich earthy aroma and acidic finish. Suitable for Gueuze, Fruit Lambics and Faro." [previously, Wyeast #3278 contained only *Brettanomyces* but under the new number designation, #3278B, this is a blend of a *Saccharomyces* and *Brettanomyces* yeasts along with a lactic bacteria; in my experience, it produces an extremely fruity beer at first, but then, over the course of six or nine months, develops some of the classic horsey aromas associated with Lambic/Lambiek beers;] |
| **Yeast Culture Kit Company** | | |
| M 3220 Brettanomyces | | [this yeast needs to be used along with (at the least) a strain of *Saccharomyces* and a lactic bacteria to attempt to make something similar to Belgian Lambic/Lambiek beers;] |
| M3200 Pediococcus | | [a lactic bacteria which can be used along with M3220 and a *Saccharomyces* yeast to make something similar to Belgian Lambic/Lambiek beer;] |

# REFERENCES

1. deLange, A. J., "Understanding pH and Its Application in Small-Scale Brewing - Part II: Measurement Techniques," *Brewing Techniques*, 5 (1), 44-57 (Jan/Feb 1997).

2. Daniels, R. and S. Hamburg, "Scroll Through Brewing Software," *Zymurgy*, 17 (1), 46-50 (Spring 1994).

3. Hough, J. S., D. E. Briggs, R. Stevens, and T.W. Young, *Malting and Brewing Science*, Vol. 1 (Chapman and Hall, London, 1982), 249.

4. Donaghue, J., " Testing Your Metal - Is Aluminum Hazardous to Your Beer?," *Brewing Techniques*, 3 (1), 62-65 (Jan/Feb 1995).

5. Hitchcock, E., "Planispiral Wort Chiller," *Brewing Techniques,* 2 (3), 9 (May/Jun 1994).

6. Schmidling, J., Jack Schmidling Productions, personal communication, January 1993.

7. Davison, D., Davison Manufacturing Company, Greenfield, Wisconsin, personal communication, January 1996.

8. Lemon, J., Lemon Creek Winery, Berrien Springs, Michigan, personal communication, September 1996.

9. Fix, G. J., "Science in the Service of the Brewer's Art," presented at the American Homebrewers Association Conference, Denver, Colorado, June 1994.

10. Fix, G. J., *Principles of Brewing Science* (Brewers Publications, Boulder, 1989), 142.

11. DeClerck, J., *A Textbook of Brewing,* Vol. 1 (Chapman and Hall, London, 1957), 305.

12. Hough, J. S., D. E. Briggs, R. Stevens, and T.W. Young, *Malting and Brewing Science*, Vol. 2 (Chapman and Hall, London, 1982), 514.

13. DeClerck, J., *A Textbook of Brewing*, Vol. 1 (Chapman and Hall, London, 1957), 333.

14. Hough, J. S., D. E. Briggs, R. Stevens, and T.W. Young, *Malting and Brewing Science*, Vol. 2 (Chapman and Hall, London, 1982), 525.

15. Aquilla, T., Homebrew Digest #2030 post.

16. Noonan, G., *Scotch Ale* (Brewers Publications, Boulder, Colorado, 1993), 95.

17. DeClerck, J., *A Textbook of Brewing*, Vol. 1 (Chapman and Hall, London, 1957), 395.

18. Saltukoglu, A. and J.C. Slaughter, "The Effect of Magnesium and Calcium on Yeast," *Journal of the Institute of Brewing*, 89, (1983).

19. Frane, J., personal communication, February 1995.

20. Hough, J. S., D. E. Briggs, R. Stevens, and T.W. Young, *Malting and Brewing Science*, Vol. 2 (Chapman and Hall, London, 1982), 698.

21. DeClerck, J., A *Textbook of Brewing*, Vol. 1 (Chapman and Hall, London, 1957), 432.

22. Hough, J. S., *The Biotechnology of Malting and Brewing*, (Cambridge University Press, Cambridge, 1985), 136.

23. Foster, T., "Clear Beer Please," *Beer and Brewing Vol. 9* (Brewers Publications, Boulder, Colorado, 1989), 60.

24. Stroud, S., Homebrew Digest #2123 post.

25. Hough, J. S., D. E. Briggs, R. Stevens, and T.W. Young, *Malting and Brewing Science*, Vol. 2 (Chapman and Hall, London, 1982), 458-461.

26. Fix, G. J., DME Brewing Services, Arlington, Texas, personal communication, July 1993.

27. Papazian, C., *The New Complete Joy of Homebrewing* (Avon Books, New York, 1991), 103.

28. Foster, T., "Clear Beer Please," *Beer and Brewing Vol. 9* (Brewers Publications, Boulder, Colorado, 1989), 57-58.

29. Foley, Tim., J.E. Siebel and Sons, Chicago, Illinois, personal communication, January 1996.

30. Miller, D. G., *The Complete Handbook of Home Brewing* (Storey Communications, Pownal, Vermont, 1988), 193.

31. Papazian, C., T*he New Complete Joy of Homebrewing* (Avon Books, New York, 1991), 103-104.

32. Hough, J. S., D. E. Briggs, R. Stevens, and T.W. Young, *Malting and Brewing Science*, Vol. 2 (Chapman and Hall, London, 1982), 832.

33. Korzonas, A. R., "When Fermentation Rears Its Dirty Head," *Brewing Techniques*, 4 (3), 50-54, (May/Jun 1996).

34.  Fix, G. J., *Analysis of Brewing Techniques* (publication pending by Brewers Publications, Boulder, Colorado, 1997).

35.  Fix, G. J. and L. Fix, *Vienna, Märzen, Oktoberfest* (Brewers Publications, Boulder, Colorado, 1991), 71-72.

36.  Nay, E.V., Brewer's Digest, 29 (5), 51, (1954).

37.  Hough, J. S., D. E. Briggs, R. Stevens, and T.W. Young, *Malting and Brewing Science*, Vol. 2 (Chapman and Hall, London, 1982), 635.

38.  Baker, C. D. and S. Morton, *Journal of the Institute of Brewing*, 83, 348, (1977).

39.  DeClerck, J., *A Textbook of Brewing*, Vol. 1 (Chapman and Hall, London, 1957), 334-339.

40.  Hough, J. S., D. E. Briggs, R. Stevens, and T.W. Young, *Malting and Brewing Science*, Vol. 2 (Chapman and Hall, London, 1982), 523-524.

41.  Knull, G. W., "Trouble With Trubless Fermentations," *Brewing Techniques*, 4 (5), 14-19, (Sept/Oct 1996).

42.  Noonan, G., *Brewing Lager Beer*, (Brewers Publications, Boulder, Colorado, 1986), 70.

43.  Hough, J. S., D. E. Briggs, R. Stevens, and T.W. Young, *Malting and Brewing Science*, Vol. 1 (Chapman and Hall, London, 1982), 139.

44.  Daniels, R., "A Cereal Called Rye," *Zymurgy*, 17 (4), 93, (Special Issue 1994).

45.  Hough, J. S., D. E. Briggs, R. Stevens, and T.W. Young, *Malting and Brewing Science*, Vol. 1 (Chapman and Hall, London, 1982), 232-235.

46.  Winship, K., "Hops Through the Years," *Zymurgy*, 13 (4), 9-11 (Special Issue 1990).

47.  Preis, F. and W. Mitter, "The re-discovery of first wort hopping," *Brauwelt International* (Brauwelt/Verlag, Nuremburg, Germany, 1995)  No. 4, 1995.

48.  Hough, J. S., D. E. Briggs, R. Stevens, and T.W. Young, *Malting and Brewing Science*, Vol. 2 (Chapman and Hall, London, 1982), 404.

49.  Haunold, A., Hop Researcher, U.S. Department of Agriculture-Agricultural Research Service, Corvallis, Oregon, personal communication, June 1991.

50.  Olson, R., and G. Lewis, HopUnion, U.S.A., personal communication, December 1995.

51.  Rigby, F. H., "A Theory on Hop Flavor of Beer," *American Society of Brewing Chemists Proceedings*, 1972, 36-50.

52.  Hough, J. S., D. E. Briggs, R. Stevens, and T.W. Young, *Malting and Brewing Science*, Vol. 2 (Chapman and Hall, London, 1982), 401.

53.  Haley, J. and T. L. Peppard, "Differences in the Utilization of Hop Oils During the Production of Dry-Hopped and Late-Hopped Beers," *Journal of the Institute of Brewing*, 89, 1983.

54.  Jakob, S., Brewmaster, Forschungsbräurei, Perlach, Germany, personal communication, February 1997.

55.  Maier, J., Chairman - Scientific Commission, Hans-Pfulf Institute fur Hopfenforschung, Hüll B Wolnzach, Germany, personal communication, November 1996.

56.  Hough, J. S., *The Biotechnology of Malting and Brewing*, (Cambridge University Press, Cambridge, 1985), 47.

57.  Taylor, K., "The Effects of Brewing Water Ions," *The New Brewer*, (May/June 1984).

58.  Fix, G. J., *Principles of Brewing Science* (Brewers Publications, Boulder, 1989), 20.

59.  Moll, M., Chapter 1 in Pollock, J. R. A, ed., *Brewing Science*, Vol. 3 (Academic Press, London, 1987), 118.

60.  Moll, M., Chapter 1 in Pollock, J. R. A, ed., *Brewing Science*, Vol. 3 (Academic Press, London, 1987), 290.

61.  Briggs, D. E., Chapter 4 in Pollock, J. R. A, ed., *Brewing Science*, Vol. 3 (Academic Press, London, 1987), 481.

62.  Hough, J. S., The Biotechnology of *Malting and Brewing*, (Cambridge University Press, Cambridge, 1985), 44-45.

63.  Hough, J. S., The Biotechnology of *Malting and Brewing*, (Cambridge University Press, Cambridge, 1985), 48.

64.  Hough, J. S., D. E. Briggs, R. Stevens, and T.W. Young, *Malting and Brewing Science*, Vol. 2 (Chapman and Hall, London, 1982), 820-822.

65.  Hough, J. S., D. E. Briggs, R. Stevens, and T.W. Young, *Malting and Brewing Science*, Vol. 2 (Chapman and Hall, London, 1982), 779.

510

66. Miller, D. G., *Dave Miller's Homebrewing Guide*, (Storey Communications, Pownal, Vermont, 1995), 58.
67. Compton, J., Chapter XV in Broderick, H. M., ed., *The Practical Brewer* (Master Brewers Association of America, Madison, Wisconsin, 1977), 293.
68. Piesley, J.G. and T. Lom, Chapter XI in Broderick, H. M., ed., *The Practical Brewer* (Master Brewers Association of America, Madison, Wisconsin, 1977), 204
69. Hough, J. S., D. E. Briggs, R. Stevens, and T.W. Young, *Malting and Brewing Science*, Vol. 2 (Chapman and Hall, London, 1982), 648.
70. Hough, J. S., D. E. Briggs, R. Stevens, and T.W. Young, *Malting and Brewing Science*, Vol. 2 (Chapman and Hall, London, 1982), 657.
71. Mellem, J., "Fine Your Way to Clear Beer," *Zymurgy*, 18 (5), 46-50 (Winter 1995).
72. McConnell, D., The Yeast Culture Kit Company, personal communication, December 1996.
73. "The Secret of Success" Lallemand Website, http://www.lallemand.com/
74. Hough, J. S., D. E. Briggs, R. Stevens, and T.W. Young, *Malting and Brewing Science*, Vol. 2 (Chapman and Hall, London, 1982), 538-539.
75. Hough, J. S., D. E. Briggs, R. Stevens, and T.W. Young, *Malting and Brewing Science*, Vol. 2 (Chapman and Hall, London, 1982), 635.
76. Hough, J. S., D. E. Briggs, R. Stevens, and T.W. Young, *Malting and Brewing Science*, Vol. 2 (Chapman and Hall, London, 1982), 539.
77. Donhauser, H., Brewmaster, Paulaner Bräuhaus, Munich, Germany, personal communication, February 1997.
78. Rajotte, P., presentation at The Spirit of Belgium, Washington, D. C., November 1994.
79. Walsh, A., Homebrew Digest #2086 post on Ester Formation.
80. Nay, E.V., *Brewer's Digest*, 29 (5), (1954), 51.
81. "Jim's Fermentation Hints," Lallemand Website, http://www.lallemand.com/
82. Hough, J. S., D. E. Briggs, R. Stevens, and T.W. Young, *Malting and Brewing Science*, Vol. 2 (Chapman and Hall, London, 1982), 569-572.
83. Hough, J. S., D. E. Briggs, R. Stevens, and T.W. Young, *Malting and Brewing Science*, Vol. 2 (Chapman and Hall, London, 1982), 593-594.
84. Pickerell, A. T. W., A. Hwang, and B. C. Axcell, "Impact of Yeast-Handling Procedures on Beer Flavor Development during Fermentation," *ASBC Journal*, 49 (2), 1991, 87-92.
85. Fix, G. J., "Sulfur Flavors in Beer," *Zymurgy*, 15 (3), 40-44 (Fall 1992).
86. DeClerck, J., *A Textbook of Brewing*, Vol. 1 (Chapman and Hall, London, 1957), 50.
87. Peddie, H., "Ester formation in brewery fermentations," *Journal of the Institute of Brewing*, 96, 327-331, (1990).
88. Palmer, A., et al., "Ester control in high gravity brewing" *Journal of the Institute of Brewing*, 80, 447-454, (1974).
89. Anderson, R., et al., "Quantitative aspects of the control by oxygenation of acetate ester concentration in beer obtained from high-gravity wort," *Journal of the Institute of Brewing*, 81, 296-301, (1975).
90. Lentini, A., S. Takis, D. B. Hawthorne, and T. E. Kavanagh, "The Influence of Trub on Fermentation and Flavour Development," *Proceedings of the 23rd Convention - Australian Institute of Brewing*, 89-90 (1993).
91. Hough, J. S., D. E. Briggs, R. Stevens, and T.W. Young, *Malting and Brewing Science*, Vol. 2 (Chapman and Hall, London, 1982), 607-608.
92. Fabbri, B., personal communication, January 1996.
93. McGee, H., "The Curious Cook: More Kitchen Science and Lore," (MacMillan Publishing Co.).
94. Hough, J. S., D. E. Briggs, R. Stevens, and T.W. Young, *Malting and Brewing Science*, Vol. 1 (Chapman and Hall, London, 1982), 238-244.
95. Bradee, L. H., Chapter IV in Broderick, H. M., ed., *The Practical Brewer* (Master Brewers Association of America, Madison, Wisconsin, 1977), 50-53.
96. Jelenc, P., personal communication, November 1995.
97. *Zymurgy*, 17 (4), (Special Issue 1994).
98. Papazian, C., *The New Complete Joy of Homebrewing* (Avon Books, New York, 1991), 97.
99. Jarry, C., "Sprucing Up Your Homebrew," *Zymurgy*, 17 (4), 54-55, (Special Issue 1994).
100. Seitz, P., "Brewing Better Belgian Ales," *Zymurgy*, 18 (1), 50-57, (Spring 1995).

101. DeClerck, J., *A Textbook of Brewing*, Vol. 1 (Chapman and Hall, London, 1957), 334-339.
102. Hough, J. S., D. E. Briggs, R. Stevens, and T.W. Young, *Malting and Brewing Science*, Vol. 2 (Chapman and Hall, London, 1982), 458.
103. Fix, G. J., *Principles of Brewing Science* (Brewers Publications, Boulder, 1989), 121.
104. DeClerck, J., *A Textbook of Brewing*, Vol. 1 (Chapman and Hall, London, 1957), 303-307.
105. McFarlane, W. D. and M. B. Millingen, "The Aromatic Amino Acids in Alcoholic Fermentations," *American Society of Brewing Chemmists Proceedings*, 1964, pp.41-48.
106. Awford, B.B., *Technical Quarterly* (Master Brewers Association of America, Madison, Wisconsin, 1977),14, 129.
107. Hough, J. S., D. E. Briggs, R. Stevens, and T.W. Young, *Malting and Brewing Science*, Vol. 2 (Chapman and Hall, London, 1982), 667.
108. Hough, J. S., D. E. Briggs, R. Stevens, and T.W. Young, *Malting and Brewing Science*, Vol. 2 (Chapman and Hall, London, 1982), 752-754.
109. Coors, J. H., Chapter XII in Broderick, H. M., ed., *The Practical Brewer* (Master Brewers Association of America, Madison, Wisconsin, 1977), 243-246.
110. McNeill, R., Brewmaster/Owner, McNeill's Pub, Brattleboro, Vermont, personal communication, November 1995.
111. Fix, G. J., *Principles of Brewing Science* (Brewers Publications, Boulder, 1989), 73.
112. Fix, G. J., *Principles of Brewing Science* (Brewers Publications, Boulder, 1989), 190.
113. Hough, J. S., D. E. Briggs, R. Stevens, and T.W. Young, *Malting and Brewing Science*, Vol. 2 (Chapman and Hall, London, 1982), 595.
114. Hoffmann, S, *Brauwelt International* (Brauwelt/Verlag, Nuremburg, Germany, 1985).
115. Fix, G. J., "Diacetyl: Formation, Reduction, and Control," *Brewing Techniques*, 1 (2), 23, (Jul/Aug 1993).
116. Guinard, J. X., *Lambic*, (Brewers Publications, Boulder, Colorado, 1990), 86.
117. *Zymurgy*, 10 (4), (Special Issue 1987).
118. Fix, G. J., *Principles of Brewing Science* (Brewers Publications, Boulder, 1989), 142-147.
119. Hough, J. S., D. E. Briggs, R. Stevens, and T.W. Young, *Malting and Brewing Science*, Vol. 2 (Chapman and Hall, London, 1982), 611.
120. Donhauser, S. and D. Wagner, "Zymotechnical factors and beer quality", *Brauwelt*, (No. 1/96), p.18.
121. Dickenson, C. J., *Journal of the Institute of Brewing*, 86, 134, (1979).
122. Meilgaard, M., Chapter VI in Broderick, H. M., ed., *The Practical Brewer* (Master Brewers Association of America, Madison, Wisconsin, 1977), 113.
123. Lentini, A. et al., "The influence of trub on fermentation and flavour development." *Proceedings of the 23rd Convention - Australian Institute of Brewing*, 89-95, (1993).
124. Heresztyn, T., "Formation of substituted tetrahydropyridines by species of Brettanomyces and Lactobacillus isolated from mousy wines," *American Journal of Enology and Viticulture*, 37, 127-131, 1986.
125. Jelenc, P., private correspondence, July 1994.
126. Fix, G. J., *Principles of Brewing Science* (Brewers Publications, Boulder, 1989), 71.
127. Guinard, J. X., *Lambic*, (Brewers Publications, Boulder, Colorado, 1990), 50.
128. Thomlinson, T., "India Pale Ale, Part II," *Brewing Techniques*, 2 (3), 20, (May/Jun 1994).
129. Fix, G. J., *Principles of Brewing Science* (Brewers Publications, Boulder, 1989), 124.
130. Renner, J., " Tips and Gadgets: 30-cent Beer Engine," *Zymurgy*, 18 (3), 33-34, (Fall 1995).
131. Westemeier, E., personal communication, January 1996.
132. Fix, G. J. and L. Fix, *Vienna, Märzen, Oktoberfest* (Brewers Publications, Boulder, Colorado, 1991), 88-92.
133. Daniels, R., "Beer Color Demystified," *Brewing Techniques*, 3 (4,5,6), (Jul/Aug, Sep/Oct, Nov/Dec 1995).
134. Korzonas, A., "Reviews: Using Hops," *Zymurgy*, 18, (1), 89-90, (Spring 1995).
135. Rager, J., "Calculating Hop Bitterness in Beer," *Zymurgy*, 13 (4), 53-54, (Special Issue 1990).
136. Hall, R. D., "Factors Affecting the Efficient Utilization of Hops," *Proceedings of the European Brewing Convention, Copenhagen*, 1957, 314-326.
137. Liddil, J., Letter to the Editor response, *Zymurgy*, 19 (5), 9, (Winter 1996).
138. Raines, M., "Methods of Sanitization and Sterilization," *Brewing Techniques*, 1 (2), 30-33, (Jul/Aug 1993).

512

139. Haunold, A and G. B. Nickerson, "Factors Affecting Hop Production, Hop Quality, and Brewer Preference," *Brewing Techniques*, 1 (1), 21, (May/June 1993).
140. Haunold, A., Hop Researcher, U.S. Department of Agriculture-Agricultural Research Service, Corvallis, Oregon, personal communication, February 1997.
141. Fix, G. J., *Principles of Brewing Science* (Brewers Publications, Boulder, 1989), 137.
142. Engan, S., Chapter 3 in Pollock, J. R. A, ed., *Brewing Science*, Vol. 2 (Academic Press, London, 1981), 93-157.
143. Perpette, P., lecture at Spirit of Belgium 1994.
144. Gilliland, R. B., Chapter 1 in Pollock, J. R. A, ed., *Brewing Science*, Vol. 2 (Academic Press, London, 1981), 7-13.
145. Moll, M., Chapter 1 in Pollock, J. R. A, ed., *Brewing Science*, Vol. 3 (Academic Press, London, 1987), 61-62.
146. Moll, M., Chapter 1 in Pollock, J. R. A, ed., *Brewing Science*, Vol. 3 (Academic Press, London, 1987), 119-142, 175.
147. Moll, M., Chapter 1 in Pollock, J. R. A, ed., *Brewing Science*, Vol. 3 (Academic Press, London, 1987), 173-174.
148. Moll, M., Chapter 1 in Pollock, J. R. A, ed., *Brewing Science*, Vol. 3 (Academic Press, London, 1987), 182-186.
149. Moll, M., Chapter 1 in Pollock, J. R. A, ed., *Brewing Science*, Vol. 3 (Academic Press, London, 1987), 190-201.
150. Moll, M., Chapter 1 in Pollock, J. R. A, ed., *Brewing Science*, Vol. 3 (Academic Press, London, 1987), 283-287.
151. Hough, J. S., D. E. Briggs, R. Stevens, and T.W. Young, *Malting and Brewing Science,* Vol. 2 (Chapman and Hall, London, 1982), 531.
152. Van Valkenburg, D., Homebrew Digest V2 #024 post, and personal communication February 1997.
153. Potter S., Homebrew Digest V2 #024 post.
154. Stuecheli, J., personal communication, December 1996.
155. Fermcap™ product literature from J. E. Siebel Sons' Company.
156. Sovcik, P., Homebrew Digest #2329 post.
157. Hudston, H. R., Chapter VII in Broderick, H. M., ed., *The Practical Brewer* (Master Brewers Association of America, Madison, Wisconsin, 1977), 118-119.
158. Moll, M., Chapter 1 in Pollock, J. R. A, ed., *Brewing Science*, Vol. 3 (Academic Press, London, 1987), 48.
159. Hough, J. S., *The Biotechnology of Malting and Brewing*, (Cambridge University Press, Cambridge, 1985), 86.
160. deLange, A. J., Homebrew Digest V2 #016 post.
161. Fix, G. J., *Principles of Brewing Science* (Brewers Publications, Boulder, 1989), 18.
162. deLange, A. J., Homebrew Digest V2 #024 post.
163. Alexander, S., Homebrew Digest V2 #017 post
164. Cotterill, J., Homebrew Digest #1149 post.
165. Fix, G., Homebrew Digest #1598 post.
166. Franz, D., Librarian and Archivist, Anheuser-Busch, St. Louis, Missouri, personal communication, December 1995.
167. Draper, D. and M. Hibberd, "The Prime Directive," *Brewing Techniques*, 4 (4), 18, (Jul/Aug 1996).
168. Hough, J. S., D. E. Briggs, R. Stevens, and T.W. Young, *Malting and Brewing Science*, Vol. 1 (Chapman and Hall, London, 1982), 268.
169. Jelenc, P., personal communication, July 1994.
170. Ensminger, P. A., "Light and Beer" *Zymurgy*, 19 (3), 39-43, (Fall 1996).
171. Brockington, D., "West Coast Amber Ale," *Brewing Techniques*, 3 (6), 36-44, (Nov/Dec 1995).
172. Foster, T., *Porter*, (Brewers Publications, Boulder, Colorado, 1992), 40.
173. Lodahl, M., "Old, Strong, and Stock Ales," *Brewing Techniques*, 2 (5), 23, (Sep/Oct 1994).
174. Engan, S., Chapter 3 in Pollock, J. R. A, ed., *Brewing Science*, Vol. 2 (Academic Press, London, 1981), 135-143.
175. Hough, J. S., D. E. Briggs, R. Stevens, and T.W. Young, *Malting and Brewing Science*, Vol. 1 (Chapman and Hall, London, 1982), 208.

176. DeClerck, J., *A Textbook of Brewing*, Vol. 1 (Chapman and Hall, London, 1957), 79.
177. Foster, T., *Pale Ale*, (Brewers Publications, Boulder, Colorado, 1990), 59.
178. Bernstein, L. and I. C. Willox, Chapter II in Broderick, H. M., ed., *The Practical Brewer* (Master Brewers Association of America, Madison, Wisconsin, 1977), 18.
179. Bouckaert, P., *"Brewery Rodenbach: Brewing Sour Ales,"* posted to Lambic Digest #846.
180. Thomlinson, T., "India Pale Ale," *Brewing Techniques*, 2 (2), 26, (Mar/Apr 1994).
181. Noonan, G. J., *Scotch Ale*, (Brewers Publications, Boulder, Colorado, 1993), 92.
182. Hudston, H. R., Chapter VII in Broderick, H. M., ed., *The Practical Brewer* (Master Brewers Association of America, Madison, Wisconsin, 1977), 121.
183. Eckhardt, F., *The Essentials of Beer Style* (Fred Eckhardt Associates, Portland, Oregon, 1989), 90.
184. Jackson, M., *The New World Guide to Beer* (Running Press, Philadelphia, Pennsylvania, 1988), 66.
185. Jackson, M., *Beer Companion* (Running Press, Philadelphia, Pennsylvania, 1993), 172-173.
186. Foster, T., Porter, (Brewers Publications, Boulder, Colorado, 1992), 6-15.
187. Harrison, J., *Old British Beers and How to Make Them* (Durden Park Beer Circle, London, 1991), 8-9, 32-34, 45.
188. Jackson, M., *Beer Companion* (Running Press, Philadelphia, Pennsylvania, 1993), 25.
189. Fix, G. J., "Explorations in Pre-Prohibition American Lagers," *Brewing Techniques*, 2 (3), 28-31, (1994).
190. Renner, J., "Reviving the Classic American Pilsner," *Brewing Techniques*, 3 (5), 70-71, (Sep/Oct 1995).
191. Jankowski, B., "The Bushwick Pilsners," *Brewing Techniques*, 2 (1), 38-43, (Jan/Feb 1994).
192. Davison, D., "Eisbock: The Original Ice Beer," *Zymurgy*, 18 (3), 37-42 (Winter 1995).
193. Protz, R., "Straight up - it's real lager," *What's Brewing*, Feb 1997, 12.
194. Deschner, R., "The Regal Altbiers of Düsseldorf ," *Zymurgy*, 17 (5), 52-56 (Winter 1994).
195. Jackson, M., *Beer Companion* (Running Press, Philadelphia, Pennsylvania, 1993), 244-249.
196. Mosher, R., "Potions!," *Zymurgy*, 17 (4), 62-64 (Special Issue 1994).
197. Rahn, P. and C. Skypeck, "Traditional German Steinbier," *Zymurgy*, 17 (4), 16-18, (Special Issue 1994).
198. Toney, M., Brewmaster, Brimstone Brewing Company, Baltimore, Maryland, personal communication, January 1996.
199. Hilton, J. F. and G. H. Salazar, Hops - *The Essence of Beer and The U.S. Hop Market Report*, (S. S. Steiner, Inc., Milwaukee, Wisconsin, 1993).
200. Grant, B., "Hop Varieties and Qualities," *Zymurgy*, 13 (4), 24-26, (Special Issue 1990).
201. Olson, R. and G. Lewis, HopUnion, U.S.A., personal communications, January-June 1996.
202. Hough, J. S., D. E. Briggs, R. Stevens, and T.W. Young, *Malting and Brewing Science*, Vol. 2 (Chapman and Hall, London, 1982), 405-410.
203. Slosberg, P., "The Road to American Brown Ale," *Brewing Techniques*, 3 (3), 36, (May/Jun 1995).
204. Sierra Nevada Brewing Company informational brochure.
205. Protz, R., *Real Ale Almanac* (Neil Wilson Publishing Ltd., Glasgow, Scotland, 1993).
206. Hall, G., Brewmaster, Goose Island Brewing Company, Chicago, Illinois, personal communication, December 1993.
207. Van Valkenburg, D. "A Question of Pedigree - The Role of Genealogy in Hop Substitutions," *Brewing Techniques*, 3 (5), 56-57, (Sep/Oct 1995).
208. Marketing Literature titled *Hopfen aus Deutschland/Hops from Germany* (Centrale Marketinggesellschaft der deutschland Agrarwiertschaft mbH.).
209. Schnitzler, J., Brewmaster, Zum Uerige, Düsseldorf, Germany, personal communication, July 1995.
210. Van Valkenburg, D, personal communication, December 1996.
211. Blum, P., Archivist and Historian, The Stroh Brewery Company, personal communications, February-March 1997.
212. Hashimoto, N., Chapter 6 in Pollock, J. R. A, ed., *Brewing Science*, Vol. 2 (Academic Press, London, 1981), 347-405.
213. Fix, G. J., *Principles of Brewing Science* (Brewers Publications, Boulder, 1989), 45.
214. Meilgaard, M., Chapter VI in Broderick, H. M., ed., *The Practical Brewer* (Master Brewers Association of America, Madison, Wisconsin, 1977), 105-111.

514

215. Gilliland, R. B., Chapter 1 in Pollock, J. R. A, ed., *Brewing Science*, Vol. 2 (Academic Press, London, 1981), 36-37.
216. Mosher, R., "A Turn-of-the-Century British Account of Selected 19th Century Belgian Brewing Methods," *Brewing Techniques*, 2 (6) 46-49 (Nov/Dec 1994).
217. Jackson, M., *The New World Guide to Beer* (Running Press, Philadelphia, Pennsylvania, 1988), 66.
218. Aquilla, T., "The Biochemistry of Yeast: Debunking the Myth of Yeast Respiration and Putting Oxygen in Its Proper Place," *Brewing Techniques*, 5 (2) 50-57 (Mar/Apr 1997).
219. Barstow, O. D. L., Research Assistant to Michael Jackson, London, England, personal communication, April 1997.
220. Jankowski, B., "American Porters - Marching to Revolutionary Drummers," *Brewing Techniques*, 5 (2) 34-43 (May/Jun 1997).
221. "Of Brewing Butt-Beer, called Porter," *The London and Country Brewer* (1744, 5th edition) 221-222. *Courtesy of The Stroh Brewery Company.*
222. Maurice, A., "A Practical Treatise on Brewing the Various Sorts of Malt Liquors," (London, 1819, 6th edition) xix-xx. *Courtesy of The Stroh Brewery Company.*
223. *The London and Country Brewer* (1750 edition) 276. *Courtesy of The Stroh Brewery Company.*
224. Scheer, F. M., "Homebrew - What it really contains," *Zymurgy*, 13 (5) 30-34 (Winter 1990).
225. "Technotes: Crown Caps Absorb Oxygen," *Zymurgy*, 17 (5) 21 (Winter 1994).
226. Richman, D., *Bock*, (Brewers Publications, Boulder, Colorado, 1994), 30-34.
227. Charalambous, G., Chapter 4 in Pollock, J. R. A, ed., *Brewing Science*, Vol. 2 (Academic Press, London, 1981), 213.
228. Hough, J. S., D. E. Briggs, R. Stevens, and T.W. Young, *Malting and Brewing Science*, Vol. 2 (Chapman and Hall, London, 1982), 476-478.
229. Hough, J. S., D. E. Briggs, R. Stevens, and T.W. Young, *Malting and Brewing Science*, Vol. 1 (Chapman and Hall, London, 1982), 295.
230. Scandrett, C., Homebrew Digest #2401 post on "Phenols."
231. Sleigh, G., *The Brewer's Assistant* (Bath, 1815), 90-105. *Courtesy of The Stroh Brewery Company.*
232. deLange, A. J., Homebrew Digest #2403 post on Mash pH.
233. Fix, G. J., Homebrew Digest #1080 and #1513 posts.

# GLOSSARY

**AAUs**. Alpha acid units.

**ABV**. Alcohol by volume.

**ABW**. Alcohol by weight.

**Acetaldehyde**. An intermediate product that yeast make in the production of ethanol (ethyl alcohol). In the presence of oxygen, ethanol can be oxidized to acetaldehyde. It has a distinctive green-apple aroma.

**Acetic acid**. An acid very commonly encountered in spoiled beer. It is produced by a number of different aerobic bacteria (and by some yeasts in small amounts). It is commonly called vinegar.

**Acidification**. The addition of acids to steeping or mash water or to the mash directly to lower the pH, subsequently minimizing polyphenol extraction.

**Adjuncts**. Starch sources used in all-grain or partial-mash brewing that do not have their own enzymes and must be mashed with malt or another source of enzymes.

**Adsorption**. The process of one type of particle sticking to another type of particle. Typically, it refers to the adsorption of proteins or yeasts by finings.

**Aeration**. The addition of air to wort in an effort to dissolve oxygen into it.

**Aerobe**. An organism (usually bacteria, in a brewing sense) that requires air.

**Aerobic**. Requiring air.

**Airlock**. A device that allows fermentation gasses to escape, but prevents air from entering a container.

**Airspace**. More accurately called headspace (because it is often filled with carbon dioxide, not air), this is the non-liquid space at the top of a bottle, keg, or fermenter.

**Airstone**. A device for making very small bubbles. It is usually made of stainless steel, plastic, or (as you can guess from its name) porous stone. It increases the surface area of the gas (air, oxygen, or carbon dioxide, depending of the application) so that it dissolves into the liquid more efficiently.

**Alcohol** by volume. The percentage of alcohol as a ratio of alcohol volume to beer volume. Alcohol by volume is related to alcohol by weight by the following formula (because alcohol weighs less than beer: ABV=ABW*1.25.

**Alcohol by weight.** The percentage of alcohol as a ratio of alcohol weight to beer weight. Alcohol by weight is related to alcohol by volume by the following formula (because alcohol weighs less than beer: ABW=ABV/1.25.

**Alcohol tolerance.** A measure (usually very general, like "high" or "low") of how sensitive a yeast strain is to alcohol. A strain with a low alcohol tolerance will die or go dormant from lower alcohol levels than a strain with a high alcohol tolerance.

**Aldehydes.** Oxidized alcohols. They give stale aromas to beer their presence is always considered a fault. Acetaldehyde is the aldehyde of ethanol, but there are corresponding aldehydes for most alcohols.

**Ale.** Originally, an unhopped malt beverage, but in modern terms, it is beer that is fermented with ale yeast at warmer temperatures.

**Ale yeast.** Yeast that ferment sluggishly at colder temperatures if at all and are only able to partially ferment raffinose (they split a fructose molecule off the end, but leave the remaining melibiose).

**Alkalinity.** A measure of how the water will react to the addition of acid.

**All-grain.** A brewing method or beer made using no malt extract, only malts and adjuncts.

**All-malt.** Beer made only from malt (no adjuncts or refined sugars).

**Alpha acid unit.** The percentage of alpha acid of a particular hop sample multiplied by it's weight in ounces. Three ounces of 5% Alpha Acid hops is 15 Alpha Acid Units or AAUs. It was first proposed as a measure of bittering by Dave Line. They are equivalent to Homebrew Bittering Units or HBUs.

**Alpha acids.** The most important of the bittering acids in hops. Alpha acids are soluble in hot water and wort, but unless they are isomerized (the atoms in their molecules re-arranged), they are only very slightly soluble in cooled water or wort.

**Amino acids.** A group of nitrogen-containing compounds, which are important yeast nutrients. They are the building blocks of proteins. Wort gets its amino acids primarily from the malt.

**Anaerobic.** Literally, "without air." Fermentation (by yeast) is an primarily an anaerobic process. *See also Crabtree effect.*

**Apparent attenuation.** The percentage of specific gravity loss from before the addition of yeast (original gravity) to the end of fermentation (final gravity). It differs from the real attenuation in that the yeast produce alcohol which is lighter than water and therefore throws-off the measurement. The way to determine real attenuation is rather complicated (and, for our purposes, unnecessary): boil-off the alcohol and bring the volume back up with water; measure the FG and calculate the attenuation.

**Aroma hops.** This can be interpreted two ways. In this book, it always means hops added to give the beer aroma. However, some books and magazines refer to low-alpha acid hops as "aroma hops" and you might read: "only aroma hops are used by this brewery" - this simply means that this brewery only uses low-alpha hops for bittering.

**Astringent.** A drying feeling imparted usually on the roof and sides of the mouth by polyphenols (tannins) in the beer.

**Attemperation.** The process by which freshly rehydrated dry yeast is gently brought to pitching temperature by slowly adding wort to the rehydrated yeast until the volume has quadrupled. It is important because simply dumping yeast that has been rehydrated in 104° F (40° C) water to 68° F (20° C) wort will temperature shock the yeast - many cells will die and the survivors will tend to ferment sluggishly.

**Attenuation.** *See Apparent attenuation.*

**Autolysis.** This sometimes occurs when yeast are starved for food. The yeast excrete an enzyme that breaks down the cell walls of their neighbors. The resulting effect on the beer is a sulfury or rubbery aroma and flavor.

**Balance.** Usually the relative strengths of bitterness and maltiness in a beer. In fruit or spiced beers, the balance can refer to the relative strength of beer and non-beer flavors/aromas.

**Balling.** A scale for measuring the weight of the wort relative to the weight of a solution of sucrose in water. 12 degrees Balling represents 100 grams of sucrose/water solution of which 12 grams are sucrose.

**Beechwood aging.** A method of shortening the lagering time when using a very flocculent yeast in which strips of sanitized beechwood are put into the bottom of the lagering tanks. After the flocculent yeast settles on the larger surface area provided by the beechwood strips, more of the yeast is exposed to reduce acetaldehyde, diacetyl, and other byproducts of the primary fermentation.

**Beer.** A malt beverage. In modern terms, both ale and lager are beer. Incidentally, once yeast has been added to the wort, brewers refer to it as beer.

**Beer engine.** A pump used for dispensing Real Ale in a traditional manner (without carbon dioxide pressure).

**Beerstone.** Mostly calcium oxalate, it is a brown crust that, over time, forms in kettles and fermenters.

**Bitter wort.** Wort after hops have been added.

**BJCP.** Beer Judge Certification Program. A program of certifying and ranking beer judges, involving a written examination, scoring test beers, and gaining points by helping run BJCP Registered competitions (judging, stewarding, organizing, etc.).

**Black malt.** A very dark roasted malted barley.

**Black Patent malt.** *See Black malt.*

**Blowoff.** A method of brewing in a closed fermenter in which the foam that forms during fermentation is directed out of the fermenter via a tube.

**Blowoff tube or hose.** The tube used to divert the foam formed during fermentation out of the fermenter.

**Body.** The perception of thickness or thinness of a beer.

**Boil gravity.** The specific gravity of the wort during the boil.

**Boiling hops.** Another name for bittering hops.

**Bottle brush.**  A device for cleaning dirty bottles.

**Bottle filler.**  A device for filling bottles.  It has a valve in it which allows the starting and stopping of flow of beer into the bottle.

**Bottle tree.**  A tree-like drying rack for bottles.

**Bottle-conditioned.**  Beer that has been naturally carbonated in the bottles via fermentation.

**Bouquet.**  The aroma of the beer.  Some refer to the aromatic character of the hops as "bouquet" and the aromatic character of the malt as "aroma."

**Break.**  The coagulated protein-polyphenol complexes that form during the boil ("hot break") or during chilling ("cold break").

**Brewers' degrees.**  The specific gravity of the wort or beer if you remove the leading "1" and decimal point.  In other words, a wort with a specific gravity of 1.045, has 45 brewer's degrees.  Also referred to as "points" and "excess gravity."

**Brussels/Bruxelles Lace.**  The lacy webbing of foam that lingers on the sides of a glass.

**Candi sugar.**  The Belgian term for rock candy sugar.  White candi sugar is equivalent to sucrose (table sugar) and dark candi sugar is simply caramelized sucrose.

**Capper.**  A device for affixing a bottlecap to a bottle and making a seal that holds pressure.

**Caramel malt.**  A malt that is made by raising the temperature of wet green malt to a temperature during which the enzymes in the malt convert the starch to sugars, in effect mashing the grain "in the husk."

**Carboy.**  A large, glass or ceramic, narrow-mouthed bottle.

**Cask-conditioned.**  Beer that has been naturally carbonated in the cask via fermentation.

**Chalk.**  The common name for calcium carbonate.

**Chill haze.**  Protein-polyphenol complexes that stay in solution at warm temperatures, but precipitate into a haze at cooler temperatures.

**Chlorophenols.**  Unpleasant compounds formed via reactions between chlorine and phenolic compounds.

**Chocolate malt.**  A malt made by roasting malt till it is dark, but not black.

**Clarity.**  The absence of haze.

**Closed fermentation.**  A fermentation method in which the fermenter is sealed.  Sometimes, but not necessarily, a blowoff tube is affixed to the top of the fermenter to divert the foam created during fermentation out of the fermenter.  If a blowoff tube is not used, there must be sufficient headspace to accommodate the foam created.

**$CO_2$.**  Carbon dioxide.

**Cohumulone.**  The second most important of the alpha acids (after humulone).

**Cold break.**  The coagulated protein-polyphenol complexes that are formed when hot wort is cooled.

**Conditioning.**  This is primarily carbonation, but in lagers and stronger beers many other chemical and biological reactions take place which decrease undesirable compounds such as DMS and acetaldehyde.

**Coolship.**  A shallow, wide tank used for cooling beer.  Due to sanitation concerns, coolships are no longer in use except in very traditional breweries, often where a lactic bacteria fermentation is an accepted component of the beer character (e.g. Lambic/Lambiek breweries).

**Corker.**  A device for forcing a cork into a bottle.

**Copper.**  A British term for the kettle.

**Copper finings.**  A British term for finings that are used in the kettle (primarily Irish Moss and Bentonite).

**Counterflow chiller.**  A device for chilling hot wort in which the cooling liquid (usually water) flows in hoses or cylinders surrounding hot wort in a tube.  Typically the wort and cooling liquid flow in opposite directions, hence "counterflow."

**Counterpressure bottle filler.**  A device for filling bottles with carbonated beer in which the bottle is first pressurized with carbon dioxide.

**Crabtree effect.**  An effect where yeast respiration is repressed in favor of fermentation despite the availability of oxygen.  Glucose or fructose levels in excess of 0.4% induce the Crabtree effect as well as other sugars (maltose, mannose, or galactose) but to a lesser extent[83].

**Cropping.**  The harvesting of yeast.  A "top-cropping" yeast is one that flocculates to the top of the ferment and can be skimmed off, whereas a "bottom-cropping" yeast is one that does not and is harvested from the bottom of the fermenter.

**Crystal malt.**  *See Caramel malt.*

**Decant.**  Pour off the liquid and leave the solids behind.

**Decoction mash.**  A method of all-grain brewing in which portions of the mash are removed from the main mash, heated to boiling and returned to the main mash in order to raise the temperature of the main mash.  A "decoction" is one of those portions of removed mash.

**Dextrins.**  Large unfermentable carbohydrates.  During mashing, starch is converted to fermentable and unfermentable carbohydrates.  The fermentable carbohydrates are known as "sugars" and the unfermentable ones as "dextrins" (which include oligosaccharides, megalosaccharides and higher dextrins).

**Dextrose.**  Another name for glucose, "brewer's sugar," or "corn sugar."

**Diacetyl.**  A compound created by yeast and then usually reabsorbed if the yeast are given the opportunity.  It imparts a butterscotch or buttery aroma and flavor to the beer.  It can also be created by certain bacteria.  It is acceptable in ales at low levels and is unpleasant in both ales and lagers at high levels.

**Diacetyl rest.**  A method in which the temperature of a mostly-fermented lager is raised from typical lager fermentation temperatures up into the range of 55 to 65° F (13 to 18° C) for two to ten days.

**Dimethyl sulfide.**  A sulfur compound that is formed primarily during the boil. It imparts a cooked-corn or parsnip aroma and is acceptable at low levels in lagers and Kölschbiers and considered a fault in all other ales.

**Dirty head.**  The brown part of the foam that forms during the early part of fermentation.

**Dissolved oxygen.**  The level of oxygen that is dissolved in the wort or beer.

**DME.**  *See Dried malt extract.*

**DMS.**  *See Dimethyl sulfide.*

**DO.**  *See Dissolved oxygen.*

**Dormant.**  Usually refers to the state of yeast that is not dead, but no longer actively biologically interacting with the beer.

**Dried malt extract.**  Wort that has been dehydrated to about 3% moisture and powdered.

**Dropping.**  A method of separating fermenting beer from the break and dirty head by racking the beer from the primary fermenter into a secondary fermenter.  During this racking, the beer may optionally be aerated.

**Dry yeast.**  Yeast that has been dehydrated to a very low moisture level.  It is most certainly still alive and should be refrigerated, not frozen.

**Dryhopping.**  A method of imparting hop aroma to a beer by adding hops directly to the fermenter.

**Dryhops.**  The hops used in dryhopping.

**EBC.**  Stands for European Brewing Convention, but usually used in reference to the color measurement method adopted by this body.

**Endosperm.**  The main, starchy, part of a malt kernel.

**Enteric bacteria.**  Bacteria that is found in the gut of mammals.

**Enzymes.**  Specialized proteins which act as catalysts in biological or chemical reactions.

**Erlenmeyer flask.**  A triangular laboratory flask.

**Essential oil.**  The part of the hop lupulin that provides aroma (essence).

**Esters.**  Compounds built from alcohols and organic acids which provide fruity and other aromas/flavors.

**Ethanol.**  Ethyl alcohol, a.k.a. "grain alcohol." It is the primary alcohol in alcohol-containing beverages.

**Excess gravity.**  *See Brewer's degrees.*

**Exothermic.**  A reaction which produces heat.

**Extract.**  The soluble part of the mash.

**Fatty acids.**  Organic molecules which are the building blocks of fats and other lipids.  Some of them can be quite aromatic and impart off-aromas to the beer.

**Fermentation.** The biological process by which yeast turn wort into beer. In simple terms, it is primarily the conversion of sugars into alcohol and carbon dioxide, but in reality it is a complex process also involving esters, higher alcohols, amino acids, fatty acids, aldehydes, diacetyl, and sulfur compounds, just to name a few.

**Fermentation lock.** *See Airlock.*

**Fermenter.** The vessel for containing the beer during fermentation.

**FG.** *See Final gravity.*

**Final gravity.** The specific gravity of the beer when fermentation is complete.

**Fining.** Clarifying.

**Finings.** Clarifying agents.

**Finishing hops.** Hops added at the very end of the boil, which add mostly aroma to the beer.

**First wort hopping.** A method of imparting hop character to beer by adding the hops to warm wort instead of adding them after the boil has begun.

**Flaked.** Grains that have been heated with microwaves and then pressed through heated rollers. They may not be added to the wort without mashing or they will give the beer a haze from unconverted starch.

**Flavor hops.** Hops added with roughly 10 to 20 minutes remaining in the boil. They add mostly hop flavor to the beer.

**Floatation tank.** A tank used to separate wort from trub.

**Flocculation.** Clumping into "flocs" or "clumps." It can refer to the clumping of yeast during fermentation or the clumping of protein-polyphenol complexes.

**Flocculent.** A yeast that has a strong tendency to clump into large groups is said to be "highly-" or "strongly-flocculent."

**Foam-negative.** Decreasing head retention.

**Foam-positive.** Improving head retention.

**Food-grade.** Approved for food contact. On plastic containers and tubing, look for "FDA-approved" or "NSF-approved for Food Use."

**Fructose.** A simple, 6-carbon sugar that is a minor component of wort unless added deliberately.

**Full-boil.** A method of brewing where the entire wort is boiled at once. *See also Partial-boil.*

**Fusel alcohols.** *See Higher alcohols.*

**Glucose.** A simple, 6-carbon sugar that is a minor component of wort itself (unless added deliberately) but is the most common building-block of larger sugars such as sucrose, maltose, maltotriose, etc.

**Glycogen.** A carbohydrate which is used by yeast to store energy.

**Golden syrup.** A British term for invert sugar syrup.

**Grain bag.** A mesh bag for steeping crushed malts and/or grains.

**Gravity.** Short for specific gravity.

**Green beer.** Beer that is not yet ready for consumption. From the time yeast is pitched into wort till the time it is ready for consumption, brewers refer to it as green beer.

**Grist.** Crushed malts/grains.

**Grits.** Just the starchy part of the grain.

**Gusher.** A bottle or keg that produces a fountain of foam upon opening.

**Gypsum.** The common name for calcium sulfate.

**Handpump.** *See Beer engine.*

**Hardness.** Primarily a measure of the calcium and magnesium in water.

**Haze.** Cloudiness. It may come from chemical or biological sources or may be temperature dependent *(see Chill haze).*

**HBU.** Homebrew Bittering Unit. *See Alpha acid unit.*

**HDPE.** High-density polyethylene. White HDPE is usually food-grade.

**Headspace.** The non-liquid space at the top of a bottle, keg, or fermenter.

**Higher alcohols.** Alcohols that are more complex (have longer-chained molecules) than ethanol.

**High-gravity beer.** Beer made from a high original gravity (greater than 1.060 or so).

**High-kilned malt.** Malts, such as "Vienna," "Munich," "Amber," "Aromatic" and "Brown," that are kilned at higher temperatures than Pale malts.

**Homebrew Digest.** A digested mailing list for beer and brewing on the Internet.

**Hop back.** A device for separating hops from wort.

**Hop bag.** A mesh bag for containing hops during the boil (an alternative to a hop back).

**Hop character.** A rather nebulous term that has been used to describe everything from hop aroma to hop flavor to the quality of the bitterness imparted by hops. In this book, it is used to refer to both hop aroma and flavor together.

**Hop extract.** An extract of the bittering part of the hops. It imparts no aroma.

**Hop oil.** The aromatic part of the hops. It imparts no bitterness.

**Hop pellets.** Whole hops ground into a powder and pressed into pellets.

**Hop plugs.** Whole hops pressed into large "pellets," each approximately 1/2 ounce in weight.

**Hopped wort.** Wort after hops have been added.

**Hops.** Flowers of the perennial climbing vine, *Humulus lupulus.*

**Hose clamp.** While a hose clamp can refer to those stainless steel clamps used to secure a hose to a hose barb (like a radiator hose clamp), in this book, it refers to a plastic or metal device for pinching a hose to regulate the flow of liquid.

**Hot break.** The coagulated protein-polyphenol complexes that are formed when wort is boiled.

**Hot-Side Aeration.** The introduction of air when wort is hot.

**HSA.** *See Hot-Side Aeration.*

**Humulone.** The most important of the alpha acids. Isomerized humulone (isohumulone) is the primary bittering agent in beer.

**Hydrogen sulfide.** A byproduct of fermentation. It is commonly known as "the rotten egg" smell.

**Hydrometer.** A device for measuring the specific gravity of wort or beer.

**IBU.** *See International Bittering Unit.*

**ID.** Inside Diameter.

**Immersion chiller.** A wort chiller in which cold water is run through a coil of tubing that is immersed in hot wort.

**International Bittering Unit.** A measure of bitterness in milligrams per liter of isohumulone.

**Infusion mash.** A method of mashing in which the temperature of the mash is raised by infusions of boiling or hot water.

**Invert sugar.** Sucrose that has been partially broken down into its component glucose and fructose.

**Irish Moss.** A kettle fining agent made from red seaweed which helps coagulate protein in the boil.

**Isinglass.** A post-fermentation fining agent used primarily to help flocculate yeast.

**Isohumulone.** Isomerized humulone. Humulone is not very soluble in cool wort, but it is soluble in hot wort. Isohumulone is considerably more soluble in cool wort, which is why it is important to isomerize humulone during the boil: so that it stays in solution and provides bitterness.

**Isomerized.** A compound with the same chemical formula, but a re-arranged molecular structure.

**Kettle finings.** Clarifying agents used in the kettle (i.e. in the boil).

**Kräusen.** (n.) The foam that forms on the top of the beer during fermentation. (v.) To perform kräusening.

**Kräusening.** The addition of actively fermenting beer to finished beer to add carbonation.

**Lacing.** *See Brussels/Bruxelles Lace.*

**Lactic acid.** An organic acid produced by several varieties of beer-spoiling bacteria.

**Lactose.** Milk sugar. It is unfermentable by cultured brewer's yeast.

**Lag time.** The from when the yeast is pitched till when active fermentation begins (a kräusen begins to form).

**Lager.** A beer fermented with lager yeast at cooler temperatures and cold-conditioned.

**Lager malt.** A very pale malt typically used to brew lagers. It is another name for "Pilsner malt."

**Lager yeast.** Yeasts that are able to ferment at lower temperatures and are able to fully ferment raffinose (whereas ale yeasts are only able to split a fructose molecule off the end and leave melibiose unfermented).

**Lagering.** The cold storage of lagers important for many processes such as the reabsorption of diacetyl by yeast.

**Läuter.** Literally, "to clarify." In brewing terms, läutering (usually written without the umlaut) is the separation of the wort from the husks and other insoluble parts of the malts and grains. In extract brewing, the mashing and läutering has been done for you by the malt extract manufacturer.

**Läuter tun.** A tub-like vessel with a perforated bottom or containing perforated tubes, used for läutering by all-grain and partial-mash brewers.

**LDPE.** Low-density polyethylene. Often food-grade, LDPE is slightly more permeable than HDPE.

**Leaf hops.** A misnomer. Whole hop flowers are often called leaf hops, possibly because the petals of the hop flowers resemble leaves.

**Lipids.** A group of fatty or fat-like organic compounds including fatty acids, fatty oils, fats (glycerol esters), waxes, sterols and esters of fatty acids with other groups (e.g. phospholipids). Some lipids are important for yeast nutrition (e.g. sterols are important to cell membrane formation) whereas others may yield off-flavors and aromas. Some lipids are foam-positive (improve head retention) but the vast majority of them are foam-negative.

**Liquid yeast.** Technically, this refers to yeast that is purchased suspended in a liquid media, but in this book, I use the term to also refer to yeasts purchases on solid media (slants, stabs, etc.) to distinguish them from dehydrated yeasts (dry yeasts).

**Liquor.** The brewer's term for water.

**Lovibond.** A scale for measurement of beer and malt color.

**Lupulin.** The yellow sticky substance found in hop lupulin glands. Of all the compounds that lupulin contains, of primary importance to brewers are alpha, beta, other soft resins, and essential oils.

**Lupulin glands.** The glands at the base of hop petals which contain lupulin.

**Lupulone.** The primary beta acid.

**Malt.** Most commonly, it is a short version of "malted barley" but often it is also used to mean "malt extract."

**Malt extract.** Basically, this is dehydrated wort. It may be a syrup (about 20% water) or a powder (about 3% water), hopped (containing isomerized alpha acids) or unhopped, and is available in many colors.

**Malting.** The process of germinating, drying, and (optionally) roasting grains into malts.

**Malto-dextrin.** A processed product used to add dextrins (unfermentable carbohydrates) to the wort in an effort to increase mouthfeel and decrease fermentability (increase FG).

**Maltose.**  The most common sugar in wort.  Each molecule of maltose is made up of two glucose molecules and it is fully fermentable.

**Maltotriose.**  Another common wort sugar, it is made up of three glucose molecules and is fully fermentable.

**Mash.**  The mixture of crushed malts, grains, and brewing water, during which the enzymes from the malt convert complex molecules (such as large proteins and starches) into simpler molecules (such as amino acids, smaller proteins, fermentable sugars and dextrins).  In extract brewing, mashing and läutering has been done for you by the malt extract manufacturer.

**Mash tun.**  The vessel used in all-grain or partial-mash brewing for holding the mash.

**Mashing.**  *See Mash.*

**Media.**  The liquid or solid on which yeast is grown or stored.

**Melanoidins.**  Important flavoring compounds formed from reactions between carbohydrates and amino acids during malt drying, wort boiling, and malt extract storage.  They are more abundant in high-kilned malts and are extremely important to the flavor of many beer styles such as Oktoberfest and Munich Dunkel.

**mg/l.**  Milligrams-per-liter (equivalent to ppm or "parts-per-million" when discussing ion concentrations in water).

**Micro-aerophilic.**  Life forms (typically bacteria) that prefer small amounts of air.

**Noble hops.**  A much-debated label given to a group of hops said to give superior aromatic qualities to beer.

**Nose.**  In brewing terms, the aroma of the beer.

**OD.**  Outside diameter.

**OG.**  Original gravity.

**Open fermentation.**  A method of fermentation in which the fermenter may be opened to skim the foam the forms.

**Original gravity.**  The specific gravity of the wort just before the yeast is added.

**Overcarbonated.**  Having too much carbonation.

**Overprimed.**  A beer that has had too much priming sugar added (usually leads to overcarbonation).

**Oxidation.**  A chemical reaction in which one substance is oxidized (loses electrons) while another substance is reduced (gains electrons).  (Please note that "reduced" here is in the chemical sense and is not synonymous with "decreased.")  In brewing, quite commonly free oxygen is involved and thus minimizing oxidation of wort compounds is most easily accomplished by decreasing the amount of oxygen that is introduced into hot wort (when the oxidation reactions are much more rapid) or finished beer.  Oxidation of wort compounds results in darkening, loss of hop aroma, stale aromas, and harsh flavors.

**Oxygenation.**   The intentional introduction of oxygen into cooled wort to provide dissolved oxygen for the yeast to use.  Some oxidation (see above) of wort compounds is unavoidable, but if done at cool temperatures, the yeast consume the oxygen before noticeable damage is imparted to the wort.

**Pale Ale malt.**   A pale malt (slightly darker than lager malt) commonly used as the base malt in brewing ales.

**Pale malt.**   Sometimes used to mean Pale Ale malt, other times it is used as a general term for  both Pale Ale and Lager/Pilsner malts.

**Papain.**   An enzyme extracted from papaya fruit that breaks large and medium-sized proteins down into amino acids and small proteins (at the expense of head-retaining, medium-sized proteins in the beer).

**Partial boil.**   A brewing method in which only part of the water is used during the boiling of the malt extract (usually due to kettle capacity) and then adding this concentrated wort to sanitized water in the fermenter.

**Partial mash.**   A brewing method in which part of the fermentables come from mashing malted grains and part from malt extract.

**Pasteurization.**   The process of sanitizing (not sterilizing) something by heating it to a moderate temperature for a definite period of time or to a high temperature for a short time followed by a quick cooling (flash pasteurization).

**Pasteur effect.**   A phenomenon in which yeast abandon fermentation and revert to respiration caused by the introduction of oxygen.  Note that the Pasteur effect is in competition with the Crabtree effect (see above) so that the introduction of oxygen does not necessarily mean that the yeast will display this effect.

**Permanent hardness.**   Related primarily to the amount of sulfate in the water because calcium is not precipitated as calcium sulfate. *See also Temporary hardness.*

**Permeable.**   Capable of allowing gasses or liquids to pass.

**pH.**   Literally, "potential of hydrogen."  It is a logarithmic scale from 0 to 14 which represents the acidity or alkalinity of a solution.

**Phenolic.**   Hydrocarbons that are characterized by what is known as an "aromatic ring."  There are many phenolic compounds associated with brewing including hop alpha acids, polyphenols (commonly referred to as tannins) from the malt husks and woody parts of the hops, and 4-vinyl guaiacol (the source of one of the characteristic aromas of Bavarian Weizens).

**Pilsner malt.** *See Lager malt.*

**Pitch timing.**   The timing of the yeast addition.  It is important not only so fermentation starts quickly, but also because starved yeast produce higher amounts of undesirable compounds.

**Pitching.**   Adding yeast to the wort.

**Pitching rate.** The amount of yeast added per volume of wort. In general, when using fresh, rehydrated, dry yeast, 1 gram of dry yeast per gallon of ale wort is sufficient. For lagers and high-gravity beers, two to four times that rate is recommended.

**Plato.** A scale for measuring the weight of the wort relative to the weight of a solution of sucrose in water. 12 degrees Plato represents 100 grams of sucrose/water solution of which 12 grams are sucrose. It is said to be more accurate than the Balling scale.

**Points.** A term used for specific gravity contributions that appears to have been introduced (to the best of my knowledge) on the Homebrew Digest. If a particular ingredient is said to contribute "24 points-per-pound-per-gallon," then this means that a pound of this ingredient in a gallon of water would produce a specific gravity of 1.024, or "24 points." It is equivalent to "excess gravity" and "Brewers' degrees."

**Polyclar.** A trade name for PVPP.

**Polyphenols.** Various phenolic compounds with multiple hydroxyl groups. They are commonly called tannins, which originates from the fact that polyphenolic compounds are used for tanning animal hides.

**Powdery.** Describes yeasts that do not form a firm, compact mass at the bottom of the fermenter or bottle after settling. These types of yeasts generally take longer to settle and tend to be more attenuative than strains that flocculate strongly.

**ppm.** Parts-per-million. Equivalent to mg/l when discussing ion concentrations in water.

**Precipitate.** To fall out of solution or suspension. The most common example of precipitation in brewing is that of calcium carbonate flakes forming when you boil water that has a high temporary hardness.

**Primary fermenter.** The first fermenter. For ales, I recommend that only a primary fermenter be used because the benefits of transferring the beer to a secondary fermenter usually do not outweigh the risks.

**Priming.** The addition of a measured amount of sugar to beer that has finished fermenting. This addition of sugar is done just prior to bottling or kegging so that the renewed fermentation produces carbonation.

**Priming bucket/carboy.** A vessel used to mix priming sugar with the beer in preparation for bottling. It is also called a "bottling bucket." This separate container for priming is recommended so that the priming sugar can be mixed into the beer well without disturbing the settled yeast in the fermenter.

**Priming sugar.** The sugar used for priming.

**Primings.** Another name for priming sugar.

**Proteolytic.** A general name for enzymes that cut proteins into smaller proteins and amino acids.

**PVPP.** Polyvinylpyrrolidone. It is a post-fermentation fining.

**Racking.**  The transfer of beer or wort from one container to another, leaving the sediment behind.

**Racking cane.**  A long, stiff, food-grade tube used for siphoning beer or wort, which has a device on the inlet such that the liquid is not drawn off the very bottom so that sediment (yeast, break, etc.) is prevented from being transferred.

**Real Ale.**  Ale that has been naturally carbonated in the container in which it is delivered (cask or bottle) and which is served without any extraneous $CO_2$ pressure (i.e. via handpump, gravity, electric pump, or air pressure).

**Rehydration.**  The process by which dry yeast are allowed to re-absorb water. It should be done for 15 to 30 minutes in water (not wort) that has been boiled to sanitize and then cooled to between 90° and 110° F (32° and 43° C).

**Repitching.**  Reusing yeast that has already fermented a batch of beer.

**Rice syrup solids.**  Dehydrated sugar syrup made from rice.

**RO water system.**  Reverse osmosis water system. This type of water "filter" produces virtually mineral-free water.

**Roasted barley.**  Unmalted barley that has been roasted to a dark brown color.

**Roasted malt.**  Malted barley that has been roasted. It can vary in color from amber to black.

**Rouse.**  To swirl, stir, shake, or pump yeast that has flocculated back into suspension.

**Ruh beer.**  Beer in which fermentation is almost complete and that is ready for lagering.

**Runnings.**  The liquid part of the mash after läutering (the wort coming out of the läuter tun).

**Sanitized.**  Boiled or treated with sanitizers such that virtually all undesirable microorganisms have been killed. Even with extremely good sanitation techniques there are still many live bacteria, wild yeasts, and molds in our wort, but complete sterilization is practically impossible. The key to clean, tasty, stable beer, is to use adequate amounts of healthy, vigorous yeast so that they outcompete the undesirable microorganisms.

**Secondary.**  *See Secondary fermenter.*

**Secondary fermenter.**  A second fermenter recommended for lagers and fruit beers so that beer destined for a lengthy fermentation can be removed from the dead yeast and (hot and cold) break.

**Silica gel.**  A polymeric hydrogel (or xerogel) fining made from sodium silicate.

**Skunked.**  Beer that has been exposed to light such that a significant amount of the isohumulone in the beer has been converted to mercaptans which give the beer an aroma exactly like skunk. Brown glass provide slightly more protection from skunking than green or clear, but a few hours in bright sunlight or a few days under fluorescent lights will skunk beer even in brown glass. Fermenting beer is also susceptible to skunking so that fermenters should be kept in the dark.

**Slant.** A method of storing yeast on a solid media in a cylindrical tube where the tube was tilted on an angle during cooling so the media is on an angle, which makes the surface area larger.

**Slurry.** The thick paste of yeast at the bottom of a starter or fermenter.

**SMM.** *See s-methyl methionine.*

**S-methyl methionine.** A sulfur compound found in malt that is the precursor of DMS. It is driven off by heat, so that paler malts (such as Pilsner/Lager malt) will be higher in SMM than more highly kilned malts (such as Pale Ale, Vienna, or Munich malts).

**Solubility.** The limit of how much of a substance (gas or solid) can dissolve in a particular liquid.

**Sparge.** The addition of water to the top of the grain in the läuter tun in order to rinse the sugars out of the grains.

**Sparging.** *See Sparge.*

**Sparkolloid®.** A polysaccharide in a diatomaceous earth carrier used as a fining agent (usually by winemakers).

**Specific gravity.** The weight of a liquid relative to that of water.

**SRM.** A scale for measurement of beer color.

**Starter.** A "miniature batch of beer" which is recommended for growing up larger quantities of yeast for adding to the main wort.

**Steeping.** The soaking of malts and grains that don't require mashing (such as crystal malt and roasted barley) in water to extract their sugar, color, and flavor.

**Sterile.** Completely without life (including spores).

**Sterilization.** A virtually unachievable level of sanitation (for our kitchens/home breweries) in which all living microorganisms have been killed (including their spores). The only practical means for sterilization in the kitchen is the pressure-cooker, but except for starters (and even for starters it's not absolutely necessary), it is overkill.

**Stuck fermentation.** A condition where the yeast have stopped fermenting earlier than expected.

**Suckback.** The sucking of airlock liquid into the fermenter by the contraction of the cooling headspace. S-shaped airlocks are immune to this problem.

**Sucrose.** A simple sugar made up of a glucose and fructose molecule. Usually derived from sugar cane or sugar beets, it is what we commonly call "table sugar."

**Supersaturated.** An unstable condition where the solubility limit of a substance is exceeded. In other words, more of something has been dissolved in a liquid than should normally be possible. This condition is usually the result of heating or raising of pressure, followed by cooling or lowering of pressure.

**Sweet wort.** Wort before hops have been added.

**Tannins.** *See Polyphenols.*

**Temperature shock.**  A sudden change in temperature (usually downward).  It can apply to glass carboys for example (where the result is a large pile of glass shards) or to yeast (where the result is a large number of dead yeast and sluggish fermentation by the survivors).

**Temporary hardness.**  Related primarily to the amount of bicarbonate/carbonate in the water.  It is called "temporary" because the hardness (which is due to calcium) can be reduced somewhat via boiling, which causes calcium carbonate to precipitate out of solution, lowering the hardness.

**Terminal gravity.**  The specific gravity when fermentation is complete.

**Tertiary.**  Literally: "third."  It refers to a third-stage fermenter.

**Toasted malt.**  Malted barley which has been toasted (either commercially in a kiln or at home in an oven).  It contains starch which means it must be mashed.

**Torrified.**  Puffed.  Many grains are available in torrified form, alas, all must be mashed.

**Treacle.**  The British term for molasses.

**Trub.**  Dead/dormant yeast and coagulated protein (hot and cold break) - pronounced TROOB.

**Turbid.**  Cloudy.

**Ullage.**  Headspace, especially in a cask.

**Underaerated.**  Insufficient aeration (i.e. not enough dissolved oxygen).

**Undercarbonated.**  Insufficient carbonation.

**Underpitching.**  The addition of too little yeast for a given volume of wort.

**Unfermentable sugars.**  Sugars that are too complex for our yeast to ferment.  Note that many wild yeasts and bacteria can still ferment these sugars, so their fermentability is relative to the yeast that you are pitching.

**Unflocculent.**  Yeast that do not clump together and rise to the top of the fermenter or sink to the bottom

**Utilization.**  The percentage of the alpha acids that actually make it to the beer glass.

**v/v.**  A ratio of volumes.  In brewing, usually referring to alcohol percentage.

**Vegetal.**  Smelling like vegetables, especially cooked ones.

**Viable.**  Able to reproduce.

**w/w.**  A ratio of weights.  In brewing, usually referring to alcohol percentage.

**Whirlpool.**  A device used to separate hops and break from the wort.

**Whole hops.**  Whole hop flowers as opposed to hop pellets, plugs, or extracts.

**Wild yeast.**  Uninvited yeast other than our cultured yeasts.

**Wort.**  Unfermented beer. "Beer" before the yeast has been added.

**Wort chiller.**  A device for cooling hot wort in preparation for the addition of yeast.

**Wort spoiling bacteria.**  A group of various bacteria which do their damage during the lag time and which are later killed by the alcohol in the beer.

They are the second most common source of cooked-vegetable aromas (after SMM conversion to DMS).

**Yeast.** Roughly: unicellular non-photosynthetic fungi.

**Yeast energizer.** A mixture of a variety of nutrients necessary for yeast health.

**Yeast nutrient.** Other than a few exceptions, simply diammonium phosphate.

**Yeast washing.** The process of separating yeast from trub by repeated rinsing with water and decanting.

**Zymurgy.** The study of fermentation - pronounced ZYE-mer-gee.

# ABOUT THE AUTHOR

Al Korzonas has been critically tasting and researching beer since 1979, after his first trip to Britain, Belgium and Germany. He holds Bachelor's and Master's Degrees in Electrical Engineering and supports his homebrewing habit by working as a software developer at Lucent Technologies – Bell Labs Innovations. Al has worked as a technical editor for Zymurgy magazine and is currently a technical consultant. He is a frequent contributor to the Homebrew Digest, Brewer's Forum, Lambic Digest, JudgeNet, and Advanced Topics in Brewing electronic "newsletters," and has written several articles for Zymurgy and Brewing Techniques. Al is an active member of the Chicago Beer Society (1996 AHA Homebrew Club of the Year), Brewers of South Suburbia, Urban Knaves of Grain, and Headhunters homebrew clubs, has achieved the rank of Master Judge in the Beer Judge Certification Program, and is a member of the BJCP scoresheet and style guideline subcommittees. A serious homebrewer since 1987, Al's beers have earned him over one hundred ribbons at homebrew competitions throughout the US including several in the American Homebrewers Association National Competition. His 7-Grain E.S.B. was selected Champion Beer at the 1995 CBS Midwest Invitational Brew-Off both by popular vote and by Michael Jackson. Al lives in Palos Hills, Illinois with his wife Karen and is owner of Sheaf & Vine, which publishes books, provides brewing consultation, and sells specialty brewing supplies.

# B

# C

sodium, 169, 310
softened, 7
softener, 7
solvent-like aroma, 300
sour, 28, 257
sour flavor, 313
sparging, 41, 43
sparkler, 404
Sparkolloid, 109
Special B malt, 135
Special Bitter, 405
special enzymes, 209
Specialty Beer, 440
specialty grains, 367
specific gravity, 30
spices, 209
spicy aroma, 300
spruce, 211
spruce aroma, 301
SRM, 71, 130
stab, 183
stale aroma, 301
starter, 80, 183
starter media, 371
starters, 55
steeping, 36, 38, 43, 75, 91, 107, 132,
        139, 366
Steinbier, 440
sterilization, 365
Sticke, 436
Stout
    Dry, 420
    Foreign-Style, 420
    Imperial, 420
    Oatmeal, 421
    Sweet, 421
stoves, 44
stovetop cleanup, 388
strong, 3
Strong Export Bitter, 406
stuck fermentation, 271
style guidelines, 326
suckback, 9, 52, 98
sucrose, 85, 119
sugar
    absorbing water, 386
    brown, 198
    candi, 206

corn, 85
dextrose, 198
fructose, 198
glucose, 198
invert, 198, 207
lactose, 188, 212, 216
sucrose, 198, 206
syrup, 207
table, 85, 198
testing for, 381
wort similar, 207
sulfate, 169, 172, 257, 308
sulfate and bitterness, 374
sulfur aroma, 301
sulfur dioxide, 200
super attenuators, 179
supplies, 3
SureScreen™, 46
swan neck, 404
sweaty aroma, 302
sweet, 257

# T

tall, narrow fermenters, 273
tannins, 40, 87, 91, 96, 102, 103, 105,
        107, 108, 151, 165, 167, 171
temperature compensation, 33
temperature control, 56
temperature shock, 73, 98
terminal gravity, 130
tetrahydropyridines, 293
thermometer, 29
tin, 100, 170
toasted malt, 138
toffee aroma, 302
tomato plant aroma, 302
too dark, 305
too light, 306
topping-off, 78
topping-up, 380
Traditional German Bock, 428
Trappist Ale, 421
Trappist Ales
    non-Dubbel/Tripel, 422
treacle, 343
Tripel, 422
troubleshooting, 23, 263

# Z